Brief Contents

Contents

Part 2   **Manufacturing and Service Flow Issues 135**

Preface

Welcome to *Process Management: Creating Value along the Supply Chain; Text & Cases.* The past 25 years has been characterized by tremendous change in the areas of purchasing, transportation, production, information systems, and supply chain management. These changes have created significant changes in the processes used for product design, manufacturing, and distribution, and in the way companies manage their relationships with suppliers and customers. Companies have evolved from being strictly internally focused with adversarial supplier relationships and only a passive regard for customers, to what we commonly see today—significant efforts placed identifying customers and end-product users with the goal of continually satisfying their needs; and building long-term, mutually beneficial relationships with suppliers and customers in order to collaborate to better serve customers. When process collaboration or integration is performed correctly, supply chains become formidable competitive entities, customers get what they want and continue to return, and all of the companies along the supply chain benefit.

The objective of this textbook is to encourage readers to think about the key processes companies use to purchase, make, and deliver products and services successfully, and how these processes are integrated within a supply chain framework. This textbook would be most useful for a Process Management class in an undergraduate supply chain management curriculum, as an upper-level Operations Management class or elective, as an MBA class in Process or Operations Management, or as a business-oriented course in Industrial Engineering. Most supply chain management degree programs have a course entitled Process Management, and this text is specifically suited for this class. This text is designed around the eight key value-creating supply chain processes listed in Chapter 1. Managers, too, will find this textbook extremely useful in creating strategies for improving their firms' competitive positions. Some of the unique things included in this text are: 21 easy-to-difficult cases spread throughout the sections and provided on the student and instructor CD-ROMs, three chapters addressing the concepts of flow management, a chapter on lean thinking, a chapter on returns management, and a chapter on future trends in process management. We think these and the other chapters will be a valuable source of information for business and engineering students and practicing business managers.

Part 1, Creating Customer-Driven Process Strategies, includes an introductory chapter discussing the concept of process management and how it is used as a way to create value along the supply chain, a product design chapter, and two chapters discussing the relationship between a firm and its customers. Chapter 1 introduces the eight key supply chain processes, while the core concepts in Chapters 2, 3, and 4 include customer and supplier input in the new product design process, designing an effective customer relationship management (CRM) process, CRM technologies, a framework for managing customer service, and integrating customer service in the supply chain. There are three cases focusing on customers and customer service issues to accompany Part 1.

Part 2, Manufacturing and Service Flow Issues, includes chapters on forecasting and inventory management, and then three chapters that are unlikely to be found in any other similar textbook: these are Managing Material Flows, Managing Customer and Work Flows, and Managing Information Flows. These important chapters introduce the concepts of flow management and the processes required to manage flow within the firm and between the firm and its trading partners. The key concepts discussed in Part 2 include the demand management process; collaborative planning, forecasting and replenishment; collaborative inventory management; material flow mapping; flow analysis; customer flow mapping; service delivery system design; managing work flows along the supply chain; and automating process management. Accompanying Part 2, there are four cases addressing these issues.

Part 3, Lean Production Systems, presents three chapters discussing a number of issues regarding lean thinking. Chapter 10 presents an introduction to lean production systems and lean thinking, while the other two chapters discuss the order fulfillment process, logistics network planning, strategic sourcing, and supplier relationship management. There are six cases dealing with lean thinking, logistics, and supply issues associated with Part 3 that we hope you will find thought-provoking.

Part 4, Quality Issues and Process Performance, contains three chapters. Chapter 13 discusses the basics for managing and controlling quality within the supply chain, while Chapter 14 presents a discussion of the very popular Six Sigma methodology for improving quality. Chapter 15 closes this section with a discussion of returns management. Core topics in this section include the quality improvement process; Six Sigma tools, initiatives, and challenges; developing a returns management strategy; and designing the returns network. There are five cases which are most appropriate for Part 4, discussing issues related to these topics.

Part 5, Looking to the Future, is the closing section and chapter, and discusses supply chain process integration and future trends in process management. Key topics in this chapter include internal process integration, supply chain process integration, and future trends in integration and process management. There are also three cases for this section. This final section, along with cases for each of the parts, can be found on the CD-ROM accompanying each text.

We hope you agree that this unique combination of process management topics will keep readers interested and challenged. The Instructor CD-ROM that comes with the text contains Part 5 and Part 6 (cases), sample syllabi, PowerPoint slides, sample tests, answers to all of the end-of-chapter discussion questions and problems, and teaching notes for all of the cases.

We welcome your comments and suggestions. Please email them to Dr. Joel D. Wisner at joel.wisner@unlv.edu.

Acknowledgments

We greatly appreciate the efforts of a number of people at Thomson/South-Western. Without their feedback and guidance, this textbook would not have been completed. Charles E. McCormick, Jr., Senior Acquisitions Editor, kept the project moving and kept the authors inspired. Taney Wilkins and Julie Klooster, our original and current Development Editors, handled all of our daily questions and problems (thanks so much for putting up with us!). Larry Qualls, Sr. Marketing Manager, is continuing to spread the news about this textbook. Kim Kusnerak, Content Project Manager, was responsible for getting the manuscript ready to print. And Erin Donohoe, Production Technology Analyst, has also helped to get the manuscript in final form.

Joel Wisner would also like to thank all of the wonderful people at Hanken, the Swedish School of Economics and Business Administration in Helsinki, Finland, where he spent his sabbatical during the fall of 2005, and was graciously allowed the use of an office to work on this textbook. Specifically, he wishes to thank Dr. Anders Tallberg, Dr. Karen Spens, Oana Velcu, Ogan Yigitbasioglu, Gyöngyi Kovács, and Monica Stark for all of their help and inspiring conversations.

Additionally, we wish to thank all of the reviewers who kindly gave their time to this project and helped to improve the final product. These people are:

Layek Abdel-Malek	*New Jersey Institute of Technology*
Robert Ash	*Indiana University Southeast*
M. Khurrum S. Bhutta	*Nicholls State University*
Stanley E. Fawcett	*Brigham Young University*
Cristina Gimenez	*Universitat Pompeu Fabra*
John D. Hanson	*University of San Diego*
Janet L. Hartley	*Bowling Green State University*
John Hironaka	*California State University, Sacramento*
Stella Hua	*Western Washington University*
Ling Li	*Old Dominion University*
Greg Magnan	*Seattle University*
Santosh K. Mahapatra	*Clarkson University*
Daniel S. Marrone	*Farmingdale State University of New York*
Tobias Schoenherr	*Eastern Michigan University*
Daniel Glaser-Segura	*Our Lady of the Lake University*
Pedro M. Reyes	*Baylor University*
Tim Vaughan	*University of Wisconsin—Eau Claire*

Finally, we would like to thank the case contributors, whose cases are an invaluable contribution to the textbook. We apologize if we have failed to thank any other contributors, and we want you to know that your efforts were also greatly appreciated.

About the Authors

Joel D. Wisner is professor of Supply Chain Management at the University of Nevada, Las Vegas. He earned a BS in Mechanical Engineering from New Mexico State University, an MBA from West Texas State University, and a Ph.D. in Supply Chain Management from Arizona State University. Prior to his academic career, Dr. Wisner worked as an engineer in the oil industry in West Texas and the Louisiana Gulf Coast. His research interests are in quality assessment and improvement strategies along the supply chain. His articles have appeared in numerous journals, including *Journal of Business Logistics, Journal of Operations Management, Journal of Supply Chain Management, Journal of Transportation, Production and Operations Management Journal,* and *Quality Management Journal.* Dr. Wisner also coauthored the textbook *Principles of Supply Chain Management,* also published by South-Western. More information about Dr. Wisner can be found at his Web site: http://www.scsv.nevada.edu/~wisnerj.

Linda L. Stanley is an adjunct professor for Arizona State University. Previously, she was a visiting professor at Arizona State University West and associate professor and chair of the Management Department at Our Lady of the Lake University in San Antonio, Texas. She earned a BA at California State University, a BS in Accounting at Arizona State University, and a Ph.D. in Business Administration also at Arizona State University. Before her academic career, Dr. Stanley worked in the mortgage banking and savings and loan industries. Her research interests include internal service quality, purchasing performance, and the buyer/supplier relationship. She has published articles in several journals, including *Journal of Operations Management, Journal of Supply Chain Management,* and *Journal of Business Logistics.* Dr. Stanley has coauthored two other books, *Transportation and Logistics Management* and *Effective Supply Management Performance,* both due out in 2007.

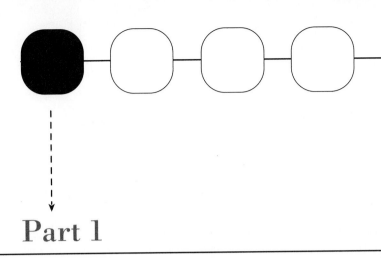

Part 1

Creating Customer-Driven Process Strategies

Chapter 1:

INTRODUCTION TO PROCESS MANAGEMENT

"The best companies understand what customers are willing to pay for a certain kind of vehicle, and then figure out how to produce such a vehicle and still return a profit. And that's why product and process design are such critical factors at the beginning phase of a new vehicle's life cycle." [1]

"A process-managed enterprise makes agile course corrections, embeds Six Sigma quality and reduces cumulative costs across the value chain. It pursues strategic initiatives with confidence, including mergers, consolidation, alliances, acquisitions, outsourcing and global expansion." [2]

Learning Objectives

After completing this chapter, you should be able to:

- Define and discuss process management, using examples.
- Understand the business value of process management.
- Describe the eight processes linking organizations along the supply chain.
- Discuss the importance of process management in services.
- Describe why quality management and Just-In-Time are important process management activities.
- Describe how processes are modeled and improved, and how firms measure process performance.
- Discuss the use of information technologies to integrate supply chain processes, and discuss other trends in process management.

Chapter Outline

Introduction

Processes and Process Management Defined

Process Management and Supply Chain Management

Eight Key Supply Chain Processes

Inventory and Process Management

Lean Thinking and Process Management

Quality and Process Management

Business Process Management—Formalizing Process Improvement

Measuring Process Performance

Trends in Process Management

Process Management in Action   *HP's Portal Strategy*

The Telecommunications Infrastructure Division of Hewlett-Packard (HP) is a single part of one of the world's largest corporations, but it also is a sizeable and rather complex business in its own right. This division—which makes control stations for wireless networks—revolves around a "project center" in Cupertino, California, where a group of workers coordinate all of the tasks involved in building and delivering these network control systems to HP customers around the world.

When a wireless network operator orders an HP base controller, the project center is expected to give the salesperson handling that transaction instant feedback on the availability and expected delivery date for the equipment. The project center also must make sure that the delivery date is no more than two days after the customer places the order.

"The challenge for the project center is figuring out how to keep track of exactly what is going on throughout the entire supply chain," says Andre Kuper, process technology manager with HP's Supply Chain Services Group. "They are pulling data from at least five different ERP systems, and communicating with multiple organizations, each of which has its own unique business processes."

This past spring, Kuper's Supply Chain Services Group, which in effect does business process and information technology consulting for HP's various business units, launched a pilot project that it expects will make the project center's job easier, and ultimately make HP's Telecommunications Infrastructure Division a more profitable enterprise. The centerpiece of this project is an enterprise portal platform that Kuper refers to as "an information backbone."

HP leases this portal infrastructure from Global Factory, located in Santa Clara, California. Since connecting to the Global Factory Network, Kuper estimates that HP's project coordinators spend at least 50 percent less time on mundane tasks, such as verifying that they have current information before inquiring about the status of a particular order. "With the portal, we have moved into a collaborative environment," Kuper says. "Instead of arguing over whether we are looking at the right documents, we are proactively working to make sure we are meeting customer demand."

That simple change also has allowed the division to create more effective business processes. "The end result is that everyone is performing fewer nonvalue-added tasks," Kuper says. "That means we can process orders faster, which ultimately should increase revenue by allowing our project coordinators to handle more orders simultaneously."

Source: Hill, S., "See the Whole Chain," *Manufacturing Systems* (MSI), V. 19, No. 10, 2001. Used with permission.

Introduction

In today's highly competitive global marketplace, organizations must continually assess, adjust, and redefine themselves to win new orders, please existing customers, and stay competitive. Large new markets have opened up in China and Russia, for instance, and many smaller markets in developing countries are continually opening and growing as political climates change. Many foreign organizations are coming to the United States and other highly developed nations and adding competition, while domestic firms are constantly seeking to expand into new product areas and new markets to improve profitability. These dynamic conditions create a need for organizations to be continually reducing costs, improving responsiveness, and improving quality, while designing new and exciting products to meet constantly changing customer requirements.

For most organizations, becoming and then staying competitive is like hitting a swiftly moving target. Firms must study their customers, determine what their needs are now, and anticipate what their needs will be in the future. Then they must develop or adjust processes, products, and services to meet current and (hopefully) future customer needs. Processes are woven throughout all organizations and represent unique ways that organizations provide what their customers want. **World-class businesses** manage processes in part by successfully managing inventories, creating long-lasting and mutually beneficial partnerships with suppliers and customers, establishing effective information and communication systems to connect with stakeholders, utilizing Just-In-Time (JIT) practices, and instituting quality management programs to create and deliver products and services customers want, leading to long-lasting success in the marketplace.

Today, managers taking a strictly functional view of the organization run the risk of creating silos of competence, while ignoring the value suppliers and customers bring into the firm in terms of shared information and knowledge of markets, products, and technologies. Successful organizations collaborate with their trading partners, blending functional groupings and firm boundaries to find the most effective solutions to a host of process issues. Process management along the supply chain thus improves the competitiveness of all participating organizations.

These and other related process management topics will be addressed in detail in this and other chapters in the textbook. While some of the topics may appear similar to those found in many Operations Management texts, the differences come about from the collaborative or integrative nature of supply chain process management. This chapter presents the foundation for the remainder of the text, leading the reader through short discussions of the topics comprising the remaining chapters in the textbook.

Processes and Process Management Defined

Our individual and work lives are filled with **processes** that need to be managed, from getting up in the morning, getting the kids off to school, and arriving to work on time, to hiring the right individual for an open position, organizing a meeting, making products customers will buy, and delivering products to customers in a timely fashion. Many processes are trivial and require minimal time and effort to be managed, while others can be monumental, requiring significant effort and resources over a long period of time to be managed successfully. In this text, we will be concerned with processes linking businesses and their supply chain trading partners, and how these are managed.

Through the years, a number of themes have emerged for business processes: their management, analyses, and improvement. Thus, it is beneficial here to review several definitions to establish a common ground for discussion throughout the remainder of the text. Several business process definitions follow:

> • *"A network of activities performed by resources that transform inputs into outputs."* [3]

- *"A set of logically related tasks or activities performed to achieve a defined business outcome."*[4]
- *"The collection of activities and operations involved in transforming inputs, which are the physical facilities, materials, capital, equipment, people, and energy, into outputs, or the products and services."*[5]
- *"A collection of activities and decisions that produce an output for an internal or external customer."*[6]

As alluded to in the previous definitions and shown in Figure 1.1, a business process consists of a set of linked activities or elements designed and performed by internal and external suppliers to create valued goods, services, and decisions for internal and external customers. Collectively, these processes ARE the business and need to be managed. Process activities may be performed for instance by suppliers, employees, customers, manufacturing equipment, and computers. Processes may start small or large, formally or informally, and deliberately or naturally; they can also be successful or unsuccessful. Successful processes ultimately keep employees, stockholders, and customers satisfied, creating value for the firm and its products. Unsuccessful processes can be harmful to businesses and are either changed, retired, or left to create long-term problems or distractions. These sets of activities underlie every aspect of an organization, including top-level planning, communication, management of employees, and design of products, as well as the management of supply chain relationships.[7]

Process decisions must continually be made in organizations regarding, for example, which activities to perform in-house and which to outsource, the best mix of people and technology, how to change an existing assembly process when current quality levels are deteriorating, implementing a new service to accommodate customer requests, or determining how to reduce manufacturing costs to stay competitive. In today's business environment, materials, technologies, customer tastes, and competition change rapidly, causing demand to change and processes to become obsolete much faster than in years past. Thus, as processes are created within an organization, an emphasis on continuous process evaluation leading to **process improvement** or replacement must also be created, to maintain business success. Over the course of a typical workday, employees can be seen discussing overnight problems as they begin their workday, talking to suppliers about scheduled deliveries, observing quality measurements and comparing these to desired standards, resolving customer complaints, and mapping

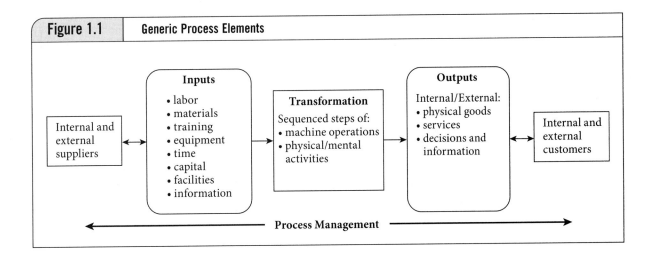

Figure 1.1 | **Generic Process Elements**

"Don't worry. We've worked out every
step of this process right up to the
point before you land."

out plans for a new product or service marketing campaign. All of these activities are, or are closely linked to, a business process.

It can also be seen from the discussion so far why the measurement of **productivity** (defined in very simple terms as outputs divided by inputs) plays such a large role in many organizations, as they seek to gauge process performance and keep the business competitive. The adage, "you can't improve what you can't measure" applies to the management of all business processes. In describing a firm's performance, it makes sense to monitor productivity, along with other performance measures, of many processes, by measuring the costs of process inputs and the value or quantity of process outputs. Monitoring processes in this way and using other performance measures allows managers to keep track of the firm's performance over time, and also provides clues as to where weaknesses lie in the organization. Performance measurement is thus a process management activity that can involve many constituents from both within and outside the organization.

Today, the term **business process management** (BPM) has become a wide-ranging business philosophy regarding design, analysis, and improvement of business processes. Journals such as the *Business Process Management Journal* are devoted entirely to this topic. In the business software industry, BPM is a very hot topic, and a number of software applications of BPM are available.[8] Adept managers realize that businesses are a collection of interrelated processes, and that managing core business processes effectively is paramount to long-term success.

Process Management and Supply Chain Management

Widespread and frequent changes in consumer demand, due in many cases to rapid technological changes and competitive pressures, have prompted organizations to move from a strictly internal focus on business processes to a more external sharing and coordination of key processes along the supply chain. This sharing or integration of business processes, beginning with a firm's primary goods and service suppliers and extending to the firm's most valued customers, allows each participant within the supply chain to learn the actual purchase plans of customers; to share new product design and development plans with suppliers; to jointly develop better ways to purchase, build, and deliver products; and to reduce stockout, inventory carrying, and delivery costs. With time, the integration of these key processes can also extend to second- and third-tier suppliers and customers, covering many participants within a product's supply chain.

Business process integration took on an even greater level of importance during the 1990s, as manufacturers changed their business practice from vertically integrated organizations to greater outsourcing of materials, parts, and services. Reengineering of existing products and processes and new approaches to product design and development also occurred. As a matter of fact, Hammer and Champy's book, *Reengineering the Corporation: A Manifesto for Business Revolution,* addressed the topic of **business process reengineering** (BPR), or the radical redesign of business processes to achieve improvements in cost, quality, and service, and actually became a best seller in the early 1990s.[9] Additionally, manufacturers greatly simplified product bills of materials and parts modularization, which helped simplify product and process design while decreasing inventory levels.

As the practice of **outsourcing** became widespread in many industries, the reliance on outside suppliers to lower product costs while providing high levels of service and product quality also grew, resulting in a greater emphasis on improving buyer-supplier relationships. Thus, organizations began to realize the importance and potential benefits of jointly managing business processes with their supply chain partners in order to improve quality, supplier responsiveness, and final product delivery to meet the needs of end customers at a reasonable cost. Outsourcing can also be troublesome, though, when companies give up control of core processes. Today, some companies are even buying back or redeveloping competencies that were earlier discontinued. For instance, in September 2004, J.P. Morgan announced it was terminating a seven-year technology outsourcing deal with IBM. It decided to take its tech services back because they were strategically too important to leave to an outsider.[10]

The integration of key business processes regarding the flow of materials from raw material suppliers to the final customer has developed into a concept known as **supply chain management**. Key business process integration is thus the essence of supply chain management. Today, companies are working harder than ever to integrate processes with suppliers and customers. Managing and coordinating these key business processes within a network of supply chain members requires a great deal of trust and cooperation. The Global Supply Chain Forum, a supply chain management research group at The Ohio State University, identified eight key processes that should be integrated across participants in a supply chain.[11] The following section presents and discusses in more detail these primary supply chain processes.

Eight Key Supply Chain Processes

Identifying which business processes should be jointly managed along the supply chain is an important issue. To achieve successful supply chain process integration and all of the associated benefits, supply chain partners must reach a shared understanding of the key supply chain processes. Table 1.1 lists the eight supply chain processes identified by The Global Supply Chain Forum, which form the foundation for much of this textbook. The processes are briefly discussed here.

Table 1.1	The Eight Key Supply Chain Processes	
PROCESS	**DESCRIPTION (CHAPTER)**	**ASSOCIATED ACTIVITIES**
Customer Relationship Management	Creating and maintaining customer relationships (3)	Identify and categorize key customers; tailor products and services to meet the needs of customer groups.
Customer Service Management	Interacting with customers to maintain customer satisfaction (4)	Manage product and service agreements with customers; design and implement customer response procedures.
Demand Management	Balancing customer demand with supply capabilities (5)	Forecast demand; plan or adjust capacity to meet demand; develop contingency plans for imbalances.
Order Fulfillment	Satisfying customer orders (11)	Design logistics network to deliver products on time.
Manufacturing Flow Management	Making products to satisfy target markets (7, 8, 9)	Design manufacturing and service processes to create products customers want; determine process flexibility.
Supplier Relationship Management	Creating and maintaining supplier relationships (12)	Identify key suppliers; establish formal relationships with key suppliers; further develop key suppliers.
Product Development and Commercialization	Develop new products frequently and get them to market effectively (2)	Develop sources for new ideas; develop cross-functional product teams, including customers and suppliers.
Returns Management	Manage product returns and disposal effectively (15)	Understand legal issues; develop guidelines for returns and disposal; develop returns network.

Source: The Global Supply Chain Forum, The Ohio State University, http://www.fisher.osu.edu/centers/scm.

Customer Relationship Management Process

This process provides the structure for creating and maintaining successful relationships with customers. Firms that know their customers, and understand which ones are the most important, can design strategies and assign resources to maximize value for these key customers and, in turn, maximize the firm's profitability. Two definitions of customer relationship management (CRM) are provided here:

- "The infrastructure that enables the delineation of and increase in customer value, and the correct means by which to motivate valuable customers to remain loyal—indeed to buy again." [12]
- "… an interactive process for achieving the optimum balance between corporate investments and the satisfaction of customer needs to generate the maximum profit." [13]

Based on these definitions, the general idea of CRM is thus to manage the firm's customer base so that customers remain satisfied and continue to purchase goods and services. Since customers are not all the same, firms must segment their customers and provide different sets of products and value-enhancing services to each segment to maximize long-term profitability. A successful CRM program is both simple and complex—it is simple in that it involves treating customers right and making them feel they are valued. It is complex in that it also means finding ways to identify the firm's customers and their needs, and then designing strategies such that all customer contact activities are geared towards creating customer satisfaction and loyalty. The customer relationship management process is covered in Chapter 3.

Customer Service Management Process

Today, customer service is often poor, and represents one area where organizations can create a significant competitive advantage, provided customer service processes are designed and managed correctly. The customer service management process provides the structure for delivering products and services to customers, and attending to customer needs. Appropriate response procedures are developed for common events, questions, or complaints. Information systems, software, and websites are designed to relay information to customers, and customer service employees are trained to provide information and services that customers want.

One customer service definition covers most of the subprocesses in customer service management; it is the "Seven R's Rule." [14] Providing the seven R's means having the *right* product, in the *right* quantity, in the *right* condition, at the *right* place, at the *right* time, for the *right* customer, at the *right* cost. A **perfect order** is one where all seven areas are satisfied. This definition can be applied to any business, product or service, and customer. Poor performance by the firm in any of the seven areas results in poor customer service. Consequently, competitive advantage can be created by routinely satisfying the seven R's. The customer service management process is covered in Chapter 4.

Demand Management Process

The demand management process seeks to balance customer demand with the firm's capacity. To accomplish this, the firm must use effective demand forecasting techniques, and then translate demand forecasts into the desired level of procurement, production, and distribution. Forecasts can be short- or long-term oriented, simple or complex, and qualitative or quantitative. To minimize forecast error, customers can share their planned future purchase quantities, actual sales data, or promotion and new product plans with their suppliers.

Today, systems such as **collaborative planning, forecasting, and replenishment** (CPFR) have become quite popular as a tool for reducing forecast error. The objective of CPFR is to optimize the supply chain by improving demand forecast accuracy; delivering the right product at the right time to the right location, and consequently reducing inventories across the supply chain; and avoiding stockouts while improving customer service. This can be achieved only if the trading partners are willing to work closely together and share information and risk through a common set of processes.

Demand management also involves developing contingency plans for the occasions when demand/capacity imbalances exist. Even when accurate forecasting and good capacity management techniques are used, there are still many occasions when these imbalances exist. Organizations can try to reduce demand during busy periods using several short-term demand management techniques. These include raising prices during busy periods to curtail or move excess demand to less busy periods, or segmenting demand to facilitate better service (for instance, express versus regular checkout counters).

Alternately, firms can try to stimulate demand through use of off-peak pricing and aggressive marketing campaigns. In manufacturing and service environments, firms can also adjust capacity by hiring or laying off employees and cross-training employees, and service providers may use customers to perform part or all of the service. Demand management process activities are covered in Chapter 5.

Order Fulfillment Process

The order fulfillment process provides for the delivery of products and services to customers, which requires the internal integration of marketing, manufacturing, and logistics such that customers get what they want, on time, at a competitive price. Successful firms know their customer requirements and have a good logistics network so that products are delivered where and when they are needed, at a low cost. The logistics network potentially consists of production and warehousing facilities, retailing facilities, suppliers, customers, and the transportation modes utilized by an organization. Facility sizes and locations, supplier and customer locations, and the various modes of transportation used all impact the ability to deliver products and services to customers.

Transportation, for instance, is what allows products to move from point of origin to point of consumption throughout the supply chain. For international supply chains, the transportation function is even more critical. Providing adequate transportation and storage, getting items through customs, delivering products to foreign locations in a timely fashion, and transportation pricing can all impact the ability of a firm and its supply chain to serve a foreign market competitively. In many cases, firms are forced to use outside agents or **third-party transportation services** to move items domestically or into foreign locations effectively. Supplier and customer locations impact where production facilities, warehouses, and retail facilities are located. Using foreign suppliers and entering foreign markets can greatly complicate the order fulfillment process. Frequent communication with customer relationship management and demand management functions is also necessary to ensure that capacities and facility locations are adequate to meet customer demand and that customer requirements are being met on a continuing basis. The order fulfillment process is covered in Chapter 11.

Flow Management Process

The flow management process is responsible for making the product or service and managing production inventories, customers, and information. This involves designing the manufacturing or service processes to achieve the desired flexibility to meet ever-changing customer requirements. Decisions here include how and where to store and move incoming and work-in-process materials, how to design and manage customer queues, how to schedule products and servers, the type of manufacturing or processing equipment to use, the level of technology to employ, and how and where to store finished goods. Aiding in all of these decisions is the use of information systems; thus, information flow is also included in the broad topic of flow management. Other issues impacting flow management decisions include personnel hiring and training, quality procedures, manufacturing postponement, outsourcing, environmental compliance, automation, product and service customization, reverse logistics, and customer service goals.

Decisions within the flow management process are coordinated with other internal processes such as customer service management, order fulfillment, and supplier relationship management. Firms, for instance, must know how long customers are willing to wait once an order is placed, and the level of product quality and customization desired. Manufacturing and customer processing requirements will also impact purchase order frequency and supplier selection. Flow management process activities are covered in Chapters 7, 8, and 9.

Supplier Relationship Management Process

Companies in all parts of the globe today are realizing the importance of developing win-win, long-term relationships with a relatively small number of key suppliers. It is critical that firms develop strong relationships and partnerships with suppliers based on a strategic perspective, and then manage these relationships to create value for all participants in the supply chain. These activities constitute the supplier relationship management process. Successful partnerships with key suppliers can contribute to product innovations, cost containment, and quality improvement, and have the potential to create long-term competitive advantage for the firm. Selecting the right supply partners and successfully managing these relationships over time is thus strategically important, and as it is often stated, "a firm is only as good as its suppliers."

Most firms operate with too many suppliers, and in fact, many newly employed supply managers and executives reduce supplier bases to increase leverage on the remaining suppliers, resulting in lower prices along with better quality and service levels. For example, in one of the most stunning corporate turnarounds in recent history, Mr. Carlos Ghosn, named CEO of Nissan Motor Co. in 2000, halved the number of suppliers and cut purchasing costs as part of the revival plan to return Nissan to profitability. Today, Nissan has overtaken Honda as the second biggest automaker in Japan, and leads all automakers worldwide, with an 11.1 percent operating margin.[15] In most cases, firms establish performance criteria to rank suppliers and then utilize the best suppliers while curtailing use of the suppliers that are not performing well. Other related activities include further developing key suppliers through training and knowledge sharing, developing compatible information systems, including supplier representatives on new product development teams, and use of key suppliers to develop second-tier suppliers. Suppliers are also typically evaluated on a periodic basis to achieve continuous improvements in cost, quality, and service. The supplier relationship management process and related activities are covered in Chapter 12.

Product Development and Commercialization Process

Designing and producing new products that customers want, and doing it frequently and efficiently, is a requirement for continued success in competitive industries. Product life cycles are constantly shortening as customers demand new products and better versions of old ones. The product development and commercialization process must maintain close contact with customer relationship management as a source for new product and product improvement ideas. Additionally, a manufacturing representative is typically involved in new product development, along with representatives of other internal functions, thus enabling **concurrent engineering**. In this way, designing the manufacturing process or service delivery system simultaneously with the design of the product enables firms to reduce new product development cycles, design the distribution infrastructure and marketing plans, and speed time to market. A new development in improving new product design is the simultaneous design of product, process, and supply chain, referred to as **three-dimensional concurrent engineering**.

Personnel from the product development and commercialization process frequently interact with suppliers to obtain feedback on materials and components used in new product designs, and with order fulfillment to discuss how new product introductions will likely impact the distribution system. Bringing marketing and customer relationship management into the design stage also enables the use of effective promotion strategies and existing marketing channels. The product development and commercialization process is covered in Chapter 2.

Returns Management Process

While often overlooked, managing product returns effectively can be a source of additional customer satisfaction and product improvement ideas. In many cases, proper disposal of product returns may also be a legal requirement. Close contact with product development and commercialization and manufacturing flow management is necessary to provide feedback from product returns due to quality defects and poor fit with customer expectations. Managing **reverse supply chains**, or the product returns process, is today becoming a significant concern. For example, product returns cost U.S. suppliers more than $100 billion in 2003. A case in point is the Home Shopping Network—it ships more than 32 million packages each year, of which 6.4 million are typically returned. [16]

In some cases, concentrating on the speed of the product returns process can help to maximize the possibilities for product reuse or resale. In other cases, centralizing the returns process can aid in reducing the cost of product returns. Finding the right product return strategy among supply chain participants is the objective of an effective reverse supply chain strategy. Retailers, for instance, can share product return and complaint data with manufacturers, with the aim of improving product offerings and customer satisfaction. Additionally, a number of third-party reverse supply chain service providers are available to assist firms in managing their product returns processes.

Another objective of returns management should be to ultimately reduce or eliminate product returns. The firm must therefore develop a performance measurement system to be used as a feedback mechanism, one that effectively tracks returns, warranty repairs, product dispositions, and customer complaints in areas such as operating and maintenance instructions. This information can be used to find and fix product and service problems. Product returns, complaints, and information requests typically come through the customer relationship management or customer service management processes.

Decisions within the product returns process include how to receive, inspect, process, dispose, and route a product return. Possible process actions include repairing, remanufacturing, recycling or reselling products, or disposing of products in an environmentally acceptable manner. The returns management process and related activities are covered in detail in Chapter 15.

In this section, we have attempted to illustrate the importance of supply chain processes and how they are typically integrated both internally and externally with other supply chain members. All processes and personnel interacting with the product must communicate and work together to maximize product value as products move along the supply chain. For example, purchasing must coordinate procurement plans with production planning, manufacturing, and marketing, and then interact with suppliers, warehousing, and transportation providers to ensure that supplies, components, services, and other purchased items are available when and where they are needed. Manufacturing interacts with product design personnel, capacity planners, salespeople, and logistics providers in order to deliver products on time to customers. When products are returned or repaired frequently, this information eventually makes its way back to product designers who make design changes, leading to manufacturing process changes. Compatible information and communication systems overlay all of these processes, allowing effective coordination activities to occur inside the firm and along the supply chain, until products are delivered to the end customer. Process management thus overlays the entire firm and all of its supply chain trading partners. Inventory management plays a significant role within a number of the key processes briefly described above, and this topic follows.

Inventory and Process Management

Inventory management is certainly one of the most critical activities of an organization and its supply chain, directly influencing how effectively supply chain trading partners produce and deliver goods and services. Inventories act as a buffer between all of the sources of demand and supply inside and outside the organization. Too much inventory is costly in terms of **inventory holding costs** (such as warehousing, material handling, shrinkage, obsolescence, labor, and capital costs), while too little inventory causes stockouts, which can be expensive in terms of lost productivity, lost sales, and lost future business. Ineffective communication between buyers and suppliers and infrequent delivery of materials, combined with production based on poor forecasts along a supply chain, results in either too little or too much inventory at various points of storage and consumption, also known as the **bullwhip effect**. Consequently, firms are forced to hold safety stocks of purchased items and finished goods to avoid stockouts.

Developing flexible production schedules and using integrated planning and control systems to meet delivery due dates while minimizing waste across the organization and its supply chains are indeed complex problems. Continued investments in better forecasting, scheduling, planning, and inventory management systems are occurring in many organizations to keep inventory costs under control while meeting the ever-expanding requirements of customers. Particularly among supply chain partners where close, interdependent relationships between buyers and suppliers exist, and where stockouts can create compounded problems downstream, meeting delivery due dates while minimizing inventory cost is a challenging problem. The e-Commerce Perspective feature profiles Ace Supply's use of a flexible e-catalogue to help it keep better control of its inventories.

Inventory management processes thus overlay all of the units and functions within the organization, its suppliers and customers, and other members of the supply chains where physical goods are purchased, stored, moved, or manufactured. These processes are typically classified as either independent demand or dependent demand inventory management processes. **Independent demand** is the external demand for finished products and replacement parts created by market conditions, whereas **dependent demand** is the internal demand for raw materials, parts, and components that are necessary for building finished products and supplying services.

Processes used to manage independent demand inventory include creating ordering policies, developing inventory review systems, classifying inventory by importance, and making safety stock determinations. Inventory management processes used for dependent demand include aggregate planning, master production scheduling, material requirements planning, lot sizing, scheduling and sequencing, distribution requirements planning, and enterprise resource planning. Inventory management processes and related activities are discussed in Chapter 6.

Lean Thinking and Process Management

The lean philosophy is much more than a process. It is, rather, a collection of processes and philosophies emphasizing the reduction of waste throughout a productive system, along with continuous improvement, and the synchronization of material flows within the organization and eventually including the organization's immediate

e-Commerce Perspective

Ace Supply's e-Catalogue Helps Manage Inventories

HVAC wholesale distributor, Ace Supply, based in Eagan, Minnesota, for years produced its own catalog using a word-processing application. It was a labor-intensive, time-consuming process, and because of that, the company only printed new catalogs once every couple of years. When Ace Supply began looking for a cost-effective way to improve the efficiency of its catalog process, the wholesaler determined that outsourcing wasn't the answer.

"There are many companies that offer catalog development for people, but they're costly and then you're constrained to that third party to compile your information into their catalog format," says Greg Vogel, technical and information services manager at Ace Supply. "Oftentimes they require you to provide all the materials and data you would like to have compiled. With that in mind, we figured that if we had to provide the data and information, we might as well find something that will let us compile the catalog ourselves, and display it in the media we wanted."

What the company found was Catalog Builder™ software from Computer Pundits Corp. It has been using this software for nearly five years now, which puts Ace Supply a step ahead of the pack when it comes to modern catalog design and distribution. Catalog Builder is a catalog management system for building, designing, and maintaining catalogs in-house. Pulling from a single database, Catalog Builder can be used to generate print catalogs, PDF files, and searchable CD-ROM and e-commerce catalogs. Ace Supply uses Catalog Builder to generate its own searchable digital catalogs (with hyperlinked Table of Contents) that customers can access 24/7 on the Ace Supply website or browse on CD.

Catalog Builder users construct their catalog database by importing information such as part numbers, product descriptions, pricing, and so on, from their inventory management system, then modify and expand on it as necessary with images, specifications, and even benefit statements if desired. Once this task is complete, users select the information they want displayed and choose fonts, colors, and other design elements to create the customized look and feel of their catalog.

The setup process is a one-time deal. All of the output formats—print, PDF, CD-ROM, e-commerce, whole catalogs, and minicatalogs—will be generated from this single database. Modifications and additions can be made continuously. And by synchronizing the database with the inventory management system using Catalog Builder's Update Feature, changes in pricing or availability are automatically updated.

According to Vogel, the ease of dealing with changes in list pricing has had the largest impact on the wholesaler's ability to provide customers with convenient access to up-to-date product information. "The No. 1 benefit to us at Ace Supply has been that when list prices change, I can update Catalog Builder and simply generate new catalogs on demand," he explains.

Source: Batham, P., "Keeping It Current," *Supply House Times,* V. 47, No. 8, 2004, pp. 92–93. Used with permission.

suppliers and customers. The primary topic of discussion within the lean philosophy is Just-In-Time (JIT). With JIT systems, supplies and assemblies are "pulled" through the system when and where they are needed. When problems are encountered, the process is stopped until the problem is solved. Because reductions in throughput time allow things to get where they need to be on time, JIT activities are all connected to this objective. JIT is an important aspect of supply chain management, since in effect supply chain management seeks to incorporate JIT elements across the entire supply chain to get products where they are needed on time, and at the desired quality and price. As stated recently by the vice president of freight management at Pennsylvania-based Penske Logistics, a logistics provider for firms such as PepsiCo, Inc., who require JIT deliveries, "In a JIT environment, leading-edge technology and optimized transportation are very important; but they are not the customer's number one requirements. The customer's primary concern above all else is having a provider that can flawlessly execute the process and deliver on time, every time."[17]

Many firms implement multiple JIT processes based on available resources, product requirements and production characteristics, customer needs, and supplier and logistics capabilities. Companies that have begun to implement JIT processes find it easier to expand these efforts over the long term into an effective supply chain management program. The Global Perspective feature profiles Delphi's JIT supply chain management system.

While Henry Ford initially used and discussed manufacturing activities that are today referred to as parts of the overall JIT philosophy,[18] Mr. Tai'ichi Ohno and several of his colleagues at Toyota are given credit for coining the terms Lean Production and Just-In-Time, and widely communicating the practices to other manufacturing organizations, beginning in the 1970s. JIT processes include a set of activities related to waste reduction (reducing excess inventories, scrap losses, and reworks, for instance), the creation of JIT partnerships with buyers and customers, the design of JIT layouts, the creation of JIT manufacturing schedules, the use of continuous improvement efforts, and gaining the commitment of workers. In many cases, implementing and refining these processes can be very time consuming, and a number of companies have given up on JIT because the touted benefits were not realized quickly enough. However, far more firms have experienced the significant value-enhancing benefits of JIT. These topics are discussed in Chapter 10.

Quality and Process Management

To ensure continued business success, firms must strive to offer better customer service and higher quality products and services to customers at competitive prices. Thus, managing and improving quality is a continuous effort in most competitive organizations. As with lean thinking, company-wide quality management and improvement (also termed **Total Quality Management** or TQM) is a philosophy encompassing a collection of processes that seek to assess and improve quality continuously to please customers, reduce costs, and, ultimately, create competitive advantage for the firm. It is also an integral part of all lean production programs, since continuous improvement methods refer to the use of TQM. Particularly when one considers that a primary objective of lean thinking is to deliver products at the desired level of quality, where and when they are needed, then the need for an effective TQM program becomes apparent. TQM also involves the coordinated efforts of the firm along with its supply chain partners, since incoming supply costs and quality ultimately impact products and services created by the firm and delivered to its immediate customers and ultimately, the end customer.

Most effective TQM programs employ a number of quantitative and philosophical or qualitative processes aimed at creating products and services that will please the customer. Although the list of people and their contributions are abbreviated here, the set of TQM processes have been collected from a number of people and organizations

Global Perspective

Delphi's JIT System

Delphi's Supply in Line Sequence (SILS) Center in the United Kingdom runs from the Vauxhall supplier park at Ellesmere Port, which was built to support a massive car plant producing the Astra and new Vectra. It not only builds and sequences its own assemblies, but also schedules and sequences products from other first-tier suppliers. It supplies 33 groups covering 3,400 part numbers, and employs 230 people. Products made in 85 locations are consolidated and sequenced through the SILS Center—the largest such operation in Europe.

Clearly, this approach gives Vauxhall a huge operational advantage in maintaining the leanness of its own operations. It deals with a single supplier taking complete responsibility for meeting Vauxhall's schedules over a huge range of products. By supplying components, subsystems, and modules to the line in the order they are needed, lineside storage is reduced by up to 20 times and Vauxhall is relieved of the complexities of replenishment.

Delphi simplifies logistics further by pre-configuring many of the other first-tier suppliers' products, including glass and exhaust systems, and generators and batteries (some of which Delphi makes itself).

So how does the supply chain work between the manufacturer, Delphi, and partner suppliers? Each morning, Vauxhall broadcasts to suppliers a ten-day indication of the planned vehicle build sequence. This allows Delphi to plan its own manufacturing and to send pick-up schedules to its suppliers. According to Graham Bell, Delphi's European director for marketing and planning, Delphi aims to share advanced notification with its suppliers at monthly intervals; this is refined into firmer numbers on a weekly basis.

Delphi is piloting a new web-based system to replace traditional methods like electronic data interchange (EDI)—it allows suppliers to receive order information from Delphi and confirm quantities and timings of dispatches over a standard web browser. When components arrive at the SILS Center, they go into short-term storage ready for sequencing or module assembly.

Vehicle specification is confirmed only as the finished body enters the assembly hall. From here, Delphi has only two to four hours to configure, sequence, and deliver the components, subsystems, and modules, in some cases holding under four hours' stock. Delphi handles line deliveries on special dollies and tracks work-in-progress. Replenishment signals come direct from operators on the line.

"We are trying to move towards the Japanese style that says, let's have our core suppliers as partners, with resident engineers from our suppliers in our technical centers working alongside our own engineers. As we identify issues up front, we can design them out rather than trying to manufacture around them or test them in when we go into production." This process has allowed the company to get its shipped quality tightly under control.

An operation so smooth and lean could have come out of a textbook.

Source: Gregory, A., "Chain of Fitness," *Works Management,* V. 56, No. 4, 2003, p. 24. Used with permission.

starting after World War II, including, for example, Walter Shewhart (statistical process control techniques), W. Edwards Deming (his Theory of Management), Philip Crosby (his book *Quality is Free),* Joseph Juran (his Quality Trilogy), and the U.S. Malcolm Baldrige Quality Award.

In order to improve processes, organizations must first assess process performance. Managers therefore identify processes that are critical to achieving quality objectives, determine how to monitor process performance, gather data and utilize the appropriate TQM tools, and finally, create policies for collecting process performance information and monitoring quality over time. Managers in world-class organizations also work to create a firm culture where quality improvements are encouraged and employees are empowered to make changes that will result in improved product and service quality. Quality and performance measurement topics are discussed in Chapters 13 and 14.

Business Process Management—Formalizing Process Improvement

Business process management (BPM) is a term used to describe a structured approach to process assessment and organizational improvement, typically involving the use of commercial software applications. This approach has gained momentum over the past ten years or so, as managers realize they must continually reassess and reinvent the organization to satisfy changing customer requirements and stay ahead of the competition, and as information technologies have been developed in this area. In a recent business executive survey, 85 percent of respondents indicated they would have a BPM solution underway within 18 months.[19] Additionally, information technology has made it much easier to communicate the necessary process information between internal functions and supply chain partners. The two definitions of BPM that follow will serve to clarify the term:

1. *"... a structured approach to analyze and continually improve fundamental activities such as manufacturing, marketing, communications and other major elements of a company's operation."*[20]
2. *"A systematic, structured approach to analyze, improve, control, and manage processes with the aim of improving the quality of products and services."*[21]

It thus can be seen that BPM looks at the entire organization and seeks significant improvements in how the work gets done. To make process improvement a reality, employees throughout the firm must work together and be empowered to examine, question, and change processes within the firm and between supply chain trading partners. Tools such as **benchmarking** are also commonly used to study how things are done well in other firms and potentially use the same methods. Other improvement tools are also commonly included in BPM programs, such as reengineering and Six Sigma.

The common theme throughout many BPM programs is that software applications are utilized, processes are selected, performances are monitored, problem areas are identified, solutions are generated and implemented, and finally, performances are again monitored to provide feedback on the process solutions so that refinements can be made, if needed. Initial process solutions often tend to be radical departures from the ways things were done in the past, and are significantly impacted by the firm's culture and its drivers for change. As mentioned earlier in this chapter, the radical rethinking of business processes has also been termed business process reengineering (BPR) and can involve the complete dissolution of some processes, along with the initialization of others. Several surveys have identified a number of drivers for change; these include globalization, changing technologies, business crises, the threat of future competition, and changing regulatory environments.[22]

Service Perspective	*American Suzuki Motor Corp.*

American Suzuki Motor Corp. serves its customers through a network of 1,700 dealerships in 49 states. Whether it's a motorbike, automobile, outboard engine, or any other Suzuki product, Suzuki's promise is the same: If there's a problem with the product during the warranty period, take it back to the dealer, and the dealer will fix it. It's good customer service, but it's also a hostage to fortune. If the dealer does a lousy job or takes too long to get Suzuki's approval to undertake a warranty repair, then it's Suzuki's name that suffers. But giving too much autonomy to dealers, to self-authorize repairs, for example, is like signing a blank check: Fix what you like, and just send Suzuki the bill. This potential combination of expensive repairs, tight sales margins, and requirements for rapid response form a particularly unholy trio.

It's a dilemma, and to resolve it, American Suzuki turned to a business intelligence solution from Hyperion. Called the Self-Authorization Project by American Suzuki, the solution feeds data relating to warranty claims into a server. Hyperion's software then analyzes and presents the results in a dashboard format.

Key metrics include warranty repair costs by vehicle and dealer, defects per vehicle, total claim analysis by region and district, duplicate repairs by vehicle (the number of times the same fault is fixed), and externally sourced customer satisfaction data. To gain self-authorization of warranty repairs, says Suzuki Data Warehouse Specialist Claire Ashby, a dealer must meet a certain number of criteria, including speed with which it undertakes repairs, accuracy and timeliness of its warranty billing process, and extent to which a fault stays fixed.

"It's not exactly the kind of dashboard that people were talking about a few years back, but it offers the same functionality," says Ashby. "It collects information, presents it on a single screen, and allows drill down for detail on specific issues." A traditional dashboard has all the needed information ready to go, concedes Srikant Gokulnatha, Hyperion director of product marketing and strategy. "The dashboard in use at Suzuki has a richer ability for drill downs, to see data in different contexts. It lets end users customize the data view based on their own requirements."

And the benefits are clear. Customer service improved, potential for overcharges was minimized, productivity of head office employees was boosted, and best of all, there's the prospect of increased market share. What's more, as Suzuki implements other projects, cross-analyses become possible. For example, explains Ashby, a subsequent project to monitor dealer performance permits Suzuki to look at underperforming dealers and examine how well their warranty claims have been processed.

Source: Wheatley, M., "Scorecards, Dashboards Are Two Different Things," *MSI*, V. 22, No. 9, 2004, p. 32. Used with permission.

To facilitate these initiatives, BPM and BPR software solutions have become popular as firms seek to monitor and improve specific processes, and then track changes to these processes. As shown in the Service Perspective feature, American Suzuki uses BPM software developed by Hyperion to monitor the warranty repairs process at its 1,700 U.S. dealerships. Many other BPM applications have also been developed for various industries. For example, BPM software is available for the airline industry to help airlines detect less profitable bookings, reduce overbookings, and increase passenger loads.[23] Electronic banking services use BPM solutions that offer information reporting and payments and collection capabilities, among other services.[24] Government agencies in the United States are also beginning to embrace BPM to deliver services electronically, in response to pressures from the Government Paperwork Reduction Act and the Freedom of Information Act.[25] Finally, BPM solutions are available to assist companies with their make-versus-buy decisions in the areas of network, data, product development, product maintenance, and customer support.[26] These are just a few examples of the many process management software tools available today. Business process management and business process reengineering is discussed in detail in Chapters 9 and 14.

Measuring Process Performance

The overarching objective in process management is to achieve successful process outcomes, be it the creation of products and services that customers want and find useful; the hiring of the right personnel; making decisions that effectively solve problems; or successfully repairing, returning, or recycling products. When processes do not achieve the intended outcomes, managers and users want to be notified, so redesigns, repairs, or rethinking can occur to fix problems or otherwise get processes back to desired performance levels. To accomplish this, performance measurement systems must be in place to continually test or monitor process outputs and compare them to desired outcomes or standards. When managing supply chains, process performance can be greatly complicated by things such as the geographic distance between trading partners, the number of times materials or products change hands, processing variations, the differing goals of trading partners, and the information that must pass between various organizations when moving parts and products among supply chain partners.

Several points must be considered when designing effective performance measurements:[27]

1. Link measures to the firm's vision and goals—measures should support firm goals and tie process improvements to things the firm cares about.

2. Measure what customers care about—performance measures can help to translate customer requirements into product and process characteristics.

3. Output isn't everything—performance measures should also monitor the quality, cost, and timing of outputs along with the volume to get a complete picture of a process.

4. Effectiveness trumps efficiency—similar to point 3, measurement systems should be concerned with process methods, or the way things are done, rather than simply how much or how often something is done. For example, monitoring and rewarding table turnover per shift for restaurant servers encourages servers to hurry customers to finish their meals, which may send the wrong message to customers.

5. More measurements are better—to get a complete picture of process performance, organizations should be monitoring a suite of measures, all linked to organizational goals.

Like business process management, another set of activities gaining in popularity is **business performance management**, the "other" BPM. Business performance management refers to a formal set of process analytic activities supported by information technologies that address financial and operational performance. Recently, a group of suppliers, consultants, and analysts formed the BPM Standards Group to accelerate the adoption of successful performance measurement projects and to establish performance standards in a number of industries. Tom Akright of St. Louis, Missouri–based Nestlé Purina, says they are already seeing the benefits of its BPM program. The company recently went from the bottom third of the American Customer Satisfaction Index ranking of companies in its industry to number one. And it ranks among the best in its market segment in processes like order entry and accounts payable. It has also been named Wal-Mart's "Vendor of the Year" for three consecutive years.[28] These and other performance measurement topics are discussed in Chapters 13, 14, and 15.

Trends in Process Management

In order to find new customers, continually please existing customers, and maintain or improve competitiveness, organizations are always on the lookout for new and better ways to plan, design, implement, integrate, and improve processes. These topics are discussed in the textbook's final chapter, which can be found on the CD accompanying the text. For firms actively managing their supply chains, coordinating and integrating key processes is particularly important for long-term success. Today, more and more business between supply chain partners is being conducted in cyberspace, using software applications with increasing levels of functionality. However, this virtual supply chain creates problems in areas such as security and remote access by internal users, third-party service providers, and supply chain partners. Coordinating customer-facing processes with supplier-facing processes can also be a challenge, particularly in a volatile demand environment such as seasonal products, or when selling complex, make-to-order custom products. In his research, Radjou discusses the use of **composite processes**, or technology-enabled, cross-organizational process flows designed to share and act on changes in demand.[29] Composite processes thus facilitate integration efforts along the supply chain. Typically, a composite process is activated by a customer activity, such as the receipt of a request for quote (RFQ) or a product complaint. In the case of an RFQ, the manufacturer can check for availability of the parts or products requested, submit purchase orders to suppliers for the unavailable parts, generate a price quote for the job, and then submit it to the customer, all in a matter of hours rather than days or weeks.

Several trends in process management include **business process outsourcing** (BPO); environmental, health, and safety factor concerns in the supply chain; use of **collaborative environments** (CEs); **automated decision systems**; and the use of **radio frequency identification** (RFID) tags and other technologies to manage processes and link physical products to the Internet. A number of years ago, process outsourcing concentrated on routine processes such as billing or collections, whereas today the trend is towards the outsourcing of processes that could be deemed strategic in nature, or core activities, such as in information systems management, purchasing, or human resources management. Offshore BPO is also becoming very popular, with India frequently being selected as the foreign destination.[30]

Environmental, health, and safety (EHS) managers are today collaborating with other functions within the firm and with supply chain partners to increase customer retention, revenue generation, cost reduction, and asset utilization. Leading companies realize the business value of EHS factors, and are taking advantage of the synergies between environmental excellence and supply chain excellence. EHS professionals today are moving beyond their traditional roles of ensuring environmental compliance and managing risks and are making contributions to profitability, resource productivity, innovation, and growth among supply chain partners.[31]

Collaborative environments allow two or more participants to communicate and coordinate processes to accomplish a shared objective. These environments use a combination of communication technologies such as instant messaging, email, chat rooms, mobile communicators, whiteboards, and web conferencing capabilities. As organizations and supply chains grow and encompass more global regions and greater numbers of trading partners, and particularly as travel budgets shrink and concerns for safety increase, the need for collaborative environments increases. For example, in the New York offices of IBM, email and Internet servers were taken down during the blackout of 2003, which disrupted 50 million people in the eastern United States and Canada; however, employees were still able to communicate with colleagues on IBM's Sametime® instant messaging technology. [32]

Automated decision systems combine artificial intelligence and decision support systems. These systems typically make actual decisions in real time, often without any human intervention, after analyzing data from other inputs for a particular customer or situation. Some have referred to these systems as "smart BPM systems." Some examples of decisions made by automated decision systems include what price to charge a hotel or airline customer, whether a loan or insurance policy should be approved, or how a delivery truck can be rerouted. These are decisions that are typically made frequently and require quick turnaround, and are used across a variety of industries. LendingTree.com, for example, uses automated decision systems to decide which participating banks are most likely to issue a loan, and then to propose four loan deals that customers can consider. [33]

Radio frequency identification (RFID) technology enables a device to read data stored on chips at a distance, without requiring line-of-sight scanning. While this technology has existed for quite some time, recent cost decreases, technology advances that have greatly reduced their size, and requirements for their use by large customers such as Wal-Mart and Albertsons have enabled many supply chain participants to start thinking about or testing the use of RFID tags. The potential benefits include greater product visibility across the supply chain, better inventory management, easier product tracing and recalls, and reduced product tampering. Some of the problems facing this technology include the design of RFID tags and readers that will work well under variable environmental conditions, conflicts with other sources of wireless transmissions, and the lack of a standard for transmission protocols. Getting the right data onto RFID tags in the first place and then deploying middleware to access or filter the data as products move along the supply chain is also a significant problem. As Jon Brendsel, VeriSign's director of electronic product code network services, says, "If I put a tag within the read field of an antenna, the reader reads it a couple hundred times a second. You need a middleware layer which knows that the first time it sees it, it's an event, and the next 10,000 times it's just garbage." [34]

Many firms today are also extending the Internet to link to physical assets, products, and devices. For example, Caterpillar uses MineStar®, a Global Positioning System that tracks the location and status of all Caterpillar machines in a mining site, allowing mining firms to prevent equipment failures and boost productivity. Michelin sells eTires, which allow commercial users to track air pressure and tire temperature, reducing downtime and increasing fuel efficiency. A survey in 2003 though, found that only 35 percent of those surveyed knew the identity of their physical assets and even fewer knew their physical assets' location or status. Further, almost half did not see the value in collecting asset data. [35] This attitude is bound to change soon though, as firms face growing pressure to provide capabilities for asset tracking. These and other topics are discussed in Chapter 16, which can be found on the CD accompanying the text.

SUMMARY

This chapter has introduced the concept of process management by first defining what processes are and then discussing how they are jointly managed within the firm and among supply chain trading partners. There are eight generally recognized supply chain processes which were introduced in this chapter. These processes form the foundation for the textbook, and are discussed fully in later chapters. Additionally, a number of other process management concepts were introduced and will be discussed throughout the text. Several trends in process management were also introduced. Along with introducing these process management activities and concepts, this chapter has attempted to explain the importance of collaborative process management and how firms can improve competitiveness through effective process management along their supply chains.

KEY TERMS

automated decision systems, 20

benchmarking, 17

bullwhip effect, 13

business performance management, 19

business process integration, 7

business process management, 6

business process outsourcing, 20

business process reengineering, 7

collaborative environments, 20

collaborative planning, forecasting, and replenishment, 9

composite processes, 20

concurrent engineering, 11

dependent demand, 13

independent demand, 13

inventory holding costs, 13

outsourcing, 7

perfect order, 9

processes, 4

process improvement, 5

productivity, 6

radio frequency identification, 20

reverse supply chains, 12

supply chain management, 7

third-party transportation services, 10

three-dimensional concurrent engineering, 11

Total Quality Management, 15

world-class businesses, 4

DISCUSSION QUESTIONS

1. What is a process? Define the term and provide an example.

2. What impact would effective process management have on costs? Profits? Productivity?

3. Define the term supply chain management, and discuss how collaborative process management can aid in the management of supply chains.

4. List and briefly describe the eight key supply chain processes.

5. Define bullwhip effect, and describe how process management can reduce the bullwhip effect.

6. Define independent and dependent demand.

7. What is lean thinking, and what does it have to do with process management?

8. Describe the JIT processes.

9. What are the TQM processes, and how is TQM related to lean thinking?

10. What is BPM, and how is it different from process management?

11. Describe BPR and the differences between BPM and BPR.

12. Why is it important to continually monitor process performance?

13. Describe the term business performance management.

14. List and describe three trends in process management.

INTERNET QUESTIONS

1. Go to the BPM Standards Group website and determine what the organization's goals are, who the founders were, and what types of activities they are doing now. Provide some examples.

2. Go to The Ohio State Global Supply Chain Forum website and discuss its research efforts with respect to the eight supply chain processes.

3. Search on the terms *BPM solutions* and *BPR solutions* and report on the number, types, and manufacturers of software available.

INFOTRAC QUESTIONS

Access http://www.infotrac-thomsonlearning.com to answer the following questions:

1. Use InfoTrac to search on the terms *Taiichi Ohno* and *Toyota Production System*. Write a term paper using your findings, and include a bibliography.

2. Using InfoTrac, write a paper on the value of effective process management, using business examples. Include a bibliography.

REFERENCES

McAdam, R. and D. McCormack, "Integrating Businesses for Global Alignment and Supply Chain Management," *Business Process Management Journal,* V. 7, No. 2, 2001, pp. 113–130.

Wisner, J., G. Leong, and K. Tan (2005), "*Principles of Supply Chain Management: A Balanced Approach,*" South-Western, Mason, OH.

ENDNOTES

1. Harbor, R., "Profit Comes from Product, Process Design," *Automotive Industries,* August 1, 2002, p. 2.

2. Business Editors, "BPMI.org Endorses Landmark Book 'Business Process Management: The Third Wave,'" *Business Wire,* November 13, 2002.

3. Anupindi, R., S. Chopra, S. Deshmukh, J. Van Mieghem, and E. Zemel, *Managing Business Process Flows,* Upper Saddle River, NJ: Prentice-Hall, 1999.

4. *APICS Dictionary,* 8th ed., Falls Church: American Production and Inventory Control Society, Inc., 1995.

5. Evans, J. and W. Lindsay, *The Management and Control of Quality,* 5th ed., Mason, OH: South-Western, 2002.

6. Devane, T., *Integrating Lean Six Sigma and High-Performance Organizations: Leading the Charge Toward Dramatic, Rapid, and Sustainable Improvement,* San Francisco: Pfeiffer (An Imprint of Wiley), 2004.

7. Smith, H. and P. Fingar, "The Humble Yet Mighty Business Process," *Darwin Magazine,* February 2003, pp. 1–4.

8. See for instance applications by HandySoft, QPR, Savvion, SmartDraw, and many others.

9. Hammer, M. and J. Champy, *Reengineering the Corporation: A Manifesto for Business Revolution,* New York: Harper Business, 1993.

10. Hamm, S., "Is Outsourcing on the Outs?" *Business Week,* October 4, 2004, p. 42.

11. Croxton, K., S. Garcia-Dastugue, D. Lambert, and D. Rogers, "The Supply Chain Management Processes," *International Journal of Logistics Management,* V. 12, No. 2, 2001, pp. 13–36.

12. Dychè, J., *The CRM Handbook: A Business Guide to Customer Relationship Management,* Upper Saddle River: Addison-Wesley, 2002.

13. Shaw, R., "CRM Definitions – Defining Customer Relationship Marketing and Management," appearing in *Customer Relationship Management,* edited by SCN Education B.V., the HOTT Guide Series, The Netherlands, 2001.

14. Shaprio, R. D. and J. L. Heskett, *Logistics Strategy: Cases and Concepts,* St. Paul, MN: West Publishing Co., 1985.

15. Bremner, B., G. Edmondson, C. Dawson, D. Welch, and K. Kerwin, "Nissan's Boss: Carlos Ghosn Saved Japan's No. 2 Carmaker. Now He's Taking on the World," *Business Week,* October 4, 2004.

16. Morton, R., "Return to Sender," *Logistics Today,* V. 44, No. 11, 2003, p. 33.

17. Moyer, L. and P. Burnson, "Pepsi-Penske Partnership Satisfies Consumer Demand," *World Trade,* V. 16, No. 9, 2003, p. 42.

18. Ford, H. and S. Crowther, *My Life and Work,* Garden City, NY: Garden City Publishing, 1922.

19. Surmacz, J., "BPM May Push Excel Aside," *Darwin Magazine,* September 17, 2003.

20. Zairi, M., "Business Process Management: A Boundaryless Approach to Modern Competitiveness," *Business Process Re-Engineering & Management Journal,* V. 3, No. 1, 1997, pp. 64–80.

21. Elzinga, D., T. Horak, L. Chung-Yee, and C. Bruner, "Business Process Management: Survey and Methodology," *IEEE Transactions on Engineering Management,* V. 24, No. 2, 1995, pp. 119–128.

22. Armistead, C., S. Machin, and J. Pritchard, "Approaches to Business Process Management,"4th International Conference of the European Operations Management Association, 1997, Barcelona, Spain; Hill, F. and L. Collins, "The Positioning of BPR and TQM in Long-Term Organizational Change Strategies," *The TQM Magazine,* V. 10, No. 6, 1998, pp. 438–446.

23. Kontzer, T., "Sabre Deals for Better Tools," *InformationWeek,* October 11, 2004, pp. 15–16.

24. "Recent Rollouts," *Bank Systems & Technology,* V. 41, No. 9, 2004, p. 50.

25. Editors, "Aberdeen Group: Business Process Management Is the Key to Efficient Government," *Business Wire,* March 25, 2002.

26. "Caneum Closes up 13.64% to Close at $2.50 After Research Enrollment," *Financial Wire,* September 30, 2004, p. 1.

27. Drickhamer, D., "Don't Fool Yourself with Metrics," *Industry Week,* V. 253, No. 10, 2004, p. 85.

28. Violino, B., "Getting Better All the Time," *Optimize,* May 2004, pp. 110–113.

29. Radjou, N., "A New Way to Balance Demand and Supply," *Supply Chain Management Review,* V. 8, No. 5, 2004, pp. 26–35.

30. Barnes, P., "Good Going," *Financial Management,* October 2004, pp. 31–32.

31. Fiksel, J., D. Lambert, L. Artman, J. Harris, and H. Share, "The New Supply Chain Edge," *Supply Chain Management Review,* V. 8, No. 5, 2004, pp. 50–60.

32. Fontaine, M., S. Parise, and D. Miller, "Collaborative Environments: An Effective Tool for Transforming Business Processes," *Ivey Business Journal Online,* May/June 2004, pp. 1–7.

33. Davenport, T., "Decision Evolution: Automated Systems Are Helping Businesses Make Decisions More Productively and Consistently," *CIO,* V. 18, No. 1, 2004, pp. 1–5.

34. Margulius, D., "The Rush to RFID," *InfoWorld,* V. 26, No. 15, 2004, pp. 36–41.

35. Radjou, N., "The X Internet Invigorates Supply Chains," *Industrial Management,* V. 46, No. 1, 2004, pp. 13–18.

Chapter 2:

NEW PRODUCT DEVELOPMENT—CREATING ORDER WINNERS

"Design is not the province of engineering, not even of engineering and manufacturing jointly. Instead, representatives of every stage in a product's life cycle, from materials employed in its manufacture to its ultimate disposal, participate in setting its design specifications."[1]

"The manufacturer is creating an environment where the supply chain plays a greater role in the design and innovation of the product."[2]

Learning Objectives

After completing this chapter, you should be able to:

- Describe the product development process.
- Understand the quality function deployment process.
- Define integrated product development and concurrent engineering.
- Describe technology advances in new product development.
- Understand the role of suppliers in new product development.
- Describe the fit between product development and process development.
- Know the four basic process designs.
- Understand mass customization.
- Perform a break-even analysis.
- Describe the trends in service design.
- Understand the enablers of good product and service design.

Chapter Outline

Process Management in Action
Building Better Diesels

Over the past decade, as diesel engines have grown in popularity, competition between manufacturers of midrange diesels powering larger pickup trucks, vans, and sport utility vehicles has heated up considerably, with diesels chosen as an option by nearly half of buyers who purchase vehicles rated at 8500 lb (3825 kg) and higher.

To meet tough federal EPA emissions standards and maintain its position as a leading designer and manufacturer of midrange diesels, International Truck and Engine Corp. (Warrenville, Illinois) embarked upon a multiyear program to lower emissions and improve fuel economy. In 1994, the company introduced its Next Generation Diesel (NGD) engine program that brought International's low-pressure common rail fuel system technology to the market. International developed the 7.3-L V-8 diesel engine used for International vehicles and for Ford Motor Co. (Dearborn, Michigan), which sells the engine under the Power Stroke® Diesel brand name for the Ford F-Series Super Duty pickup trucks, Econoline vans, and Excursion SUVs. More recently, International began work on its Next Generation Diesel II (NGD II) program to deliver new V-6 and V-8 midrange diesel engines that will allow the diesel engine and vehicle manufacturer to expand into new markets. The new V-8 is used in International's medium trucks, and it will be offered in Ford's 2003 F-Series Super Duty pickup trucks and the Excursion model.

Refining manufacturing engineering and process design enabled International's Engine Group to achieve an industry-leading average machine uptime level of 85 percent, a cornerstone to meeting the company's production and financial goals. Specific operational objectives included continuous improvement of customer satisfaction, increased machining and assembly uptime, maximized use of work-hours, quality improvements, and simplification of products and processes. Management also determined that the group's machining operations would focus only on those parts over which it had specialized expertise: crankcases, cylinder heads, camshafts, crankshafts, and connecting rods.

Maintaining flexibility would be key to the company's success. The new engine program had to adapt the plant's layout to allow for a completely new assembly system, two new connecting rod lines, new block and cylinder head machining systems, and for reconfiguring the crankshaft and camshaft lines to accommodate the new 6.0-L engine design. This had to occur while continuing to produce current model engines at near-record levels. The Indianapolis plant's new layout improves its two-shift, straight-time capacity level to about 250,000 engines a year while adding improvements in quality, efficiency, and cost.

Involving suppliers early on during engineering changes marks International's corporate culture, according to its managers, and the built-in flexibility designed into the systems made the Indianapolis plant's updates all the easier. Simultaneous engineering and using single-source suppliers also played an important role in achieving International's desired results.

A third-party logistics company handles much of the plant's inventory, enabling the plant to trim inventory, reduce costs, and free up valuable space to accommodate the new engine program. In 1998, the plant turned inventory over just 23 times annually, and by 2002 the facility reached a rate of 63 inventory turns. To accomplish its goal of 82 inventory turns, the plant worked closely with suppliers and carriers to develop daily deliveries, instead of weekly deliveries, and one local supplier is now delivering three times a day to the plant. In addition, the plant uses a strategy referred to as routes, or sweeps. Carriers make stops at multiple suppliers in the same geographic area, pick up quantities of material on a daily basis, and then deliver the material to a Materials Distribution Interface (MDI), a third-party logistics center located less than five miles from the plant, enabling it to minimize freight costs and inventory.

At the MDI center, material is consolidated into smaller shipments and delivered to the plant at multiple times during the day. This strategy improves the plant's profitability because suppliers own the material until it is delivered from the MDI to the plant's 32 docks, and the process resulted in a 60 percent decrease in standard order-to-shipment lead time.

Introduction

Developing new or redesigned products and services quickly is a source of competitive advantage for many firms. In fact, in many industries at least 40 percent of revenues are generated from products introduced in the previous year. Innovative companies that are first in the marketplace are known to generate high revenue streams initially and edge out their competitors. However, an organization must be able to take a customer's "must haves" and desires and integrate these criteria into its products and services. Customers are increasingly demanding better quality and reliability in new products.

The product development process is complex because firms must also consider many things including the cost of design and production, supply and distribution channels, and quality goals, as described in "Building Better Diesels." What processes do some firms have in place that give them an edge over their competitors? The most successful have a number of practices in place, starting with an effective new product development process.

To remain competitive, however, companies are under increasing pressure to come up with innovative designs and then adapt those designs to foreign markets. Companies must understand not only their local markets, but how new products can be adapted in other countries. Take, for example, General Motors (GM), which has consolidated new product development to save money but must create designs that will meet local needs and desires. More about GM's challenges can be found in the Global Perspective feature.

Improvements in technology to aid the product and process design process are also being developed at a rapid pace. Software is now available to enable concurrent engineering, design for manufacturing and assembly, and early supplier involvement in the product development process.

These developments make for an exciting but demanding time for those involved in designing new products and services. These topics and more will be discussed in the following sections to further understand the new product development process. The chapter begins with a discussion of the process to develop new products.

General Motors (GM) is the largest car maker in the world, manufacturing more than 9 million cars annually in 33 countries. With a company this size, meeting demand and managing capacity can be difficult challenges. For example, while GM lost more than $3 billion in 2005, more than half its sales came from outside the United States, where it sold its second highest volume of cars. In 2006 the automaker was unable to keep up with demand in central and eastern Europe and was seeking to buy an old Daewoo Romania plant to add 200,000 units of annual capacity for its line of entry-level vehicles.

Meeting the needs of customers with different needs in 33 countries is also a challenge. In the past, GM was extremely decentralized, with redundant designs and divisions competed against each other, and with costly results. For instance, in Europe it had designed the Saab 9-3 convertible. However, manufacturing was unable to use the same convertible top previously developed for the Pontiac G6 because design specifications were different. The differences also caused problems because the Saab's convertible top could not be built using production equipment at GM's U.S. plants.

In the past two years, GM has been revamping its methods to handle global production, which has been the same for many years. The automaker has consolidated new product development into six design and engineering centers across its four global regions of North America, Europe, Asia Pacific, and Latin America/Africa/Middle East. Each center will be managed by a senior executive that will have autonomy over the program, within GM specifications. The company's goal is to reduce the number of product architectures (the number of models) by half, thereby reducing cots. Thus, GM is looking for ways to share designs across markets, and rename the same product from market to market. This approach is expected to save GM money on components, cut product development and prototyping costs, and cut specific vehicle program costs. To keep costs down, any variation in product specifications from preset standards will have to be approved by GM's Automotive Product Board. The question is whether the new approach will meet customer desires. However, the focus appears to be on cost savings.

GM's vice president for global program management, Jon Lauckner, has said the company has already realized savings on the next generation of mid-size cars because it has eliminated engineering and manufacturing costs due to duplication of design efforts and the need for new plants and tooling. Robert Kruse, executive director of vehicle integration, says the company estimates a $1 billion savings alone for the line of mid-size cars.

Sources: GM 2005 Annual Report; Hamprecht, H., "GM Wants to Buy Romanian Plant; Automaker Seeks More Capacity in East to Build Chevrolets," *Automotive News Europe,* July 24, 2006, p. 3; Chappell, L., "GM Expects Big Development Savings," *Automotive News,* August 8, 2006, p. 3; Stein, J., "GM Launches Global Product Plan; Automaker Wants to Standardize Designs, Engineering," *Automotive News Europe,* October 3, 2005, p. 24.

The New Product Development Process

There are several stages in the product design and development process, as shown in Figure 2.1. Typically, multiple functions within an organization are involved in the development and launching of new products and services, including design engineers,

Figure 2.1	New Product Development Process

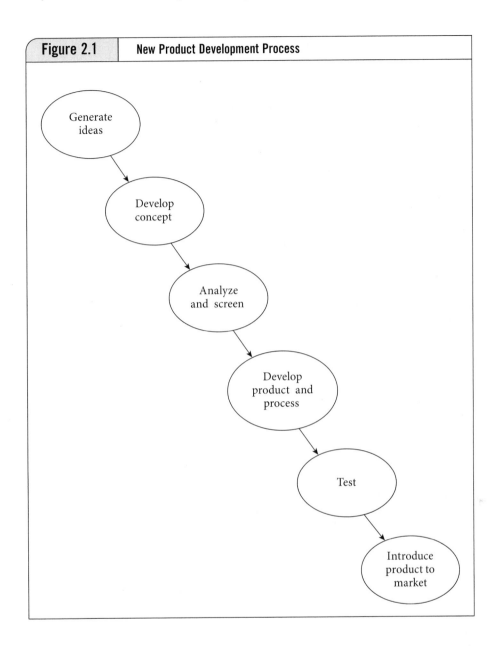

marketing, finance, and manufacturing or service operations. The process begins with the generation of a new product idea or redesign of an existing product.

Generating Product Ideas

Many manufacturing organizations and some service providers have research and development teams devoted to what's known as **basic research**—finding ways to increase the number of product innovations and then converting that research into commercial applications. For example, McDonald's Corporation, the leading global foodservice retailer, operates a test kitchen to develop new product ideas for its stores around the world. Research and development may also be outsourced to independent companies such as IDEO, a U.S. firm headquartered in Palo Alto, California, which designed such products as the Oral-B® toothbrush for kids and stand-up toothpaste for Crest®.[3]

Employees are also a good source of ideas. 3-M, a Minnesota–based diversified technology company, actively encourages its employees to offer new product suggestions. Other companies utilize **skunkworks** to develop new products. Skunkworks are teams that develop new products, usually in a short timeframe, outside the normal rules of an organization.[4] Teams consist of a small group of experts that may develop new technologies or applications that will be used later to further develop new products in a more traditional manner. These projects may be done in secrecy or without the support of top management, although the team normally has the unwritten approval of its immediate managers. Maryland-based Lockheed Martin Corporation, famous for designing aeronautics and space systems, was contracted to develop a 12-seat supersonic jet for Supersonic Aerospace International using its skunkworks team concept.[5]

Lastly, ideas for new products and services may also develop through contact with other sources, such as business customers, consumers, and suppliers. These ideas may surface as salespeople develop working relationships with their business clients. Marketing also spends time gleaning information through focus groups and surveys. Some organizations form **kaizen investigative teams** to get at the true needs and wants of the customer.[6] The word *kaizen* is Japanese for continuous improvement. These cross-functional teams visit customer sites, observing the customer using its products and asking lots of questions. Insights from these visits are used to discover unmet customer needs that may not have been verbally communicated. As organizations work more closely with their suppliers, ideas for new product components or the redesign of existing components that will increase quality or innovation often emerge during exchanges and meetings. Whatever the source, ideas should initially be screened based on the organization's manufacturing or service mission, strategy, and objectives.

Developing the Concept

If an idea appears to be a good "fit" with a company's strategy, mission, objectives, and financial capabilities, it is further developed. As you have probably figured out by now, determining what customers really want and then translating that into product/service technical requirements that are meaningful to the designers and producers is a difficult process. Traditional methods have focused more on the capabilities of the design engineers and less on the customer. However, one technique developed in the 1960s and commonly used in manufacturing today is **quality function deployment** (QFD), which helps with planning and communication among those involved in the design process. Companies must be customer-focused for this process to work successfully. Many companies use QFD, including Ford, Procter & Gamble, AT&T, 3M, and Hewlett-Packard. The steps in QFD include:

1. Develop a list of high-level product requirements or technical characteristics derived from surveys of customer needs.

2. Determine the product concepts to satisfy these requirements, and select the ones that will benefit the customer the most.

3. Benchmark competitors to compare the performance and desirability of competitors' products.

4. Translate customer requirements into measurable engineering requirements.

5. Develop engineering targets for the product design.

6. Partition the product concept into its subsystems or assemblies, and determine the product's technical requirements to each subsystem or assembly.

7. Derive assembly or part characteristics and specifications from subsystem/assembly requirements.

8. Develop the manufacturing process steps to meet these assembly or part characteristics.

9. Develop setup requirements, process controls, and quality controls to assure achievement of these critical assembly or part characteristics.

Customer needs are determined during the concept development stage where the design team begins by analyzing the research results collected from the customer in the form of focus groups, surveys, or on-site visits with business customers. The team then creates a document, called the **house of quality**, which is a series of tables assembled together that show the translation of customer requirements into the product attributes, the technical specifications (how the product will be built), an evaluation of how competitive the product will be, and a technical evaluation of the product against its competitors. At the top of the "house" is a "roof" that indicates the correlations between a product's technical requirements. Customer requirements must be translated into measurable design targets. For example, what does "easy to close" mean to the designers of a car door? Figure 2.2 illustrates a partially completed house of quality for a DVD player, which includes:

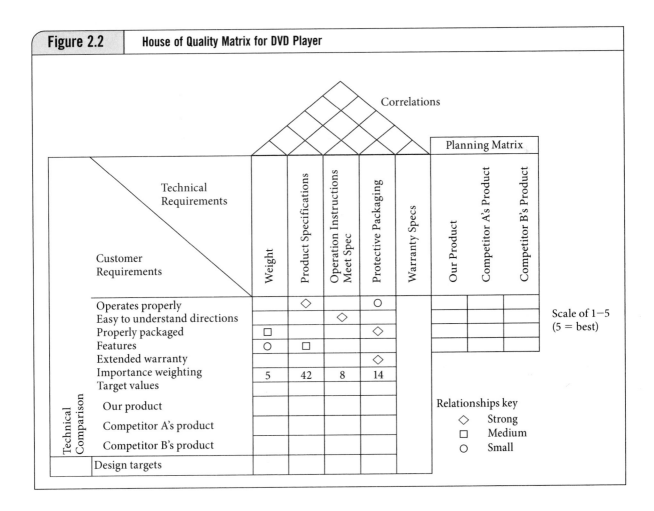

Figure 2.2   House of Quality Matrix for DVD Player

1. Rows, which indicate the quality demanded by the customer;

2. Columns, which show the technical characteristics and target values of the product;

3. An evaluation of the interrelationships between customer requirements and technical requirements;

4. A competitive assessment or planning matrix, found on the right side of the matrix; and a

5. Technical evaluation against competitors, which is at the bottom of the house.

Generally, a new product team starts with a house of quality to convert customer requirements into technical requirements. As shown in Figure 2.3, a **design matrix** is created to convert the technical requirements into the features of key product parts. These product features are then used to determine the process that will be used to manufacture these parts using an **operating matrix**. Finally, the characteristics of the manufacturing process are converted into more specific operational tasks and control procedures using a **control matrix**.

There are multiple benefits attributed to using a house of quality, including improved products, processes, and services. A house of quality also provides direction for

| Figure 2.3 | QFD Process |

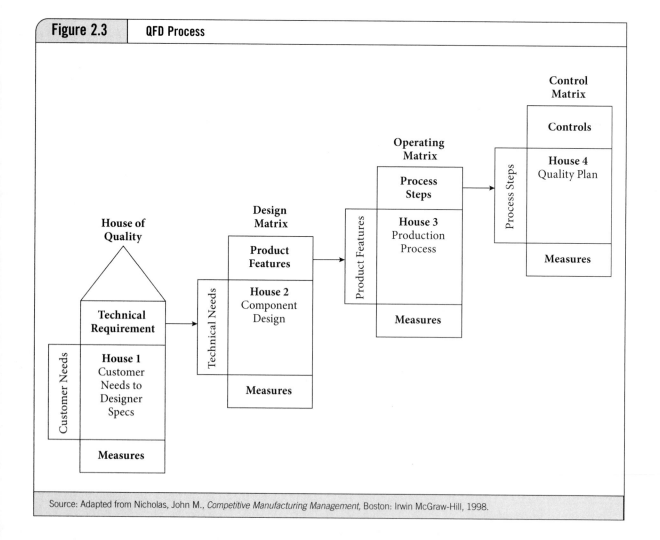

Source: Adapted from Nicholas, John M., *Competitive Manufacturing Management,* Boston: Irwin McGraw-Hill, 1998.

the design process and keeps teams focused. Management can easily do peer reviews of the design activities because they have a visual graphic of the design information. Lastly, the process to create the house of quality has been documented, which can be used if future product improvements are needed.[7]

GCC Rio Grande, a Mexican cement company with customers in New Mexico, Texas, and Arizona, used QFD to set itself apart from the competition. Traditionally the cement industry is riddled with price wars because cement is considered a commodity. GCC Rio Grande wanted to reinvent itself as a solutions provider and increase business through relationship-building with its customers and value-added services. The company determined, through site visits, the customers' unspoken needs as well as services that would prompt customers to buy from it. GCC Rio Grande then used the house of quality to translate product and service features into technical specifications. As a result of QFD, the company developed product training programs for its customers and customer support training programs for its employees. It also plans to develop a new line of cement products. Most importantly, it developed more loyal customers because it provided marketing and technical solutions.[8]

Product Screening

Once the product idea is more fully developed, a **business case** should be prepared for review and approval by a formal screening team for larger companies, or by the owner/president if the company is smaller. The business case, a written justification for approving the new product or service idea, is based on data collected with respect to the expected target market, any environmental constraints, projected market trends, a cost analysis, and projected profit. (More on cost analysis is covered later in this chapter in the section on break-even analysis.)

As shown in Table 2.1, many issues must be considered before the product or service idea moves to the next stage of development. The more complete the product concept—including the reasons why this new product or service is important along with its benefits to the customer—the greater the chance of success of moving to the next stage of the development process. Screeners will generally consider three basic issues: Is there a market for this product, will the company be competitively positioned to make a profit, and are the revenue and cost estimates realistic and acceptable?

Design Phase

If a project is authorized, it goes into a "design phase," where design engineers make up detailed drawings of the new product and develop prototypes, either with actual physical models or by using computer-aided design. Tests then are done to simulate the actual use of the product. This process, known as **design-build-test**, may be repeated more than once if the product doesn't stand up to performance specifications. At the same time, tools and equipment should be developed to support the production process, referred to earlier as part of concurrent engineering.

For service providers, the method of delivery, or **delivery system**, is developed at the same time as the new service concept because they really can't be separated. Customers are generally brought into the process for feedback on whether the new service idea (1) is easily understood, (2) will have a positive impact on them, (3) will provide some added benefit not experienced with other services, and (4) will generate sales revenue. Various pricing options may be tested at this time to determine the salability of the service.

Service blueprinting, a method similar to flowcharting, is often used to describe and evaluate a new or redesigned service process. A service blueprint visually distinguishes

Table 2.1	Screening Process Issues

Product Marketability
- Is there a need?
- Will customers buy this product?
- Can this product actually be made?
- What technologies will be required?
- Do we have the expertise in-house or a qualified supplier to make this product?

Product Competitiveness
- What are the product's competitive strengths?
- How are we going to compete? (price, performance, innovativeness, reliability)
- Can we sustain a competitive advantage?
- Is this product in line with our overall strategy?

Financial Considerations
- Do we have realistic sales, revenue, and cost estimates?
- Are product costs acceptable?
- Are development costs affordable and acceptable?
- What is our break-even point and is it acceptable?
- What is our expected return on investment and is it acceptable?
- What is our expected profit over the product's life cycle?

Source: Adapted from Crow, Kenneth, "Assessing the Feasibility of a New Product," retrieved November 4, 2004, from http://www.npd-solutions.com/feasibility.html.

between the activities of the service provider contact person and those that are "behind the scenes." Figure 2.4 provides an example of a typical experience at a fast-food restaurant, with each activity mapped on the service blueprint. Below the "line of visibility" are those activities unseen by the customer. A service blueprint can be the starting point for identifying and addressing potential problems in the delivery process. A more detailed discussion on service blueprinting can be found in Chapter 8.

Product Introduction

Pilot production occurs once the design-build-test phase is successfully completed. At this point, the product is produced on a limited basis to determine if full-scale production is possible. Once pilot production is complete, production is ramped up slowly until a consistent level of quality is maintained; then volumes are increased to a full-scale launch of the product.

Similarly, a new service is thoroughly tested and a marketing plan is developed and tested. A full-scale launch of the service takes place through introduction to the entire market. Generally, a post-launch review is important to decide if any adjustments are necessary.

Reducing New Product Development Cycle Time

Because of increased pressure from customers and competitors to rapidly introduce new products, a number of practices have been adopted by manufacturers. These are described in the following paragraphs.

Figure 2.4	Service Blueprint of a Fast-Food Restaurant

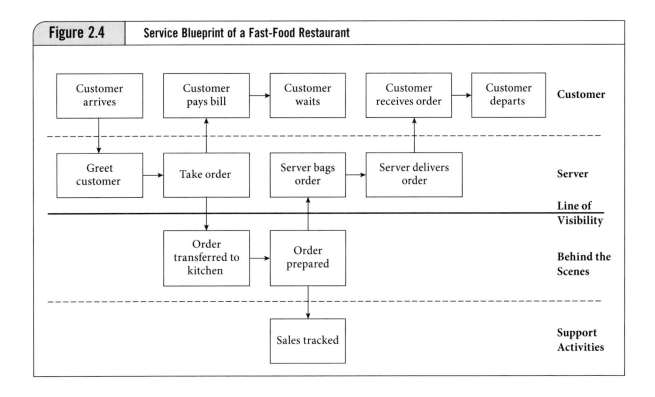

Integrated Product Development

Integrated product development is a practice based on the idea of simultaneously designing products and their manufacturing and support processes. It is a relatively new practice but has been found to shorten the design cycle time, increase company performance, and improve competitiveness. Also known as **concurrent engineering**, all involved parties—which may include engineering, marketing, operations, and supply management—work together from the beginning of a new product design project to ensure that quality, cost, marketing, and operational goals are met. As a result, the concerns of all interested parties are incorporated from the beginning of the process. The needs of the customers are also integrated into the process early, resulting in products that meet their needs but also are within the capability of manufacturing and its suppliers.

In the past, manufacturability, reliability, and supportability of the product were determined *after* the product had been designed. Changes were then made to the design to improve its competitiveness, once any feedback from market research was obtained. This approach was found to extend the design cycle time, which limited the number of new product introductions, and increased product development cost.

Since approximately 75 to 80 percent of the cost of a product is set during the design stage, it's important to get product designs right the first time. Integrated product development can reduce or eliminate design changes and product rework, as well as shorten the development process. Connecticut-based General Dynamics Electric Boat Corporation, developer and builder of modern submarines for the U.S. Navy, completely revamped its organizational structure and business processes to support concurrent engineering when it faced severely declining sales. As a result, design cycle time was reduced by 35 percent. Much of the reduction was due to fewer change orders during construction and elimination of much of the approval process for ship drawings by the Navy. For example, in the past only 5 percent of a new ship's drawings were completed prior to construction. Once concurrent engineering was in place, more than half of the drawings were completed prior to construction, reducing product costs attributed to change orders. The dramatic reduction in design cycle time was also possible because cross-functional teams were created to include the Navy. Because of the Navy's active role on the design/build team through involvement at team meetings and electronic access to design data, the need for approval of a new ship's drawings was reduced by about two-thirds. [9]

Concurrent engineering teams begin by developing a design of the product and its characteristics using input from stakeholders. A product functional analysis is performed, so that "how the product is supposed to work" is incorporated into the design. An agreed-upon list of common product priorities is also developed to keep the team on target. In contrast to traditional new product development, the process for manufacturing the product is determined concurrently with the product design. Any key suppliers that are designing major product components are involved from the start of the project.

Some companies have moved to the next level, called **three-dimensional concurrent engineering** (3-DCE), where the design of the product, process, and supply chain are considered simultaneously. [10] It has been argued that concurrent engineering is critical where time-to-market pressures are imperative. However, it is not enough to provide an organization with a sustainable competitive advantage. Supply chain design issues must be formally considered at the same time, or problems related to logistical support, quality control, and production costs will typically occur late in product development. Last-minute decisions tied to designing the supply chain place the organization in the reactive and costly position of fixing unanticipated problems as it is trying to introduce a new product. During the 1990s California-based Intel, for example, implemented 3-DCE by continually developing and launching new products based on new processes. The designer and manufacturer of chips, boards, systems, and software building blocks to the computing and communications industries then integrated supply chain design through its suppliers by fostering relationships with smaller start-up companies that could improve its processes and create a competitive advantage. [11]

Design for Manufacture and Assembly

When creating new products, design engineers and marketing personnel study the usability of the product. At the same time, manufacturing personnel become involved in the new product design process as they determine how production of a new product can be produced and controlled more easily, otherwise known as **design for manufacture and assembly** (DFMA). The types of materials to use, the means to shape and form materials, any machining processes, tooling changeovers, and quality control are some of the issues under consideration. DFMA calls for the current skills of the workforce and suppliers, as well as the capability of the existing processes, to be incorporated into the manufacturing process. However, one should not take precedence over the other.

The reduction in the number of parts used per product, through use of **modularity**, has been a result of the increased use of DFMA. The payoffs of modularity include working with fewer suppliers (translating to lower material costs), fewer inventory items (resulting in lower inventory carrying costs), fewer assembly steps (translating to lower labor costs), faster product assembly (equating to higher levels of productivity), and increased product reliability. Whirlpool Sweden used DFMA and lowered manufacturing costs considerably by reducing the number of parts of its microwave ovens and standardizing several parts. As a result, parts were reduced by 29 percent, assembly time was reduced by 26 percent, and cost savings were more than expected. [12]

Advances in Technology

Because multiple tasks are performed at the same time using integrated product development strategies, new advances in technology have made the process easier. **Computer-aided design** (CAD) is one software program that uses computer graphics to design component parts with great precision. Washington-based Boeing, for example, designed the Boeing 777 by integrating the wishes of passengers and airlines for the first time ever. Engineers relied entirely on the computer to virtually "assemble" and test the plane using CATIA, a 3-D CAD program. [13]

There are several advantages to using CAD. Copies of the product designs can be passed on to others involved in the new product development process, such as purchasing/supply management, suppliers, or marketing. These systems can also perform engineering analyses of product weight, part volumes, and stress tests. Multiple alternative designs can be compared quickly to determine the best one. As a result, designers are more productive and revised drawings are fewer.

DFMA software is also available to improve new product development. Deere & Company, the world's leading manufacturer of agricultural and forestry equipment based in Illinois, bought DFMA software in 2002 to reduce parts cost and improve the reliability of its products. [14] As a result, parts have been consolidated into better, multifunctional designs. Design engineers can also compare the cost of producing a new design to the costs of the old assembly processes. Lastly, engineers are able to use the software to select the most cost-efficient materials and processes.

New Product Development along the Supply Chain

Today the design of new products and services often extends beyond one organization to include business customers, suppliers, and consumers. The extent of involvement will depend, to a great extent, on an organization's strategy. In the case of business customer or consumer involvement, some companies take a **customer focus**, meaning that the customer drives all strategic marketing decisions. All dimensions of a new product offering are tested using customer feedback before introduction to the market. Marketing gathers consumer research through tools such as surveys, interviews, and focus groups to determine consumer preferences. For business customers, marketing may also visit the business customer's facilities to determine their needs, review past customer complaints, and analyze product quality performance reports. Products are then created and tested based on those preferences. Once the product is introduced into the market, the organization monitors customer satisfaction and makes any necessary adjustments.

However, some organizations take a **product focus**. This innovation strategy is based on the belief that the customer doesn't necessarily know what he or she wants, or what is available. Thus, these innovators develop products or services and then attempt to create a market for them. An argument for this approach is that if Thomas Edison had taken a customer focus, he would have simply made larger candles rather than design the light bulb. Bausch & Lomb, an eye health company based in New York, is well-known as an innovator. It introduced the first soft contact lens in 1973 and is constantly inventing new materials and engineering new technologies and processes to improve eyesight. [15]

More and more, manufacturers are also bringing suppliers into the design process as they increasingly outsource components and subassemblies, a form of early supplier involvement. Some reasons for this phenomenon include the potential for shorter product development times, more modularization, lower production costs, higher levels of quality, and access to the supplier's technological capabilities. Manufacturers today are focusing more on what they do best, which may no longer be manufacturing, but rather final assembly of the finished product or even "virtual" manufacturing where no direct involvement in the manufacturing process occurs. As costs have skyrocketed, manufacturers turn more and more to smaller manufacturers with nonunion workforces, or overseas suppliers with extremely low cost structures, to make at least part of the finished product. These trends make it fairly evident that the design of the supply chain becomes even more important. Thus, suppliers must be able to meet the manufacturer's varied requirements based in part on what the customer wants, and in part on what the designers think the customer wants.

This approach requires a great deal more integration and collaboration among trading partners and is especially visible today in the automotive, aerospace, and telecommunications industries. Caterpillar Inc., an Illinois manufacturer of construction and mining equipment, started integrating suppliers into its design process several years ago. Before, the company would design each part for a new product, and then hand over the part specifications to one of three contracted suppliers for production. Terry Gramlich, commodity manager at Caterpillar, says, "All three suppliers now look at the total (product) concept and they all have the simple objective of designing a system that will work." [16]

Companies are also forming strategic alliances, sharing information and colocating suppliers in their manufacturing plants to create innovative and competitive products. These changes, however, require a major shift in thinking. Key functions within the customer organization must "buy in" to supplier integration.

Suppliers may be involved at the planning, design, or production stages of new product development. Commonly referred to as **early supplier involvement**, the degree of supplier involvement at each of these stages will vary based on company cultures, supplier capability, the buyer-supplier relationship, the nature of the product, and competitive conditions. In some instances the supplier may simply be involved at the production stage and is given the complete design specifications to make the part. This is a common practice when the part is considered a commodity item. Suppliers may also be brought in at the product planning stage as a consultant to the project for their feedback but with no direct authority. A third level of involvement increases the supplier's responsibilities to a more formal level, where the supplier helps design, develop prototypes, and test the new product. Finally, suppliers may be given full responsibility to design and develop a component or module based on performance specifications developed by the customer. At this level, the customer and supplier have an excellent relationship and the customer knows the supplier's design will be a good fit into the finished product.

To determine the extent suppliers should be integrated into the design process, manufacturers generally develop a set of performance measures to assess the supplier's capabilities. [17] Important questions to consider include:

- Does the supplier have the necessary in-house expertise to meet the new product's performance requirements?

- Can the supplier meet performance targets in the areas of cost, quality, and delivery?
- Can the supplier meet new product development schedule deadlines?
- Does the supplier have the flexibility and capacity to meet production requirements?
- Does the supplier have the processes in place to meet the manufacturing requirements?

Companies including California-based Alventive, a product life cycle management software company, have created online software with a suite of products that support the early supplier involvement process. With Alventive's Design-to-Order Solution, for example, product design files can be developed and shared online in real time between a customer and its suppliers. As manufacturers receive design requests from their customers, they can also decide how much of the design to keep in-house and how much to bid out to one or more suppliers. [18]

Process Selection

As mentioned earlier in this chapter, the process used to manufacture a product or deliver a service should be designed at the same time the product is designed to gain optimal performance and reduce time to market. Organizations generally match the production process to the product based on two criteria:

- Expected level of output, and
- Variety of products or services the system will be expected to handle.

Higher levels of product and service variety can be found in more customized operations, although some companies may offer both high- and low-volume processes. For example, most banks offer ATM machines, which provide two or three services, but at a higher speed than standing in line and transacting with a live teller. Inside a bank, however, customers may take advantage of a full menu of services, including teller service, access to safe deposit boxes, new accounts, and loans, but at slower service speeds. Thus, as product and service variety increases, production speed or level of output will tend to decrease. With greater product variety, more general-purpose equipment will be used and employees will be more highly skilled with higher levels of education. As shown in Table 2.2, production processes can be separated into four general types:

1. **Job Shop.** Job shop processes are generally found in organizations offering custom products or services. Thus, volumes are low but flexibility in accommodating the customer is high. The workers are generally highly skilled operators of one or more pieces of equipment, and equipment used in the process is flexible. Custom furniture and printing jobs are two examples of products made in a job shop environment.

2. **Batch.** Batch processes are found in organizations where less customization is provided to customers than in a job shop environment. Some flexibility is needed but equipment is more specialized and automated than in a job shop. Workers are also less skilled than in a job shop setting. For example, banks that process customer checks and bakeries operate in a batch environment.

3. **Assembly Line.** Much higher volumes are generated on an assembly line than in a batch environment, with little flexibility. Equipment is dedicated to one or two

Table 2.2	Process Choices			
	JOB SHOP	**BATCH**	**ASSEMBLY LINE**	**CONTINUOUS**
Volume	Very low	Low–Medium	High	Very high
Product Variety	Very high	High	Low–Medium	Very low
Equipment Flexibility	Very high	Medium	Low	Very low
Employee Skills	Very high	Medium–High	Low	Low
Manufacturing Example	Tooling for manufacturing	Candy making	Auto assembly	Oil refinery
Service Example	Mortgage banking	Bank check processing	Cafeteria	No application

Source: Adapted from Hayes, R., and Wheelwright, S., *Restoring Our Competitive Edge: Competing Through Manufacturing*, New York: John Wiley and Sons, 1984, p. 209.

tasks and must have a high degree of precision. In general, workers can be trained easily because they are limited in their tasks and equipment is highly automated, but there are exceptions. For example, while automobile assembly and a cafeteria line require less employee training, surgeons require extensive education and training. However, all three are performed using an assembly line approach.

4. **Continuous Production.** In a continuous system, there is almost no variety and equipment is dedicated to one task. The labor force requirements are generally small and workers on the line can be easily trained. Utilities, such as phone service and electricity, are delivered on a continuous basis.

In developing a production process, service providers are also concerned about the trade-off between the efficiency or cost of the process and the ability to generate higher sales. Generally, service processes with low customer contact are very efficient but offer fewer opportunities to increase sales. As discussed in the Service Perspective feature, McDonald's has added self-service in the form of touch-screen order pads for customers. However, this process reduces the actual customer contact with an employee, who could make suggestions for additional purchases such as, "Would you like fries with your order?"

Mass Customization

Mass customization, the high volume production of customized products, was developed to reach worldwide markets. The idea was to create enough variety in a company's product line so that just about any consumer could find what they wanted at a reasonable price. Firms do this by postponing final production and delivery of those customized touches until the last minute. Vans Inc., an outdoor apparel and shoe retailer owned by VF Corporation, for example, lets customers design their shoes online, receiving their order in six weeks or less. The e-Commerce Perspective feature on page 42 provides an inside look at Vans' mass customization process. While fairly common in the service sector, manufacturers started adapting their production systems to mass customization around 1990. In the European automotive market alone, Mercedes-Benz, BMW, VW, and Renault expect to quadruple the number of car models currently offered, to 1700, by 2010 through mass customization.[19] In order to accomplish this, however, organizations must follow three general design principles.

Service Perspective

Customer-Driven Service at McDonald's

IDEO collaborated with McDonald's on the first generation of a new service system in its Lone Tree restaurant, south of Denver. The new system allows McDonald's customers to place their orders without assistance, providing improved flexibility, speed, accuracy, and convenience to both McDonald's customers as well as its crews. The system consists of touch-screen self-order kiosks at the front counter and in the children's PlayPlace area that have been fully integrated into the McDonald's physical environment, operational flow, and brand message.

Customers place their orders using an icon-based system and pay at the kiosk or at the pick-up counter. After placing their orders, customers pick up their food at the counter by showing the order number on their printed receipts. In the PlayPlace area, parents can place and pay for their orders while supervising their children. A McDonald's crew member then delivers the food to their table.

This new model needed to work within the popular and highly efficient system in use today. The completed design spanned the entire ordering experience and not just the kiosks themselves. The team updated the restaurant's graphics, signage, counters, and crew uniforms, and created nine self-order kiosks with a fully developed icon-based menu system. All design elements plus the in-store layout of the new service experience were arranged to complement the traditional experience of ordering at the counter.

The work began with a national survey of all kinds of quick-serve and self-serve experiences and distilled behavioral patterns of McDonald's customers to guide the design work. Since its launch and after thousands of transactions, the new service has had a high customer adoption rate with virtually no lines.

Source: "Customer-Driven Service for McDonalds," retrieved on October 21, 2004, from http://www.ideo.com. Reprinted with permission.

First, products must consist of independent modules that can be assembled in multiple configurations without too much trouble and at a low cost. Wisconsin-based direct merchant Lands' End, for example, has teamed with Archetype Solutions Inc., a software provider, to offer custom-fit chinos through its online catalog. U.S.-based customers can select their style and fit preferences, enter details about their body shape, and receive a pair of custom-made pants in their mailbox two to four weeks later.[20] Lands' End saves largely in inventory carrying costs because it avoids stocking up to 2.8 billion garments in various styles and sizes. Each pair of chinos is individually fashioned by a contract manufacturer and then shipped directly to the consumer. Orders are transferred electronically each day to Archetype, which designs the jeans and transmits the orders to a contract manufacturer in Mexico.

Secondly, the manufacturing and service processes should be designed into independent modules that can be moved around to accommodate various forms of distribution. The contract manufacturer for Lands' End uses a modular manufacturing process with eight machines to make the pants one pair at a time.

Finally, the supply chain needs to be designed so that it can supply the "basic" product quickly and at a low cost to the supply chain member customizing the product.

e-Commerce Perspective

Closer Connections

Back in the 1960s, when Vans Inc. started out as a shoe outfitter for the surf and skateboard crowd, its customers could walk into a shop in Southern California with their favorite surf shorts, jeans, or even a piece of carpet and order sneakers made of the same fabric. Now at Vans.com, web surfers can custom-design shoes thousands of different ways and be striding in style in six weeks or less.

Mass customization isn't a new idea. The PC industry pioneered the model about five years ago, other footwear and apparel companies have tried it, and automakers have been chasing it for several years. "We're continuing to see a trend of moving away from a make-to-stock strategy in manufacturing and fulfillment to a make-to-order or configure-to-order strategy," says Mike Dominy, a senior analyst with the Yankee Group.

Vans' online initiative, which began in the spring of 2004, is different in a few ways. For one thing, the company is drawing on its heritage of treating each customer as an individual and responding directly to his or her present-day needs. "We kept hearing from customers who would e-mail us or write us, saying, 'I remember the day . . . ,'" says Jody Giles, VP and CIO of Vans, which in June 2004 was bought by VF Corp. for $396 million. And every tailored pair of shoes Vans sells is made thousands of miles away in a Chinese factory, then shipped nearly direct to the customers who've ordered them.

The strategy is working. The company's annual e-commerce sales equal those of about five Vans retail stores, with custom shoes being the No. 1 sellers online. The Vans brand is all about individual flair, but the IT, product development, marketing, and overseas factory staffs who worked on the project at first weren't sure they could tailor their e-commerce and back-end systems to support online customers' desire to express their creativity. Like many apparel and footwear manufacturers, Vans outsources almost all of its manufacturing to China. "How do you do a one-off custom order all the way in China?" Giles says. Custom shoes are loaded for delivery to buyers on the same UPS truck that brings them into Vans' distribution center. "It is a true cross-dock operation," CIO Giles says.

Accepting an order was the easy part. "The hard part was getting the order information from our Web site through our ERP system to generate a unique purchase order that would then be sent to China," Giles says. And once the shoes were made, how quickly could Vans get them to buyers, factoring in a long boat ride, customs paperwork, and Vans' distribution-center processes?

For Vans, the answer was in the Vans Factory Exchange, a web-based purchase-order system that's integrated with the company's J.D. Edwards & Co. supply chain software and linked electronically to a factory in Guangzhou, China. The software is built on an IBM iSeries AS/400, which provides capacity on demand, giving Vans a cushion to handle order spikes. Those systems have been generating standard footwear purchase orders since the company began its web operations in 1999. The new custom orders rely on a web services link from Vans Factory Exchange back to the shop.vans.com site to view a picture of the shoe to be made, which serves as the bill of materials. Vans also had to modify its distribution-resource-planning process to handle custom inventory that would pass through, but never be stocked in, its distribution center.

This means the supply chain must be flexible enough to deliver the final product quickly and at reasonable cost to the end customer. In the case of Lands' End, online technology enables speedy delivery of the orders to the contract manufacturer. Manufacturing for its U.S. market takes place in Mexico, a close location, so customer shipments can be delivered back to the United States quickly. Finished chinos are shipped in bulk to a distribution center for customs clearance. While at the distribution center, the pants are sorted, packaged, and mailed to the customer directly.

Break-Even Analysis

In the decision to launch a new product or service, management generally considers its financial feasibility during the screening process. They need to determine the expected return on their investment—when they expect to make a profit and the expected profit over the life of the product.

From an operations viewpoint, managers may have more than one process option in producing a product or service and they must decide which process is more cost effective. For example, managers may have to decide whether to use existing technology, adopt newer technology, or outsource production to a third party.

These decisions are often based on the cost trade-offs among the various options and **break-even analysis** is one quantitative technique used by management. One form of break-even analysis considers the relationship between fixed costs, variable costs, and profit. The results of the calculation provide the approximate sales volume required to cover fixed and variable costs. Any production below the break-even point will not be profitable; any production above the break-even point will be profitable. The other form of break-even analysis looks at the costs of alternative production processes to decide at what production ranges each alternative is most cost efficient.

To perform a break-even analysis, managers must have access to certain information, including:

- Volume, or projected level of production, based on expected sales.
- Fixed costs of production, or those costs that remain constant, such as investment in plant, equipment, and overhead.
- Variable costs of production, or those costs that vary depending on the number of units produced, including labor and materials.
- Expected sales price of the new product or service.

To determine the volume of sales where management expects to earn a profit, we can find the point where profit will equal zero, or the break-even point. The formula used to find the break-even point is:

Total Revenue = Total Cost
or, TR = TC

Where:

Total Revenue = Sales Price $\times$ Volume Produced
or, TR = p $\times$ v
and
Total Cost = Fixed Costs + Variable Costs
or, TC = fc + vc

Where:

p = sales price per unit
v = volume produced
fc = fixed cost, and
vc = variable cost per unit produced

Example 2.1 provides an example of how break-even analysis works. The solution can also be illustrated graphically as shown in Figure 2.5.

Using a second form of break-even analysis, we can look at different processes to determine which one is more cost effective, depending on expected volume of production. The trend today is to outsource production unless there are concerns such as protecting proprietary knowledge or patents, or the loss of control. Generally, companies decide to outsource if it is cheaper and it gives them greater flexibility. However, companies also want to ensure the quality will be the same or even better than if they produced it themselves. Thus, suppliers are screened carefully for quality as well as for their reliability and experience.

The formula to calculate the break-even point between two or more processes is:

$$TC_1 = TC_2 = TC_3 = \ldots TC_z$$

The case of Susan and Bob's gourmet dog boutiques, as discussed in Example 2.1, evaluates two alternative processes for adding the new line of dog food. This problem and solution is shown in Example 2.2 and Figure 2.6.

Example 2.1   **Finding the Cost-Profit Break-Even Point**

Susan and Bob own several boutiques that cater to dog lovers with upscale tastes. They create, make, and sell gourmet dog treats. Recently, they have considered adding a line of gourmet canned dog food. They estimate the costs to add new production equipment will be $25,000 and the additional labor and material costs will be $0.75 per can. They plan on selling each can for $2.00.

SOLUTION:

Given that:

Price, p = $2.00 per can of dog food
Fixed cost, fc = $25,000
Variable cost, vc = $0.75 per can of dog food

The break-even point is: $\dfrac{fc}{p - vc} = \dfrac{\$25,000}{\$2 - \$0.75} = 20,000$ cans

Following is the solution using Excel:

Input		Results	
		Alternative 1	
Fixed Costs	$ 25,000.00	Contribution/Unit	$ 1.25
Variable Costs	$ 0.75	Break-Even Point	
Selling Price/Unit	$ 2.00	(units)	20,000
Desired Profit	$ -	Profit Point (units)	20,000

Susan and Bob need to sell more than 20,000 cans to make a profit.

Figure 2.5	Cost-Profit Break-Even Analysis

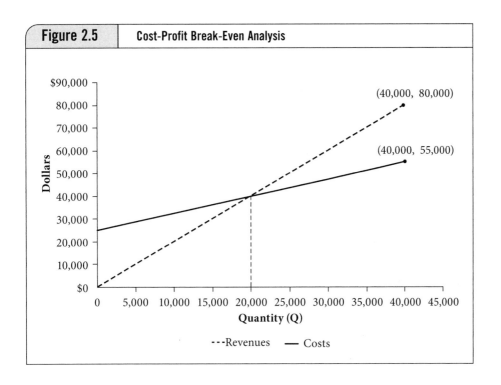

Example 2.2   Finding a Make vs. Buy Break-Even Point

Bob and Susan are considering whether to manufacture the gourmet dog food themselves or outsource the process to a contract manufacturer. They have been in contact with a local manufacturer that will produce and deliver the dog food to a central distribution center for $1.25 per can. Bob and Susan estimate it will cost them about $2,000 in legal fees to draw up the contract.

SOLUTION:
The break-even point Q is found by setting the costs of the two options equal to each other.

Total cost to make = Total cost to buy

$$\$25,000 + \$0.75Q = \$2,000 + \$1.25Q$$
$$\$23,000 = \$0.50Q$$
$$Q = 46,000 \text{ cans}$$

In other words, if Bob and Susan expect to sell less than 46,000 cans of dog food, they should outsource the manufacture of the dog food to the contract manufacturer. If they expect to sell more than 46,000 cans of dog food, it will be cheaper to manufacture the dog food themselves. The solution is also shown using Excel below and graphically in Figure 2.6.

	Input				Results	
	Alternative 1		**Alternative 2**			
Fixed Costs	$ 25,000.00	Fixed Costs	$ 2,000.00	Break-Even		
Variable Costs	$ 0.75	Variable Costs	$ 1.25	Point (units)	46,000	

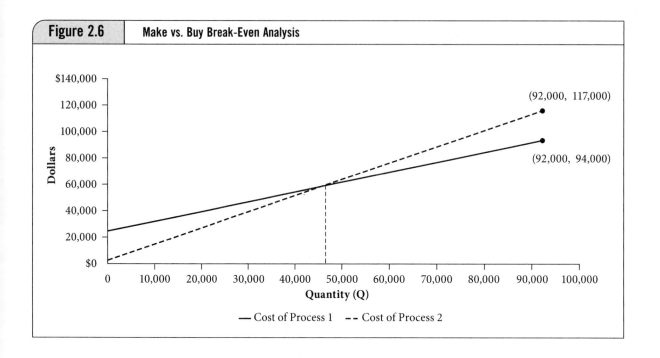

Figure 2.6 | **Make vs. Buy Break-Even Analysis**

Special Issues in Service Design

A great deal of the previous discussion has focused on the design and development of manufactured products. However, much of the U.S. and other highly developed economies are now based in the service sector. Services and their processes have unique characteristics that make them more difficult to design. First, services have both "substantive" and "peripheral" components. In a restaurant, for example, the substantive component would be the food and the peripheral component would be things like the surroundings or ambience, the friendliness of the wait staff, the music, and table presentation. Some of these elements are intangible, such as atmosphere and treatment by the service provider, but are just as critical to the experience as the tangible elements. Second, the customer plays a direct role in the design and delivery process. Service providers frequently offer a "menu" of services from which to choose, such as options offered in the design and delivery of a vacation package or a visit to a day spa. In these cases the customer provides instant input in making service selections and then provides feedback to the service provider as the service is delivered.

Third, the service may take place in a matter of minutes or last over an extended period of time. Use of the ATM machine requires a few minutes. However, in the case of financial planning, customers make the final decisions on various initial investment options and then have continual involvement in managing their portfolios over many years.

Lastly, it is difficult to remove the variability inherent in service delivery because in most instances, people are involved. While manufacturers can set tight product specifications, this is not easily done in a service environment. Services try to mitigate service variabilities through training programs, and setting strict specifications and standards. However, variability is needed and actually encouraged for customized services.

Service organizations also have generally not been known for innovation. Compared to manufactured products, services are frequently underdesigned or designed in an inefficient manner because service providers don't develop a clear strategic direction and they don't have formal design processes.[21] New services also tend to be more difficult to design and initially more time-consuming as the service provider tries to determine the role and integration of its customers into the service delivery process.

Still, a number of changes in services are occurring at a more rapid rate than ever before. Advances in technology have created multiple service delivery options for consumers and, in many cases, improved quality perceptions. For instance, Verizon Communications Inc., a New York–based provider of wireless and broadband services, now offers Internet-based as well as cell phone service. Southwest Airlines has kiosks located in airport terminals, which allow passengers to obtain their boarding passes before passing through security; alternatively, a passenger may download a copy of his or her boarding pass at home via the Internet. And Kentucky-based Papa John's Pizza now takes delivery orders via the Internet. These examples are just a few of the many ways technology used in service product design has changed our lives in recent years.

The level of service innovation generally runs along a continuum, from simple style changes, which alter the appearance of the service, to completely new services. As shown in Table 2.3, McDonald's Corporation has implemented both incremental and dramatic design changes since its inception. There are many other examples, however. Shopping malls periodically go through style changes—an incremental improvement—by changing the flooring, décor, storefronts, and lighting in order to update its look and attract new customers. U.S. home improvement retailer Home Depot has developed both extensions in its service lines and a new service in its existing markets. By adding kitchen design centers to its stores—a service line extension—it became more competitive with independent designers. However, Home Depot also created EXPO, a start-up business chain of upscale retail stores, in the 1990s to target customers who are remodeling their home but want more assistance, with high-end materials and appliances.[22]

Table 2.3	Innovations in Service Design—McDonald's Corporation
INCREMENTAL INNOVATIONS	**EXAMPLE**
Small Changes in Service Style	Nutritional information added to food wrappers
Improvements in Service	Inside dining added in the 1970s; drive-up window service added
Extension in Service Line	Healthy choice foods such as salads and bottled water added to menu
MAJOR INNOVATIONS	
New Service in Current Market	Nontraditional U.S. locations added in gas service stations such as Chevron and Amoco
New Service in New Market	Expansion worldwide with country-specific menus

Source: Adapted from Johnson, S. P., Roth, A. V., and Chase, R. B., "A Critical Evaluation of the New Service Development Process," *New Service Development* by Fitzsimmons and Fitzsimmons, Thousand Oaks, CA: Sage Publications, 2000, p. 19.

Service providers have also developed other delivery methods at the service design stage. For example, some companies use mass customization, standardizing the first steps of their process and delaying the customization of their service as late as possible. This approach is common in a hospital setting, where a patient goes through a battery of tests a few days before surgery, is admitted to the hospital through a standardized procedure, is prepped for surgery, and then finally receives a "customized" surgical procedure.

Companies may also **modularize** their service, allowing a customer to choose from various packages of features. When planning a cruise to Alaska, you may get to choose whether you want to include hotel accommodations in Seattle before the cruise begins; add optional additional-cost outings such as a float-plane trip to the glaciers during the cruise; or include a four-day land package that includes the train trip, sightseeing, and accommodations to Denali National Park after the cruise.

However, whether designing new products or services, a number of factors come into play before these development projects can be successful. Some of these aspects are discussed further in the next section.

Effective Product and Service Design

Support from senior management must be visible and continuous throughout the design phase. Management should keep the project in the forefront of other company employees and back the project through a strong marketing case.[23] Market research that helps an organization understand the desires of the target customer group is essential but not always executed well, often resulting in new product and service failures. Generally, market research needs to be conducted early in the process, beginning with a well-designed market research plan. Marketing should set clear objectives before beginning its research and have a good feel for the size of the market.

From a manufacturer's or service provider's standpoint, information technology systems can also support the new product and service development process in a number of ways. As discussed in Chapter 3, more companies than ever before are using **customer relationship management systems** and **data mining** or **web mining** to unlock customer preferences. Marketers use data mining software to help retailers identify hidden patterns of behavior or common interests among their customer group. Web mining is similar although it uses customer data collected from websites. More and more companies are using **spyware**, which collects information without the user's knowledge. This information might be used, for example, to predict whether customers will buy a new product based on past purchases. Information technology systems also speed the flow of information between members of the organization, promote conceptualization of new ideas, and possibly speed up the feedback process.

High-performing cross-functional teams can also improve the design process, resulting in faster completion times and thus fewer labor hours invested in the project. Generally, successful teams exhibit a great deal of coordination and cooperation among the members. Team members understand the benefits of the project to their company and why they are involved. Project members are also highly qualified, with a strong commitment to and enthusiasm for the project. Each team member contributes through his or her unique capabilities and strengths and offers fresh perspectives. Wisconsin-based Harley-Davidson has been using cross-functional teams for years, resulting in higher quality in-demand motorcycles than their competitors. "They're responsible for the success of the motorcycle in the marketplace," says Leroy Zimdars, Director of Supply Chain Management. [24]

A more formalized process will generally improve the design process and result in more successful new products and services. There are three reasons for this. First, creating written guidelines provides direction for projects. A company might decide, for example, that all product ideas should be screened by one centralized committee that determines which projects should get the "green light" to move forward. Second, learning from past projects can be incorporated into the formal process, improving the current project's chance for success. Lastly, a routine can develop from a formal process, improving the learning curve and speeding up the development process. This last advantage is particularly important for companies that focus on continuously introducing new products to gain a competitive advantage.

Of course, without appropriate resources, both financial and human, new product and service projects have little chance of success. Companies can improve the process by allocating financial resources early in the product development phase. Then, the company should allow enough time for the design and development of the new product or service to more adequately meet customer specifications. Lastly, dedicated project teams will ensure the project is completed in a timely manner.

SUMMARY

As shown in this chapter, the development of new products and services is a complex process but critical to maintaining a competitive advantage for most companies today. Service providers are coming up with new delivery venues that are aided by advances in technology. Manufacturers are also using technology as well as cross-functional teams to ramp up the introduction of new products at an even faster pace. This chapter introduces the new product development process as well as new tools and technologies that are available to organizations today.

To make the process successful, businesses need designers who can take ideas from many sources and turn them into a workable "solution" that will satisfy their target market. Organizations also need production and delivery processes that are adaptable to new product specifications and can ramp up quickly to meet customer demand. Lastly, teamwork is essential and often involves others outside the organization, including customers and suppliers. This chapter placed particular emphasis on the changing role of suppliers in the new product development process.

KEY TERMS

basic research, 29

break-even analysis, 43

business case, 33

computer-aided design, 37

concurrent engineering, 35

control matrix, 32

customer focus, 37

customer relationship management systems, 48

data mining, 48

delivery system, 33

design-build-test, 33

design for manufacture and assembly, 36

design matrix, 32

early supplier involvement, 38

house of quality, 31

integrated product development, 35

kaizen investigative teams, 30

mass customization, 40

modularity, 36

modularize, 48

operating matrix, 32

pilot production, 34

product focus, 37

quality function deployment, 30

service blueprinting, 33

skunkworks, 30

spyware, 48

three-dimensional concurrent engineering, 36

web mining, 48

DISCUSSION QUESTIONS

1. Describe the stages of new product and service development.

2. Name at least three sources of new product and service ideas.

3. Describe the quality function deployment process.

4. How do organizations use the house of quality to improve customer satisfaction in a new product or service?

5. What are some factors companies consider when screening a new product or service idea?

6. Why have firms integrated their new product development to include cross-functional teams?

7. Describe the concurrent engineering process and its benefits.

8. What is design for manufacture and assembly (DFMA)?

9. What are the advantages of modularizing products?

10. What is the impact of the design and development stage on a product's total cost?

11. Describe the advances in technology that have made the design process faster and resulted in better quality.

12. Why are suppliers today more involved in new product development? What role can the supplier play in the process?

13. What factors should an organization consider when integrating suppliers into its new product development process?

14. What criteria do organizations use to match the production process to the product?

15. Describe the four generic production processes. Provide an example of a company that operates with two or more production processes.

16. What are the design principles behind mass customization?

17. How does the design of services differ from that of manufacturing?

18. What factors help improve the product or service design and development process?

SPREADSHEET PROBLEMS

1. Frank's Framery designs and manufactures picture frames. Frank, the owner, is introducing a new frame. He has fixed costs of $10,000 and each frame will cost $4 to build. He plans to sell the frames to retailers for $10 each.

   a. What is Frank's break-even point?

   b. If Frank sells 2,500 frames, what will be his profit?

2. A start-up toy company is trying to decide whether to manufacture its newest board game in-house or outsource it to a contract manufacturer. Cost data are as follows:

OPTIONS	FIXED COST	VARIABLE COST
Manufacture in-house	$9,000	$12.00
Source to contract manufacturer	$1,000	$15.00

   At what range of demand should each option be chosen?

INTERNET QUESTIONS

1. Go to the Society of Concurrent Product Development website and determine what the organization's goals are, who the founders were, and what types of activities they are doing now. Provide some examples.

2. Search on the term *mass customization*. Find three websites and write a report about companies that apply the design principles described in this chapter to mass customization. Describe your findings and include a bibliography.

3. Use the Internet to search for the term *data mining* and determine at least three uses for data mining.

INFOTRAC QUESTIONS

Access http://www.infotrac-thomsonlearning.com to answer the following questions:

1. Use InfoTrac to search for the terms *teams* and *new product development*. Write a term paper on the benefits of teams in the new product development process using your findings, and include a bibliography.

2. Use InfoTrac to search for the terms *DFMA* and *software*. Write a paper on ways DFMA software improves the product development process and provide company examples. Include a bibliography.

REFERENCES

Chase, Richard B., Jacobs, F. Robert, and Aquilano, Nicholas J. (2004), *Operations Management for Competitive Advantage,* McGraw-Hill, Boston, MA.

Nicholas, John M. (1998), *Competitive Manufacturing Management,* Irwin McGraw-Hill, Boston, MA.

Scheuing, Eberhard E., and Johnson, Eugene M., "A Proposed Model for New Service Development," *The Journal of Services Marketing,* Spring, Vol. 3 (2), 1989, pp. 25–34.

Stevenson, William J. (2002), *Operations Management,* 7th edition, Irwin McGraw-Hill, Boston, MA.

ENDNOTES

1. Hunt, V. Daniel, author of *Re-Engineering: Leveraging the Power of Integrated Product Development.*

2. Bruggeman, John, Vice President of Marketing for Alventive Inc., in Sofranec, Diane, "Giving Customers What They Want, When They Want It," *Computer-Aided Engineering,* V. 20, No. 1, January 2001, p. 46.

3. Visit http://www.ideo.com for some of its innovative ideas.

4. For more information, go to http://www.worldwidewords.org/qa/qa-sku1.htm.

5. Lunsford, J. Lynn, "Two Groups Vie to Build a Supersonic Business Jet: Key Is to Lower the 'Boom' and Expand Route Map for Globe-Trotting CEOs," *Wall Street Journal,* October 11, 2004, p. A–1.

6. "A Shift toward Innovation," *The Manufacturer.com,* V. 15, July 2004, retrieved on November 1, 2004 from http://www.themanufacturer.com.

7. ReVelle, Jack B., John W. Moran, and Charles A. Cox, *The QFD Handbook,* John Wiley and Sons, 1998.

8. Hearon, H. and G. Mazur, "Using QFD to Improve Technical Support to Make Commodity Products More Competitive," 14th Symposium on QFD, QFD Institute, 2002, pp. 1–10.

9. More on General Dynamics can be found in the case study "CSC Works with General Dynamics to Build Digital Design Solution" at http://www.csc.com/industries/aerospacedefense/casestudies/1266.shtml.

10. Fine, C. H., *Clockspeed,* Reading, MA: Perseus Books, 1998.

11. Fine, Charles H., "Clockspeed-Based Strategies for Supply Chain Design," *Production and Operations Management,* V. 9, No. 3, 2000, p. 221.

12. "Whirlpool Sweden Invests in Better Designs," *Training & Management Development Methods,* V. 15, No. 3, 2001, pp. 945–947.

13. "Catia-based Design of Boeing 777–200LR Goes to Factory Floor," *MSI,* V. 22, Issue 4, April 2004, p. 24.

14. "John Deere Selects DFMA Software from Boothroyd Dewhurst," retrieved on November 3, 2004, from http://www.dfma.com/news/Deere.htm.

15. Visit http://www.bausch.com to learn more about Bausch & Lomb's innovation strategy.

16. Porter, Anne Millen, "At CAT, They're Driving Supplier Integration into the Design Process," *Purchasing,* V. 120, March 7, 1996, p. 38.

17. Handfield, Robert and Ernest Nichols Jr., *Supply Chain Redesign,* Upper Saddle River, NJ: Prentice-Hall, 2002.

18. Sofranec, Diane, "Giving Customers What They Want, When They Want It," *Computer-Aided Engineering,* V. 20, January 2001, pp. 45–47.

19. Kern, Lawrence, "Getting Designs Right the First Time," *Machine Design,* V. 75, October 23, 2003, p. 96.

20. Drickhamer, Dick, "A Leg Up on Mass Customization," *Industry Week,* September 1, 2002, retrieved on November 2, 2004, from http://www.industryweek.com.

21. Froehle, Craig R., Aleda V. Roth, and Richard B. Chase, "Antecedents of New Service Development Effectiveness: An Exploratory Examination of Strategic Operations Choices," *Journal of Service Research,* V. 3, No. 1, 2000, pp. 3–17.

22. Howell, Debbie, "Home Depot Alters Expo Mix to Reach More Mass-Like Demographic," *DSN Retailing Today,* V. 41, No. 2, 2002, p. 3.

23. Edgett, Scott, "The Traits of Successful New Service Development," *The Journal of Services Marketing,* V. 8, No. 3, 1994, pp. 40–49.

24. Brunelli, Mark, "How Harley-Davidson Uses Cross-Functional Teams," *Purchasing,* V. 127, Issue 7, November 4, 1999, p. 144.

Chapter 3:

CUSTOMER RELATIONSHIP MANAGEMENT

Brand ambassadors can be very effective in building and maintaining brand loyalty among customers. All employees who have contact with customers play the role of brand ambassadors. As they provide customers with the "brand experience," employers must ensure that their personnel are aware that they are the human face of the company. [1]

Empower your customers—let them help themselves, which for the most part is what customers want. [2]

Learning Objectives

After completing this chapter, you should be able to:

- Understand the value of the customer relationship management (CRM) process.
- Discuss how to segment customers, and describe why this is important.
- Consider the design and improvement of a CRM program.
- Describe a number of CRM program performance metrics.
- Describe how CRM programs vary based on the firm's competitive strategy.
- Describe several CRM process software solutions, and discuss the value of these products.
- Understand the importance of information privacy for CRM programs.
- Describe some of the latest trends in CRM.

Chapter Outline

Process Management in Action

How to Fire Your Customers

Though it may seem counterintuitive, letting customers go can help your company grow. That's because some customers, even those who pay fully and on time, can be a drain on your business. If you're like most business owners, you have a few marginal customers who draw your attention away from more profitable accounts. You might even have clients that cost more to serve than they pay for your product. The solution, however, involves more than identifying the right customers to cull and building up the courage to say, "Thanks for your business, but we don't want it anymore." Dump a paying customer without tact and diplomacy, and they could turn into your archenemy.

Robert Bracey faced a hard decision when he acquired his current firm, Quartet Service Corp., in July 2002. At the time of its acquisition, the provider of outsourced IT and telecom services was growing exponentially on the top line, but bleeding on the bottom. To stanch the losses, Bracey performed a rough cost-benefit analysis on each of Quartet's customers; within two months, he cut ten of the worst performers, representing 7 percent of his total clients. After trimming, Quartet prospered. "We went from losing a huge amount of money to making money almost instantly," says Bracey. Monthly profitability now ranges from 5 to 20 percent.

Deciding who to cut is easier if you conduct account reviews on an annual or semiannual basis, says Richard Pridham, president of Agili-T Group Inc., a Montreal-based consulting firm specializing in managing customer relationships. Begin by looking at both top-line sales and margins, and also at underlying support costs such as marketing, acquisition, customer support, and administration. Next, evaluate the lifetime value of a customer. Today's unprofitable customer may be on a high-growth curve leading to big profits in the future, or may be worth clinging to if he or she attracts other clients through word of mouth or comprises an impressive name on your client list. "It could be your flagship account in a new market that you're trying to develop and you're willing to live with some of the trade-offs, like a loss leader," says Pridham. Finally, don't neglect to speak to your frontline staff, who can shed light on whether retaining a client is more hassle than it is worth.

Get all that right, and your bottom line can grow. When handled correctly, firing customers can increase revenue as well. Bracey discovered as much when sales rose 50 percent in the year after culling his customer base, thanks in part to positive word of mouth from fired customers. Bracey explained his cuts honestly to clients, either in person or over the phone, and then spent a considerable amount of time helping them locate alternative suppliers. Bracey saved himself grief not only by acting diplomatically, but also by being swift. "Many companies try the attrition approach," says Pridham, referring to the too-common practice of simply ignoring bad customers' calls and hoping they'll go away. "This makes the relationship even more acrimonious." The result: an angry ex-customer, which can have disastrous effects on your company. Instead of generating bad feelings by ignoring the problem or slacking on service, speak to the client personally. Senior management should be involved on both sides, says Pridham: "You don't want your sales rep telling their purchasing guy that you don't want to do business anymore." Discuss your challenges and see if the relationship can be salvaged. If not, explain your reasons for letting them go. Your goal should be maintaining maximum goodwill—after all, even if you've just ended the relationship, you may want it back one day.

Source: Baillie, S., "How to Fire Your Customers," *Profit,* V. 22, No. 5, 2003, pp. 72–74. Used with permission.

Introduction

Customer relationship management (CRM) is concerned with managing the relationships between a supplier and its buyers of goods and services. All businesses want to satisfy their customers, make profits, and grow their customer base by identifying new customers and continuing to satisfy existing ones. Thus, many successful companies seek to identify existing and potential new customers, determine their needs, and use internal resources and competencies to satisfy those needs, which increase the value of their products and services. Consequently, satisfied customers return and also tell others, creating even greater demand and the potential for more new customers. In today's high-tech global economy, though, competitors abound, making the task of finding new customers and keeping old ones a continuous battle. Businesses that do the best job of managing customer relationships create a competitive advantage, making the job of finding and keeping customers much easier.

Today, the emphasis is turning more towards retaining existing customers, particularly the most profitable ones, since retaining existing customers is far less expensive than finding new ones. Since the mid-1990s, a number of studies have confirmed that small increases in customer retention (also referred to as decreases in **customer churn**) often result in large increases in profits. This has spawned a tremendous interest among firms today in investing in CRM activities and software applications.

However, many customers might actually be losing money for the firms who sell to them. In situations such as this, firms may consider "firing" these customers through either raising the prices or making the products and services these customers purchase, less desirable. **Firing a customer**, if handled diplomatically, can generate not only greater overall profits, but also greater levels of sales through word of mouth. As shown in the opening Process Management in Action feature, Quartet Service Corp. found ways to successfully fire some of its customers.

Whenever a product or service is delivered to a customer, the process of customer relationship management, or CRM, begins. If companies can make products customers want and deliver them at the desired time, in the right condition, for the right price, then customers are at least initially satisfied. After the sale, customers may require information, repairs, and parts, and this too requires attention by the firm to successfully manage customer relationships. Further, when marketing products and designing new ones, communication with existing customers can prove to be valuable.

Segmenting and marketing to existing customers can be a useful sales tool if firms can identify purchase histories of customers and then tailor marketing efforts to appeal to various customer groups. Simply put, attracting and serving customers profitably is the primary objective of all CRM processes.

Starting during the 1990s and continuing today, CRM has also become known as a technology tool or software application, and this has brought about several problems that continue to plague some organizations. CRM application providers sell software to automate marketing and customer service processes, and in some cases firms pay exceedingly high prices for these products in the hope that they will generate greater sales and more profits. In fact, annual CRM software investments in the United States are expected to reach $11.4 billion by 2008.[3] Many of these applications, though, have failed to accomplish the desired results, and some have even succeeded in scaring customers away. And a significant percentage of these applications have failed to recover the initial investment in terms of increasing sales to existing customers or decreasing marketing and customer service costs.

In too many cases, managers view these applications as a quick and easy way to improve sales to existing customers, while neglecting activities customers regard as value enhancing. Many firms have learned the true meaning of CRM the hard way—that technology alone can't endear customers to a product or company; employees and their actions do. CRM software applications can only achieve the desired benefits when they are used as a facilitating mechanism for CRM. The right plan, people, policies, and techniques, when coupled with a good CRM software application, can become an effective process for finding and serving customers and creating significant competitive advantage for the company and its trading partners. Taken in these contexts, CRM has two distinct meanings that can be successfully integrated to achieve business results:

- It is a process seeking to maximize customer satisfaction, revenue, and profitability by attracting customers and then delivering behaviors, products, and services that satisfy them.
- It is a collection of technologies that assist and integrate the CRM activities.

Therefore, care must be taken in both the design aspects of the CRM activities and the selection and implementation of CRM technologies. This chapter discusses these important aspects of the CRM process.

Designing an Effective CRM Process

Any successful CRM process must begin with the identification of the firm's key competencies or success factors, and an understanding of how these can be leveraged by the CRM process. CRM failures are often due to a firm simply adopting ideas or purchasing applications without understanding the impact these will have on the firm. For instance, improvements in handling customer requests at a call center (discussed further in Chapter 4) may reduce call center costs, but have minimal effect on the firm's overall customer service levels or customer satisfaction. Ill-advised businesses might invest in a CRM software package and then spend months or years redesigning certain activities to coincide with process automations in the software. Conversely, other businesses can spend millions of dollars customizing CRM software to automate existing business activities, without first considering the impact these changes are likely to have on the firm's products, services, or sales efforts.

Firms with successful CRM programs realize that in the final analysis, customers must benefit in some way. Organizations decide which elements of CRM are beneficial when considering the technologies available; specific strategies that will likely lead to the greatest increases in competitive advantage; and activities that make sense, given the customers being served, their needs, the firm's resources and capabilities, and the existing competition. Table 3.1 provides some examples of business activities, tools, and strategies that are part of many typical CRM processes.

CRM tools have the capability to capture and analyze information generated from the various activities shown in Table 3.1. By centralizing this information and providing a system whereby users throughout the organization can access, update, and organize information and then generate customized reports, managers can devise strategies for improving customer response times, design services to meet specific customer needs, devise marketing campaigns to improve sales to customer segments, deliver products and services to the most profitable customers, and reduce costs associated with unprofitable customers. As discussed in the Global Perspective feature, Procter & Gamble is

Table 3.1	Examples of CRM Activities, Tools, and Strategies	
ACTIVITIES	**TOOLS/ANALYTICS**	**STRATEGIES**
Sales lead/territory management Channel management Account and contact management Customer request management Field service and dispatch support Customer call routing and management	Packaged business applications • Key activity automations—data capture, reporting, user inquiry capabilities • Preconfigured activities • Configurability—enables users to customize application	Customer centric approaches • Segmentation of customers • Tailoring services to fit customer segments • Coordinating departments to better serve customer segments
Direct marketing and campaign management	Data storage—customer information and other custom data in secure data fields	Prospecting and cross-selling • Targeting customer segments using tailored marketing methods • Cross-selling to various customer segments
Pricing, promotions, and revenue management	Data inquiry—allows easy access to sales, service, and marketing information	Tracking customer profitability and dealing with underperforming customers
Order management	Performance management tools—tracking and reporting of key activity metrics	Capturing customer and demand information and feeding it back to each business function
	Analytics—allows for fast and flexible queries; can create new queries, create reports	

Source: Adapted from Bligh, P., and D. Turk, *CRM Unplugged: Releasing CRM's Strategic Value*, Hoboken, NJ: John-Wiley & Sons, 2004.

doing a very good job of designing a CRM plan that uses technology in order to increase the flexibility of the various applications, since its customer base is so diverse. It is letting its customer needs drive the type of CRM program being developed, instead of letting the software application drive the design of the program.

Many CRM programs are not necessarily formal programs at all, but rather a collection of small activities, implemented at various times, and aimed at improving some aspect of the organization's operations such as sales, marketing, or customer service. In each case, these activities are seen as increasing customer value while addressing some strategic capability of the firm. For instance, in June 2002, U.S. passenger air carrier Southwest Airlines began retiring its plastic boarding cards and started using an automated system that issued paper boarding cards at several locations within each airport. Improving customer check-in and boarding service in this way meant that Southwest customers stood in fewer lines, resulting in less time spent waiting. Additionally, this reduced airplane turnaround time (a strategic imperative at Southwest Airlines) as well as costs. Both Southwest and its customers benefited from this activity.[4]

In their book, *CRM Unplugged: Releasing CRM's Strategic Value*, Philip Bligh and Douglas Turk recommend that companies answer three questions prior to implementing any CRM idea:[5]

1. What is the value being added and for which customers?
2. Does it strengthen or dilute the firm's strategy?
3. What is the expected effect on the firm's profitability?

The litmus test thus encompasses three requirements—customers must perceive value in any CRM initiative, the initiative must support or advance the firm's strategy, and any investment in CRM must pay for itself by reducing costs or improving revenues. CRM activities that address all three requirements in a positive manner have the best chance of keeping the most profitable customers satisfied and coming back,

Global Perspective

Procter & Gamble's Global CRM Initiative

With more than 5 billion end consumers in more than 160 countries, Procter & Gamble (P&G) has long had an enviable global reach. The Cincinnati-based packaged goods manufacturer literally makes products with brand names from A to Z, and sells them all around the world in stores that range from giants like Wal-Mart to mom-and-pop outfits operating off the back of a truck.

But such reach, while a blessing for brand recognition, has often presented a challenge when it comes to interacting with retailers. Until recently, P&G kept track of its diverse customer base through an equally diverse array of local (often homegrown) systems. That lack of integration meant a retailer such as Wal-Mart might receive conflicting product and promotion information about Crest® toothpaste from a legacy trade funds system in Cincinnati and a homegrown shipment reporting system in Guangzhou, China. If the two systems had different SKUs for the same product, it would lead to confusion and extra work for Wal-Mart if the retailer attempted to roll up its data on worldwide Crest sales. And for P&G, the more variety in its systems, the harder it was for the company to dispense consistent information to its retailers about its nearly 300 brands, not to mention plan promotions and execute a sales strategy.

"As customers become more global, our ability to understand, interact, and manage our business is limited by a nonintegrated platform," says Robert Scott, vice president of IT for P&G's Global Market Development Organization (MDO). Faced with aging IT systems in the late 1990s, P&G decided to take the plunge and launch a worldwide customer relationship management initiative.

CRM is not a term to be tossed around lightly in a company as vast as P&G—especially since its global offices operate with varying degrees of technological sophistication. In a developing market like China, for example, retailers are much more likely to sell small packets of Tide® than the 100-ounce containers that dominate the shelves in North America. The cost of business therefore has to be lower, leaving less money for technology initiatives. So P&G had to figure out how to manage CRM technology on a global level, making it broad enough to traverse the world but flexible enough to help get products on the shelves in far-flung places. By choosing a single platform that could be scaled down for the smaller markets, P&G was for the first time trying to treat its retail customers consistently, whether those customers were selling Folgers® in Fort Worth or Downy® in Dublin.

Scott says three factors drove P&G's CRM efforts. First, P&G needed integrated systems to eliminate inconsistencies in product data and simplify the process of synchronizing internal data with customers' systems. Second, P&G spends hundreds of millions of dollars annually on customer incentives to encourage retailers to stock and sell P&G products. Without a reliable way of managing those promotion dollars in all countries, it was tough to track which incentives were successful and which were bombs. Third, the company had streamlined its field sales force in the 1990s yet still wanted to make sure that retail plans formulated at the company's headquarters reached stores quickly.

Enter CRM. P&G decided to use Siebel because, according to Scott, Siebel made it possible for P&G to build a global integrated platform that was also configurable for specific markets. So far, P&G's CRM efforts fall into three categories: retail execution, trade funds management, and product management. In the past decade, P&G has begun to use multifunctional customer teams at headquarters—which rely on data gathered by a lean team of sales reps—to care

Continued

for key accounts. Reps who visit stores relay information such as product placement and out-of-stock situations to the customer teams. Reps—or third-party temps—used to collect data ad hoc: writing it down, faxing, rewriting it.

The CRM system now lets P&G's sales force gather that data in North America and parts of Western Europe with laptops, handhelds, or tablet PCs and send it electronically back to P&G's databases. "In near real-time we can assess whether or not we're having problems with key sales fundamentals that ultimately will impact sales," says Scott. Now P&G can collect data such as what items are out of stock in a particular retailer and get that data into the hands of those responsible for filling the shelves.

The new system helps reps collect information faster so that they can visit more stores, and more store visits translates into higher sales. In fact, Scott attributes a 3 to 5 percent sales volume increase to the CRM efforts. And because cost controls mean that P&G is learning to do more with fewer people—the company says it reduced its sales force "substantially" when it introduced the customer teams—the more efficiently those people can work, the better. The CRM efforts have saved the company 10 to 15 percent on retail selling costs and allowed P&G to increase sales coverage by 15 to 20 percent.

P&G won't say exactly how much it spends annually on promotions and incentives that encourage retailers to stock and sell P&G products, but Scott estimates it to be hundreds of millions of dollars globally. That's a significant chunk of change, but in P&G's pre-CRM days there was no electronic tool to ensure adherence to global standards for managing that expense. Each country often had its own tools, ranging from simple Excel spreadsheets to complex legacy systems. "Some were very good; some were a disaster—but it was very local," says Scott.

Now P&G has begun using its CRM tools to plan and execute promotions, set budgets, trigger payment requests, and get payment status. The system also allows P&G to record a history of promotions. "When we start planning promotions, we do it with a smarter knowledge around what we've learned in the past," says Erik J. Verrijssen, associate director of IT. "We found there was opportunity to get more bang for the buck and really make sure that we have more efficiency in spending that money by understanding what worked and what didn't work."

With a product list as extensive as P&G's, getting consistent product data—sizes, descriptions, prices, and images of new products—from headquarters to retailers around the world remains a perennial challenge. The more efficiently that happens, of course, the faster the products can get onto the shelves and into shopping baskets. By using Siebel eConsumer Goods to manage its data, P&G is able to more easily deliver product information in a standardized format to Transora, a consumer packaged goods industry exchange. Retailers using the same standards can plug into Transora and download product data. This standards-based data sharing lets P&G efficiently deliver precise product information uniformly to its retailers—no easy task given the U.S. market is home to 7 varieties of Tide®, at least 10 other P&G laundry products, and more than 20 other major categories, such as pet food and oral hygiene. It's hard to overstate the significance of this uniform delivery. Using industry standards reduces the time-consuming process of filling out forms for both P&G and retailers.

P&G thinks of its upcoming efforts as "closing the loop" between sharing data with and gathering data from its customers, and using that information to make smarter, faster business decisions. Tim Butler, North American MDO CIO, believes that CRM's true power lies not merely in collecting and storing specific sales or promotional data but in capturing something less tangible but ultimately more important: conversations with customers about business strategies that will help P&G improve its business processes. Says Butler: "When you can use something like CRM to pull together the knowledge you have on a customer with the systemic transactional data, that's where you really start to see the whole CRM picture coming into view." Before, he says, business strategy plans were often captured "on napkins, in people's heads, or not at all."

Source: Moore, M., "300 Brands, One Strategy; When your reach is as vast as Procter & Gamble's, building a worldwide view of your customers is a matter of thinking globally and acting locally," *CIO*, V. 16, No. 22, 2003, p. 1. Reprinted through the courtesy of *CIO*. Copyright © 2007 CXO Media, Inc.

keeping the firm focused on achieving its strategic objectives, and developing long-term competitive advantage for the firm. Company personnel must therefore be aware of the strategies being employed by top management and how a CRM initiative links to these strategies, the customer segment impacted by the initiative and finally, the expected outcome.

A formal customer relationship management implementation model should look similar to what is shown in Figure 3.1. A discussion of each element shown in the model follows.

Identifying Competitive Strategies

All organizations utilize some combination of the following three strategies to gain competitive advantage:

1. *Differentiation*—Competing using a **differentiation strategy** means that products and services are unique in some way that differentiates them from similar competitor offerings. Running Room, for example, is a Canadian chain of stores that sells running gear. What differentiates the company from the large sporting goods outlets is that it also sells wellness—it offers running clinics and practice runs for all ages and abilities of customer—and its revenues are growing at approximately 27 percent per year.[6]

   In most cases, differentiation is perceived by customers as meaning greater levels of product and service quality. Consequently, CRM activities among firms competing using differentiation should address some aspect of product and service quality. In the previous example, Running Room is offering services to its customers that differentiate it from its competitors, and this appears to be paying off. The company might also want to consider use of in-store kiosks, announcing upcoming running events, or use of direct mail or email to advertise products of interest to various customer groups like marathon runners or casual runners.

2. *Low Cost*—Many firms commonly compete by using a **low-cost leadership strategy**. For instance, Dell Computers has experienced great success using its low-cost strategy for selling computers, and is busy translating that strategy into customer services. Dell now offers certification programs for its own hardware, and has small business training programs such as financial management and time management using e-learning applications. It is thus serving its primary market of individual consumers and small businesses in an effective, low-cost manner.[7]

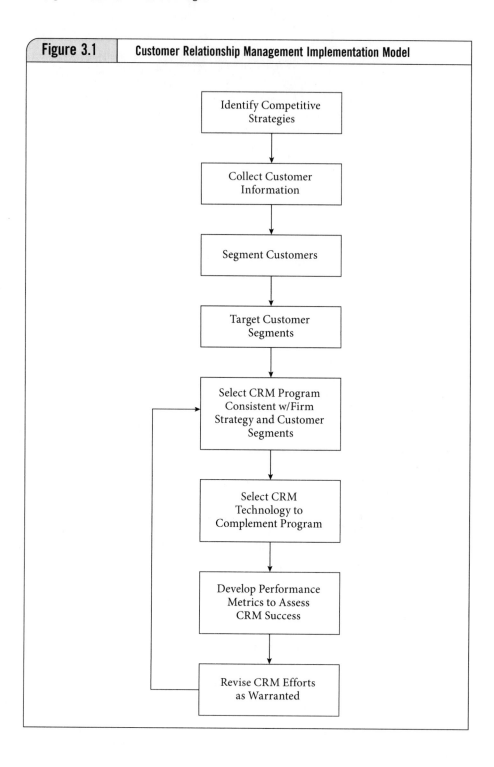

Figure 3.1 | **Customer Relationship Management Implementation Model**

3. *Response*—Competing using a **response strategy** means using a quick, reliable, and/or flexible response to customer demand. Companies that can deliver purchased products on time are considered reliable, whereas companies that can deliver right away offer quick response. Allowing the rerouting of an order in midstream would be considered use of a flexible response strategy. U.K.-based

CD WOW!, an online CD, DVD, and game retailer, has made a success out of selling products at low cost and getting them to customers reliably. For example, if customers order multiple CDs, CD WOW! mails them separately (for free) so they will fit into mail slots, precluding customers from having to pick packages up from post offices. To increase sales, CD WOW! is developing revenue-sharing associations with large businesses. These associations allow businesses to offer CD WOW! products to its employees at a price significantly lower than if the person visited a CD WOW! site directly. These associations have led to revenue growth for CD WOW! without any advertising costs. [8]

Recalling that CRM is one of the top two or three priorities for supply chain management, it is not surprising that companies such as those mentioned put significant effort into managing their customer relationships. Many companies combine two or all three of the competitive strategies previously described to attract and keep customers. Southwest Airlines, for example, has become one of the largest, most profitable U.S. passenger air carriers by focusing on low fares, on-time flights, and a culture of fun; it is thus combining and using all three competitive strategies. It is no coincidence that in 2003, Southwest Airlines was named the most admired airline and the second most admired company by *Fortune* magazine. [9]

Depending on the strategy or combination of strategies employed, firms must first look to their competitive strategies and those of their supply chain trading partners when considering any CRM initiative. CRM applications for low-cost leaders should help to lower costs; for the differentiation strategy, they should help to further differentiate products and services; and for firms concentrating on response, CRM applications should coincide with some type of response characteristic. CRM implementations must either support or advance the firm's strategies to create customer satisfaction and ultimately be successful. Additionally, CRM activities must be focused on the right customers. This topic is discussed in the following sections.

Collecting Customer Information

Identifying customers and constructing a customer database is necessary prior to selecting any specific CRM activity for implementation. Collecting customer information requires searching internal sources such as customer service, accounting, field sales, catalogue sales, marketing, and warranty or repair services. This can be a very time-consuming task for companies that have not already collected much customer information, or for companies that have collected information but are storing it in various databases. Information should be collected and aggregated on each of the following over time. [10]

- *Customer Transactions*—purchase histories, prices paid, delivery dates, return histories;
- *Customer Contacts*—sales calls, service requests, company-initiated contacts;
- *Descriptive Information*—demographic information such as age, education, and profession; and
- *Response to Marketing Stimuli*—how customers responded to company-initiated contacts.

Information can be found and collected from many sources, including warranty cards, complaint cards, company websites, point-of-sale information-gathering activities, call center logs, sales representative logs, warranty repair logs, marketing mailing lists, and a host of other customer-contact sources throughout the organization. Information may already be available on separate databases throughout the organization, requiring the centralization of customer data into one database, in order to provide a single view of each customer.

Firms having direct contact with end customers, such as retailers and banks, generally have the easiest time collecting and organizing customer information, while companies with little or no direct contact with end customers, such as manufacturers, have a more complicated data collection and organization problem. While a manufacturer's direct customers (such as retailers) are certainly important, requiring one customer database, its indirect customers (end-product consumers) must also be marketed to, requiring another customer or consumer database.

As shown in the previous Global Perspective feature, Procter & Gamble is doing a good job managing its worldwide corporate retailers' needs with its CRM efforts. To communicate with and generate information from end users, though, Procter & Gamble and other manufacturers today are relying more and more on their websites. Japanese electronics manufacturer Panasonic (also marketed under the name Matsushita), for example, uses its website to offer consumers before- and after-sales support and information, a range of accessories to purchase, special offers on upcoming products, a download center for manuals and software, and a subscription to the company newsletter. Suk Bhupal, manager of European Web Activity at Panasonic, says that the number of users of its website has doubled every year for the past three years. As Bhupal explains, "A lot of companies want people to come to their site to push products at them. Our approach is more, this is Panasonic, how can we help you?" [11]

Segmenting Customers

Obviously, firms try very hard to market products to people or companies who will respond by making purchases. **Customer segmentation**, or grouping customers within a firm's existing customer database, allows the company to design specific CRM initiatives that will satisfy its customers, provide personalized services to the most profitable customers, and allow marketing efforts to be targeted to specific sets of customers. Segmenting customers can be tricky and prove dangerous, though, when not thought out properly. Today, customers can move through different behaviors, segments, and product choices very quickly. Understanding what connects customers to products or segments is extremely important, while categorizing customers based on age, gender, or income level can be very problematic. A 19-year-old, single, female student working part-time at a sandwich shop and living in a shared apartment, for instance, has seemingly nothing in common with a 47-year-old, married, male engineering manager with two kids who lives at a country-club housing development. But both buy Bruce Springsteen CDs, eat sushi, enjoy bike riding, and shop at Target. Thus segmenting these two customers based on their similarities can be much more effective than other segmentation techniques.

Satisfying and marketing to profitable customers, while reducing the costs of serving unprofitable or low-profit customers, is certainly a primary objective in any CRM initiative, and thus becomes one of the primary ways to segment customers. Other types of segmentation include identifying groups of customers with similar needs, geographical locations, buying attitudes, or buying habits. This has also been referred to as **niche segmentation**. Finally, the ultimate form of segmentation is **individual segmentation**, which has become easier in recent years due to advances in communication and tracking technologies.

Segmenting Customers by Profitability

Dr. Philip Kotler, a leading marketing authority, defines a **profitable customer** as "a person, household, or company that over time yields a revenue stream that exceeds by an acceptable amount the company's cost stream of attracting, selling, and servicing that customer."[12] An automobile buyer, for instance, might represent tens of thousands of dollars in car purchase and service profits over the buyer's lifetime, to an automobile manufacturer. Similarly, an individual credit card user might represent thousands of dollars in profit value over that user's lifetime, to the issuing company. Thus, segmenting customers based on profitability makes sense when deciding which customers the company should pursue, satisfy, and try to retain. The Boston Consulting Group, for example, has found that bank customers who regularly pay their bills online are twice as profitable for the bank as other accountholders. As a result, banks that are successful in having customers adopt online bill paying are achieving a competitive advantage in financial services.[13] Example 3.1 provides an illustration for calculating current year customer profitability.

The term **customer lifetime value** (CLV) is also used as a way to segment customers based on current and projected future profitabilities.[14] Firms assign a profit figure to each customer by summing the revenues of all the products and services purchased over time, less the cost of marketing to and maintaining that customer, such as the costs of direct mail and sales calls and the service costs for each customer (the one-year calculation is shown in Example 3.1). Additionally, the firm forecasts future purchased quantities, profit margins, and marketing costs for each customer, discounts these back to the current date, and then adds this projected profit quantity to the current profit amount. Obviously, CLV cannot be known with certainty, as it varies based on how long the customer is retained, and the size of future purchases. Still, given these CLV figures, marketing departments can then decide which customers to target

---

Example 3.1   Calculating Customer Profitability

Grebson's Golf Shop desires to monitor the profitability of all its customers so that current email, mail, and promotional efforts can be directed towards its best customers. The owners, Phyllis and Bob, have been experimenting with the calculation and have adopted the one shown in the following table for their profitability calculation. The table shows the annual profit calculations for 2004 for Mr. John Adams, one of their best customers, and Ms. Joan Brown, one of their most costly customers.

	JOHN ADAMS	JOAN BROWN
Total Revenue	$ 2,186.42	$ 72.45
Costs of Goods Sold	$ 1,339.81	$ 63.76
Maintenance, Processing, Mailing Costs	$ 180.00	$ 60.00
Marketing Costs	$ 25.00	$ 25.00
Profit	$ 641.61	($ 76.31)

Using this information, the Grebsons decide to take Ms. Brown (and others like her) off their mailing and email lists and curtail any promotional activities such as telemarketing and free or discount promotions to these customers. For their most profitable customers, like Mr. Adams, they decide to design and mail specific catalogues and advertisements for the items and services these customers purchased over the year, while offering a number of promotional items to attract them to the golf shop more often.

with future promotions, and how much they should be spending to acquire new customers and retain existing customers.

Unprofitable customers can prove to be a severe drain on the firm's resources. If these customers are not handled appropriately, they can turn into an enemy of the business and be quite harmful to the firm's reputation. For example, Mr. Brad Anderson, CEO of North American electronics retailer Best Buy Co., seeks to separate the "angels" from the "devils" among his 1.5 million daily customers. Best Buy's angels are those customers boosting profits the most by buying HDTVs, portable electronics, and newly released, high-priced CDs, while their devils are customers that, for example, return purchases and then buy them back at returned-merchandise prices, or demand that Best Buy match rock-bottom price quotes. Other devils buy up loss leaders and then turn around and sell them for a profit on eBay. Through careful identification of good and bad customers in their database, Best Buy is stocking more merchandise and providing more appealing service to its angels, while cutting back on promotions and sales tactics that tend to lure the devils. [15]

Thus, as discussed here, segmenting customers by profitability allows firms to focus their customer relationship management efforts where they will achieve the greatest benefit while reducing marketing costs, thus shedding unprofitable customers. Figure 3.2 presents one way to segment and analyze customers by products and profitability. Segmenting customers in this way allows firms to design methods for managing both customers and products. One mistake firms make is to equate sales with profitability. This can be very costly—if a product is unprofitable (represented by Quadrants III and IV in Figure 3.2), then every one of these units sold to a customer of any type represents a *loss in profits*.

Segmenting Customers by Niche

Organizations can also identify and target a number of market niches for tailoring their marketing and customer relationship management efforts. These might include niches based on industry, firm size, geography, customer psychographics, demography, or behavior. **Psychographics** refers to customer lifestyle choices or personalities. Some firms identify customers based on geography such as in local or **neighborhood marketing**,

Figure 3.2	Customer Profitability Analysis Matrix	
	Profitable Customers	**Unprofitable Customers**
Profitable Products	BEST CUSTOMERS (Quadrant I)	PROFIT POTENTIAL CUSTOMERS (Quadrant II)
Unprofitable Products	SLOW LEAK CUSTOMERS (Quadrant III)	WORST CUSTOMERS (Quadrant IV)

Source: Petro, T., "Profitability: The Fifth 'P' of Marketing," *Bank Marketing*, V. 22, No. 9, 1990, pp. 48–53.

where customer segments can be viewed as having similar income levels or ethnic traits. Banks, fast-food outlets, and grocery stores, for instance, might offer different products and services that appeal to these neighborhood segments. The East West Bank, for example, a full-service commercial bank in California, has grown quickly by concentrating on serving ethnic Chinese living in their Californian communities. Employees speak Chinese and English, all interactive systems are trilingual (Mandarin, Cantonese, and English), and most employees come from Chinese backgrounds. [16]

Segmenting markets by gender can often lead to problems, as briefly discussed earlier—do it wrong, and firms risk offending or alienating customers. However, many firms are segmenting by gender successfully. Home improvement retailer Home Depot, for instance, invested considerable effort in understanding its stores' women customers, who account for about 50 percent of sales. One thing it found through its research was that women focus more on projects and outcomes and less on specific products and their features. Consequently, Home Depot installed design showrooms with room "vignettes," and trained salesclerks to check that customers had everything they needed for a project. They have also launched "do-it-herself" workshops to appeal to women customers. The Bank of Montreal recognized the best way to promote its services to women was to create a more gender-balanced workplace. It created a Task Force on the Advancement of Women in the early 1990s, and today the percentage of women executives at the bank has increased fourfold. Additionally, its customer research reveals that women are more loyal to the bank than men and have placed a larger share of their assets with it. [17] And finally, U.S. apparel retailer Gap's Banana Republic chain is opening its first stores catering to women no taller than five feet, four inches, called Banana Republic Petites. [18]

Another type of niche segmentation is **income segmentation**. Identifying and catering to customers with large disposable incomes can generate significant profits. The Marriott Vacation Club for example, identified the need for a different luxury vacation product after extensive customer research. Many of its affluent customers wanted a second or third vacation home, but didn't want the maintenance obligations of full-time home ownership. So it rolled-out the Ritz-Carlton Club in 1999, a shared-ownership property that shares amenities with existing Ritz-Carlton resorts. The Club attracts new high-income customers and keeps its existing affluent customers "in the family" with a product that offers every convenience and luxury offered by the Ritz. [19]

Firms are also expending significant effort to identify and better serve customers with similar needs. Wachovia Corporation, the 4th largest bank holding company and one of the largest brokerage firms in the United States, is developing a specialty group to serve the legal community. The idea is to sell financial services, investments, and insurance products to law firms and their customers. Currently, Wachovia has relationships with 500 law firms and 3,000 lawyers, and it expects those numbers to grow substantially as news of its specialty services spreads. It plans on establishing additional groups to focus on professionals, business owners, corporate executives, emerging markets, and people with inherited wealth. [20] Microsoft is also trying to think differently about customer segments; it has begun to market to small businesses, recognizing their needs for more products like Small Business Server and the small business edition of Office. Internet networking equipment maker Cisco is also studying the small business market segment and introduced a number of small business-specific products in 2004. [21] Several automakers are designing cars to appeal to young, childless, urban, fashion-conscious customers—these buyers want cars that are small, cheap to run, and have as much interior space, technology, and character as possible. Examples are the DaimlerChrysler Smart, the Peugeot 1007, the Fiat Punto, and the Toyota Aygo. Even though these small cars generate small profits, the car companies are hoping that as their consumers' lifestyles change, they will purchase bigger cars within the same brand.[22] And in yet another example, Procter & Gamble is now marketing products to teenage boys—these include hair care, antiperspirant/deodorant, and personal cleansing products that were launched in early 2004.[23]

Segmenting Customers Individually

Given the capabilities of computers and software to enable better database investigations, firms today are expending more effort in understanding each customer's needs, characteristics, and profitability, such that marketing and service efforts can be tailored to individual customers or very small groups. The idea is to offer the right services or products to the right customers at the right time, referred to as **individual marketing** or **one-to-one marketing**. This has appeal to both businesses and customers because, alternately, firms must design promotions and marketing strategies aimed at an "average customer" among a large group of customers. Thus, understanding individual customer needs or those of small clusters and designing products, services, and marketing strategies to appeal to these customers is the objective of individual segmentation.

To segment individual customers successfully, firms must be able to predict who is going to buy next, what they are going to buy, and when they will buy it. U.S. pharmacy giant CVS Pharmacy, for instance, has over 50 million customers carrying its Extra Care loyalty card, giving CVS perfect visibility into its best customers, and allowing it to determine how each of these customers shops. The company communicates tailored news and special offers to these customers, based on their purchasing histories, and has even rearranged some of its stores based on this information.[24] Florida-based frequent buyer program provider S&H Solutions, the company that made the S&H Green Stamps of old famous, has updated its rewards program and, in the process, created a means of tracking individual preferences for its grocery store partners. Shoppers earn S&H Greenpoints® at a number of grocery stores in the northeastern United States, and can redeem their points at an online catalog store. The company's 7.5 million members swipe their cards at partner grocery stores, which identifies them for special offers on brands their shopping history shows they buy. Shoppers can collect 10 Greenpoints for every dollar they spend. John Durkin, vice president of operations at Foodtown Stores in New Jersey, says the program gives his stores a unique opportunity to understand its customers. "We know who our customers are, what they spend, and what they spend it on."[25]

This type of segmentation and marketing is particularly important with business-to-business markets. In these cases, building a relationship with and successfully serving just one customer can mean millions of dollars in additional revenues for the seller. For example, the Public Sector Business Unit of Dell Computers realized a few years ago that it had identified a key business contact in only 31 percent of its highest profit segment customers. Consequently, over a several year period, Dell used telemarketing to increase its key business contacts to 90 percent of this segment's database. Dell then used email and other methods of communication to make offers and generate responses from these key contacts.[26]

A number of businesses are also attempting to identify and appeal to small, specific groups of customers. Firms that are flexible enough to successfully match customers with the products they will buy, stand to create many long-term, profitable customer relationships. Shaw's Supermarkets, which operates stores throughout New England, has developed the ducklings program to attract mothers with children younger than five. There is no fee; to join, customers sign up for the Shaw's reward card program, either online or in stores. Members receive complimentary issues of *Duckling*, a seasonal magazine with parenting tips, educational articles, and product coupons, only redeemable at Shaw's. Shaw's is thus able to track purchases of individual customers and appeal to this group, in part, through its ducklings program. [27]

Targeting Customer Segments

Following segmentation activities, firms must decide which customers to target with CRM-oriented communications, promotional materials, and marketing programs, along with the most appropriate communication channels to use. Referring again to Figure 3.2, note that the firm's best customers (Quadrant I) purchase the firm's most profitable products and services, while costing the firm the least in terms of selling and servicing or maintenance costs. Thus, CRM initiatives for these customers should focus on maintaining and cultivating successful relationships over the long run, through careful attention to customer service, while seeking to increase sales of additional products and services to these customers. A firm's worst customers (Quadrant IV) purchase only unprofitable or low profit margin products and require high maintenance or service costs; CRM efforts for this group should focus on firing these customers diplomatically, to maintain the firm's reputation. Slow leak customers (Quadrant III) are potentially good customers who buy unprofitable products. Products in this category might be repriced, repackaged, repositioned, or removed from the market, while CRM efforts should focus on marketing more profitable products and services to these customers. Finally, Quadrant II customers buy the most profitable products, but cost the firm too much to maintain and service. CRM efforts for these customers should focus on reducing maintenance and service costs or increasing the prices for the products and services these customers buy.

Generally speaking, CRM initiatives should either seek to move customers and products into Quadrant I, or remove the products and customers from future business dealings. A good rule of thumb to apply is a version of the 80/20 rule—most of the firm's profits are generated by a relatively small group of customers; these customers are the ones who should then receive the most service and attention. Targeting customer segments typically involves use of the Internet, telemarketing, direct mail, and/or direct sales for communication purposes.

Using the Internet to Target Customer Segments

Targeted email marketing campaigns cost very little for the firms doing them and the results are all too evident each day as we access our home and business email accounts. Most of us spend the first five or ten minutes of our day deleting unwanted or junk emails. But the very low cost of distribution is attractive to businesses, and if customers are first asked to "opt-in" or agree to receive messages, then this can be an effective way to target customers for CRM purposes without alienating them. This method, along with other forms of electronic communication with customers, is referred to as **e-CRM**. The e-Commerce Perspective feature discusses Volvo's e-CRM initiatives.

Even though response rates to marketing emails can be extremely low, the very low distribution costs still make this channel quite attractive. According to Peter Steyn, director of sales and marketing for global Internet research company Neilsen/ NetRatings, "If you add up all the time that the average Joe is exposed to all the different media, we'd estimate that 30 percent of that is exposure to the Internet. However,

| e-Commerce Perspective | *e-CRM Initiatives at Volvo* |

Historically, many consumers' perceptions of Volvos likely mirrored those of Dudley Moore in the movie "Crazy People." Moore's character played an advertising executive who has a breakdown and decides there should be truth in advertising. He comes up with the immortal line, "Volvos. They're boxy, but they're good."

The Swedish car manufacturer is working to change that perception, introducing a wider selection of vehicles and attracting a more diverse group of consumers. Database marketing is a key part of the company's plan to retain its loyal customer base and draw new drivers into the fold. Phil Bienert, manager of CRM and e-business for Volvo Cars of North America LLC, recently talked with *Direct* magazine about the firm's online and traditional initiatives.

DIRECT: How important is CRM to your marketing mix?

BIENERT: I think the writing is on the wall that relying entirely on mass marketing to drive your business is just very inefficient. All you have to do is look at the ratings on network TV. At Volvo, CRM and e-business don't report to national advertising like they do at most companies. From a strong foundation and belief in owner loyalty grew a philosophy of believing in CRM, [an idea] that "Gee, if we need to take care of our owners, we need to know who they are, and we need to have some sort of discipline and rigor and analytics behind that." To best serve the people we've identified through the analytics, we need to have mass customization of our marketing activities. And so, even though we're owned by Ford, we're still a small Swedish car company. We don't have the sort of budget of a Ford or a Toyota or a Chevrolet. So we have to do things differently and more efficiently.

DIRECT: What's the backbone of your relationship marketing strategy?

BIENERT: The thing we have, first and foremost, is the database. Everything—segmentation, clustering—springs from that. It's a customer database managed by Harte-Hanks. We have your standard paper-based direct marketing, which can be anything from a launch campaign to a loyalty effort for owners. Direct mail volume varies between 1 million and 2 million pieces per year, depending on if we're in a launch mode or not. We have loyalty clubs. The Volvo Saved My Life Club [meets] a need owners showed us they had. A couple of times a month we'd get these letters from customers who were just writing to say, "Hey, I was in a horrible car crash. Here's the pictures, here's the situation. The police said if I hadn't been in a Volvo I'd be dead. I just want to thank you for making Volvos." They were so moving. We started recognizing that writing letters to us was an outlet for the customers. We felt we owed them the club. It's a way for people to share their stories. The owners love it. The same thing with the High Mileage Club. It was an outlet for the owners to say, "Hey, look, I'm still at Volvo." You've got to own a car for a long time to put 2 million miles on it. But those people are just as valuable from an owner perspective as those who are flipping cars every four years.

DIRECT: How heavily does Volvo use the Web to communicate with its audience?

BIENERT: We do a huge number of e-mail marketing campaigns to prospect hand-raisers and owners. We have an e-newsletter program for both owners and prospects. We used to have a Volvo owners' magazine and we transitioned a lot of that content to electronic format. This year is going to be our most active in terms of really trying to convert a lot of our owners to e-communications. It's something our CEO Vic Doolan is very enthusiastic about. He came up with the idea [to send] every new owner of a Volvo a "Welcome to the brand" video e-mail, personalized by vehicle, just to say "Thanks, we're glad you're here, we're glad you're part of the family. If there's anything we can do, let us know." Right now our e-newsletters are customized based on vehicle owned, years of ownership and region of the country. We add some other profiling from the existing segmentation models we have. We're going to put our new segmentation models that we're working on into that. And basically we have more than 60 different versions of the e-newsletter. [Between] owners and prospects, [the circulation is] not massive right now. I'd say [it's around] 100,000.

DIRECT: Have you discovered anything unusual about your customer base through the segmentation and modeling you've done?

BIENERT: Some people will say, "How do you segment Volvo owners? They're all the same." And for years and years, when we were only selling a sedan and a wagon, trying to segment Volvo owners was a moot point. We knew who they were and they pretty much all looked the same. But since Volvo has expanded from selling just a couple of cars to selling at this point nine-plus vehicles—we have an SUV, a convertible, a flagship luxury sedan, cars we've never had before—we've had to start [taking] a much more serious look at segmentation. The first work we did was back in 1998 when we were launching the S80, our flagship sedan. Nobody was quite sure how to do something like that at Volvo. They never had anything like it before. And that's when Volvo did the first of their vehicle-specific data models. It was more of a targeting model, saying, "OK, if our research on this product says this type of customer should be buying it, how do we look at our existing database, knowing that nobody on the database—as far as we know— owns a car like that?" Today, when we roll out new cars, we do launch-oriented models, whether it's owners or conquest modeling for new products. But the segmentation we're working on now, which I think is the most interesting, is really getting into our database and [seeing] where the clusters are. Now that we've been selling these different types of cars for four or five years, these people are active on the database. It's not the same old customer anymore. We're finalizing our latest round of segmentation and what's most interesting to me is how much the Volvo owner database has changed. [Since] I came to Volvo four years ago the S80 and the XC70 have been on the market for a while. We've introduced an all-new S40, the S60 and a sporty core sedan to replace the old, boxy S70. The face of a Volvo customer has changed and, yes, we still have core families— high-income, highly educated families—but we're starting to [see] different groupings. There are clusters of younger people. It's not all families. We're seeing some atypically high-income people buying Volvos. It's not one-size-fits-all at Volvo anymore.

when you look at share of adspend, we estimate it's still only about one to 1.5 percent." This is partly due to the low cost, but also partly because businesses are hesitant to use the Internet. Steyn says it is the concern about measuring the Internet and obtaining data that is holding most advertisers back.[28] In the United Kingdom, though, e-CRM will have taken 13 percent of the direct marketing expenditures by 2005, and it was already a £525 million industry by the end of 2003.[29]

Besides the cost advantage, there is also a time advantage when using email advertising. Peter Larsen, a managing director at global mobile media specialist Enpocket, explains that while it may take six weeks to design and deploy a piece of direct mail, it takes only six hours to do the same thing using email. "This has a total advantage in terms of cost. Ease of deployment is a major advantage, as is ease of personalization," he says.[30]

Another advantage is the ease of response for first-time and repeat customers. Responding to traditional advertisements or messages requires customers to contact a call center or to find the firm's webpage comment or order form, while responding to emails requires only the click of a mouse. Still, some customers may prefer to be communicated with in other ways, and firms must try to better understand customers and how they should be targeted. Taking a more comprehensive view of customer needs, France-based Société Générale (SG), for example, turned to email personalization and customized web experiences to increase online leads and improve conversion rates. The solution has "… dramatically impacted our own marketing culture and has made the Web a key marketing communication channel," says Oliver Chedeville, vice president of market research and development at SG. SG is now able to reengage clients who drop an application prior to completion—an efficiency that has resulted in a 30 percent increase in online application rates. As a result, it has boosted online revenues, cut service costs, and significantly increased its online channel's ROI.[31]

One complication with email communications is that most people have multiple email addresses and utilize spam blockers, resulting in messages that either don't reach the target audience or reach them multiple times, aggravating customers and causing unsubscribe or opt-out messages to be returned. A number of messages can also be incorrectly identified as spam and blocked, creating **false positive blocking**. For instance, California-based Ferris Research estimates that false positives cost U.S. businesses $3.5 billion in 2003. John Nugent, director of strategic services at DoubleClick, a New York-based provider of digital marketing services, says its company sends out 2.5 billion emails per quarter, and its research shows that 19 percent do not reach the intended recipients.[32] Firms may not even be able to determine the cause of delivery failures. These reasons include decay (the recipient is no longer at the address), poor quality (incorrect address), system failure (server down), or use of spam prevention software. Updating and cleaning email addresses, another problem, can prove somewhat costly for users, too. Andy Ridings, data account director for Insight, a global business-to-business IT provider based in the United Kingdom, says it is more expensive to process an email address than it is to serve it. "It is not in the client's best interest to spend 20p (pence) per record to ensure the e-mail has the correct syntax, when it only costs between 0.5p and 2p to serve the e-mail."[33]

Using Telemarketing to Target Customer Segments

Telemarketing refers to the use of salespeople who use the telephone to identify and qualify potential new customers. Marketing strategies can then be employed to sell products and services to these potential customers and also to cross-sell the firm's other products. Telemarketers can contact many more people per day compared to a field salesperson (perhaps 50 versus 5 customers), and they can be used to give more attention to neglected accounts, or to follow up on other sales leads obtained through other sources. Today, the telemarketing industry accounts for well over $100 billion in annual sales in the United States.

In many cases, telemarketing is reducing the amount of customer contact needed by field sales personnel, allowing them to spend their time calling on larger or more important accounts. As technologies advance and customers become more accustomed to doing business over the phone and Internet, telemarketing systems may play a larger role in marketing and CRM programs. Medienhaus, a leading Austrian media company, has determined that it costs only about one-tenth as much to cross-sell services to customers using telemarketing when compared to direct marketing or door-to-door selling. And telemarketing can be twice as successful if handled correctly. It uses a campaign management system created by Siebel Systems to unify customer information across a very diverse set of customer groups to better understand its customers, improve telemarketing campaigns, and reduce complaints from priority customers. [34]

Telemarketing, though, has some very negative connotations. People often see phone contact from business marketers as intrusive, and in the United States this has resulted in the National Do-Not-Call Registry, initiated in late 2003. Enforced by the U.S. Federal Trade Commission, the national registry was created to make it easier for consumers to avoid telemarketing calls they don't want. Consumers can register a phone number online at http://www.donotcall.gov, and within three months, most telemarketing calls will stop (companies can still call for up to 18 months once a customer makes a purchase). [35] According to a Harris Interactive poll, 92 percent of people who placed a number on the registry reported they were receiving fewer calls. In fact, in just the first two months of registrations, over 48 million U.S. phone numbers were added to the registry. [36]

The Do-Not-Call legislation has had a large negative impact on many U.S. businesses. For instance, in the newspaper publishing industry, telemarketing has been relied upon heavily to increase subscriptions. This is no longer the case. Virginia-based news and information company Gannett saw U.S. subscriptions acquired via telemarketing decline by over 33 percent in 2004. [37] Additionally, circulation for the Tribune's *Los Angeles Times* newspaper declined over 8 percent in 2004, due in part to its cutback in telemarketing. [38]

Particularly when customers receive telemarketing calls from salespeople who know nothing about the customer or their needs (referred to as **cold calls**), consumer resistance and frustration regarding these calls increases. However, when telemarketing calls are in response to a requested call obtained through direct sales calls, emails, or advertisements, the calls are viewed in a positive light and result in a sale much more frequently. In an article published in *Target Marketing Magazine*, Mitchell Lieber suggests six keys to successful telemarketing, as shown in Table 3.2. Lieber suggests that telemarketing is most successful when customers believe there is a good reason for the call, when the offer sounds good to the customer, when the customer has prior knowledge about the call and the offer, and when the telemarketer is thoughtful and engaging.

Using Direct Mail to Target Customer Segments

Direct mail involves sending an announcement, offer, or some other type of hardcopy communication to a customer's or potential customer's address. Direct mail is used to produce prospective customer leads, to sell to existing customers, to enhance customer relationships, and to inform or educate recipients. Each year, millions of

Table 3.2	Six Keys to Successful Telemarketing
1. **Have a good reason for the call, from the customer's perspective.**	There must be a high perceived value from the customer, in terms of both style and substance, to have a successful outcome.
2. **Construct a great offer that appeals to the individual consumer.**	Businesses must be creative and design an offer that is better than their competitors' offers.
3. **Introduce the company and the offer before calling.**	Use some form of direct marketing other than telemarketing to introduce the product and company before the call.
4. **Empower salespeople to engage in meaningful dialogue.**	Train telemarketers to sound as if they are not reading a script; use call guides and suggested questions; empower telemarketers to provide structure to their conversations.
5. **Call the right person with the right offer.**	Design offers to appeal to specific customer segments; use database management and modeling applications to achieve better results.
6. **Use the golden rule of sales.**	Do unto others as you would like done unto you. Place yourself in the position of the customer.

Source: Lieber, Mitchell, "Six Ways to Conduct Successful Telemarketing in a Do-Not-Call World," *Target Marketing,* V. 2w7, No. 10, 2004, pp. 107–109.

pieces of direct mail are sent to addresses obtained from purchased or internally generated mailing lists. Internet access companies send out computer disks and offers of free time on the Internet, auto repair shops send out reminders for oil changes, grocery stores send out their latest advertisements, department stores mail tailored catalogs to customers, and hotels mail advertisements for reduced price rooms and amenities. Direct mail, while expensive, allows firms to more closely target various market segments and to personalize offers sent to specific customers. The response rates have been found to be virtually identical for both business and consumer direct mail—about 11 percent as of 2004. In-house mailing lists provide the best response rates, while use of rented lists and directories has response rates that are lower.[39] Consequently, this type of response rate can generate large profits for companies using direct mail.

Recently, the U.K.-based telecom Interoute designed a direct mail campaign to reach CIOs in the United States. Nick McMenemy, CMO at Interoute, says, "They're the most contacted segment on earth. They're busy, used to receiving junk, and they're good at screening calls." Their strategy consisted of two direct mail pieces—a teaser flyer featuring the British Union Jack, followed by an MP3 player with the same Union Jack motif and a 30-second audio message from an Interoute representative with a British accent. The campaign had a 19 percent response rate and generated over $250,000 worth of new business, with a cost of about $40,000.[40]

Use of direct mail is increasing today in the United States, due in part to the Do-Not-Call registry. According to a survey by *Direct* magazine, use of direct mail increased from 25 to 45 percent of the respondents' total marketing budgets from 2003 to 2004. Additionally, respondents reported higher revenues from direct mail campaigns when comparing 2003 to 2004. Specialty retailer The Sharper Image Corp. of California, for example, increased catalog circulation by 13 percent for the first six months of 2004 and realized a 21 percent boost in catalog-generated revenue. Using direct mail to prospect for new customers is also increasing in importance. Marketers spent 62 percent of their budgets on consumer acquisition in 2004 versus 58 percent in 2003 and 46 percent in 2002. [41]

As discussed in this section, building supply chain relationships with the right customers using personalized emails, telephone calls, and direct mail has been shown to be much more effective than simply talking "at" large audiences using mass-marketing channels, and is the foundation for all successful CRM programs. The next section provides information on selecting the most appropriate CRM program.

Selecting a CRM Program Consistent with Firm Strategy

As mentioned earlier, the three strategic imperatives for firms are differentiation, low cost, and response. Since one of the primary objectives of CRM is to achieve high levels of customer satisfaction and loyalty, CRM programs should support or advance the firm's strategy while satisfying and retaining key customers in order to achieve long-term success. Some firms may be tempted to deviate from their core competencies in an effort to increase customer revenues; however, this can be a drain on the firm's resources and may still not achieve desired outcomes. Additionally, CRM program failures may actually result in lower customer satisfaction levels and permanent loss of customers. Several CRM programs or initiatives are discussed next.

Customer Loyalty Programs

Customer loyalty programs (also called frequency programs or company clubs) reward repeat customers with discounts, credits, cash, and prizes, depending on the value and frequency of the repeat purchases. In recent years, customer loyalty programs have become widespread among even the smallest of businesses as firms have realized that repeat purchases can create brand loyalty and that brand loyalty results in successful customer relationships. Brand loyalty can be generated by combinations of good customer service, high product quality, customization, and other product or service characteristics. If designed effectively, loyalty programs are seen by customers as a valuable complement to the base product or service. Loyal customers generate more sales for businesses through frequent word-of-mouth advertising; additionally, loyal customers often buy a wide range of the firm's products. These initiatives can be a powerful way to attract potential high-value, long-term customers; gather purchase data over time; keep customers interested; and attract new customers from competitors while creating a direct pipeline to customers for marketing purposes.

The cost, information generated, and perceived value of a customer loyalty program can vary greatly, and can be designed to integrate well with a firm's differentiation, low-cost, or response strategy. For a small business such as a barbershop, a punch-card system might be used to track customer purchases, with a reward of a free haircut after ten paid haircuts. At the other end of the spectrum might be a casino that uses a registered loyalty card to track customer information, with product offerings, discounts, and gifts automatically generated when certain casino spending hurdles are reached.

Charlie Brown's Steakhouse, for instance, is a New Jersey–based regional restaurant chain with over 40 units. It has experienced 13 consecutive years of sales increases, and one measure of the chain's success is its customer loyalty program, called the Handshake Club. With over 750,000 members, the club accounts for about 35 percent of Charlie Brown's annual sales. Members earn one point for each food dollar spent, and when customers reach 200 points, they are mailed two $10 vouchers. Members also receive a voucher on their birthday. Charlie Brown's competes on value, and this simple program appears to be working quite well. [42] Another example is Harrah's Entertainment, one of the world's largest casino operators. Harrah's loyalty card customers swipe their cards 100 million times per day from 28 globally dispersed casinos. This information is fed to a computer in Memphis, Tennessee, and each morning Harrah's knows which customers should be rewarded with free show tickets, dinner vouchers, or room upgrades. "We can see how much money is going through a machine, how frequently it pays out, how much it pays out, and what type of player is on it, male or female, and what age they are," says Tim Stanley, CIO at Harrah's in Las Vegas. "We're trying to figure out which products sell, and we're trying to increase our customer loyalty." Harrah's enormous data warehouse holds 30 terabytes, or roughly three times the number of characters in the U.S. Library of Congress. It recently spent $10 million upgrading its computer system and keeps detailed records on 30 million people. [43]

The popularity of loyalty programs has spawned several problems for both providers and customers. Customers are literally swamped with company club programs, making it difficult to carry cards and discern the value and differences in them. Many companies are consequently searching for better ways to package, market, and price their programs. To better manage the loyalty program process, service companies specializing in loyalty program management have been created. Georgia-based TSYS Loyalty manages programs for some of the top issuers of loyalty programs in the United States. Its objective is to counsel program providers such that companies receive maximum benefit from the program, while providing value to cardholders.

Fees are also making their way into many loyalty programs, and these can be viewed very negatively by cardholders. For instance, Diners Club International announced plans in 2004 to add a 95-cent handling fee for every 2,000 points redeemed in its Club Rewards program; Air Canada charges a $25 fee to redeem miles in its Aeroplan program; and American Express charges up to $50 to transfer points into an airline frequent flyer program. These and other companies argue that their reward program administration costs are increasing, but many customers view these charges as a reversal in commitment to the customer relationship, potentially resulting in customer defections. "Your message becomes, 'Yes, we love you, but don't become too much of a burden to us, or we might change our minds,'" says Bill Hanafin, of The COLLOQUY Group, a consulting arm of Ohio-based Frequency Marketing, Inc. [44]

Customer Service Initiatives

Customer service is seen as a high priority among firms where customer retention, customer loyalty, and customer profitability are important. If firms are in the process of developing a CRM program, then customer service aspects ought to be a primary component of the design considerations. This is such an important aspect of the customer–supplier relationship that it deserves an entire chapter of discussion in this text—Chapter 4. While many definitions for **customer service** exist, the term generally refers to the provision of information, help, and/or technical support to customers in a way that meets or exceeds customer expectations. Firms can provide reactive and proactive customer service to customers through use of call centers, websites, and printed materials. Well-designed customer service initiatives at companies can go a long way towards maintaining or improving customer relationships, retaining customers, and finding new ones through word-of-mouth communications.

Reactive customer service occurs when customers with a problem contact the firm and the firm helps to solve the problem. This includes handling product returns, mechanical problems with the product, technical questions about the product's operation, requests for product information, and requests for product repairs. Call center technicians and customer service desk personnel are trained to provide an array of information on a host of product-related questions and problems. For most businesses this type of customer service is expected, and when it is not available or adequately performed customers become dissatisfied. Thus, poorly designed or delivered reactive customer service can be extremely damaging to customer relationships. Example 3.2 provides a real example of a customer's complaint regarding poor reactive customer service. The bank in the example appears to have lost this customer's loyalty.

Proactive customer service is much more difficult for businesses to provide, but when designed well it often exceeds customer expectations and significantly benefits the CRM process. Proactive customer service entails anticipating customer needs and problems and delivering solutions prior to the time when requests and complaints occur. This can take the form of providing answers to frequently asked questions in product pamphlets or on company websites, mailing out automobile recall notices, or warning customers of probable wait times. Recently for instance, e-banking customers have

---

Example 3.2   An Example of Poor Reactive Customer Service

Here is an online chat room discussion found on the Internet regarding a complaint about an e-bank's inability to provide good reactive customer service:

I have had an e-plan with current account, credit card, savings account and mortgage since April 2000. I have been happy with the product offering which I find very competitive. I am also reasonably satisfied with the technology, which I believe is above average. It is a shame that their customer service is so appalling.

For a start, it is difficult to speak to a member of the staff when you need to, as they seem to be struggling with demand. On the other hand, whenever I have had a problem, I have been frustrated by the unskilled staff. Not only do they not seem to have been trained to a decent standard, but they also lack the ability to perform basic banking transactions, which invariably need to be done by the "banking department."

As an example of the problems you could face, I recently tried to send money abroad through a SWIFT payment. Not only was the money not received on time, but it was "lost" for a month. During that period of time, I made multiple calls and there was always an answer: "We'll find out and call you back." They never did.

Eventually, after speaking to one of their managers, I was refunded my money. The only explanation provided was that the person that had filled in the form had made a mistake in the foreign bank's address. No official apology was issued. I could mention a couple of examples similar to the above.

I am shocked and concerned to realize that my money is being manipulated by extremely unreliable staff. I am very uneasy every time I ask these guys to perform a transaction. This is not what I would expect from a serious bank. It is a shame that a fantastic product is being ruined by poor customer service. I will stay with them for some time, but they will have to improve if they want to have me as a customer in the medium term.

been the subject of "phishing" scams, wherein consumers get a fraudulent email directing them to a legitimate bank website. Once in the site, though, consumers are directed to a different and fraudulent site, which asks for personal account information. A number of banks with e-commerce capabilities have been the recipient of this type of scam and have taken steps to educate their customers of the potential threat, while patching security holes in their websites.[45] More on proactive service is presented in the Service Perspective feature.

Customization Capabilities

Allowing customers to customize the products and services they buy creates a uniqueness that is appealing to many customers. Thus, unwanted complexity, traits, and add-ons can be avoided, while desired functions or attributes can be retained for each individual customer, creating greater feelings of ownership and consequently satisfaction. This is quite easy for service providers, and getting easier for manufacturers as well.

For many forms of information services, this is also called **versioning**. Using the latest digital printing presses, catalog and magazine publishers can offer versioning to personalize their publications and appeal to individuals or very small market niche segments. Perhaps marketing has found that first-time customers who buy running shoes typically buy exercise clothing for their second purchase. In this case, catalogues can be printed with exercise gear on the front cover. The pages of the catalogue can also be designed to highlight exercise gear, and letters accompanying the catalogue mailings to first-time running shoe buyers can mention the current sale of exercise gear. Catalogue versioning such as this can typically achieve a 50 percent rebuy rate from first-time buyers.[46] Global specialty coffee retailer Starbucks does a great job of offering customized coffee drinks, and encourages employees to use their own discretion when customizing services for customers. These types of tailored services tend to engage customers and create very positive word-of-mouth advertising.

For many manufacturing companies, **mass customization** (as discussed earlier, in Chapter 2) has enabled firms to offer customized products while keeping production costs under control. While some initial attempts at mass customization were unsuccessful, such as Levi's custom-fitted jeans and toy maker Mattel's customized "friends of Barbie" dolls, companies like Wisconsin-based clothing catalogue retailer Lands' End and Nike appear to be succeeding at custom-ordered goods manufacturing. Even though the garments cost more at Lands' End and take longer to arrive than standardized equivalent products, about 40 percent of its shoppers choose customized garments, and reorder rates are 34 percent higher than for buyers of standard-sized clothing.[47]

Building Customer Communities

Today, firms can create **customer communities** using the web to build a network of customers to facilitate communication or the exchange of ideas between customer members and also with company personnel. This helps to foster relationships between customers and the company, creating more of a personal or family environment. Engaging customers in these communities also makes it harder for customers to "leave the family." For instance, motorcycle manufacturer Harley-Davidson has developed Harley Owners Groups, or HOGs, through its website, where Harley owners can share their experiences and ideas. This direct online information sharing is also sometimes referred to as **viral marketing** or **bottom-up branding**.[48]

Service Perspective

Call Center Trends in the Banking Industry

With rising call center operating costs and legal limitations on outbound calling, the focus of call centers has changed, says Pare Ravesi, senior product marketing manager for ATG, located in Cambridge, Massachusetts. "A dramatic trend in the past two years has been the change in focus from customer acquisition to customer retention," says Ravesi. "Companies are now focused on 'How do I sell more to my existing customers?' and 'How do I retain more customers?'"

To reduce costs while maintaining quick response and quality service, Ravesi says many banks are turning to self-service applications. "Banks were the early adopters of self-service with ATMs," says Ravesi. "They sought ways to provide increased service and differentiation, but without the increased cost burden."

Ravesi says many organizations are now turning to "proactive service," which allows banks to communicate with customers and prospects in a way that reduces the number of inbound contacts, as well as the peaks and valleys of call times, and also lowers costs. "Proactive service increases customer satisfaction by communicating with the customer before they contact you," says Ravesi. "For example, if you can communicate the status of a mortgage application before the realtor or customer contacts you, you can increase their satisfaction, reduce your cost per transaction and show better customer service."

Ravesi believes that proactive service and self-service are major areas of growth that will reduce the cost per contact as well as the cost associated with traditional call centers. "Further, it will reduce the number of agents needed and free up agents to engage in more high value and high worth interactions with customers and prospects," she says.

Ravesi offers this advice: "If you already have a call center, review and analyze the facts: customer retention rates, talk times, wait times and service levels. Look at your competition. Are you aligned, are you behind or are you leading? Leading the service curve is the way to differentiate your business and that may mean replacing some older technologies with some of the newer self-service, lower cost solutions. However, if you are just considering launching a call center, check out alternative technologies first," says Ravesi. "Many online self-service solutions are very affordable, easy to deploy and easy to maintain. A self-service oriented website can be more efficient and less costly than five live call-center agents."

"Customers will embrace an online channel with varying degrees of acceptance," Ravesi says. "By deploying such a solution, you can create an environment in which call center agents are able to focus their attention on the high-value, high-worth customers, and you can integrate your online and Web systems so that when your customers go to your website, you can present them with personalized and relevant information that will differentiate your organization from your competitors."

Web communities also provide companies with real-time access to customers and their ideas and concerns, and give company personnel opportunities to interact one-on-one with customers. Customer ideas can sometimes find their way into future product designs, and company personnel can answer questions and share news about products, product operating information, or new uses for old products. Marketing personnel must be careful, though, not to use web communities as a way to openly market products, since customers may cease using the community if it is perceived as another marketing channel. Salesnet, a Massachusetts-based supplier of CRM systems, practices what it preaches; in a recent online community project, it created an e-learning portal called mySalesnet, which empowers customers to share best practices with Salesnet as well as other CRM customers. Anthony Nelson, Salesnet chief customer officer, says, "We recognize we'll only be successful if our customers are successful. We need to understand their world, the business drivers, and devote resources at the highest level." [49]

As we've seen, businesses have access to a number of CRM programs and initiatives, which have shown to be quite successful in building and maintaining valuable customer relationships. Some can be implemented for very little cost, while others can require very large expenditures for training, computer systems, and other equipment. As companies begin identifying customers, their purchase habits, and the strategies for remaining competitive, suitable and compatible CRM programs can be utilized. Along with these programs, technologies to deliver CRM programs (referring back to Figure 3.1) must also be considered, and this topic follows.

Selecting a Compatible CRM Technology

Many CRM efforts today are driven by technology. Depending on the number of customers a firm has, the profit contributions of each customer, and the specific CRM program employed, technology usage will vary. Wal-Mart has no desire to contact each of its millions of customers individually; however, it can use the Wal-Mart website to express appreciation, ask for feedback, and initiate customer-oriented programs. On the other hand, a custom home builder communicates directly with customers and may utilize a computer software application to enable customers to visualize certain home design alternatives. In all cases though, firms should consider the most appropriate CRM technology only after a customer relationship initiative has been identified. CRM technologies can be both expensive and time consuming, while potentially doing a poor job of operationalizing a CRM idea.

While CRM technology investments are growing, companies are finding it difficult to utilize these investments to create a competitive advantage. A survey compiled in 2004 by New York-based consulting firm Marakon Associates found that 56 percent of U.S. business respondents had invested in CRM technologies, yet only 16 percent rated their companies as doing a commendable job with it. "Clearly, these efforts have not paid off for many companies," says David Meer, head of Marakon's customer value group. "Either the research investments have not produced insights that lead to a meaningful advantage over competitors, or the companies are unable to act on the insights collected." [50] Companies should identify the desired benefits of any CRM investment and use these as the yardstick to assess CRM success. Additionally, firms should try to stick to their plan while working closely with application providers to minimize any implementation or upgrade problems. Finally, once a CRM program is working well, businesses should avoid the tendency to introduce changes and complexity to the program. The old adage, "If it ain't broke, don't fix it," applies to all CRM implementations.

CRM technologies have matured over the past ten years, but implementation failure rates remain high—as much as 75 percent according to the Meta Group, an information technology research and consulting company (now part of Connecticut-based Gartner, Inc.). [51] Some of the reasons for failure include:

- the inability to create an enterprise-wide CRM strategy,
- the difficulty in integrating CRM applications with legacy systems, and
- lack of an approach to analytics. [52]

Thus, some of the same failures that plagued ERP systems several years ago are seen today with many CRM system implementations. Companies with many disparate CRM applications are now trying to integrate these throughout the organization to allow better internal communications and to present one face to the customer. Most of the ERP system vendors offer their own compatible CRM applications and are also working on housing a firm's existing CRM applications within their ERP system. Lastly, many companies suffer from not knowing what to do with all the customer information floating around the organization. This lack of an **approach to analytics** has caused firms to miss out on marketing or customer service opportunities. Other complicating issues include the idea that different segments of the organization view customers differently, have dissimilar customer processes, different marketing and distribution channels, and diverse systems to contend with. One company may have many existing CRM applications providing different services to different segments of customers. And managers must always remember that CRM technologies are only enablers, not a substitute for a well-designed and delivered CRM initiative. If the plan does not allow the firm to ultimately serve customers better, then the best technology implementation in the world will not help the firm at all.

While it has already been mentioned that CRM failure rates are quite high, there have been many very successful CRM application implementations. For example, Mascot International, Europe's fourth largest workwear manufacturer, installed mySAP CRM in 2003 to automate its sales transaction processes online and to integrate with its back-office SAP system. Now, orders are processed faster and with greater accuracy, resulting in faster order cycle times and a 40 percent reduction in order-entry errors. Additionally, since the implementation, its cost of service has decreased by 12 labor-hours per day and its sales revenue growth has increased by 7.5 percent per year. KLM Royal Dutch Airlines installed E.piphany Marketing in 2003 to track customer information. Flight attendants can now use the information to recognize their Platinum members by name and membership status. The system has allowed KLM to achieve response rates to marketing campaigns of 5 to 12 percent, well above the industry average. Additionally, its customer base has grown by 20 percent and annual revenue from known customers has increased by 5 percent. [53]

CRM software products are also expanding into government, education, and other not-for-profit organizations. For instance, in 2005, former software manufacturer PeopleSoft installed a CRM solution for Mexico's national tax service, at the time the biggest single client engagement in PeopleSoft's history. The recruiting process at universities is very competitive, and CRM providers are helping universities to replace their manual, paper-oriented campaigns with intelligent, advanced analytics and call center CRM products. [54] The Golden Key International Honour Society uses a hosted CRM system from Florida-based Aplicor to track its business partner transactions, aid in the development of marketing programs aimed at business partners, and to monitor the value of the services provided to its partners. The system enabled Golden Key to increase annual partnership revenues by 41 percent, improve employee productivity by 17 percent, and reduce new staff training time by 33 percent. [55]

Developing CRM Performance Metrics

Measuring the performance of all of the CRM activities, both initially and then periodically after implementation, is extremely important, given the historically poor performance of many CRM initiatives to date. Given that initial monetary outlays can be very high and that training and implementation activities can require significant time investments, not to mention the possibility of damage to valuable customer relationships resulting from poorly designed or executed CRM initiatives, performance monitoring should be viewed as a necessary CRM element. CRM performance metrics should measure customer satisfaction and customer loyalty associated with use of the particular program. Initially, companies should establish baseline measurements to serve as a basis for comparison once the various CRM initiatives are in place. Then, as the CRM program matures and expands, the organization can periodically assess performance as a means for reviewing the success of each new activity, as well as reviewing performance of the activities already in place. When weaknesses or performance gaps are identified, firms should revise CRM efforts to treat these problems.

In his book *Beyond Customer Satisfaction to Customer Loyalty*, Mr. Keki Bhote, one of the instrumental people behind Motorola's Six Sigma program and in part responsible for Motorola receiving the prestigious Malcolm Baldrige National Quality Award (Motorola won in 1988 and again in 2002), recommends that companies generate customer information prior to embarking on any customer loyalty program.[56] He recommends use of focus groups, input from customer-contact personnel, and one-on-one, in-depth, key customer interviews.

Focus groups are an assembled group of customers giving their opinions to company personnel regarding various product, service, or proposed CRM initiative strengths and weaknesses. Customer contact personnel can also provide valuable insights and ideas regarding CRM initiatives, since they are in a position to know about customer needs and specific product or service problems. Finally, spending time with key customers (the ones responsible for the largest percentages of profits) in their own environment is by far the best way to obtain feedback regarding products, services, and programs.

Once the CRM initiative(s) have been designed and implemented, use of the same customer inputs as previously described along with surveys and information captured using information technologies are recommended to determine levels of customer satisfaction and customer loyalty. Mail surveys can be used and are inexpensive and fast; however, they tend to suffer from poor response rates and are biased towards those customers who are dissatisfied. Telephone surveys are more effective than mail surveys, although they are more expensive, time consuming, and prone to customer hang-ups. Additionally, call center comments, website company contact emails, trade show customer comments, and prepaid survey postcards contained in product packages can be used to gauge customer satisfaction with CRM efforts. Table 3.3 describes several metrics that can be useful for measuring CRM program success.

Measuring the performance of CRM programs and finding positive results will help create a more proactive, customer-centric organization, and will enable the firm to justify further CRM program investments. The American Automobile Association's (AAA) Mid-Atlantic U.S. franchise uses response rate and costs to sustain membership as metrics to track the success of their marketing campaigns. After employing SAS business intelligence software to improve its membership modeling and marketing capabilities, it was able to raise response rates among existing members by as much as 92 percent. Additionally, it was able to reduce the cost of sustaining the membership in its insurance program by 92 percent.[57]

Table 3.3	CRM Performance Metrics
PERFORMANCE METRIC	**DESCRIPTION**
CRM return on investment	Additional profit generated/$ program investment
Conversion efficiency	# new customers generated/$ program investment
Maintenance ratio	# customers retained/# customer defections
Defection rate	# customer defections/total # customers
Top management commitment	Senior manager time spent on CRM activities
Key customer metrics	Can be measured using: # key customers (those exceeding an annual profitability value) # key customers/total # of customers Avg. key customer annual profitability Avg. key customer longevity Avg. key customer satisfaction survey rating Percent of key customer complaints successfully resolved Percent of key customers defected

Revising and Improving CRM Efforts as Warranted

Inevitably, organizations will find that at least some CRM initiative outcomes fall short of expectations, particularly with initial program implementations. According to Mr. Patrick Harris, Director of Information Technology at New York-based Sealing Devices, a manufacturer of various products for original equipment manufacturers in the aerospace, defense, and electronics industries, and also a CRM program award winner, "You can't just install, train, and expect everything to work flawlessly. You need to continually reevaluate your sales processes and continually tweak the CRM system to support the processes."[58] Companies also find they must continually be considering ways to improve their CRM programs just to stay even with the competition and maintain customer loyalty. The desire to improve CRM programs also occurs as improvements in CRM technologies emerge.

Some CRM programs are changing to reduce the administrative and equipment costs associated with some initiatives. According to a recent study by global technology consultant Booz Allen Hamilton, 71 percent of CFOs stated they were in the process of cutting nonessential funding, including the CRM budget. Thus, these companies must discover ways to increase the value of remaining CRM initiatives. For example, the Yankee Group, a global leader in communications and networking research and consulting, found that one of the biggest expenditures for CRM is connecting customers with the company information they need. If companies can automate tasks like order management and billing, while seamlessly connecting users to the information needed, the results are increases in productivity and first-call resolution, which translate to lower costs. CRM self-service tools can also reduce the time it takes to assist customers and solve problems, also reducing costs. "Eighty percent of CRM costs are in the process of solving the customers' problems," says Brian Kelly, executive vice president of marketing and product strategy for KANA, a California-based provider of customer service technology solutions.[59]

Retooling or revising a CRM program involves monitoring program performance metrics, comparing the results to desired objectives or standards, and then making changes when the standards are not met or exceeded. Additionally, if the firm is in frequent contact with customers, previously undiscovered needs or problems can be uncovered and then dealt with through changes or additions to CRM activities. The CRM planning process should also identify and prioritize innovative CRM ideas that can be tested and evaluated. Sufficient resources must be applied to these experiments or trial runs to evaluate their success and applicability to a larger or system-wide implementation. These small-scale initiatives can produce valuable insights into ways of improving customer relationships and profitability. Some of these ideas may also fail, but will provide valuable insights about what will and will not work.

Kentucky-based horse racing company Churchill Downs, Inc. is trying out a new idea to improve the likelihood of higher CRM returns. It has developed a sponsorship with computer and electronics manufacturer Gateway to provide high-definition plasma televisions in strategic locations at its horse racing tracks to show standard and slow-motion replays of the races for its customers. In return, Gateway gains valuable marketing territory and visibility in front of millions of track customers. Certain Churchill Downs loyalty club customers will also receive opportunities to enter sweepstakes for new Gateway products. Atique Shah, vice president of CRM at Churchill Downs, says, "It takes a lot of courage and vision on both sides to get this done. And Gateway is really working toward ways to help us improve the customer experience."[60]

Privacy Issues in CRM

Since many CRM solutions depend to a large degree on storage and analysis of a large volume of customer information, there is an obvious privacy issue pertaining to the amount of personal information contained in these data banks and how it is used. Indeed, there are various privacy issues present in all of the steps of the CRM model just discussed, and shown in Figure 3.1. While this is certainly not a new concern, the nonstop nature of marketing emails, combined with the ability of business websites to gather user information unwittingly and sell it to third parties, has thrust the privacy issue to the forefront in the minds of many customers, associations, and lawmakers. In a survey of Internet information privacy undertaken by Forrester Research, 61 percent of Internet users in the United States reported that they do not purchase online because of privacy concerns.

Interesting, too, is that business purchases of **clickstream tracking software** (software that enables the storage of each request for information made by a visitor to a website) was expected to reach $6 billion by 2006, according to Jupiter Research.[61] This software creates **cookie files** that store clickstream information captured on a website as users interact with the site. Companies can then share and consolidate cookie information gathered from numerous websites. Unfortunately, hackers can also intercept cookie files and gain access to consumer identity information. While this type of identity theft is illegal, it nevertheless occurs at an ever-increasing rate.

Websites have an ethical obligation to allow visitors to decide whether their personal information can be collected and used, and there is currently a fairly large number of quickly changing and vague state, federal, and international privacy rules and regulations, making compliance a difficult thing for many companies. Some of the current regulations in the United States include the Health Insurance Portability and Accountability Act, the Gramm-Leach-Bliley Act, the Sarbanes-Oxley Act, and California's SB 1386 identity protection bill. Also, the Global Internet Freedom Act and the Online Privacy Protection Act are slowly winding their way through the U.S. Congress.

Still other European Union and Canadian laws are forcing companies to deal with the issue of information privacy.

Many businesses post their privacy policies, and customers need to look for this information prior to making a website purchase or inquiry. Some websites allow users to **opt-in**, or give their consent regarding the use of personal data, as well as to **opt-out**, or explicitly forbid the use of personal data by the website company. For companies today, an important issue with respect to information privacy is to control all of the customer data. Technologies have made it easy to collect and store tremendous amounts of customer data. This data is then distributed across the organization, and in many cases among partner networks. To control this information, firms must create an inventory of all sensitive data in the organization and establish policies related to its use and protection. For example, AXA Financial Services, located in New York, has built a database that consolidates customer information from multiple applications and systems within the company. Each customer record has an embedded indicator that describes the customer's privacy preferences. This database is linked to every legacy application at AXA. AXA also uses a web-monitoring tool to ensure the information on its web pages and its use of cookies complies with the firm's privacy policies. [62]

A number of industry trade associations have developed self-regulation policies and guidelines in order to avoid or minimize government legislation. A few of these organizations follow:

- *The Online Privacy Alliance (http://www.privacyalliance.org):* A cross-industry coalition of more than 80 global companies and associations committed to promoting the privacy of individuals online. The Alliance is an ad hoc organization whose sole purpose is to work to define privacy policy for the new electronic medium and to foster an online environment that respects consumer privacy.

- *The Direct Marketing Association (http://www.the-dma.org):* The DMA's Privacy Promise to American Consumers took effect for all DMA member companies that market to consumers on July 1, 1999. The Privacy Promise seeks to "raise the bar" for privacy practices by ensuring that DMA members adhere to certain privacy practices, and by challenging all non-DMA industry members to meet this high standard as well.

- *The World Wide Web Consortium (http://www.w3c.org):* The Platform for Privacy Preferences Project (P3P), developed by the World Wide Web Consortium, is emerging as an industry standard providing a simple, automated way for users to gain more control over the use of personal information on websites they visit. At its most basic level, P3P is a standardized set of multiple-choice questions, covering all the major aspects of a website's privacy policies. Taken together, they present a clear snapshot of how a site handles personal information about its users.

Some Recent Approaches to CRM

As new and faster analytical and data storage technologies emerge, new CRM capabilities and ideas are also discovered. While these technologies cannot replace the necessary customer contact and high service levels required of CRM, they can certainly enable the firm to do more for customers and do it faster, with fewer resources. Several of these recent technologies impacting CRM initiatives are discussed next, along with several other trends in CRM.

Voice over Internet Protocol

Voice over Internet Protocol, or VoIP, is a method for taking analog audio signals (such as talking on the telephone) and turning them into digital data that can then be transmitted over the Internet. Firms can use VoIP to turn voice communications into simply another network application that can integrate with other real-time applications such as instant messaging and web and video conferencing, and to enable collaboration among various units of the firm or between the firm and its business partners. VoIP can merge web, email, and phone conversations in a contact center to greatly improve customer service, and it can also integrate with ERP and other applications to enable instant virtual meetings and dramatically speed up decision-making processes. Email and voice calls can sit together in one inbox accessible from a PC, PDA, or cell phone. Most people agree that converting to VoIP in organizations is inevitable; some are integrating with VoIP gradually, while others are installing complete system-wide applications. [63]

Social Network Technology

For field sales personnel, closing a deal may depend on who you know; and **social networking technology** helps salespeople figure out who knows who at a prospect organization. Social networking applications allow firms to search for relationships to accounts and contacts within their existing CRM system. According to Lynda Radosevich, vice president of communications at Visible Path, a social networking application provider, "The impact of leveraging these trusted relationships results is tracked in the CRM system and creates a rigorous means of measuring a company's relationship capital." [64]

Self-Service CRM

Self-service CRM applications, aided by **Voice Extensible Markup Language** or VoiceXML, can greatly increase productivity while satisfying customers, particularly at call centers. VoiceXML uses standards for building telephone speech applications to improve the effectiveness of touchtone customer service capabilities. Today, these systems handle only a small portion of customer calls, perhaps 20 percent, but according to Steve Tran, cofounder of BeVocal, a California-based provider of hosted speech solutions, "I see the next ten years really shifting that balance on its head." [65]

Outsourced CRM

Firms that want to deploy CRM initiatives quickly but do not possess the capability, equipment, or personnel to do so are turning to externally hosted or **on-demand CRM** services. Businesses can also outsource CRM initially for testing purposes, while saving on implementation costs. If the particular initiative shows promise, then the firm can deploy it in-house as a long-term solution, with greater confidence in its performance and capabilities. "It's not a panacea," Unisys's Rich Jaso says. "On-demand by definition will never give you the type of access to data, the type of mining, the type of integration that you need in order to truly do a world-class CRM. But over the next couple of years, you're going to see huge increases in on-demand types of services." [66]

The "Curse" of Cheap Data Storage

Companies have always tried to gather information about customers, and today's data storage capabilities make that possible as never before. "A decade ago, the biggest data centers in the U.S. had 10 terabytes (10 trillion bytes) of storage, and there were only five or ten of them. Today we have customers with two or three petabytes

(3000 terabytes)," says Gil Press, senior director of open software at EMC, a Massachusetts-based manufacturer of disk storage systems. This space has enabled firms to gather more information than they now know what to do with, and the available microprocessors and database software applications have yet to catch up in terms of processing capabilities. "The situation we're in is like having a dam that's filling up with water, getting bigger and bigger, and we're trying to get water out of it with a straw," says James Gray, manager of Microsoft's San Francisco Bay Area Research Center.[67]

Even with the latest storage technologies, the demand for more storage is quickly outpacing the industry's ability to deliver. Storage shipments in 2004 topped 22 exabytes (22,000 petabytes) of hard-disk space. That is four times the space needed to store everything mankind has EVER said, and it is twice the amount sold in 2002. This growth in demand for data storage is expected to continue, as prices keep falling and as data processing capabilities keep improving. "Companies want to look at all the data. They want atomic level data," says Sanju Bansal of Virginia-based MicroStrategy, whose software analyzes customer data. However, managing data in this way has become very difficult. In some cases, large dataset queries overload computers, bogging them down for hours or even days at a time. At Premier, an alliance of 200 hospitals headquartered in San Diego, some queries were so complex that its IBM system couldn't return an answer in any amount of time. So, in 2003 it started using a specialized online transaction processing system from Netezza, a data warehouse appliance company located in Massachusetts, that could analyze its data 15 times faster than the IBM system, making queries much more manageable.[68] However, the problem of just what to do with all of that data and storage capability remains an area of investigation for many companies and business researchers.

RFID Tracking

Radio frequency identification devices (RFIDs) are just now beginning to be used to track loyalty program members' transactions. RFID devices can communicate with point-of-sale systems, providing a convenient, inexpensive alternative to magnetic strip and smart card payment systems. A number of trials have recently been completed using RFID devices. Texas-based Integrity For You, Inc., a customer retention program provider, is in the process of launching an RFID-based loyalty system for U.S. restaurants that will allow frequent diners to be identified upon entering a restaurant, enabling them to receive personalized services and special offers. Plans are already underway to expand this system to other retailers. Another system being piloted by several European banks is an RFID tag attached to a loyalty card for elite-level banking customers. When the member enters the bank, the card triggers an instant text message to an employee cell phone as an alert of the customer's presence. The bank can then pull up CRM information such as how they like to be addressed, their accounts, and their transaction histories. Paired with an effective loyalty strategy, RFID may prove to be a very effective CRM initiative.[69]

Personal Knowledge Banks

According to Richard Watson, director of the Center for Information Systems Leadership at the University of Georgia, the future of CRM lies in giving customers total control over information about their past purchases and preferences. Termed **personal knowledge banks** or **customer managed interactions**, customers could be allowed to compile a record of all their interactions across an entire industry and supplement this data with current preferences and plans for future purchases. For example, a person could store information of all the CDs they ever purchased in their personal knowledge bank and make it available to a music retailer, who could make purchase recommendations for new CDs. Thus, suppliers could have a much better picture of the customer's preferences, and their lifetime value. Benefits also include the ability to provide timely and relevant communications, reduced marketing costs, the ability to track market trends in real time, and access to new ideas for products and services. Currently, only one firm, Information Answers, is developing the architecture and services to enable personal knowledge banks. But some people like Richard Watson believe this market will be "even bigger than CRM."[70]

SUMMARY

As evidenced in this chapter, customer relationship management is an enormous area of concentration for many organizations actively managing their supply chains. CRM programs typically involve the hiring and training of personnel and the investment of significant (sometimes huge) sums of money to implement a set of CRM initiatives and software applications. This chapter primarily focused on the CRM model as shown in Figure 3.1, beginning with identifying a competitive strategy, collecting customer information, segmenting customers, targeting customer segments for marketing purposes, and then finally selecting a CRM program consistent with the firm's strategy. Once the CRM program has been designed an appropriate technology must be identified and used, and then performance metrics can be developed to monitor CRM success and guide continuous improvements. The chapter concluded with a discussion of customer information privacy and its impact on CRM, as well as some current trends in CRM.

KEY TERMS

approach to analytics, 81

bottom-up branding, 78

clickstream tracking software, 84

cold calls, 73

cookie files, 84

customer churn, 56

customer communities, 78

customer lifetime value, 65

customer loyalty programs, 75

customer managed interactions, 87

customer segmentation, 64

customer service, 76

differentiation strategy, 61

direct mail, 73

e-CRM, 69

false positive blocking, 72

firing a customer, 56

focus groups, 82

income segmentation, 67

individual marketing, 68

individual segmentation, 64

low-cost leadership strategy, 61

mass customization, 78

neighborhood marketing, 66

niche segmentation, 64

on-demand CRM, 86

one-to-one marketing, 68

opt-in, 85

opt-out, 85

personal knowledge banks, 87

proactive customer service, 77

profitable customer, 65

psychographics, 66

radio frequency identification devices, 87

reactive customer service, 77

response strategy, 62

social networking technology, 86

telemarketing, 72

versioning, 78

viral marketing, 78

Voice Extensible Markup Language, 86

Voice over Internet Protocol, 86

DISCUSSION QUESTIONS

1. What are the three basic competitive strategies, and how might you expect CRM initiatives to vary with these strategies?

2. What sort of customer information is typically collected when segmenting customers, and how is this information usually obtained?

3. What is customer segmentation, and why is it important?

4. Define niche segmentation.

5. Discuss the term *profitable customer* and why it is so important when segmenting customers or designing marketing campaigns.

6. What is customer lifetime value, and how can it be used in the design of marketing initiatives?

7. Why might a company want to "fire" some of its customers?

8. Discuss the meaning of neighborhood marketing, and provide some examples of firms that might do this.

9. Can segmenting markets by gender be done successfully? Explain.

10. Can individual marketing really be done successfully? Explain.

11. How can Figure 3.2 be used in designing a CRM program?

12. Describe e-CRM.

13. How does false positive blocking affect e-CRM?

14. Compare telemarketing to the use of field sales personnel for CRM purposes.

15. Discuss customer loyalty programs and their use as a CRM initiative.

16. Discuss the effect of fees charged to customers using loyalty cards.

17. Compare reactive and proactive customer service.

18. Define and discuss versioning as it is used in CRM.

19. Why do CRM technology investments have relatively high failure rates?

20. How should performance metrics be used in CRM program implementations?

21. Discuss your feelings and experiences about online identity theft and online information privacy.

22. Discuss two of the trends in CRM that sound most interesting to you and provide some examples of how they might be used.

23. Why is it that the current huge data storage capabilities can be considered a problem with CRM?

INTERNET QUESTIONS

1. Go to http://www.donotcall.gov and describe the history, administration, and value of the site.

2. Go to a search engine like Google, and search the web for CRM application providers and report on the most current products and providers that are listed.

3. Go to the World Wide Web Consortium (http://www.w3c.org) and report on the current laws that are being considered in the U.S. Congress regarding information privacy. Discuss the impact on CRM programs.

 ## INFOTRAC QUESTIONS

Access http://www.infotrac-thomsonlearning.com to answer the following questions:

1. Write a paper regarding online information privacy in the United States and Europe.

2. Search on *RFID* and *CRM programs* and write a paper describing some of the current uses of RFID in CRM.

3. Firing customers is a very "hot" topic in CRM. Use InfoTrac to find some current examples of companies who have successfully fired some of their customers. See if you can find some examples of companies who did this poorly.

REFERENCES

Bergeron, B. (2002), *Essentials of CRM: A Guide to Customer Relationship Management,* John-Wiley & Sons, Hoboken, NJ.

Bligh, P., and Turk, D. (2004), *CRM Unplugged: Releasing CRM's Strategic Value,* John-Wiley & Sons, Hoboken, NJ.

Croxton, K., Garcia-Dastugue, S., Lambert, D., and Rogers, D., "The Supply Chain Management Processes," *International Journal of Logistics Management,* V. 12, No. 2, 2001, pp. 13–36.

Winer, R., "A Framework for Customer Relationship Management," *California Management Review,* V. 43, No. 4, 2001, pp. 89–105.

Wisner, J., Leong, G., and Tan, K. (2005), *Principles of Supply Chain Management: A Balanced Approach,* South-Western, Mason, OH.

ENDNOTES

1. St. George, D., "Branding from Inside Out," *Australasian Business Intelligence,* October 8, 2004.

2. Quote from Pare Ravesi, senior product marketing manager for ATG, in Sablosky, T. L., "'Hello! This is your call center. I'm evolving into a more dynamic channel for banks to interact with their customers.' If your call center could ring you up, that is probably what it would say," *Bank Marketing,* V. 36, No. 8, 2004, pp. 30–35.

3. Editorial, "The Real Customers for CRM," *CFO, The Magazine for Senior Financial Executives,* Fall 2004, p. 17.

4. Southwest Airlines press release, June 17, 2002, website address http://www.southwest.com/about_swa/press/prindex.html.

5. Bligh, P. and D. Turk, *CRM Unplugged: Releasing CRM's Strategic Value,* Hoboken, NJ: John-Wiley & Sons, 2004.

6. Cornell, C., "Marathon Man," *Profit,* V. 23, No. 2, 2004, pp. 36–41.

7. Dolezalek, H., "The State of the e-Learning Market," *Training,* V. 41, No. 9, 2004, pp. 20–27.

8. "CD Wow: Cheap and Cheerful," *New Media Age,* November 27, 2003, p. 24.

9. Rezak, C., "Playing for Keeps," *T & D,* V. 58, No. 10, 2004, pp. 93–96.

10. Winer, R., "A Framework for Customer Relationship Management," *California Management Review,* V. 43, No. 4, 2001, pp. 89–105.

11. "Strategic Play—Panasonic: First Contact," *New Media Age,* August 26, 2004, p. 18.

12. Kotler, P., *Marketing Management,* Upper Saddle River, NJ: Prentice Hall, 2000.

13. Schneider, I., "Online Banking Moves the Needle," *Bank Systems & Technology,* V. 41, No. 4, 2004, p. 11.

14. Winer, R., "A Framework for Customer Relationship Management," *California Management Review,* V. 43, No. 4, 2001, pp. 89–105. Also see Hughes, A. M., "How to Compute Your Customer Lifetime Value," listed on the Database Marketing Institute's website at http://www.dbmarketing.com/articles.

15. McWilliams, G., "Minding the Store: Analyzing Customers, Best Buy Decides not All Are Welcome," *Wall Street Journal,* November 8, 2004, p. A1.

16. Shanmuganathan, P., M. Stone, and B. Foss, "Ethnic Banking in the United States," *LIMRA's MarketFacts Quarterly,* V. 23, No. 4, 2004, pp. 22–28.

17. Marjo, J., "What Women Want: Gender-Based Marketing Is a Risky Business, But It's a Risk Companies Can't Afford Not to Take," *CMA Management,* V. 77, No. 8, 2004, p. 18.

18. "Retail Detail," *Business Week,* February 7, 2005, p. 10.

19. Baumann, M., "High-End Offerings the Result of In-Depth Research," *Hotel and Motel Management,* V. 219, No. 9, 2004, p. 36.

20. Ackermann, M., "With Legal Group, Wachovia Back in Segmentation Game," *American Banker,* V. 169, No. 156, 2004, pp. 7–10.

21. Clancy, H., "Slicing and Dicing," *CRN,* July 19, 2004, p. 22.

22. Bold, B., "Breaking into the Small Time," *Marketing,* November 3, 2004, p. 14.

23. Van Arnum, P., "P&G Taps a Niche Market—Personal Care for Teenage Boys," *Chemical Market Reporter,* V. 266, No. 13, p. FR6.

24. Bloom, J., "It's Not What You Know About Customers, But How You Use It," *Advertising Age,* V. 75, No. 45, 2004, p. 26.

25. Barker, J., "New Life," *Incentive,* V. 178, No. 11, 2004, pp. 34–37.

26. Yensen, K., "Data Critical," *Target Marketing,* V. 27, No. 10, 2004, pp. 117–120.

27. Wilson, M., "Make Way for Ducklings," *Chain Store Age,* V. 80, No. 5, 2004, p. 126.

28. Bowman, J., "The Advertising Lag," *Media,* November 5, 2004, p. 11.

29. Rigby, E., "The Revolution Masterclass on Electronic CRM," *Revolution,* November 2004, pp. 66–69.

30. See note 28 above.

31. Bailor, C. and E. Favilla, "Quick Wins," *Customer Relationship Management,* V. 8, No. 10, 2004, pp. 54–56.

32. Derrick, S., "How to Get From A to B," *Revolution,* October 2004, pp. 56–60.

33. "Special Report—Email Marketing: Cutting Corners," *Precision Marketing,* October 29, 2004, p. 21.

34. "Medienhaus Closes 40 Percent More Business Using Siebel Sales," *Business Wire,* November 8, 2004.

35. More information about the U.S. Do-Not-Call Registry can be found at http://www.ftc.gov/donotcall.

36. Davidson, P., "FTC's Do Not Call Registry Puts Telemarketing Jobs on the Line," *USAToday.com,* September 10, 2003.

37. Cardona, M., "Newspapers '05 Outlook Gloomy," *Advertising Age,* V. 75, No. 50, 2004, p. 8.

38. Myerhoff, M., "Telemarketing Limits Blamed for Slip in Newspaper Sales," *Los Angeles Business Journal,* November 8, 2004.

39. "Special Report—Research Index: The Law of Averages," *Precision Marketing,* December 3, 2004, p. 15.

40. Van Camp, S., "British Marketer Targets U.S. Execs with the Royal Treatment," *Brandweek,* V. 45, No. 144, 2004, p. 32.

41. Levey, R., "Prospects Look Good," *Direct,* December 1, 2004.

42. Frumkin, P., "Charlie Brown's: Sales Gains Reflect Emphasis on Quality, Value," *Nation's Restaurant News,* V. 38, No. 50, 2004, pp. 4–5.

43. Lyons, D., "Too Much Information," *Forbes,* V. 174, No. 12, 2004, p. 110.

44. Hanafin, B., "Sincerely Yours," *Credit Card Management,* V. 17, No. 10, 2004, p. 46.

45. Ramsaran, C., "Catch of the Day: Banks Face New Phishing Scams," *Bank Systems & Technology,* V. 41, No. 12, 2004, p. 13.

46. Valentino, G., "Get Them Back," *Target Marketing,* V. 27, No. 12, 2004, pp. 21–24.

47. Schlosser, J., "Cashing in on the New World of Me," *Fortune,* V. 150, No. 12, 2004, pp. 244–249.

48. See for instance, Snyder, P., "Wanted: Standards for Viral Marketing," *Brandweek,* V. 45, No. 26, 2004, p. 21 and Dunne, D., "Bottom-Up Branding," *Marketing,* V. 109, No. 22, 2004, p. 10.

49. Powers, V., "Tail of Two: CRM CCOs," *Customer Relationship Management,* V. 8, No. 11, 2004, p. 34.

50. Marshall, J., and E. Heffes, "Customer Assessment Efforts Seen Wanting," *Financial Executive,* V. 21, No. 1, 2005, p. 10.

51. The Meta Group was acquired by Connecticut-based Gartner in 2005.

52. Chan, J., "Toward a Unified View of Customer Relationship Management," *Journal of American Academy of Business,* V. 6, No. 1, 2005, pp. 32–39.

53. Krell, E., "The 2004 CRM Elite," *Customer Relationship Management,* V. 8, No. 9, 2004, pp. 30–37.

54. Compton, J., "It's Not Business as Usual," *Customer Relationship Management,* V. 8, No. 12, 2004, pp. 32–38.

55. See note 52 above.

56. Bhote, K., *Beyond Customer Satisfaction to Customer Loyalty: The Key to Greater Profitability,* New York, NY: AMA Membership Publications Division, 1996.

57. See note 52 above.

58. See note 52 above.

59. Ledford, J., "Reducing CRM's Total Cost of Ownership," *Customer Relationship Management,* V. 8, No. 8, 2004, p. 15.

60. Krell, E., "Churchill Downs Bets on Its Brand," *Customer Relationship Management,* V. 9, No. 2, 2005, p. 26.

61. Sipior, J., B. Ward, and N. Rongione, "Ethics of Collecting and Using Consumer Internet Data," *EDPACS,* V. 332, No. 11, 2004, pp. 1–14.

62. Vijayan, J., "Privacy Potholes," *Computerworld,* V. 38, No. 11, 2004, pp. 36–37.

63. Erlanger, L., "The 411 on VoIP," *InfoWorld,* V. 26, No. 23, 2004, pp. 42–49.

64. Bailor, C., "10 Technologies That Are Reinventing the CRM Industry," *Customer Relationship Management,* V. 8, No. 12, 2004, pp. 44–48.

65. See note 63 above.

66. See note 63 above.

67. See note 43 above.

68. See note 43 above.

69. Capizzi, M., R. Ferguson, and R. Cuthbertson, "Loyalty Trends for the 21st Century," *Journal of Targeting, Measurement and Analysis for Marketing,* V. 12, No. 3, pp. 199–213.

70. Mitchell, A., "Personal Knowledge Banks Will Be Marketing's Oxygen," *Marketing Week,* November 11, 2004, p. 30.

Chapter 4:

CUSTOMER SERVICE MANAGEMENT

"Profit in business comes from repeat customers, customers that boast about your project or service, and that bring friends with them."

W. Edwards Deming

"There is only one boss. The customer. And he can fire everybody in the company from the chairman on down, simply by spending his money somewhere else."

Sam Walton

Learning Objectives

After completing this chapter, you should be able to:

- Define customer service, and describe its contributions to firm success.
- Understand how customer behaviors and expectations influence elements of customer service.
- Describe several customer service strategies.
- Explain how customer service audits are conducted.
- Define customer service quality, and explain how it is measured and improved.
- Describe some of the trends in customer call centers.
- Understand the importance of customer service integration throughout the supply chain.

Chapter Outline

Introduction

Customer Service Defined

Customer Behavior and Expectations

Customer Perceptions and Satisfaction

A Framework for Managing Customer Service

Integrating the Customer Service Process along the Supply Chain

Process Management in Action

TFE, Inc. Is Taking Care of Business 24/7

Situated in the back corner of an unassuming industrial park in Fort Wayne, Indiana, TFE, Inc., also known as Transmission & Fluid Equipment, seems like a calm, collected, and tan-colored business that may or may not do anything dynamic. Only the foolish would judge this book by its cover. From within, the concrete warehouse roils with power transmission and fluid power intensity, focused on one thing: servicing its customers the best it can.

Open early and late (6 A.M.–10 P.M.) Monday through Friday, TFE is always accessible (customers have the sales staff's emergency contact numbers to use at any time) and ready to provide hose, bearings, or motors to its client accounts. "Chris himself has driven up to drop product for us in the middle of the night," says Chad Conley, vice president of Indiana Phoenix, Inc., a concrete mixer builder in Avilla, Indiana. "If we have a problem, they are always there to help."

Chris Hughes, co-owner and president of TFE, is proud of his company's 24-hour emergency service. "A lot of our customers work through the night, with third shifts and that sort of thing," he says. "We just want to be there for them during all their active hours. We build a pattern of being there when they call us for any kind of emergency. We feel that helping someone at 3 A.M. may have them think of us at 3 P.M., during regular hours, too." TFE's policy is for its salespeople to have their emergency phone numbers—home or cell phone—on their business cards. If customers need something, they are calling someone they know and have worked with. From that call, the help is on its way.

For TFE, in order to do a good job for its suppliers, the distributorship has to focus on them, become their outlet in this area, and not dilute the vendor's presence in the area. "We've stuck very close to our roots with the power transmission products such as bearings, electric motors, and chain sprockets, as well as the fluid power side, including hose and hydraulic fittings," says Hughes. "We are proud of the lines that we have; they are some of the best names in the industry. We've not sold ladders or safety glasses and that kind of extra equipment in the past, like our competitors are now, and we haven't wanted to stray from that."

Gates Rubber Corp., a hose, belts, and hydraulic hose manufacturer in Denver, has anointed the distributorship a certified hydraulic hose assembly fabricator, and TFE distributes the manufacturer's full industrial hose and hydraulic hose product line. "Gates has a broad product line, so we can take care of any customer that comes our way," says Hughes. "They have high-quality products, in which we pride ourselves. We feel like we are an extension of their factory in this area, providing just-in-time service as well as stocking product for customers ranging from a large OEM to a small contractor. We've had a great relationship with them."

In 2001, TFE opened a second location in Indianapolis—a gamble for the distributorship that prides itself on a concentrated presence. But the gamble has paid off, as the location has done so well for TFE that the operation is already moving into a building twice the size of its original space. Along with customers spending money on contracts and deliveries, TFE's counter area has had a good walk-in trade. As long as TFE has been in business, the distributorship has had a counter, and the space in Indianapolis is no exception. Because the company has so many accounts whose product buying doesn't include the counter space, the area's sales figures are harder to figure, but Hughes says the counter accounts for about 3 percent of the company's $10 million in sales. "It's not a big number, but it's a huge service for our customers," says Hughes. "Some customers who don't normally use the counter, like an account that may have regular deliveries, may find one morning or afternoon to be short one thing that they need right then. They benefit from being able to come in and pick up that one V-belt at 9 P.M. that night."

Continued

The distributorship's extra-long counter hours, second Indiana location, 24-hour emergency service, and can-do attitude are definite benefits for its customers, says Hughes. "We just try to service our customers the best way we can, and if someone needs something any hour of the day, we're there for them," states Hughes. "We try to stock for our customers what they are buying and have it here for them to access any time during the day or night." And all that comes from a small distributorship behind the modest glass doors of a tan building in a low-key industrial park in northern Indiana.

Source: Griffiths, K., "Taking Care of Business 24/7," *Industrial Distribution*, V. 93, No. 8, 2004, p. 40. © Reed Business Information. Used with permission.

Introduction

Customer service can be one of those things like product quality—as consumers, we may not be very good at defining what it is, but we know when we don't get it. Companies today spend a great deal of time, money, and effort trying to deliver great, or at least acceptable, customer service. Consumers see this occurring in most of the maturing markets around the world as global competition increases and as emerging technologies create faster, more efficient ways to deliver various customer service activities.

Many companies are doing an extremely effective job of delivering great customer service, and they are benefiting in terms of competitive advantage and financial rewards as a result. Several of these world-class customer service providers are profiled in this chapter. TFE, Inc. is one such example, and is profiled in the opening Process Management in Action feature. Too often, though, companies experience great difficulties designing customer service capabilities that please customers and create loyal buyers who return for additional purchases and tell others about the great service they received. Most of us, unfortunately, can vividly recall many examples of poor customer service, such as the cashier who contentedly discusses the previous night's reality TV show with his fellow employee while disgruntled customers wait to pay for their purchases, and the physician who overloads her appointment schedule with no regard for the time patients must wait to be seen. And evidence points to a worsening of customer service in most industries around the world.

The **American Customer Satisfaction Index** (ACSI), produced by the Ross Business School at the University of Michigan, shows a general decrease in customer satisfaction in the United States since its inception in 1995, due lately to waning satisfaction in the retail industry, high gas prices, and the large volumes of traffic on e-commerce websites. As a matter of fact, for the 12-year period from 1995–2006, average customer satisfaction across all industries in the United States was down almost 7 percent.[1] And it's not just a problem in the United States. Just read the Service Perspective feature about a shopper's view of customer service in the United Kingdom.

Conversely, when great customer service is encountered, it is often so unexpected we find ourselves wondering if there was some mistake! It can make such an impression that we search for reasons to go back and experience the service again. Delivering great customer service is one of the key success factors businesses can have. If designed and delivered well, customer service creates opportunities for long-term customer

Service Perspective

A New Year, But the Same Lousy Service

We never hear the end of retailers applauding themselves for the high standards they achieve in the provision of customer service. Most of these claims are, of course, complete rubbish. Anybody with eyes and ears in their head knows this, and anyone who has been to a shop anywhere else in the world will have something with which to compare UK standards. I sometimes wonder why UK retailers don't just admit their service is woeful and play to their real strengths, such as low prices.

You might be thinking that I have recently had a bad experience while shopping, but you would be wrong. I have had several. From trying to explain to retail staff that I want them to honor the multi-buy offer they are so prominently advertising, to explaining to others that they should be charging the price marked on the product rather than another price entirely, and walking out of shops because I am being ignored while staff chat about Coronation Street or delayed while I am offered a dozen things I didn't ask for at the checkout, I can honestly say I have had my fill of customer service.

It could be argued there are so many reasons for retailers' failure to live up to their service promises that a solution can never be found, but perhaps it could be a New Year's resolution to try. Paying staff better wages might be a good start. Retailers are fond of complaining they are being ruined by wage demands, but they obviously aren't. And if they were more generous to their staff, might that not be reflected in their loyalty and effort? It doesn't matter how many systems are in place to help staff provide better service if they all leave the job before they're taught how they work.

And an acknowledgement that the initiatives designed to make customers spend more money are quite transparent would be good, too. When shoppers are visiting multiple retailers in one trip, the constant, clumsy pressure applied to make them spend more can become tiring very quickly. No shop is an island.

Is it any wonder that a growing number of people are now shopping on the Internet? Happy new year.

Source: "A New Year But the Same Lousy Service," *In-Store,* January 12, 2005, p. 13. Used with permission.

loyalty. Most successful companies are good at providing customer service because they have managed the customer service process well—they've identified their customers along with their expectations and requirements, worked hard at developing the skills and procuring the equipment necessary to deliver products and services such that customers are satisfied, thought about how technology can enhance customer service performance, and have developed effective methods for tracking and improving customer service over time.

This chapter provides a framework for designing, implementing, and improving customer service activities both internally and among supply chain trading partners. The chapter begins by defining customer service, and then presents generalized discussions of customer behavior, expectations, and satisfaction. This is followed by the customer service management framework and concludes with a discussion of the integration of the customer service process along the supply chain.

Customer Service Defined

Along with the growth in popularity of customer service initiatives, a large number of customer service definitions have surfaced—some good, and some bad. Providing a good working definition of just what customer service is can create a solid foundation and direction for the design and delivery of high-value customer service activities in organizations. A number of the better customer service definitions follow:

- The activities that support orders, including application, advice, configuration, order processing, handling, post-sale communication, and special services. [2]
- A series of activities designed to enhance the level of customer satisfaction before, during, and after a purchase. [3]
- The collection of activities performed in filling orders and keeping customers happy, or creating in the customer's mind the perception of an organization that is easy to do business with. [4]

These definitions clearly demonstrate that customer service is a process, a set of intangible activities—some specific and some vague—designed to take care of customer needs before, during, and after the sale.

Logistics plays a vital support role in customer service performance, since this function is so involved in moving, storing, and distributing products in response to a customer order. As a matter of fact, the customer service definition offered in Chapter 1 (the Seven R's Rule) has its origins in logistics literature. The definitions above include order processing and after-sale activities and services, such as delivery, which are certainly aligned with the logistics function. The topic of logistics customer service will be discussed in Chapter 11.

As alluded to in one of the previous definitions, customer service can be something the firm provides prior to the sale, during the sale, and after the sale. These are also referred to as pretransaction, transaction, and posttransaction elements of customer service (see Table 4.1). A discussion of these elements follows.

Pretransaction Elements

Pretransaction customer service elements occur within the firm prior to, or apart from, the sale of products and services. They involve the firm's ability to support various customer service activities, allowing the firm to position itself such that it can provide good customer service. These elements include the development of customer service policies, how they will be deployed and monitored within the firm, and how they will be communicated to customers. Also included in this category are the assignment of decision-making responsibility for customer service and the selection of software applications that enable customer service policies and directives to be followed. Examples might include the use of CRM and ERP software applications as discussed in Chapter 3. Finally, the hiring, training, and use of customer service personnel is included among the pretransaction elements. The overall objective of the pretransaction elements is to *prepare the firm* for effective customer service.

Transaction Elements

The **transaction customer service elements** are associated with and occur during the **order cycle**, defined as the time from initiation of the customer order until the product or service is delivered to the customer. Transaction elements assist the firm in the

Table 4.1	The Elements of Customer Service

CUSTOMER SERVICE CATEGORIES	ACTIVITIES
Pretransaction Elements	**Customer service policies** – defines customer service for the customer, including guarantees, warranties, and return policies. Sets standards and performance metrics.
	Customer service communication – communication of policies to customers through websites, pamphlets, TV, and other media forms.
	Customer service authority – determines customer service decision-making authority at all levels in the firm.
	Information system deployment – selection of software applications to store, analyze, and use customer information to meet customer needs.
	Personnel – hiring and training of customer service personnel and policies or structures (such as call centers) associated with these employees.
Transaction Elements	**Safety stock and excess service capacity** – enables timely delivery of products and services during periods of unforeseen demand increases.
	Substitute products – allows firms to satisfy customers when the desired product is unavailable.
	Order entry – correctly enter order and communicate to production.
	Order status – determine status of order and relay information to customer.
	Order expediting – hasten the manufacturing and/or delivery processes to reduce order cycle time.
	Warehousing and product delivery – determine the most effective and efficient distribution of product or service to customer.
Posttransaction Elements	**Warranty and maintenance services** – repair and maintain products during and after warranty period.
	Product operating information – provide operating and troubleshooting information to customers, and update as needs arise.
	Parts and installation – order and install new and replacement parts.
	Follow-up, complaints, and returns – after-sales communication, resolution of customer complaints, and handling product returns.

Source: Based in part on Stock, J., and D. Lambert, *Strategic Logistics Management,* New York, NY: McGraw-Hill, 2001.

successful delivery of purchased products and services. These elements include the holding of work-in-process and finished goods safety stock to reduce stockouts, the presence of excess service capacity to enable the firm to respond quickly to unexpected demand, the presence of substitute products for times when stockouts do occur, the determination of order status, and the activities of order entry, order expediting, ware-housing, and delivery. The objectives of customer service transaction elements are to provide service flexibility and to enable the firm to consistently deliver **perfect orders** (recall from Chapter 1 that a perfect order occurs when the seven R's are satisfied).

Posttransaction Elements

Posttransaction customer service elements are activities that occur after the product or service has been sold. These activities include warranty and maintenance services, product operating information, parts and installation, following up with customers after the sale, and dealing with customer complaints and product returns. In some cases, as in the automobile industry, posttransaction elements (maintenance and repairs) can be a profit-generating activity for the firm. Some of these activities can also be very expensive, such as when firms must dispose of toxic waste materials in an environmentally acceptable fashion. The objective of the posttransaction elements is to create an ongoing and successful after-sale relationship with customers. Many of these activities mark the beginning of customer relationship management efforts, as described in Chapter 3.

Customer Service Failures

When any of the customer service activities described are neglected or performed poorly, a **customer service failure** is likely, which can lead to additional costs and possibly loss of goodwill, customer defections, and reduced future sales revenues. Examples of customer service failures include stockouts, unwillingness to honor customer service policies, lost orders, late deliveries, employee indifference to customer needs, and unsatisfactory resolution of customer complaints. Thus, customer service failures occur as a result of some aspect of customer service being unavailable, slow, or unacceptable. The U.S. Postal Service, for example, is doing a good job of reducing customer service failures, as shown in the Service Perspective feature.

Some of the more obvious ways organizations can try to minimize customer service failures are through more effective hiring practices, increased general communication training of customer contact personnel, and better design and management of other activities in the three customer service categories shown in Table 4.1. Regardless of the level of preparation, though, customer service failures will occur, making it necessary for firms to be proactive and have well thought-out recovery plans in all processes involving customers. In fact, research has shown that getting customers to articulate their problems and then solving the problems quickly has an enormous impact on customer retention. Research executed by TARP (Technical Assistance Research Program) at Harvard University found, for instance, that when the financial loss to a customer due to product or service failures was more than $100, only 9 percent of those who did not articulate their problem remained brand loyal, while 54 percent of those who articulated their problem and were satisfied with the solution continued to buy the product.[5]

"This is the You-Must-Be-Wrong
Department, formerly known
as Customer Service."

Service Perspective

Reducing Service Failures at the U.S. Postal Service

It's not easy to tell Bob Otto, USPS chief technology officer, that something can't be done. "Failure is not in my vocabulary," he says. One of his subordinates describes him as "the iron man." Another says perfection is his goal.

He is widely credited with turning a department that was in shambles into one of the government's top IT operations. In just a few years, Otto has overseen the development of sophisticated self-service tools for customers and employees, the replacement of an outdated infrastructure, and the overhaul of the organization's financial systems. "He's changed the nature of information technology in the Postal Service," says Chief Financial Officer Richard Strasser.

Otto wears his success on his walls. Technology awards and framed magazine articles line his office. He became the Postal Service's chief information officer in January 2001. Two years later, he also took on the role of chief technology officer. Since he was appointed CIO, Otto has earned 17 awards for projects he has done or managed.

"I've been antsy all my life," Otto says. "I look at everything as an opportunity. My lifetime is short, and if I don't try to do as many things as I can, I'm going to miss out on life. I don't want to look back with regrets." The size and complexity of the Postal Service present enough challenges to hold his attention. And Otto likes the people and the culture, a sentiment he expresses with fervor. "We believe that this company is our company," he says. "You want to make a difference; you want to do something to help."

More important than his work ethic is his strategy, says George Wright, manager of USPS finance and administrative systems, who has worked with Otto as a boss, contractor, peer, and now subordinate. "I don't have the time, the energy, or the hours to work for someone who doesn't know where they're going," Wright says. "Bob, because of his direction-setting activity, eliminates 90 percent of the nonsense you have to deal with in a corporate environment."

Charts and graphs in bright colors hang in rows on the walls of the conference room next to Otto's office. The most telling, he says, is a bar graph showing the average number of daily technology failures that affect customers. The massive Postal Service infrastructure—which includes 225,000 personal computers, 600 applications, and 1,000 websites—encompasses about 1 trillion potential failure points. In fiscal 2000, some part of that infrastructure broke down on average more than 200 times daily. Now the average is less than 20.

As coach of his dream team, Otto focuses on the basics. His credo of "standardize, centralize, simplify" guides everything the department does, such as giving users a single logon for all systems and consolidating servers into two facilities, a decision that helped winnow the number of contractors the department pays from 1,000 to 64.

If a system comes with a long manual, Otto doesn't want it. When he took over, many Postal Service departments had their own technology employees because they didn't trust the organization-wide IT department. "I centralized all that," he says. "After a couple months, they saw they were getting better service, and they didn't care who worked for them."

Like any good coach, Otto takes pride most of all in the team he's assembled. "I wanted people who were customer focused," he says. "If you weren't customer focused, you weren't going to be a manager." Even with his key team members in place, recruiting, mentoring, and succession planning remain top priorities. The best part of the job, he says, is taking someone who believes they have reached their peak, pushing them and watching them exceed their own expectations. As he says, "I just really believe that we are the best at everything."

Source: Kersten, D., "Winning Season," *Government Executive*, V. 37, No. 2, 2005, pp. 31–33. Used with permission.

Table 4.2	**A Stepwise Approach to Service Recovery**
1. **Break the silence and listen for complaints**	Many customers just don't like to complain. Create an organization that can uncover service failures and customer problems.
2. **Anticipate needs for recovery**	Develop recovery plans and procedures for all potential failures, then train employees to use the procedures.
3. **Train employees**	Develop the skills of good communication, creative thinking, quick decision making, and customer empathy among customer contact employees.
4. **Empower the front line**	Allow frontline employees to act quickly and decisively to solve customer problems.
5. **Act fast**	Act quickly and effectively once the service failure has occurred to make the best impression and increase the likelihood of customer retention.
6. **Close the loop**	Permanently fix the condition that led to the customer service failure.
7. **Measure the failure costs**	Measure and record the costs to recover from and to fix the problem; this can be used as a justification for further service improvements.

Source: Based on Hart, C., J. Heskett, and W. Sasser, "The Profitable Art of Service Recovery," *Harvard Business Review,* July–August, 1990, pp. 148–156.

Thus, firms need to develop ways to facilitate customer feedback to find out as quickly as possible when a failure occurs. Examples include using questions by servers (e.g., "Is everything OK?") during service delivery, providing toll-free complaint numbers, using customer comment cards to uncover problems, offering rewards for suggestions, using focus groups, and interviewing customers who no longer buy the product or use the service (known as defecting customers). Once a failure is detected, company personnel in a position to remedy the situation must be empowered to act. These frontline personnel need to show empathy towards the customer, while taking effective and quick actions to fix the situation. It is imperative that organizations anticipate and prepare for service failures and design the proper **service recovery** actions into each customer service element. The R.J. Gators Florida Sea Grill & Bar chain based in Jupiter, Florida, for example, has instituted a "110% Program" as a way of handling customer service recoveries. If guests have any problems with service, the food, delays, or cleanliness, 10 percent is taken off the bill. And, on the customer's next visit, 100 percent is comped on any item. "We just want to walk our talk and create a guarantee to our guests," explains Mitch Timotio, vice president of the restaurant chain. "But, more importantly, to let our employees know that these things occur, and if they occur this is our way to make us sharper and more customer focused."[6] Table 4.2 describes an effective plan for service recovery.

Customer Behavior and Expectations

Customer behavior can be defined as the mental and physical activities that result in decisions to purchase and use products and services. These behaviors are impacted by customer needs and wants. In order for organizations to create a competitive advantage, they must be able to understand how customer needs and wants vary, the factors that influence these needs and wants, and the decisions they make to satisfy them. **Customer needs** are characterized by a desire to make an unsatisfactory condition better, such as the need for acceptable housing, food, and transportation. **Customer wants**, on the other hand, are characterized by the desire to make an already satisfactory condition better, such as wanting a bigger house, better food, or a more fuel-efficient car.

Customer needs can vary based on a customer's culture, gender, age, perceptions, and past experiences, just to name a few. For instance, as people age, their need for healthcare and household services increases; women need different styles of clothing than men; and people in China most likely have different food needs than those in Mexico.

Customer wants are influenced by factors such as their financial resources; the organizations and groups they belong to; their cultural influences; and their environmental surroundings, such as the local economy, availability of technology, and laws governing behavior. Thus, as personal wealth increases, customers are likely to want more expensive goods and services; religious or peer-group affiliation might influence customers' desire for various products; the influence of customers' cultures can impact their desire for products; and the availability of computers and the Internet influences a customer's knowledge of and desire for products.

Purchases are important to customers, and perhaps even more so to the companies who sell the products. Thus, to the employees selling products and providing various customer services, it is important to understand the motivations behind each customer purchase. These purchases can have varying levels of emotional attachments for each of the customers. In many cases, it can also be difficult for company personnel to understand or even notice this attachment, given a large customer base and the number of customer interactions taking place with each server every day. Firms that can identify the wants and needs of customer groups and then build this knowledge into customer service training programs are likely to provide higher levels of customer service, leading to a competitive advantage in the marketplace. The Wachovia Bank of Charlotte, North Carolina, typically has higher customer satisfaction than its peers because it listens to its customers and makes a point of acting on what the customer is saying. Ms. Gwynne Whitley, head of Corporate Customer Service Excellence for Wachovia, explains, "Our customers are at the center of everything we do, and we are focused on satisfying our customers at every level of the company. We recognize that to be successful, we need to keep our customers happy."[7]

Customer Expectations

Aside from their needs and wants, customers are also influenced to purchase goods and services based on their expectations. When customers transact business, they may have numerous expectations concerning the products themselves—their quality attributes and pricing—as well as the level of customer service. In a supply chain setting, supply managers may have varying expectations regarding a product they are about to purchase from a supplier, along with the associated services provided.

Both consumer and business customer expectations can be formed and modified by such things as firsthand experiences, word-of-mouth communications of previous performance of the products and service personnel, the selling firm's and the product's reputation, advertisements, and guarantees. Promises and commitments coming from field sales personnel also can greatly influence the business customer's expectations. In some cases, sales personnel may be setting their companies up for failure by overstating product performance or overcommitting support just to sell product. Later, when actual performance falls short of the seller-enhanced customer expectations, customer relationships can be damaged or destroyed.

Over time, there has been a continuously increasing level of expectations related to product and supplier capabilities, due largely to the influx of competitors in almost every industry and market, and the associated rising levels of product and service quality. Product suppliers who adequately meet customer expectations one year may find they lose customers the following year to companies who have raised overall customer expectations by reducing product prices and/or improving quality and service characteristics.

If organizations can categorize customers in terms of their expectations, then they can design product attributes and elements of customer service to cater to these different expectations. In a now-landmark paper where classifications of customers and their expectations were developed, Gregory Stone discussed four types of customers: [8]

1. *The economizing customer*—wants to maximize the value received, given the time, effort, and money expended. Product or service pricing is a major determinant for sales to this type of customer. When restaurants advertise early-bird specials, they are trying to attract this type of customer.

2. *The ethical customer*—feels morally obliged to buy from socially or environmentally responsible firms. The firm's social or environmental reputation is a large factor when successfully servicing this type of customer. Firms often advertise their social and environmental activities, such as donations to charity or recycling waste materials, to attract ethical customers and influence their expectations.

3. *The personalizing customer*—wants recognition and conversation from the selling firm's personnel. Training frontline employees to greet customers using their names is one method for appealing to personalizing customers. Computer applications are available that enable personnel to offer these and other types of personalized experiences to customers.

4. *The convenience customer*—wants products and services fast, and is willing to pay extra for the convenience. These customers may shop at a neighborhood market or corner convenience store to avoid cashier queues or congested parking lots, even if the cost of goods is somewhat more. Home delivery would also be a desirable service for these customers.

Firms need to consider ways to design products and services to appeal to some or all of these customer classifications. Fast-food restaurant chain Wendy's, for instance, has a super value menu to attract economizing customers. It sells salads and advertises a customer suggestion toll-free phone number to attract ethical customers. Food orders are shown on LED order boards in the drive-through lanes to attract personalizing customers, and single queues and drive-through lanes are used to attract convenience customers. Many other examples exist where companies are trying to attract and serve the four customer groups.

Customer Perceptions and Satisfaction

Customer perceptions of products and services before, during, and after the sale ultimately drive their overall level of satisfaction with the products and services. Perceptions are based on an individual's interpretation of the information received from the product, the service, and the environment. Obviously, companies hope that high-quality products, reasonable prices, and great service will lead to positive customer perceptions, customer satisfaction, increased customer retention, and finally increased market share and profits. But this is not always the case.

Perceptions can be influenced by a number of seemingly non-product-related things, including the five senses (sight, smell, hear, touch, taste), experiences with a similar product, the setting or context of the item, and prior expectations. For instance, a television in a doctor's office can reduce perceived wait times; poor service and cold food at a restaurant can negatively influence perceptions of future service and food quality at the same or similar restaurants; first-class seating on an airline compared to economy-class seating might influence perceptions of the service received; and an advance flood of advertising might increase the expectations about a newly released movie. In all of these examples, businesses either directly or indirectly influence customer perceptions and, in turn, customer satisfaction.

Perceptual Biases

Every day, consumers are bombarded with stimuli geared towards influencing their wants and perceptions. As a result, most consumers have developed a selective internal screening mechanism to ignore certain stimuli while seeking out others. People ignore some TV commercials while paying close attention to others; they look at electronics retailer ads if they are interested in purchasing a camera; and they pass by some stores in a mall while they enter others. These are examples of **selective exposure** and **selective attention**. Consequently, only a small percentage of the enormous quantity of marketing communications actually reaches the typical consumer.

Consumers also interpret various marketing communications, product information, or stimuli differently, based on their predisposition and personality. People intent on having a bad service experience will most likely find problems and complain loudly, regardless of the efforts by company personnel; those who have purchased a large and powerful SUV might tend to ignore warnings about gas price trends and low resale values; and others who smoke might distort or ignore health warnings regarding prolonged smoking and secondhand smoke. These are examples of **selective interpretation** and **perceptual distortion**.

Because of the way these perceptions can alter customer opinions and purchases, companies must be mindful of how perceptual biases can be influenced. Pleasant music, comfortable furniture, and other pleasing environmental attributes, when combined with product attributes such as low cost, high quality, and good service, can go a long way towards keeping customers happy and returning for future purchases.

Customer Satisfaction

Philip Kotler, a distinguished marketing professor, defines **customer satisfaction** as a person's feelings of pleasure or disappointment resulting from comparing a product's perceived performance or outcome, relative to his or her expectations.[9] Thus, if the actual outcome exceeds initial expectations, then customers are satisfied. And, the greater the difference is, the larger the impact on satisfaction. Many companies routinely initiate strategies aimed at creating greater product and service satisfaction, since consumers who are only "satisfied" may switch to other sellers when something better materializes. For instance, eastern U.S. grocery store chain Giant Food Stores is placing a state-of-the-art grocery store in Philadelphia, Pennsylvania, that will feature a free-standing kiosk where shoppers can pull recipe ingredients, check on card savings, find food locations, and place advance deli orders for pickup. Shoppers will use handheld scanners as they shop, allowing them to keep running tallies of their expenses, and they will self-scan and bag their own groceries when they are ready to check out. [10]

As mentioned earlier in the chapter, expectations are influenced by marketing ads, guarantees, promises, and previous experiences. Businesses must be wary not to raise the bar of expectations too high, though, since actual performance may not live up to customer expectations, resulting in dissatisfaction and potential customer defections. For example, a one-hour photo processing shop better be able to deliver its service within one hour or customers will be unhappy. However, a firm that routinely opens up for business earlier than advertised will exceed expectations and create customer satisfaction for those arriving early.

Some of the most successful companies are periodically raising customer expectations and delivering better performance to match, creating a formidable competitive weapon. The Process Management in Action feature profiles Tech Systems, a company that has set the customer service standard for its industry. Hyundai Motor Co. is another example. It has caught up with Honda and Toyota in terms of quality, based on the number of customers complaining within the first 90 days of car ownership. Just a few years ago, no one took Hyundai Chairman Chung Mong Koo seriously when he said that they would increase quality levels to rival Toyota. Today, with Hyundai's quality performance and industry-best warranty (ten years for the drivetrain and five years for everything else), sales and profits are growing steadily. [11] These and other companies have found a very positive relationship between customer satisfaction and profitability.

In a now-famous article by Dr. James Heskett and his colleagues, the **service-profit chain** was proposed, linking the internal environment to employee satisfaction, which leads to customer service value, customer satisfaction, customer loyalty, and finally profitability. [12] Since that time, there have been numerous examples of companies successfully exploiting this chain of associations or relationships. We have already seen the service-profit chain utilized successfully by Tech Systems as discussed in the Process Management in Action feature. In another example, U.S. retail giant Sears found that a 5 percent improvement in staff attitude created a 1.3 percent increase in customer satisfaction, an increase of 0.5 percent in sales growth, and an increase in profitability. Furthermore, the information was used to launch a related initiative that returned more than $200 million in additional revenues through the value creation process. [13] Much of the remainder of this chapter provides a discussion of the management of the customer service process, which is based in part on the service-profit chain.

A Framework for Managing Customer Service

As we've shown in this chapter, customer service, while often provided to customers by well-intentioned firm policies and employees, is nevertheless subject to interpretation by customers, and is not unlike hitting a moving target with each customer interaction. Managers may certainly be trying various customer service–enhancing initiatives, but quite often may find the actual impact on the bottom line to be less than anticipated. By viewing customer service as a process, businesses can create a framework for managing and improving their customer service performance.

Process Management in Action   *Going to Extremes*

Imagine a company that takes the adage "the customer is always right" and adapts it to the integrated systems industry: If it messes up, it pays the customer. Imagine a company that doesn't charge for servicing a potential client so it can demonstrate its capabilities. Imagine a company that tells its employees, "You tell us what we can do to make you happier." Imagine all that, and you now have some insight into Tech Systems of Duluth, Georgia. "Up through 1997 essentially we would try to compete for just about any piece of business that was out there," Darryl Keeler, Tech Systems' president says. "We were a fairly small company, and not very proactive about finding opportunities." Then the company had a negative experience that turned out to be the best thing that ever happened to it, according to Keeler.

"It was a three-day weekend," Keeler recalls. "We had a client who had a problem with a camera system. They lost all the cameras on their parking deck. I talked to our guy on call, who said we didn't have to worry about it because our contract said we didn't need to respond until Tuesday [which would have been the next regular business day]." Realizing that three days would be a long time to wait, Keeler went to see the client on Saturday to see if he could help, but by then they had identified the problem on their own and fixed it themselves.

A few weeks later the client called Tech Systems, and asked them to come in for a meeting. "She fired us," Keeler says. "She told us she had been in a terribly vulnerable position at that point. She said, 'I know what the contract said, but instead of doing the thing right you should have done the right thing.' She was 100 percent correct. It was an eye-opening experience. We had always perceived ourselves to be among the best service providers in town, but we were really no different than anyone else. We decided to take what had happened and turn it into something positive."

From that time on, Tech Systems vowed to change its business philosophy to be service-oriented, not sales-oriented. "We began to measure service in hours instead of days and weeks," Keeler says. "If we weren't successful, we began to pay the client. That was the beginning of FOCUS."

FOCUS, the acronym for "For Our Clients' Ultimate Satisfaction," is one of the cornerstones of Tech Systems' current business philosophy. It was designed to guarantee that clients' expectations are always met or exceeded. In essence, FOCUS is a program designed to help Tech Systems reach its goal of developing long-term partnerships with its clients. It provides escalating levels of benefits—including technical, economic, and educational—based on the clients' level of investment with Tech Systems.

"The creation of FOCUS turned us from a security integration company to a service-based company," Keeler says. "We are not a company out looking for a sale; we are looking to build relationships with our clients. It's not a list of benefits; it's a philosophy and a way of doing business."

"It's an attitude, not a product," says senior vice president Clark. "Delivering that attitude to customers is what has been responsible for our growth. Customers talk to each other. They want you in a place you are not currently in because they see what you have to offer and they want it. We've had to go to other states to meet their needs."

Ron Luchene, a vice president based in Raleigh, North Carolina, came on board in 1997 to open the first branch office. Luchene has seen firsthand how FOCUS and the overall service-based model led to growth. "We have clients in markets that we service today coming to us

Continued

and asking if we have a presence, say, in Indiana. When we say 'no,' they say we need to hire someone because they want us there."

One of the main reasons FOCUS works so well is that Tech Systems' employees truly buy into the philosophy and different way of doing business. "People don't like working for us," Clark says. "They either love it or hate it. Ours is a very extreme place. You need to really be into it, or it doesn't feel good at all. We have a large, core group of individuals that absolutely wouldn't work anywhere else. We have spent years being very radical with our approach to customer service. It finally occurred to us that we only had two assets. Our clients were one, but the other was our employees. We needed to be more radical with our employees."

The result is an employee base that will "go the extra mile" for the customers as well as for fellow employees. It's a two-way street. When an employee does something special, Tech Systems rewards him or her for the effort. Its STAR program allows anyone (fellow employees or even clients) to nominate an employee for doing something special. When the employee receives the award, he or she receives an engraved trophy and a day off from work. The STAR recipient also is honored with a black shirt with a gold company logo, which only STAR award recipients are allowed to wear. When an employee reaches five STAR awards he or she receives a check for $500.

In a corporate environment dedicated to fanatical service, the STAR awards were developed to remind people that they are doing exemplary work. "There is something magical that happens. There is an ingredient that occurs just because we've created an environment where people can be their absolute best. We encourage them to do that and they do. They become people who do miraculous things," Clark says. "That's what has made us so great."

When you put together employees who are motivated to do the best they can for the client with a program like FOCUS that backs it up, the result is a tight one-on-one relationship with each and every client. In fact, the fanatical service model makes every customer need personal. "If a client called and needed a quote on Christmas day we would have someone capable and willing to do it," Keeler says. "We have determined what our best opportunities are and once we develop that relationship, there are no obstacles to that. Ever. We do whatever is necessary to make things right. If a client's system is down or has a problem, we see our own company as being in jeopardy. That is our greatest challenge, to get in front of someone and show them it is possible to be unique in this industry. Once we do that, almost 100 percent of the time we win the opportunity with that client."

Source: Hodgson, K., "Going to Extremes," *SDM,* V. 34, No. 11, 2004, pp. 38–43. Reprinted with permission from *SDM* magazine. © 2004.

Figure 4.1 is a representation of the customer service framework. Initially, and as just alluded to, organizations must prepare for the provision of effective customer service by evaluating (and improving, if need be) internal employee satisfaction.

Evaluate and Improve Employee Satisfaction

Employee satisfaction is derived from the internal work environment, including comfort factors, hiring and training practices, motivational factors and the reward system, equipment and technologies utilized, and job design. The impact of employee satisfaction on employee service performance, productivity, and other measures of performance has been the subject of many research efforts. Among other things, the research has

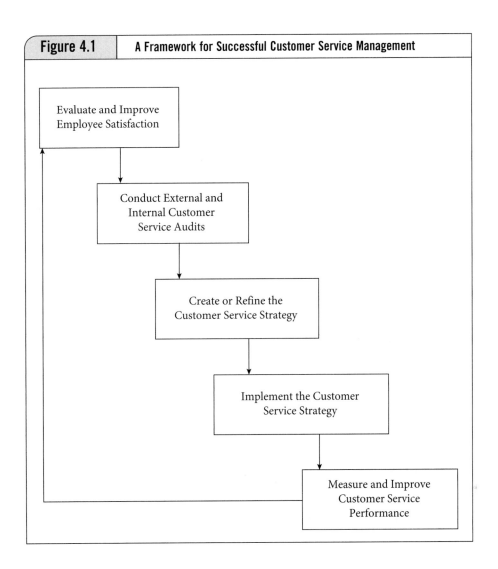

Figure 4.1 | **A Framework for Successful Customer Service Management**

Evaluate and Improve Employee Satisfaction

Conduct External and Internal Customer Service Audits

Create or Refine the Customer Service Strategy

Implement the Customer Service Strategy

Measure and Improve Customer Service Performance

found strong evidence that overall job satisfaction is a critical link to employee service performance. This is sometimes referred to as the **happy productive worker hypothesis**. [14] Reuters, a London-based global information provider, introduced an employee satisfaction improvement initiative in 2003 in an effort to turn around the company's fortunes following a difficult year in 2002. Afterwards, workers could nominate coworkers to receive up to 1,000 points, redeemable for online merchandise and travel awards, for demonstrating commitment to four characteristics: being fast, accountable, service driven, and team oriented. As a result of the recognition program, Reuters' share price, revenues, and customer satisfaction improved. [15]

Typically, managers place much of their attention on either the organization's top performers or on those who are the poorest performers. The majority of the firm's workforce, though, falls somewhere in between. These workers can often be neglected in terms of additional training, tools, and other productivity-enhancing resources. Rosalind Jeffries, president of Performance Enhancement Group Inc., a consulting firm from Bethesda, Maryland, terms this group "Steady Eddies" and warns that these dependable contributors may leave the organization if neglected. Additionally, Jeffries explains, productivity can also be adversely impacted, unless managers use some simple strategies concerning their Steady Eddies, to improve employee satisfaction:[16]

1. Let them know their ideas are appreciated.
2. Ask them for their input.
3. Say "thanks" and show you personally care about them.
4. Give them time on your calendar.

Employee satisfaction surveys are a useful tool for determining where an organization's strengths and weaknesses are, with respect to developing and maintaining high levels of job satisfaction. Additionally, these surveys can themselves create higher levels of satisfaction. According to research completed in the hotel industry, more than 20 percent of hotels that administered employee surveys experienced an improvement in overall employee satisfaction by greater than 10 percent for the following year. The hotels that experienced the greatest satisfaction improvement were found to utilize the following common strategies:[17]

1. Commitment to measurement – Surveys help identify and prioritize problems, as well as offer insights into solutions. It also shows a focus on employees.
2. Allocation of time and resources to act on feedback – These hotels interpret the survey findings, develop and implement action plans, and then communicate the results. Employees are involved in developing and implementing the plans.
3. Alignment of management incentives to satisfaction – Employee satisfaction levels are used in determining managers' performance appraisals and monetary rewards.
4. Employee communication – Managers meet with employees throughout the year to update them on progress towards solving problems. Human resource personnel meet with workers to validate problems identified in the survey.
5. Demonstration and implementation of actions that really matter – Hotel managers show a commitment to taking effective action quickly to get the job done.

Figure 4.2 provides an example of a typical web-based employee satisfaction survey that can be distributed to employees in an email.

Conduct Customer Service Audits

Once the firm is satisfied it is making progress towards developing a satisfying work environment, it can begin to identify customer service requirements. This can best be accomplished through use of an initial external customer service audit using focus groups, interviews, and/or surveys. Information regarding customer service requirements can also be gathered from existing customer information databases (such as records of complaints, repair work, call center comments, and comment card information). This initial customer service audit is necessary to identify a set of service characteristics that are important to customers as well as their performance expectations for each characteristic. Once a number of valued service characteristics and performance expectations are identified, the firm can then determine customers' overall satisfaction with each of these identified service characteristics. This is accomplished through use

Figure 4.2	Employee Satisfaction Survey

1) Please describe your position with the company: [text field]

2) How long have you worked for the company?

-- Select Here -- ▼

Please indicate how much you agree or disagree with each of the following statements:

	Strongly Disagree	Disagree	Undecided	Agree	Strongly Agree
3) I have full access to the information and tools I need to get my job done.	○	○	○	○	○
4) I am familiar with the mission statement of the company.	○	○	○	○	○
5) I am familiar with the mission statement of my department.	○	○	○	○	○
6) I participate in decision making that affects my job.	○	○	○	○	○
7) Management has created an open and comfortable work environment.	○	○	○	○	○
8) I know my job requirements and what is expected of me on a daily basis.	○	○	○	○	○
9) I have received the training I need to do my job efficiently and effectively.	○	○	○	○	○
10) I receive additional training to enable me to do my job better.	○	○	○	○	○
11) Management recognizes my contributions and makes good use of my abilities and skills.	○	○	○	○	○
12) I am treated with respect by management and the people I work with.	○	○	○	○	○
13) I am encouraged to develop new and more efficient ways to do my work.	○	○	○	○	○
14) I and my fellow employees work well together and get the job done.	○	○	○	○	○
15) Management is flexible and understands the importance of balancing my work and personal life.	○	○	○	○	○
16) I would recommend that others work for this company.	○	○	○	○	○
17) I am rewarded well for the work I do for the company.	○	○	○	○	○
18) Overall, I am a satisfied employee.	○	○	○	○	○

19) What changes, if any, do you feel need to be made in your department to improve working conditions?

[text field]

20) What changes, if any, do you feel need to be made in the company to improve working conditions?

[text field]

Source: Based on survey templates available at SurveyConsole.com, QuestionPro.com, and SurveyShare.com.

of follow-up external customer service audits. The need for this two-phase external customer service audit is explained in the following paragraphs.

Determining customer service satisfaction can be tricky without first knowing customer service requirements. For example, asking customers to rate their satisfaction with "speed of service" on a 5-point scale might result in an average rating of 3.8. Is this good or bad? Without first knowing the customer requirements for speed of service, it is impossible to interpret these findings. Additionally, speed of service may not even be a valued service characteristic for this firm. On the other hand, if the firm knows that speed of service is highly valued by customers and that the average customer requirement is 4.5 for speed of service, then a frame of reference exists, and a rating of 3.8 suddenly seems inadequate. Firms must therefore determine customer service characteristics and requirements prior to embarking on any service improvement initiatives or service satisfaction measurements.

Thus, to proceed, businesses must first identify important customer service characteristics along with the average performance requirements for each characteristic. One approach for determining the relative importance of a number of customer service characteristics is to ask the survey respondents or interviewees to rank order a number of potential characteristics. Additionally, respondents should be directed to allocate a total of 100 points to the list of service characteristics based on their relative importance, allowing companies to determine how much more important one factor is relative to another. A final list of five to ten customer service attributes, with their associated customer requirements, can then be identified for use in follow-up audits and any corresponding improvement initiatives.

Internal customer service audits are also necessary to review the firm's current customer service policies and practices. Once both the external and internal audits are completed, organizations will be able to identify gaps between the services customers require and the services the firm is currently providing. These gaps would then be used to guide any improvement strategies.

One final topic to consider in customer service audits is the type of customer surveyed. Does the firm want to survey all customers, the most profitable ones, or some other segment, such as women customers? Perhaps the firm should choose to ignore the assessments of unprofitable customers, and concentrate on providing the desired service elements of one or more segments of customers instead. Depending on the objectives of the customer audits, firms may want to look at specific customer segments and their requirements, as well as the average customer's requirements. The McAlister's Deli restaurant chain, which serves the southeastern United States, realized it had two distinct types of customers when it started surveying them—those who ate in, and those who used takeout. Today, it has a better understanding of its customers, and it uses customer segment feedback to drive specific areas of improvement. As a result, it is improving its brand loyalty and generating greater annual sales increases.[18] Both external and internal customer service audits are described in more detail in the following sections.

The External Customer Service Audit

Most **external customer service audits** are of the follow-up variety, and are typically employed for two reasons: (1) to identify any changes in customer service requirements from the previous audit and (2) to determine current customer service performance of the firm and, ideally, its competitors as well. It is important to understand that ever-changing environmental conditions such as new competition and technological advances can dramatically impact customer service requirements from one year to the next. Thus, external customer service audits should be an ongoing process to monitor not only the success of any service changes the firm has undertaken, but to identify changing customer requirements and potential performance changes on the part of competitors.

On the actual survey instrument, customers should be directed to convey their satisfaction with the firm's performance on each customer service element (using a 5-point Likert scale or something similar), and then to make the same assessments for the firm's major competitors. Some surveys also ask respondents to list the percentage or volume of business allocated to the firm and each of its major competitors, and to supply demographic information such as the type of customer (commercial or individual), income or sales volume, and geographic location. Satisfaction surveys should also ask for free-form comments throughout the survey, to cover areas not treated by the questions. A sample customer satisfaction survey is shown in Figure 4.3. (Given the desired survey elements discussed in this section and differences that may exist from industry to industry, readers are encouraged to identify the strengths and potential weaknesses, if any, in the survey.)

Results from the external customer service audit will identify strengths and weaknesses regarding the firm's customer service capabilities. It will also allow firms to see improvements, if any, from the previous audit and the ensuing service improvement initiatives. Areas of strength can be communicated to customers via marketing campaigns and thus become a competitive advantage for the company. Weaknesses need to be dealt with quickly and effectively, and this can be aided with the use of an internal customer service audit (discussed next). McDonald's has seen a remarkable turnaround in its business since 2001, based in part on its surveys of customer satisfaction. Satisfaction reached a low point in 2001 when customer surveys showed it was losing customers to its rivals Burger King and Wendy's, and also because customers were switching to healthier alternatives such as the sandwich chain Subway. Complaints about the food, dirty restaurants, and indifferent staff were growing, along with a general concern about obesity and junk food. Since then, salads and other lighter meal options have been added to menus and more money is being spent on remodeling existing locations. McDonald's is also changing its training practices and getting into the sandwich business. Today, it is the world's biggest salad seller and its business is flourishing again. [19]

The Internal Customer Service Audit

The **internal customer service audit** allows the organization to review its current customer service measures, policies, and practices. Making changes in these areas—to improve customer service capabilities when weaknesses are identified from the customer satisfaction survey—becomes the basis for new customer service strategies. The internal customer service audit should provide information on the following topics:

- *Measures* – How are different functions within the firm actually measuring customer satisfaction? Do these measures support the external customer service characteristics? How are these measures reported and communicated? Have performance improvements in the internal measures led to external performance improvements?

- *Policies* – What customer service policies exist within each function of the organization? Are they effectively communicated to employees? Are these polices related to the external customer service requirements? Have these

Figure 4.3	Customer Satisfaction Survey

Dear Customer: Thank you for purchasing from us, and giving us the opportunity to serve you. Please help us serve you better by taking a couple of minutes to tell us about your purchase and the service that you have received so far. We appreciate your business and want to make sure we meet your expectations. Enclosed, you will find a token of our appreciation for returning this survey.

1. Thinking about your most recent customer service experience with our company, the quality of service you received was:
___ Poor, ___ Unsatisfactory, ___ Satisfactory, ___ Very Satisfactory, ___ Superior

If you indicated that the customer service was poor or unsatisfactory, would you please describe what happened?

The process for getting your concerns resolved was (check one):
___ Poor, ___ Unsatisfactory, ___ Satisfactory, ___Very Satisfactory, ___Superior

If you indicated that the problem resolution was poor or unsatisfactory, would you please describe what happened?

2. Now please think about the quality (features, benefits) and cost of your recent purchase from our company. Which characteristic best describes your feeling about the product?
___ Poor, ___ Unsatisfactory, ___ Satisfactory, ___ Very Satisfactory, ___ Superior

If you are not at least satisfied, would you please take a few minutes to describe why?

3. Customer Service Representative – The following items pertain to the customer service representative you spoke with most recently. Please indicate whether you agree or disagree with the following statements:

	Strongly Agree	Agree	Neutral	Disagree	Strongly Disagree
The customer service representative was very courteous.					
The customer service representative handled my question quickly.					
The customer service representative was very knowledgeable.					

Are there any other comments about the customer service representative you would like to add?

4. Our Competition – The following questions pertain to the company that you think is our best competitor. Please indicate whether you agree or disagree with the following statements.

Name of our best competitor:	Strongly Agree	Agree	Neutral	Disagree	Strongly Disagree
Our customer service is better than our competitor's.					
The product you purchased is better than our competitor's.					
Our customer service representatives are better than our competitor's.					

5. Overall satisfaction.

	Very Satisfied	Somewhat Satisfied	Neutral	Somewhat Dissatisfied	Very Dissatisfied
Considering our total package of customer service, product quality, and cost, how satisfied are you?					

Thank you very much for your feedback. We sincerely appreciate your honest opinion and will take your input into consideration when providing products and services in the future. If you have any additional comments or concerns about this survey, or if you want to discuss a problem further, please contact: [MANAGER_NAME] [ADDRESS, CONTACT INFO.].

Source: Based on survey templates available at SurveyConsole.com, QuestionPro.com, and SurveyShare.com.

policies contributed to improvements in customer satisfaction, or are they inhibiting improvements in customer satisfaction?

- *Practices* – How often are external customer service audits performed? Are the audit findings used in any of the firm's reward systems? Are the external audit findings communicated throughout the firm? Are improvement initiatives routinely designed and implemented based on external customer service audit results? Are resources readily available to support the customer service improvement initiatives? Are these activities supported and encouraged by top management? Does the firm track the cost and the value created by these initiatives?

The overall objective of the internal customer service audit is to identify any inconsistencies between the firm's view and practice of customer service and the actual requirements of customers. Integrating the two can be problematic. For example, managers and their employees might think the firm's customer service attributes are very good, when in fact customers are saying something entirely different. In other cases, employees may simply have no idea of their company's customer service performance or the cost of providing it. All of these disconnects between the company and its customers are likely to be identified with an effective audit of the firm's customer service measures, policies, and practices, once the external audit has been completed. When identified, these problems can then be resolved through the design of the right customer service strategy. U.S. financial institution Bank of America, for example, measures customer satisfaction with an ongoing survey and communicates results every quarter throughout the company. Its quality improvement program is based on findings from this survey. Since implementing the survey and improvement efforts in 2001, it has seen customer satisfaction improve by 25 percent. Today, Bank of America's business model is focused on customer service, which drives its strategy for making improvements and developing unique products that appeal to its diverse customer base.[20]

Gathering the initial information regarding customer service measures, policies, and practices is likely to be a time-consuming activity, and organizations should make use of interviews with functional managers. Once established, updates can be accomplished with relative ease. Internal customer service audit information is likely to highlight inconsistencies in how customer service is regarded in different departments and how polices are carried out and communicated to customers. It is important for the firm to present a unified face to the customer, and audits can be the first step in that direction.

The internal customer service audit should also assess the costs and value of the current strategies employed to improve customer service capabilities. Strategies may need to be refined, redeployed, or discontinued based on findings from the external audit. Internal and external audit information can also be used when benchmarking the competition's customer service attributes. The following section discusses the formation of customer service strategies, based on information obtained during the customer service audits.

Creating a Customer Service Strategy

Effective customer service strategies are based on the knowledge of how customers define service, their perceptions of current customer service levels, and the experiences the firm has had in designing and delivering customer service. Thus, trying to improve customer service will be both costly and ineffective unless internal and external customer service audits are a regular business activity. The objective of all customer service strategies should be to create value through optimum service levels, leading to long-term competitive advantage and improved profitability. The optimum service level may not be the highest attainable, nor the most expensive, but a level that will adequately satisfy customers. The most profitable customers will most likely receive the highest levels and the most frequent customer service, whereas unprofitable customers may receive very little in the way of service.

It is also important to understand the law of diminishing returns as it applies to customer service. As customer service levels increase overall for the organization, the incremental value and benefit created by even higher levels of customer service becomes smaller. Eventually, the cost of adding additional customer service capabilities overcomes any additional value generated. At some point, the firm might actually be decreasing its profitability by continuing to improve customer service. Businesses can develop this cost/profit relationship by observing what happens when certain unplanned service failures occur (such as strikes, accidents, shortages, quality failures, weather interruptions, etc.). Sales to various customer segments before and after these events can provide insight into the variations of specific service elements and their impact on sales and specific customer segment profitability. Figure 4.4 shows the relationship between investments in customer service and the impact on profitability. What this figure refers to is that for firms providing low overall levels of customer service, investments to improve service should provide a positive impact on profitability.

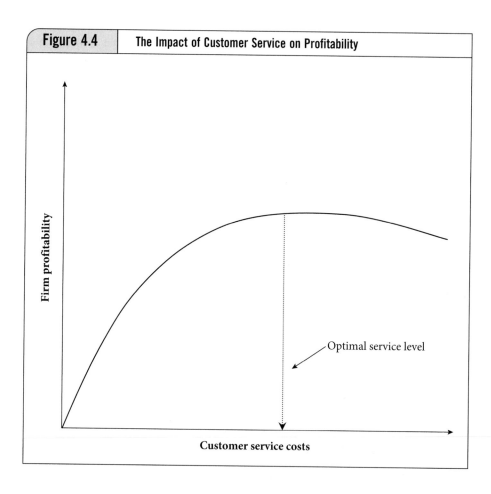

| Figure 4.4 | The Impact of Customer Service on Profitability |

But, as customer service levels increase, further investments to improve service will result in increasingly smaller impacts on profitability. At some point, investments in customer service improvements will result in overall profit reductions for the firm.

In general, effective service strategies concentrate on delivering high-quality customer service and value, foster achievement within the organization, and are aligned with the company's mission. Each of these is briefly discussed next.

High-Quality Customer Service

Delivering **high-quality customer service** is achieved through attention to four basic service principles:

1. *Reliability* – Companies keep their promises; their services are accurate and dependable.
2. *Recovery* – Companies must be able to adequately fix things in a quick, meaningful way when they go wrong.
3. *Fairness* – Companies respect customers and treat them in a fair and ethical way.
4. *Wow factor* – Companies add unexpected touches to the service, meant to impress customers, as in "Wow! This is great!"

Find companies delivering excellent customer service and you'll most likely find ample evidence of all four of these service quality principles. Company culture should encourage these beliefs and reward and otherwise support employees who deliver service performance in these areas. Commitment to these four principles creates high-quality customer service. MinuteClinic, for example, a quick-care health clinic located in a number of CVS Pharmacies and Cub Food stores in the Minneapolis-St. Paul, Minnesota area, provides treatment for common ailments such as strep throat and ear infections. No appointment is necessary and it is open seven days per week. No visit takes more than 15 minutes, and most services cost $44, although most insurance companies cover MinuteClinic visits. "If the nurse practitioner is with another patient, our customers simply take a beeper—like those used in restaurants—and they can go elsewhere in the store to shop for groceries, clothes, or household items," says Linda Hall Whitman, CEO of MinuteClinic. Its nurse practitioners use a software program that guides evidenced-based diagnosis, treatments, and billing. Patient records are kept in the database and are accessible from any MinuteClinic location on a real-time basis. Since opening in May 2000, MinuteClinics have treated 150,000 patients with greater than 99 percent customer satisfaction.[21]

Creating Value with Customer Service

When customer service meets or exceeds customer expectations, it makes customers feel they are getting their money's worth and perhaps even better. They desire to return and make future purchases. This sense of value provides firms with a competitive advantage, and in many cases may be very easy to provide to customers. For instance, a quick-change oil business that provides a copy of the newspaper, a TV, and free coffee to patrons who are waiting to have their automobile's oil changed is providing extra value to the actual service. Additionally, if it performs extra services, such as checking the air filter and the wiper blades, the service value is increased even more. Finally, since many people view waiting time as lost earnings potential, getting customers in and out quickly also creates service value. Utah-based Internet clearance retailer Overstock.com recently began a service at its website that is creating a lot of interest among its customers. A problem with many Internet shopping sites is that customers will frequently abandon online shopping carts due to problems encountered with navigating the site. To counteract this problem, when Overstock.com's website detects a customer having difficulty with their purchases, a pop-up window will invite the customer to a text chat-room where a customer-support agent is located. The agent can answer questions and even complete the checkout process for the customer by plugging in shipping and billing information or redoing an order. "We see it as a service we are providing to customers, like a personal shopper at Nordstrom's," says Tad Martin, vice president of merchandising and operations at Overstock.com. He finds that customers accept the invite about 10 percent of the time, or about 25,000 times per month. [22]

Fostering Achievements in Customer Service

Service strategies should include training to develop skills required by customers. Managers should also allow service providers in the organization to use creativity when solving problems. Additionally, successful service recoveries should be communicated to other service providers in the organization, while unsuccessful recoveries should be viewed as an opportunity to find a more successful solution. Successful, innovative customer service activities exhibited by employees should also be rewarded. According to U.S. human resource consulting firm Hewitt Associates' 2003 Variable Compensation Measurement Report, which summarized pay-for-performance practices at 111 U.S. companies, 63 percent thought the benefits of their plans outweighed the costs. And 57 percent reported unexpected favorable outcomes, including increased employee productivity and morale. [23]

Aligning Customer Service with the Mission

Firms must be serious about committing to providing good and even great customer service. As Leonard Berry says in his book, *On Great Service*, firms must live their service strategy. Hiring and training the right people, providing the right technology, and using effective performance measures and reward systems, among other things, gives life to service strategies. [24] Mission statements should contain language pertaining to customer service and this commitment should filter down through the firm's hierarchy. Here are two examples of company missions that contain customer service language:

1. From Churchill China, a major UK manufacturer of ceramic tableware: *To be a leading provider to the tabletop market and deliver value through excellence in design, quality, and customer service.*

2. From Sainsbury's, a leading UK food retailer with banking interests: *Our number one job is to serve our customers well. This means we must look to provide a consistent level of good customer service across all our activities whether this is customer contact, product availability, food quality, or banking services.*

In both cases, the commitment to customer service is clearly stated and easily accessible at the companies' websites.

A customer service strategy for a firm is the collective customer service practices and policies that are derived from the company's mission, the customer requirements, the customer service practices of the competition, and previous experiences with customer service initiatives. It is an organizing principle that directs employees to provide services that benefit customers. Thus, customer service strategies define the ongoing management of customer service for a business. As competition increases and products and services change, customer requirements change and, consequently, customer service strategies must also change. To create loyal customers who generate long-term repeat purchases, a number of commonly used customer service practices have been employed. Several of these are described next.

Customer Service Departments

While customer service departments have existed for many years, and may at one time have been repositories for disgruntled employees armed with a company policy manual, a curt smile, and a line that went something like, "We're sorry, but that is against company policy," today **customer service departments** are staffed with a collection of innovative and knowledgeable people and in many cases are viewed as a competitive weapon. Customer service departments create a focal point for service assessment and improvement, and can be the drivers for creating a service culture in the organization. The customer service department can create and maintain an emphasis on service quality, and add a sense of formality to the firm's customer service strategy. NorVergence, an information technology solution provider based in New Jersey, provides "white glove" treatment to its customers through its large and growing customer service department. "With our White Glove customer service, we handle each call thoroughly, answering all questions about services and products and resolve issues facing our customers," says Rashan Thompson, Assistant Vice President of Customer Service at NorVergence. "It's this level of professionalism at NorVergence that attracts both customers and customer service professionals alike." In addition, it has a client management department that contacts customers to provide updates on the status of their orders and installations, and gathers feedback from customers for analysis. These contacts also reduce inquiry calls made to the Customer Service Department. [25]

Innovative customer service departments provide direction and coordination to customer service assessment and improvement efforts. It oversees the internal and external customer service audits; creates the strategic service plan; and establishes funding, timelines, and responsibilities for implementation of service activities. It also helps set up project teams for specific customer service improvement initiatives, and serves as the collection point for service improvement ideas that come from employees in the organization. When initiatives are implemented, the customer service department helps design performance metrics and then assists in monitoring actual performance, taking the appropriate actions to further refine and improve performance. Finally, it creates customer service progress reports, summaries, and plans, and communicates these throughout the organization and to customers and the general public.

Of critical importance is the selection of department personnel. They must be motivated to get the job done, possess a service mentality, have the necessary product knowledge and skills, and be well-respected within the organization. The department manager should report to top management and communicate frequently with marketing, production, and human resource department managers (who might also be members of a long-range customer service steering committee that aids in the creation of customer service strategies). The department should have a support staff to collect information, provide hands-on help with daily service issues, and to help carry out initiatives designed by the department and perhaps a broader customer service steering committee.

Temporary **customer service teams** can also be created with the help of the customer service department, and can consist of executives, department managers, design engineers, and other personnel, to react to a significant customer service problem. For example, while global conglomerate General Electric (GE) had not made small appliances since the early 1980s, news of old GE coffeemakers causing fires created the need for an innovative customer service solution, involving customers in both North and South America. GE formed a cross-functional team of GE managers to study the problem and implemented a meaningful solution that would satisfy its customers. It conducted a media blitz to publicize a toll-free phone number consumers could call to see if their coffeemaker was hazardous. GE manned the call center 24/7 with hundreds of specifically trained English-, French-, and Spanish-speaking operators. When a suspect coffeemaker was found, packaging was delivered to the consumer and overnight shipping company Airborne Express was contracted to handle doorstep pickups. Customers were also paid $10 for their inconvenience when the repaired or replaced coffeemakers were returned to the owners. "The part of the program that makes this recall unique is that from the customer standpoint, the process costs nothing and it's completely hassle-free," said Chip Keeling, GE's spokesperson for the recall. "They don't have to pay for a phone call, provide packaging, or go to the post office. In terms of customer service, we're seeing a higher level of customer satisfaction than we expected, based on previous recalls."[26]

The customer service department plays an important role in educating all employees on the importance of customer service and in providing assistance to others in the organization, such that frontline workers can do the majority of the work and thus "own" the particular service improvement process.

Customer Contact Centers

Today, customer call centers are more aptly named **customer contact centers** because they integrate all of the methods customers can use to contact a business, including telephone, mail, comment cards, email, and website messages and chat rooms. For most large firms, these contact centers are open 24/7. In some cases, contact center automation technologies allow a small staff to handle a large volume of customer calls, and in cases where most customers are asking for similar information, firms have found it more efficient to add automated systems such as interactive voice response, speech recognition, and call routing systems. In many contact centers, this **automated agent** handles about 70 percent of all calls coming in to the contact center.[27] Automated agents have more responsibility than ever before due to cost reduction efforts and enable real agents to spend time more effectively handling more complex questions or problems.

In many organizations today, the customer contact center has become the focal point for developing, monitoring, and improving customer service strategy, in essence replacing the customer service department previously discussed. And the recognized value of contact centers is increasing rapidly. Contact center employees commonly hear about the value of optimizing customer interactions and improving customer satisfaction. For instance, a 1 percent increase in first-call resolution can improve customer satisfaction by 6 percent; and one hour of contact center training can drop the cost per customer contact by more than three cents.[28] When these savings are multiplied over many thousands of customers, the impact can be significant.

But too often, it is difficult for customers to complain or request more information. Comment cards must be placed in plainly visible locations, and toll-free contact center phone numbers should be printed on all of the firm's catalogues, mailings, websites, and comment cards. Customer contact center personnel can undertake proactive methods to seek out customer feedback and solve problems by making follow-up calls to customers who have recently purchased a product or service, or who complained at an earlier time and were given assurances that their complaint would be resolved. New technologies, better training, and full-enterprise awareness of the value of a well-managed customer contact center are allowing businesses today to differentiate themselves from their competitors, create loyal customers, and find new ones.

Customer Participation and Self-Service

Allowing customers to participate in the service itself provides customers with the opportunity to somewhat customize their service. Customer participation also involves the customer to a greater degree with the company, increases the productivity of service providers, and can improve customer satisfaction. Services that involve customers are becoming more common as firms try to find ways to reduce labor costs.

Self-service is one form of the **customer participation approach**. It requires a standardized service that can be administered with little or no company assistance. Examples of self-service processes include automated bank teller machines, automated information obtained during customer telephone calls, website purchases and queries, refueling at most gas stations, and the ever-more-popular customer self-checkout stations at retail locations. Self-service can be very appealing to customers, since it allows them to decide when to access the service, how long to interact, and the precise service desired. However, customer training or indoctrination may be needed, and this involves careful thought when designing printed directions, and may also have to involve a company employee to monitor customers. Problems with instructions and accessing assistance from employees can lead to lower levels of customer satisfaction, so self-service processes must be effectively designed and closely monitored.

Customer participation can also represent much greater customer involvement in the service process. A visit to the doctor, dentist, or hairstylist involves the consumer to some degree, in relaying information to the service provider in order to customize and expedite the service. One benefit to customer participation is that customers take more responsibility in the process. Organizations, for example, may decide to take ownership of purchased products at the seller's location in order to provide more custom-tailored delivery services (in logistics parlance, this is termed **FOB origination**). If the products are damaged while in transit, it becomes the responsibility of the buyer to replace or fix them. Additionally, some customer segments may desire higher levels of customer participation than others, and this is yet another reason for segmenting and understanding the needs of various customer groups.

Web-Based Customer Service Applications

In many cases and as briefly noted in the self-service discussion, a well-designed company website can enable customers to obtain answers to their questions or receive additional information, eliminating the need for interaction with customer service personnel. Companies commonly post answers to frequently asked questions and provide catalogues and installation, assembly, operating, and troubleshooting manuals on their websites. Other e-service solutions can respond to customer queries by interpreting questions and then delivering answers from a knowledge database. These automated e-services largely eliminate emails, cost much less than providing traditional call center answers, and can raise customer satisfaction levels. Additionally, they can handle up to 90 percent of the typical customer queries received by companies. For example, Sony Computer Entertainment Europe uses an e-service provider to handle about 47 percent of its PlayStation® queries automatically, and has a large impact on inbound phone calls. Good website management can also make use of e-service records to see what customers are asking for, and further develop customer relationships.[29] The e-Commerce Perspective feature profiles BTService, a provider of a web-based warranty service for the U.S. home building industry.

e-Commerce Perspective

A Web-Based Warranty Service for Home Builders

If there's one area where even good builders blow it with their buyers, it's warranty service. Perfect customer relationships can be damaged in a hurry if their new homes are not delivered defect-free and warranty service requests are not handled efficiently.

Developed jointly by Illinois-based Kimball Hill Homes and software maker BuildTopia, BTService is a web-based warranty service management application that promises to change how builders close out their jobs and offer follow-up care. The software is available either as a stand-alone application or as part of the larger BTBuilder™ home builder management package.

The product provides customer/warranty-service managers, warranty technicians, subcontractors, and home buyers with their own screens, accessible from any web browser. The users see only information that pertains to them: Service managers use their screen to log service requests and assign items to a specific service technician, and technicians use their screen to manage their open service requests and assign items to subcontractors. The customer's screen can be integrated with the builder's own website, creating a secure warranty-service portal for buyers.

According to Kimball Hill, a web-based platform offers many advantages over conventional warranty-service applications. Home buyers can attach notes directly to their service request and enter multiple service items in one request from their service portal. The requests flow from the buyer's machine into the service manager's screen, where they can be processed for repair or rejected as non-warranty items. Buyers are notified automatically by email whenever their request is assigned a disposition code, and they can track all of their requests online.

Likewise, when a technician assigns an open item to a subcontractor, the subcontractor is contacted immediately, either through the BuildTopia system if he or she is a member, or by email if not. The system lets builders track subcontractor performance. Subcontractors who aren't performing can be easily culled out and their items reassigned so that the buyer always receives prompt service.

Customer service reps and technicians can drill into the buyer information and view or make corrections to any information, except the project address. If BTService is used as part of the larger BuildTopia BTBuilder system, notes and incidence logs originating all the way through the sales and construction process will be available as background information to the technician.

Source: Stoddard, J., "Webbed Warranties," *Builder*, V. 27, No. 12, 2004, pp. 305–306. Reprinted with permission from *Builder* magazine. © Hanley Wood.

Web-based service applications have also opened up opportunities for technology-assisted selling. Today the role of the field salesperson provides added value as a customer service representative by enabling current information to be provided about the company's products and services in the field, and by allowing company resources such as marketing information, training, logistics information, diagnostic information and collaborative planning initiatives to be made available to customers. From the customer's perspective, web-based services have greatly simplified the product search, order, and payment processes.

Outsourcing Customer Service

As technologies improve and become less costly, customers find they no longer need to communicate directly with customer service personnel to obtain information. Instead, they find what they need using automated contact center services, web services, or e-services. In an environment such as this where most questions can be answered using automated applications, there would not be significant labor costs associated with many customer services, and consequently the company's desire to outsource the customer service function would not be that great. In other cases, though, customer contact centers and other customer support personnel represent a significant expense for the organization, and lately have been considered a prime target for outsourcing as a means for reducing costs and even improving customer service performance.

Because of the potential value of customer service activities and the real possibility of damaging valuable customer relationships, firms tend to be cautious when considering an outsourcing solution, and in some cases will pay handsomely to firms with a reputation for providing high-quality customer services for clients. For example, in 2004, global communication services provider Sprint signed a $400 million five-year agreement with IBM Global Services to help the company improve customer service in both its wireline and wireless operations. Among other arrangements, IBM will provide new e-commerce and web applications for Sprint customers, help accelerate new product deliveries, and aid Sprint in improving its overall business practices.[30] In Canada, many of the largest electric and gas utilities have outsourced their entire customer service function. Accenture Business Services for Utilities, a North American customer service provider, lists as clients Canadian utilities such as BC Gas, BC Hydro, and Enmax. BC Hydro claims it will save $250 million over a ten-year period and improve customer satisfaction by turning over its customer service responsibilities to Accenture.[31]

Other companies remain unconvinced of the value of **outsourcing customer service**. For instance, Nationwide Building Society, a banking, insurance, and investment provider in the United Kingdom lists commitment to its employees, the high value of customer service, and risk to its reputation as the three main reasons it has decided against customer service outsourcing.[32]

Lately, there has been much discussion in the press regarding outsourcing of call center activities to offshore companies, particularly to service companies located in India. India-based Infosys Technologies' (global provider of IT consulting services) workforce in India grew by over 75 percent from September 2003 to September 2004, and Meta Group Inc., a U.S. research firm (now part of Connecticut-based Gartner Research), estimated that offshore outsourcing by U.S. businesses will grow about 20 percent per year through 2008. One consequence from this increase in outsourcing is that wages are increasing in India in the neighborhood of 15 percent per year, forcing Indian offshore companies to add more sophisticated services so they can justify charging higher fees.[33] An interesting discussion of offshore outsourcing appears in the Global Perspective feature.

Another form of customer service outsourcing involves the creation of a **virtual call center** (mentioned briefly in the Global Perspective feature). With this type of arrangement, an organization's call center agents can be located anywhere, while the center can be managed and utilized as a single entity. Using the virtual call center model allows staffing resources to be optimized, employee retention and satisfaction to increase, call center costs to decline, and perhaps most importantly, allows management control to be retained (in contrast to offshore outsourcing of an entire business function). Today,

Global Perspective

Offshore Outsourcing of Customer Contact Centers

There is no bigger topic in the customer service market these days than that of outsourcing; more specifically, offshore outsourcing. Walk into any contact center and you'll hear the same fears—that management has mostly let "enlightened" customer service go by the wayside, in favor of simply doing it cheaper. These fears may be based on assumptions that cheap offshore labor equates with low quality.

Now put on your customers' shoes for a minute. When you have a service request or problem, do you care if the agent:

- Works for a third-party service provider?
- Is physically seated in an international location?
- Is physically seated at a remote (e.g., home) location?
- Has an accent or an unfamiliar (e.g., foreign) name?

The answers that just about any honest customer will give are no, no, no, and no.

Customers care about quality of service and efficiency of service. Period.

In other words, offshoring will succeed if it results in a more productive customer service operation. This means higher quality and lower cost. One without the other will not be successful. But both together will continue to succeed.

Technology is enabling this success. Moving agents offshore has never been all that difficult. The challenge has been moving the infrastructure—in particular the telephony and IT systems that support the contact center. Today on-demand computing and voice over IP are rapidly making both trivially easy. Within the next 24 to 36 months legacy call centers that are hanging on only because it's too expensive to move the boxes and the telephone lines will no longer have a reason to exist. Forward-thinking companies, such as JetBlue, are doing this today. Their call centers aren't centers at all; they're wherever the reps happen to be, and wherever the company wants them to be, whether it's in the sales rep's kitchen or in Bangalore.

So does this mean that everything's going offshore? Of course not. Look at the automobile industry as an example. What will happen over time is not mass migration, but equilibrium. Inefficient local companies will shutter some operations, but efficient foreign companies will establish new ones. Some jobs will be lost, but many more will be gained. Smart companies will recognize that the right strategy involves a blending of resources, and that there are big advantages in having the agents situated where they can be supervised, trained, and managed without racking up thousands of frequent flyer miles.

Offshoring has advantages and disadvantages. The companies that are most successful in understanding both will achieve maximum benefit. And customers will ultimately be more satisfied as a result, regardless of who is answering the phone and where they happen to be sitting.

Source: Selland, C., "Offshore Versus Onshore Contact Centers," *Customer Relationship Management*, V. 8, No. 6, 2004, p. 24. Used with permission.

global home improvement retailer Home Depot uses about 1,400 remote call center agents who are supplied by its outsourcing partners. It has been steadily increasing its virtual call center agents and plans to continue this trend. Before going virtual, global office product retailer Office Depot's call center attrition rates were about 60 percent per year, whereas today they are in the teens. "Attendance is also up," says Julian

Carter, Director of Operations at Office Depot in Del Ray Beach, Florida. "On the productivity side, the biggest thing we see is a reduction in absenteeism." He estimates the company has cut costs by 30 to 40 percent per call by virtual outsourcing.[34]

Hopefully, the firm is able to identify a customer service strategy that is a good match between what its customers are saying they want, what the firm is capable of doing, and what competitors are not currently doing very well or at all. A well-conceived and implemented service strategy can serve the company well for a very long time, requiring only minor technical adjustments over time for continued effectiveness.

Implementing the Customer Service Strategy

Referring again to Figure 4.1, once the firm has decided on a customer service strategy and the activities to be included in this strategy, the necessary resources must be committed to implementing the activities, including the hiring and training of personnel, procurement of equipment and software applications, and the assignment or construction of facility space. Obviously, management must support the overall customer service strategy, be willing to provide the financial resources required, and be committed to seeing the strategy through the implementation phase prior to realizing any of the potential benefits. This organizational commitment, though, may be the most difficult implementation issue management faces. For example, the strategy may require speed of delivery, but the firm's culture and bureaucracy may create sluggishness. The strategy may require service providers to think outside the box, but the prevailing fear in the organization results in employees who won't take action without first obtaining management approval. Organizational leaders, then, must look at the culture and structure required to enable service strategy success, and be willing to make any required changes. To achieve long-term success, management must communicate what changes will occur, why and how they will occur, and who will be affected. Additionally, management must demonstrate its support throughout the life of the service strategy by providing continual communication along with the required initial and continuing resources.

Start with a Pilot Project

Depending on the required investment and probability of success, the firm may choose to start small, with a **pilot customer service initiative**. Piloting enables management to assess the impact of the initiative on customer satisfaction, the real costs involved, and the changes in structure required. A number of problems will likely surface and allow employees involved to work through the problems and refine the system prior to any organizational customer service strategy rollout. Surveys can be used to assess customer and employee satisfaction after the pilot project is implemented. It is during this time that the required resources, costs, benefits, and merits of the customer service strategy will become clear, allowing the firm to make a final decision regarding whether or not to go ahead with full implementation.

Provide the Necessary Training, Equipment, and Leadership

Training is one of the more critical issues with any new customer service strategy. Service delivery personnel may be skilled in several functions, but may be required to perform others, using equipment unfamiliar to them. Education and equipment training needs must be assessed and provided. Hiring personnel with the required training levels may also be an option, particularly if this knowledge doesn't already exist within the organization. Supervisory roles must be established along with a transitioning period for jobs that will change and middle management power that might be affected. The firm must decide who is going to teach, who is going to coach, and who is going to make decisions and solve problems when they arise.

Measuring and Improving Customer Service Performance

The final step in implementing a customer service strategy is to develop performance standards and the accompanying measurements to assess ongoing performance. Management sets service performance standards for all of the activities that make up the service strategy based on factors such as the type of customer and their service requirements, the distribution channel, and the product or service involved. Standards for each service activity should be quantitative and measurable. Performance standards must then be communicated to the service activity providers. Reward systems should also be considered that will encourage employees to meet and exceed the performance standards.

Measures of actual customer service performance should be conducted frequently for each of the activities comprising the overall customer service strategy, and compared to the accompanying standard. Ideally, performance should be measured each time a service is provided. In some cases, though, this might not be possible. The time it takes a customer service representative to answer a telephone call once the customer has been put on hold can be monitored using automated applications. Measuring every customer's satisfaction at a restaurant, though, can be time consuming and impractical. In this case, random monitoring is typically employed. Performances can thus be collected, averaged over time, and compared to the service standards. When negative variances are found between an actual performance and the standard, corrective actions can be taken to improve performance. Some potential customer service measures are shown in Table 4.3, and are organized according to the classifications shown in Table 4.1. Each measure should have a performance standard that is determined and periodically revised as conditions merit.

Monitoring customer service performance should incorporate several methods, including use of complaint or suggestion systems, customer satisfaction surveys, ghost or mystery shoppers, and customer interviews. Firms should try to make it easy for customers to provide feedback, complaints, or suggestions, such as providing space for comments on company websites, placing complaint/suggestion forms where customers regularly interact with service personnel, providing surveys with invoices or products, calling customers who recently purchased a product or service, and establishing a toll-free customer service hotline. These have all been previously discussed in this chapter, with the exception of the use of mystery shoppers.

Using Mystery Shoppers to Monitor Service Performance

Many companies hire professional **mystery shoppers** who pose as customers in order to assess the customer service performance of employees and the work environment. Mystery shoppers gather performance information and document employee behaviors, and then create summary reports that are sent to management. These reports indicate how long, for example, the customer had to wait for service, the type of greeting used, the willingness of the service provider to answer questions or solve problems, and the server's knowledge of the products and services. While the mystery shoppers conduct covert observations, employees are typically told in advance about the likelihood of mystery shopper visits, and how the information collected will be used. This enables the firm to maintain employee trust.

Mystery observations can yield a full picture of job performance and the work environment, and can be an ideal method for identifying the underlying causes of performance problems. Skilled observers can uncover workplace tools and other items that

Table 4.3	Customer Service Performance Measures
Pretransaction Measures	Percentage of queries answered satisfactorily
	Time to answer customer query
	Number of sales calls made
	Number of technical skills acquired
	Hours of training completed
	Number of new product/service meetings attended
	Number of existing products/services reviewed
	Number of customer service improvements implemented
	Safety stock levels for each product
Transaction Measures	Time to seat customer
	Time to acknowledge customer order
	Time to fill customer order
	Number of deliveries made
	Order cycle time
	Percentage of on-time deliveries
	Percentage of orders unfilled (stockouts)
	Percentage of shipments with errors
	Percentage of orders expedited
	Number of orders traced
	Percentage of customers complaining during transaction
	Percentage of emergency orders handled satisfactorily
Posttransaction Measures	Percentage of invoices with errors
	Percentage of returns/adjustments
	Number of product/service complaints
	Percentage of shipments damaged
	Number of warranty services performed
	Number of service requests
	Percentage of operating queries answered satisfactorily

Source: Based on Lambert, D., J. Stock, and L. Ellram, *Fundamentals of Logistics Management*, New York, NY: McGraw-Hill, 1998, p. 66.

help to create superior job performance, as well as things that hinder performance. Ineffective work flows, processes, and communication patterns can also be identified. Additionally, observers can assess employees' mastery of training regimens and uncover differences in behaviors among excellent, average, and poor service employees.

Mystery shoppers have been used for decades in the restaurant business; however, they are gaining popularity today for gathering information on customer contact centers, hotels, conference facilities, office environments, and many other service functions and businesses. McDonald's, a leader in the use of mystery shoppers, claims the program has had a significant impact on same-store sales since it was re-initiated in 2002. Every domestic outlet receives a visit monthly. By the end of 2005, the McDonald's program encompassed all 30,000 of its worldwide locations. Jeff Hall, president of the Mystery Shoppers Providers Association based in Dallas, Texas, estimates that 70 to 80 percent of quick-service operators are using some type of anonymous visit program. He says that a 25-unit chain would spend between $15,000 and $25,000 annually on a program involving one visit per store per month. And most of these companies insist that the programs are worth the investment. [35]

The Captain D's restaurant chain in the United States uses its own unique mystery guest program. "We recruit local businesspeople to come in and fill out a form, and then we reimburse their meal," says Gary Wilson, senior vice president for Captain D's. Its goal is to mystery shop each restaurant six times per month. The 579-unit chain spends about $250,000 per year on the program. "Franchisees are required to participate, and they get billed for the program each time a shopper comes in," explains Mr. Wilson. Shopper reports are filed via email, allowing the store to get feedback immediately so that managers can make improvements quickly. Positive comments earn employees gift certificates and other rewards. [36]

Atlas-Butler Heating & Cooling services company of Columbus, Ohio, mystery shops each service technician once per year. Every technician knows that they'll be mystery shopped, and the visit is viewed as a training opportunity. Select customer homes are fitted with miniature cameras and customers provide feedback to management that is later shared with the service technician. The service manager and technician also review the videotapes of the service call. They have found that the level of customer service has been greatly enhanced, and the technicians say they enjoy learning how to improve their service capabilities. [37]

A number of third-party mystery shopper services have also sprung up in the past few years. Bare Associates based in Fairfax, Virginia, administers mystery shopper programs for hotels and major conference facilities. These people will register for a conference and stay at the conference hotel, observing the registration services, transportation to the site, bell services, hotel check-in, maintenance, audiovisual equipment, food and refreshments, restrooms, and security. When they are ready to leave, they contact the manager to review their findings and discuss areas in need of improvement. Star employees are also singled out at that time. [38]

Improving Customer Service Performance with TQM

Once the methods for measuring service performance are in place and standards of performance have been established, measurements can be compared against standards. When a performance shortfall is identified, creative, effective, value-added solutions can be designed and corrective actions taken. This type of continuous performance monitoring followed by periodic improvement initiatives is the application of **total quality management** (TQM) to customer service activities. While the topic of TQM will be covered in detail in Chapter 14, it will be briefly discussed here, particularly the use of fishbone diagrams.

The identification of potential service failure causes can be facilitated with the use of a **fishbone diagram** that is used to tabulate potential causes of a particular problem in the areas of *manpower*, *machinery*, *materials*, and *methods*, termed the 4 M's of the fishbone diagram (these four areas have been found to contain the vast majority of all business problem causes). Figure 4.5 shows a fishbone diagram with potential problem causes for the long wait times experienced by customers.

To use the tool as shown in the figure, managers and employees brainstorm potential causes of the long wait times in each of the four areas. The next step would be to determine sub-causes of each of the primary causes. For example, under the Materials section, "run out of food" is listed as one of the potential causes of the long wait problem. (The sub-causes are identified by asking the question "why?" to each of the causes.)

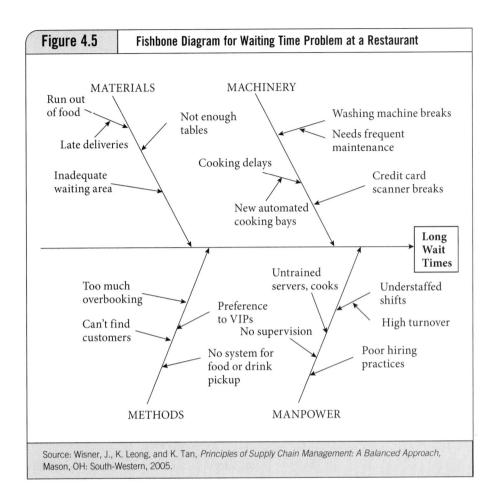

Figure 4.5 | **Fishbone Diagram for Waiting Time Problem at a Restaurant**

Source: Wisner, J., K. Leong, and K. Tan, *Principles of Supply Chain Management: A Balanced Approach*, Mason, OH: South-Western, 2005.

In this case, it is suggested that the restaurant runs out of food because food suppliers frequently arrive late.

The final step is to then investigate the legitimacy of each of the causes. For the restaurant example, this would require monitoring the frequency of late food deliveries, and whether the late deliveries actually caused additional waiting time for customers. For a period of time, the restaurant should monitor delivery performance and determine the relationship to customer wait times. If late deliveries are found to be a significant cause of the customer wait time problem, the restaurant staff should implement a solution to the problem (perhaps by either changing food suppliers or improving the performance of the existing suppliers through better supplier management). Each of the causes are thus investigated until the majority of the overall wait time problem is identified and solved (there may be several contributing causes for this problem).

Integrating the Customer Service Process along the Supply Chain

In the previous section, we discussed the customer service process, from evaluating and improving employee satisfaction, conducting customer service audits, creating the customer service strategy, implementing the strategy, and concluding with measuring and improving the performance of the customer service strategy. In a supply chain setting, where trading partners are trying to collaborate and jointly manage supply chain processes, the final step in the customer service process is to share information and make joint decisions regarding customer service activities with key supply chain customers, in order to maximize customer service value and ultimately provide end customers with their required products and services in such a way that it creates a sustainable competitive advantage. Key supply chain customers will want their products and services delivered in ways that will allow them to provide maximum service value to their customers.

A number of collaboration efforts involve the use of software applications and the Internet to better manage the flow of information and make decisions regarding how best to serve customers. Tourism Vancouver in Canada, for example, represents approximately 1,000 businesses in the Vancouver area, and is busy collecting and dissecting information to design marketing packages to promote the city prior to the 2010 Olympics. It recently traded in its old DOS-based systems and installed Microsoft's Navision software and SharePoint® Services to allow representatives who are traveling abroad to access the data they need over the Internet, and to allow member organizations to upload information and interface with other systems that house things like web content imagery. In this way, Tourism Vancouver hopes to make their marketing package design process much more efficient, collaborative, and valuable to its members.[39]

Key supply chain customers will most likely have varying service requirements and the firm itself will have higher customer service performance standards for its key customers as well. External customer service audits with key supply chain trading partners will give firms a chance to compare notes on expectations, capabilities, and existing problems, and then jointly design service improvements where any performance gaps are found. Existing customer relationship management (CRM) programs with these customers should also assist the firm in monitoring its customer service capabilities and performance over time. Both parties can discuss any expected changes that are likely to occur in the upcoming planning period, and how this will impact relationship requirements. Customer service strategies with key supply chain customers will most likely include more activities and higher performance standards, and will require more communication and information sharing when compared with other, more traditional supplier–customer relationships. When combined with an effective CRM program, the customer service management process will enable the firm to offer the types of customized services that result in long-term supply chain success.

With respect to measuring and improving customer service activities, the firm and its trading partners can discuss and agree on performance standards, how performance is to be measured and how often, and how the findings will be communicated. Over time, as supply chain partnerships mature and as end-customer requirements for product speed, flexibility, quality, and cost change, then supply chain capabilities along these lines will also have to change in order to remain competitive. This will undoubtedly mean that customer service capabilities along the supply chain will have to improve, even as costs have to be decreased.

SUMMARY

This chapter presents a comprehensive discussion of the customer service process, beginning with defining the term *customer service* and describing a number of customer service elements that take place prior to, during, and after the sale. When customer service does not meet customer expectations, a service failure occurs, and a firm's recovery from poor service is an important determinant of customer satisfaction. Customer service elements should be based in part on customer needs, wants, and expectations. Customer perceptions are impacted by the firm and its products, along with other environmental factors, and these have a relationship with customer service. These relationships are all explored in the chapter.

Customer service management entails the design, control, and improvement of the customer service process. A framework for customer service management is presented, and the framework is based in part on the service-profit chain. The framework includes a section on employee satisfaction and its impact on customer satisfaction, conducting customer service audits, delivering high-quality customer service, creating value with customer service, use of customer participation, customer contact centers, and outsourcing customer service. The framework concludes with discussions of implementing customer service strategies, and measuring and improving service performance. The final section of the chapter presents a discussion of integrating the customer service process along the supply chain.

KEY TERMS

American Customer Satisfaction Index, 96

automated agent, 120

customer behavior, 102

customer contact centers, 120

customer needs, 103

customer participation approach, 121

customer satisfaction, 105

customer service departments, 119

customer service failure, 100

customer service teams, 119

customer wants, 103

external customer service audits, 112

fishbone diagram, 128

FOB origination, 121

happy productive worker hypothesis, 109

high-quality customer service, 117

internal customer service audit, 113

mystery shoppers, 126

order cycle, 98

outsourcing customer service, 123

perceptual distortion, 105

perfect orders, 99

pilot customer service initiative, 125

posttransaction customer service elements, 99

pretransaction customer service elements, 98

selective attention, 105

selective exposure, 105

selective interpretation, 105

self-service, 121

service-profit chain, 106

service recovery, 102

total quality management, 128

transaction customer service elements, 98

virtual call center, 123

DISCUSSION QUESTIONS

1. Define customer service. Provide a definition that is geared towards the Dean's office at your university.

2. Describe the pretransaction, transaction, and posttransaction customer service elements that might exist at the Dean's office at your university.

3. Define customer service failure, and provide an example for a grocery store.

4. What are customer needs and wants, and why are they important to the topic of customer service?

5. What are the four types of customers as described in this chapter? Which one best describes you? Which clothing retailer would you most likely visit?

6. Define customer satisfaction. Describe a recent satisfying and unsatisfying product or service experience.

7. What does the service-profit chain propose? Provide an example from your own experiences.

8. What does the happy productive worker hypothesis refer to?

9. Fill out the employee satisfaction survey shown in Figure 4.2 for your current job (or a previous one) and score your answers (1 point for Strongly Disagree and 5 points for Strongly Agree). Additionally, fill out the customer satisfaction survey shown in Figure 4.3 for a company you frequent. Discuss the results of the surveys.

10. What are external and internal customer service audits used for?

11. Should firms always strive to provide the highest levels of customer service possible? Explain.

12. What does high-quality customer service refer to?

13. Describe the responsibilities of a customer contact center.

14. What are the advantages of self-service?

15. Why would companies want to outsource the customer service function?

16. What are virtual call centers, and what are their advantages?

17. Why might the use of a pilot customer service initiative be a good idea?

18. Describe some customer service performance measures that might be useful for the professor teaching this class.

19. What are mystery shoppers, and why might they be used?

20. How are fishbone diagrams used for improving customer service?

21. How does the customer service process change when the firm is dealing with its supply chain customers?

INTERNET QUESTIONS

1. Go to the American Customer Satisfaction Index (ACSI) website (http://www.theacsi.org) and discuss how the index has changed over the years since 1995. Which industry has the highest level of customer satisfaction?

2. Go to the Albertson's grocery store website (http://www.albertsons.com) and see if you can find out if customers are using the scanners discussed in this chapter to enrich their shopping experiences.

3. Think of a well-known company that prides itself on delivering high levels of customer service. Go to its website and see if you can find its mission statement. Does it contain any language about customer service?

4. Go to the website of the Mystery Shopper Association (http://www.mysteryshop. org) and report on its membership, reach, job opportunities, and any new developments in the use of third-party mystery shop firms.

INFOTRAC QUESTION

Access http://www.infotrac-thomsonlearning.com to answer the following question:

1. Use InfoTrac to research and write a paper on one of the following topics:

- The relationship between employee satisfaction and customer satisfaction (the happy productive worker hypothesis).
- Customer service failure and recovery methods.
- Innovations in self-service or customer participation—include a discussion of Internet self-service.
- Mystery Shopping—discuss the history of its use, third-party providers, and any new innovations.

REFERENCES

Berry, L. (1995), *On Great Service,* The Free Press, New York, NY.

Bowersox, D., D. Closs, and M. Cooper (2002), *Supply Chain Logistics Management,* McGraw-Hill/Irwin, New York, NY.

Fitzsimmons, J., and M. Fitzsimmons (1994), *Service Management: Operations, Strategy, and Information Technology,* Irwin McGraw-Hill, New York, NY.

Kotler, P. (2000), *Marketing Management,* Prentice-Hall, Upper Saddle River, NJ.

Metters, R., K. King-Metters, and M. Pullman (2003), *Successful Service Operations Management,* South-Western, Mason, OH.

Lambert, D., J. Stock, and L. Ellram (1998), *Fundamentals of Logistics Management,* McGraw-Hill, New York, NY.

Stock, J., and D. Lambert (2001), *Strategic Logistics Management,* McGraw-Hill, New York, NY.

Czinkota, M., et al. (2000), *Marketing Best Practices,* Dryden Press, Orlando, FL.

ENDNOTES

1. Interested readers can go to http://www.theacsi.org for more information about the ACSI.

2. FiveTwelve Group website definition, http://www.fivetwelvegroup.com.

3. http://www.ecommerce.etsu.edu/Glossary.htm.

4. Johnson, J., D. Wood, D. Wardlow, and P. Murphy, Jr., *Contemporary Logistics,* Upper Saddle River, NJ: Prentice-Hall, Inc., 1999.

5. Goodman, J. and S. Newman, "Understand Customer Behavior and Complaints," *Quality Progress,* V. 36, No. 1, 2003, pp. 51–56.

6. Prewitt, M., "Speed, Sincerity the Keys to Resolving Complaints," *Nation's Restaurant News,* V. 39, No. 38, 2005, pp. 142–143.

7. Wachovia Corporation press release, "Wachovia Outpaces Peers in Customer Satisfaction for the Fourth Consecutive Year," *PR Newswire-FirstCall,* February 15, 2005.

8. Stone, G., "City Shoppers and Urban Identification: Observations on the Social Psychology of City Life," *American Journal of Sociology,* July 1954, pp. 36–43.

9. Kotler, P., *Marketing Management,* Upper Saddle River, NJ: Prentice-Hall, 2000.

10. Amir, N., "A Giant Step Forward," *Chain Store Age,* V. 82, No. 5, 2006, pp. 120–121.

11. Ihlwan, M., L. Armstrong, and M. Eidam, "Hyundai: Kissing Clunkers Goodbye," *BusinessWeek,* May 17, 2004, p. 45.

12. Heskett, J., T. Jones, G. Loveman, W. Sasser, and L. Schlesinger, "Putting the Service-Profit Chain to Work," *Harvard Business Review,* V. 72, No. 2, 1994, pp.164–175.

13. Kittredge, J., "Process Management and Cost Management: Collaboration or Opposition?" *Cost Management,* V. 18, No. 5, pp. 23–31.

14. Fisher, C., "Why Do Lay People Believe That Satisfaction and Performance Are Correlated? Possible Sources of a Commonsense Theory," *Journal of Organizational Behavior,* V. 24, No. 6, 2003, p. 753.

15. Rauch, M., "Motivating the Masses," *Incentive,* V. 179, No. 2, 2005, pp. 26–29.

16. Anonymous, "Are You Neglecting Your 'Non-Star' Employees?" *HR Focus,* V. 82, No. 2, 2005, pp. 11–13.

17. Barsky, J., C. Frame, and J. McDougal, "Variety of Strategies Help Improve Hotel Employee Satisfaction," *Hotel and Motel Management,* V. 219, No. 21, 2004, pp. 8–9.

18. Bailor, C., "Effectively Serving Multiple Customer Types," *Customer Relationship Management,* V. 8, No. 11, 2004, p. 51.

19. "Special Report: Big Mac's Makeover—McDonald's Turned Around," *The Economist,* V. 373, No. 8397, 2004, p. 88.

20. Cox, D. and J. Bossert, "Driving Organic Growth at Bank of America," *Quality Progress,* V. 38, No. 2, 2005, pp. 23–27.

21. Walker, T., "Quick-Care Centers Rapidly Becoming an Option for Health Plan Executives," *Managed Healthcare Executive,* V. 14, No. 10, 2004, pp. 11–12.

22. Prince, M., "Technology (A Special Report): Help (May Be) on the Way," *Wall Street Journal,* March 21, 2005, p. R–13.

23. Smilko, J. and K. Van Neck, "Rewarding Excellence Through Variable Pay," *Benefits Quarterly,* V. 20, No. 3, 2004, pp. 21–25.

24. Berry, L., *On Great Service,* The Free Press, New York, NY: The Free Press, 1995.

25. "NorVergence Increases Hiring in Customer Service Department; Technology Company Quadruples Number of Staffers to Better Serve Customers," *PRNewswire,* April 15, 2004.

26. Farber, B. and J. Wycoff, "Customer Service: Evolution and Revolution," *Sales and Marketing Management,* V. 143, No. 5, 1991, pp. 44–49.

27. Moreno, F., "Don't Ignore Your Other Workforce: The Automated Agent," *Customer Inter@ction Solutions,* V. 22, No. 12, 2004, pp. 60–64.

28. Alban, O., "Optimizing Customer Experiences: Bridging Front-Office Contact Centers and Back-Office Departments," *Customer Inter@ction Solutions,* V. 22, No. 12, 2004, pp. 50–53.

29. "NMA OUTSOURCING: Customer Call Centres," *New Media Age,* October 28, 2004, p. 10.

30. Senia, A., "Sprint Expands Outsourcing Relationship with IBM," *America's Network,* V. 108, No. 12, 2004, p. 13.

31. Smith, D. and L. Tanner, "Will Utilities Plug In?" *Electric Perspectives,* V. 29, No. 2, 2004, pp. 22–29.

32. "Nationwide Chief Explains Offshore Rejection," *Supply Management,* V. 9, No. 20, 2004, p. 38.

33. Thibodeau, P., "Offshoring Fuels IT Hiring Boom in India," *Computerworld,* V. 38, No. 42, 2004, p. 8.

34. Bednarz, A., "Users Grow Virtual Call Centers," *Network World,* V. 22, No. 4, 2005, pp. 25–26.

35. Garber, A., "No Mystery: Shopping the 'Shops' Gains in Popularity," *Nation's Restaurant News,* V. 38, No. 50, 2004, pp. 39–41.

36. See note 35 above.

37. Murphy, M., "Customer Service: Mi Casa, Su Oficina," *Air Conditioning, Heating & Refrigeration News,* V. 223, No. 16, 2004, p. 23.

38. Welch, S., "Conference Confidential," *Successful Meetings,* V. 54, No. 3, 2005, pp. 36–38.

39. Khanna, P., "Tourism Agency Missing Collaboration Boat," *Computing Canada,* V. 31, No. 1, 2005, p. 22.

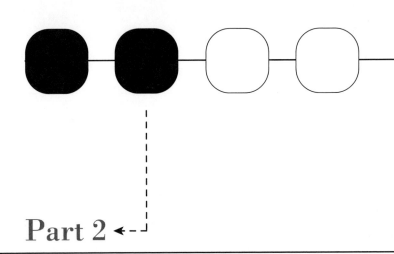

Part 2

Manufacturing and Service Flow Issues

Chapter 5:

DEMAND MANAGEMENT AND FORECASTING

While in the last decade or so we have experienced many improvements in our demand planning, we expect to tap into many other opportunities in the future, particularly in the area of integrating closely our planning process with our customers. [1]

As business-forecasting processes continue to be refined, more emphasis than ever is placed on collaborative forecasting. Processes such as collaborative planning, forecasting and replenishment; vendor-managed inventory; and co-managed inventory are now becoming a mandate of many major retailers. [2]

Learning Objectives

After completing this chapter, you should be able to:

- Explain the role of demand management and forecasting in an organization.
- Describe the demand management process.
- Identify the components of a forecast.
- Understand qualitative and quantitative forecasting methods.
- Determine the accuracy of a forecast.
- Describe the collaborative planning, forecasting and replenishment process.

Chapter Outline

Introduction

Demand Management Defined

Types of Demand

The Forecasting Process

Forecasting Methods

Forecast Accuracy

Collaborative Planning, Forecasting and Replenishment

Process Management in Action
Right Place, Right on Time

Making sure products are at the right place at the right time is especially important when you're dealing with seasonal items and perishable food. That's why Gertrude Hawk Chocolates and Sunsweet Growers Inc. are spending their IT dollars on new supply chain software that will help them forecast demand, schedule production, and better manage inventory.

At candy maker and retailer Gertrude Hawk Chocolates, timing is everything. Too little chocolate on the shelves in the weeks leading up to Easter means missed sales, but too much is just as disastrous. For years, store managers were able to draw on their experience to analyze and predict seasonal sales with some certainty, taking into account the time of year, weather, and previous year's sales quantities. But the nearly 70-year-old company's growth from 36 to 70 retail stores throughout the United States in the last five years and an expanded list of about 400 products in peak seasons was too much to handle.

To resolve the problem, the chocolatier decided one buyer at headquarters should oversee the procurement of products. But the job soon proved too complex for just a spreadsheet. "It became a headache trying to forecast between 80 and 90 items weekly in stores," says Bruce Cottle, CIO at Gertrude Hawk Chocolates. The inefficient system meant the company had less time to plan for its year-round products, which sometimes went out of stock.

All that has changed since the company automated forecasting and demand planning in November at its 60 permanent and 10 seasonal stores with John Galt Solutions Inc.'s ForecastX Demand Engine. The chocolatier can check daily sales data sent from point-of-sale systems in each store. The ForecastX Demand Engine also is linked to an SQL database that serves as a repository for historical sales information, which helps the company determine future demand. The system ties into the company's SSA Global Technologies Inc.'s enterprise resource planning (ERP) software, so sales data can be used in financial and other back-office applications.

Now the chocolatier can more closely pinpoint how much chocolate and other products need to be shipped to store shelves. Armed with more exact forecasts, the company also is better able to determine, for example, how much raw materials it needs to buy.

Sunsweet's supply chain processes also had relied for too long on manual processes and cumbersome spreadsheets. The $250 million-a-year grower-owned co-op, which produces a third of the world's prunes as well as other dried fruits, has complex scheduling and planning needs. In its 825,000-square-foot plant in Yuba City, California, fruit packs range in size from an ounce to 50 pounds and are labeled in 20 languages.

To optimize demand, inventory, and production planning, Sunsweet is implementing Zemeter® from Supply Chain Consultants. Already the company has more information at its fingertips so its five planners can more quickly build demand forecast reports, says Tom Garland, director of supply chain at Sunsweet. The software can calculate inventory levels and run them against predefined business rules; if levels hit preset thresholds, the system can automatically issue alerts to appropriate personnel. "Before, you'd have to go through reams of paper to identify those issues," he says.

Sunsweet chose Supply Chain Consultants over its ERP vendor, SAP. All things being equal, SAP would have been its choice, says Harold Upton, vice president of strategic business processes at Sunsweet. But the IT team that evaluated contenders concluded Supply Chain Consultants' software was easier to use and would be faster to implement.

Continued

The company is about halfway through the implementation. Sunsweet already has cut the number of production lines to 10 to 15 stock-keeping units or less, so there are fewer machines, packaging, and other changeovers on lines and more efficient use of labor and equipment. It also has cut production overruns from 30 percent to about 12 percent.

Source: Beth Bacheldor, "Right Place, Right Time," *Information Week,* August 16–23, 2004, p. 55. Copyright © 2004 by **CMP Media LLC**, 600 Community Drive, Manhasset, NY 11030, USA. Reprinted from *Information Week* with permission.

Introduction

Every company wants the most accurate forecast, or prediction of future sales. Sales forecasts are used to plan for purchases of inventory, hiring of personnel, and budgeting cash flows. As a result, sales forecasts have an effect not only on the inventory levels of both finished goods and raw materials, but also on manufacturing and delivery lead times, and ultimately customer satisfaction. As shown in the opening Process Management in Action feature, when the product line increases, forecasting can become a real headache. When managers underforecast, products may not be available to sell. However, high forecasts result in excess amounts of product held in inventories, with the associated costs of carrying inventory and price markdowns and inevitably lower profits.

Inaccurate forecasts often occur because of distortion of information in the supply chain. For example, customers may overorder when trying to meet expected demand. Nokia retailers in Europe in 2002, for example, were running out of cell phones based on unexpected consumer demand. As a result, they ordered too many phones. Nokia, basing its forecast on retail orders rather than actual sales data, misread the market and overproduced.[3]

Companies may also buy more than immediately necessary because of unexpected promotions or incentives offered by a vendor, a practice known as **forward buying**. These miscues typically occur because companies not in direct contact with the consumer do not receive real-time sales data. As a result, a phenomenon known as the bullwhip effect, introduced in Chapter 1, occurs. Some companies like Wal-Mart have reduced the bullwhip effect by providing point-of-sale data directly to their supply chain partners (a more detailed description on the bullwhip effect can be found in Chapter 10). In addition, Wal-Mart has eliminated forward buying practices and negotiated fixed-price contracts with suppliers.

However, companies must first have an established forecasting process before they can move to collaborative forecasting among supply chain members. They also must have clear objectives for each forecast. In other words, how will that forecast be used? All parties involved need to understand the connection between the forecast and any resulting decisions that are made. For example, if Target plans to sell bedspreads at a discount in September, that information must be shared with the manufacturers, logistics providers, and anyone else involved. All partners should develop a forecast for bedspreads together and then jointly develop a plan of action based on the forecast.

Gertrude Hawk Chocolates, profiled in the opening feature, provides one key example of why forecasting and demand management are key processes to the successful operation of a company. This chapter will first focus on the role of the demand planning and forecasting process in an organization. Several forecasting methods will be introduced, along with some ways to measure forecast accuracy. Collaborative planning, forecasting and replenishment, an important recent initiative designed to reduce the bullwhip effect, will be discussed later in this chapter.

Demand Management Defined

Demand management has been defined, in a broad sense, as "the process that balances customer requirements with supply chain capabilities,"[4] and "those activities that range from determining or estimating the demand from customers, through converting specific customer orders into promised delivery dates, to helping balance demand with supply."[5] One way companies have tried to balance demand and supply has been to carry more than enough inventory to meet the customer's needs. However, the high costs of carrying that inventory have forced companies to move toward leaner operations. Subcontracting and the use of overtime or temporary labor are other means to increase capacity to meet demand in the short term. For instance, department stores usually hire temporary workers for the busy Christmas season. Firms also try to manage customers' demand patterns. Price discounts may be offered during slow periods to increase demand. Restaurants, for example, offer "early bird specials" to entice people to dine during off-peak hours. There is, of course, the chance that demand may exceed supply. Many services, such as airlines, doctors, and dentists, use a reservation system to control the flow of customers into their establishments.

However, firms must still develop an effective forecasting process to plan for expected customer demand. As shown in Figure 5.1, the first element of the demand management process is **forecasting**: Firms estimate resource requirements by identifying and quantifying all sources of demand. There are a number of methods companies use to forecast demand, and some of these methods will be discussed in more detail later in this chapter.

Ideally, firms use the forecast to plan operations and coordinate the purchase of incoming materials, products, and supplies. Forecasts should also be given to marketing so it can develop a sales plan for the next 6–18 months. In the best organizations, sales and operations coordinate their plans, known as **sales and operations planning**. Once the planning stages are complete, common everyday activities take place, including order entry, communicating delivery dates to customers, confirming the status of current orders, and relaying information on any changes to orders. Resource estimates are then made based on demand forecasts.

Several advantages are to be found using the demand management process. First, it can be used to coordinate the flow of demand through the supply chain. More on coordination in the supply chain can be found later in a discussion of collaborative planning, forecasting and replenishment. The demand management process can also be used to assess the contribution to profit for an organization's products and customers based on existing capacity constraints. Lastly, firms can use the process to manage the relationships with other members in the supply chain and find ways to motivate suppliers to efficiently manage their demand flows.[6] The result of the demand management process is a projection of requirements over the **planning horizon**.

Within an organization, the demand management process has an impact on several key departments. Several functions should be involved in the process, including:

- *Field Sales.* Responsible for pricing, promotion, distribution, and display of finished goods to retailers, field sales personnel manage the relationship with

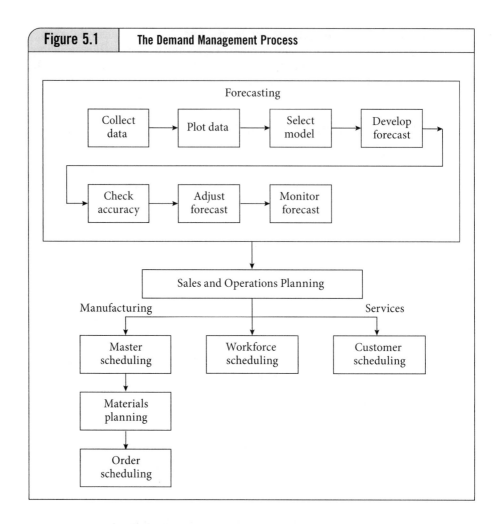

| Figure 5.1 | The Demand Management Process |

the company's trading partners. The sales staff also provides sales projections for the next year to management for planning purposes. These sales projections provide input to the forecasting process and, as a result, need to be accurate.

- *Marketing.* Marketing builds brand awareness and has ultimate responsibility for the success or failure of a product based on new product introductions, packaging, special promotions, and price analysis. Marketing may also collect individual customer data through the use of **customer relationship management** (CRM) software. CRM data provides clues as to new product and service requirements, and expected demand, based on customer requests. (More on customer relationship management was found in Chapter 3.) Marketing provides feedback on the effect of market share trends on demand. This department also should have information on the competition, in terms of similar product launches and promotions.

- *Finance.* The finance department, which controls and reports revenues and costs, is in a position to identify the risks and opportunities within the organization's profit and loss (P&L) statements. It also uses forecast information to plan the budget for the upcoming year, including machine, labor, and overhead requirements.

- *Supply Management.* Supply management oversees the procurement of materials, parts, components, and finished goods for the organization. As a result, personnel are responsible for managing the relationship with an organization's network of suppliers to ensure a specified level of quality and delivery at the lowest price. They are also responsible for determining any supply risks or opportunities, and that information should be an input to the demand management process. Supply management is also in a position to share demand data with its suppliers over the planning horizon. Thus, it needs to be kept in the loop in the demand planning process.

- *Manufacturing and Service Operations.* People in operations manage the production or service delivery process. Thus, feedback to the demand management process includes information on machine and labor capacity constraints. Operations then uses forecasts to make plans for its labor force such as adding shifts, planning overtime, and budgeting for additional equipment. Manufacturing also uses these plans to estimate future capital expenditures such as adding locations or expanding the capacity of existing locations.

- *Distribution.* The responsibility of distribution is to fill customer orders and monitor and manage inventory, seasonal trends, and special promotions to ensure on-time delivery of finished goods. Ideally, it should receive a projection of an organization's shipping needs based on forecasts to estimate capacity needs and utilize its labor force most efficiently. Distribution can also use the information from demand planning to level out its load in picking and shipping orders from the warehouse. For example, if a business operates in a seasonal environment, advance planning allows distribution to arrange orders in advance rather than waiting for the customer's orders.

- *Transportation.* This department moves the goods from the organization's distribution centers to the customer's distribution centers or retail outlets. Transportation personnel use forecasts from demand planning to manage the relationships with its transportation carriers more efficiently. They also use the information to manage the company's own fleet, the yard, and trailers more effectively.

Notice these parties could all be integrated into the demand management and forecasting process, depending on the nature of the organization. Some companies develop cross-functional demand management teams that include departments affected by the forecasting process to improve operational performance. In this manner, all organizational issues are considered in the forecasting and planning stages.

The next sections will further explain the demand management process beginning with a general discussion of forecasting. The various types of demand will be explained, followed by a look at various methods companies use to predict demand, and then followed by a discussion of forecast accuracy.

Types of Demand

Demand can be divided into three categories:

Independent demand. The demand for any finished product by a customer in the supply chain is defined as **independent demand**. Any product consumers buy, including refrigerators, CDs, or furniture, can be classified as independent demand. Typically retailers are responsible for estimating this type of demand and then sharing it with other supply

Service Perspective	*What Makes Wal-Mart Tick*

When the Wal-Mart IT leader analyzed the transaction data of stores along the coast of North Carolina in the days leading up to Hurricane Isabel last fall, she expected to see a spike in sales of emergency supplies. And she found what she was looking for: Sales of bottled water tripled from their normal levels, sales of tarpaulins and manual can openers increased seven times, and spotlight purchases leapt by a multiple of 16.

But there were surprises, too. Spam® flew off the shelves at seven times its normal volume. Sales of Vienna sausages quintupled. Perhaps most tellingly, there was a tripling in sales of Kellogg's Pop-Tarts. "We didn't expect to see that happen, but those of us with small children understood it immediately!" Dillman laughed.

Dillman shared the anecdote during a presentation she gave at A.G. Edwards & Sons' 2004 Retailing Science/Technology Conference, held in Miami in late January. The story was to illustrate Wal-Mart's recent efforts in improving its predictive technology. Although Wal-Mart certainly is no stranger to demand forecasting, it has recently redoubled its efforts to use POS data. The discoveries made during the Hurricane Isabel analysis, Dillman said, will help Wal-Mart better stock its shelves for similar extreme-weather events in the future.

Wal-Mart's technological approach is firmly planted in self-reliance. Outsourcing and offshore development have almost no place in Wal-Mart's IT strategy, Dillman explained. As such, the retailer demands versatility from its IT associates so they can handle whatever challenges arise. Each Wal-Mart IT associate must be proficient in two or three programming languages, and be knowledgeable in more than one business area.

One of the reasons Wal-Mart's IT personnel are able to do such heavy lifting is because all of the retailer's business units share the same source code. The result is a powerful, elegant economy of uniformity. When a change is made to the code of one business unit, it can be rapidly duplicated to all the other business units. "If we decide tomorrow we need to develop a new report, we can do the change across the entire enterprise in a week or less," Dillman said. "Our systems' uniformity gives us great speed."

The speed Dillman describes can be seen in Wal-Mart's POS. The merchant maintains more than 136,000 POS units across ten countries, yet Wal-Mart is able to update its POS software platform twice a month.

What's next: Naturally, much of Wal-Mart's IT development efforts focus upon the retailer's widely publicized initiative to RFID-enable its supply chain. Wal-Mart wanted its top 100 suppliers to begin RFID-tagging Wal-Mart shipments at the pallet and case level by the beginning of 2005.

When asked how many RFID tags would be needed to meet Wal-Mart's demand for case- and pallet-level tagging, Dillman noted that the suppliers affected by Wal-Mart's ultimatum ship a combined one billion cases to the retailer every year. Wal-Mart began its own RFID rollout with three Dallas-area distribution centers, which support 185 Wal-Mart and Sam's Club locations, and will continue the enterprise-wide deployment from there.

Wal-Mart also is beginning to look at item-level tagging. Dillman said that the first items to be tagged with RFID will be items with high price points and/or high shrinkage. She identified electronics, video, pharmacy, and jewelry as good areas to begin item-level tagging.

Source: Scheraga, Dan, "What Makes Wal-Mart Tick," *Chain Store Age,* March 2004, pp. 49–50. Reprinted by permission from *Chain Store Age* (March 2004).

chain members. Data used to forecast demand is generally collected from the retailers' **point-of-sale (POS) data**, sales/marketing intelligence, and operations department records of pending customer orders. Wal-Mart has been using POS data for years but is always looking for ways to improve the power of prediction through improved technology. The company's newest efforts include the use of radio frequency identification tags (RFID), which can hold a great deal more information than bar codes. RFID tags also capture more recent and accurate information. More on Wal-Mart's efforts can be found in the Service Perspective feature. Sales and marketing is responsible for estimating sales based on several sources, including (1) existing contracts, (2) direct feedback from customers, (3) focus groups, and (4) customer surveys. Operations also provides information on demand for finished goods or services, service parts, supplies, intra-organizational de-mand (demand from internal departments), and promotional inventory requirements.

Derived demand. **Derived demand** comes from intermediaries in the supply chain, such as wholesalers and distributors. They forecast the number of lots needed to meet the needs of other intermediaries in the supply chain. A **lot** might be the number of boxes or containers, which contain a certain number of items. Intermediaries may use some or all of the following types of demand data to develop their sales and production plans:

- Customer forecasts based on simple moving averages of recent sales,
- Actual consumer purchases based on weekly or daily raw POS data,
- Withdrawals from customer warehouses, and
- Customer orders. [7]

Dependent demand. **Dependent demand** items are the raw materials, parts, and compo-nents used to manufacture a product. The forecast for dependent demand is typically deter-mined from customer orders for finished goods and input from sales. Manufacturers often use **material requirements planning (MRP) software** to determine future needs of dependent demand items over the planning horizon. The topic of MRP is covered in Chapter 9.

The forecasting process described in this chapter is typically used for independent demand and derived demand and is discussed further in the following sections. Depen-dent demand is typically estimated based on the forecasts and outstanding contracts for independent and derived demand, and is typically covered in introductory opera-tions management courses.

The Forecasting Process

As shown in Figure 5.1, forecasting begins with the collection of historical data, if available, and plotting that data in graphical form to determine any significant pat-terns. Forecasting requires continuous monitoring and revision to be effective.

Forecasters start with a **base demand**, which is generally the average sales demand before considering other factors. Those other factors may include seasonal effects, up-ward or downward trends, cyclical patterns, promotions, or random effects.

Seasonal effects are recurring upward or downward changes in demand within a year. For example, the demand for snow skis generally peaks in November after the first snow-fall and then declines in March. **Cyclical patterns** are like seasonal variations, but they last longer and occur every several years, not months, and reflect economic conditions.

Trends are long-range changes in sales over an extended time period. An upward trend indicates increasing sales. Manufacturers of cell phones, for example, continue to experience an upward trend in sales and that trend is expected to continue at least through 2010.[8] Trends are generally tied to changes in demographics or consumer preferences. For example, demand for bottled water in restaurants was practically unheard of in the 1970s. Since then, the demand for bottled water has continued to grow as consumer concerns over the safety of tap water, the perceived health benefits of bottled water, and the "snob appeal" factor have increased.[9]

Marketing often initiates **promotions** through special advertising and pricing schemes and are especially important to consumer products industries, which may sell 50 percent or more of all goods based on promotions. Sales generally increase immediately after a promotion, followed by a decline in sales after the promotion ends. Promotions often occur on a regular basis at the same time each year. If the promotions are predictable, they are considered seasonal. For example, the department store industry typically offers "white sales" of linens and towels in January. Unusual or unexpected promotions are tracked separately. To improve forecast accuracy, it is important for marketing to share upcoming promotions with their supply chain partners.

Lastly, **random effects** are impossible to predict and occur at irregular times. For example, natural disasters such as hurricanes in Florida are often the reason for unusual demand patterns.

Forecasters then select the method most appropriate for the identified pattern and calculate the forecast based on historical data. Optimally, forecasters will develop more than one forecast and select the method that provides the most accuracy. Software such as SAS® Forecasting Solutions and DecisionPro has greatly improved the forecaster's ability to use the "best" forecast. More on forecasting methods can be found later in this chapter.

Companies may estimate their forecasts by either a top-down or decomposition approach, or a bottom-up or aggregation approach. In the **top-down approach**, management develops a forecast for each **stock-keeping unit** (SKU) and then divides that total demand across its locations. For example, if a company expects to sell 20,000 units and it has five distribution centers, it would allocate a percentage of demand to each center based on historical figures. This approach is highly centralized and works when demand is stable, when the company uses national promotions, or when changes in demand are fairly uniform throughout the market. New Jersey-based Nabisco Biscuit Company, for example, uses a top-down approach. The snack products manufacturer begins with a national production forecast for each product, based on a national product promotion schedule and information collected from finance and marketing, for the next four-week sales period. Weekly forecasts are then created and given to each distribution center.[10]

With a **bottom-up approach**, managers develop forecasts for each regional location and then aggregate them, or roll them up into one national-level forecast. This approach works best when demand patterns vary from region to region. However, as might be obvious, the bottom-up approach will require a higher level of record keeping and the impact of national promotions may be harder to determine. Companies may also combine these two methods or change from one method to another. Swiss-owned Syngenta Crop Protection, producer of fungicides, herbicides, and insecticides, switched from a top-down to a bottom-up approach in 2002 to improve its forecasting process. More on Syngenta can be found in the Global Perspective feature.

The forecast is then used over the planning horizon and adjusted as new information is gathered from the sales force, forecast analysts, or customers. For example, computer manufacturers reexamined their expected market share when, in late 2004, IBM announced it was selling a majority stake in its desktop and laptop computer

Global Perspective   *Forecasting Processes from the Ground Up*

Syngenta Crop Protection is a $6.2 billion business globally. With 19,000 employees in 90 countries, including 4,300 in the North American Free Trade Agreement (NAFTA) region, the company is headquartered in Basel, Switzerland. Syngenta sells its fungicides, herbicides, and insecticides to distributors and dealers, who then sell to growers.

In the past, Syngenta employed a top-down business planning process for generating sales goals and production targets whereby the company's finance group would generate quarterly sales estimates and set targets for the sales staff. On the manufacturing side, the company's production planners would determine how much of each SKU to produce. The catch, of course, was that without accurate demand forecasts, the company found itself loading up on inventory to ensure that it could meet fluctuations in customer demand and minimize orders lost due to out-of-stock product.

SPREADSHEETS OFFER CLOUDED VISIBILITY

The company made an initial move to get at forecast numbers using Excel spreadsheets. Once a month, Syngenta's central office would create a spreadsheet for each business unit, with volume and price forecasts, and email the document to a contact within the unit who had been tapped to do the forecasting. The business units would revise the figures and email them back to the central office, where another staffer combined all the numbers for manual uploading into the company's enterprise resource planning (ERP) system.

This approach had several shortcomings: First, the company was updating its forecasts only once a month, but changes in the market might require daily revisions to production plans. In addition, the spreadsheet forecasts reflected sales estimates made by business unit heads and excluded insights that could be provided by field reps and their local district managers. And finally, this manual process did not allow the company to identify and manage gaps between the forecast and sales plan, and forecasters did not have ready access to such information as sales to date, current inventories, or marketing plans.

Around the beginning of 2002, Syngenta began looking for a more effective tool for forecasting that would overcome these shortcomings. The company's requirements included, among others, that the tool support Syngenta's sales and operations planning (S&OP) process cycle at the business unit, country, and NAFTA levels; allow gap, exception, and assumption management; allow for multiple languages and currencies; and meet the needs of the various functions that would be using the forecast. They eventually settled on ForecastX by John Galt Solutions.

A NEW PROCESS

Syngenta's formal S&OP process, as it stands now, works like this: At the beginning of the month, the company's crop managers (CMs) enter their sales forecasts for each SKU. Those forecasts get rolled up to the business unit level, and by the end of the first week of the month the business units develop, and commit to, their own forecasts, which may or may not conform to the CMs' forecasts (both are shown in the Collaborator report). Once all those data are entered, in the second week of the month the brand managers review the sales and demand forecasts, and then input their product supply requirements, which are fed into the ERP system and used by the company's supply chain function to plan production.

In the third week of the month, the company's S&OP meeting brings top executives together to review the current supply and demand plan against the annual budget. Based on any trends occurring with supply and demand, or in the marketplace, the S&OP meeting could produce changes in the sales plan, which can then be entered into Collaborator.

Continued

Finally, toward the end of the month, district managers enter their seasonalized invoiced sales forecasts into the system, in part based on feedback from sales reps out in the field. The district managers' input feeds up the chain to the CMs, and the process begins again.

Despite the challenges, Richard Herrin, manager for NAFTA planning and forecasting, says that the forecasting initiative appears to be paying off already in that, combined with other project initiatives, the company has been able to achieve inventory reduction targets and has focused attention on tracking and reducing top-line and product mix forecast error.

Source: Reese, Andrew K., "Forecasting Processes from the Ground Up," *Supply & Demand Chain Executive,* August/September 2004, retrieved online at http://www.sdcexec.com/. Reprinted with permission.

operations to Lenovo Group Ltd., China's largest maker of computers.[11] The forecast is compared to actual sales to measure the accuracy of the forecast. If the performance of the forecast is not acceptable, the forecast is adjusted or parameters are changed.

Forecasting Methods

Companies may use qualitative models or quantitative models, but generally some combination of both results in the most accurate forecasts. When organizations use qualitative forecasting methods, there are no formal mathematical models used to forecast demand.

Qualitative Forecasting Methods

Qualitative forecasts are based on management judgment and opinions and are commonly used in long-range planning or when only limited information is available. For example, companies often use qualitative methods for new product introductions. These methods include:

- **Sales Force Estimates**: The sales force should be closest to the market; it therefore provides good intelligence on customer needs. However, forecasts may be politically motivated or based on performance expectations.

- **Consumer Surveys**: Marketing may develop a survey on consumer opinions of existing products, their expected future buying habits, or new product ideas. The results are then analyzed using a variety of statistical techniques.

- **Delphi Method**: A series of questionnaires is developed to establish consensus on future events or long-term demand forecasts. Experts, drawn from internal and external sources, answer these surveys. Results are compiled and a summary is returned to each participant. The participants are then allowed to modify their initial responses. This process is repeated until some consensus is reached. The advantage of the Delphi Method is that participants do not physically meet, avoiding "group think."

- **Jury of Executive Opinion**: Senior management executives meet and develop the forecast. These individuals provide considerable expertise, but "group think" may occur if one or two dominate the meeting.

Time Series Methods

The most popular quantitative forecasting techniques companies use are **time series methods**, because they are relatively easy to understand. In forecasting, a time series consists of observations of actual demand over a given time period. Time series methods use historical data of actual demand to predict future demand, based on the assumption that the past is a good predictor of the future. This means that companies must have accurate records of past sales and a good idea of their demand patterns. Time series models are particularly useful for short-term forecasting. The most commonly used time series forecasting methods are simple moving, weighted moving average, and exponential smoothing.

Simple Moving Average Method

When demand is relatively stable over time, the **simple moving average forecast** is a fairly reliable forecasting method. At least two previous periods of actual demand are averaged together to predict the following period's demand. Averaging smoothes out or dampens the random changes in demand that occur within one period. As more past periods of demand are averaged together, the forecast becomes smoother. As a result, the forecast responds more slowly to changes in demand.

To calculate the forecast, the following formula is used:

$$F_{t+1} = \frac{\text{Sum of last } n \text{ demands}}{n} = \frac{A_t + A_{t-1} + A_{t-2} + \cdots + A_{t-n+1}}{n}$$

where

F_{t+1} = forecast for Period $t+1$
n = number of periods used to calculate moving average
A_t = actual demand in Period t

Example 5.1 provides an example of the simple moving average method.

Weighted Moving Average Method

When using the simple moving average, each of the past n-periods of demand is weighted equally. However, it may be better at times to weight the more recent periods more heavily since what influenced these periods may be more likely to influence the

---

Example 5.1   Simple Moving Average Forecasting Method

J&J Enterprises sells garden supplies to local nurseries. Jack and Jill, the owners, are estimating demand for one of its products, a 4-inch spade, and have the following sales records for the past eight months.

MONTH	SPADE SALES
January	420
February	370
March	425
April	490
May	450
June	440
July	350
August	420

Calculate the forecast for September using a three-period and six-period simple moving average.

Continued

SOLUTION:

The three-period simple moving average forecast for September is calculated based on demand for spades for the past three months, using the following formula:

$$F_{Sept} = \frac{F_{June} + F_{July} + F_{Aug}}{3} = \frac{440 + 350 + 420}{3} = 403.33 \approx 404 \text{ spades}$$

The six-period simple moving average forecast for September is calculated on demand for spades for the past six months:

$$F_{Sept} = \frac{425 + 490 + 450 + 440 + 350 + 420}{6} = 429.17 \approx 430 \text{ spades}$$

An Excel spreadsheet can also be used to calculate the forecast and is shown in Figure 5.2.

Figure 5.2	Simple Moving Average and Microsoft Excel

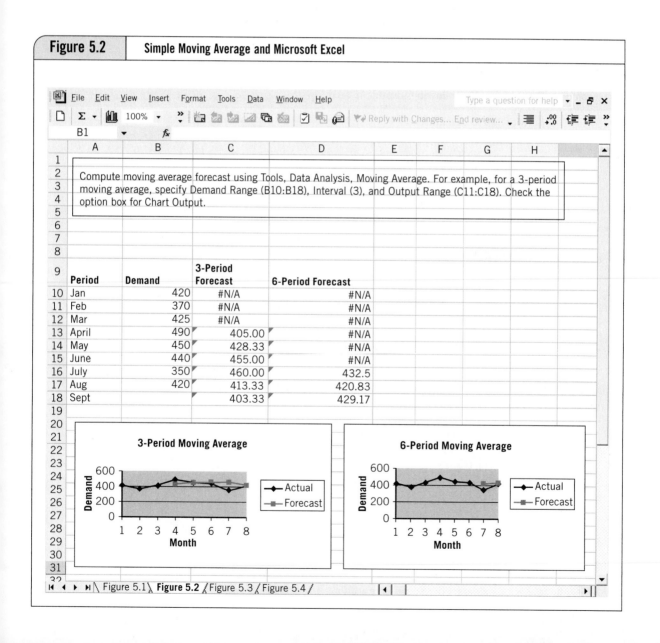

upcoming forecast period than what influenced earlier periods. This is called a **weighted moving average forecast**. Often the weights are assigned based on the forecaster's past experience, and the knowledge of how various weights will impact forecast error. The sum of the weights should always equal 1.0. The forecast is calculated using the following formula:

$$F_{t+1} = \text{Weighted sum of last } n \text{ demands}$$
$$= w_1 A_1 + w_2 A_{t-1} + w_3 A_{t-2} + \ldots + w_n A_{t-n+1}$$

where

F_{t+1} = forecast for Period $t+1$
n = number of periods used in determining the moving average
w = weights assigned to each Period (with $\Sigma w = 1$)
A_t = actual demand in Period t

Example 5.2 provides an illustration of the weighted moving average method.

Exponential Smoothing Method

A slightly more sophisticated forecasting method is **exponential smoothing**, which is used when there is little evidence of seasonality or trends but more recent demand is an indicator of future demand. To calculate the forecast, the difference between the previous period's forecast and actual demand is weighted and added to the previous period's forecast. The weight is called the **smoothing constant** and *must* be between 0 and 1. As the smoothing constant approaches 1, more weight is placed on the previous period's actual data. Thus, the forecast is more responsive to changes in demand as the smoothing constant increases. Forecasters often determine the value of the smoothing constant based on past experience, but may also test different values to find the most accurate forecast.

An advantage of this method is that less demand data is needed—a forecaster can start with two past periods and begin forecasting. The first-period forecast is commonly estimated based on a qualitative method, or simply set equal to the first-period's actual demand. Another advantage is that exponential smoothing has a good track record for successful forecasting. As a result, this is a popular forecasting method.

There are two alternative formulas to calculate the exponential smoothing forecast, which result in the same answer:

$$F_{t+1} = F_t + \alpha(A_t - F_t) \quad \text{or}$$
$$F_{t+1} = \alpha A_t + (1-\alpha)F_t$$

where

F_{t+1} = forecast for Period $t+1$
F_t = forecast for Period t
A_t = actual demand for Period t
α = smoothing constant ($0 \le \alpha \le 1$)

Example 5.2   Weighted Moving Average Forecasting Method

Using the data from Example 5.1, Jack and Jill calculated the forecast for September using a three-period weighted moving average. The weights of 0.5, 0.3, and 0.2 were assigned to the most recent, second most recent, and third most recent periods, respectively.

SOLUTION:
$$F_{Sept} = 0.2(440) + 0.3(350) + 0.5(420) = 403$$

An Excel spreadsheet can also be used to calculate the forecast and is shown in Figure 5.3.

Figure 5.3	Weighted Moving Average and Microsoft Spreadsheet

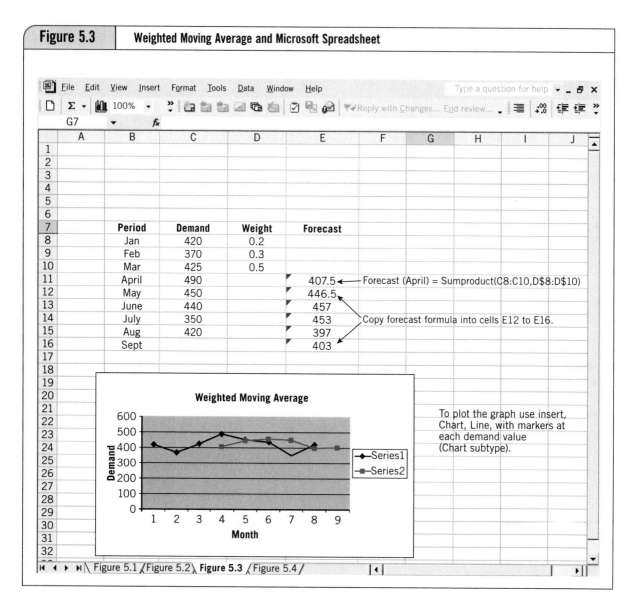

	Period	Demand	Weight	Forecast
	Jan	420	0.2	
	Feb	370	0.3	
	Mar	425	0.5	
	April	490		407.5 ← Forecast (April) = Sumproduct(C8:C10,D$8:D$10)
	May	450		446.5
	June	440		457
	July	350		453 ← Copy forecast formula into cells E12 to E16.
	Aug	420		397
	Sept			403

Weighted Moving Average

To plot the graph use insert, Chart, Line, with markers at each demand value (Chart subtype).

Example 5.3 provides an illustration of exponential smoothing. Note that when α is set equal to 1, the formula reduces to $F_{t+1} = A_t$.

Trend-Adjusted Exponential Smoothing Method

The exponential smoothing method can also be adjusted for a trend. As described earlier, a trend is a consistent upward or downward movement in demand over time. In **trend-adjusted exponential smoothing**, there are two smoothing constants, α and β. The α value smoothes the forecast, while the β value adjusts for a trend. β, similar to α, *must* be between 0 and 1. Higher values of β mean the forecaster has placed more emphasis on changes in recent trends, while a small weight smoothes out a current trend. Forecasters set the weights for α and β based on past experience and trial and error. The trend-adjusted exponential smoothing method also requires the forecaster to set initial values for the first-period forecast and the trend. If the forecaster has access to several periods of demand data, it will be easier to set initial values.

There are three equations for this method:

1. **Smoothing initial forecast:** $F_t = \alpha A_{t-1} + (1-\alpha)(F_{t-1} + T_{t-1})$
2. **Smoothing the trend:** $T_t = \beta(F_t - F_{t-1}) + (1-\beta)T_{t-1}$
3. **Trend-adjusted forecast:** $TAF_t = F_t + T_t$

where

F_t = exponentially smoothed average in Period t
A_t = actual demand in Period t
T_t = exponentially smoothed trend in Period t
α = smoothing constant $(0 \le \alpha \le 1)$
β = smoothing constant for trend $(0 \le \beta \le 1)$

Example 5.4 provides an illustration of trend-adjusted exponential smoothing.

Associative Forecasting Method

Linear regression may be used for both time series forecasting to estimate a trend and when the forecaster sees a causal relationship between one or more factors, or **variables**, and expected sales. Expected sales—the **dependent variable**—are linearly related to one or more **independent variables**. In **linear trend forecasting**, the independent variable is time. In **linear regression analysis**, the independent variable is some causal factor. For example, the demand for new starter homes built by U.S. homebuilder KB Homes—the dependent variable—would be expected to be affected by family income, interest rates, and KB Homes' advertising expenditures.

For one independent variable, the theoretical relationship between the dependent and independent variables is shown by the following equation:

$$Y = a + bX$$

where

Y = forecast or dependent variable
X = independent variable
a = Y-intercept of the line
b = slope of the line

Example 5.3   Exponential Smoothing Method

Using the data from Example 5.1, Jack and Jill calculated the forecast for September using the exponential smoothing method and a smoothing constant of $\alpha = 0.3$.

SOLUTION:
To calculate the forecast for September, begin with the forecast for January. Assume that January's forecast is equal to 420 (the demand for January).
Given:

$F_{Jan} = 420, \alpha = 0.3$
$F_{Feb} = F_{Jan} + 0.3(A_{Jan} - F_{Jan}) = 420 + 0.3(420 - 420) = 420$

Similarly, calculate the forecast for March:

$F_{Mar} = F_{Feb} + 0.3(A_{Feb} - F_{Feb}) = 420 + 0.3(370 - 420) = 405$

Continue to calculate the rest of the months (April through September) using the same formula.

Continued

The final forecast for September is:

$$F_{Sept} = F_{Aug} + 0.3(A_{Aug} - F_{Aug}) = 412.65 + 0.3(420 - 412.65) = 414.86 \text{ or } 415 \text{ spades}$$

The solution using a Microsoft Excel spreadsheet is found in Figure 5.4.

The coefficients, a and b, are calculated as follows:

$$b = n\frac{\Sigma(xy) - \Sigma x \Sigma y}{n\Sigma x^2 - (\Sigma x)^2}$$

$$a = \frac{\Sigma y - b\Sigma x}{n}$$

where

x = independent variable values
y = dependent variable values
n = number of observations

Figure 5.4 **Exponential Smoothing and Microsoft Excel Spreadsheet**

Compute forecast using Tools, Data Analysis, Exponential Smoothing. Specify the Demand Range (B11:B19), Damping Factor (.70), Output Range (C11:C19), Check the Option Box for Chart Output.
Note: The damping factor is 1 - alpha; the forecast for January is the actual demand for January, however, the software output returns the January forecast as #N/A.

Period	Demand	Forecast
Jan	420	#N/A
Feb	370	420
Mar	425	405
April	490	411
May	450	434.7
June	440	439.29
July	350	439.503
Aug	420	412.6521
Sept	--	414.8565

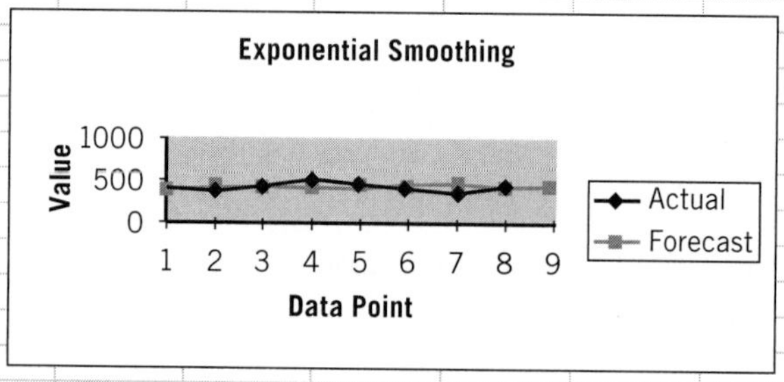

Figure 5.1 Figure 5.2 Figure 5.3 Figure 5.4

Three other measures are often used to determine whether a linear relationship exists between the independent and dependent variables. The **sample correlation coefficient**, r, is a measure of the strength and direction of the relationship between the independent variable and the dependent variable. It ranges from -1 to $+1$; as the value of r approaches 1, it means *increases* in the independent variable result in *increases* in the dependent variable and the better fit of the regression line to the data. The opposite

---

Example 5.4   Trend-Adjusted Exponential Smoothing Method

Jack and Jill (see Example 5.1) own a lawn and garden store. They believe there is an upward trend in the sales of one of their products, a titanium rake. They have collected the following sales data.

MONTH	RAKE SALES
January	1,900
February	2,100
March	2,000
April	2,300
May	2,500
June	2,250
July	2,700
August	2,800

Using this data, Jack and Jill calculate the forecast for September using trend-adjusted exponential smoothing. They use $\alpha = 0.3$ and $\beta = 0.5$. Assume the smoothed forecast for January was 1,900 rakes and the smoothed trend was 150 rakes.

SOLUTION:

To calculate the forecast for September, begin with the forecast for February.

Smoothing the forecast: $F_{Feb} = 0.3(A_{Jan}) + (1-0.3)(F_{Jan} + T_{Jan}) = 0.3(1,900) + 0.7(1,900 + 150)$
$$= 570 + 1,435 = 2,005 \text{ rakes}$$

Smoothing the trend: $T_{Feb} = 0.5(F_{Feb} - F_{Jan}) + (1-0.5)T_{Jan} = 0.5(2,005 - 1,900) + 0.5(150)$
$$= 52.5 + 75 = 127.5 \text{ rakes}$$

Trend-adjusted forecast for February: $TAF_{Feb} = F_{Feb} + T_{Feb} = 2,005 + 127.5 = 2,132.5 \text{ rakes}$

The forecast for March is:

Smoothing the forecast: $F_{Mar} = 0.3(2,100) + (1-0.3)(2,005 + 127.5) = 630 + 1,492.75 = 2,122.75 \text{ rakes}$

Smoothing the trend: $T_{Mar} = 0.5(2,122.75 - 2,005) + (1-0.5)127.5 = 58.875 + 63.75 = 122.625 \text{ rakes}$

Trend-adjusted forecast for March: $TAF_{Mar} = 2,122.75 + 122.625 = 2,245.375 \text{ rakes}$

This process continues for each month. The forecast for September is:

Smoothing the forecast: $F_{Sept} = 0.3(A_{Aug}) + (1-0.3)(F_{Aug} + T_{Aug})$
$$= 0.3(2,800) + (1-0.3)(2,566.6 + 101.4) = 840 + 1,867.6 = 2,707.6$$

Smoothing the trend: $T_{Sept} = 0.5(F_{Sept} - F_{Aug}) + (1-0.5)T_{Aug} = 0.5(2,707.6 - 2,566.6) + 0.5(101.4)$
$$= 70.5 + 50.7 = 121.2$$

Trend-adjusted forecast for September: $TAF_{Sept} = 2,707.6 + 121.2 = 2,828.8 \text{ rakes}$

The complete solution is shown in Figure 5.5 using Microsoft Excel.

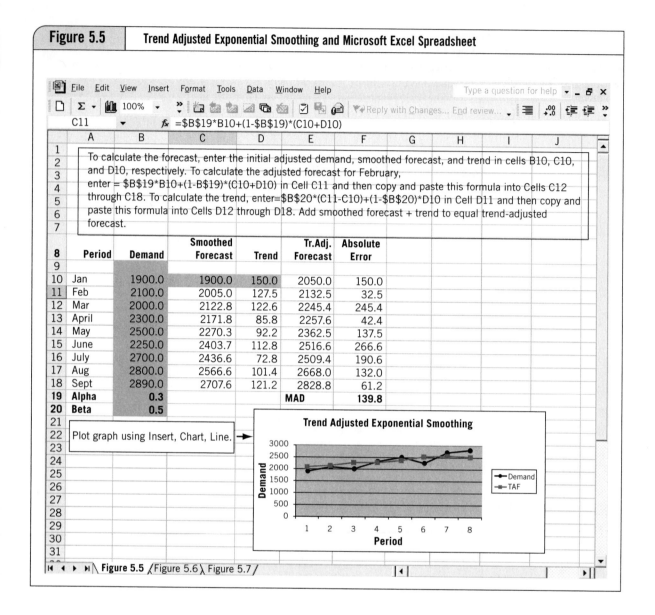

Figure 5.5 | **Trend Adjusted Exponential Smoothing and Microsoft Excel Spreadsheet**

is true as the value of r approaches -1; *decreases* in the independent variable result in *increases* in the dependent variable. If the value of r is 0, there is no relationship between the independent and dependent variables. The formula to calculate r is:

$$r = \frac{n(\sum xy) - \sum x \sum y}{\sqrt{[n\sum x^2 - (\sum x)^2][n\sum y^2 - (\sum y)^2]}}$$

where

r = sample correlation coefficient
x = independent variable values
y = dependent variable values
n = number of observations

The **sample coefficient of determination**, r^2, is a measure of the variation in the dependent variable that can be explained by the independent variable. The value of r^2 falls between 0 and 1. As the value of r^2 approaches 1, it indicates the variations in the dependent variable and the forecasts are more closely related. The value of r^2 can simply be calculated by squaring the sample correlation coefficient.

To measure how well the dependent variable data cluster around the regression line, the **standard error of the estimate**, s_{yx}, is calculated. It measures the deviation or error, or the difference between actual demand and the regression line estimate. The forecaster should choose the independent variable(s) that will result in the smallest standard error of the estimate, an indicator that the forecast is the most accurate. One equation to calculate the standard error of the estimate is:

$$s_{yx} = \sqrt{\frac{\sum(y - y_c)^2}{(n - 2)}}$$

where

y = dependent variable values
y_c = computed value of the dependent variable from the regression equation
n = number of observations

Example 5.5 provides an illustration of linear trend forecasting and Example 5.6 illustrates linear regression analysis.

Multiple regression is used when there are several explanatory variables used that explain demand, as with the KB Homes example earlier. The multiple regression equation is similar to the simple regression model:

$$Y = a + b_1X_1 + b_2X_2 + b_3X_3 + \cdots + b_nX_n$$

where

X_n = nth explanatory or independent variable
a = constant
b_n = regression coefficient of the independent variable X_n

The formulas to calculate the multiple regression forecast are complex and outside the scope of the textbook. Again, commercial software programs are available to solve these equations, including Microsoft Excel®, SPSS, and SAS.

Simulation Forecasting Method

A simulation forecasting method mimics consumer preferences that result in demand for specific products. The advantage of simulation is that a wide range of scenarios can be created and explored. However, it is also the most sophisticated forecasting method, and as a result it is used much less frequently than other methods. One company that uses simulation is Union Electric Company of Missouri. It uses simulation to predict power usage for its residential customers. [12]

To begin the process, historical data is drawn from a firm's information system as a basis for the simulation. Multiple forecasting methods are then used, including time series and associative models, to predict the effect of store promotions, new product introductions from rivals, new competition, etc. A more detailed discussion is beyond

Example 5.5   Linear Trend Forecasting

Demand for MP3 players has continued to grow as consumers replace or supplement their CD and cassette players. Cherry, a manufacturer of the P-Pod, expects growth in the MP3 market to continue. Demand for the past year is shown in the following table.

MONTH	DEMAND (000s OF UNITS)	MONTH	DEMAND (000s OF UNITS)
1	43	7	54
2	42	8	50
3	39	9	56
4	45	10	58
5	51	11	64
6	48	12	62

1. Using least squares regression analysis, what is the trend line?
2. What is the forecast for Period 13?
3. What is the sample correlation coefficient?
4. What is the coefficient of determination?

SOLUTION:

PERIOD (x)	DEMAND (y)	x^2	y^2	xy
1	43	1	1,849	43
2	42	4	1,764	84
3	39	9	1,521	117
4	45	16	2,025	180
5	51	25	2,601	255
6	48	36	2,304	288
7	54	49	2,916	378
8	50	64	2,500	400
9	56	81	3,136	504
10	58	100	3,364	580
11	64	121	4,096	704
12	62	144	3,844	744
$\Sigma x = 78$	$\Sigma y = 612$	$\Sigma x^2 = 650$	$\Sigma y^2 = 31{,}920$	$\Sigma xy = 4{,}277$

$$b = \frac{n\Sigma(xy) - \Sigma x \Sigma y}{n\Sigma x^2 - (\Sigma x)^2} = \frac{12(4{,}277) - (612)(78)}{12(650) - (78)^2} = 2.09$$

$$a = \frac{\Sigma y - b\Sigma x}{n} = \frac{612 - 2.09(78)}{12} = 37.42$$

1. The trend line is $Y = 37.41 + 2.09X$
2. To forecast demand for Period 13, we substitute $X = 13$ into the trend equation.

   Forecast for Period $13 = 37.41 + 2.09(13) = 64.58$ or $64.58 \times 1{,}000 = 64{,}580$ P-Pods.
3. The sample correlation coefficient (r) is:

$$r = \frac{n(\Sigma xy) - (\Sigma x)(\Sigma y)}{\sqrt{\left[n\Sigma x^2 - (\Sigma x)^2\right]\left[n\Sigma y^2 - (\Sigma y)^2\right]}}$$

$$= \frac{12(4{,}277) - 78(612)}{\sqrt{\left[12(650) - (78^2)\right]\left[12(31{,}920) - (612)^2\right]}} = \frac{3{,}588}{3{,}817.61} = 0.9398$$

4. The sample coefficient of determination (r^2) is: $r^2 = (0.9398)^2 = 0.8832$

The sample correlation coefficient, r, is close to 1.00, so there appears to be a strong positive relationship between sales of P-Pods and time. The coefficient of determination, r^2, indicates that almost 94 percent of the demand for P-Pods can be explained by time. The solution using a Microsoft Excel spreadsheet is shown in Figure 5.6.

(Note—Answers obtained using Excel may vary from those obtained in this and other examples, due to rounding.)

Figure 5.6   Forecasting a Trend Line Using Regression and Microsoft Excel Spreadsheet

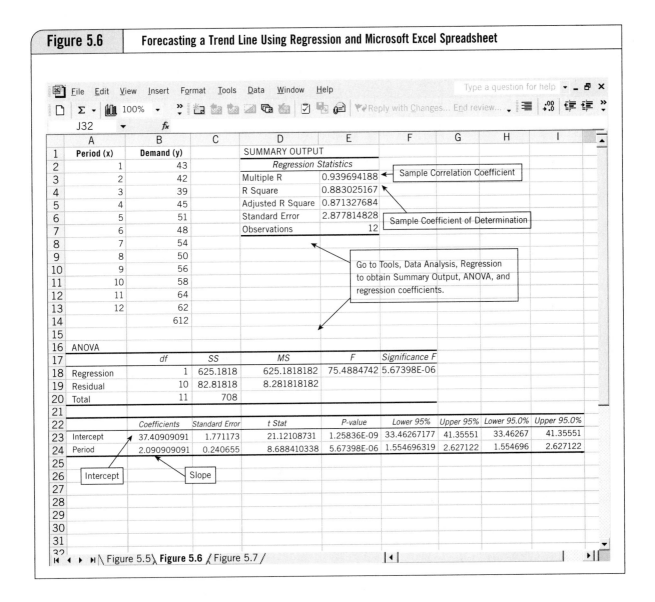

Example 5.6   Simple Regression

Jim and Jane own a Christmas tree lot in Portland, Oregon, selling and delivering Douglas fir trees directly to customers. They feel that artificial tree sales in Oregon have an impact on their sales. They have collected the following data for the past ten years.

YEAR	ARTIFICIAL TREE SALES (x)	TREE LOT SALES (y)
1	36,000	115
2	33,000	104
3	40,000	100
4	42,000	95
5	39,000	89
6	44,000	80
7	56,000	76
8	61,000	74
9	55,000	61
10	63,000	57

1. Determine the linear relationship between artificial tree sales and Jim and Jane's Douglas fir tree sales.

2. If artificial tree sales in Oregon are 66,000 in Year 11, how many Douglas fir trees should Jim and Jane expect to sell?

3. What is the sample correlation coefficient?

4. What is the coefficient of determination?

SOLUTION:

YEAR	TREE LOT SALES (y)	ARTIFICIAL TREE SALES (x)	x^2	y^2	xy
1	115	36,000	1,296,000,000	13,225	4,140,000
2	104	33,000	1,089,000,000	10,816	3,432,000
3	100	40,000	1,600,000,000	10,000	4,000,000
4	95	42,000	1,764,000,000	9,025	3,990,000
5	89	39,000	1,521,000,000	7,921	3,471,000
6	80	44,000	1,936,000,000	6,400	3,520,000
7	76	56,000	3,136,000,000	5,776	4,256,000
8	74	61,000	3,721,000,000	5,476	4,514,000
9	61	55,000	3,025,000,000	3,721	3,355,000
10	57	63,000	3,969,000,000	3,249	3,591,000
	$\Sigma y = 851$	$\Sigma x = 469,000$	$\Sigma x^2 = 23,057,000,000$	$\Sigma y^2 = 75,609$	$\Sigma xy = 38,269,000$

$$b = \frac{n\Sigma(xy) - \Sigma x \Sigma y}{n\Sigma x^2 - (\Sigma x)^2} = \frac{10(38,269,000) - (469,000)(851)}{10(23,057,000,000) - (469,000)^2} = -0.0015$$

$$a = \frac{\Sigma y - b\Sigma x}{n} = \frac{851 - (-0.0015)(469,000)}{10} = 155.45$$

1. $Y = 155.45 - 0.0015X$

2. In Year 11, Jim and Jane should expect to sell

$Y = 155.45 - 0.0015(66,000) = 56.45 = 57$ trees

3. The sample correlation coefficient (r) is:

$$r = \frac{n(\Sigma xy) - (\Sigma x)(\Sigma y)}{\sqrt{\left[n\Sigma x^2 - (\Sigma x)^2\right]\left[n\Sigma y^2 - (\Sigma y)^2\right]}}$$

$$= \frac{10(38{,}269{,}0000) - (469{,}000)(851)}{\sqrt{\left[10(23{,}057{,}000{,}000) - 469{,}000^2\right]\left[10(75{,}609) - 851^2\right]}} = -0.8932$$

4. The sample coefficient of determination (r^2) is:

$$r^2 = (-0.8932)^2 = 0.7978$$

Since r is close to 1.00 and negative, there appears to be a strong negative relationship between tree lot sales and artificial tree sales (when one goes up, the other goes down). The coefficient of determination, r^2, indicates that almost 80 percent of demand for tree farm trees can be explained by artificial tree sales. The solution using a Microsoft Excel spreadsheet is shown in Figure 5.7.

the scope of this text, but books addressing this topic include *Modeling Risk: Applying Monte Carlo Simulation, Real Options Analysis, Forecasting and Optimization Techniques* by Jonathan Mun and *Corporate Planning, Human Behavior and Computer Simulation* by Roy Nersesian. [13]

Forecast Accuracy

Ultimately, companies want to develop an unbiased forecast that is the most accurate. **Forecast bias** occurs when a forecast has a tendency to be either consistently higher or lower than actual demand. When forecasts are inaccurate, the costs of doing business increase. Lost sales occur when inventory levels are too low, resulting in customer dissatisfaction and a loss of goodwill. Firms spend more money to hold inventory if sales forecasts are overly optimistic. As a result, inventory is sold at reduced prices, resulting in lower revenue streams.

To mitigate these problems, companies need to test a number of forecasting models and measure the forecast error in each model to find the "best historical" forecasting model. This is an ongoing process because sales patterns may change over time. The forecast error for a given period of time is simply the difference between what actually took place and the corresponding forecast for that same period, or:

$$e_t = A_t - F_t$$

where

e_t = forecast error for Period t
A_t = actual demand for Period t
F_t = forecast for Period t

To compare forecasting methods, however, a manager should look at multiple past periods to determine the historical forecast accuracy. The simplest and most common calculation to compare forecasting methods is the **mean absolute deviation** (MAD), which averages the absolute value of the forecast errors over a given period of time. Absolute values of the errors are used so that negative errors do not "cancel out" the positive ones when averaging errors over time. As a result, errors are equally

Figure 5.7

Regression Analysis Using Excel

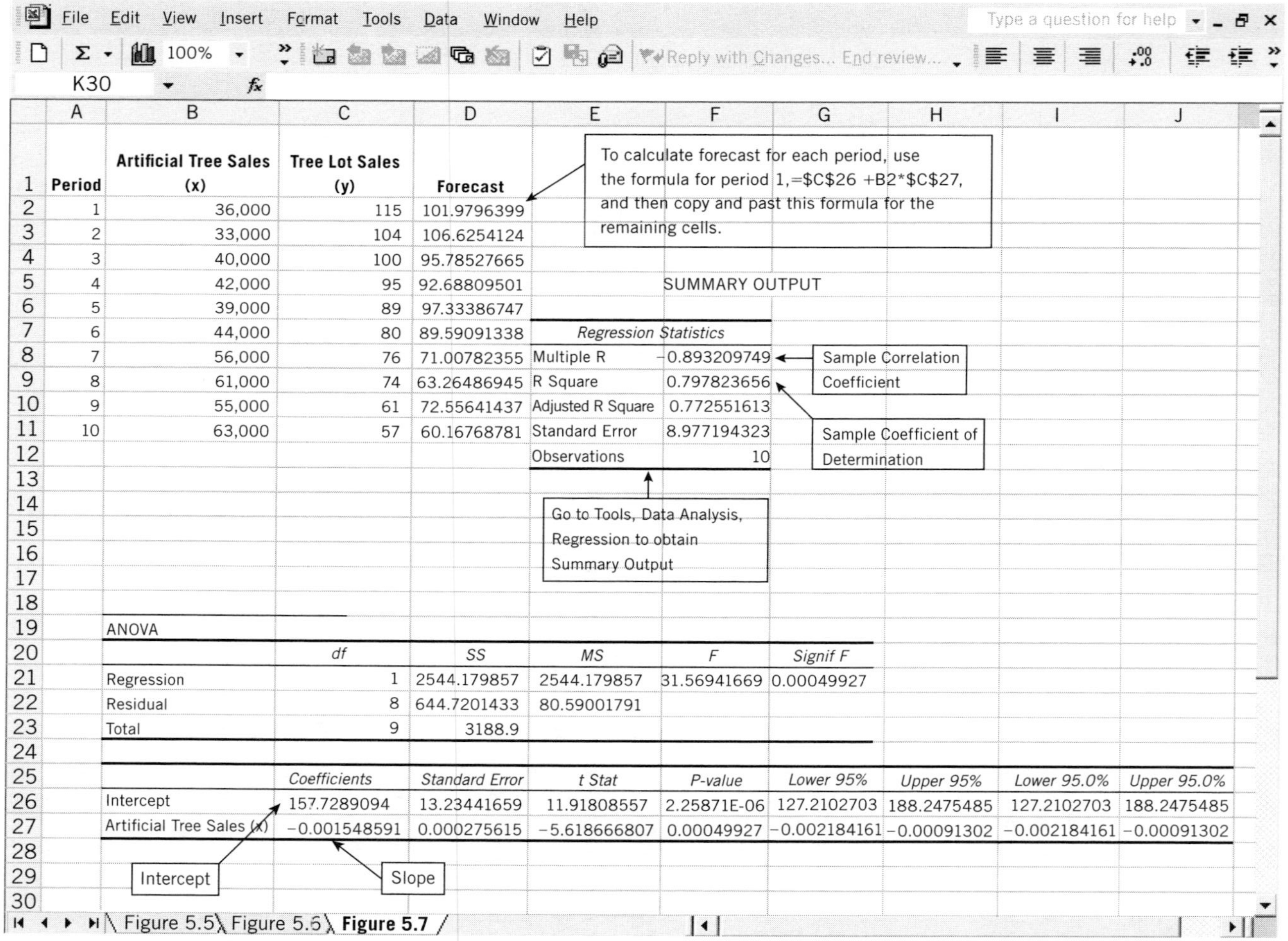

Excel spreadsheet — File Edit View Insert Format Tools Data Window Help

To calculate forecast for each period, use the formula for period 1, =C26 +B2*C27, and then copy and past this formula for the remaining cells.

	A	B	C	D
1	Period	Artificial Tree Sales (x)	Tree Lot Sales (y)	Forecast
2	1	36,000	115	101.9796399
3	2	33,000	104	106.6254124
4	3	40,000	100	95.78527665
5	4	42,000	95	92.68809501
6	5	39,000	89	97.33386747
7	6	44,000	80	89.59091338
8	7	56,000	76	71.00782355
9	8	61,000	74	63.26486945
10	9	55,000	61	72.55641437
11	10	63,000	57	60.16768781

SUMMARY OUTPUT

Regression Statistics

Multiple R	−0.893209749	← Sample Correlation Coefficient
R Square	0.797823656	
Adjusted R Square	0.772551613	
Standard Error	8.977194323	← Sample Coefficient of Determination
Observations	10	

Go to Tools, Data Analysis, Regression to obtain Summary Output

ANOVA

	df	SS	MS	F	Signif F
Regression	1	2544.179857	2544.179857	31.56941669	0.00049927
Residual	8	644.7201433	80.59001791		
Total	9	3188.9			

	Coefficients	Standard Error	t Stat	P-value	Lower 95%	Upper 95%	Lower 95.0%	Upper 95.0%
Intercept	157.7289094	13.23441659	11.91808557	2.25871E-06	127.2102703	188.2475485	127.2102703	188.2475485
Artificial Tree Sales (X)	−0.001548591	0.000275615	−5.618666807	0.00049927	−0.002184161	−0.00091302	−0.002184161	−0.00091302

Intercept — Slope

Figure 5.5 / Figure 5.5 / Figure 5.7

considered, whether they are over- or underestimations of demand. The MAD is similar to the standard deviation in that it measures the dispersion of actual demand to the expected forecast. In comparing forecasting methods (or the weights or alphas of one method, along with other methods), a manager looks for the method that results in the lowest MAD. The calculation is:

$$\text{MAD} = \frac{\Sigma |e_t|}{n}$$

where

$|e_t|$ = absolute value of the forecast error for Period t
n = number of periods of evaluation

Another commonly used method is the **mean absolute percentage deviation** (MAPE). This method provides an estimate of the magnitude of forecast error. To calculate the MAPE, the monthly absolute forecast error divided by actual demand is summed, then divided by the number of months used in the forecast to derive an average, and lastly multiplied by 100. The formula to calculate MAPE is:

$$\text{MAPE} = \frac{\Sigma [|e_t|/A_t]}{n}(100)$$

where

e_t = forecast error for Period t
n = number of periods of evaluation
A_t = actual demand for Period t

The **running sum of forecast errors** (RSFE) provides a measure of forecast bias. When the RFSE is positive, it indicates managers are generally underestimating demand. As a result, not enough inventory was typically on hand to satisfy demand. On the other hand, a negative RFSE indicates managers are, as a rule, overestimating demand, ordering too much inventory and spending too much money on carrying costs. An RSFE of zero does not indicate an accurate forecast—since positive and negative errors will cancel each other out—but rather indicates an unbiased forecast. The formula to calculate RSFE is:

$$\text{RSFE} = \Sigma e_t$$

where

e_t = forecast error for Period t

A second method of determining bias in a forecast is the use of a **tracking signal**. The tracking signal measures whether a particular forecasting method is accurately predicting the changes in demand, and is the number of MADs the forecast is above or under actual demand. To calculate the tracking signal the following formula is used:

$$\text{TS} = \text{RSFE/MAD}$$

There are two methods to calculate MAD: (1) a simple average of all absolute errors to date (as shown earlier) or (2) a weighted average of MADs, using exponential smoothing, as shown here:

$$\text{MAD}_t = \alpha |e_t| + (1 - \alpha)\text{MAD}_{t-1}$$

where

$|e_t|$ = absolute value of the error for Period t

The second method requires less historical data but the smoothing constant (α) must be estimated, thus requiring some management experience and judgment.

A tracking signal is initially calculated and then updated for each month and plotted on a **control chart**. The control chart limits are set based on the number of MADs above or below zero. If the tracking signal falls outside the control limits, it may be time to use a different forecasting method. For example, a manager may decide to set the limits based on $+/-4$ MAD. For example, if TS $= 4$, this means that the RSFE is four times the MAD. Managers thus wish to set limits based on an RSFE of $+/-4$ times the MAD. Table 5.1 shows the percentage of tracking signal points that would be included for a range of 1 to 4 MADs.

Acceptable control limits depend on the item forecasted. Higher volume and higher revenue items should be monitored more frequently. However, the amount of human resources available should be considered. Whenever the control limits are more narrowly set, personnel spend more time investigating tracking signals that fall outside the limits. Example 5.7 provides an example of measuring forecast accuracy using a tracking signal.

Table 5.1	Percentage of Tracking Signal Points within Control Limits	
	CONTROL LIMITS	
NUMBER OF MADs	**EQUIVALENT NUMBER OF STANDARD DEVIATIONS**	**% OF POINTS WITHIN CONTROL LIMITS**
+/- 1	0.80	57.62
+/- 2	1.60	89.04
+/- 3	2.40	98.36
+/- 4	3.20	99.86

Example 5.7   Forecast Accuracy

Jim and Jane have tracked demand and forecast for tree farm trees over the past ten years, as shown in the following table. They have asked you to calculate MAD, MAPE, RSFE, and the tracking signal to determine the quality of their forecasts. Assume the control limits for the tracking signal are $+/-4$ MADs.

PERIOD	ACTUAL DEMAND	FORECAST DEMAND
1	115	102
2	104	107
3	100	96
4	95	94
5	89	97
6	80	90
7	76	71
8	74	63
9	61	73
10	57	60

SOLUTION:

The solution for Example 5.7 using Microsoft Excel is shown in Figure 5.8. Note that the tracking signal falls within $+/-4$ MADs. Thus, the forecast method appears to be appropriate.

| Figure 5.8 | Calculation of Tracking Signal Using Excel |

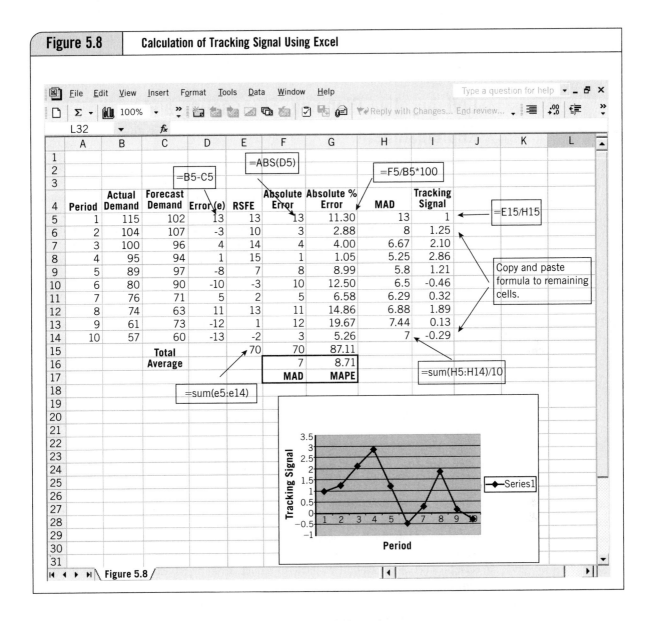

Regardless of the attention paid to forecasting, there will always be a certain amount of over or underforecasting of actual demand. Thus, organizations need to develop contingency plans for those times when demand varies from the forecast. In the short term, airlines "pay" customers to take a later flight in the event of an oversale. Restaurants periodically change their menu items to generate business because many customers want variety. Grocery chains will offer in-store specials to move unsold perishable product at the end of its shelf life.

Forecast accuracy is also subject to the underlying motivations of personnel inside and outside an organization. Sales associates, for example, may underforecast to ensure that they meet or exceed their sales quotes. On the other hand, operations personnel lean toward overforecasting to ensure they meet delivery deadlines. As a result, some form of collaboration is important to mitigate these factors and improve forecast accuracy. A collaborative planning, forecasting and replenishment process improves forecast accuracy even further by using real-time data and including input from supply chain partners and is discussed further in the next section.

Collaborative Planning, Forecasting and Replenishment

As implied in these definitions of demand management and forecasting, collaboration is essential among internal functional areas and supply chain partners to obtain accurate customer feedback, which is then used to develop the forecast. Demand planning that incorporates supply chain management by involving suppliers and customers in the process is known as **collaborative planning, forecasting and replenishment** (CPFR®). A formal definition of CPFR has been developed by the Voluntary Interindustry Commerce Standards (VICS): "A business practice that combines the intelligence of multiple trading partners in the planning and fulfillment of customer demand. CPFR links sales and marketing best practices, such as category management, to supply chain planning and execution processes to increase availability while reducing inventory, transportation and logistics costs."[14] Through collaboration, less inventory is needed as a protection against uncertain demand, lead times can be shortened because less unnecessary product is manufactured, and sales tend to increase because the correct amount of product is available at the right place. Ultimately profits should be higher and costs lower. Using a simplified example of CPFR, if a buyer collaborates with a trusted supplier and agrees to purchase exactly 1,000 units of a part over the upcoming quarter, then the supplier knows *exactly* how many units to produce for the buyer—no safety stock is required and there is no forecast error. Consequently, the purchase price should reflect the fact that no safety stock is produced. This also means that the bullwhip effect will be mitigated for the second- and third-tier suppliers. Additionally, the buyer knows that the supplier will deliver exactly that many units and can plan appropriately.

CPFR is a fairly new idea, but large global companies like Wal-Mart, Procter & Gamble, Warner-Lambert, Kimberly-Clark, and Nabisco have proven that collaboration reduces costs in the supply chain. The Coca-Cola Bottling Company of Charlotte, North Carolina, for example, uses CPFR software to determine how much to make of each product. As a result, it was able to reduce inventory levels in half and at the same time improve customer service. Because inventories were reduced, it was able to close facilities, significantly reducing capital expenditures. More on Coca-Cola can be found in the Process Management in Action feature.

Wal-Mart has been the leader in collaboration efforts and encourages others in the retail sector to adopt similar practices. As a result of Wal-Mart's efforts, a set of consumer goods industry guidelines was adopted by the Voluntary Interindustry Commerce Standards (VICS) Association in 1996.[15] VICS is a not-for-profit organization dedicated to improving the efficiency of the supply chain by developing high-level strategic standards. VICS also developed a process model and updated it in 2004,[16] which further divides CPFR into four stages: strategy and planning, demand and supply management, execution, and analysis (see Figure 5.9, on page 167).

The strategy and planning stage involves two steps:

1. *Collaboration Arrangement* – includes setting business goals for the relationship, setting parameters for the scope of the collaboration, and determining roles and responsibilities.

Process Management in Action

Collaborative Forecasting Lowers Coke's Inventory

When Coca-Cola came only in little green bottles and was the soft drink maker's single brand, replenishing stores was a simple matter. Drivers loaded their trucks with product and dropped whatever was needed at the businesses on their route.

The environment at Coke's bottlers and distributors today is far more complex, as evidenced by Coca-Cola Bottling Co. Consolidated in Charlotte, North Carolina (CCBCC), CCBCC is Coca-Cola's second-largest bottler in the United States and one of the highest per-capita soft drink bottlers in the world. It bottles, packages, and distributes 13,000 SKUs to 200,000 customers throughout 11 Southeastern states, delivering more than 125 million cases of product each year. Nearly all of its customers engage in frequent promotions and aggressive discounting—often with little or no notice to the bottler—that can result in dramatic swings in volume for particular products. With five bottling plants and 60 distribution centers, knowing what to produce and how much to ship to which locations are critical issues.

Before implementing a collaborative demand planning and forecasting system from Manugistics two years ago, these issues were "pain points" for the bottling company. "We were very efficient at producing product, but we really didn't know what we should be making," says Brian Wieland, director of demand planning at CCBCC.

The result was that the company suffered sporadic stockouts while holding too much inventory overall. Additionally, as the company continued to grow and as Coca-Cola introduced more new products, CCBCC was facing the expense of adding 10 to 15 new warehouses to its then already large network of 73. Since warehouses average $5 million each, this represented a huge capital investment.

DEMAND VISIBILITY

The project drove a fundamental change in the way CCBCC managed its business. Previously, forecasting and production had been completely decentralized, says Wieland. Each manufacturing plant created its own forecasts and scheduled production and delivery to its associated distribution centers based on that. Forecasts typically looked out four weeks and were updated weekly by that plant's sales and marketing personnel. There was no visibility between plants or distribution centers, so an inventory surplus in one location could not easily be shifted to make up for a shortage elsewhere.

CENTRALIZED PLANNING

Under the new system, forecasting, production, and replenishment are managed by a centralized planning group based at the Charlotte headquarters. The current process begins with the marketing and customer-development group feeding in price plans from the company's largest customers—"those that in a given week can run us out of stock if they have a big ad," says Wieland. Estimated demand from other customers, along with known promotions and price points, also is input, as is information about new product introductions or other system-wide events. Wieland notes that Coca-Cola has added about 150 new items in the past year, including Vanilla Coke®, Fanta® drinks, and Dasani® water products. "Under the old system," he says, "it would have been impossible to plan all those new items and to manage all the required changeovers to our production lines."

Every Thursday the forecast is updated and sent to the area sales managers, who are aligned with specific distribution centers. They review the forecast, making notes and modifications as far as four weeks out. These modifications are based on new or changing promotions among

Continued

their customer base and on specific local knowledge, such as a fair coming to town or foul weather that may prompt people to stock up on bottled water.

"With the Collaborate application, our sales managers are able to provide local intelligence to the system, and they also can see their forecast accuracy in the past as well as any adjustments they already have made," says Wieland.

REALITY CHECK

On days subsequent to the Thursday update, sales managers also can send messages to demand analysts and go in and make changes to the forecast based on more current information. "We want to get the information in there as soon as possible because we rerun the plan every night to bring in that day's changes in inventory positions," says Wieland. These changes reflect inventory that was shipped from the distribution centers on that day as well as what was received from the plants, but it does not incorporate point-of-sale information. The demand plan drives production and scheduling, which is locked in three days out. Distribution is planned every day, with shipments going out in the evening for next-day delivery.

GOALS MET

Already the benefits from this project are significant and have met or exceeded CCBCC's initial goals, Wieland reports. Overall inventory has been reduced by about half.

Forecast accuracy has improved 10 to 20 percent and now is above 90 percent accurate, Wieland says. Finally, the company has achieved significant reductions in capital expenditure. Not only did CCBCC refrain from spending approximately $50 million on new warehouses, it actually closed more than a dozen existing facilities—a process that is ongoing. "We cut the inventory so much that we get a lot more efficient use of our warehouse space," says Wieland.

Source: "Forecasting Tool Lowers Coke Bottler's Inventory," *Global Logistics and Supply Chain Strategies,* November 2004. Available at http://www.supplychainbrain.com. Reprinted by permission of Keller International Publishing, publishers of Global Logistics & Supply Chain Strategies, Great Neck, New York.

2. *Joint Business Plan* – names any important events that will affect the planning process, such as store openings/closings, product promotions, product introductions, or inventory policy changes.

The demand and supply management stage continues the cycle, including:

3. *Sales Forecasting* – consumer demand is predicted using point-of-sale data and other available information. The forecast may be generated by one or more supply chain partners.

4. *Order Planning/Forecasting* – product ordering and delivery needs are set based on the sales forecast, current inventory levels, and lead times.

The execution stage involves:

5. *Order Generation* – the forecast is translated into committed orders by the purchasing/supply management department.

6. *Order Fulfillment* – orders are produced, shipped, delivered, and stocked for purchase by consumers.

| **Figure 5.9** | Collaborative Planning, Forecasting and Replenishment Process |

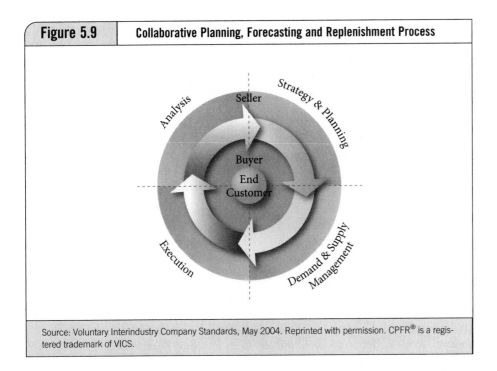

Source: Voluntary Interindustry Company Standards, May 2004. Reprinted with permission. CPFR® is a registered trademark of VICS.

Lastly, the analysis stage includes:

7. *Exception Management* – the review of any situations that fall outside the present conditions.

8. *Performance Assessment* – analyzing the achievement of business goals, uncovering trends, and developing alternative strategies based on key performance metrics.

A study conducted by Massachusetts-based consultants AMR Research cited some best practices as the key to successful CPFR.[17] First, companies must have an integrated forecast/demand planning organization. In other words, each supply chain partner must, *together*, develop an effective set of practices to manage demand. Integration will, of course, require a high level of trust among supply chain partners and a commitment to implement joint plans.

A sales and operations planning (S&OP) process should also be implemented to match supply and demand each month. The process involves determining the production level needed for a product family in order to meet the demand forecast, given the organizational strategy and any resource constraints. Strong cross-functional teamwork between sales and operations is required to optimize the planning process.

As mentioned earlier, S&OP helps keep a company in line with changing conditions in the marketplace. Software companies such as Georgia-based Logility and California-based Oracle offer integrated software with real-time information to help companies process any demand information and develop "what-if" scenarios. However, regular meetings among all parties involved in the demand management process are critical to avoiding mismatches between demand and supply. Samsung Electronics of South Korea, for example, greatly improved its profitability by combining its sales and manufacturing processes over the course of four years with the help of software from Virginia-based i2 Inc.[18]

Additionally, supply chain partners should operate with common demand numbers. For example, business customers can provide feedback on such things as plans for advertising and promotional campaigns, new store openings, or store closures. Suppliers may provide information on new product introductions. With access to this type of information, supply chain partners are able to improve their planning process over the planning horizon. Each supply chain partner then develops its demand forecast independently. If significant discrepancies occur, partners can negotiate any changes to finalize a forecast. During the late 1980s the demand manager for 3M, a global diversified technology company with headquarters in Minnesota, had consolidated customers' demand expectations for the following year. He found that combined demand exceeded 200 percent of total market potential. [19] Thus, data must be analyzed carefully.

Lastly, performance must be measured on a regular basis. Performance should be shared and then adjustments made for improvement. Metrics may include return on investment and sales growth at a macro level, and inventory turnover, sales forecast accuracy, order cycle time, and inventory level at a micro level.

There are, of course, challenges to adopting CPFR because the process requires frequent communication and information sharing, changes in internal operations, additional costs, and because trading partners often do not trust one another. To make the switch requires the long-term commitment of top management. Funds must also be allocated to the CPFR project, and initially firms may limit these efforts to large suppliers. As well, retailers and their suppliers must be willing to work together. An important ingredient for success is that information technology systems, business processes, data collection, and organizational structures must be aligned.

SUMMARY

The demand management and forecasting process is an important element of customer relationship management and is critical to all parts of an organization. Forecasting and demand management is used to develop budgets, allocate resources, make hiring and layoff decisions, and schedule work and people. If done properly, effective planning can result in better use of resources and, as a consequence, a more competitive organization. Too, a demand management and forecasting process is most effective when there is a collaborative effort among multiple functions within an organization, including marketing, operations, finance, and supply management, among others.

The demand management process begins with forecasting. Multiple methods are available to improve forecasting, including qualitative and quantitative techniques. Qualitative techniques provide the insight and experience of management while quantitative techniques use historical data and apply mathematical methods. A balance of both methods generally results in the most accurate forecast. The forecast is then used as a basis for marketing and operations planning and for everyday decisions. Forecasts are updated as market conditions change.

Collaborative planning, forecasting and replenishment is a relatively new supply chain approach that brings together an organization and its suppliers and customers. Rather than acting in isolation, firms across the supply chain share demand, production, and forecasting information to optimize inventory movements and reduce costs. While still in the early adoption stage, firms have found significant advantages to CPFR, including lower inventories and improved customer service.

KEY TERMS

base demand, 143

bottom-up approach, 144

collaborative planning, forecasting and replenishment, 164

control chart, 162

customer relationship management, 140

cyclical patterns, 143

demand management, 139

dependent demand, 143

dependent variable, 151

derived demand, 143

exponential smoothing, 149

forecast bias, 159

forecasting, 139

forward buying, 138

independent demand, 141

independent variables, 151

linear regression analysis, 151

linear trend forecasting, 151

lot, 143

material requirements planning (MRP) software, 143

mean absolute deviation, 159

mean absolute percentage deviation, 161

planning horizon, 139

point-of-sale (POS) data, 143

promotions, 144

random effects, 144

running sum of forecast errors, 161

sales and operations planning, 139

sample coefficient of determination, 155

sample correlation coefficient, 153

seasonal effects, 143

simple moving average forecast, 147

smoothing constant, 149

standard error of the estimate, 155

stock-keeping unit, 144

time series methods, 147

top-down approach, 144

tracking signal, 161

trend-adjusted exponential smoothing, 150

trends, 143

variables, 151

weighted moving average forecast, 149

DISCUSSION QUESTIONS

1. What is demand management and why is it important to companies today?

2. Describe the process of demand management.

3. What is the purpose of forecasting in the demand management process?

4. Describe the forecasting process.

5. What is the difference between top-down and bottom-up forecasting? What are the advantages and disadvantages of each method?

6. What is the difference between qualitative and quantitative forecasting? Why should companies combine both qualitative and quantitative forecasting?

7. Identify and describe three qualitative forecasting methods.

8. Describe the most appropriate time to use the following forecasting methods:

   a. simple moving average

   b. weighted moving average

   c. exponential smoothing

   d. adjusted exponential smoothing

   e. linear regression

   f. multiple regression

9. What are the sample correlation coefficient and coefficient of determination? What is the purpose of these two measures?

10. Why is it important to monitor forecast accuracy?

11. Describe the following measures of forecast accuracy:

    a. mean absolute deviation (MAD)

    b. mean absolute percentage error (MAPE)

12. What is a tracking signal?

13. Describe the continuous planning, forecasting and replenishment process.

14. Why have some companies implemented CPFR? Why have some companies found it difficult to adopt CPFR?

15. What are the stages in the continuous planning, forecasting and replenishment process?

16. What is the sales and operations planning (S&OP) process?

SPREADSHEET PROBLEMS

1. Sales for greeting cards at Dottie's Gift Shop for the past five weeks are as follows:

WEEK	SALES (# OF CARDS)
1	440
2	410
3	385
4	450
5	420

a. Forecast sales for Week 4 using the three-period simple moving average.

b. Forecast sales for Week 4 using the three-period weighted moving average and weights of .60 for the most recent month, .30 for the next most recent month, and .10 for the third most recent month.

c. If actual card sales for Week 6 were 425, what would be the forecast for Week 7 for each of these models?

d. Compare the accuracy of these two models using the mean absolute deviation (MAD). Which model would you recommend?

e. Compare the accuracy of these two models using the mean absolute percent error (MAPE). Which model would you recommend?

2. The owner of a barber shop would like to use exponential smoothing to forecast demand for haircuts. However, he wants to compare the forecast accuracy of a high versus a low α value. The data he has collected for the past six weeks is as follows:

WEEK	DEMAND (HAIRCUTS)
1	33
2	36
3	32
4	38
5	39
6	34

a. Calculate the forecast for Weeks 2–6 using an α value of .80.

b. Calculate the forecast for Weeks 2–6 using an α value of .20.

c. Compare the accuracy of the two forecasts for Weeks 2–6 using the calculation of mean absolute deviation. Which model would you recommend to the owner?

3. The manager of the Rest Easy Motor Lodge has kept track of room registrations for the past eight quarters. The data is shown in the following table.

QUARTER	REGISTRATIONS
1	3,120
2	3,500
3	3,300
4	3,730
5	3,510
6	3,890
7	4,100
8	4,140

a. Plot the monthly data using Excel. Do you notice any patterns?

b. Calculate a trend-adjusted exponential smoothed forecast for Quarters 2 through 9 using $\alpha = 0.4$ and $\beta = 0.6$. Assume the smoothed forecast for the first quarter was 3,300 room registrations and the smoothed trend was 200 room registrations.

c. Calculate the forecast for Quarter 9 using linear regression. (Hint: The independent variable is time.)

d. Calculate the MAD for each method using Quarters 2–9. Which method provides the more accurate forecast? Why?

4. The tax collector for Mercy County, Alabama, has collected the following data on annual home sales and property taxes collected for the past seven years:

YEAR	ANNUAL HOME SALES (x)	PROPERTY TAXES COLLECTED (y)
2001	2,590	$ 987,000
2002	2,796	993,000
2003	2,980	1,023,000
2004	3,123	1,054,000
2005	3,069	1,072,000
2006	3,350	1,081,000
2007	3,529	1,093,000

a. Using linear regression and Excel, predict the amount of property taxes that will be collected in 2008.

b. Calculate the sample correlation coefficient and the coefficient of determination using Excel or other forecasting software. Are annual home sales a good predictor of collected property taxes? Why/why not?

5. The forecast results generated by two forecasting methods are as follows:

MONTH	ACTUAL SALES	FORECAST – METHOD 1	FORECAST – METHOD 2
1	592	570	660
2	611	585	632
3	735	603	634
4	767	696	735
5	822	746	794
6	901	799	853
7	946	870	933
8	952	923	990

Compute the RSFE, MAD, MAPE, and the tracking signal for each forecasting method (assume the control limits are +/− 2 MAD). Calculate the MAD as the average of the absolute value of the forecast errors. Which method is better? Why?

INTERNET QUESTIONS

1. Go to the Institute of Business Forecasting website at http://www.ibf.org/ and determine the organization's goals and its current types of activities. Provide some examples.

2. Search on the term *business forecast software*. Find three software websites and compare and contrast the features of each software package. Write a report about your findings.

3. Go to the Voluntary Interindustry Commerce Standards (VICS) website at http://www.vics.org. What is the purpose of the organization and how is it involved in collaborative planning, forecasting and replenishment?

INFOTRAC QUESTIONS

Access http://www.infotrac-thomsonlearning.com to answer the following questions:

1. Use InfoTrac to search for the terms *forecasting* and *supply chain*. Write a term paper on the ways forecasting has changed because companies are taking a supply chain management approach. Include a bibliography.

2. Use InfoTrac to search for the terms *CPFR* and *software*. Write a paper on ways CPFR software improves demand management and provide company examples. Include a bibliography.

REFERENCES

Bowersox, Donald J., David J. Closs, and M.Bixby Cooper (2002), *Supply Chain Logistics Management*, McGraw-Hill, Boston, MA.

Stitt, Brad, "Demand Planning: Pushing the Rest of the Company to Drive Results," *The Journal of Business Forecasting*, V. 23, No. 2, Summer 2004, pp. 2–11.

Vollmann, Thomas E., William L. Berry, D. Clay Whybark, and F. Robert Jacobs (2005), *Manufacturing Planning and Control for Supply Chain Management*, 5th ed., McGraw-Hill Irwin, Boston, MA.

Wisner, Joel D., G. Keong Leong, and Keah-Choon Tan (2005), *Principles of Supply Chain Management: A Balanced Approach*, Thomson South-Western, Mason, OH.

ENDNOTES

1. Miller, Steven and Krista M. Liem, "Collaborative Forecasting: Goodyear Tire and Rubber Company's Journey," *The Journal of Business Forecasting Methods and Systems*, V. 23, No. 3, Fall 2004, pp. 23–27.

2. Sadarangani, Nareshand and John A. Gallucci, "Using Demand Drivers for a Collaborative Forecasting Process," *The Journal of Business Forecasting Methods and Systems*, V. 23, No. 2, Summer 2004, pp. 12–15.

3. "Nokia Feels the Squeeze from Shortage," *Off the Record Research*, November 13, 2003.

4. Lambert, Douglas M., "The Essential Supply Chain Management Processes," *Supply Chain Management Review*, September 2004, p. 21.

5. Vollmann, Thomas E., William L. Berry, D. Clay Whybark, and F. Robert Jacobs, *Manufacturing Planning and Control for Supply Chain Management*, Boston: McGraw-Hill Irwin, 2005.

6. Mentzer, John T. and Mark A. Moon, "Understanding Demand," *Supply Chain Management Review*, V. 8, No. 4, May/June 2004, pp. 38–45.

7. Kiely, Daniel A., "Synchronizing Supply Chain Operations with Consumer Demand Using Customer Data," *The Journal of Business Forecasting*, V. 17, No. 4, Winter 1998/1999, p. 3.

8. Goldstein, Michael, "R.I.P PDA?" *Successful Meetings*, V. 53, No. 9, August 2004, p. 24.

9. See http://www.nrdc.org/water/drinking/bw/chap2.asp for more information on the growth of the bottled water industry.

10. Barash, M., and D. Mitchell, "Account-Based Forecasting at Nabisco Biscuit Company," *Journal of Business Forecasting*, V. 17, No. 9, Summer 1998, pp. 3–6.

11. "Growth of Global PC Market Forecast to Ease," *The Boston Globe*, December 9, 2004. Available online at http://www.boston.com.

12. Weigel, Peter J. and Reuven R. Levary, "Using Simulation to Estimate the Uncertainty in Union Electric Company's Residential Customer Forecast," *International Journal of Computer Applications in Technology*, V. 12, No. 2/3/4/5, 1999, pp. 225–232.

13. The full references are: Mun, Jonathan, *Modeling Risk: Applying Monte Carlo Simulation, Real Options Analysis, Forecasting, and Optimization Techniques*, New York, NY: John Wiley & Sons, 2006; and Nersesian, Roy L., *Corporate Planning, Human Behavior and Computer Simulation*, Westport, CT: Quorum Books, 1990.

14. VICS, *CPFR: An Overview*, p. 5. Available at http://www.cpfr.org.

15. Crum, Colleen and George E. Palmatier, "Demand Collaboration: What's Holding Us Back?" *Supply Chain Management Review,* January/February 2004, pp. 54–61.

16. Voluntary Interindustry Commerce Standards, *CPFR, An Overview,* May 2004. Available online at http://www.vics.org.

17. O'Marah, Kevin, "Best Practices for Collaborative Forecasting," *ARM Research Report,* March 2002.

18. Bowman, Robert J., "Best Practices Minimize the 'Luck Factor' in SC Planning," *Global Logistics & Supply Chain Strategies,* January 2004. Available at http://www.glscs.com.

19. See note 15 above.

Chapter 6:

INVENTORY MANAGEMENT

Out of stock. Whether referring to semiconductor chips or potato chips, these are dreaded words for those in charge of far-flung and increasingly complex chains.[1]

Supply costs are the second largest expense for hospitals after personnel costs. Managing materials, supplies, and associated costs consumes 15 to 30 percent of net patient revenues.[2]

Learning Objectives

After completing this chapter, you should be able to:

- Appreciate the value and the costs of inventory, for the firm and its supply chains.
- Describe the various types of inventory.
- Understand the role of inventory in the order fulfillment process.
- Describe the methods used for managing and controlling dependent and independent demand inventories.
- Understand the role of information systems in managing inventory.
- Describe the role and importance of inventory management along the supply chain.

Chapter Outline

Introduction

The Types of Inventory

The Functions of Inventory

Inventory Costs, Risks, and Value

Independent Demand Inventory Management

Dependent Demand Inventory Management

Collaborative Inventory Management along the Supply Chain

Measuring Inventory Management Performance

Process Management in Action

The Roller Lifter Supply Chain

Everywhere we look, it appears that our established American industrial firms are under attack from more nimble and responsive competition. It comes equally from new small domestic start-up firms and from foreign companies entering our domestic markets. These firms can challenge the existing model in several areas of apparent weakness. They are less prone to follow our time-honored business tradition. They can be faster and, because they are relatively new, can operate with less structure and bureaucracy. Our well-established system has too many separate layers and transactions. The flow of goods, material, and information is hampered by the fact that the atmosphere between the parties is more adversarial than it needs to be.

The supply group at Chrysler selected one of the simplest parts that went into a car, and then used it as an example of how complicated supply chains really are. The group selected a mundane little part called a roller lifter, a two-inch-long machined metal component used in the valve train of an engine. If the roller lifter fails, the intake or exhaust valve fails to open or close and the engine misses or loses power. In addition, its failure pushes the emissions system out of legal compliance. In other words, this is a critical and vital part. The device was purchased from Eaton Corp., which sold it to Chrysler for about $2 each.

This one simple part is actually made up of 12 subcomponents, including springs, seals, washers, and roller bearings. As the end user, Chrysler had paid no real attention to where these subcomponents came from because it was assumed that Eaton either made most of them or closely controlled them. Actually, Eaton mainly did the final machining and assembly of the part.

When investigating the origin of all 12 subcomponents, it turned out that this single part from one supplier actually was a complicated web of parts that came from 33 individual companies. That massive figure was rolled into a thing that cost less than $2. The supply chain includes the raw material used in making steel, the drawing of wire to make springs, and the ball bearings. Just for fun, every single item was traced, including the raw materials used in making this relatively simple part.

We started with raw materials that naturally come from the earth. Our first raw material supplier for the roller lifter, the American Colloid Company, is one of the world's leading suppliers of bentonite clay. That's a commodity that appears in thousands of products, including auto parts, building materials, diapers, and even kitty litter. Imagine the feeling in Detroit that we were in some small way competing with kitty litter manufacturers for a commodity.

After the American Colloid people scoop up the bentonite that will eventually form part of the roller lifter, they ship it to their plant in central Michigan for processing. When they've finished, the refined clay is sent to a foundry about 100 miles away. The foundry uses lots of other raw materials in a process to anneal, blast, grind, machine, and heat-treat the housing of the roller lifter and ship it to Eaton to be assembled and sent to Chrysler.

But the chain isn't finished. Lots of other subcomponents are involved. Plungers come from two sources, one in Ohio and one in Australia. Add a retainer from Connecticut, a bearing from Tennessee, and cast sockets from Missouri, along with clips from Japan, springs from Ohio, and leak test fluid from Illinois. It all ends up in an Eaton plant near Detroit for final assembly.

By this point, you might be amazed by the complicated chain of events. So were we. The whole process involved no fewer than 33 companies. The seemingly simple act of building one small part for one engine turned out to be incredibly complex. Now multiply this for every part in a car (there are more than 5,000 parts in a finished car), and you can see why the auto industry touches so many companies and employees around the country. It is truly a massive extended enterprise that employs more people than any other manufacturing industry.

The fact so amazed our staff that we started to call all the suppliers involved along the chain to see if they knew what was happening to their product. We called one of our distant suppliers who made one component of the roller lifter. When he found out that we were calling from Chrysler, he said, "Gosh, my wife loves her Grand Cherokee!" So we questioned whether he knew if his part had a critical role in his wife's safety. We told him the thing he made went to a guy who did something else with it and then sent it to someone else, who did another thing with it, and then sent it to one of our engine plants—and if that part didn't work, his wife's engine would die.

He said, "Nope. I never know where the stuff goes after I ship it." That comment is indicative of what happens all the time. Smaller companies almost never know that their product is ultimately going to Chrysler or any other large manufacturer. That's because the different tiers in the supply chain typically don't communicate with each other through any medium other than purchase orders.

The management of these companies rarely ever has a clue about where they fit into the bigger picture. They run their companies from a perspective that they are isolated—and if they do know their place in the chain, they often assume they have no real impact on it. More often than not, the commercial system forces companies to remain distant and separate themselves from each other. The companies make a product and ship it to someone else. The communication is limited and seldom involves anything more than shipping or pricing information. When management does get involved, it often turns negative because it usually means that problems exist. This is a consistent trait of adversarial management culture: The managers rarely get involved unless there is a problem.

This illustrates the problems that exist in the way we currently manage the enterprise of business. It shows how seemingly unrelated companies travel through time without really knowing how they affect other companies. This remoteness is complicated by the fact that companies are all independent from each other in purpose, mission, management, planning, and communication.

Because we value our independence so dearly in this country, our businesses operate with a fierce sense of separation and single-mindedness. That is one reason acquisitions are favored over alliances. We seem to have a natural inclination to run our own show and look like we are in control of our own destiny. As the roller lifter story shows, the truth is that companies are much more interrelated than their management might want to believe or might even know.

Source: Stallkamp, T., "Ending Adversarial Commerce," *Supply Chain Management Review*, V. 9, No. 7, 2005, pp. 46–52. Used with permission.

Introduction

As described in the opening Process Management in Action feature concerning a cheap, small auto part at Chrysler, inventory management can be an extremely complex issue for most companies, as well as their many direct and indirect supply chain trading partners. In many cases, businesses are not even aware of the impact their products and associated delivery characteristics have on their customers' products and inventory levels. Since inventory costs can account for a large portion of a firm's total costs, effectively managing inventories is often cited as a primary requirement for maintaining competitiveness, reducing costs, and restoring or improving profitability. Thus, inventory management plays an extremely important role in the overall success of the supply chain.

Every company that carries inventories has the potential for inventory-related problems. Too little inventory can lead to stockouts, idle workers and facilities, disgruntled customers, and lost sales. Too much inventory leads to storage problems, shrinkage losses, inventory write-downs, and higher inventory carrying costs. Battles over the "right" levels of inventory to carry occur on a daily basis in organizations. Production personnel want plenty of raw materials to keep machines running; supply management personnel want to purchase large quantities of material to obtain quantity discounts; and sales personnel want plenty of finished goods inventory to close the sale. Conversely, finance managers, inventory managers, and other company executives see the impact of all this inventory on the firm's costs and put pressure on personnel to continuously reduce inventory costs. What tends to happen is that firms go through periods of gradual inventory growth followed by periods of sudden and deliberate inventory reductions as managers try to reengineer the firm, reduce costs, and improve profits. These large swings in inventory levels contribute to the bullwhip effect and can also add considerable costs to an organization's bottom line.

Consequently, firms must develop effective internal and external inventory control procedures. **Internal inventory control** includes methods used to manage inventories from the time parts and materials reach the facility until the time that finished goods are packaged and ready for delivery to customers. This chapter begins with a discussion of basic inventory terms, followed by a detailed presentation of internal inventory control topics, including both independent demand and dependent demand inventory management discussions. **External inventory control** refers to the collaborative inventory management activities occurring between the focal firm and its supply chain trading partners, as purchased parts and materials make their way to the firm and as finished products are delivered to customers. These topics are covered towards the end of the chapter. Over time, companies and their supply chains must seek to continuously improve competitiveness through improvements in these inventory management activities. It then becomes necessary to design inventory management performance measures, and these are discussed as the final topic of the chapter.

It is important to understand the impact inventories have on all firms within a supply chain. In Part 1 of this book, inventories were discussed as one of the enablers of customer relationship management. In Part 2, the current segment, we are spending a large amount of time and space discussing how inventories play a role in forecasting, layout design, location analysis, and information system design. In Part 3, inventories will be discussed as an important consideration when designing logistics systems and lean manufacturing systems, and when purchasing items from suppliers. And finally, in Part 4, inventories again play a large role in discussions of quality management, process analysis, and returns management. Inventory thus cuts across functional and organizational boundaries, and is a global concern that all companies and their trading partners must eventually come to appreciate and control.

The Types of Inventory

Inventories are typically classified into four types—raw materials; work-in-process; finished goods; and maintenance, repair, and operating supplies. Each type is defined as follows:

1. **Raw materials**: Raw materials consist of purchased assemblies, parts, and materials that are delivered by suppliers and used in the manufacture of finished products or services. Raw materials might include things like paint, auto engines, nuts and bolts, wood, hotel bathroom soaps, and fast-food hamburger buns—at an auto manufacturer, a construction company, a hotel, or a fast-food restaurant, respectively. These can be delivered to and stored in off-site warehouses, in stockrooms located within the facility, directly at the point of use, or some combination of all three.

2. **Work-in-process (WIP)**: WIP inventories are items that are in some intermediate processing stage, on their way to becoming finished products. Once raw materials have been delivered and put into the production process, they become WIP inventories. These include items on an automobile assembly line, partially completed houses, hamburgers on the grill, and raw oil being refined into its various product forms. In a manufacturing facility, WIP inventories can be stored on pallets close to processing centers, or possibly on automated overhead racks that move throughout the facility.

3. **Finished goods**: Finished goods are exactly what the name implies—completed products ready for delivery to business customers or consumers. When WIP inventories are completed, they become finished goods and can be stored in a designated area within the facility, on a warming tray, or in one of several geographically dispersed distribution centers.

4. **Maintenance, repair, and operating (MRO) supplies**: MRO inventories are those items that are consumed by the business or used to support manufacturing and service processes. Examples of MRO inventories include machine tools and greases, cleaning supplies, office supplies, and employee bathroom and lunchroom supplies. MRO items do not become part of finished goods; rather, they are purchased by the firm and consumed by the firm.

Each of the inventory types described creates costs for the firm, but can also add significant value if managed effectively. All four types of inventory play an important role in the production of high-quality, low-cost products; smoothly running equipment; competitive supply chains; and satisfied employees and consumers. The objective of inventory management should be to find an optimal quantity for each inventory item, considering its cost, availability, importance to the firm, the inventory speed or flexibility desired, and inventory function. The various functions of inventory follow.

The Functions of Inventory

In some respects, inventory is considered a *necessary evil* in organizations— necessary in that without it, firms cannot make, sell, and deliver products and services; evil in that inventories cost the firm and its supply chain partners money. Inventories ensure high levels of customer service and keep internal processes operating, but managers must decide what level of inventory is enough and which functions of inventory are required. Inventories serve many necessary functions within an organization, which are listed in Table 6.1.

Anticipation inventories are held with the intent of fulfilling demand during periods of expected high demand, such as holidays like Christmas or Valentine's Day, or the period following an advertising campaign. Ideally, the firm accurately forecasts demand for these periods, purchases or produces the anticipated quantities of stock, and then uses or sells all of it.

Table 6.1	The Functions of Inventory
Anticipation Inventory	Inventories that are accumulated by organizations in anticipation of some <u>known future event</u>, such as the Christmas holiday or an advertising campaign.
Cycle Inventory	Inventories that result from the purchase or production of batches or "lots" of product. Batch sizes are meant to satisfy demand for a specific time period or cycle.
Hedge Inventory	Inventories that are accumulated to protect the firm from some <u>potential future event</u>, such as a sudden surge in purchase prices, a labor strike, or foreign government upheaval.
Safety Stock	Inventories that are held to protect against unexpected demand and lead time increases, which could cause the firm to stock out.
Transportation Inventory	Inbound and outbound inventories that are owned by the firm, but have not yet reached their destination.

Cycle inventories are created when the firm purchases or produces a quantity or lot size large enough to last until the next purchase or production period. By considering the purchase order cost or the production equipment setup cost and the inventory carrying cost, the firm can determine the optimal purchase or production lot size (as with the EOQ determination, which will be discussed shortly).

Hedge inventories are used when the firm desires to hold inventory as a protection from some potential future event such as a sudden upsurge in purchase prices or an unforeseen shortage of some commodity or part. For countries like the United States that depend on oil imports from countries in the Middle East, there have occasionally been events that have caused gasoline shortages or sudden spikes in prices. As a hedge against these potential problems, some firms have opted to stockpile supplies of gasoline. The U.S. government continues to stockpile oil in the Strategic Petroleum Reserve for the same reason.[3]

Safety stocks are commonly held by firms as a "backup" to satisfy demand when purchase or production quantities are late in arriving, when machinery breaks down, or when demand is higher than anticipated. Firms can opt to hold safety stocks of raw materials, WIP, or finished goods. Inventory management strategies often include plans for reducing safety stocks as a way to reduce overall inventory carrying costs.

Transportation inventories are those inventories owned by the firm and in transit either inbound to the firm or outbound to the firm's customers. If a firm purchases parts from a supplier, for example, and chooses to use its own vehicle to transport the shipment to the firm, then the parts become transportation inventory and create inventory carrying costs while in transit. These costs become considerable for high cost items traveling a long distance.

As shown in Figure 6.1, the total adjusted business inventories-to-sales ratio in the United States has been falling steadily for the period 1996 to 2005. While this could indicate better inventory management practices, it could also indicate that firms are reducing inventory levels to keep costs contained, while allowing stockout situations to increase. The figure might also be somewhat misleading in that the U.S. Census Bureau stated that sales for December 2005 were up 7 percent from the previous year, while inventories were up 4.3 percent for the same period. Thus, while the inventory-to-sales ratio may indeed be falling, many companies are finding that inventories are still up

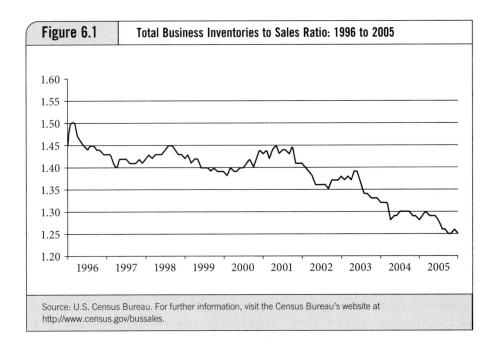

Figure 6.1 | **Total Business Inventories to Sales Ratio: 1996 to 2005**

Source: U.S. Census Bureau. For further information, visit the Census Bureau's website at http://www.census.gov/bussales.

from the previous year, and that inventory problems are increasing. For example, Mr. Scott Phillips, director of purchasing at Pennsylvania-based specialty gas distributor Airgas Products, recently noticed a steady increase in the firm's inventories. He pointed to increased sales, recent acquisitions, product-line expansions, and logistics issues as the reasons. In fact, in a recent survey of 497 U.S. businesses, 61 percent indicated they were holding more inventory currently than in the past.[4] More discussion of these topics is provided in the following section.

Inventory Costs, Risks, and Value

Inventory costs are considerable for many organizations, particularly for large manufacturing firms such as Illinois-based Deere & Company and large retail firms such as Wal-Mart. Reducing total inventory costs has thus become a corporate-wide strategic imperative at many businesses, since as inventory costs are reduced, profits are increased on a dollar-for-dollar basis (not counting any costs incurred for the resources used to reduce inventory levels). This impact on profits can be enormous for firms with large inventories. At Deere & Company, the Commercial and Consumer Equipment (C&CE) Division undertook an inventory and customer service optimization strategy starting in 2001. Between 2001 and 2003, the C&CE Division reduced and avoided inventories totaling $890 million, which in turn increased shareholder value added by $107 million per year (shareholder value added is net operating profit after tax minus the cost of capital from the issuance of debt and equity).[5] Unfortunately though, as inventory levels and costs are reduced, the risk of stockouts increases due to the uncertainties of customer demand and supplier deliveries. In a well-managed supply chain, however, the stockout risk can be mitigated through use of shared forecast and sales information between customer, seller, and supplier, as described in Chapter 5. The various costs of inventory are presented and discussed next.

Order Costs

Order costs are the administrative costs associated with purchasing items. These include the labor and paperwork costs to select a supplier, write a purchase order, process it through the company, transmit it to the supplier, receive the order, inspect it, and then process the invoice. Production **setup costs** can also be thought of as a type of internal order cost; these include writing the production order, preparing equipment for a production run, and setting up the labor for the processing. An average order cost or setup cost might be in the neighborhood of $100 to $200, although using the Internet for e-purchasing, corporate procurement cards (or p-cards as they are often referred to), and automated purchasing practices that use bar code scanners and interconnected information systems can reduce order costs considerably. A 2003 Purchasing Card Benchmarking Study found the average order cost when using the p-card was $20 compared to an average traditional purchase order cost of $80. Additionally, the study found that p-cards contribute to a 74 percent reduction in purchase order lead times.[6]

Inventory Carrying Costs

Inventory carrying costs, also called **inventory holding costs**, are the costs incurred when firms must store inventories. These include storage costs, which are building rent and depreciation costs; maintenance and energy costs; warehouse personnel costs; handling and equipment depreciation costs; and shrinkage costs. These costs can be quite large for firms with a network of company-owned warehouses. Additionally, inventory carrying costs include **lost opportunity costs** or **capital costs**, which are the monies the firm gives up by having capital tied up in inventory and the land, buildings, and equipment used for storage purposes. If the firm normally makes a 20 percent return on its invested capital, then this would be included in inventory carrying costs. Finally, inventory carrying costs are incurred while the firm is transporting purchased items inbound to its storage, manufacturing, or retail facility, or transporting finished goods outbound to its distribution centers or to fill customer orders. Shrinkage, or cargo theft, has become quite a problem in the U.S. retail industry during transportation between warehouses and retail locations. The FBI and industry executives stated it amounted to more than $10 billion in 2004 for retailers, which adversely impacts carrying costs.[7] Also, while goods are in transit, they are in essence being stored in trucks (or planes, ships, or trains). In-transit time increases the time that capital is tied up in inventory, and therefore impacts inventory carrying costs. This topic is covered in Chapter 10.

Stockout Costs

When the internal or external demand for materials or products cannot be met, a **stockout cost** is encountered. When customers cannot buy an item, a lost sale, lost goodwill or damage to the firm's reputation, lost future sales, and possibly a cost to process a backorder results. Backordering incurs administrative costs, expediting costs, and shipping costs. In a supply chain setting, stockout costs can be very expensive for both the buyer and the seller, particularly if the seller is a sole supplier of a strategic product to a highly valued buyer. In some cases, a sizeable late delivery penalty might be charged to the supplying company. Generally, stockout costs can be difficult to estimate, since damage to a firm's reputation and lost future sales cannot easily be determined.

Inventory managers have long wrestled with quantifying the cost of a stockout, since the cost is a function of a customer's initial and future response to the stockout.

Customers may substitute the item with a similar one, leave and return later, demand that the item be backordered and delivered later, or may leave and purchase the item elsewhere. Research performed by Drs. Zinn and Liu to determine consumers' actual responses to retail stockouts found that consumers substituted the item 62 percent of the time, backordered the purchase 15 percent of the time, and simply left the store 23 percent of the time.[8] If firms can generate this type of customer information, then stockout cost can more accurately be estimated and compared to the cost of carrying safety stock. Otherwise, managers are left to use trial-and-error methods when setting safety stock levels. The Process Management in Action feature points out how the fairly recent hurricanes Katrina and Rita in the greater U.S. Gulf Coast region elevated the awareness of the need for safety stocks and inventory contingency planning.

Process Management in Action   *The True Impact of Hurricanes*

How much inventory is enough? That's a question many are asking (once again) in the wake of Katrina and Rita.

There was a time when more than enough inventory was considered an asset. Safety stock ruled. Then less became better. Materials handling advancements made companies more efficient. Meanwhile, automatic data capture and software tracked inventory, eliminating large quantities of it.

But that doesn't mean there's less inventory to handle today. Quite the opposite. According to economist, Dr. James Haughey, inventory volume has risen 21 percent since 1999. However, the inventory-to-sales ratio has dropped significantly. Ten years ago it was 1.47, and 2005 will finish at about 1.3.

So while there's much more inventory in the supply chain, we are operating at quite lean levels given the balance of supply and demand and our abilities to manage it. Then Katrina and Rita created a great imbalance.

Early in 2005, Steve Sensing of third-party logistics provider Ryder had this to say: "The way we break it down is there needs to be two to six weeks of inventory across the entire supply chain. The higher range is for product being made in Asia, and the lower range is for product from the U.S. and Mexico." That's a good start, but it only tells part of the story going forward.

Dr. James Tompkins of Tompkins Associates made a great observation: "Contingency planning is no longer just contingency planning. Instead, contingency planning is part of your strategy." And that has a great ring of truth. Based on what happened with Katrina and Rita, it seems only natural to elevate contingency planning. Being prepared can go a long way toward coping with such events.

The last time contingency planning was elevated to this level was immediately following 9–11, when people felt most vulnerable. Then we settled back into more traditional concerns. It's time to break out of that, and move contingency planning into your supply chain strategy. And from that, appropriate inventory levels will most likely become apparent. That's the true impact of Katrina and Rita.

Source: Forger, G., "The True Impact of Katrina and Rita," *Modern Materials Handling*, V. 60, No. 10, 2005, p. 5. Used with permission.

Purchase Costs

Purchase cost is the actual cost of the items bought from suppliers. In many inventory examples, the purchase cost per unit is considered constant regardless of the inventory management policies used; however, when suppliers offer a purchase quantity discount, then the purchase cost becomes variable and is a function of the order quantity. The impact of quantity discounts on inventory policies is discussed later in the chapter. Many firms also consider other costs in evaluating the total purchase cost, including transportation cost, tariffs and duties, return of parts cost, repair cost, late delivery costs, and follow-up costs. This is sometimes referred to as **total landed cost**.

Inventory Risk and Value

As we have somewhat alluded to already, holding too little inventory increases the risk of a stockout and its associated costs. To reduce this risk, the firm can employ more accurate forecasting techniques and use collaborative planning and forecasting techniques with customers to reduce demand uncertainty and the corresponding need to carry safety stock. Ultimately, managers must compare the cost of carrying safety stock to the cost of stocking out.

Alternately, increasing inventories *by the right amount* means that more customers will be served in a timely fashion, creating happy end customers, repeat sales, and potentially more profits in general for all supply chain trading partners. This is the value of inventory, and cannot be taken lightly. Too often managers become fixated on reducing inventory costs as part of a firm-wide cost reduction effort, only to find that stockouts have increased and customers have started complaining or are just leaving. Many recent studies show that average stockout rates for retailers are about 8 percent, and as high as 17 percent for promotional items.[9] Firms that can increase performance by employing better forecasts, better collaboration with supply chain trading partners, and more responsive delivery systems can improve the value of their inventories without necessarily increasing safety stock or overall inventory levels.

Aside from demand uncertainties that increase the risk of a stockout, the uncertainties in delivery timing, delivery quantities, and product quality from suppliers can increase the risk of raw material stockouts in the firm's internal operations. These potential stockouts can be mitigated by carrying more raw material safety stock (which is expensive), or by finding and building relationships with more reliable suppliers. Alternately, managers can help to develop or improve the capabilities of existing suppliers and their distribution systems. Recently, **radio frequency identification** (RFID) devices have been used to monitor the progress of orders through warehouses, transportation networks, and even on retail shelves to improve order timing and inventory levels. RFID tags have become inexpensive and can even be placed on single units, so that RFID signals can be picked up and transmitted to computer systems to monitor real-time location information. As the inventory levels decline, decisions can be made to order or move items to avoid stockouts. The e-Commerce Perspective feature profiles a futuristic grocery store in Germany where RFID, along with a number of other technologies, is being used to track inventories and reduce stockouts.

In a supply chain, one potential costly problem associated with forecasting and inventory levels is the **bullwhip effect**. While this term has been mentioned already several times in this text, it is nevertheless important to understand the relationship between the bullwhip effect and inventories. Even though end-item demand may be relatively stable, forecasts of demand combined with additions of safety stock for the end-item

e-Commerce Perspective

The Supermarket of the Future—Here Today

At the Metro Future Store in Rheinberg, Germany, technology partners are testing the use of RFID, wireless networks, Personal Shopping Assistants, and other advanced electronics in a real, working store environment to set standards for the supermarket of the future. Enter the Metro Future Store, and the future begins now. On its list of surprises: a Personal Shopping Assistant (PSA) that displays your shopping list and shows you exactly where each product can be found; a produce scale that "sees" what product you are weighing; electronic digital price "tags" on store shelves that can be changed every hour, if needed; video display screens throughout the store showing today's specials, which can be changed by the minute; a wine aisle in which a computer matches the perfect wine selection for tonight's dinner—and then guides you to the bottle's location via a beamed display on the floor. And there's no need to empty the cart's contents onto a conveyor at checkout—just hand the PSA to the cashier and pay.

Meanwhile, RFID tags are tracking product, from distribution center to back room to store shelf to checkout. No, this is not your ordinary supermarket. Electronic shelf labels display current prices of goods on the shelf. Unchanging information, such as the product name, is printed on a paper label affixed beneath the LCD display. From a computer in the back room or store headquarters, prices can be changed within seconds. In fact, all 40,000 SKUs in the Future Store can be changed in less than one hour. Shoppers collect their Personal Shopping Assistant as they enter the store. The computer is activated by a store employee and personalized with the swipe of the customer's loyalty card. The PSA can display the customer's shopping list, downloaded from home before leaving for the store, and can direct the customer to the aisle and location where each product will be found. Electronic display screens throughout the store offer static promotions or video animation on store specials, unadvertised sales, or just product promotion. Displays are changed via the store's wireless data network.

Although RFID is used primarily in the supply chain, it also provides customer benefits in the store. While many of the store's vendors are now attaching RFID tags to pallet loads of products, the store itself is tagging some primary packages: Procter & Gamble's Pantene® Pro-V® line of hair care products, Kraft's Philadelphia® cream cheese, and Gillette®'s Mach 3 razors and blades. With RFID, the movement of products through the supply chain can be identified, right to the store shelf and on through checkout, if the primary package is tagged. Stockouts can be prevented, since a smart shelf can notify the backstore of the need for replenishment. According to Metro Distribution Logistics (MDL), goods can be reordered according to demand, and the number of wrong deliveries is considerably reduced.

Before delivery to the Future Store, goods are sorted by case load onto pallets in a central warehouse by MDL. The cases and the pallet are each given a smart chip that contains the bar codes of the products in each case and the number of the pallet. Warehouse employees read this data into an electronic RFID merchandise-management system, which is connected to the Future Store. As the store requires replenishment, the loaded pallets are moved to the exit zone of the central warehouse, where an RFID transceiver, or gate, records the identification of the products. At this point, the inventory management system changes the products' status from "in storage" to "in transit."

When goods are received at the Future Store, employees transport the pallets from the truck through yet another RFID gate at the store's back entrance. The reader can identify as many as 35 tags per second. Now, the products' status becomes "received in-store." Most product is then stored temporarily in the back room. Each storage location is equipped with a smart chip.

Continued

As each case is loaded onto a shelf, the case chip and shelf chip are read via a handheld reader and matched. Employees now know exactly where every product is stored.

As goods are moved to the sales floor, the cases move through another RFID gate, where the chips are read and the products' status is now changed to "on shelf." When the employee has emptied the case onto the shelf, the smart chip is removed and deactivated before the empty case is moved to the back room.

While RFID is the most prominent technology being tested at the Future Store, it is not the only one. State-of-the-art information media and electronic personal devices are providing customers with a customized shopping experience. The Future Store uses a number of technologies for communication with the customer. The information systems make shopping easier, faster, more convenient, and decidedly more interesting. Among those features, customers can take advantage of a Personal Shopping Assistant, or PSA; information terminals; intelligent scales; electronic shelf labels; smart shelves; electronic advertising displays; and expedited checkouts.

The products that are RFID-tagged, such as the Gillette Mach 3, sit on smart shelves equipped with RFID readers. The shelf tracks product movement and can alert the back room when stock is running low, before a stockout occurs. Two deactivation terminals are placed at the store's front doors so that customers can render the RFID tags lifeless before going home with their purchases.

The shopper can self-scan articles as he or she puts them into the cart, thus receiving additional product and price information. The PSA includes a built-in EAN bar code scanner. Items scanned are then displayed on the PSA's screen, along with the price. Then, at the checkout, the customer simply hands the PSA to the clerk, who prints out a price list and tally. There is no need to empty the cart's contents onto the conveyor for scanning.

At checkout, shoppers have three options. First, customers without a PSA can do a conventional checkout by emptying the contents of the cart onto a conveyor, with the cashier scanning each item. Or, customers can scan items into a PSA and then just hand the PSA to the cashier. Products then go directly from the cart to bags or boxes. Or, shoppers can do a self-checkout, scanning each item and placing it directly into an open plastic bag, which is sitting on a scale. If the weight of the item added to the bag does not match what was scanned, a store attendant is notified that there is a problem. Payment in all options is the same: cash or debit/credit card.

Source: Falkman, M., "Future Store Shows Off Tomorrow's Technology," *Packaging Digest*, V. 42, No. 7, 2005, pp. 40–43. Used with permission.

manufacturer tend to cause the corresponding supplier forecasts to become larger. As suppliers also add safety stock to their resulting forecasts of the manufacturer's demand, then the forecasts of second- and third-tier suppliers become larger still. This pervasive safety stock amplification problem can add significant inventory costs to the supply chain, resulting in more expensive end items for consumers. Additionally, inventory buildups resulting from the bullwhip effect among supply chain trading partners are usually followed by fewer and smaller orders, leaving companies overstocked and facing markdowns to unload slow-moving products, and also forcing production slowdowns to reduce inventories. Ultimately, involving the firm's key customers and suppliers in forecasting, purchasing, and production decisions along with sharing information regarding forecasts and safety stock levels can reduce the bullwhip effect. (Some additional means to reduce the bullwhip effect can be found in Chapter 10.)

Independent Demand Inventory Management

Independent demand refers to the firm's external demand for its finished products. Firms typically use quantitative techniques to forecast this demand, and then translate these forecasts into production plans, human resource plans (together these are also called **aggregate plans**), and eventually purchase plans. If the firm is a retailer, then the independent demand forecasts translate directly into purchase plans. When making purchase plans, the firm must decide *when to order* and *how much to order,* and these and other related inventory management topics are covered in the following sections. If the firm is a manufacturer, then the independent demand forecasts are translated internally, into all of the parts, components, and materials that comprise the finished item. These items are referred to as **dependent demand** items, because their quantities are completely dependent on the quantities of the finished goods required. For example, if a bicycle manufacturer determines its upcoming annual demand forecast for bicycles is 10,000 (independent demand) and decides to make that amount, then this means it must manufacture 20,000 bicycle rims and purchase 10,000 bicycle seats (dependent demand items). Managing this transformation process and the many dependent demand items are discussed in the dependent demand inventory management segment later in this chapter.

Deciding How Much and When to Order or Produce

Management's decision regarding *how many* units to order at one time is based on a knowledge of **total inventory costs** (the sum of inventory carrying costs, order costs, stockout costs, and purchase costs). The general idea is to find an order quantity that will minimize total annual inventory costs. The decision of *when* to order is based on knowledge of how long orders take to arrive (**order cycle time**) and how many units are likely to be demanded during the order cycle time period. One very basic model in use that provides information for these decisions is the economic order quantity model, which follows.

The Economic Order Quantity Model

The basic **economic order quantity** (EOQ) model determines the order quantity that will minimize the sum of the annual inventory holding cost and the annual order cost. The model is based on the following assumptions:

- Daily demand is constant.
- Each order arrives in a single delivery at the desired quantity and quality.
- The order cycle time is known and constant.
- Order costs are known and constant.
- Inventory carrying costs are known and constant.
- There are no purchase quantity discounts.

Given these assumptions, it is easy to see that no stockouts can occur and no backorders are needed, since the firm knows *exactly* when stock levels will be depleted, and knows with certainty that an order will be delivered *exactly* when it is expected. Also, since no purchase quantity discounts are allowed, the annual purchase cost will remain constant regardless of the ordering policy. Thus, the relevant total annual inventory cost reduces to the sum of the annual inventory carrying cost and the annual order cost. While these assumptions are obviously unrealistic, many firms still use the EOQ calculation when ordering from suppliers, due to its simplicity and ability to determine an order quantity that comes close to minimizing inventory costs. The practice of using a minimum total cost order quantity has been around for decades, and many automated inventory control systems include an EOQ calculation routine.

As shown in Figure 6.2, the economic order quantity, Q, arrives every Q/d days (where d is the constant and known daily demand), and is depleted at a constant rate equal to d. The order cycle time is constant and equal to L, thus the **reorder point**, ROP (the inventory on hand that will be necessary to satisfy demand during the order cycle time period), is simply equal to $d \times L$. No safety stock is required, and the new order will arrive exactly when the inventory on hand reaches zero. Finally, the average inventory level is Q/2, which is the average of the maximum inventory, Q, and the minimum inventory, zero. With this information, it is possible to calculate the annual order cost, O, which is:

$$O = \frac{D}{Q}S$$

where

> D = annual demand (units/year)
> Q = economic order quantity (units)
> S = cost of one order ($)

The annual inventory carrying cost, I, is:

$$I = \frac{Q}{2}iC$$

where

> Q = economic order quantity (units)
> i = carrying cost per unit plus lost opportunity cost,
>   expressed in terms of %/year
> C = purchase cost of one unit ($/unit)

The total annual inventory cost for the EOQ model is then O + I.

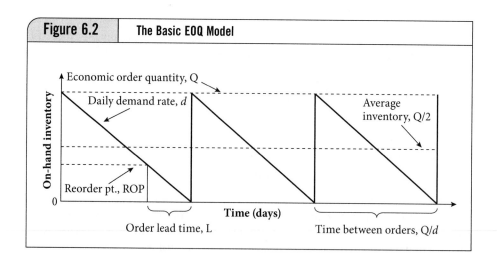

| **Figure 6.2** | **The Basic EOQ Model** |

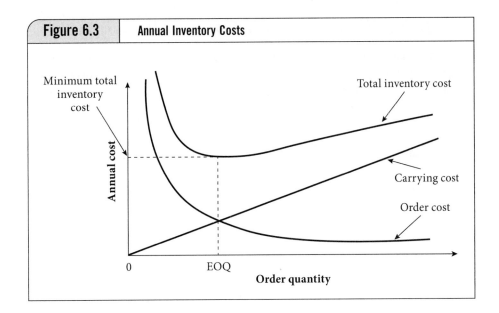

Figure 6.3 | **Annual Inventory Costs**

Figure 6.3 shows the relationship between the annual order cost, the annual inventory carrying cost, and the total annual inventory cost. The minimum total annual inventory cost and the EOQ are found at the point where the annual order cost equals the annual inventory carrying cost. Thus, the expression for the EOQ can be found as follows:

$$\frac{D}{Q}S = \frac{Q}{2}iC, \ \ \text{or}$$

$$Q^2 = \frac{2SD}{iC}, \ \ \text{or}$$

$$EOQ = \sqrt{\frac{2SD}{iC}}$$

Note also the flatness of the total inventory cost curve around the minimum point. This characteristic is what makes the EOQ model **robust**, allowing firms to use the EOQ even though demand, order lead time, order cost, and carrying cost may be only estimated and not necessarily constant. Example 6.1 solves the general inventory problem for a company such as a retailer, illustrating all of the relevant equations.

The Economic Production Quantity Model

If the firm manufactures end items rather than, or in addition to, buying them from suppliers, then the **economic production quantity model** is an appropriate model to use, and is illustrated in Figure 6.4. In this case, inventory gradually builds up over time at a rate equal to the daily production rate less the daily demand rate. This is illustrated in the figure by the upward-sloping line during the period *t*. When the full manufacturing lot size is produced, then inventory gradually declines at the daily demand rate, until a production order is placed and the production cycle once again commences.

In this model, the same assumptions from the EOQ model apply. Here, the annual setup cost (as opposed to the annual order cost in the EOQ model) is set equal to the annual inventory carrying cost to solve for the optimal production lot size or **economic production quantity** (EPQ). The average inventory level, as with the previous example, is

Example 6.1   Solving a Standard Inventory Problem for a Retailer

The Hayley-Girl Beret Company would like to determine optimal inventory policies for ordering berets from its beret supplier. Fred, the owner, assumes that beret demand is constant and equal to 5,000 berets per year. The order cost is $100, the carrying cost plus opportunity cost is 30 percent per year, the purchase cost is $40 per beret, and the order lead time is 7 days. The optimal order quantity in whole units is:

$$EOQ = \sqrt{\frac{2SD}{iC}} = \sqrt{\frac{2(100)(5,000)}{.3(40)}} = \sqrt{83,333.3} \approx 289 \text{ units}$$

The annual order cost is:

$$O = \frac{D}{Q}S = \frac{5,000}{289}(100) = \$1,730.10$$

The annual inventory carrying cost is:

$$I = \frac{Q}{2}iC = \frac{289}{2}.3(40) = \$1,734.00$$

Note here that O and I are not equal, as should be the case. This is because the EOQ has been rounded off to a whole number of units, as would be the case in a real situation. The total annual inventory costs are then:

$$T = O + I = \$1,730.10 + \$1,734.00 = \$3,464.10$$

This does not include the annual purchase cost of $200,000, which remains constant regardless of the order policy. The number of orders the Hayley-Girl Beret Company will make per year is:

$$n = \frac{D}{EOQ} = \frac{5,000}{289} \approx 17 \text{ orders}$$

The number of days between orders is:

$$t = \frac{\text{days per year}}{n} = \frac{365}{17} \approx 21 \text{ days}$$

The reorder point is:

$$ROP = dL = \frac{5,000}{365}(7) \approx 96 \text{ units}$$

So, the optimal order policy is for Fred to order 289 berets whenever the on-hand inventory reaches 96 berets. Seven days later the order will arrive, just as the stock of berets is running out. Fred should check on-hand inventory every 21 days.

the maximum level minus the minimum level (zero), divided by two. The maximum inventory level is:

$$\text{Max} = pt - dt$$

where

p = production rate per day
t = length of production run in days
d = usage rate per day

Also, the production quantity, Q, can then be expressed as:

$$Q = pt, \text{ or } t = Q/p$$

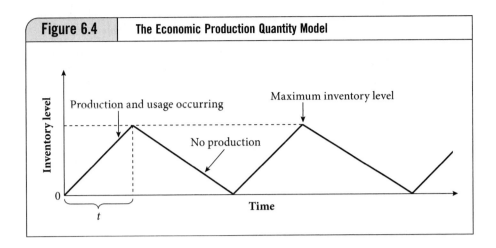

Figure 6.4 | **The Economic Production Quantity Model**

So, substituting for t, we can express the maximum inventory as:

$$\text{Max} = p\left(\frac{Q}{p}\right) - d\left(\frac{Q}{p}\right) = Q - Q\left(\frac{d}{p}\right) = Q\left(1 - \frac{d}{p}\right)$$

and the average inventory as:

$$\text{Average} = \frac{\text{Max}}{2} = \frac{Q}{2}\left(1 - \frac{d}{p}\right)$$

Now, the annual inventory carrying cost can be shown as:

$$I = \frac{Q}{2}\left(1 - \frac{d}{p}\right)iC$$

where

$i =$ carrying cost per unit plus lost opportunity cost, expressed in terms of %/year

$C =$ production cost of one unit ($/unit)

The annual setup cost is:

$$O = \frac{D}{Q}S$$

which is the same expression shown for the EOQ model, except that S now becomes the cost of one setup. Setting I = O allows us to derive the expression for the EPQ:

$$\frac{Q}{2}\left(1 - \frac{d}{p}\right)iC = \frac{D}{Q}S, \text{ or}$$

$$Q^2 = \frac{2DS}{\left(1 - \dfrac{d}{p}\right)iC}, \text{ and}$$

$$\text{EPQ} = \sqrt{\frac{2DS}{\left(1 - \dfrac{d}{p}\right)iC}}$$

Example 6.2 illustrates solutions to the general production problem for manufacturing firms.

> ## Example 6.2   Solving the General Production Problem for a Manufacturer
>
> The Blakeman Sports Ball Company desires to determine the optimal production lot size for basketballs. Its demand forecast for the upcoming quarter is 4,000 basketballs, or an average daily demand of approximately 44 basketballs (assuming the plant operates 365 days per year). The manufacturing process can produce about 500 balls per day. The setup cost is $50, the cost to make one basketball is $3, and the opportunity cost of holding inventory is 30 percent per year. Thus:
>
> $$EPQ = \sqrt{\frac{2DS}{\left(1 - \frac{d}{p}\right)iC}} = \sqrt{\frac{2(4,000)(50)}{\left(1 - \frac{44}{500}\right)(.3)(3)}} = \sqrt{\frac{400,000}{(.912)(.3)(3)}}$$
>
> $$= \sqrt{487,330} \approx 698 \text{ basketballs}$$
>
> The Blakeman Company should make basketballs in lot sizes of 698. It will take about 1.4 days to produce that many basketballs (or 698/500), and the maximum inventory level will be 698 − 44(1.4), or about 636 basketballs, assuming that each day it ships or sell 44 basketballs. The stock keeper would need to order another production run when the existing stock level reaches an amount equal to what would be sold during the setup time (if the setup time was two hours, for example, then the ROP would be about (44/8)2, or 11 basketballs, assuming the company was open for eight hours per day).

As mentioned earlier, knowing how much to order from suppliers or from the firm's own production process is certainly important from an inventory management perspective, since having too much inventory is costly from a carrying cost perspective, and having too little results in stockouts, lost sales, and perhaps even production plant shutdowns. It is also important from a supply chain management perspective, since being unable to supply a key customer's order can result in stockouts for them as well. And, ordering in an unpredictable or random fashion from key suppliers results in the bullwhip effect. The following segment discusses several extensions of the EOQ model.

Extensions of the EOQ Model

Allowing Purchase Price to Vary

One of the more common extensions of the EOQ occurs as the purchase price is allowed to vary, as when quantity discounts are offered. In the real world, this can occur if a supplier offers a price discount for larger than normal purchase quantities. In this case, the **quantity discount model** can be used, and is illustrated in Figure 6.5. The supplier may offer several discounted prices, depending on the purchase quantity, resulting in several total cost curves, as shown in Figure 6.5. Managers must consider each of the purchase prices, along with the impact on total annual costs, when determining the optimal purchase quantity. The relevant equation for the annual inventory cost then becomes:

$$T = O + I + P$$

where

$$O = \text{annual order cost}$$
$$I = \text{annual inventory carrying cost}$$
$$P = \text{annual purchase cost}$$
$$\text{(Note: P is calculated as the purchase price}$$
$$\text{per unit times the annual demand)}$$

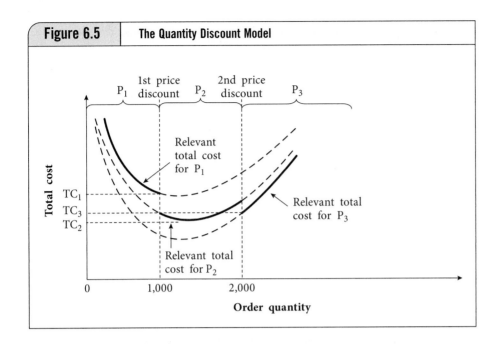

Figure 6.5 | **The Quantity Discount Model**

In the figure, two discounts are offered, resulting in three potential purchase prices—P_1 is the purchase price per unit if fewer than 1,000 units are purchased; P_2 is the purchase price corresponding to a purchase quantity between 1,000 and 1,999 units; and P_3 is the unit price paid when ordering 2,000 or more units at one time. Thus, three total cost curves are shown, with the solid lines corresponding to the actual total cost when various quantities are ordered. In this case, note that if fewer than 1,000 units are ordered, then the corresponding EOQ cannot be used, since that quantity is greater than 1,000. The minimum total inventory cost occurs when P_2 is used to calculate an EOQ that happens to fall within the corresponding discount range.

Example 6.3 illustrates the determination of the optimal order quantity using several purchase quantity discounts. Note that in this example, the optimal purchase quantity was not one of the calculated EOQs. The savings in annual purchase cost more than offset the additional carrying cost when using the first discounted price of $65 per unit and ordering 500 each time an order is placed. A final note regarding discounted pricing might be warranted. Firms may opt to purchase fewer items and forego a quantity discount to reduce obsolescence costs and theft, or because they don't want to use precious storage space. Also, companies today are moving toward greater use of "everyday low pricing" (which means no unit price discounts) to avoid inventory buildups and sell-offs, which also reduces the bullwhip effect.

Allowing Variations in Demand

If annual and hence daily demand is said to vary, then the possibility of a stockout exists, and inventory policies must include the use of safety stocks. Demand in this case is specified using a probability distribution. Managers can still calculate an EOQ using the average annual demand, and this quantity can still be ordered; however, the reorder point, or ROP, will have to include safety stock to guard against unexpected increases in demand during the order cycle time. Figure 6.6 presents the **probabilistic demand reorder point model**, where the variable demand situation is illustrated. This model still assumes the purchase lead time to be constant, however, the time between

Example 6.3   Finding the Optimal Order Quantity when Quantity Discounts Are Offered

The Ceejay Software Company purchasing agent needs to determine the lowest cost order quantity for a particular high-selling software product. The manufacturer is offering several pricing incentives to encourage bulk buying. The pricing alternatives are $75 per unit for 1–499 units purchased, $65 per unit for 500–999 units purchased, and $60 per unit for 1,000 or more units purchased. Ceejay's average order cost is $75 per order, the forecasted annual demand for the product is 850 units, and its inventory carrying cost rate is 35 percent per year. The purchasing agent first calculates the EOQ for each of the three purchase prices:

$$EOQ_1 = \sqrt{\frac{2(850)(75)}{0.35(75)}} \approx 70 \text{ units}$$

$$EOQ_2 = \sqrt{\frac{2(850)(75)}{0.35(65)}} \approx 75 \text{ units}$$

$$EOQ_3 = \sqrt{\frac{2(850)(75)}{0.35(60)}} \approx 78 \text{ units}$$

Since only EOQ_1 is a valid order quantity (both of the other quantities would result in the original $75 per unit pricing), the purchasing agent must use EOQ_1 to calculate T_1, the annual inventory cost for the $75 per-unit alternative, and then the minimum order quantities when calculating the other two annual inventory costs. The total annual inventory costs are then:

$$T_1 = O_1 + I_1 + P_1 = \frac{850(75)}{70} + \frac{70(0.35)(75)}{2} + (850)(75)$$

$$= \$911 + \$919 + \$63,750 = \$65,580$$

$$T_2 = \frac{850(75)}{500} + \frac{500(0.35)(65)}{2} + (850)(65) = \$127.5 + \$5,688 + \$55,250 = \$61,066$$

$$T_3 = \frac{850(75)}{1,000} + \frac{1,000(0.35)(60)}{2} + (850)(60) = \$64 + \$10,500 + \$51,000 = \$61,564$$

So, it is seen that the best inventory management alternative is to purchase 500 units each order, so that the purchase price will be $65 per unit, resulting in a total annual inventory cost of $61,066.

orders varies, since orders are made whenever the inventory on handa reaches the reorder point level. The order policy for this situation thus becomes *order the EOQ whenever the reorder point is reached.*

The probabilistic demand ROP is determined by the following:

$$ROP = \text{lead time demand} + \text{safety stock} = d(L) + Z(\sigma_L)$$

where

d = average daily demand
L = order cycle time
Z = number of standard deviations
σ_L = standard deviation of lead time demand

Note that this formulation for the ROP is somewhat different than the ROP used with the classic EOQ model. In that model, the ROP was simply set equal to the order

Figure 6.6	The Probabilistic Demand Reorder Point Model

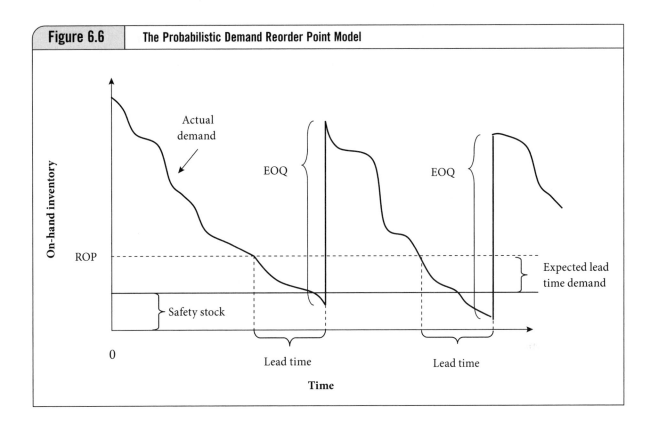

cycle time demand, d × L. Now, with variable demand, a safety stock component must be added to the ROP to ensure that the firm will not stock out while waiting on an order to be delivered. The level of safety stock used depends on the desired **service level**. Service level is generally defined as the percentage of the area under the demand distribution that is covered by, or to the left of, the ROP, as shown in Figure 6.7. The value for Z is then determined based on the desired service level. Assuming a normal distribution of lead time demand, Appendix 1 can be used to find the appropriate Z, given a desired service level. Figure 6.7 illustrates these concepts. Note that if the ROP from the classic EOQ is used with variable demand, then the corresponding service level would be 50 percent, and we would expect to stock out 50 percent of the time while waiting on an order to be delivered. Example 6.4 provides an example calculation of the probabilistic demand ROP.

Allowing Variations in Both Demand and Lead Time

An even more realistic model is when both demand and order cycle times or lead times are said to vary. In this case, both the daily demand and the order cycle times are assumed to be normally distributed about their means. Combining demand variability with cycle time variability greatly increases the variance of the joint distribution along with the safety stock needed to ensure a given service level. The new ROP will thus reflect this safety stock increase. The expected demand during the order lead time is then the average daily demand multiplied by the average order cycle time, and the variance of the cycle time demand is the sum of the variances of the daily demand and the order cycle time. The standard deviation of the order cycle time demand is then:[10]

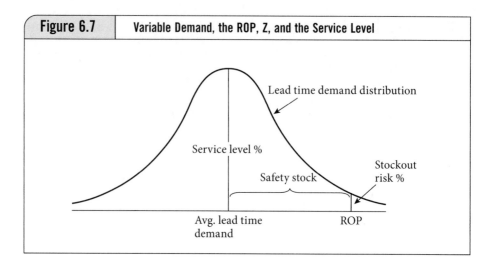

Figure 6.7   **Variable Demand, the ROP, Z, and the Service Level**

$$\sigma_{d\mathrm{LT}} = \sqrt{\overline{\mathrm{L}}\sigma_d^2 + \overline{d}^2\sigma_\mathrm{L}^2}$$

where

$\overline{\mathrm{L}}$ = average order cycle time
$\overline{d}$ = average daily demand
σ_d^2 = variance of daily demand
σ_L^2 = variance of order cycle time

The **probabilistic demand and cycle time ROP** can then be written as:

$$\mathrm{ROP} = \overline{d}(\overline{\mathrm{L}}) + \mathrm{Z}\sqrt{\overline{\mathrm{L}}\sigma_d^2 + \overline{d}^2\sigma_\mathrm{L}^2}$$

The Z in the ROP calculation is again found in Appendix 1, given a desired service level. Example 6.5 provides an example calculation of the probabilistic demand and cycle time ROP.

Example 6.4   **Calculating the Probabilistic Demand ROP**

John and Janie's Hawg Heaven store sells Harley-Davidson® accessories, and they want to calculate an appropriate ROP for many of their items. Their Harley t-shirts are one such example. The annual forecast for these t-shirts is 4,500 shirts. The lead time for t-shirt purchases is always six days. The daily demand for Harley t-shirts varies, and John and Janie have calculated the standard deviation of lead time demand to be approximately 15 shirts. They desire to have a 95 percent service level. Assuming their store is open 300 days per year, then:

$$\mathrm{ROP} = d(\mathrm{L}) + \mathrm{Z}\sigma = \frac{4{,}500}{300}(6) + 1.64(15) = 90 + 25 = 115 \text{ shirts}$$

The Z-value was found using Appendix 1, and searching for an area under the curve as close as possible to 0.95. The safety stock corresponding to a 95 percent service level is 25 units. John and Janie's order policy should then be to order the EOQ whenever the stock of t-shirts falls to 115 shirts.

Example 6.5   Calculating the Probabilistic Demand and Lead Time ROP

The Jay and Stella T-Shirt Depot desires to use an ROP for the various t-shirts it sells, and one shirt has an annual demand forecast of 4,500 shirts. The purchase order lead time varies, with an average of six days and a standard deviation of two days. The daily demand also varies, with an average of 15 shirts per day and a standard deviation of 3 shirts per day. It would like to maintain a 95 percent service level. The ROP would then be:

$$ROP = \overline{d}(\overline{L}) + Z\sqrt{\overline{L}\sigma_d^2 + \overline{d}^2\sigma_L^2} = 15(6) + 1.64\sqrt{6(3)^2 + (15)^2(2)^2}$$
$$= 90 + 1.64(30.89) \approx 141 \text{ shirts}$$

The safety stock for this situation is 51 shirts, and the order policy is to order the EOQ whenever the stock level gets down to 141 shirts.

ABC Inventory Classification

The **ABC inventory classification** approach is used to help companies manage their independent demand inventories. The idea is to pay closer attention to items accounting for a larger percentage of the firm's annual sales. Typically, the Class A items (the most important) represent about 20 percent of inventory SKUs and account for perhaps 70 to 80 percent of the firm's annual sales. These items should be monitored closely and have adequate levels of safety stock to ensure the highest service levels. Class B items account for approximately 15 to 20 percent of annual sales and represent 25 to 30 percent of inventory SKUs. The B items are moderately important and can be monitored less closely, with lower levels of safety stock. Class C items are the least important to the firm, representing about 50 to 60 percent of the inventory SKUs while accounting for only about 5 percent of sales. Service levels can be low for these items and this group represents an area where large savings in inventory carrying costs can be realized (through safety stock reductions). Class C items should only be checked periodically, and safety stock levels should be very low, perhaps even zero. Many companies today use the ABC method to reduce safety stock inventories and get rid of poor selling items, while reducing the number of suppliers. In the Service Perspective feature, a number of cost saving advantages are found in warehousing through use of the ABC method.

Example 6.6 illustrates the ABC inventory classification approach. Notice that the inventory SKU and sales breakdowns do not necessarily represent *exactly* the 80/20 percentages previously mentioned. These are only guidelines. It should be fairly intuitive in which category each inventory item should be placed. For numerous reasons, managers may want to place a B item, for instance, on the A or C list.

Order Quantities and Safety Stock among Supply Chain Partners

In the previous discussions, the general objective was to minimize the focal firm's total annual inventory costs, which led to the use of the EOQ or the EPQ, and several reorder point formulations, depending on assumptions regarding demand and order cycle time. Safety stock was held to help the firm avoid stockouts when demand was larger than expected or order cycle times were longer than expected. Applying these policies leads each firm to act independently to minimize its own annual inventory costs. When

Service Perspective

Using the ABC Inventory Classification

All SKUs are not created equal. The key to streamlining inventory is finding out what should be closely managed and what should be let go. Too much inventory is a costly liability, but too little risks stockouts and customer dissatisfaction. The goal is to achieve a delicate balance. "You cannot arbitrarily reduce inventory without affecting customer service," explains Jim Tarr, principal of ACA Group management consultants. "You must instead change business processes to enable higher service levels with less inventory." Without basic business policies that allow effective inventory management, no sophisticated computer system can bring inventories under control.

Tarr says excess inventory is caused primarily by misalignment and variability—whenever supply (inventory) and demand (incoming orders) don't match. Late or missing vendor deliveries, inaccurate inventory records, and quality issues, among other things, lead to variability and misalignments. Warehouses manage these variables by holding safety stock—"just–in–case" inventory—but holding too much cuts into the bottom line.

"The number one reason for misalignment is inventory inaccuracy," claims Tarr, "so improving inventory accuracy is the number one way to reduce inventory." The more misalignment is minimized, the less safety stock will be needed. Reducing all misalignment is a harrowing, if not impossible, task. A good start, suggests Tarr, is conducting an ABC classification of SKUs using order history data collected through a warehouse management system.

ABC classifications of inventory do much more than just help with cycle counting. Once inventory records are accurate and every SKU has an ABC designation, it's time to manage ABCs within the network. David Malmberg, principal at CGR Management Consultants, regularly conducts seminars on inventory management for the Manufacturing Management and Technology Institute in Palo Alto, California. Prior to his consulting and academic work, Malmberg served as vice president of purchasing and inventory management for Merisel, a distributor of computer products. At Merisel, he stepped up to a big challenge. "Our philosophy was to stock every SKU in all of our nine warehouses. As a result, we had a lot of dead stock." Malmberg noticed redundancies. "We had 18 [printer] cable suppliers," he says.

Malmberg sorted SKUs based on their ABC classifications. He noticed that 10 percent of SKUs accounted for 65 percent of sales. He discovered he could rank suppliers the same way—by their individual contributions to overall sales. By combining ABC classifications of SKUs with that of suppliers, Malmberg developed what he calls a supplier/SKU decision matrix. He eliminated suppliers and SKUs contributing the least value. He didn't just haphazardly remove SKUs. Whenever a SKU was eliminated, arrangements were made to replace it with a similar SKU from a top-performing supplier or source it from a distributor.

Malmberg's next task was to reconsider the company's stocking logic. "Our warehouses were bursting at the seams. There were proposals to add new warehouses." Instead of adding new warehouses, Malmberg decided to slim down current ones by evaluating which SKUs to carry and where to carry them. "We stocked A items at all nine warehouses, and B and A items at master warehouses," says Malmberg. Merisel operated three master warehouses—on the West Coast, East Coast, and Midwest. "In addition to A and B items, we also stocked C items in our Midwest master warehouse, making it a super master warehouse." Slow movers were only stocked in the super master warehouse. By applying ABC stocking logic to its distribution strategy, Merisel was able to consolidate safety stock into one warehouse, resulting in a 25 percent space reduction in the network. Merisel also reduced SKUs from 20,000 to 12,000. Who knew mastering inventory ABCs could do so much?

Source: Aichlmayr, M., "The Quick, the Dead, and the Slow Movers," *Transportation & Distribution*, V. 43, No. 2, 2002, pp. 38–41. Used with permission.

supply chain partners such as the firm's key suppliers and customers are considered, though, the inventory objectives and strategies may be altered somewhat. Safety stock levels tend to be significantly less, since supply chain partners use collaborative planning, forecasting and replenishment (as discussed in Chapter 5). Order lead times and demand quantities tend to be more predictable and reliable, reducing the need for safety stock. In essence, the general idea behind actively managed supply chains is that cooperation, information sharing, inventory visibility, and planning collaboration causes demand and lead time to behave similarly to the assumptions used with the classical EOQ model. Thus, the bullwhip effect is found to be less pervasive when supply chain partners are considered, resulting in fewer inventory management problems and lower total inventory costs.

Another general theme in actively managed supply chains is that firms act to **globally optimize the supply chain**, thus minimizing total supply chain inventory costs while satisfying the service requirements of supply chain members. Orders tend to be more frequent, resulting in smaller order quantities since many supply chains make use of vendor-managed inventories, electronic ordering and shared databases, shorter geographic distances between buyer and supplier, a need for better customer service, and a desire to reduce average inventory levels to reduce costs. Buyer–supplier contracts or agreements among supply chain partners cover many of these inventory issues and reduce the level of variation found in the "typical" marketplace. And variation is precisely what causes inventory problems to be created and costs to increase. The ABC inventory classification method previously discussed can also be applied to supply chain management. In Example 6.6, Nik might have decided to try more proactive supply chain management techniques with the suppliers of his A items, instead of just increasing the safety stocks of those items.

Lean Principles

Because of the attention placed on reducing process variance and inventories in actively managed supply chains, trading partners commonly employ Just-In-Time purchasing, production, and logistics techniques and continuous improvement of processes. Taken together, these activities describe **lean principles**. Initially developed by Toyota beginning in 1950, with its Toyota Production System, lean principles have become an important aspect of supply chain management. Chapter 10 is devoted entirely to this topic.

There are many examples of firms that are successfully managing their supply chains and seeing benefits from reduced supply chain inventories and stockouts. For example, in 2001, global fashion retailer Liz Claiborne Inc. was struggling to manage a global supply chain with 250 million units of product sourced from 3,000 factories in 35 countries. Just a few of the problems it faced were shipment delays, strikes, security issues, the weather, capacity problems, and equipment failures. Today, while its supply chains are still very complex, Claiborne's mastery of supply chain inventory control

---

Example 6.6   Using the ABC Inventory Classification Method

Nik's Gourmet Restaurant Supply Store has a number of inventory items, and the owner wants to make sure he has the right inventory policies in place for each item. The following ten items are a representative group of stock items.

ITEM SKU	COST/UNIT ($)	FORECASTED ANNUAL DEMAND	PROJECTED ANNUAL SALES ($)	PERCENT OF SALES (CLASS)
000325	26.45	3,750	99,187.50	33.8 (A)
001026	12.40	2,500	31,000.00	10.3 (B)
000977	4.35	6,240	27,144.00	9.1 (B)
000265	2.79	260	725.40	0.2 (C)
001236	145.99	150	21,898.50	7.3 (B)
000635	345.00	300	103,500.00	34.5 (A)
000079	87.35	30	2,620.50	0.9 (C)
001166	146.80	50	7,340.00	2.4 (C)
000439	55.20	100	5,520.00	1.8 (C)
000237	37.16	25	929.00	0.3 (C)

Total: $299,864.90

SOLUTION:

Based on these findings for the upcoming year, Nik classified items 000325 and 000635 as A items; 001026, 000977, and 001236 as B items; and 000265, 000079, 001166, 000439, and 000237 as C items. Nik then decided to increase the safety stocks of the A items, and do away with the safety stock of the C items.

---

has allowed it to cut its inventory levels by an average of seven to ten days of demand. In 2006, it was placed on the Massachusetts-based research service provider Aberdeen Group's roster of International Logistics Best Practice Winners. In another example, a few years ago Black & Decker, the power tool manufacturer, had operations in 11 countries and markets in 100 countries, but was struggling to meet its customers' service requirements while controlling inventory costs. With the help of a supply chain software application, it was able to cut inventory expenses across all levels of its supply chains, while improving service levels for its customers.[11]

Dependent Demand Inventory Management

As described earlier, every time a unit of product is produced, an internal demand within the manufacturer for the raw materials, parts, components, and subassemblies that comprise the finished product is created. The quantities of parts required for these end items are *dependent* on the number of units of end items produced. To manage these dependent demand items, most firms require some type of system to keep track of when production orders and purchase orders need to be created, and how many should be made or purchased, in order to meet the demand for finished goods. This can be accomplished with the use of a material requirements planning system, and this segment follows.

The Material Requirements Planning (MRP) System

Figure 6.8 presents a schematic of a **material requirements planning** (MRP) system. The MRP system is a software application that has been available since the 1970s, but can still be quite expensive for firms with many manufactured products and complicated product designs. Briefly, an MRP system performs an analysis of the firm's existing internal conditions and reports back what the production and purchase requirements are for a given finished product manufacturing schedule. These systems have been extremely popular over the years, and have been touted by MRP system software providers and customers to provide better customer service, better demand responsiveness, lower inventory levels, and higher capacity utilization when compared to informal, passively managed inventory systems. Aside from the cost of the software, there are potentially large training and hardware expenditures, and implementation periods can take anywhere from a month or two to a year or two. And, as with any software application, the *garbage-in, garbage-out rule* applies. This means that in order for the system to work properly, accurate and updated data must be made available continuously to the MRP system. Otherwise, the system will produce inaccurate outputs, which are not worth much to the organization and can even be quite damaging in terms of stockouts or excess inventories.

Figure 6.8	An MRP System Schematic

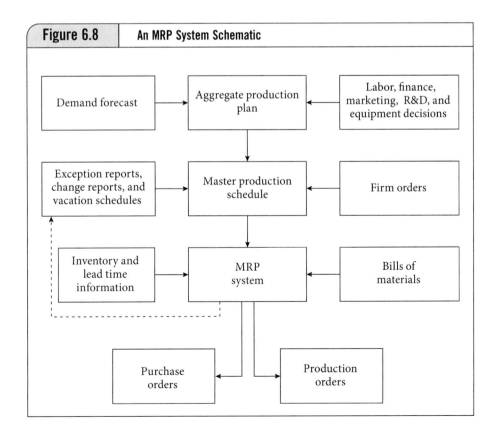

Companies must also be willing to change how they do things in order to accommodate the requirements of the MRP system. In fact, one of the primary reasons MRP system implementations fail is because users simply underestimate the requirements of the MRP system. The MRP must be implemented as an entire system for it to successfully achieve its objectives of component manufacturing and purchase order management. A comprehensive study of MRP implementations completed in 2002 confirmed the importance of data accuracy, user support, and training when implementing MRP systems. Significant benefits from use of MRP were also documented, including improved customer service, better production scheduling, and reduced manufacturing costs.[12]

MRP Inputs

The MRP inputs are the master production schedule, current inventory and lead time information, and bills of materials information.

Master Production Schedule

The **master production schedule** (MPS) specifies the end products to be made, the dates they need to be completed, and the quantities required. This usually takes the form of a daily or weekly production schedule for each product, which then become inputs to the MRP. The MPS is based on the aggregate production plan, existing customer orders, and current information regarding the capacity of the manufacturing facility. Since work center capacities vary based on human resource deployment and equipment used, the MPS personnel must know how changes in human resources will likely vary over the coming months and year, and what equipment will be coming online or going out of use due to scheduled maintenance and historical breakdown information. Some of the newest automated manufacturing systems have MPS capabilities, but in many cases, an office of MPS personnel with intimate knowledge of the firm's production characteristics performs the production scheduling activity by hand.

Wise Foods, the largest regional snack food manufacturer on the U.S. East Coast, is a good example. The company boasts that its Pennsylvania snack food manufacturing facility is the largest under one roof. But until recently, scheduling for the

"Now all we need is another 10,000 gigs to store all the information my program will generate."

26 potato-related and 20 corn-related production lines was done manually by three people and took anywhere from three to four hours *every day*. "This little silo had all the knowledge of how that's done," said Neil Bixler, director of IT for Wise. The three planners had the knowledge of how to make the schedule work, such as what fryer makes a better kettle chip than the others. "It was all in their heads," Bixler added. By the end of 2003, Wise decided it had to automate the process. With help from JRG, a supply chain services provider, Wise went live with a new software production scheduling system in May 2004. Scheduling now takes two of the planners less than an hour each day, setup times have been reduced by 35 percent, inventory levels have been more accurate, and most importantly, customer satisfaction measures have doubled.[13]

As the capacity of a production facility changes due to unforeseen changes in the workforce or production equipment, the MPS must then be revised. Additionally, as customer orders come in from field salespeople and regional distribution centers, the information can be compared to existing MPS quantities, allowing for further revisions in the production schedule. These and other revisions to the MPS must be made far enough in advance for the production processes to respond. This requires the MPS to use a **frozen time period** or **time fence**, wherein no changes are allowed to the weekly production schedule. This time period is at least as long as the lead time required to purchase parts and assemble the mid-level components and finished product.

The **aggregate production plan** provides an annual production plan for each product family to the MPS personnel. As shown in Figure 6.8, the aggregate plan is decided upon by the firm's top managers, based on existing marketing plans, financial capability, human resource plans, capacity plans, and a forecast of demand for each product family. The MPS personnel then split up, or disaggregate, the annual production plan, turning it into weekly production requirements for individual products (the MPS). Each week, the MPS extends its frozen weekly production schedule for the set frozen time period, and projects a working schedule for the remaining portion of the year. This is known as a **rolling production schedule**.

Inventory and Lead Time Information

Other inputs to the MRP include accurate inventory and lead time information for all raw material, work-in-process, and finished goods. The MRP system must know how long it takes for all incoming parts to be purchased and for each manufacturing process to be completed. The system must also know exactly how many units of each purchased part, each manufactured component and assembly, and each finished product exist on the shop floor and in the warehouse. This information can be particularly problematic, since as suppliers are replaced, product designs change, and items move into and out of the warehouse and production facility lead time and inventory levels change. If these changes are not updated in the MRP as soon as they occur, the MRP system becomes subject to the garbage-in, garbage-out rule. In many companies this is an ongoing problem, causing periods when the MRP system must be shut down and information updated.

Bills of Materials

For each product on the weekly production schedule, a **bill of materials** (BOM) exists. Simply put, the BOM is a *recipe* for that product. It indicates all of the raw materials, parts, components, subassemblies, and assemblies required to manufacture a product. It also indicates how many of each part are required, the parts that go into each subassembly or assembly, and the order of assembly. The simplest form a BOM can take is the **product structure diagram**, shown in Figure 6.9.

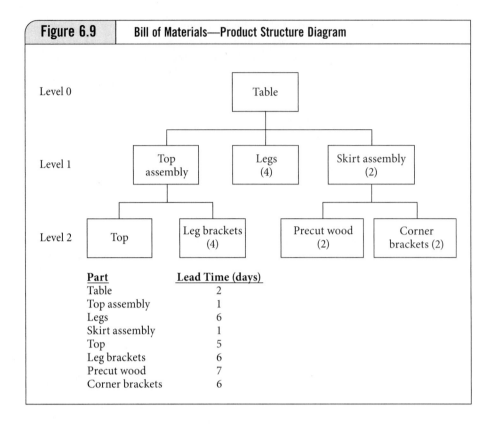

Figure 6.9   Bill of Materials—Product Structure Diagram

Part	Lead Time (days)
Table	2
Top assembly	1
Legs	6
Skirt assembly	1
Top	5
Leg brackets	6
Precut wood	7
Corner brackets	6

The MRP then breaks down or *explodes* the BOM, determining the parts and production processing required at each level of the BOM. The requirements for the level 0 item (the finished product) are determined first by subtracting the current inventory level of the finished product from the master production schedule requirement. The level 1 item requirements are determined next in the same fashion, and this progresses until all of the item levels are completed. For instance, when viewing Figure 6.9, it can be seen that for a net requirement of 50 tables, the company must make 50 top assemblies and 100 skirt assemblies, and it must purchase 200 legs (the 4 in parentheses under "Legs" signifies that four legs are required for each table; similarly, two skirt assemblies are required for each table, and two corner brackets are required for each skirt assembly, for a total of four corner brackets for each table).

The BOM along with item lead time information can be used to determine the minimum frozen time fence, as previously discussed. The lead times for all of the items in the BOM in Figure 6.9 are shown. Using a bottom-up approach, it can be seen that it will take eight days to finish a skirt assembly (it will take a minimum of seven days to purchase the wood and corner brackets, with one more day to finish the skirt assembly). During this same period, the legs can be purchased (six days), and the top assembly can be completed (six days to purchase the top and leg brackets, and one day to finish the assembly). The final table assembly will take two additional days, for a total purchase and production lead time of ten days. The frozen time fence for this table should then be at least ten days, and possibly longer if the purchase order and production lead times are subject to any variance. Increases in the MPS within this time period would require expediting, and cost the firm more money.

MRP Outputs

The outputs of the MRP consist of the purchase orders, the production orders, and work center capacity feedback information, which is fed back to the MPS personnel in the form of missed due dates, changes to process capacities, and other information impacting the production facility's ability to make product. The purchase orders and production orders are read directly from the MRP's **planned order release** computations for each item in the BOM. These computations determine the feasibility of the MPS. Computing the planned order releases for each item in the BOM follows.

The MRP Part Records

Each item in the BOM must be associated with a **part record**, as shown in Table 6.2. Since eight items appear in the Table BOM shown in Figure 6.9, then eight part records must be created in the MRP system for this product. Table 6.2 illustrates the calculations of the planned order releases for four of the eight parts. The rule to remember when following the generation of numbers in the part records of Table 6.2 is *the planned order releases of the assembled part (also called the "parent") determines the gross requirements of the constituent parts (the "children").*

The Level 0 Part Record

The first part record completed must always be the Level 0, or finished product (in this case, a table). The gross requirements entries for the Level 0 item are the MPS quantities for the frozen time period. If any production orders are already in progress, then their scheduled deliveries are shown in the scheduled receipts row (in this case, ten units are shown as scheduled receipts for day 1). Note that these part records are a snapshot in time; thus, the only scheduled receipts shown are those of an order already in progress as of the beginning of the current week. The end-of-period on-hand inventory is the sum of the previous period inventory and the scheduled receipts for the period, less the gross requirements for the period. For period 1, the on-hand inventory would then be 30 + 10 − 10 = 30 tables. For period 3, the on-hand inventory is initially projected to be 20 − 20 = 0 tables. However, the safety stock requirement (or SS) is 15 tables, so the net requirement is 15. The required lot size, though, is ten, so only multiples of ten are made. Thus, in period 1, a planned order release for 20 units is created, which will be ready by period 3 (the lead time, or LT, is stated as two days). In period 3, the updated on-hand inventory is then 20 tables. Since in the current period (period 1) none of these 20 units is in progress, this order is not shown as a scheduled receipt in period 3. In similar fashion, planned order releases are also generated in periods 3, 6, 7, and 8.

The Skirt Assembly Part Record

Now that the planned order releases of the table have been calculated, the gross requirements for the skirt assembly (as well as the other two Level 1 items) can be determined. Since two skirt assemblies are required for each table, the gross requirements for skirt assemblies are twice that of the planned order releases for tables. The projected on-hand inventories are then determined, and when this number falls below zero (no safety stock is required) a planned order release is generated. For skirt assemblies, the lot size is lot-for-lot (LFL), meaning that just enough to maintain zero inventories is assembled when an order is placed. Planned order releases are generated in periods 2, 5, 6, and 7.

The Corner Bracket and Precut Wood Part Records

Note that two of each of these parts is needed for each skirt assembly. Consequently, each planned order release for the skirt assembly is multiplied by two to determine the

Table 6.2		Sample MRP Part Records for Table in Figure 6.9

Table – Level 0		1	2	3	4	5	6	7	8	9	10
Gross requirements		10	10	20	0	20	0	0	20	10	15
Scheduled receipts		10									
Projected on-hand inventory	30	30	20	20	20	20	20	20	20	20	15
Net requirements				15		15			15	5	10
Planned order releases		20		20			20	10	10		

$Q = 10; LT = 2; SS = 15$

			x^2		x^2			x^2	x^2	x^2		
Skirt Assembly – Level 1		1	2	3	4	5	6	7	8	9	10
Gross requirements		40	0	40	0	0	40	20	20	0	0
Scheduled receipts		20									
Projected on-hand inventory	25	5	5	0	0	0	0	0	0	0	0
Net requirements				35			40	20	20		
Planned order releases			35			40	20	20			

$Q = LFL; LT = 1; SS = 0$

			x^2			x^2	x^2	x^2			
Corner Bracket – Level 2		1	2	3	4	5	6	7	8	9	10
Gross requirements		0	70	0	0	80	40	40	0	0	0
Scheduled receipts				60	60						
Projected on-hand inventory	90	90	20	80	140	60	20	10	10	10	10
Net requirements								30			
Planned order releases		30									

$Q = 30; LT = 6; SS = 10$

			x^2			x^2	x^2	x^2			
Precut Wood – Level 2		1	2	3	4	5	6	7	8	9	10
Gross requirements		0	70	0	0	80	40	40	0	0	0
Scheduled receipts					150	50					
Projected on-hand inventory	92	92	22	22	172	142	102	62	62	62	62
Net requirements											
Planned order releases											

$Q = 50; LT = 7; SS = 20$

gross requirements for these two parts. One planned order release for corner brackets is needed in period 1, and no planned order releases are need for precut wood.

The outputs of the MRP system can now be seen in Table 6.2. The table's final assembly area is told when to assemble tables, and how many are needed. The skirt assembly work center is also told when and how many skirt assemblies to make. Finally, the buyers of the firm are told when to purchase corner brackets and precut wood and how many to purchase. Also, if it had turned out that more precut wood, for instance, was needed in period 6, then there would not be enough remaining time to generate a purchase (notice that the lead time is seven days). In this case, a precut wood purchase would have to be expedited and an exception report would be generated and transmitted to the MPS personnel, so that upcoming table production quantities could be revised. Alternately, a shift of production floor personnel or equipment might be made to accommodate the additional capacity requirements.

The Distribution Requirements Planning (DRP) System

The **distribution requirements planning** (DRP) system allows the firm's regional distribution centers and local warehouses (and indirectly, customers) to communicate actual orders to the MRP and to allow the firm to look ahead and anticipate when orders will need to be placed, just as with the MRP. As retailers and other customers order goods from a manufacturer, orders are filled from a warehouse. When the warehouse's ROP is reached, an order is generated for a specific quantity from the distribution center. Eventually, the distribution center's ROP for that item is reached, and an order is transmitted to the factory. A planning system is thus needed to manage the movements of stock into and out of each of these facilities to avoid stockouts or excess stock situations in factories and warehouses, and to plan ahead for changes in demand and hence required delivery vehicle and warehouse capacities.

A few years ago, Ohio-based fashion retailer Limited Brands started thinking about giving its distribution system a makeover after some 400 semitrailers showed up unexpectedly at its distribution center parking lot, which was built for 150 vehicles. "It was one of our worst supply chain disasters ever," said Paul Matthews, senior vice president of supply chain transformation. Today it is using DRP-based technologies to increase inventory visibility, and to link supply-side data on trucks and inventory with demand-side forecasts. The system is enabling it to synchronize sales and marketing with finance, transportation, and other operations.[14] As a matter of fact, according to a recent study by Colorado-based distribution service provider ProLogis Global Solutions, creating a network that can deliver on customer demands while minimizing costs is the number one challenge facing supply chain executives.[15] Hopefully, some of the readers are beginning to realize that DRP systems connected to MRP systems are essentially creating customer-driven or supply chain pull-oriented systems, which is what JIT or lean systems seek to create, and this gets back to the long-term goals of actively managed supply chains. Today, many fully implemented enterprise resource planning (ERP) systems contain MRP and DRP modules. ERP systems are discussed at length in Chapter 9.

The **DRP record** is similar to the MRP part record. The demand profile at each warehouse is translated into a demand forecast for each period, and this replaces the gross requirements used in the MRP. The forecast requirements are subtracted from the warehouse's on-hand inventories and planned receipts. Net requirements are generated as safety stock levels are reached, and planned shipping quantities are generated based on the delivery lead times (similar to the planned order releases in the MRP). The planned shipping quantities for all warehouses are then aggregated into one set of

Table 6.3	Warehouse DRP Record

Warehouse No. 6											
Product: Table		1	2	3	4	5	6	7	8	9	10
Forecast requirements		2	4	3	6	5	4	8	0	3	5
Shipments in transit			30								
Projected on-hand inventory	6	4	30	27	21	16	12	4	4	31	26
Net requirements										2	
Planned shipments								30			

Q = 30; LT = 2; SS = 3

Projected order to factory or distribution center

time-phased requirements for a central distribution center or the manufacturing facility. A DRP record is shown in Table 6.3.

The DRP planned shipping quantities are important sources of information for the manufacturing facility. The master production scheduling function can use the information to adjust future MPS quantities to better meet actual demand. It also allows the firm's top planners to compare the information used in preparing the aggregate plan to the various marketplace demand characteristics throughout the year, as well as to indicate the firm's ability to satisfy demand. And finally, when inventories are in short supply due to unforeseen changes in overall demand, material availability, or manufacturing capacity, the DRP can be used to inform warehouses when shipments will be arriving, and for allocating units among the firm's warehouses or its most important supply chain customers.

Ideally, finished goods arrive on distributor and retailer loading docks at precisely the right time and with the right quantity. As with many other supply chain management strategies, Wal-Mart is leading the way by providing its suppliers point-of-sale (POS) data for each store, updated several times daily, to allow suppliers to its DRP-based systems to adjust their distribution quantities, as well as their manufacturing plans based on what is actually selling and where. For example, Florida-based Litehouse Foods, a dressings and sauce maker, uses demand-planning software to compare POS data from Wal-Mart against its forecasts. This allows Litehouse to adjust its deliveries to Wal-Mart distribution centers to avoid overstocks and thus spoilage of product. "Having access to every item's performance at every store for every day for the past two years enables Wal-Mart and the supplier to jointly manage their business at the lowest level of detail," says Wal-Mart spokeswoman Christi Gallagher.[16] As shown here, companies that make use of DRP systems can adequately plan ahead to reduce inventory levels and stockouts, as well as maximize customer service levels.

The Manufacturing Resource Planning (MRP II) System

Once MRP and DRP systems became operational and users saw the benefits of this information for planning, purchasing, and manufacturing control purposes, a desire by personnel in various functional areas of the firm was created to use the MRP as a planning tool on a much larger scale. The initial expansion of the MRP was for capacity requirements planning purposes. However, organizations determined that if cost information could be attached to each of the BOMs, then the projected financial requirements to achieve the aggregate plan could be determined. Marketing personnel might use the MRP system to find the impact on the production facility of a planned promotional campaign. Human resource personnel could use the MRP system to generate the projected labor requirements for the firm's short- and long-term expansion plans. Shop floor managers might use the MRP system for overtime or undertime planning and worker scheduling purposes. Lastly, manufacturing engineers could use the system to help plan facility expansion requirements. The desire to perform these look-ahead activities or use what-if scenarios for planning purposes was the impetus for the development of the **manufacturing resource planning (MRP II)** system.

Today, most MRP II systems have a simulation capability to allow users to perform what-if analyses and gain an understanding of likely outcomes when capacity or production timing decisions are made. Other modules are also included with MRP II systems, enabling various functional area personnel to interact with the MRP II system using a central database. Production, marketing, human resource, and finance personnel can then work together to develop a feasible aggregate plan based on available funds, equipment, advertising plans, and labor. In this way, all functional areas have a vested interest in achieving the aggregate plan. Starting in the United States in the early 1990s and continuing today, many MRP II systems have been integrated into system-wide ERP applications. However, the functionality of MRP II systems remains, whether it is a stand-alone system or part of a larger ERP system. In many countries, use of MRP II is still in its infancy. The Global Perspective feature profiles a Greek company's recent experiences when implementing an MRP II system.

The Capacity Requirements Planning Function

One of the most important features of the MRP II system is the **capacity requirements planning** capability. Given MPS quantities, the planned order releases from the MRP, the current shop load, part routing information, and processing and purchasing lead times, the short-range capacity requirements can be developed for the entire production facility. Initially, the MPS may be found to be infeasible given the shop's current workload and the capacity of each work center. If this is the case, the choices are either to increase capacity or reduce the MPS. The MRP II system generates **load reports** for each work center for a series of time periods. These load reports compare the required capacity for the given MPS with the projected available capacity. Given this information, production managers can determine if workloads need to be shifted to later periods, overtime needs to be scheduled, or work needs to be contracted out. Ultimately, a feasible production schedule and capacity plan is decided upon.

As the actual work begins, reports generated by the MRP II system aid in monitoring the progress of work and allow managers to adjust capacities to keep the flow of work on schedule. However, even when a feasible schedule is indicated by the load reports, variances in processing and parts delivery times can still cause production system delays and bottlenecks, requiring further capacity adjustments or expediting, or simply resulting in some late work orders. In actively managed supply chains, a firm may have a number of key customers. The capacity requirements planning capability of its MRP II system thus allows the firm to ensure timely planned deliveries to these key customers.

Extensions of MRP II

MRP II systems have found applications in large-scale services that require complex scheduling of materials and workers, and have a need to perform analyses of market

HAI, a Greek state-owned company, has about 3,000 employees and an estimated annual sales turnover of $130 million with an inventory level of $30 million. Its mission is to provide aircraft and engine maintenance services, and other products and services, to a broad range of global customers and the Greek Armed Forces. HAI was established in 1975 and today ranks among the largest and most advanced aviation support centers in Europe.

The operational activities of HAI cover three main areas—maintenance (aircraft, engines, electronics), integrated training programs, and manufacturing (aero structures and electronics). HAI's operational activities are supported by research and development activities, material supply and warehouse facilities, quality assurance, and a precision-measuring laboratory.

Before installing the new MRP II system, HAI used different uncoordinated systems to estimate and plan the material requirements and control production (which produced an excessive level of materials). The increasing competition demanded a new integrated system to cover the entire production planning and control process. The main external factors promoting the installation of the new MRP II system were the requirements demanded by its major customers for better support, and the increasing competition in the marketplace driven by pressure on costs and manufacturing lead time.

The decision to implement MRP II was taken after the strategic objectives had been set at the senior level within the business. MRP II implementation was part of the overall strategic direction to increase HAI's competitiveness through better production and inventory control. Furthermore, the duration of the implementation process (about ten months) and the configuration of the project team (mainly top management) meant that the implementation project was given high priority.

The selected software was a proprietary MRP II package from a vendor that appeared to cover the business's needs. The software was developed to meet the specific requirements of the aerospace industry, which meant that the software needed a limited number of minor modifications.

The implementation of the MRP II system was based on a rapid implementation methodology adopted by the chosen supplier, due to HAI senior management desire for a quick realization of the planned benefits derived from the MRP II system. There appeared to be an excessive emphasis on completion rather than a focus on achieving the potential benefits of the MRP II system. The short implementation timescale did not give an opportunity to HAI to train all the affected personnel before the new MRP II system went operational.

The MRP II system required a large resource commitment for implementation. The functional capabilities of the system included material management, production planning, sales, financial accounting, quality control, and human resources and enterprise controlling, all of which were computerized. The vendor provided an implementation plan and there was coordination with the steering committee and the individual project teams. Generally, top management showed a positive attitude concerning the overall implementation effort, mainly due to the fact that it was already familiar with computer-based systems for production planning and inventory control.

A project steering committee had been established and its main mission was to ensure a successful implementation, evaluating the overall process and coordinating the individual project teams. The steering committee provided a strategic dimension to the implementation phase and specific operational issues were the responsibility of individual project teams.

The managers involved in the implementation effort attended an MRP II education session in order to be more knowledgeable about the overall system. During the implementation, more employees were involved in an education and training effort. The overall education and training session lasted about ten days and was arranged by the software supplier.

Following the implementation phase, HAI used multiple performance criteria to measure manufacturing schedule performance, production delivery performance, cost of manufacture, and customer supply performance.

HAI had chosen to employ an independent consultant to oversee and facilitate the implementation of the MRP II system. The use of the consultant benefited HAI with an objective assessment of the overall project progress, giving early identification of potential problems and recommending appropriate corrective actions that could be fed to the individual project teams.

With regard to BOM, the main problem related to accuracy. Although an effort of "cleaning up" the BOM files before entering them to the new system had been undertaken, HAI was facing some problems with the accuracy of the BOM. The lack of an integrated training program for all the affected personnel caused a misunderstanding of how critical accurate data input was, and the appropriate work was not done. This caused considerable extra remedial work to correct data entry errors.

The MRP II implementation benefits included better production scheduling, reduced component shortages, better inventory control, reduced delivery lead times, reduced production lead times, reduced overtime, better cost estimating, improved customer satisfaction, and improved financial position.

Source: Towers, N., A. Knibbs, and N. Panagiotopoulos, "Implementing Manufacturing Resource Planning in a Greek Aerospace Company: A Case Study," *International Journal of Operations & Production Management*, V. 25, No. 3/4, 2005, pp. 277–289. Used with permission.

alternatives, for example. Large resort/hotel complexes are one such example. MRP II systems can be used for tracking food supplies at a number of a resort's restaurants; for growth and hiring plans; and possibly to analyze the impact a large concert would have on the resort's hotel rooms, restaurants, and other amenities. Foxwoods Resort and Casino in Connecticut has 29 food and beverage outlets, 11 casino service outlets, 5 restaurant service outlets, 5 casino lounges, and 5 production kitchens requiring 3,700 food and beverage items in its sprawling 4.7 million square foot facility. At one time, all of the food service processes were controlled manually, which negatively impacted productivity, speed, consistency, and accuracy. In January 2005, Foxwoods went live with an automated food and beverage inventory and recipe control process to better manage its food service operations. When fully deployed, the system will collect data from the POS system and feed it to the company's ERP and MRP II systems for purchase orders, warehouse accounting, and other financial applications. The system will ultimately be used to create orders, maintain inventories, execute requisitions and transfers, manage production, maintain recipes, and provide food costing analyses.[17]

Since a key characteristic of MRP II systems is storing information centrally to provide interaction capabilities with functional units at a manufacturing center, the next evolution was towards the integration of business functions throughout the *entire global organization*. This is what is commonly referred to as an enterprise resource planning (ERP) system, and this topic is discussed in detail in Chapter 9.

Collaborative Inventory Management along the Supply Chain

In actively managed supply chains, controlling supply chain inventories effectively as parts are sold to manufacturers and as finished products are distributed to retailers can result in significant cost and customer service benefits to all supply chain participants, including end customers. In many cases, though, supply chains are becoming longer, slower, and more complex as companies and their global markets continue to grow. This has tended to make supply chain inventory management more problematic. Steve Wood, supply chain manager for Siemens Canada, a designer and marketer of electronics products, estimates that his company's safety stock has had to increase 7 to 8 percent just to satisfy customers' demands for specific delivery times. "It always comes back to customers saying, 'I can call your competition and get it there tomorrow. Why can't I call you and get that?' And there's only one answer to that," he says. Jim Hutchinson, vice president of supply chain integration for Brown-Forman Beverages of Kentucky, admits that it's hard to be both global and lean. He said they recently added seven days of demand to their safety stock of Jack Daniels whiskey in the United Kingdom because of variability in transportation times. "Sometimes we could get bookings and sometimes we couldn't. And sometimes [our shipments] would get bumped."[18]

As mentioned in several of the previous chapters in this text, close supply chain relationships, collaborative forecasting with customers and suppliers, and frequent open communications can add visibility to supply chains and reduce the bullwhip effect, which greatly reduces inventory problems and the need for safety stock. Several other topics not yet discussed that are related to supply chain inventory management follow.

Continuous Replenishment Programs

With its origins in strategies used by Japanese manufacturers in the 1980s, the primary objective of **continuous replenishment** is to increase inventory speed as it flows from supplier to buyer. It is also sometimes referred to as **efficient consumer response**. Today, the most common strategy to increase speed or reduce delivery lead times is to utilize the Internet to transmit orders from buyer to supplier. For example, bar codes on products or case cartons are scanned at a retailer and transmitted to its MRP system. When the reorder point is reached, an order is electronically generated and sent via the Internet to the supplier's order receiving system, whereby the order is filled and transported to the buyer. Radio frequency identification (RFID) tags are also used to track products and generate orders electronically to suppliers. One advantage with the use of computer-to-computer transfer of information is the system of **continuous inventory review**. Computer systems will know instantly when a reorder point is reached, causing an order to be generated exactly when desired, and not when someone notices that inventory levels are getting low. This further reduces the likelihood of stockouts as well as the required safety stock.

The long-term purpose of quick response is to create a just-in-time replenishment system that can respond quickly to customer order variations. Eventually, quick response is implemented both externally and internally among key supply chain participants to improve work-in-process flow and reduce internal lead times, improve finished goods delivery times, and to better serve supply chain and end customer needs. This just-in-time characteristic is also one of the lean production principles, the topic of Chapter 10. Quick response strategies reduce the need for forecasts and safety stock since supplies can more closely match demand. Consequently, average inventory levels are reduced, along with their associated carrying costs. The trend towards quick response is particularly evident in the consumer packaged goods industry today. According to a U.S. Grocery Manufacturer's Association 2005 survey, retailers are requesting more floor-ready displays, customized packaging, and store-ready cross-docked pallets than before; they are requiring shorter order cycle times; and they are implementing zero tolerance policies for late shipments.[19]

Vendor Managed Inventories and JIT II

Developing and maintaining long-lasting and trusting relationships with suppliers provides the buyer with many benefits, and these are discussed at length in Chapter 12. As a firm and its key suppliers become more continuous replenishment–oriented, one extension of the buyer–supplier relationship can be the creation of **vendor managed inventories** (VMIs). Wal-Mart and now many other companies have found that allowing suppliers to monitor internal inventories of *their own products* at the buyer's location and then deciding when and how much to order results in fewer stockouts, fewer ordering problems, faster order cycle times, and less overall inventory carrying costs for the buyer. Benefits accrue for the suppliers, too. The Boeing/Alcoa VMI relationship is one example. As demand grew for airplanes, Boeing and Alcoa started working together to reduce forecasting and delivery problems. VMI was the result. Today, Boeing sends ERP-generated weekly forecasts and inventory counts to Alcoa. It's up to Alcoa to decide if delivery safety lead time is required, and if it needs to group several orders in its production runs.[20]

Some readers may have witnessed VMI occurring in a smaller scale at convenience stores. The distributor pulls up daily or semi-daily, checks stock on the shelves, fills the space for the products needing more stock, and even changes the products or the positioning of products on the shelves. Later, the store receives an invoice for the items left at the store. No one at the store is required to count items, contact the distributor, or make an order. In this scenario, everyone wins: The store rarely runs out of anything and it doesn't have to spend time and money managing inventories; the distributor gets to maximize its sales while providing a great service to the buyer, thereby assuring itself of continued business; and the end users (like you and me) know that whenever they go in looking for something, it will most likely be there.

In some supply chain settings, a further progression of the buyer–supplier relationship is occurring, and this is termed **Just-In-Time II** (JIT II). A concept created by Mr. Lance Dixon of the Massachusetts-based audio manufacturer Bose Corp. in the late 1980s, JIT II requires a strong bond and a large degree of trust between buyer and supplier. A representative of the supplier is housed in the buyer's purchasing department, acting as both buyer and supplier representative (similar to the VMI strategy), but also participating as an integral member of the buying organization's new product development and value engineering/value analysis teams. For all intents and purposes, this individual is a full member of the buying firm's purchasing department. JIT II is also commonly referred to as **supplier colocation**. Since suppliers have more expertise on the products they sell than their customers do, they can suggest modifications or alternate components during the product design phase that customers would not know about. As with the VMI strategy, use of JIT II creates better service, lower costs, and fewer inventory management problems for the buyer, and the higher level of commitment from both sides means continued sales for the supplier and a great opportunity to participate in new project designs and to supply new products to the buyer. An abbreviated list of JIT II users includes Gulfstream Aerospace, Harley-Davidson, Honeywell, IBM, Maytag,

Motorola, Siemens, Varian, and Westinghouse. "Most companies have five to ten in plants, but some have dozens," says Lance Dixon.[21]

Measuring Inventory Management Performance

No discussion of inventory management would be complete without talking about the tracking of inventory management performance. While the topic of performance assessment is covered in detail in Part 4 of this textbook, it must be mentioned here as well to emphasize the importance of inventory control. Hopefully by now the reader appreciates the role inventory plays along the supply chain and the "doubled-edged sword" of inventory management—inventories are necessary to provide customer service, but inventory carrying costs can account for a large portion of a supply chain's total costs.

Specific measurements must be in place to assess inventory management performance both internally and externally as the firm interacts with its key supply chain members. The dual objectives of maximizing customer service while minimizing inventory costs require close and frequent attention to the policies and tools used when purchasing, processing, and distributing raw materials, work-in-process, and finished products. Stockouts and excessive inventory carrying costs can become a financial burden to all sizes and types of organizations, and represent an even greater concern for companies trying to maintain and improve supply chain performance and competitiveness.

As an example, the Materiel Management Directorate (MMD) of the Canada Revenue Agency (CRA), known for administering Canada's tax laws, has the authority to purchase goods and services for all CRA clients. In 2000, it began to implement a performance measurement system to assess the effectiveness of its material management services. The feedback from this system allowed the MMD to improve decision making, provide proactive problem correction, and achieve continuous improvement. It developed a balanced set of performance measures to provide information on financial performance, asset management, client satisfaction, employee morale, and business results. Performance targets were established based on external benchmarks. Today at the MMD there is little variance between budget and expenditures; clientele are generally satisfied with the services they receive; employee satisfaction has improved; and significant improvements have been realized in service deliveries, cost savings, and asset management.[22]

In another example, a recent study performed by Robert Yokl, president of Pennsylvania-based consultant Strategic Value Analysis in Healthcare, found that for at least one-third of U.S. hospitals, inventories were excessive for a number of reasons. These included stocking out-of-date and low-usage items, carrying too much safety stock, lengthy reorder cycle times, double stocking, and poorly determined economic order quantities. One of Strategic Value Analysis' hospital clients established an inventory reduction program that took the following steps—it generated a list of products that hadn't moved in three months, and then held on to the more critical ones while disposing of or returning the rest; items that were stored for only one department were transferred to the using department; and it analyzed usage patterns and discovered it could order many items more often and in smaller quantities. As a result, the hospital was able to reduce inventories by over $92,000 in the first three months of the program without impacting its service capabilities.[23]

Once the internal inventory performance measures are in order, it's time to begin working on external measures to better integrate supply chain processes. Indeed,

Dr. Thomas Speh, professor of marketing and logistics at Ohio's Miami University, asks, "If you don't have good internal measures, how can two companies work together?" The challenge in designing effective supply chain performance measures is in establishing relationships, connectivity, and trust. Again Speh asks, "We have the technology to share, but are we willing to do it?" Maureen Strahan, vice president of global supply chain operations at computer products firm Hewlett-Packard, believes that performance measures drive behavior. Each of its business units has its own supply chain and if one unit is doing something well, it can then leverage it across all the others.[24]

Finally, as effective supply chain relationships become solidified and as internal performance is continually monitored and improved, measuring inventory performance along with other indicators of performance across the network of supply chain participants becomes extremely important in ensuring customer satisfaction, long-term competitiveness, and continued economic success. Peter Bolstorff, CEO of Minnesota-based SCE Limited and one of the co-developers of a widely-used model of supply chain performance, recommends a number of supply chain–oriented performance measures, and some of these are shown in Table 6.4.[25]

All of the measures shown in Table 6.4 are directly or indirectly related to supply chain members' abilities to manage inventories. The final measure, cash-to-cash cycle time, provides an overall view of the number of days of working capital tied up in managing supply chain inventories. For this measure, inventory days of supply can be calculated as:

$$IDS = \frac{\text{Avg. Inventory \$}}{\text{Annualized cost of goods sold}/365}$$

Table 6.4	Supply Chain Performance Measures*
PERFORMANCE MEASURE	**DESCRIPTION**
Delivery performance	Total on-time and full orders/Total orders
Order fulfillment lead time	Average time from customer authorization of sales order to receipt of product
Backorder duration	Average order fulfillment lead time for customer orders not filled in full
Other lead time measures: 　Manufacturing lead time 　Warehouse lead time 　Shipment lead time	Average manufacturing order start date to order ship date Average warehouse order receipt date to ship date Average warehouse ship date to customer receipt date
Supply chain response time	Average time to respond to an unplanned 20% increase or decrease in demand without a service or cost penalty
Total supply chain management cost	Average fixed and operating costs associated with SCM. Includes order management, customer service, warehousing, transportation, purchasing, supplier management, supply/demand planning, inventory holding, IT costs, and returns/warranty management costs.
Cash-to-cash cycle time	(Number days of inventory + Number days receivables outstanding) – Number days payables outstanding

*Measures must be averaged across all supply chain participants. Measures are based in part on Bolstorff, P., "Measuring the Impact of Supply Chain Performance," *Logistics Today*, December 2003, p. 6.

the days receivables outstanding can be calculated as:

$$DRO = \frac{\text{Avg. Receivables \$}}{\text{Annualized Revenues}/365}$$

and the days payables outstanding can be calculated as:

$$DPO = \frac{\text{Avg. Payables \$}}{\text{Annualized Materials Costs}/365}$$

Cash-to-cash cycle time is commonly viewed as one of the best overall measures of supply chain performance, when averaged across all of a supply chain's members. It encompasses a number of contributing activities such as supply chain speed, quality, and cost.

SUMMARY

This chapter introduced a wide range of inventory management topics, all of which are important to the continued success of firms and their supply chain constituents. The objective of the chapter was to illustrate the processes, benefits, and challenges of inventory management, beginning with a general discussion of the types and functions of inventory, continuing with discussions of independent and dependent demand inventory management methods, and ending with discussions of collaborative inventory management practices and the importance of monitoring the performance of inventory management inside the firm and among its supply chain trading partners. Effective inventory management practices can provide a competitive weapon for an organization and its supply chains, or they can create a continuing depletion of assets and customers if ignored or designed and implemented poorly.

KEY TERMS

ABC inventory classification, 197

aggregate plans, 187

aggregate production plan, 203

anticipation inventories, 179

bill of materials, 203

bullwhip effect, 184

capacity requirements planning, 209

capital costs, 182

continuous inventory review, 212

continuous replenishment, 212

cycle inventories, 180

dependent demand, 187

distribution requirements planning, 207

DRP record, 207

economic order quantity, 187

economic production quantity, 189

economic production quantity model, 189

efficient consumer response, 212

external inventory control, 178

finished goods, 179

frozen time period, 203

globally optimize the supply chain, 199

hedge inventories, 180

independent demand, 187

internal inventory control, 178

inventory carrying costs, 182

inventory holding costs, 182

Just-In-Time II, 213

lean principles, 199

load reports, 209

lost opportunity costs, 182

maintenance, repair, and operating (MRO) supplies, 179

manufacturing resource planning (MRP II), 209

master production schedule, 202

material requirements planning, 201

order costs, 182

order cycle time, 187

part record, 205

planned order release, 205

probabilistic demand and cycle time ROP, 196

probabilistic demand reorder point model, 193

product structure diagram, 203

purchase cost, 184

quantity discount model, 192

radio frequency identification, 184

raw materials, 179

reorder point, 188

robust, 189

rolling production schedule, 203

safety stocks, 180

service level, 195

setup costs, 182

stockout cost, 182

supplier colocation, 213

time fence, 203

total inventory costs, 187

total landed cost, 184

transportation inventories, 180

vendor managed inventories, 213

work-in-process (WIP), 179

DISCUSSION QUESTIONS

1. Why is inventory considered a "necessary evil"?

2. List and describe the five functions of inventory.

3. What are the four types of inventory costs?

4. How can the risk of a stockout be reduced?

5. List some of the causes of stockouts.

6. Discuss the relationship between the bullwhip effect and inventory, and what can be done to manage it.

7. Define independent and dependent demand, and provide examples of each.

8. What are total inventory costs comprised of?

9. Why does the EOQ only seek to minimize annual order costs and annual inventory carrying costs? What happened to stockout cost and purchase cost?

10. Why is the EOQ model described as "robust"?

11. How does the quantity discount model differ from the EOQ?

12. Explain the order policy used when demand is allowed to vary.

13. What determines the level of safety stock to be used in the variable demand reorder point level?

14. What is the idea behind ABC inventory classification?

15. What can be said about order lead times and safety stock in actively managed supply chains?

16. In a few sentences, explain what an MRP system is and what it does.

17. Where do the numbers in the MPS come from?

18. What is a frozen time period or time fence in the MPS?

19. What is a rolling production schedule in the MPS?

20. Why is accurate inventory and lead time information so important to the MRP?

21. What is a BOM, and why is it important to an MRP system?

22. What is the MRP part record rule?

23. What does the DRP do?

24. Why are DRP planned shipping quantities so important?

25. What were the drivers behind the development of MRP II?

26. Describe several ways that various functional groups might use an MRP II system.

27. How does the MRP II system perform capacity requirements planning?

28. Define the term *quick response* and describe its connection to supply chain management.

29. Discuss the benefits of vendor managed inventories.

30. JIT II and supplier colocation, now being practiced in many large organizations, provides ample benefits to buyer and supplier. Discuss these.

PROBLEMS

1. Debbie Jenkins owns a neighborhood hot dog stand, and wants to determine some good order policies for hot dogs. She estimates her annual demand to be constant and equal to 10,000 hot dogs. Her order cost is $20, her carrying cost plus opportunity cost is 40 percent per year, her purchase cost is $0.20 per hot dog, and her order lead time is two days.

   a. What is the optimal order quantity?

   b. What is the annual order cost?

   c. What is the annual inventory carrying cost?

   d. How many orders per year will Debbie make?

   e. How many days are there between orders?

   f. What is the reorder point?

   g. What is the optimal order policy?

2. Grebby Golf Tees makes high-end golf tees for professional golfers, as well as the economy tees that all other golfers use. Their demand forecast for the upcoming professional season is 3,500,000 tees, or an average daily demand of approximately 14,000 premium tees, given that the plant operates 250 days per year. The Grebby tee manufacturing process can produce about 22,000 tees per day (for either premium or economy tees). The setup cost for premium tees is $100, the cost to make one tee is $0.08, and the opportunity cost of holding inventory is 25 percent per year.

   a. What is the EPQ for premium tees?

   b. How many days will it take to make the production run?

   c. What will the maximum inventory level be?

3. Perkin's Rodeo Tack & Boots sells gear to rodeo industry customers and Greg, the owner, has been offered discounts for the purchase of some alligator-hide boots from his long-time boot supplier. The pricing alternatives for the alligator boots are $62 per pair for 1–99 units purchased; $57 per pair for 100–299 units purchased, and $54 per pair for 300 or more units purchased. Perkin's average order cost is $25 per order, the forecasted annual demand for alligator boots is 1,200 pairs, and the inventory carrying cost rate is 24 percent per year.

   a. Calculate the EOQ for each of the three purchase prices. Which EOQs are valid?

   b. Which purchasing alternative should Perkin's take? What is its total annual inventory cost?

4. Roy and Gayle's Fix-It Shop purchased a new automated inventory control software application, and it wanted to put ROPs on all of its purchased tools and supplies. After forecasting the demand for items for the upcoming year, the shop was ready to start calculating ROPs. Three of the items are shown in the following table, along with the forecasted annual demands, purchase lead times, lead time demand standard deviation levels, and desired service levels. Calculate the ROPs for the three items and their safety stock levels. Assume the store is open 365 days per year.

ITEM	ANNUAL DEMAND	LEAD TIME	STD. DEV. OF LEAD TIME DEM.	REQUIRED SERVICE LEVEL
Duct Tape	2,300 rolls	12 days	6 rolls	99%
Super Glue	1,800 bottles	6 days	4 bottles	90%
Hammer	650 hammers	21 days	3 hammers	80%

5. Bob was just hired as the new purchasing manager at Laura's Furniture, and he decided to recalculate all of their ROPs since he noticed that many of the suppliers' delivery times varied substantially from one order to the next. Bob asked Mary Jane, his buyer, to recalculate the first one he calculated (a desk) to make sure he did it correctly. Bob also wanted to know the safety stock required. The upcoming annual demand forecast was 950 units. The purchase order lead times varied, with an average of 18 days and a standard deviation of 6 days. The daily demand also varied, with an average of three units per day, and a standard deviation of five units per day. The company tries to maintain a 98 percent service level. Determine the ROP and safety stock for the desk, as Bob did.

6. Classify the following items using the ABC inventory classification approach. Which items should be monitored most closely, and which ones should have the least amount of safety stock?

ITEM	COST/UNIT ($)	FORECASTED ANNUAL DEMAND
1	6.40	1,700
2	7.80	7,500
3	17.49	6,240
4	44.00	260
5	105.99	150
6	345.00	300

7. Using the product structure diagram and the other information shown in the following table, complete the part records for each of the parts. Note that "LFL" means lot-for-lot, or to simply make or buy whatever is needed. Note also that Part D appears in two places, but must be combined into one part record. Also, what are the purchase and production plans so far?

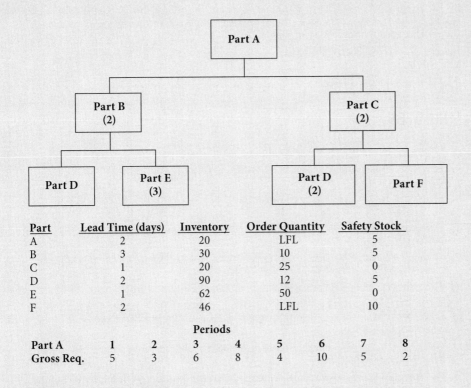

Part	Lead Time (days)	Inventory	Order Quantity	Safety Stock
A	2	20	LFL	5
B	3	30	10	5
C	1	20	25	0
D	2	90	12	5
E	1	62	50	0
F	2	46	LFL	10

			Periods					
Part A	1	2	3	4	5	6	7	8
Gross Req.	5	3	6	8	4	10	5	2

INTERNET QUESTIONS

1. Go to http://www.inventoryops.com and report on three inventory topics covered on the site.

2. What is the latest hog and pig inventory in the United States? Is the number increasing or decreasing?

3. Visit http://www.e-z-mrp.com and report on the characteristics of E-Z MRP™.

INFOTRAC QUESTIONS

Access http://www.infotrac-thomsonlearning.com to answer the following questions:

1. Write a report on the relationship between RFID technologies and inventory management in warehousing and across the supply chain.

2. Write a report on the history of the EOQ formula, and give some real-world examples of it being used today.

3. Discuss the development of MRP and its evolution to MRP II and then ERP. Provide company examples.

REFERENCES

Anupindi, R., S. Chopra, S. Deshmukh, J. Van Mieghem, and E. Zemel (1999), *Managing Business Process Flows,* Prentice Hall, Upper Saddle River, NJ.

Bozarth, C., and R. Handfield (2006), *Introduction to Operations and Supply Chain Management,* Pearson Education, Inc., Upper Saddle River, NJ.

Davis, M., N. Acquilano, and R. Chase (2003), *Fundamentals of Operations Management,* McGraw-Hill/Irwin, New York, NY.

Heizer, J., and B. Render (2006), *Operations Management,* Prentice Hall, Upper Saddle River, NJ.

Markland, R., S. Vickery, and R. Davis (1998), *Operations Management: Concepts in Manufacturing and Services,* Thomson South-Western, Mason, OH.

Meredith, J., and S. Shafer (1999), *Operations Management for MBAs,* John Wiley & Sons, New York, NY.

Stevenson, W. J. (2005), *Operations Management,* McGraw-Hill Irwin, New York, NY.

ENDNOTES

1. Patton, S., "The Perfect Order," *CIO,* V. 18, No. 20, 2005, pp. 1–5.

2. Long, G., "Pursuing Supply Chain Gains," *Healthcare Financial Management,* V. 59, No. 9, 2005, pp. 118–122.

3. Blumenthal, R., "Oil's Well that Ends Well—If the U.S. Goes Easy on Crude," *Barron's,* V. 85, No. 12, 2005, p. 12.

4. Lacefield, S., "Shippers See Inventory Rising," *Logistics Management,* V. 44, No. 10, 2005, pp. 59–62.

5. Troyer, L., J. Smith, S. Marshall, and E. Yaniv, "Improving Asset Management and Order Fulfillment at Deere & Company's C&CE Division," *Interfaces,* V. 35, No. 1, 2005, pp. 76–87.

6. Avery, S., "Purchasing Cards Pack More Punch!" *Purchasing,* V. 134, No. 17, 2005, pp. 46–48.

7. DeWeese, C., "New Trackers Help Truckers Foil Hijackings," *The Wall Street Journal,* September 29, 2005, p. B1.

8. Zinn, W. and P. Liu, "Consumer Response to Retail Stockouts," *Journal of Business Logistics,* V. 22, No. 1, 2001, pp. 49–72.

9. See, for instance, http://www.verisign.com/supply-chain-services/supply-chain-information or http://www.morerfid.com/details.php?subdetail=Report& action=details&report_id=942& display=RFID.

10. An interesting discussion of the formulation of the lead time demand standard deviation can be found in R. Ballou's *Business Logistics Management,* Englewood Cliffs, NJ: Prentice-Hall, 1985, p. 388.

11. Field, A., "Exceeding Expectations," *Journal of Commerce,* February 6, 2006, p. 1.

12. Petroni, A., "Critical Factors of MRP Implementation in Small and Medium-Sized Firms," *International Journal of Operations and Production Management,* V. 22, No. 3, 2002, pp. 329–348.

13. Wailgum, T., "How to Play with the Big Boys," *CIO,* V. 19, No. 8, 2006, p. 1.

14. Hoffman, W., "Managing a Logistics Makeover," *Traffic World,* February 6, 2006, p. 1.

15. Trunick, P., "How to Design a Cost-Effective DC," *Logistics Today,* V. 46, No. 5, 2005, pp. 42–44.

16. Gruman, G., "Supply on Demand," *InfoWorld,* V. 27, No. 16, 2005, pp. 47–50.

17. Snyder, D., "Foxwoods Sees the Wonder of a Strong Back Office Thanks to EatecNetX," *Nation's Restaurant News,* V. 39, No. 26, 2005, pp. S26–S27.

18. See note 4 above.

19. See note 4 above.

20. Micheau, V., "How Boeing and Alcoa Implemented a Successful Vendor Managed Inventory Program," *The Journal of Business Forecasting,* V. 24, No. 1, 2005, pp. 17–19.

21. Atkinson, W., "Does JIT II Still Work in the Internet Age?" *Purchasing,* V. 10, No. 17, 2001, pp. 41–42.

22. Kerr-Perrott, D., "Measuring Up," *Summit,* V. 8, No. 2, 2005, pp. 4–6.

23. Yokl, R., "Less Is More When Storing Inventory," *Hospital Materials Management,* V. 30, No. 8, 2005, pp. 2–3.

24. Richardson, H., "Does Your Supply Chain Deliver Value?" *Transportation & Distribution,* V. 44, No. 3, 2003, pp. 58–60.

25. Bolstorff, P., "Measuring the Impact of Supply Chain Performance," *Logistics Today,* December 2003, p. 6.

Chapter 7:

MANAGING MATERIAL FLOWS

"We were scheduling the plant off a clipboard. We'd pull down EDI releases from customers and say, 'OK, what do we need to ship tomorrow?' Then we'd go out to the floor and say, 'Make me this, this, and this.' It was like going to the grocery store hungry and throwing everything into the shopping cart, rather than creating a checklist of what I need for a dinner party of four."[1]

"In my own experience as a materials manager at a pet food manufacturer for instance, my job to keep stocks of raw materials to a minimum was in conflict with that of the purchasing manager, who would buy in bulk to get the cheapest possible price. A lot of companies still operate that way."[2]

Learning Objectives

After completing this chapter, you should be able to:

- Understand the concepts of material flow and why these are important to the firm.
- Describe the various types of flow analysis and the impact that flow has on the organization.
- Describe how the material flow analysis techniques are conducted.
- Understand the Theory of Constraints and how it is applied.
- Describe how plant layout and material scheduling impacts material flow.
- Describe the different types of material flow concerns in warehouses.

Chapter Outline

Introduction

Material Flow Mapping

Material Flow Analysis

Manufacturing Flexibility

Layout Design

Material Scheduling

Vehicle Scheduling and Routing

Warehouse Material Flow

Process Management in Action

Medical Material Flow at DePuy, Inc.

Surgeons work wonders today. Need a replacement for a knee, hip, or elbow? That's not a problem for modern medicine and the medical device industry. Behind these surgeries—and far, far from the public eye—are the distribution and salespeople for the medical devices used. These people are worriers. They are concerned about making sure these surgeries proceed on the day scheduled. They work wonders, too. They supply, in a timely way, the right medical devices to the right hospitals and surgeons, ensuring the surgeon isn't empty handed in the operating room. "A surgeon may schedule tomorrow's surgery for noon," says Dave Johnson, director of distribution, DePuy, Inc., "placing the order for the needed medical device today."

DePuy, Inc. is a major medical device manufacturer and distributor. Its distribution center near Bridgewater, Massachusetts, ships medical devices on a just-in-time basis directly to hospitals. DePuy does so with a high degree of accuracy, speed, and immediacy. Same-day turnaround is standard procedure for most orders.

From a relatively small distribution center (DC), just 92,000 square feet, DePuy annually ships medical devices to support over 500,000 surgeries, says Johnson. The products shipped include spine implants, surgical instruments, and replacement kits for new knees, hips, elbows, and the like.

What drives DePuy distribution to achieve a high level of excellence? Its customers, both external and internal, do. A surgeon demands a specific type and size of device to make a new knee for a patient. Others set high requirements as well. "Compliance to quality assurance procedures is common to very much of what we do," says Johnson.

The DC achieves these quality and accuracy objectives with a combination of semi-automated and mechanized systems for materials handling. The facility's semi-automated systems include horizontal carousels as well as vertical lift modules. A (horizontal) carousel and a vertical lift module (VLM) fulfill a quality control role as well. All of these storage and staging units work alongside other materials handling systems and equipment that includes narrow-aisle racks with wire-guided forklifts, conveyors, flow racks, bar code scanners, and radio frequency data communication terminals for real-time information control.

The vertical storage units and horizontal carousels together with their order selection software ensure that picking accuracy exceeds 99.9 percent, says Johnson. These systems also save floor space, he adds, as does the high-density storage capability of the narrow-aisle rack system.

Working three shifts daily on a six-day week, this DC selects orders from a total of 14,000 active DePuy stock-keeping units (SKUs). Each order averages five or six lines. The DC ships an average of 2,200 orders each night. About 70 to 80 percent of these shipments are for overnight delivery, says Johnson, making the DC the stockroom for many surgeons.

DePuy operators pick orders manually from bins through using pick tickets in the flow rack area. To ensure high picking accuracy and eliminate errors, Johnson says, he requires bar code scans several times during the picking of each item. Each night, within a time span of three to four hours, the lone carousel operator picks 500 orders. Before the use of this technology, it took five operators picking batch orders to match this one person's productivity. During the day shift, an additional 150 "emergency" orders, with three to four lines per order, are picked from the horizontal carousels. Faster moving items are staged in the carousels' golden zone for more ergonomic picking, says Johnson.

Similarly, a VLM holds some 2,000 kits of DePuy spine implants and surgical instruments. On a daily basis, orders for 150 to 250 kits are picked, and about the same number put away in the VLM. "Order selection from the VLM is a lot easier than going looking for these kits on shelving," says Johnson. With the VLM subsystem presenting the kits at a comfortable working level for picking (or for put away), there's also little fatigue for operators.

Finally, semi-automated vertical handling systems support DePuy distribution's quality control efforts. These efforts are necessary to satisfy requirements of the FDA's good manufacturing practices (GMPs) as well as to meet DePuy's ISO certification. Before the surgeon's hands can work the wonders of hip and knee replacements, DePuy distribution manages the last link in the supply chain for these surgeries. Through DePuy's use of semi-automated, mechanized, and manual material handling systems, the surgeon is not left empty-handed or without the right devices and instruments.

Source: Reprinted from Feare, T., "Just-In-Time to the Operating Room," *Modern Materials Handling,* V. 59, No. 6, 2004, pp. 18. © 2004 *Modern Materials Handling* and Reed Business Information, a division of Reed Elsevier.

Introduction

A number of different types of flow occur continuously in all organizations. For example, when a buyer initiates a purchase order, the order flows to the supplying firm via some method of communication, be it by phone, fax, mail, or web. The supplying firm responds by accepting the order and then producing the product or service ordered. While the order is being completed, the customer waits in a line or queue. When completed, the product or service is delivered to the customer, whereby the customer provides a payment to the supplier. Five different types of flow are represented in this short example. Initiating, approving, and completing a purchase order constitutes work flow; transmitting and receiving the purchase order involves information flow; manufacturing a product requires material flows; producing a service in many cases involves the flow of customers; and paying for purchases creates cash flows. In each of these cases, managing flow effectively can reduce costs while improving quality, cycle time, capacity, flexibility, and supply chain management capabilities. Ultimately, this should lead to increases in customer satisfaction, repeat purchases, profitability, and competitiveness.

At most manufacturing facilities, the idea of managing the flow of materials has been around for a long time. Henry Ford used the idea of material flow management in the early 20th century to revolutionize concepts in manufacturing. Today, Toyota has maintained a leadership position in the automobile industry by managing material flows to create extremely reliable and flexible manufacturing processes.

Generally speaking, materials and components are scheduled for processing at manufacturing and assembly operations according to a specific production strategy, desired sequence of operations, the work-in-process (WIP) inventory existing in the system, the delivery date, the packaging requirements, the customer service objectives, and the transportation and warehousing arrangements. At service facilities, customers are often part of the process and must also be sequenced or placed in queues to await the service. Customer orders are processed based on each order's service requirements, service personnel capabilities, and available server capacity. Along the way, as products and customers flow through these production systems, information is collected, manipulated, and communicated to assist in the handling of goods and people. These information flows or work flows are necessary to maintain control, and to create both fair and cost-effective production systems.

These common flows are evident in almost all organizations, and are of greatest concern to organizations seeking to improve how products and services are made and delivered to customers. World-class organizations have found ways to successfully manage all of these flows to (1) create production flexibility when demand and product selection is highly variable, (2) build lean productive systems and minimize inventories when demand is stable and product assortment is low, and (3) keep customers occupied and their wait times low, as they move through a service system. In a perfect operation, material, people, information, and work would flow in an almost uninterrupted fashion to the customer, stopping only for value-adding processes. Consequently, when problems arise within a firm, evidence of flow problems of one sort or another can usually be found. Any non-value-adding element that stops flow is a problem that must be identified and managed or eliminated. This is the essence of **flow management**.

One need only look at the opening Process Management in Action feature of DePuy to understand the importance of managing material flows. Other examples abound, including California-based Cisco Systems' inventory problems in 2001 and the New Jersey-based toy retailer Toys-R-Us' online Christmas delivery problems in 1999. Leading up to 2001, computer networking giant Cisco Systems had a market capitalization of greater than $500 billion with revenue growth in the 50 percent per year range. In August 2001, though, Cisco announced its first ever negative earnings with sales down 30 percent. It had to write off inventory worth $2.2 billion, and laid off 8,500 workers. Cisco's phenomenal growth, its willingness to let its suppliers and contract manufacturers deal directly with its customers, and a failure to foresee the large downturn in the dot-com business in 2001 led to late deliveries, duplicate orders, and a gross surplus of inventories throughout its supply chain. But Cisco weathered the dot-com bust; it developed new products, found new markets for its routers and switching equipment, and has once again become profitable.[3]

In 1999, Toysrus.com rang up an impressive $39 million for its first season of online Christmas toy sales, only to find that its delivery system was not prepared to handle such a high level of demand. Consequently, it could not honor its promise to deliver goods in time for Christmas that year. As a result of that embarrassing situation, it entered into an agreement with global Internet merchandiser Amazon.com to handle its online fulfillment needs, resulting in nearly 100 percent on-time delivery performance in subsequent Christmas seasons.[4] For both Cisco and Toys-R-Us, material flow problems were such that the supply of products did not match up well with the demand for those products, resulting in excess levels of inventory in some areas combined with stockout situations in others.

For many services, the queuing, scheduling, and processing of customers constitute important flow management considerations. To complicate matters, services are also concerned with material flows—materials that accompany the service and which are sold as part of the service product, and materials that support the provision of services. In other words, services must concern themselves with customer flow *and* product flow to maintain customer satisfaction, while simultaneously minimizing inventory costs. Manufacturing companies have a similar problem. While manufacturing firms are concerned with material flows, they also must manage customer flows when performing warranty repair and return services, or while dispensing information to customers at call centers, for example. Thus, it can be seen that most organizations routinely deal with material and customer flows, along with the other flows mentioned.

Since material, customer, work, and information flow problems are common problems found in most organizations, they are discussed and presented in Part 2 of this textbook. Chapter 7 is concerned primarily with managing material flows, while Chapter 8 discusses the flow of customers and work. Information flow encompasses a number of topics worthy of in-depth discussion and analyses, so this type of flow is discussed in Chapter 9. The topic of cash flow is beyond the scope of this text and so it is left to be covered in finance and accounting texts.

Material Flow Mapping

Chapter 6 provided a more general discussion of inventory management, and this chapter assumes readers possess an understanding of those concepts. Additionally, Chapters 10 and 11 discuss several of the more basic material flow topics as they relate to lean manufacturing and logistics, such as just-in-time concepts and transportation and warehousing. Chapter 15 also covers the flow topic of product returns management. This wide coverage of material flow is necessary for readers to gain a full understanding of the importance of material flows in the organization and its supply chains. To effectively manage material flows, an initial understanding of these flows must first be developed. Therefore, a good place to start is the mapping of material flows within a process or series of processes.

Mapping material flows within a process is the first step in understanding how a process works and integrates with other processes. This understanding is also necessary when considering strategies to improve a process. A number of terms are used to describe the mapping process, namely **process mapping, process flowcharting, process flow diagramming**, and **value stream mapping**. All of these terms essentially mean the same thing and have the same objective: to understand the material flows within a process, identify the current sequence of activities making up the process, identify and evaluate or eliminate the activities that are not adding value, and then improve the remaining process activities.

Constructing a process map should include the people directly involved in the process—managers, supervisors, frontline workers, and potentially customers. Mapping a process can become quite involved and can even result in some conflicts within the firm about what activities define a process, when they are performed, and what sequence(s) of activities take place. Process mapping can also help identify internal and external suppliers and customers, how employees fit into or contribute to the process, and how customers interact with and benefit from the process. When a process map is completed, it can be used for training purposes; to identify where performance measures should be taken; to determine where unnecessary delays and activities are occurring; and to discover where quality, cost, and productivity problems might exist.

A number of standard symbols are used when constructing a process map to improve the map's readability and visual impact, and these are shown in Table 7.1. Additionally, a simple process map for manufacturing a hypothetical testing instrument is shown in Figure 7.1, using the symbols shown in Table 7.1. The testing instrument consists of a purchased sensor board, as well as a metal box and lid, which are both fabricated from purchased sheet metal (Steps 1, 2, and 3 in Figure 7.1). The box, lid, and sensor board are assembled (Step 4), and the final product is inspected and tested in quality assurance (Step 5). If the instrument passes inspection and testing, it is packaged and labeled (Step 6) and eventually sent to the warehouse and stored until the product is distributed to customers. Units that do not pass the quality assurance stage are discarded as scrap.

Table 7.1	Process Map Symbols
SYMBOL	**MEANING**
⬭	Start or end of process.
▭	A process operation. Work is performed.
△	Delay or storage.
◇	Decision.
⟶	Physical movement or transportation.
⇢	Information flow.

Several inventory decisions occur in this manufacturing process, and these are shown as diamonds in Figure 7.1:

1. If the shop floor storage or staging area for Step 1 is empty, sheet metal is moved from the warehouse to the staging area;

2. If the staging area for Step 4 is empty, sensor boards are moved from the warehouse to the staging area;

3. If the assembled test instrument passes the quality inspection and test, finished units are sent to Step 6, otherwise, the finished units are discarded; and

4. If the Step 6 finished product storage area is full, test instruments are moved to the warehouse.

The triangles denote places where work-in-process (WIP) inventories are stored for varying lengths of time. Initially, sheet metal and sensor boards are purchased and stored in the warehouse. When the Step 1 and Step 4 staging areas need more inventory, sheet metal and sensor boards are moved from the warehouse to these shop floor storage areas. As each step in the manufacturing process is completed, the WIP inventories are stored until needed by the next step in the process. When the finished testing instrument is packaged and labeled, it is stored until a batch of packaged instruments is sent to the warehouse for storage and eventual distribution. The manufacturing process is then complete.

Subprocesses within the manufacturing process could also be mapped for more in-depth analyses. For example, the warehouse subprocess can be mapped. When purchased items arrive at the warehouse, they are inspected and checked against the invoice. Some items might be returned to the supplier if the items don't match up against the invoice, if certain initial quality requirements are not met, or if the delivery timing is incorrect. The remaining items are logged-in to the inventory control system and placed in storage, with the storage location noted. The invoice is then sent to accounting for payment or adjustment. As the stored items are requested from the shop floor, quantities are deducted from the inventory control system quantities available, and the items are

Figure 7.1	A Process Map for a Testing Instrument Manufacturer

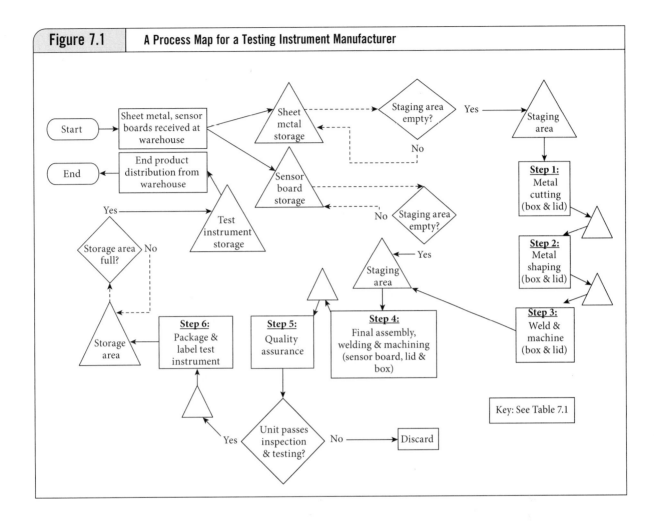

picked from storage and sent to the required areas in the shop. Additionally, as finished products fill the shop floor storage area, they are batched and sent to the warehouse. When these batches arrive at the warehouse, they are logged-in to the inventory control system and placed in storage as finished goods until customer orders are received. Units are then deducted from finished goods inventory, picked out of storage, and shipped to customers. Similarly, each of the manufacturing steps in Figure 7.1 can be mapped separately for closer analysis. The Process Management in Action feature profiles the process mapping success of Medtronic, a medical equipment manufacturer.

Material Flow Analysis

Process maps are extremely important for understanding material flows and can serve as the foundation for analyzing the material flows into, within, and out of a process. When the initial process map is complete, a number of items should become apparent, namely where inventories are delayed or stored throughout the process, the paths that inventories follow as they wend their way through the process, and the sequence of activities that make up the process. It is then possible to measure travel distances and travel times, time spent in storage and in processing, and time spent waiting on materials. It

Process Management in Action

Value Stream Mapping Success at Medtronic

Pick up just about any map of Jacksonville, Florida, and it's easy to find your way to Medtronic Inc.'s Xomed plant off I–95 south of town. Navigating the value stream mapping process that is critical to the medical products plant's impressive manufacturing achievements is a bit more challenging. Value stream mapping sounds as if it has more to do with charting a river than with producing stuff used in ear, nose, throat, and eye surgery.

Jon Swanson, director of manufacturing at Medtronic Xomed's Jacksonville plant for the past two years, recognizes that. More precise than value chain analysis, "value-stream mapping is a standardized way of documenting what's happening and a systematic way to analyze that to develop an improvement plan," Swanson stresses. "We actually look at the physical flow and map that. And then we map the information flow that links the processes together. And the whole idea is to identify what the waste is in the value stream, with the objective of eliminating the waste," explains Swanson.

Including the high-volume value streams that turn out handheld hot-wire cauteries that eye doctors use to stem bleeding during surgery, the value stream that makes two or three nerve integrity monitors per day, and the value stream that produces up to ten tiny prosthetic stapes a month for people with middle-ear problems, there are four dozen individual value streams at Medtronic Xomed in Jacksonville. Each one has been mapped at least once since April 26, 2000, the day a group of managers committed the full facility to lean manufacturing.

Value stream mapping at the Jacksonville plant is a tactical tool that allows management to identify bottlenecks and other production problems in individual value streams. "It forces you to eliminate all the things you think you know by seeing what is actually happening," Swanson stresses. For example, on the cautery line, value stream mapping helped identify fixture changeover as a production bottleneck. A technician designed a new fixture that replaces the 14 fixtures that formerly had to be rotated in and out of the line depending upon the type of cautery being produced.

Value stream mapping also is a strategic tool. "We have used it as a strategic planning tool to figure out where to go with the flow of the entire facility," says Swanson. In effect, the maps of the individual value streams get put together to produce a bigger map, not only of the entire plant's flow now (known as "current state"), but also of what management wants the flow to be (known as "future state"). For example, value stream mapping showed that the days-long process of sterilizing products—whether done at the plant or off-site—constitutes a facility-wide bottleneck that adds to lead times, inventory levels, and costs. The plant continues to evaluate alternatives even as it expects to step up the pace at which its Merocel surgical sponges move through an off-site sterilizer.

Results from value stream mapping at the Medtronic Xomed plant have been remarkable. Total production lead time, including the lead time of suppliers, has been cut to 129 days from 253 days during the last three years. Standard order-to-shipment lead time has been reduced by 50 percent during the last three years. The cost of a shipped product, including the costs of purchased materials, has fallen 38 percent during the last three years. Productivity, as measured by annual sales per employee, has increased 40 percent during the last three years. The plant's on-time delivery rate, based on the date the customer requested, is 96 percent. And the operating equipment efficiency for major production lines is 98.8 percent.

For Swanson personally, value stream mapping has "completely changed" what he thought was possible. "If someone had asked me if we could have freed up 50% of the floor space, and improved the flow rate, and improved productivity and reduce inventory, I would have said we might have been able to take one of those and improve it," he says. In contrast, "we don't think twice now about very high goals and very high expectations for the plant," he states. "These are stretch goals, and maybe we won't be able to reach them this year, but we are going to get there eventually."

Source: McClenahen, J., "Mapping Manufacturing," *Industry Week,* V. 251, No. 9, 2002, pp. 62–64. Used with permission.

is also possible to identify better routes for people, machinery, and materials throughout the facility. This information has implications for shop floor personnel and equipment capacity utilizations, personnel and machine scheduling, shop floor layout and storage capacity requirements, and a host of other things such as employee training, information system requirements, warehouse capacity and layout requirements, supplier delivery scheduling, and customer distribution scheduling.

Referring again to the test instrument manufacturing process shown in Figure 7.1, a number of process analysis questions come to mind. These questions will vary based on the process being analyzed.

- How often are supplier deliveries made to the warehouse?
- How long are inventories stored in the warehouse?
- How often are inventories moved to the shop floor?
- Where do inventories tend to stack up within the facility?
- Can purchased items bypass the warehouse and be delivered directly to the shop floor staging areas?
- How close are the six processing areas in the facility to each other?
- Are any of the six processing areas acting as bottlenecks to the flow of materials?
- Can packaged and labeled test instruments be distributed to customers directly from the shop floor storage area?
- How effective are the communications and delivery equipment between the warehouse and the three shop floor staging/storage areas?
- How often are test units discarded due to poor quality?
- Can poor-quality test units be repaired instead of discarded?
- What is the overall performance of the manufacturing process?
- What is the actual manufacturing output versus the facility's design capacity?

Answers to these questions can be found quite readily using observations and collection of data such as activity and wait times, worker and machine inactivity times, units of inventory "stored" at various locations, batch sizes, distances between activities, and the frequency and timing of inbound deliveries from suppliers and outbound deliveries to the firm's customers. The initial inquiries resulting from the process mapping exercise serve as the starting point of a **material flow analysis**. Collecting data as described here can then guide the process assessment and improvement efforts. Once the data collection phase is complete, the participants in the analysis can compare the current state of the process to a desired or ideal process state based on customer requirements, and rank order the desired process changes based on cost, implementation time, and expected benefit. Process performance measures can then be instituted to track ongoing process capability.

Some typical process changes might include things like decreasing process variability through use of standard procedures or automation; synchronizing capacity with demand by increasing process capacity, cross-training workers, and hiring part-time workers; revising process layouts to reduce material travel time; using fewer but more reliable suppliers; and postponing final assembly until customer orders are received.

Accompanying each activity in a process is a potential source of delay, production variance, and cost. As materials, parts, and products flow through the manufacturing process these problems are additive and can have a significant impact on the final product delivered to customers. Some companies are shocked when they discover the small percentage of total manufacturing cycle time that is spent adding value to products, the amount of space that is being used to store purchased and WIP materials, or the amount of idle equipment and workers on the shop floor. At a manufacturer of control panel buttons, for example, an analysis showed that while the actual manufacturing time had been reduced to just over two minutes, it was taking over 12 weeks to deliver product to customers! This equates to a ratio of value-added time to total cycle time of significantly less than 1 percent.[5]

Most companies are under increasing pressure to handle more products, with changing volumes, on flexible processes, in a shorter time frame; and all this with lower inventories, which further increases the need to continually analyze processes and their material flows. Particularly given the popularity of process outsourcing, material flows are constantly changing, requiring a continued emphasis on flow analysis. Distribution centers are a good case in point. Increasingly, manufacturers are building more centralized production facilities, consolidating regional warehouses, turning others over to third-party companies, and reducing the size of shipments to customers, while increasing delivery frequencies. The impact on distribution centers is that **throughput volumes** are increasing and unpacking and repacking activities are decreasing. Throughput in warehousing terminology is simply the rate at which packages move through the facility.[6] Additionally, there is a need for faster, automated material handling equipment and better tracking capabilities, such as the use of **radio frequency identification** (RFID) tagging. As a reminder, RFID refers to very small, inexpensive tags containing serial numbers or customer account information that can be affixed to individual products or cases. These tags carry low-power radio frequency signal transmitters that are read by mobile or fixed scanners, placed where data capture is desired. The data is fed to a host information system via wireless linkage. Items can then be tracked automatically through transport, distribution centers, and retail locations using standardized RFID tags and scanners. "You want to reduce variation where you can," says Rick Moradian, vice president of international logistics at APL Logistics of Oakland, California. "You want product to arrive on time, information to flow properly, the trucker to be at the right dock at the right time, and documents done properly. Handoffs, in particular, should be smooth."[7]

Inrange Technologies Corp., a New Jersey original equipment manufacturer, uses Avnet, a parts distributor, as a supply chain partner to help manage its material flows. Avnet serves as a liaison with local manufacturer representatives, and it maintains an on-site storage facility that moves parts to the assembly line in just-in-time fashion. Inrange shares its weekly production plan with Avnet to help plan the material pipeline. As a result, Inrange has reduced overhead costs, freed up cash, and improved flexibility to respond to changes in customer demand.[8] One of the more popular and successful

"If we process the work this way, everyone will get more exercise."

© 2000 Ted Goff http://www.tedgoff.com

material flow analysis techniques involves the use of the Theory of Constraints, the next topic of discussion.

The Theory of Constraints

Constraints in an organizational context are things that keep the firm from achieving its goals. Constraints can refer to physical things, such as material bottlenecks along the supply chain or on the manufacturing floor, or a lack of labor capacity. Constraints can also refer to procedures and behavioral constraints, such as lack of training programs, poor labor attitudes, or cultural norms that exist in the organization. A **bottleneck** is a type of constraint that acts to restrict material flow, reduce overall capacity and product output capability, increase process cycle time, and hence negatively impact customer service capabilities of the organization and its supply chain trading partners. It is important to understand that one or more bottlenecks can be found *in all firms*. As one bottleneck is discovered and fixed, the second-largest bottleneck surfaces and becomes the new primary constraint. Thus, identifying and treating process bottlenecks can be viewed as a continuous concern for the organization.

Product quality can also suffer as a result of process bottlenecks, when firms try to cut corners to make up for lost time as the result of a bottleneck. A host of other problems can also surface if bottleneck problems are not treated, such as unscheduled overtime, higher inventory levels, frequent equipment breakdowns, and constant expediting of late jobs—all of which create unnecessary costs and potential lost sales for the organization.

Identifying and improving constrained processes is the principal objective of the **Theory of Constraints** (TOC), and can be applied in supply chain, manufacturing, service, and administrative processes. The TOC has been written about and used in many business applications since the concept was popularized in 1986 in *The Goal: A Process of Ongoing Improvement,* by Eliyahu Goldratt and Jeff Cox.[9] Other terms that have been used to describe TOC are **management by constraint** and in the area of project management, the **critical path method**. Today, the TOC has come to be known as a philosophy of improvement that recognizes the fact that there will always be limitations to system performance, and that the limitations in many cases can be caused by a small number of process bottlenecks or constraints. Once solutions have been found and implemented that address these bottlenecks, system performance has been shown to generally improve.

Bottleneck activities can be found by creating time reports for various process activities for comparison purposes, or by simply looking for the telltale signs of a process bottleneck, such as inventory piling up on a warehouse dock or aisle on the shop floor, trucks waiting to be loaded or unloaded, jobs that have become backlogged, or queues of customers waiting to receive service (queuing analysis is covered in Chapter 8). Certain processes or activities can become bottlenecks for a number of reasons, including the changing designs of products, equipment wear, new workers in need of training, new suppliers or distributors, and new processing techniques and equipment. Successful managers can overcome these bottlenecks by:

- Increasing capacity at the constrained activity with better tools, workers, suppliers, or training/motivational methods;
- Designing better material routes or layouts;
- Avoiding having unconstrained resources doing unnecessary work;
- Designing effective contingency plans or procedures;
- Using performance measures that are tied to system-wide objectives to encourage global thinking;
- Performing quality checks just prior to encountering a potential bottleneck, so that defective units can be pulled from the process before bottleneck resources are applied; and
- Performing routine preventive maintenance on equipment.

Otherwise, managers must reduce their process output rate expectations to match the lower capacity of the bottleneck.

Drum, Buffer, Rope Concept

The TOC can also be explained using the **drum, buffer, rope (DBR) concept**, a popular terminology for explaining the TOC. A conceptualization of the DBR concept is shown in Figure 7.2. In the figure, the bottleneck, Machine 3, is the capacity constrained resource and determines the processing rate of the entire facility (50 units per day). This machine represents the drum, which sets the pace (the beat of the drum) for the facility. The buffer, located at Machine 3, is the inventory placed or extra work time incorporated into the schedule at the bottleneck. Inventory buffers, excess service providers, and overtime workers are used to ensure that the bottleneck resource can provide work to other downstream processes (in this case, Machine 4) even when the bottleneck process or upstream processes experience unscheduled downtime. Notice that Machines 1 and 2 have higher output capabilities than Machine 3, the constraint. This means that no inventory buffers or safety stocks are required at these machines. Even if they experience machine breakdowns or other unscheduled downtime, this is alright, since they can catch up with the constrained process, and the safety stock at Machine 3 will allow it to continue processing during this period.

Downstream of the constrained process is Machine 4. If something halts production for a time at Machine 4, this is also alright, since output from Machine 3 will accumulate at Machine 4. Then when Machine 4 is back up and running, it will quickly work through this accumulation because of its higher output capability. The rope refers to

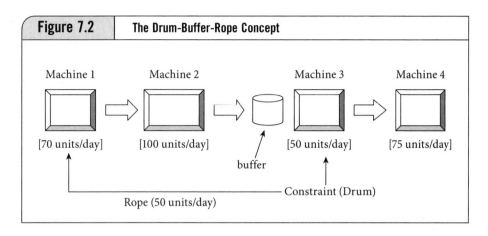

Figure 7.2 | **The Drum-Buffer-Rope Concept**

Machine 1   Machine 2   Machine 3   Machine 4

[70 units/day]   [100 units/day]   [50 units/day]   [75 units/day]

buffer

Constraint (Drum)

Rope (50 units/day)

the control or scheduling of work releases to the facility, which is derived according to the drum and the buffers. In the figure, the rope is the 50 units per day production schedule. Because the output of the bottleneck process drives the output of the entire facility, organizations must work to increase capacity at the bottleneck process in order to increase the facility's output rate. If, at some future date, technologies are added to increase the output capability of Machine 3 to 75 units per day, the new constraint will become Machine 1, and the facility's output (the rope) will be 70 units per day.

The DBR concept provides a basis for determining a production schedule that is protected from demand variabilities or stockouts. The steps in DBR production scheduling are as follows:

- Determine (forecast) the external demand requirements. This provides the ideal "drum" or processing rate objective.

- Identify the constrained resource(s) or bottleneck(s) in the system.

- Establish the production schedule in line with the most heavily constrained resource(s).

- Use time and inventory buffers at the critical bottlenecks to ensure that desired production rates for the entire system can be achieved.

- Synchronize the release of work at the constrained resources and the non-constrained resources to ensure the right amounts of materials are available at all resources when needed, no unnecessary buffers are accumulating, and that no processes are unduly impeding material flow.

The concepts of the TOC and DBR have been successfully applied in practice over the past 20 years. In a review of the TOC applications, professors Mabin and Balderstone found published reports of over 100 uses of the TOC in the 1990s by manufacturers and service organizations, including some of the world's largest and most recognizable companies as well as very small companies. Among all of the cases studied, no negative outcomes were found. The results from TOC implementations included improvements in revenue, output rate, profit, lead time, and inventory levels.[10] Today, the use of the TOC is as popular as ever. ThermoFab, a maker of plastic enclosures from Massachusetts, has used software based on the TOC since 1998 and has seen dramatic improvements in lead time, excess inventories, and delivery performance. It now delivers twice as fast as its competitors and is able to charge premium prices for its products.[11] Bescast, an Ohio-based supplier of complex casings to the aerospace industry, implemented a TOC project in 2001 and was able to reduce inventories by a third, while improving on-time delivery performance. Interestingly, the initial constraint found was not a production bottleneck, but a company mindset. "It never dawned on me that the constraint didn't have to be a physical constraint, but that it could be the way we think," said Lee Watson, Bescast president.[12] The Service Perspective feature profiles the use of TOC at Embassy Flavours, Ltd. of Canada.

The Theory of Constraints Applied to Supply Chains

Generally speaking, end-customer demand drives the pace of a supply chain, thus customer demand tends to be the drum. If a supply chain desires to satisfy customer demand, then finished goods buffers can be held immediately upstream from this demand source (at the retailer, for instance, if we are dealing with individual consumers as end customers). Additionally, one firm participating in the supply chain (a manufacturer of a key component, for example) may be more constrained than other supply chain participants, and thus could be managed as with the DBR concept. The supply chain could potentially maximize its capability to meet demand in this case by maintaining a buffer of the key component to protect against stockouts downstream of this key component manufacturer. Inventory levels at other participating organizations can be set according to the demand and buffer levels, to minimize total supply chain inventory costs.

Manufacturing Flexibility

As mentioned earlier, one objective of material flow management is increased flexibility to alter production, product design, or delivery schedules. In situations where there are many competitors, and new technology and innovative designs cause new products to be introduced frequently, demand for existing products becomes much more uncertain, which in turn means that the flexibility to respond to demand changes in a timely manner is highly desirable. Perhaps one of the better-known examples of flexibility is the often-profiled computer manufacturer Dell Inc. With its ultra-fast, low-inventory, mass-customization business model, Dell simply cannot afford to be caught in a supply-interruption situation. It has worked out a number of contingency plans to deal with potential internal and external supply interruptions. For example, when a labor lockout idled 29 U.S. west coast ports for ten days in 2002, Dell used chartered air carriers to make round trips from Asian parts suppliers to the United States, which kept Dell's manufacturing facilities up and running (a more detailed discussion of this particular Dell strategy is presented in Chapter 11).[13] On the customer side, Dell builds computers very fast (its lead time from ordering parts to customer shipment for a computer is only about eight hours), holds very little inventory, and uses highly automated computer assembly stations. As we've illustrated here, Dell must be flexible in a number of areas to remain successful.

Several terms have been used to describe manufacturing facilities when technology is used to improve material flow and manufacturing flexibility. A **flexible manufacturing system** (FMS) uses a central host computer, computer numerically controlled (CNC) machines, and a plant-wide, automated material handling system equipped with automated conveyors, automated guided vehicles (AGVs), and automated storage and retrieval systems (AS/RS) to schedule small batches of products, route and store parts, and control machining operations among carefully laid-out assembly areas for a number of similar products. This system tries to combine the benefits of highly flexible machine shop processing with highly productive (and fast) repetitive processing. The benefits of using an FMS include reductions in lead time, machining time, scrap, and piece cost, and the ability to quickly change product mix, routing, and machining sequence.

Service Perspective

Embassy Flavours and the Theory of Constraints

Martino Brambilla, owner and president of Embassy Flavours, a manufacturer of flavors for bakery applications in Canada, was ready to take his company to a new level of performance in the flavor industry. To do so, he launched an improvement program that would eventually affect all of his staff and sales force. Brambilla had read about the theory of constraints (TOC) business philosophy, and the ideas resonated loudly with his attitude towards running a business. TOC advocates actively managing the constraints present in every system, and ensures that measures used to monitor or reward directly align people's actions with an organization's goals.

Prior to TOC, staff at Embassy had 17 different measures in place. Some measures were captured for feedback, but most were used to determine staff bonuses. The measures ranged from per-shift output to the percentage of orders shipped correctly and percentage of orders shipped on time. Most of the measures had a reasonably solid foundation for existing—who can argue with measuring the rate at which orders are shipped to customers on time?

On close examination, however, seemingly small problems with certain measures actually turned out to frequently reward staff for taking actions that negatively affected the business. For example, on a day when a couple of large orders and many more small orders were to be shipped, the shipping staff would achieve a better on-time delivery performance by shipping all of the small orders and leaving the big ones until the end. If the shippers were unable to get all of the orders out, they may have actually failed to ship half of the day's potential revenues.

The sales staff was rewarded for exceeding revenue targets in existing accounts, as well as growing volumes in new accounts. Using TOC product profitability measures, it became clear that not all products earned profits for Embassy at the same rate. TOC advocates a modified form of direct costing to evaluate product profitability. This means that there are no allocations of labor or overhead. The metric used is throughput, or sales less total variable costs (typically only materials, though commissions or other variable costs may be included). For example, product A may yield $500 of throughput from $1,000 sales, while product B may yield only $250 from the same sales figure. At the same time, products are evaluated in terms of how much capacity of key limited resources (constraints) they consume. Product A may consume five times as much capacity per unit as product B, actually making it less profitable for the business. In other words, product A will generate fewer throughput dollars for a fixed amount of constraint capacity.

Brambilla decided that he didn't want salespeople, he wanted throughput people. By changing the reward basis to throughput from sales, Brambilla completely shifted the focus away from low margin, easy-to-sell products towards the products that make Embassy more money. Brambilla decided to base bonuses for all non-sales staff on a measure of late shipments that he called "sales dollar days." This measure captures the sales value of all orders that are not shipped on the due date, and averages the value over the course of a month.

Staff members in the development and quality assurance department were initially confused about their impact on achieving this measure—after all, they may not have anything to do directly with a particular order. As Brambilla explains, "The R&D staff has a great influence over our sales dollar days. As the group that initially develops the formulation, they can rationalize ingredients and use products already in stock. They have to properly notify the purchasing department on the lead times and issues regarding new raw materials."

Embassy Flavours requires scrupulous adherence to good processes in making flavors and ingredients. By tightening up the order management processes, it has been able to improve its

Continued

delivery performance while at the same time reducing the levels of inventories needed to support operations. Key in achieving these results was stripping away measures that could in any way conflict with good order flow. Embassy is now positioned to go after new opportunities in the flavor and ingredients marketplace, knowing that all employees are measured in a manner that will focus them on delivering products on time and at the best profit rate.

Source: Milroy, P., "Setting Your Sight Lines," *CMA Management*, V. 78, No. 4, 2004, pp. 16–17. Used with permission.

FMS often goes hand-in-hand with computer-aided design (CAD) systems, computer assisted manufacturing (CAM) systems, and group technology (GT) cells. Managing the entire system of interconnecting processes using central integrated computer control for planning, scheduling, and decision-making purposes is termed **computer integrated manufacturing** (CIM).

CAD refers to use of computer graphics applications for the product design process. Designers can pull up similar product designs stored in a computer database and modify them using light pens, joysticks, or similar devices. Designers can then rotate the product design three-dimensionally on a computer monitor, perform engineering design analyses, create material specifications, or cut the product in half to look inside the design. Designer productivity is greatly enhanced using CAD applications. CAM refers to the use of computers in manufacturing processes. CAM applications include welding or painting robots, **computer numerically controlled (CNC) machines** (programmable machines, such as lathes, that are capable of storing machining steps for repetitively manufactured parts), automated conveyors, and automated overhead part racks. One of the most highly regarded industrial robots is the Selective Compliance Assembly Robot Arm, or SCARA, developed in Japan over 40 years ago. The SCARA still remains the best robot for jobs involving point-to-point movements like dispensing, loading, picking and placing, assembling, and palletizing. "SCARAs are still the fastest robots," says Brian Jones, section manager of sales planning at California-based automotive parts manufacturer Denso Robotics. "We make 4-axis SCARAs that perform a standard cycle in .29 seconds and within 20 microns of repeatability. That's impressive."[14]

Group technology (GT) cells refer to groups of manufacturing workstations that are dedicated to production of similar parts or part families, requiring the same processing equipment. The machines in each workstation are physically situated close together, and may be connected by automated material handling equipment. While this manufacturing strategy has existed since the 1950s, it has come into common use more recently due to the ability of computers to search through a database of product designs and process routings, and then cluster similarly processed parts into part families. There are a number of reported advantages. In a survey of 32 U.S. companies using GT cells, the five most commonly cited benefits were (1) reduction of WIP inventories, (2) reduction of setup times, (3) reduction of manufacturing lead times, (4) reduction of material handling, and (5) improvement of output quality.[15] In a GT implementation study using Camish Machine and Mould Industry, Inc. of Turkey, the before-and-after performance measurements revealed 50 percent reductions in manufacturing lead times and WIP inventories, a 100 percent increase in on-time deliveries, and a 67 percent reduction in average setup times.[16]

Mass Customization

Generally speaking, manufacturing companies like standardization because it enables them to produce large quantities of identical product, resulting in lower purchasing costs, better equipment utilization, lower processing costs, and finally, a lower total cost per unit. Unfortunately, customers do not necessarily desire standardized products but often prefer customized products as long as the purchase price is reasonable. Firms that can figure out how to offer customized products at relatively low prices can then find themselves with fewer competitors and potentially enjoy an advantage in the market-place. As discussed in Chapter 2, companies have been able to accomplish this in recent years using **mass customization**. The idea is to design a product using standardized parts, while incorporating a degree of customized assembly, prior to delivery to customers.

Offering a number of finished product variations, and then delaying final assembly until a customer order is received is a **postponement strategy**, and is a common practice of mass customization. Manufacturers can still mass-produce parts and sub-assemblies, and negotiate large-volume purchases with suppliers to reduce costs. Numerous examples of this type of mass customization can be found in both manufacturing and services. At global shoe manufacturer Nike, for instance, customers can visit Nike.com and design a personalized pair of shoes that will be shipped directly to them. When purchasing a Dell computer, customers are required to specify the computer, keyboard, and monitor configuration they want, by visiting Dell's website or by calling Dell's customer service number. And at U.S. Italian eatery Romano's Macaroni Grill, customers can create their own pasta dishes, choosing from four types of pasta, eight sauces, and 12 toppings. Furniture and clothing manufacturers have also incorporated postpone-ment as a way to customize products while keeping costs low.

Layout Design

One of the more obvious elements impacting material flow is facility layout. Well-designed layouts can reduce product throughput time, which in turn reduces WIP inventory levels. Good layouts consider the placement of departments, work centers, equipment, materials, and workers so as to reduce non-value-adding movements and the overall distance traveled within the facility, for both products and workers, while satisfying output requirements. Poor layout design, on the other hand, can impact employee morale and productivity, as well as production costs and production lead times, and will most likely lead to significant redesign costs, as physical structures and heavy equipment are moved to accommodate layout design changes. There are a number of manufacturing facility layouts to consider, depending on product customization requirements, output desired, funds available, and the product output mix. Several manufacturing facility layouts and their design considerations are discussed next.

Product-Focused Layouts

Product-focused layouts are used to achieve high-volume output of standardized products. Processing steps are standardized and divided into relatively equal time lengths of work and then assigned to workers, permitting specialization to occur. Over time, workers become proficient in their processing activities, further reducing average product throughput time or lead time and increasing output levels. Typically, processing equipment and workers are dedicated to specific sets of tasks, and the products are similar in design, requiring the same equipment arrangements and setups. These layouts are also called **assembly lines**. Each unit of product typically follows the same sequence of processing steps, so the layout can utilize automated material handling equipment, such as conveyors, to transport products from one processing area to the next.

One of the most imitated assembly line systems in the world is Toyota's automobile manufacturing system. Its assembly lines produce high volumes of automobiles with one of the lowest defect rates in the industry. The Motomachi plant in Japan, for instance, produces about 300 automobiles per eight-hour shift—or about one car every 1.6 minutes![17] Figure 7.3 shows a simplified assembly line.

Raw materials are delivered to the line, where three workstations perform a number of processing activities until the product is completed. The workstations are located in close proximity to one another, to facilitate faster material movements. The production tasks are divided as equally as possible at each workstation, in order to balance the assembly line. **Balancing the line** achieves a number of positive outcomes. By dividing the processing work equally, an equitable work assignment is achieved for employees. It also guarantees that the firm can produce at desired output levels, and reduces the likelihood and severity of processing bottlenecks, resulting in smoother product flow and higher potential product output levels. Line balancing is based on the output levels desired, the work time available per day, the number of workers, and the assembly task times.

Assembly Line Balancing Steps

The sequence of steps required to balance an assembly line is relatively straightforward:

1. Specify the sequence of tasks to be performed, using a diagram where circles represent tasks and arrows represent the precedence relationships.

2. Determine the **takt time** (derived from the German word *taktzeit,* meaning literally "clock cycle" and also referred to as the assembly line's **cycle time**[18]) using the formula:

$$TT = \frac{\text{Daily operating time}}{\text{Average customer demand per day} + \text{Expected variability in demand}}$$

   The takt time establishes the pace of the assembly line, or how often a unit must come off the end of the assembly line.

3. Determine the minimum number of workstations required to satisfy the takt time and the output requirement per day, using the formula:

$$W_{min} = \frac{\text{Sum of all task times}}{TT}$$

4. Use a rule or heuristic to assign tasks to workstations, such that the sum of task times for each workstation does not exceed the takt time. The total number of workstations should also be as close as possible to W_{min} found in Step 3.

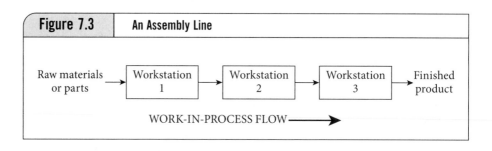

| **Figure 7.3** | **An Assembly Line** |

5. Assign all of the tasks to workstations.

6. Evaluate the efficiency of the assembly line using the formula:

$$\text{Efficiency} = \frac{\text{Sum of all task times}}{(\text{Total \# of workstations})(\text{TT})}$$

Note that (Total # of workstations)(TT) represents the total labor time utilized to produce the required output per day.

7. If necessary, use different heuristics to rebalance the line to maximize efficiency.

Example 7.1 shows an assembly line balancing problem and solution. In this example, a bicycle factory assembles a bicycle in eight assembly steps or tasks. The task times vary from one to seven minutes. The arrows in the diagram indicate the assembly order and precedence, and the circles represent the tasks. The diagram shows that Task *a* must be completed before Tasks *b, c,* or *d* can commence. Tasks *b, c,* and *d* can be completed in any order, however all three must be completed prior to the start of Task *e*. To achieve a desired output of 60 units per day, the takt time or cycle time must be one unit every eight minutes. The objective is then to group tasks so as not to exceed eight minutes of work time per unit per workstation, and to try to group tasks so that the work is evenly distributed among the workstations. The solution shown is just one potential assembly line balancing solution, since other solutions exist (such as grouping Tasks *a, b,* and *d* into Workstation 1). The efficiency is also calculated for the assembly line.

Assembly line balancing in some situations, though, can be argued to cause technical problems. For example, increasing machine utilization at non-bottleneck workstations can cause greater levels of WIP inventory to accumulate at downstream bottleneck workstations, particularly if they are subject to high process time variations. The result can actually be an increase in overall WIP and a reduction in throughput times. Cycle times or takt times, inventory carrying costs, quality, and service levels can all degrade, depending on the degree of assembly line process variabilities.

Some would argue instead for an application of the Theory of Constraints discussed earlier to balance assembly lines. As Eliyahu Goldratt, creator of the TOC said, "A plant in which everyone is working all the time is very inefficient."[19] Studies have shown that instituting an assembly line or product-focused process tends to increase worker injuries, boredom, absenteeism, turnover, and grievances, while lowering job satisfaction. For instance, repetition, high force exertion, and improper posture when using manufacturing tools can cause cumulative trauma disorders among assembly line workers. Swapping workers around in the middle of the day is sometimes done to reduce fatigue and injuries.[20] In a factory in the Netherlands, boiler manufacturer Nefit Fasto has employees walk around in circles, following a slow-moving assembly line, performing all of the assembly work on each boiler. In seven minutes, a worker completes all of the assembly tasks, then starts again on another boiler. With seven workers, they can make about 60 boilers per hour. "Standing all the time makes you more tired," says manager Theo Hendriks. With this method, employees stay fresher and do their jobs better, he explains.[21]

Assembly Line Balancing Heuristics

For all but the simplest assembly lines, assigning tasks to workstations to maximize line efficiency is an extremely complex problem. This difficulty has spawned the use of software-based **heuristic** solutions to balance most large assembly lines. A heuristic

Example 7.1   An Assembly Line Balancing Example

The Blakemaster Bicycle Company has decided to begin production of a new line of bicycles and has dedicated an area of its factory for a new production line. The processing activities are as follows, with the arrows indicating the activity sequence and precedence. The desired output per day is 60 units (including expected output variability). The Blakemaster Co. works one 8-hour shift per day, or 480 minutes. It desires to balance the new assembly line.

TASK	TIME (MIN.)
a	4
b	3
c	6
d	1
e	7
f	2
g	2
h	3
	Total 28

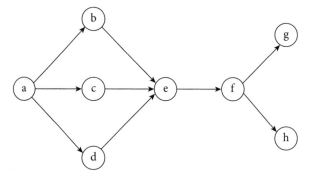

SOLUTION:

The takt time (or cycle time) is

$$TT = \frac{min./day}{units/day} = \frac{480}{60} = 8 \text{ minutes per unit.}$$

There must be at least four workstations, since

$$W_{min} = \frac{\text{tot. task time}}{TT} = \frac{28}{8} = 3.5 \text{ workstations.}$$

Grouping the activities while considering the processing sequence and the cycle time yields WS1: a, b; WS2: c, d; WS3: e; WS4: f, g, h.

WS1 a, b	→	WS2 c, d	→	WS3 e	→	WS4 f, g, h

The assembly line workstations would then appear as shown here. With this type of balance, each workstation has seven minutes of process time, and one minute of slack time, as each unit is assembled (note that the pace of the line, or the cycle time, is eight minutes per unit). The efficiency of the line is then

$$\text{Efficiency} = \frac{\text{tot. task time}}{\#WS \times TT} = \frac{28}{4 \times 8} = 0.875, \text{ or } 87.5 \text{ percent.}$$

solution does not guarantee the best solution—typically it is a procedure that yields a reasonable estimate or solution in a relatively short period of time. Estimating the number of coins in a large container, for example, might employ a heuristic such as counting the number of coins on the top layer, then estimating the number of layers in the container, to arrive at a quick, reasonable estimate.

A great number of line balancing heuristics have been proposed and tested using simulation programs over the years, and some have found their way into commercial software applications. For example, once a sequence of tasks has been specified, those tasks might then be assigned to workstations based on one of the following rules:

- Assign the largest remaining processing time first to a work center in sequential order, until the takt time is reached, then start a new work center.
- Assign the largest remaining processing positional weight first (this is equal to the task processing time plus all of the processing times of tasks depending on it), until the takt time is reached, then start a new work center.
- Assign the task with the most number of following tasks first, in sequential order, until the takt time is reached, then start a new work center.
- Assign the task with the most number of immediate followers first, in sequential order, until the takt time is reached, then start a new work center.[22]

Cellular Layouts

Group technology layouts, also referred to as **cellular layouts**, fall into the product-focused layout category as well. Parts and assemblies that are manufactured in the production facility and that require the same processing equipment are identified and grouped into part families. Manufacturing "cells" or small assembly areas are then created to process these part families. Particularly if parts are needed frequently and in large quantities, it makes sense to create cellular layouts with equipment and workers dedicated to the production of these parts. The resulting layouts can then be balanced as shown in Example 7.1 and have the same advantages as assembly lines. One caveat, though, is that designing a cellular layout may be far easier said than done, given the time and effort required to identify part families; the high purchase cost of manufacturing equipment; and the time, inconvenience, and cost of moving existing equipment into a dedicated area.

In many cases, companies introduce cellular layouts to increase output when products catch on in the marketplace, with demand growing quickly. The use of cellular layouts can also be seen as a good way to reorganize the shop floor after piecemeal expansions, which have caused material flow and inventory problems to surface. For example, Electric Box & Enclosures, Inc., a small, Alabama-based manufacturing company, started in 1988 with just a few machines. By 1997, the company had grown substantially, but haphazardly—while 1.5 percent of its products comprised over 60 percent of demand, the firm was laid out in typical machine shop fashion, with similar machines grouped in departments, for flexibility purposes. As a result, material flow problems had surfaced, causing significant quality, lead time, and inventory problems. A plan was developed to design several cellular layouts around the most popular items and the plan was fully implemented by 1999. The new layout resulted in higher output with 25 percent fewer employees, a 67 percent reduction in manufacturing lead times, and a 50 percent reduction in WIP inventory, with substantial improvements in quality.[23]

Process-Focused Layouts

Process-focused layouts are desirable when many dissimilar products are manufactured, requiring small output volumes or batch sizes. These layouts are designed for manufacturing flexibility, and are also called **intermittent process layouts**, referring to the irregular usage of processing equipment. In a typical week, some equipment may not be used at all, while other machines may be heavily utilized. Consequently, machines tend to be grouped by function in departments. Machine shops and auto repair garages are good examples of this type of production facility and departmental layout.

Due to the varied nature of demand, jobs are scheduled for processing and queued into the facility when they occur. This can result in significant wait times, depending on how busy the shop already is when demand occurs (note for instance, how long it takes to get your car repaired, when you show up at 10:00 A.M.!). Different jobs require different processing sequences within the facility, so parts, materials, and assemblies tend to be moving almost randomly within the shop. Thus, automated fixed-path material handling equipment, like conveyors or overhead racks, typically is not used. Instead, jobs are placed on pallets and moved with forklifts, placed in wheeled bins and pushed from machine to machine, or manually moved in some other fashion. This type of material handling, combined with the queuing of jobs at various processing equipment, creates relatively long lead times for jobs, along with higher WIP inventories, when compared to similar sized product-focused facilities. Process-focused facilities are built for processing flexibility but must sacrifice speed, output, and machine utilization, with high inventory carrying costs. Conversely, product-focused facilities are built to supply high volumes quickly, but sacrifice product flexibility to attain the necessary output levels.

To manage material flow in process-focused firms, the emphasis must first be on placing the most frequently used departments close to one another, so as to minimize total distance traveled (or total travel costs) for each job, and then to schedule jobs most effectively at each machine. Example 7.2 illustrates a machine shop layout analysis to minimize total job distance traveled per day (it is generally assumed that by minimizing total distance traveled, total movement costs are also minimized). In Example 7.2, a better layout was found; however, it may not be the best layout. For firms with many departments, software applications to help find the best layout are often used, since so many department combinations must be evaluated. Job scheduling also affects material flows and is discussed in the following section.

Material Scheduling

Job scheduling decisions are typically the final activity prior to actual production. Job scheduling at each machine is an important flow management activity, since the timing of material purchases and estimates of the completion date or delivery date are based in large part on the production schedule. Effective scheduling can reduce job queue times, inventory carrying costs, and job completion times, increase the capacity of the manufacturing facility, improve employee productivity, and create a competitive advantage in terms of customer service. In many scheduling situations there are trade-offs to be considered, such as whether to keep equipment heavily utilized or reduce product completion times, or finishing many small jobs versus a few long jobs. The scheduling techniques and concerns are substantially different for standardized, high-volume product-focused facilities than for low-volume, high-flexibility process-focused facilities. The scheduling techniques for both of these manufacturers are considered in the following section.

Example 7.2   A Process-Focused Layout Analysis

The Hayleyton Machine Shop has decided to analyze the job flow in its shop to see if a more effective layout can be designed to reduce average job lead time. It has six processing departments in the shop, positioned as shown in the following diagram.

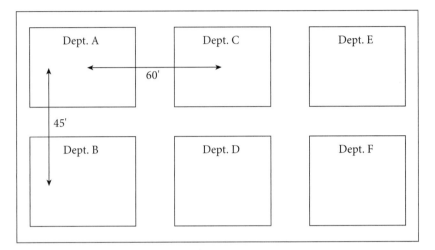

The vertical distance between departments is 45 feet, while the horizontal distance is 60 feet. To move a job from Department B to Department E would then require two horizontal moves (120 feet) and one vertical move (45 feet), for a total of 165 feet. For a typical day, the number of jobs moving from one department to the next is shown in the following matrix.

INTERDEPARTMENTAL TRIPS PER DAY

	DEPT. A	DEPT. B	DEPT. C	DEPT. D	DEPT. E	DEPT. F
Dept. A	—	6	4	5	8	10
Dept. B	2	—	9	8	0	3
Dept. C	4	2	—	0	4	4
Dept. D	2	8	4	—	6	2
Dept. E	7	4	3	6	—	2
Dept. F	8	2	0	2	4	—

SOLUTION:

Multiplying the number of trips by the correct distance for the layout shown results in the following total distance matrix, with a total distance traveled of 12,510 feet per day. For example, there are 10 trips per day between Dept. A and Dept. F, and the two departments are 165 feet apart. Multiplying these two numbers together yields 1,650 feet per day.

TOTAL DISTANCE TRAVELED PER DAY (FEET)

	DEPT. A	DEPT. B	DEPT. C	DEPT. D	DEPT. E	DEPT. F
Dept. A	—	270	240	525	960	1,650
Dept. B	90	—	945	480	0	360
Dept. C	240	210	—	0	240	420
Dept. D	210	480	180	—	630	120
Dept. E	840	660	180	630	—	90
Dept. F	1,320	240	0	120	180	—

Continued

When adding the trip distances in both directions (between A and B there are 360 trips per day, for instance), it can be seen that the following pairs of departments should be closer together: A—F, A—E, and B—C (other departments, to a lesser degree, could also be placed closer to each other). Swapping departments A and C would put all three pairs of departments closer together, but it would also put other departments further apart, making the overall impact on total distance traveled less obvious. For each change then, a new total distance must be calculated. The new layout, after swapping departments A and C, would look like this:

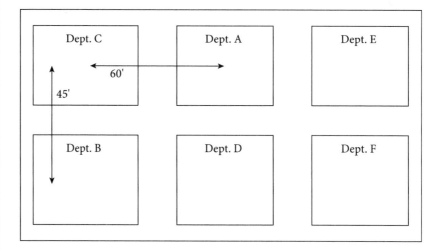

And the new total distance traveled matrix would look like this:

	TOTAL DISTANCE TRAVELED PER DAY (FEET)					
	DEPT. A	DEPT. B	DEPT. C	DEPT. D	DEPT. E	DEPT. F
Dept. A	—	630	240	225	480	1,050
Dept. B	210	—	405	480	0	360
Dept. C	240	90	—	0	480	660
Dept. D	90	480	420	—	630	120
Dept. E	420	660	360	630	—	90
Dept. F	840	240	0	120	180	—

The total distance traveled in the revised layout would be 10,830 feet per day, an improvement of 1,680 feet per day, or about 13 percent (1,680/12,510). A large number of potentially good layouts could be designed and checked, and for this reason, a number of layout software applications are available to reduce computation time.

Job Scheduling in Product-Focused Systems

Assembly line systems typically consist of automated equipment providing standardized processing to products as they pass through the line. The scheduling objective is to keep the flow of goods smooth or consistent, such that equipment and labor utilization remains high. Due to the highly repetitive nature of these systems, the processing activities, their sequence, and the approximate balance of the line are designed when the system is put in place, so these are not necessarily scheduling matters. However, several other issues are discussed next.

Many assembly line systems are used to process several models of the same product, requiring machine reprogramming and tool changes, inventory changes, and processing activity changes prior to the start of a new product model run. These are also referred to as **setup activities**. Short model runs have the advantage of lower WIP inventories (since smaller batches of product are moving through the facility) and better shop flexibility. However, for short model runs there are more frequent product model changes in a given period of time, requiring more setups. If the time required to perform a setup is long, then model run sizes must also be relatively long, which adversely impact purchasing requirements (larger quantities are required at one time), WIP levels, and finished goods storage requirements. Quality can also be a problem with long production runs. If a tool falls out of calibration, for example, during a production run, a potentially large number of units may have to be scrapped or repaired. Figure 7.4 illustrates the lot size, flexibility, and setup time trade-off.

Generally speaking then, the assembly line objective is to schedule more short production runs to increase flexibility, while reducing WIP inventories—however, to do this, setup times must be reduced. Some companies have gone to great effort to reduce assembly line setup times. For instance, Beef Products Inc., located in South Dakota, operates duplicate processing lines for some of its equipment to eliminate lost time during setups.[24] Tactics to reduce setup times also include performing setup activities externally (or off-line) while the previous production run is still in progress. Setup time reduction efforts are explored in greater detail in Chapter 10.

Aside from the production run size, the product model sequence is also a scheduling issue. Some product models may require longer and more costly setup activities, depending on the previous model produced on the line. Task times at various assembly stations can also vary substantially from model to model. Consequently, bottlenecks and line stoppages can occur if model sequences and production run sizes are not communicated throughout the facility and to suppliers in advance. Product model sequencing, then, can significantly impact total setup time and production costs. The specific model demand and corresponding production forecast play a role as well in how frequently a model run is commenced. This activity is referred to as **mixed-model assembly line sequencing**, and has been the topic of much research over the past 20 years.

At South Korean Hyundai Motor Company, for example, the mixed-model sequencing activities proceed as follows:

> *Weekly and daily production schedules are determined from a master production schedule and then distributed to each plant's production planning*

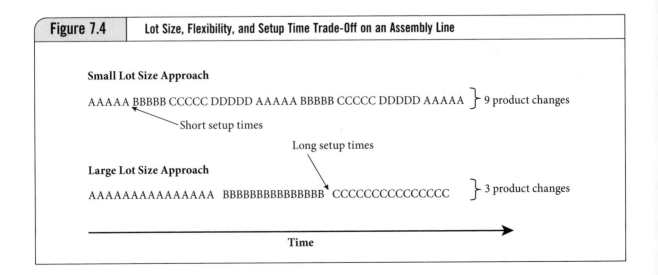

| **Figure 7.4** | **Lot Size, Flexibility, and Setup Time Trade-Off on an Assembly Line** |

Small Lot Size Approach

AAAAA BBBBB CCCCC DDDDD AAAAA BBBBB CCCCC DDDDD AAAAA } 9 product changes

Short setup times

Long setup times

Large Lot Size Approach

AAAAAAAAAAAAAAA BBBBBBBBBBBBBBB CCCCCCCCCCCCCCC } 3 product changes

Time

department. The daily sequencing lists for the assembly lines are then developed by the data processing department. The data processing department uses a heuristic sequencing approach that applies the following logic—given a daily production requirement by model type, and assuming that line balancing has already occurred, determine the sequence of model types for each assembly line that will smooth the demand for component parts and minimize the line balance delays. The models that have the closest to constant component usage rates are thus scheduled first followed by models with more erratic component usage rates. Hyundai finds, though, that it must change the model sequence frequently as time passes, due to a host of unforeseen conditions such as defective parts or temporary insufficient capacity at a processing station.[25]

Because conditions on the manufacturing floor are constantly changing, model sequencing is not an exact science. Since a typical mixed-model assembly line involves multiple lot sizes, setup times, workstation balancing variations, and varying model sequences, the problem becomes intractable from a mathematical standpoint, and an optimal line balance combined with a mixed-model sequence cannot be predetermined. Manufacturers are then left to make use of heuristic models that usually result in good sequencing solutions. Simulations of the facility have also been used with some success to design assembly lines along with determining a good work balance and mixed-model sequence. Global home appliance manufacturer Whirlpool Corporation switched from a large-batch production system to a mixed-model production system with the aid of a computer simulation and graphics animation package to iteratively test design ideas and communicate them to management. Essentially, the designers proposed a production sequence and then designed a system that would support the sequence based on the simulation. Whirlpool was able to save a considerable amount of time, cost, and redesign effort using the simulation.[26] The Global Perspective feature profiles a software company specializing in automobile assembly line model scheduling applications.

Job Scheduling in Process-Focused Systems

Scheduling work, or jobs, in a process-focused facility involves a number of complicating factors:

- If more work is accepted per day than the organization can complete per day, then WIP inventories will increase, causing more shop congestion, an erosion of the firm's output rate, and a lengthening of job completion times;

- If completion times or dates are promised to customers, then estimates of lead time for each job must be determined (considering shop congestion), and jobs must be started enough in advance to complete the job by the promised date;

- Facilities can finish more jobs per period and satisfy more customers if they work on the shortest jobs first, however, longer jobs will then ultimately be completed late or behind schedule;

- Some customers are more highly valued than others and may require earlier completion dates and be given processing priority in the shop, making it more difficult to estimate accurate completion dates for other jobs; and finally,

- Things go wrong on a daily basis, such as machine breakdowns, employee absences, poor raw material quality, and poor processing quality, causing unforeseen delays in processing.

Global Perspective   *Building Three Nissans on Two Lines*

A French software scheduling entrant in Detroit is ILOG, founded in Paris in 1987. ILOG stands for *intelligence logicielle,* or approximately, "smart software." The company has offices in the United Kingdom, Germany, Spain, Japan, and Singapore. ILOG specializes in tools used by automotive manufacturers to model the entire production cycle of their vehicles, and then optimize any portion of the manufacturing process with constraint and linear programming algorithms.

"Constraint programming can be used to solve detailed scheduling problems," said Greg Imirzian, a computer scientist and technical account manager at ILOG. "For example: In what order does the client build vehicles to optimize their production? If the company has to build 1,000 vehicles during a given period, the build order can be represented with 1,000 variables. Linear programming algorithms can be a good approach for higher-level scheduling problems. For example, if we are planning several weeks of production, how many of each type of car should we build each day."

Car manufacturers use ILOG optimization software to run their plants by planning and scheduling plant operations far enough in advance to order materials just before they are needed, so they are put swiftly into production, eliminating stockpiled inventory. The software helps balance the thousands of elements that make up a modern automotive assembly line by matching supplies, equipment, and workers to the operations. ILOG software can also schedule particular vehicles for assembly. For example, car manufacturers use the software to group their vehicles by color in order to reduce the amount of time operators need to change paints and clean equipment in paint booths.

ILOG's recent work with PA Consulting, a systems integration company based in London, enabled Nissan to build a third model car at its Sunderland, England, car factory, without adding a third production line. This plant was already touted as the most efficient car factory in Europe in 1998, when it turned out 100 Micra and Primera sedans per worker, or 7,000 vehicles per week. Then, Nissan decided to build 3,000 of its Almera model sedans there each week, too.

The conventional solution of constructing a third production line dedicated to the Almera would have cost in the hundreds of millions of dollars, so Nissan considered building the new car on its two established lines. This required developing a highly accurate scheduling system to enable different model cars to cross over one production line to another without interrupting overall efficiency.

Nissan already used its own software based on plant manager input to plan production at Sunderland, but many variables, such as part availability and tool changeover, meant that the plant adhered to its schedule only 3 percent of the time. The automaker approached ILOG to improve scheduling accuracy to accommodate the 33 percent increase in production for the Almera without building a third assembly line or major retooling. "This means deciding what vehicles Nissan will build on a given day, then deciding in what sequence those vehicles should be built, to speed up production. For example, they may decide to assemble at least three, but no more than five, consecutive five-door cars, and follow that with at least two three-door cars," explained Imirzian from ILOG.

Since implementing the software system, the Sunderland plant meets its vehicle scheduling targets 85 percent of the time. Plant management uses the scheduling tool to study the potential effect of operational or constraint changes before they are made, and no longer needs to

Continued

reschedule vehicles while they are in the storage buffers between major sections of the plant. Except for some storage and secondary tooling for the Almera, all three vehicles are made on the two Sunderland lines. The $2 million cost of the software system was paid back within three days of production.

Source: Valenti, M., "Detroit, We Are Here!" *Mechanical Engineering*, V. 123, No. 3, 2001, pp. 50–55. Article courtesy of *Mechanical Engineering* magazine; copyright *Mechanical Engineering* magazine (the American Society of Mechanical Engineers International).

The scheduling process thus includes shop-wide control measures such as input-output control techniques, along with individual job control measures such as release rules and expediting, forward scheduling, Gantt chart scheduling, and finally machine-level control techniques such as dispatching rules. These techniques are discussed next.

Input-Output Control

In many process-oriented facilities or **job shops**, determining the output capacity can be quite straightforward, and may be a matter of reviewing past daily job completion levels to arrive at a reasonable capacity estimate. Knowing this, **input-output (I/O) control** can be simply applied:

- If current WIP levels are reasonable and product flow through the shop is steady, then the daily job acceptance rate, or input, should be set equal to the shop's daily output rate;
- If the shop is currently overloaded or heavily congested and WIP is increasing at several locations within the shop, then the shop's input rate should be less than the output rate in order to reduce WIP levels;
- If the shop is currently under utilized and several work centers are idle, then the shop's job acceptance rate should be greater than the shop's job completion rate until ideal utilization rates are achieved.

In other words, when $I > O$, WIP increases; when $I < O$, WIP decreases; and when $I = O$, WIP stays constant. Over time, as technology enhancements and better flow management increase overall job shop capacity, average input levels can be allowed to increase.

For most job shops, customer orders or "jobs" spend much of the time in queues at machines, waiting to be processed. If shops are heavily loaded, jobs may spend most of their total completion time waiting in queues, ultimately leading to lengthy turnaround times and customer dissatisfaction. Shops can control input by either turning away jobs as they materialize, or by accepting jobs, assigning expected completion dates considerably longer than the work is expected to take, and then controlling the jobs' releases to the shop for processing. Unfortunately, neither of these alternatives is very appealing to job shops, which is why many tend to be bogged down with work while promising customers completion dates that tend to be unrealistic. However, as I/O control combined with other shop floor control techniques are used to improve product flow, total queue time can be decreased, improving customer service capabilities.

Forward Scheduling and Gantt Chart Scheduling

For many process-oriented manufacturing facilities, **forward scheduling** is a tactic used to control shop loading, to estimate a completion date, and to determine when a job can be released, or started in the shop. Forward scheduling means to schedule jobs forward from their arrival date at the facility. A **Gantt chart**, which is simply a timeline used for planning purposes, can be used in tandem with forward scheduling (or any other scheduling technique) to monitor and adjust job loadings at each work center, and to schedule downtime for maintenance activities, shift changes, operator days off, or other shop floor activities.

Example 7.3 illustrates the use of forward loading and Gantt chart scheduling. The priority, process time, and work center information is shown for the five jobs; the jobs are then scheduled on a Gantt chart using forward scheduling from time zero. In this example, the most-important-job-first rule is used to determine when to begin processing each job on each machine. Promise dates for job completion can be determined by looking at the completion time for each of the five jobs. Job 1 can be completed by the end of the first day (hour 8); Job 2 can be completed by the second hour of day 3 (18 hrs.); Job 3 can be completed by the fourth hour of day 1; Job 4 can be completed by the sixth hour of day 2; and Job 5 can be completed by the end of day 2. Note that use of the Gantt chart allows the scheduler to recognize, for instance, that Jobs 3 and 4 can be scheduled onto idle work centers before they are needed by higher priority jobs.

Realistically speaking, shop managers are typically not as optimistic as these schedules might imply; rather, they may add a few "safety" hours or even days to the Gantt chart completion estimates, based on personal experience with the facility and its employees, job requirements, or the value of the customers.

Preventive maintenance can also be scheduled using the Gantt chart. For example, Work center A is projected to be idle from hour 4 to hour 9; Work center B is idle from hour 1 to hour 2 and from hour 14 to hour 15; Work center C is idle from hour 0 to hour 1, hour 5 to hour 6, and hour 11 to hour 12 (we assume that other jobs will soon be scheduled at each work center, so the hours following this group of jobs may not actually be idle as shown). This idle time may be ideal for work center employees to perform scheduled maintenance or work on reducing setup times or process times.

The **makespan, average flow times,** and **average queue times** are also calculated and shown in Example 7.3. These are performance measures and are discussed in detail in the following section and are also defined in Table 7.2. Note that although Job 2 had the second highest job priority, it still finished last among the group of jobs and had a relatively long queue time. This is simply the "nature of the beast" in shop scheduling (note that it had a lower priority than Job 1, and had to wait for Work center B to be available). Also note that Job 3 was able to start immediately at Work center B, since it required only one hour of processing and was expected to be finished prior to Job 1's arrival. This illustrates the value of Gantt chart scheduling and work center loading, and is the method typically used in many shop floor control software applications.

Dispatch Rules

Dispatch rules allow machine operators to determine which job to process next from a queue of jobs waiting to be processed at various work centers. Manufacturing managers and operators use dispatch rules to prioritize jobs and continually manage queues of work at each work center, since in practice unforeseen circumstances cause job priorities to change as customer orders or jobs make their way through all of the required processing activities. Typically, a shop floor supervisor will generate a job priority report for the day, using a shop floor control software application that considers all of the jobs currently on the shop floor in various stages of completion, those due to begin that day, and the priorities of all of the jobs using the desired dispatch rule. Jobs are thus scheduled

Example 7.3   Forward Scheduling Jobs Using a Gantt Chart

The C&J Machine Shop uses a shop floor control system based on forward scheduling to determine job completion dates for its customers, and to determine when to release a job to the shop for processing. The control system generates a Gantt chart on a daily basis, along with a number of statistics. The shop is open for business eight hours per day, and there are three work centers in the shop. Activity for the most recent few days follows. The jobs waiting to be processed are listed in order of importance, and are scheduled for processing on a most-important-job-first basis.

JOB	WORK CENTER/EST. HOURS
1	A/2, B/4, C/2
2	B/3, A/3, C/6
3	B/1, C/3
4	A/2, C/1, B/5
5	C/3, A/3, B/1

SOLUTION:

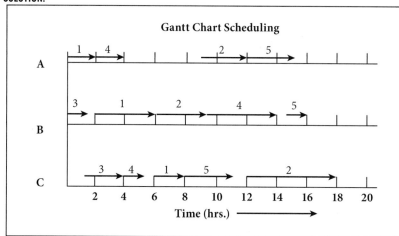

Gantt Chart Scheduling

JOB	START TIME	COMPLETION TIME	QUEUE TIME
1	0 hrs.	8 hrs.	0 hrs.
2	6 hrs.	18 hrs.	6 hrs.
3	0 hrs.	4 hrs.	0 hrs.
4	2 hrs.	14 hrs.	6 hrs.
5	8 hrs.	16 hrs.	9 hrs.

Makespan = 18 hrs.

Average flow time = (8 + 18 + 4 + 14 + 16)/5 = 12 hrs.

Average queue time = (0 + 6 + 0 + 6 + 9)/5 = 4.2 hrs.

at each machine for the day. As new jobs arrive and are released for processing, they are prioritized in real time in the control system, and queued along with the other jobs in the shop. Finally, throughout the day, machine operators must revise priorities and job processing sequences based on ever-changing conditions (a job may be pushed back in

Table 7.2	Dispatch Rule Performance Measures
PERFORMANCE MEASURE	**DESCRIPTION**
Average Flow Time	Flow time begins when a job arrives at the shop, and ends when it leaves (averaged over a group of jobs).
Average Queue Time	Flow time minus process time (averaged over a group of jobs).
Average Job Lateness	Lateness is the difference between the completion date and the due date (if it finishes early, it is still "late"; averaged over a group of jobs; there is no negative lateness).
Average Job Tardiness	Tardiness is the amount of time a job finishes beyond the due date (if it finishes early, tardiness is zero; averaged for a group of jobs).
Makespan	The total elapsed time to complete a group of jobs.

the queue for instance, if the required materials or sub-assemblies have not yet arrived from a supplier or upstream work center). A number of the more commonly cited dispatch rules are listed in Table 7.3. Examining the performance of these dispatching rules has been the topic of much research using simulated and real shop floor models under varying conditions.

In practice, simple dispatch policies concerned with each job's due date have been found to be the most popular, such as **earliest due date** (EDD) and **critical ratio** (CR). In simulation research, though, the **shortest processing time** (SPT) rule worked the best in terms of minimizing average flow time, queue time, and makespan, although long jobs end up with low priorities resulting in long queue times and tardy deliveries. Consequently, combination rules like the **truncated SPT rule** were found to perform the best for a large group of jobs in terms of minimizing **average tardiness**. In a number of studies, EDD and CR were also found to perform well in terms of **average lateness** and average tardiness. Interestingly, the **first-come-first-serve (FCFS) rule** has been found to be quite popular in real job shops, even though under controlled conditions, this rule has never been shown to perform well using any performance measure. Perhaps its

Table 7.3	Commonly Used Job Shop Dispatch Rules
DISPATCH RULE	**DESCRIPTION**
Shortest Process Time (SPT)	The job with the shortest process time is selected first.
Earliest Due Date (EDD)	The job with the earliest due date is selected first.
Minimum Slack per Operation (MINSOP)	The job with the minimum slack time per remaining operation is selected first. (Slack time is defined as time until due date minus remaining process time.)
Critical Ratio (CR)	The job with the smallest ratio of (time until due date divided by remaining process time) is selected first.
First-Come-First-Served (FCFS)	The job arriving first at a work center is processed first.
Truncated SPT	Use SPT rule until slack time (time remaining until due date minus remaining process time) reaches a predefined level for a job, then process that job next.
Most Important Job First	Jobs are prioritized based on the importance of the customer.

popularity is due to the inherent fairness attributed to FCFS processing. Understandably, the **most-important-job-first rule** was also found to be very popular in machine shops.[27] Example 7.4 compares several dispatch policies using the performance measures in Table 7.3 on a single machine.

As expected, the SPT rule performed the best in terms of average flow time and queue time (which is associated with lower WIP inventory levels), while the EDD and CR rules looked to be the best for average lateness and average tardiness (which is associated with satisfied customers). While six jobs on one machine hardly make for a real-world example, it nevertheless illustrates the usefulness of these rules. Comparison of these rules in practice requires the processing of hundreds of jobs in multiple work centers under frequently changing shop conditions.

Another complicating factor to consider when processing jobs at a machine is that setup times may be sequence-dependent. While different jobs may have significantly different setup times, some jobs may require the same setup activities. Consequently, an operator may want to group jobs together with the same or similar setup requirements to reduce overall lost time due to machine setups. Obviously, sequencing jobs in this way would significantly alter all of the performance measures discussed.

Finally, enough cannot be said regarding the constant variabilities occurring in real process-oriented manufacturing facilities. From one job to the next and even one unit to the next, variabilities can occur in processing times and setup times due to changes in operators, operator fatigue, machine tool wear, supply interruptions, and last-minute changes in customer requirements, just to name a few. Thus, for any large group of jobs in a normal job shop setting, it is simply impossible to identify the optimal processing schedule. Processing jobs becomes an ongoing activity for managers and operators throughout the day—to effectively track the progress of all jobs while doing the best to satisfy customers and control costs. Many shops use **expeditors**, whose job is to identify incoming material purchases and jobs on the shop floor that are behind schedule, and then do what is necessary to get materials delivered and jobs completed by their due dates. As a matter of fact, expeditors are in relatively high demand these days. A search on Internet job search engine Monster.com revealed a number of available expeditor jobs similar to this description:

> *Performs functions necessary to analyze and prioritize production schedules and material requirements to ensure a controlled flow of materials timed to meet production requirements. Acts as a liaison between production and materials groups to coordinate material movement between warehouse and production areas. Advises management of the status of WIP, material availability, and production problems to ensure that personnel, equipment, materials, and services are provided as needed.*

In this section we discussed managing internal material flows within the organization using various scheduling techniques. The next section focuses on the impact of vehicle scheduling and routing on material flows. This is a topic particularly important for supply chain participants that are trying to optimize material flow and integrate their efforts to create higher levels of customer satisfaction, while maintaining cost objectives.

Vehicle Scheduling and Routing

There are multiple objectives when considering vehicle scheduling and routing, including the minimization of costs (vehicle, personnel, and mileage costs), meeting

Example 7.4   Comparing Dispatch Policies at a Job Shop Work Center

Robert, a business student working at his family's machine shop for the summer, decides to compare the use of several dispatch policies at the most bottlenecked work center in the shop. On the morning of his study, there were six jobs waiting to be processed at the work center. The estimated work center process times and job due dates follow. Robert decides to compare SPT, EDD, CR, and a truncated SPT rule that switches to CR prioritization when the CR $\leq$ 1 (when slack time is less than or equal to zero).

JOB	PROCESS TIME (HRS.)	DUE DATE (HRS.)
A	8	24
B	2	36
C	6	8
D	4	12
E	10	24
F	5	6

SOLUTION:

SPT DISPATCHING:

ORDER	COMPLETION TIME	QUEUE TIME	LATENESS	TARDINESS
B	2	0	34	0
D	6	2	6	0
F	11	6	5	5
C	17	11	9	9
A	25	17	1	1
E	35	25	11	11

Makespan = 35 hrs.
Average flow time = $(2 + 6 + 11 + 17 + 25 + 35)/6$ = 16 hrs.
Average queue time = $(0 + 2 + 6 + 11 + 17 + 25)/6$ = 10.2 hrs.
Average lateness = $(34 + 6 + 5 + 9 + 1 + 11)/6$ = 11 hrs.
Average tardiness = $(0 + 0 + 5 + 9 + 1 + 11)/6$ = 4.3 hrs.

EDD DISPATCHING:

ORDER	COMPLETION TIME	QUEUE TIME	LATENESS	TARDINESS
F	5	0	1	0
C	11	5	3	3
D	15	11	3	3
A	23	15	1	0
E	33	23	9	9
B	35	33	1	0

(Note: A and E had the same due date, so A was processed first because it had the lowest process time.)
Makespan = 35 hrs. (Note that the makespan will remain constant regardless of the sequence.)

Average flow time = $(5 + 11 + 15 + 23 + 33 + 35)/6$ = 20.3 hrs.
Average queue time = $(0 + 5 + 11 + 15 + 23 + 33)/6$ = 14.5 hrs.
Average lateness = $(1 + 3 + 3 + 1 + 9 + 1)/6$ = 3 hrs.
Average tardiness = $(0 + 3 + 3 + 0 + 9 + 0)/6$ = 2.5 hrs.

Continued

CR DISPATCHING:

1st CR: A = 3, B = 18, C = 1.3, D = 3, E = 2.4, F = 1.2 (F is processed first.)

ORDER	COMPLETION TIME	QUEUE TIME	LATENESS	TARDINESS
F	5	0	1	0

(Note: CR changes based on *remaining* time until due date, so the relative priorities can change.)

2nd CR: A = 2.4, B = 15.5, C = 0.5, D = 1.8, E = 1.9 (C is processed next.)

ORDER	COMPLETION TIME	QUEUE TIME	LATENESS	TARDINESS
F	5	0	1	0
C	11	5	3	3

3rd CR: A = 1.6, B = 12.5, D = 0.3, E = 1.3 (D is processed next.)

ORDER	COMPLETION TIME	QUEUE TIME	LATENESS	TARDINESS
F	5	0	1	0
C	11	5	3	3
D	15	11	3	3

4th CR: A = 1.1, B = 10.5, E = 0.9 (E is processed next.)

ORDER	COMPLETION TIME	QUEUE TIME	LATENESS	TARDINESS
F	5	0	1	0
C	11	5	3	3
D	15	11	3	3
E	25	15	1	1

5th CR: A = −0.1, B = 5.5 (A is processed next, followed by B.)

ORDER	COMPLETION TIME	QUEUE TIME	LATENESS	TARDINESS
F	5	0	1	0
C	11	5	3	3
D	15	11	3	3
E	25	15	1	1
A	33	25	9	9
B	35	33	1	0

Average flow time = $(5 + 11 + 15 + 25 + 33 + 35)/6 = 20.7$ hrs.
Average queue time = $(0 + 5 + 11 + 15 + 25 + 33)/6 = 14.8$ hrs.
Average lateness = $(1 + 3 + 3 + 1 + 9 + 1)/6 = 3$ hrs.
Average tardiness = $(0 + 3 + 3 + 1 + 9 + 0)/6 = 2.7$ hrs.

TRUNCATED SPT DISPATCHING:

1st CR: A = 3, B = 18, C = 1.3, D = 3, E = 2.4, F = 1.2 (B is processed first, since all CRs > 1.)

ORDER	COMPLETION TIME	QUEUE TIME	LATENESS	TARDINESS
B	2	0	34	0

2nd CR: A = 2.8, C = 1.0, D = 2.5, E = 2.2, F = 0.8 (F is processed next.)

ORDER	COMPLETION TIME	QUEUE TIME	LATENESS	TARDINESS
B	2	0	34	0
F	7	2	1	1

3rd CR: A = 2.1, C = 0.2, D = 1.3, E = 1.7 (C is processed next.)

ORDER	COMPLETION TIME	QUEUE TIME	LATENESS	TARDINESS
B	2	0	34	0
F	7	2	1	1
C	13	7	5	5

4th CR: A = 1.4, D = −0.3, E = 1.1 (D is processed next.)

ORDER	COMPLETION TIME	QUEUE TIME	LATENESS	TARDINESS
B	2	0	34	0
F	7	2	1	1
C	13	7	5	5
D	17	13	5	5

5th CR: A = 0.9, E = 0.7 (E is processed next, followed by A.)

ORDER	COMPLETION TIME	QUEUE TIME	LATENESS	TARDINESS
B	2	0	34	0
F	7	2	1	1
C	13	7	5	5
D	17	13	5	5
E	27	17	3	3
A	35	27	11	11

Average flow time $= (2 + 7 + 13 + 17 + 27 + 35)/6 = 16.8$ hrs.
Average queue time $= (0 + 2 + 7 + 13 + 17 + 27)/6 = 11$ hrs.
Average lateness $= (34 + 1 + 5 + 5 + 3 + 11)/6 = 9.8$ hrs.
Average tardiness $= (0 + 1 + 5 + 5 + 3 + 11)/6 = 4.2$ hrs.

RANKING THE PERFORMANCES OF THE RULES:

AVG. FLOW TIME	AVG. QUEUE TIME	AVG. LATENESS	AVG. TARDINESS
SPT/16.0	SPT/10.2	EDD/3 & CR/3	EDD/2.5
Tr. SPT/16.8	Tr. SPT/11	Tr. SPT/9.8	CR/2.7
EDD/20.3	EDD/14.5	SPT/11	Tr. SPT/4.2
CR/20.7	CR/14.8		SPT/4.3

Based on his findings, Robert recommends use of either the EDD or CR dispatching policy at this work center to reduce average job lateness and tardiness. He will continue to measure performance of these dispatch policies, though, for a number of days to make sure of his findings.

customer delivery date requirements, maximizing driver productivity, and providing protection to the goods being transported. For services such as buses, taxis, and emergency vehicles, people are the things being transported, thus the objective would be to minimize response time and transportation time. Today, communication technologies have allowed delivery companies to offer better service with fewer drivers and vehicles. For example, Pepsi Bottling Group of Denver, Colorado, uses routing and scheduling software along with global positioning systems to optimally plan daily delivery routes for 70 vehicles, such that its highest volume customers receive priority service. The system has allowed it to improve delivery service while reducing driver overtime.[28]

For multiple pickups and deliveries, the routing and scheduling problem can be presented as a network of pickup and delivery points, as shown in Figure 7.5(a). Node 1 represents the origination/destination point (as in the manufacturing facility or the bus depot), while nodes 2, 3, and 4 represent pickup and/or delivery points. The lines connecting the nodes can represent distance, cost, or time. In Figure 7.5, the network represents a trip, or **tour**, consisting of a sequence of four stops (including the origination point).

For the simple case of one vehicle and the pickup/delivery points as shown in Figure 7.5, with the vehicle starting and ending at the origination node, the situation is called the **traveling salesman problem**. The idea is to find a route that minimizes the time, mileage, or cost objective. For these nodes, there are three unique tours to cover

Figure 7.5	A Vehicle Routing Network

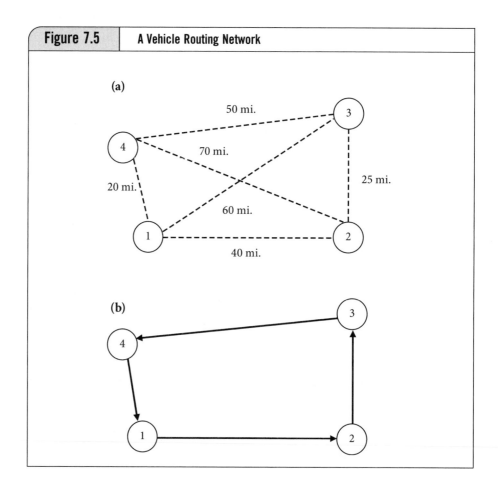

the three pickup/delivery points: 1-2-3-4, 1-2-4-3, and 1-3-2-4 (note that the distance for 1-3-2-4 = the distance for 1-4-2-3). The routing problem can also become more complicated with the use of multiple vehicles, variable demands at each node, and multiple vehicle capacities. These more general problems are called **vehicle routing problems**. If specified pickup or delivery times exist, then the routing problem also becomes a scheduling problem. When many nodes exist on a tour, then literally millions of potential routes and schedules can exist, and optimal solutions cannot be found without a great deal of computing power or time. For these large problems, or when an approximate solution is acceptable, managers often rely on heuristic solutions, three of which are described in the following sections.

The Clark and Wright Savings Heuristic

One of the most well-known heuristic methods for solving the traveling salesman problem is the **Clark and Wright savings heuristic**. The key to this procedure is the calculation of "savings" in miles (or cost) to combine two nodes into one tour, rather than have the vehicle return to the origination point and then head out to the next pickup/ distribution point. The savings is calculated in this way for all paired combinations of delivery nodes and the pairs are ranked from largest savings to smallest. The nodes for the entire tour are then linked according to this ranking. For the nodes shown in Figure 7.5, the following savings are calculated, considering the origination point and two additional nodes at a time:

1. 1-2-3-1 vs. 1-2-1, 1-3-1: savings is $[(40 \times 2) + (60 \times 2)] - [40 + 25 + 60] = 75$ mi.
2. 1-2-4-1 vs. 1-2-1, 1-4-1: savings is $[(40 \times 2) + (20 \times 2)] - [40 + 70 + 20] = -10$ mi.
3. 1-3-4-1 vs. 1-3-1, 1-4-1: savings is $[(60 \times 2) + (20 \times 2)] - [60 + 50 + 20] = 30$ mi.

Note that the pair [2,3] has the same savings as [3,2]. Ranking the node pairs, we have [2,3], [3,4], and then [2,4]. We thus link nodes [2,3] and then [3,4] to obtain the tour 1-2-3-4 shown in Figure 7.5(b) (the direction of the arrows could also be 1-4-3-2). The total distance traveled would then be 135 miles, which turns out to be the minimum distance tour.

The Cluster-First-Route-Second Heuristic

For the more general vehicle routing problem, the **cluster-first-route-second heuristic** can be used to determine a reasonably good solution. Figure 7.6(a) provides an eight-node problem, with different demand requirements at each node. Two vehicles will be used for the tours. Vehicle 1 has a capacity of 25 tons and Vehicle 2 has a capacity of 18 tons. In Part (a), the seven nodes have initially been clustered into two tours (node 1 is the origination node), taking into account proximity and vehicle capacity. Vehicle 1's tour consists of three stops and a total weight of 18 tons. Vehicle 2's tour has four stops and also requires 18 tons. The Clark and Wright savings heuristic is used to construct the sequence for each tour, resulting in a Tour 1 distance of 160 miles, and a Tour 2 distance of 210 miles, for a total distance of 370 miles.

The next step involves **tour improvement**, where one or more nodes are switched to another tour (in this case, the only other tour), such that vehicle capacities are not exceeded, and total distance of both tours is reduced. Since Vehicle 2 is already at capacity, it is only feasible to try switching one or more Tour 2 nodes to Tour 1 and Vehicle 1. Part (b) shows the revised solution. Here, node 6 was switched to Tour 1, adding ten miles and five tons to the tour. Consequently, Tour 2's load was reduced five tons and the mileage was reduced 20 miles. The resulting total distance of both tours then became

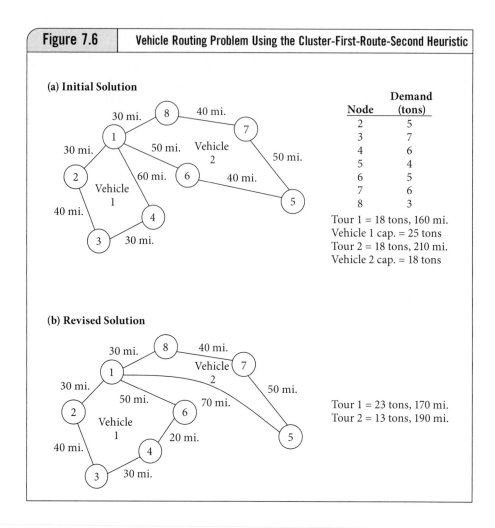

Figure 7.6 | **Vehicle Routing Problem Using the Cluster-First-Route-Second Heuristic**

(a) Initial Solution

	Demand
Node	(tons)
2	5
3	7
4	6
5	4
6	5
7	6
8	3

Tour 1 = 18 tons, 160 mi.
Vehicle 1 cap. = 25 tons
Tour 2 = 18 tons, 210 mi.
Vehicle 2 cap. = 18 tons

(b) Revised Solution

Tour 1 = 23 tons, 170 mi.
Tour 2 = 13 tons, 190 mi.

360, a savings of ten miles. No other nodes could be switched to Tour 1 due to the capacity limitation of Vehicle 1. Obviously, other factors such as geography, traffic flow, and customer value can enter into this solution, and tend to complicate the analysis.

The Concurrent Scheduler Approach

For the vehicle scheduling problem, a simple heuristic called the **concurrent scheduler approach** can also be used. The steps are as follows:

1. Put the pickups and deliveries in order by their promised arrival times.

2. Assign Vehicle 1 to the earliest promised arrival time.

3. If possible, assign the next pickup/delivery to the closest idle vehicle; if all vehicles are busy, create a new vehicle schedule and assign the pickup/delivery to that vehicle. Repeat until all pickups/deliveries are scheduled.

Example 7.5 illustrates the concurrent scheduler approach. Vehicle 1 takes the first customer. Vehicle 2 must take customer 2, since Vehicle 1 will still be handling customer 1. For customer 4, both Vehicle 1 and Vehicle 2 will be available, however since Vehicle 1 will be closer, it is assigned to customer 4. The remaining customers are assigned to vehicles similarly. By the end of the day, three vehicles will be needed.

Example 7.5   **Using the Concurrent Scheduler Approach for Vehicle Deliveries**

Mary Jane's Delivery Express assigns pickups and deliveries to its vehicles and drivers based on each morning's list of required pickups and deliveries. Today, the current customer list is as follows:

PICKUP/ DELIVERY	PROMISED ARRIVAL TIME	COMPLETION TIME	VEHICLE NUMBER
1	8:00 AM	8:45 AM	1
2	8:30 AM	9:15 AM	2 (Veh. 1 is busy)
3	9:00 AM	9:10 AM	1 (Veh. 1 is idle)
4	9:30 AM	10:00 AM	1 (Veh. 1 is closer)
5	9:45 AM	10:00 AM	2 (Veh. 1 is busy)
6	10:00 AM	10:45 AM	3 (Veh. 1, 2 are busy)
7	10:30 AM	11:00 AM	2 (Veh. 2 is closer)
8	1:00 PM	2:00 PM	2 (Veh. 2 is closest)
9	1:30 PM	1:45 PM	3 (Veh. 3 is closer)
10	3:00 PM	4:30 PM	3 (Veh. 3 is closest)

VEHICLE	SCHEDULE	START/END TIMES
1	1-3-4	8:00 AM/10:00 AM
2	2-5-7-8	8:30 AM/2:00 PM
3	6-9-10	10:00 AM/4:30 PM

To make the day's pickups and deliveries, Mary Jane schedules three vehicles for the times shown. As new customer requests are generated during the day, they are worked into the existing schedule. Obviously, for small numbers of pickups and deliveries, part-time workers must be used to avoid excessive idle time.

Other techniques exist for solving vehicle routing and scheduling problems, including use of dynamic programming, linear programming, and specialized algorithms.[29] Interested readers should look at some of the referenced articles for further discussions and appraisals of the techniques.

Warehouse Material Flow

Chapter 11 provides a good overall discussion of warehouse management, including warehouse location strategies, while this chapter introduces the idea of material flow management within warehouses. In some respects, the topics covered so far in this chapter can also apply to warehouses, since in many warehouses light manufacturing, assembly, and packaging processes are also occurring. Additionally, though, warehouses also break down shipments into individual items, store the items, retrieve them, and then combine them with other items for outbound shipments to customers. The term **distribution center** is commonly used to describe this type of warehouse. Some warehouses are very large; carry thousands of items; and use highly automated systems and equipment for moving, storing, and retrieving products; and in these warehouses, inventory flow can become difficult and costly to manage.

Even in well-managed supply chains where just-in-time deliveries are common, warehouses are a necessary element to act as a buffer between the manufacturer and the customer. As process integration and coordination between supply chain partners improves, though, warehouse activities and missions must change to remain a valued contributor to customer satisfaction. The pressure to improve order-filling accuracy and cycle time or delivery performance is continually increasing in supply chains, and this places a large burden on warehouses to improve shipping accuracy and inventory flow through better process design, layouts, use of equipment, and general warehouse operations. In addition to these changes occurring in warehousing, operating costs are already high and continue to rise, creating even further pressure to improve services while simultaneously minimizing warehousing costs. Flow management practices in warehouses have thus taken on a high level of importance when managing supply chains. Warehouse material handling has become so important for Wal-Mart, for instance, that it has mandated suppliers to begin using RFID tags on all items delivered to Wal-Mart distribution centers, on a rolling time horizon. The e-Commerce Perspective feature describes the potential problems with this mandate.

Assuming that the firm has already designed an effective warehousing network and has put in place a good pickup and delivery system, the next step is to assess inventory flows within the warehouse, and make improvements such that storing, moving, and shipping activities comprise the shortest time possible, resulting in lower inventory carrying costs, better utilization of space, potentially less required capacity, better product flow, and higher customer service levels. The obvious warehouse characteristic impacting inventory flow is the warehouse layout, so this comprises the bulk of the flow discussion for warehouses.

Warehouse Layout Considerations

Layout planning in warehouses generally involves the consideration of several basic designs, for example the U-shaped, flow-through, and modular-flow warehouse layouts. Each of these is briefly discussed next.

U-Shaped Layout

A typical **U-shaped warehouse layout** is shown in Figure 7.7. Inbound shipments arrive and are unpacked at receiving, where items are either moved to storage or to the **cross-docking** process. Eventually, items make their way to the shipping area, where they become outbound shipments to customers. Cross-docking has become an important activity in many warehouses, and refers to the activities of receiving shipments, unpacking and sorting the items, repacking the items to fill specific customer orders, and finally shipping the items out to the customers. Items thus flow in a U-shaped pattern from either receiving to cross-docking to shipping, or from receiving to storage to picking to sorting and to shipping. The advantages of a U-shaped warehouse layout include efficient utilization of receiving and shipping docks (since they can share the same dock space), dual capabilities of storage and cross-docking, and better security (since entry and exit are on the same side of the building).

Flow-Through Layout

This type of warehouse layout is designed specifically to accommodate a large volume of cross-docking, but may also have some storage capabilities for slow moving items. A simple **flow-through warehouse layout** is shown in Figure 7.8. The primary advantage of this type of layout is the dedication to cross-docking, which should result in

e-Commerce Perspective

The RFID Mandate

Reading the countless case histories, articles, and news releases about the Wal-Mart mandate to adopt RFID (radio frequency identification) for carton and pallet identification, one comes to two inescapable conclusions:

1. It's a terrible idea because the technology isn't mature, standards don't exist, and there's no ROI for suppliers.
2. It's the greatest thing since the invention of sliced bread—maybe since the cultivation of wheat—and will provide supply chain efficiencies hitherto undreamed of.

For organizations such as Wal-Mart and the U.S. Department of Defense, the benefits are clear: RFID provides automatic identification of each incoming pallet and identification of each carton as it moves down a conveyor, into or out of storage, or out onto the sales floor. While bar code labels had been used in the past, they required manual scanning. When every "touch" costs money in terms of speed and labor, the cost savings and efficiency of RFID quickly add up. For suppliers, it's a different story. For those who simply apply an RFID label at shipping, the benefit is that it gets to continue doing business with an important customer. For those that are using RFID internally, the ROI is becoming evident.

As the "flagship" of the RFID mandate, Wal-Mart is being watched most closely. Its requirement initially caused consternation, panic, and, in a few rare cases, indifference. However, according to Wal-Mart spokesperson Christi Gallagher, "We are all still in a learning phase and we're working with our suppliers to resolve problems." Some of the read failures are due to tag quality issues or failure during handling and transportation—problems that are rapidly being overcome by manufacturers.

Overall, Wal-Mart is reportedly very pleased with its RFID program. It set the goal high to challenge suppliers. Setting a lower goal would not have produced the results it has seen. Gallagher says Wal-Mart is on track to roll out RFID in 12 of its distribution centers and 500 stores, and the next 200 suppliers are on a more aggressive track to implement RFID because they will benefit from the experiences of the first 100 as well as improvements in RFID technology. The improvements in the technology can be attributed directly to the aggressive timeframes of the Wal-Mart and Department of Defense mandates.

Some companies complying with the Wal-Mart mandate are struggling just to get readable labels on their products. Others are working to move RFID back into the production process. For example, Del Monte Foods, a $3 billion-a-year food supplier based in San Francisco, had to deal with metal cans filled with liquids, two substances that are problematic for RFID labels. Tag selection and placement to achieve reliable reads were the highest priority just to get a slap-and-ship model up and running. The company did extensive testing to determine how each product should be labeled. It finally determined that placing a dipole tag (a "squiggle" antenna) over the air space between cans produced the best results.

Jack Link's, a supplier of beef jerky and other processed meat products headquartered in Minong, Wisconsin, is at the other end of the spectrum. Although not required to comply with the Wal-Mart mandate until 2006, Jack Link's realized that it had the opportunity to leverage RFID to improve its business operations. Specifically, it began employing RFID to maintain records on ingredients to simplify regulatory compliance, improve lot visibility and tracking, and streamline many distribution functions. RFID also provided the company new insights into its own processes. The major challenge facing Jack Link's was developing an infrastructure from

Continued

the ground up. The company did not have an existing bar code infrastructure, which was an additional expense, yet it avoided the complexity of integrating two different technologies into an existing database.

Still a third model is Hewlett-Packard (HP), the giant electronics and semiconductor manufacturer. HP has been using RFID internally for years, for example, in its wafer fabrication plant. HP quickly seized on the idea of labeling 100 percent of its products. This decision let HP reduce packaging line variation and take advantage of RFID for its own purposes. Because HP produces high-value items, serialized tracking has always been part of its program. RFID simply offered a better way to do what it was already doing.

According to Mark Brown, a project manager at International Paper, "Tag selection and placement will always be an issue. Always look for 'air gaps.'" But, he points out, "Tag manufacturers can create a tag that is designed specifically for impedance shift caused by dense materials or metals and liquids. You can often find two tags that will perform well but may need to use one or the other, even for similar products." International Paper is currently working with a number of high-profile clients to develop compliance programs. While RFID physics can be challenging, Brown insists, "We have demonstrated that the word 'impossible' has no place in this industry. Imagination, determination and creativity will find the answers."

While the physics of RFID is complex and requires careful study and experimentation, infrastructure may be the biggest expense many companies face. According to Stephen Schwartz, RFID systems architect for Intermec of Everett, Washington, "Most suppliers don't have the IT systems ready to accept (or take advantage of) the serialization issue. Think back to the costs associated with Y2K. This has far greater impact if the supplier wants to go beyond a 'slap-and-ship' scenario and actually use the serialization data for production tracking, recall issues, inventory control, etc. If you create billions of items each year, where will the serial numbers come from?" And there's the question of how you manage them once you've read them.

Wal-Mart's schedule to expand its own use of RFID continues more or less on schedule. The number of distribution centers has been reduced from 12 to 10 and stores from 600 to 500. However, Wal-Mart's Gallagher pointed out the initial, higher numbers were announced with the caveat "as many as . . . ." She said the lower numbers did not in any way indicate that Wal-Mart was backing away from its schedule.

better use of equipment and labor, leading to faster throughput times and, ultimately, better customer service. The obvious disadvantage is the minimal storage capability.

Modular-Flow Layout

A **modular-flow warehouse layout** is characterized by separate segments that are designed for specific warehouse applications, as shown in Figure 7.9. Large-scale warehouse operations might require a number of distinct capabilities, each suited to a specific product, volume, or customer requirement. The modular warehouse shown is capable of providing cross-docking services, along with final assembly and customization processes, short-term storage and picking services for high turnover items, and finally, long-term storage and picking services for slow-moving items.

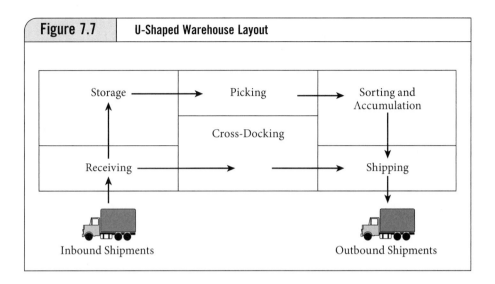

Figure 7.7 | **U-Shaped Warehouse Layout**

Along with these layout configurations, consideration of an inventory item's popularity, similarity, size, and shape can affect the layout of a warehouse, particularly when items are stored for any appreciable length of time. The **popularity storage methodology** places the fastest-moving items in the most accessible warehouse locations, resulting in less picker (the person or machine retrieving the order) travel time and decreased warehouse throughput times. In warehouses of firms that are actively managing their supply chains, throughput times and agility may be extremely important, leading to use of this storage method. Nordson, for example, a U.S. producer of precision dispensing systems for the manufacturing sector, was unhappy with its warehouse picking performance, which was averaging more than 24 hours per pick. To improve performance, Nordson changed its warehouse layout to maximize inventory flow. It re-slotted products based on movement efficiencies, eventually resulting in an average pick time of only four hours.[30]

The **similarity storage methodology** places items commonly picked together in close proximity within the warehouse. In warehouses where final assembly operations are occurring, for instance, assembly parts may be stored together to reduce picking time. As with the popularity method, the objective is to minimize total picking time. Items must be analyzed to determine common usage patterns when utilizing this method.

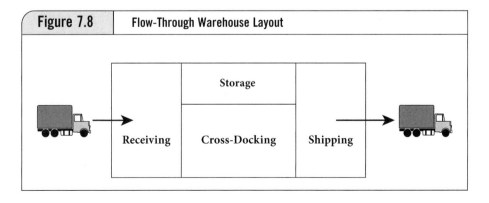

Figure 7.8 | **Flow-Through Warehouse Layout**

Figure 7.9	Modular Flow Warehouse Layout

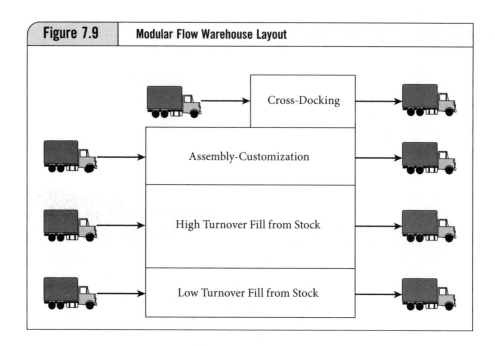

The **size and shape storage methodology** typically places heavy or bulky items in easily accessible warehouse locations. Storing these items on lower shelves, for instance, can facilitate easier handling and higher safety levels. Use of this type of storage strategy, however, can be somewhat problematic since the warehouse inventory control system must know the sizes, shapes, and weights of items that can be stored on various shelves or bins within the warehouse, and the dimensions and weight of the items themselves must also be known.

Warehouse information systems are a necessity when using any of the three warehouse storage considerations discussed here. Storing items based on popularity will result in continuously changing locations for items, as item popularity changes. In each of these storage methods, as new items are stored, as item popularity changes, and as product designs change, location requirements will indeed change, requiring a continuous attention to item characteristics and their corresponding warehouse locations. Warehouses might also use several or all three methods simultaneously. More in-depth discussions of these warehousing management systems are included in Chapter 9.

SUMMARY

Managing the flow of materials is a strategic imperative for all organizations and supply chains with significant inventories. Material flows can greatly impact the firm's costs and its ability to provide trading partners with timely, high-quality deliveries of product. In today's global economy, the flexibility to monitor process flows and rapidly adjust to changing demand patterns, technologies, and supplier offerings is a necessary competitive weapon, and can be achieved through application of the many material flow concepts discussed in this chapter. Because of the importance of material flow management, this chapter contains discussions of a large number of flow concepts including material flow mapping and analysis, manufacturing and warehouse layouts, and shop floor and vehicle scheduling. Conceptual as well as quantitative examples were provided throughout the chapter. By understanding these concepts and how they work together to create an effective organization, managers can appreciate the importance of the various material flow topics to the organization and its supply chains.

KEY TERMS

assembly lines, 239

average flow times, 251

average lateness, 253

average queue times, 251

average tardiness, 253

balancing the line, 240

bottleneck, 233

cellular layouts, 243

Clark and Wright savings heuristic, 259

cluster-first-route-second heuristic, 259

computer integrated manufacturing, 238

computer numerically controlled (CNC) machines, 238

concurrent scheduler approach, 260

critical path method, 233

critical ratio, 253

cross-docking, 262

cycle time, 240

dispatch rules, 251

distribution center, 261

drum, buffer, rope (DBR) concept, 234

earliest due date, 253

expeditors, 254

first-come-first-serve (FCFS) rule, 253

flexible manufacturing system, 236

flow management, 226

flow-through warehouse layout, 262

forward scheduling, 250

Gantt chart, 251

Group technology (GT) cells, 238

group technology layouts, 243

heuristic, 241

input-output (I/O) control, 250

intermittent process layouts, 244

job shops, 250

makespan, 251

management by constraint, 233

mass customization, 239

material flow analysis, 231

mixed-model assembly line sequencing, 247

modular-flow warehouse layout, 264

most-important-job-first rule, 254

popularity storage methodology, 265

postponement strategy, 239

process flowcharting, 227

process flow diagramming, 227

process-focused layouts, 244

process mapping, 227

product-focused layouts, 239

radio frequency identification, 232

setup activities, 247

shortest processing time, 253

similarity storage methodology, 265

size and shape storage methodology, 266

takt time, 240

Theory of Constraints, 233

throughput volumes, 232

tour, 258

tour improvement, 259

traveling salesman problem, 258

truncated SPT rule, 253

U-shaped warehouse layout, 262

value stream mapping, 227

vehicle routing problems, 259

DISCUSSION QUESTIONS

1. Why is it important to understand the flow of materials in an organization?

2. Construct a process map for a fast-food business, or a business of your choosing.

3. What are the process analysis questions that should be asked and answered for the map completed in Question 2?

4. Describe RFID and how it is used.

5. Describe the Theory of Constraints (TOC). How could this be used at a neighborhood grocery store?

6. Could the TOC be applied to management effectiveness? Explain.

7. What is the drum-buffer-rope (DBR) concept, and what does it have to do with the TOC?

8. Why is manufacturing flexibility a desirable characteristic?

9. Define mass customization and provide an example.

10. What is a flexible manufacturing system, and what are its benefits?

11. What type of manufacturing firm uses a product-focused layout? Why?

12. What is "takt time," and what is it used for?

13. What does a takt time of eight minutes mean?

14. What are the advantages and disadvantages of assembly line balancing?

15. Describe what a cellular layout is and when this would be appropriate.

16. What is a process-focused layout, and what would be an example of one?

17. What are the advantages and disadvantages of product-focused facilities compared to process-focused facilities?

18. What is the general objective when designing a process-focused layout?

19. What are the scheduling concerns at an automated assembly line or product-focused facility?

20. Describe how input-output control is used in process-focused facilities.

21. What are dispatch rules, and which one do you think is the best? Which one do you normally use when deciding which homework assignment to do next?

22. What is forward scheduling, and why is it used?

23. What is a Gantt chart, and why is it used?

24. In dispatching terminology, if I am 20 minutes early for an appointment, I am late. Explain.

25. What does the traveling salesman problem refer to, and what is the solution objective? What heuristic is typically used to solve simple traveling salesman problems?

26. What are the three basic warehouse layout configurations, and what are the advantages of each?

27. Compare the three most popular warehouse storage methodologies.

PROBLEMS

1. The Jay-Ross Bakery has decided to arrange its processes such that an assembly operation can be used to increase its baked goods output. The processing activities follow, with the arrows indicating the activity sequence and precedence. The desired output per day is 120 units (including any expected output variance). The bakery works one eight-hour shift per day, or 480 minutes. Balance the assembly line, using the information provided. Calculate the takt time, the minimum number of workstations, and the line efficiency. Note that several activities will require duplicate workstations.

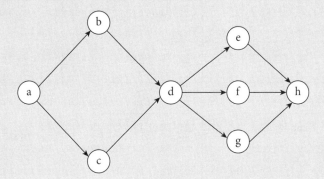

TASK	TIME (MIN.)
a	2
b	3
c	3
d	10
e	4
f	6
g	2
h	7
	Total 37 min.

2. Given that there are seven work centers, total task time of 48 minutes, a desired output of 80 units per day and two 8-hour shifts per day, what is the takt time?

3. Using the following assembly line information, construct an activity diagram using arrows to indicate sequence and precedence, calculate the takt time, calculate the minimum number of work centers, balance the line, and finally, calculate the line efficiency. What is the total worker idle time per day?

The desired output is 45 units per day. The factory is open for eight hours per day.

ACTIVITY	IMMEDIATE PREDECESSORS	TIME
A	—	6
B	A	4
C	A	2
D	A	7
E	B,C,D	3
F	E	6

4. For the information given in Problem 3, what would be the minimum takt time, if the firm put one worker at each machine (i.e., used six work centers)? What would the corresponding output be? What would the efficiency be? What would the total worker idle time per day be?

5. The Weisenheimer Travel Agency has decided to analyze the flow of employees in its office to see if a more effective layout can be designed to reduce average daily walking time. There are five departments in the office, positioned as follows:

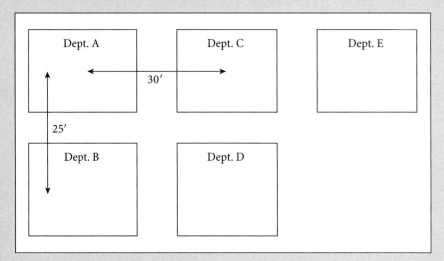

The vertical distance between departments is 25 feet, while the horizontal distance is 30 feet. To walk from Department A to Department D would then require a vertical move (25 feet) and a horizontal move (30 feet), assuming there are no hallways or diagonal movements. For a typical day, the number of employee movements from one department to the next is shown in the following matrix. Determine the total distance traveled per day, for the given process-focused facility, and then find a better layout.

	DEPT. A	DEPT. B	DEPT. C	DEPT. D	DEPT. E
Dept. A	—	10	8	22	7
Dept. B	4	—	15	8	18
Dept. C	6	10	—	0	6
Dept. D	15	9	12	—	10
Dept. E	6	14	5	14	—

6. The Russell Auto Repair Shop uses a shop floor control system based on forward scheduling to determine auto completion dates for its customers, and to determine when to release a car to the shop for repairing. The control system generates a Gantt chart on a daily basis, along with a number of statistics. The shop is open for business eight hours per day, and there are three repair centers in the shop. Activity for the most recent few days follows. The jobs are listed in order of customer arrival, and are scheduled for processing on a first-come-first-served basis. Determine what the promise times should be, along with the makespan, the average flowtime, and the average queue time.

JOB	WORK CENTER/EST. HOURS
1	A/1, B/3, C/2
2	A/2, C/3
3	B/1, A/2, C/1
4	A/3, C/2, B/2
5	C/1, B/4, A/2

7. Using the information from Problem 6, and assuming that all of the automobiles arrived at the same time, use a Gantt chart and the shortest processing time (SPT) rule whenever there is a queue at a repair center to determine the new promise times, and the makespan, average flowtime, and average queue time. Also assume that transfer times are zero.

8. Using the following information and assuming that all of the automobiles arrived at the same time, use a Gantt chart and the critical ratio (CR) rule whenever there is a queue at a repair center to determine the makespan, average flowtime, average queue time, average lateness, and average tardiness. Also assume that transfer times are zero.

JOB	WORK CENTER/EST. HOURS	PROMISE TIME (HRS.)
1	A/1, B/3, C/2	8
2	A/2, C/3	15
3	B/1, A/2, C/1	7
4	A/3, C/2, B/2	20
5	C/1, B/4, A/2	16

9. Use the Clark and Wright savings heuristic to determine an acceptable delivery route for the following network of customers, starting from location 1. Assume that any diagonal trip must pass through location 5.

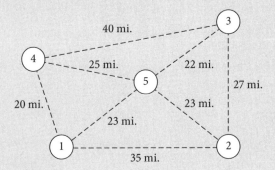

10. Josh's Furniture Delivery business delivers to a set of customers as demand dictates. The current list of deliveries for the day follows. Assuming that the customers are ranked in proximity to one another (i.e., customer 4 is closer to customer 3 than customer 5 is), use the concurrent scheduler approach to assign deliveries to vehicles such that no deliveries are late and driving distance is minimized. Determine how many delivery vehicles are needed. Also, determine each vehicle's delivery schedule, the start time, and the finish time. Assume that drive time to each customer is 15 minutes.

DELIVERY	PROMISED ARRIVAL TIME	ESTIMATED COMPLETION TIME
1	9:00 AM	9:20 AM
2	9:45 AM	10:15 AM
3	10:00 AM	10:45 AM
4	10:30 AM	11:00 AM
5	10:45 AM	12:15 PM
6	11:00 AM	11:45 AM
7	11:30 AM	12:00 PM
8	12:30 PM	2:00 PM
9	1:00 PM	1:45 PM
10	1:30 PM	2:30 PM
11	2:30 PM	3:15 PM
12	3:00 PM	4:00 PM
13	3:30 PM	4:30 PM

INTERNET QUESTIONS

1. See if you can find different examples of companies that manage material flows for businesses.

2. Find an example of a company having a material flow problem. Discuss the causes and solutions to the problem.

INFOTRAC QUESTION

Access http://www.infotrac-thomsonlearning.com to answer the following question:

1. Use InfoTrac to find current articles discussing the following topics:
   a. mass customization
   b. assembly line scheduling
   c. machine shop scheduling
   d. material flow analysis

REFERENCES

Anupindi, R., S. Chopra, S. Deshmukh, J. Van Mieghem, and E. Zemel (1999), *Managing Business Process Flows,* Prentice Hall, Upper Saddle River, NJ.

Davis, M., N. Aquilano, and R. Chase (2003), *Fundamentals of Operations Management,* McGraw-Hill/Irwin, New York, NY.

Fischer, L., ed. (2005), *Workflow Handbook 2005,* Future Strategies, Inc., Lighthouse Point, FL (particular use was made of a chapter by R. Allen, "Workflow: An Introduction").

Fitzsimmons, J. A., and M. J. Fitzsimmons (1998), *Service Management,* Irwin/McGraw-Hill, New York, NY.

Frazelle, E. (2002), *World-Class Warehousing and Material Handling,* McGraw-Hill, New York, NY.

Goldsby, T., and S. Garcia-Dastugue, "The Manufacturing Flow Process," *The International Journal of Logistics Management,* V. 14, No. 2, 2003, pp. 33–52.

Lawrence, F. B., D. F. Jennings, and B. E. Reynolds (2005), *ERP in Distribution,* South-Western, Mason, OH.

Meredith, J., and S. Shafer (1999), *Operations Management for MBAs,* John Wiley & Sons, Inc., New York, NY.

Metters, R., K. King-Metters, and M. Pullman (2003), *Successful Service Operations Management,* Thomson South-Western, Mason, OH.

Murdick, R., B. Render, and R. Russell (1990), *Service Operations Management,* Allyn and Bacon, Needham Heights, MA.

Schmenner, R. W. (1995), *Service Operations Management,* Prentice-Hall, Englewood Cliffs, NJ.

Stevenson, W. (2005), *Operations Management,* 8th ed., McGraw-Hill, New York, NY.

Waller, D. (2003), *Operations Management: A Supply Chain Approach,* 2nd ed., Thomson, London, UK.

ENDNOTES

1. Quote from Ron Lamming, Operations Manager at Kautex Textron, in Stevens, T., "Chaos to Control," *Industry Week,* V. 252, No. 10, p. 57.

2. Quote from Paul Mason of Hosca Consultants, in Meczes, R., "Make the Right Move," *Works Management,* Spring 2005, pp. 40–43.

3. Bossidy, L. and R. Charan, "Business Supermodels: What Should You Change and What Should You Keep in Your Organization?" V. 18, No. 4, 2004, p. 1.

4. Desjardins, D., "Toysrus.com Earns Title of Cyber World's Biggest Toy Store," *DSN Retailing Today,* V. 43, No. 11, 2004, pp. 22–23.

5. Meczes, R., "Make the Right Move," *Works Management,* Spring 2005, pp. 40–44.

6. Throughput is a term that is used frequently in several chapters of this textbook. It refers to a facility's average output rate. Throughput time refers to the average lead time required to turn raw materials into finished products. Thus, the terms throughput time and production lead time are often used interchangeably.

7. Langnau, L., "Room for Improvement," *Material Handling Management,* V. 60, No. 1, 2005, pp. 18–20.

8. Elliott, H., "OEMs Seek Single Point of Contact for SCM," *Electronic Business,* V. 29, No. 9, 2003, p. 37.

9. Goldratt, E. and J. Cox, *The Goal: A Process of Ongoing Improvement,* Croton-on-Hudson, NY: North River Press, 1986.

10. Mabin, V. J. and S. J. Balderstone, "The Performance of the Theory of Constraints Methodology: Analysis and Discussion of Successful TOC Applications," *International Journal of Operations & Production Management,* V. 23, No. 5/6, 2003, p. 568–596.

11. "Forget Set-Up Times and Focus on Throughput," *MSI,* V. 22, No. 2, 2004, p. 28.

12. Smith, F., "A Little TOC Goes a Long Way," *MSI,* V. 21, No. 8, 2003, p. 34.

13. Breen, B., "Living in Dell Time," *Fast Company,* November 2004, pp. 86–92.

14. Nunes, J., "SCARA Robots: Still Speedy and Dependable," *Robotics World,* V. 23, No. 3, 2005, pp. 4–5.

15. Adil, G. and D. Rajamani, "The Trade-Off Between Intracell and Intercell Moves in Group Technology Cell Formation," *Journal of Manufacturing Systems,* V. 19, No. 5, 2000, pp. 305–317.

16. Durmusoglu, M. and A. Nomak, "GT Cells Design and Implementation in a Glass Mould System," *Computers and Industrial Engineering,* V. 48, No. 3, 2005, pp. 525–536.

17. Holland, T., "Toyota Triumphant," *Far Eastern Economic Review,* V. 167, No. 32, 2004, pp. 36–40.

18. Definition found at Vorne Industrial Displays & Productivity Tools website, http://www.vorne.com.

19. Cheng, L., "Line Balancing vs. Theory of Constraints," *IIE Solutions,* V. 34, No. 4, 2002, pp. 30–32.

20. Key, W., "Assembly-Line Job Satisfaction and Productivity," *Industrial Engineering,* V. 26, No. 11, 1994, pp. 44–45.

21. Marsh, P., "The Delicate Touch of the Assembly Line: The Art of Manufacturing Part II," *Financial Times,* August 1, 2001, p. 11.

22. Goncalves, J. and J. de Almeida, "A Hybrid Genetic Algorithm for Assembly Line Balancing," *Journal of Heuristics,* V. 8, No. 6, 2002, pp. 629–642.

23. Meller, R. and R. DeShazo, "Manufacturing System Design Case Study: Multi-Channel Manufacturing at Electrical Box & Enclosures," *Journal of Manufacturing,* V. 20, No. 6, 2002, pp. 445–457.

24. Anonymous, "Custom Equipment Boosts Reliability," *Beverage Industry,* V. 96, No. 2, 2005, p. 68.

25. Duplaga, E., C. Hahn, and D. Hur, "Mixed-Model Assembly Line Sequencing at Hyundai Motor Company," *Production and Inventory Management Journal,* V. 37, No. 3, 1996, pp. 20–26.

26. Watson, E. and A. Wood, "Mixed-Model Production System Design Using Simulation Methodology," *Production and Inventory Management Journal,* V. 36, No. 4, 1995, pp. 53–58.

27. For detailed discussions of dispatch rule performance, see McKay, K., F. Safayeni, and J. Buzacott, "Job Shop Scheduling Theory: What Is Relevant?" *Interfaces,* V. 18, No. 4, 1988, pp. 84–90; Panwalker, S. and W. Iskander, "A Survey of Scheduling Rules," *Operations Research,* V. 25, No. 1, 1977, pp. 45–61; and Wisner, J. and S. Siferd, "A Survey of U.S. Manufacturing Practices in Make-to-Order Machine Shops," *Production and Inventory Management Journal,* V. 36, No. 1, 1995, pp. 1–7.

28. Deierlein, B. "Going Wireless," *Beverage World,* V. 124, No. 1756, 2005, p. 48.

29. Arunapuram, S., K. Mathur, and D. Solow, "Vehicle Routing and Scheduling with Full Truck-loads," *Transportation Science,* V. 37, No. 2, 2003, p. 170; Doll, L., "Quick and Dirty Vehicle Routing Procedure," *Interfaces,* V. 10, 1980, pp. 84–85; Dreyfus, S., "An Appraisal of Some Shortest-Path Algorithms," *Operations Research,* V. 17, 1969, pp. 395–412; Pollack, M. and W. Weibenson, "Solution of the Shortest-Route Problem—A Review," *Operations Research,* Mar/Apr 1960, pp. 224–230; Currie, R. and S. Salhi, "Exact and Heuristic Methods for a Full-Load, Multi-Terminal, Vehicle Scheduling Problem with Backhauling and Time Windows," *The Journal of the Operational Research Society,* V. 54, No. 4, 2003, p. 390; and Toth, P. and D. Vigo, eds., *The Vehicle Routing Problem,* Philadelphia, PA: SIAM, 2002.

30. Andel, T., "Nordson Goes Operation Lean, Service Heavy," *Material Handling Management,* V. 59, No. 13, 2004, pp. 35–37.

Chapter 8:

MANAGING CUSTOMER AND WORK FLOWS

"What are the barriers to improving patient flow in our hospitals? Heading the list may be the failure to recognize the importance of flow. Good patient flow may well be central to achieving the improvements in the quality of hospital care that have been so elusive."[1]

"Customers should be viewed and managed as assets of the organization to be invested in, depreciated, and replaced. In addition to the outsourcing of customers (e.g., using business partners to serve certain customer groups), companies also need to think about trading, sharing, firing, and outright selling customers."[2]

Learning Objectives

After completing this chapter, you should be able to:

- Understand the concepts of customer flow and work flow, and why these are important to the firm.
- Explain the impact that flow management has on the organization in terms of customer service, quality, costs, and productivity.
- Describe how customer and work flows are analyzed.
- Discuss how customer and work flows are managed in a firm and a supply chain.
- List some of the products that aid in customer and work flow management.

Chapter Outline

Introduction

Customer Flow Mapping

Service Delivery System Design

Demand Variability and Service Capacity Utilization

Managing Customer Queues

Managing Work Flows

Managing Work Flows in the Office

Managing Work Flows Along the Supply Chain

Process Management in Action	Cross-Training at Charlie Trotter's

Some days Matthias Merges, chef de cuisine at Charlie Trotter's, leaves his white chef's jacket at home and comes to work in a suit. He doesn't have to worry about spilling sauce on his tie, however, because he will spend the evening in the dining room, serving customers rather than cooking. Merges and the chefs at Trotter's famous fine-dining restaurant in Chicago, Illinois, take turns working the front of the house. That cross-training has broken down all barriers between the front and the back of the house and improved teamwork and efficiencies in the restaurant, said chef and owner Charlie Trotter. "I'm shocked more [restaurants] don't try to do this kind of thing," Trotter said.

Cross-training is a more common practice among fast-food and quick-service restaurants, where employees learn to make sandwiches or burritos and run the cash register. But while the practice is rare in fine-dining and casual restaurants, those who have been able to bring their chefs out of the kitchen and into the dining room say the benefits of such training are well worth the effort and planning it takes.

As leader of the kitchen, Merges spends the most time in Trotter's dining room, usually about three months. The other chefs spend about a month or more, and everyone on the cooking staff is encouraged to spend a week or more assisting the servers, the sommeliers, and the hosts. Servers also spend some time in the kitchen, helping cooks. Merges, in his six years at Trotter's, said he has seen chefs gain more composure and self-discipline after working in the dining room. "It helps the front-of-the-house, and it helps the kitchen move to a whole new level of professionalism," he said. "I don't know if some restaurants don't want to invest the time. And then some can't because they are so streamlined they cannot afford to take one person out of the back and put him in the front."

Working in the dining room, however, gives chefs a front-row seat to view how diners react to the food, Merges said. He noted that chefs in the dining room would notice if the portions on a dish are too large or too small, and they can get a better handle on pairing food with wine. Meanwhile, servers working in the kitchen gain a greater understanding of what it takes to prepare dishes. "Knowledge is power, and the more you have under your belt, the more you can provide for the guest," Merges said.

The experience gives the cooking staff a better awareness of the ebb and flow of the dining room and more respect for what their colleagues do in the front of the house, said Trotter, adding that throughout his career he has disliked the divisions between wait and cooking staffs. "I wanted to break down the barriers," he said. "I never liked that us-versus-them attitude."

Source: Berta, D., "Fine-Dining Chefs Come Out of the Kitchen, Warm Up to Patrons," *Nation's Restaurant News*, V. 38, No. 48, 2004, p. 4. Reprinted with permission from *Nation's Restaurant News*.

Introduction

For service providers and for customer service processes at goods-producing firms, effectively managing the flow of customers is an extremely important objective that can help to ensure the firm's competitiveness and long-term viability. Customer flow can represent actual persons waiting in line or being processed through a facility, phone customers on hold or trying to navigate an automated answering system, or Internet customers seeking information or purchasing goods and services online. Queues of customers represent a real paradox for managers, since, on the one hand, queues of customers are good and represent potential purchases; without these customers, businesses would cease to exist. On the other hand, long customer queues accompanied by long wait times is evidence of a flow problem, and will eventually result in disgruntled customers and lost sales.

Since each customer is unique with different attitudes and perceptions, and may require a unique service or service delivery accommodation, managing these customer flows can indeed be fraught with problems. The opening Process Management in Action feature describes how fine-dining restaurant Charlie Trotter's uses cross-training to help minimize customer flow problems. In another example, consider this story printed in an issue of the *Las Vegas Review Journal* newspaper—a gambler, who had just won a seven-figure dollar amount at a local casino, walked into a Las Vegas luxury car dealership and announced that he wanted to buy a Ferrari. The salesperson asked him to wait his turn at the back of a line of customers. The high roller persisted, saying he wanted to buy a Ferrari *now*. When he still wouldn't go to the end of the line, security was called, and he was escorted from the business. This man returned to the casino, where an employee personally arranged for him to return to the dealership. Once there, he was given the attention he originally wanted. At that point, he announced he was taking his $350,000 in cash to a dealership that would treat him better.[3] The two questions that immediately come to mind are why is there a queue of unserved customers at a Ferrari dealership in the first place, and second, why are potential cash-laden customers so easily dismissed? This is certainly evidence of a customer flow problem. To avoid these kinds of problems, organizations can manage and improve customer flow by utilizing the tools described in the following sections. These tools include customer flow mapping, service delivery systems design, service capacity utilization, server scheduling, and customer queuing policies.

A discussion of work flows is also presented in the latter part of the chapter. Work flows occur as documents, information, or tasks and are passed between recipients within an organization and between supply chain trading partners. Managing the flow of this work in parallel fashion as services and products are created and delivered to customers can greatly impact an organization's costs, customer service, quality, and productivity. As one might expect, deploying various technologies to aid in the flow of work has become common in the workplace, and a number of companies are currently developing products for organizations and supply chains to improve work flows.

Customer Flow Mapping

Many businesses concentrate significant resources on the mapping and analysis of customer flows. Somewhat similar to process mapping, use of a **customer flow map** allows the analyst to visualize the flow of customers through the service delivery system, with the objective of identifying potential problem areas related to the processing of customers. Typically, these problem areas are characterized by long, unfair, or uncomfortable waits. Customer waiting problems in restaurants, a necessary but tricky issue for services to deal with, is the subject of the Service Perspective feature.

An example of customer flow analysis at a quick-change lube shop is shown in Figure 8.1. After developing and analyzing the map of customer flows, and after talking to some of the customers, the lube shop manager identified several potential problem areas. Solutions to these problems might include:

- Better signage directing customers to the proper stall for oil changes and safety inspections,

Service Perspective

Restaurants Are Playing the Waiting Game

Fatter paychecks and harried working households have bumped up the incidence of eating out, and consequently the time diners wait for a table. That's led U.S. dining chains such as Outback Steakhouse, Bennigan's, and Bahama Breeze to devise a variety of marketing fixes, from quasi-restaurant waiting areas to advertised takeout fare, beepers, and new reservation systems—all to reduce, bypass, or eliminate the wait.

The National Restaurant Association does not keep statistics on wait times, but even casual diners can attest to longer waits and shorter fuses. Chicagoan Pat Dando won't go to casual chains anymore, especially when the wait exceeds 15 minutes. "There isn't anything that good that I would wait that long for," she said, citing the numerous times she cooled her heels another 20 minutes beyond the 20 minutes she was quoted by the host. "I'll walk out."

One method to circumvent the wait is a pseudo reservation. Some customers have been driven to make a reservation in person, then leave to go home and later return with the other guests. California Pizza Kitchen eases the process by letting customers call ahead to put their names on a priority waiting list. Cell phones have made this highly convenient. A new survey by the National Restaurant Association found that one-third of mobile phone users made restaurant reservations using their cell phones. Even more respondents, 41 percent, used their cell phones to place carryout or delivery orders.

The pre-reservation idea, however, can create as many problems as it solves. "The problem with call-ahead service is when you have consumers waiting an hour and someone walks in and gets a table right away," said Nancy Schneid, vice president of marketing for Outback Steakhouse. Waits, in fact, are such a sore subject that they are taboo as a point of differentiation in Outback's ads, handled in-house. Rather than eliminate the wait, and possibly reduce the check, Schneid said her goal is to offer hospitality during the wait with food and drink service or special "billabong rooms," hospitality rooms that are neither a bar nor a dining room, but where people can drink and eat appetizers.

Since the first Bahama Breeze opened in 1996, "we've never had a day where we've not had a wait," said Gary Heckle, president of Bahama Breeze, adding that the wait can top two hours on weekends and one hour most nights. The chain offers a tropical deck to accommodate those waiting for dinner, featuring live entertainment, drinks, and appetizers. "At Bahama Breeze people stay longer than any concept," he said. "We like to think of it as the memorable 2-hour island vacation."

Another increasingly popular way to circumvent long waits is through takeout service. Two-thirds of consumers surveyed in 1999 by the NRA said the food they purchased for takeout was worth the additional cost. The survey showed that two in five adults believe takeout service is essential to the way they live. So essential, in fact, that Outback and Bennigan's are creating dedicated entrances and marketing efforts to promote new takeout service. Brinker International's Chili's chain has had takeout since the 1970s and is now retrofitting existing units with dedicated entries, parking, and staff.

A major challenge continues to be keeping impatient diners from leaving, a task being tackled by automation. Dave Miller, president of JTECH Communications, which supplies pagers to 60,000 restaurants such as Outback and Applebee's Neighborhood Grill & Bar, said the pagers allow for a more relaxed wait, and once relaxed, customers are more likely to stay and have a greater propensity to order drinks.

To provide more accurate wait time estimates, some restaurants also have purchased automated reservation systems that calculate the wait based on the number of guests, the time, day and other criteria. Wayne Rock, vice president of product development at EZ2Get.com, said his system allowed one restaurant to increase nightly table turns from 8.5 to 13 after using the system for six months.

Source: MacArthur, K., "Fighting a Wait Problem," *Advertising Age*, V. 71, No. 24, 2000, p. 22. Reprinted with permission. © Crain Communications Inc. 2000.

- Use of a technician whose primary job is to greet customers and fill out the service order,
- Design of a more comfortable waiting area (perhaps with a television, coffee, soft drinks, and comfortable seating),
- Signage directing patrons to stay out of the garage area for safety reasons and windows to view the garage from the waiting area,
- Training technicians to ensure delivery of the invoice to customers as soon as work is completed, and
- Delivery of the car as soon as the invoice is paid.

A queuing analysis might also be performed to determine waiting line characteristics, given the number of technicians employed at various times during the day (more on customer queuing analysis is covered later in this section). This information can then be used for better technician scheduling, promotional advertisements, and demand management techniques.

Jeremiah, the service manager at John's Quick-Lube Shop, wants to see if he can improve customer service at his store. He observes customer behavior during a typical day and creates the following customer flow map describing the typical customer flows at his shop.

Figure 8.1	Mapping Customer Flows at John's Quick-Lube Shop

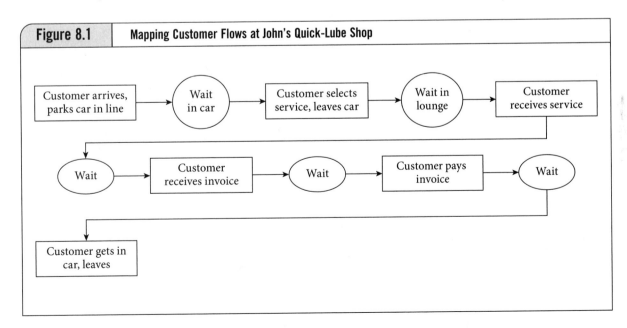

As a result of his customer flow analysis, Jeremiah notices a number of items that might be causing customer service problems:

- Customers frequently get into the oil-change line when they need an emission/safety inspection, and vice-versa.
- Customers occasionally get out of their car to find a service person.
- Customers do not sit in the lounge area—rather, they frequently wander out to the service area and talk to the automobile technicians.
- Customers occasionally complain about the lengthy wait time prior to and during the service.
- Customers occasionally notice their service is completed, and ask for their invoice.
- Customers must occasionally ask for their car after paying the invoice.

Texas-based Frost Bank recently changed its branch banks to make them more hospitable to customers, while also reducing wait times. A concierge counter serviced by an employee enables customers to get information as soon as they enter the bank. The branches provide full-service Internet terminals for their customers, and for more consultative financial services, customers are shown to a waiting room with coffee, television, and the newspaper while waiting to speak to an associate. "The branch is going to go from a transaction center to a selling spot where you go to buy financial services," says Paul Oliver, group executive vice president at Frost. "The designs that we put in place make more sense than what took place in the past."[4]

Ruby Tuesdays, a U.S. restaurant chain, uses business intelligence software to monitor such things as customer wait times at each of its locations. When the system identified one of its restaurants in Knoxville, Tennessee, with longer than normal wait and service times, corporate managers used the system to view that store's specific problem. They found that this location was constantly running at full capacity due to an economic boom that had recently hit the area. The company made changes to the kitchen layout, increasing access to food and equipment to increase kitchen capacity. Table turnover increased by 10 percent and wait times decreased.[5]

Montreal-based airline Air Canada uses a decision support system to simulate its customer check-in process, allowing the firm to study customer arrival patterns and server availability and the impact these factors have on customer wait times. This system allows managers to perform "what-if" analyses and view the impact on customer queues from unexpected problems such as flight delays caused by inclement weather, mechanical difficulties, or flight delays of other airlines. Air Canada managers can then apply various flight and employee scheduling alternatives to the problems and see the impact of these decisions prior to when they actually have to be made.[6]

Service Delivery System Design

When analyzing existing service processes or designing new ones, service system designers need to consider the objectives along with the desirable level of customer interaction for each service process. In the lube shop described in Figure 8.1, it is understandably unproductive and potentially unsafe to have customers in the garage interacting with the auto technicians as they are trying to do their jobs. Other potential problems at the garage appear to be occurring when customers cannot find someone to help them. Customers interacting with company employees, both intentionally and unintentionally, are referred to as **customer contact points**. Some service processes may require customer contact as illustrated in our garage example, when customers first arrive and then when they pay. Other processes may work best with moderate or minimal customer contact, such as when customers watch the work being performed on their cars through the window. Still other processes are best handled out of sight of customers, as with the lube shop's bookkeeping and worker training procedures. Thus, it is advisable to assess the level of customer contact and control that exists for various service processes, with the objective of separating customers from processes not designed for customer contact. This technique is termed **service blueprinting**, and is discussed next.

Service Blueprinting

Service blueprinting, introduced in Chapter 2, helps managers separate processes requiring customer contact from those not requiring customer contact. In this way, different forms of management control, personnel work methods, and tools can be employed to maximize both productivity and the level of customer service. The service blueprint is a representation of all activities constituting the service delivery process. Figure 8.2 illustrates an example of a service blueprint for the quick-change lube shop introduced in Figure 8.1.

Jeremiah, the service manager at John's Quick-Lube Shop, also wants to design the shop to provide the right level of customer contact associated with each of the business's activities. He designs the following blueprint for each service activity.

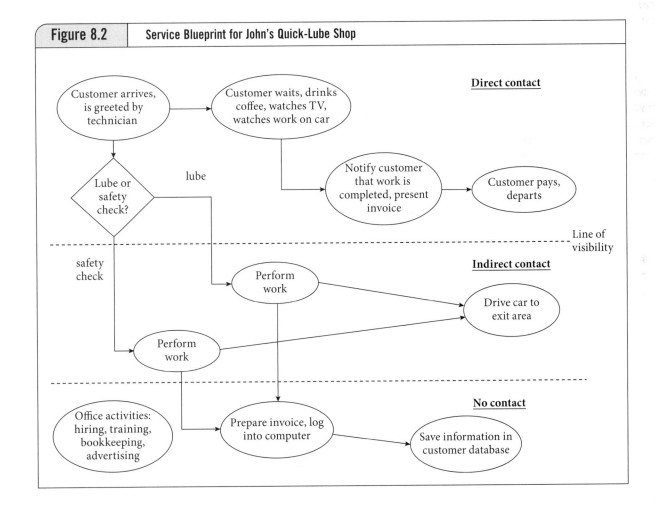

Figure 8.2 | **Service Blueprint for John's Quick-Lube Shop**

In the figure, the ovals represent activities occurring during the service, and the diamond represents a process decision. Based on management preference, customer flow, and process design, the lube service can be divided into three contact levels: activities requiring direct customer contact, those requiring limited contact (visibility), and those requiring no customer contact. Each level suggests different management control techniques and layout considerations. At the direct customer contact level, employees interacting with customers need to be trained in sales and creating or maintaining good customer relations. Self-service strategies can also be employed, as in the waiting room at the lube shop. Consideration must also be given to signage, access, parking, and customer comfort items.

At the indirect customer contact level, customers should be discouraged or otherwise prevented from directly contacting company personnel or processes in these areas. In the lube shop scenario, a wall with a window prevents customers from speaking to technicians, while allowing customers to see the work being performed on their automobiles. Hiring and training procedures for this level should concentrate on identifying and developing personnel that are technically proficient at operating the necessary process equipment. These employees may have some minor interactions with customers; thus, it might be advisable to have them undergo some level of customer relationship training. Process automation may also be a consideration, in order to increase productivity and service capacity.

Service process automation can be a double-edged sword, though, particularly when used with customer contact activities. For example, some customers view automated self-service systems with great disdain due to the learning that is required and because lower levels of personal service are provided. Most of us have encountered problems when trying to navigate self-service checkout stands; automated phone answering services; and in-store, automated product information kiosks. Shoppers at Trader Joe's, a U.S. discount food store, find little in the way of in-store technologies, and are treated to much more personal service and conversation than found at most of their competitors. On the other hand, automation that improves employee productivity without requiring a high degree of customer learning can be seen as positive by customers. The airline industry, for instance, appears to have adopted a good balance between expanded use of technology (online ticket purchases, airport check-in kiosks) and agents to serve customers personally.[7]

At the "no customer contact" level, customers must be completely separated from these process activities. In the lube shop example, some of these activities are shown. For example, hiring practices focus on identifying specialists in each of the activity areas, such as bookkeepers and other office personnel. Marketing practices in the lube shop example might utilize a customer database to contact customers every 90 days for another oil change. Employee training sessions can also be conducted here. These activities do not benefit in any way from customer involvement. A separate building or room should be used to house these personnel and activities. Information systems and other forms of office automation are typically heavily utilized to maximize back room productivity.

The service blueprint, along with the customer flow map, allows management to obtain a complete picture of the service delivery system as is, along with ideas and designs for what it should be. Jeremiah, the lube shop manager in our Figure 8.1 and 8.2 examples, should be able to use these tools to identify customer flow and service design problems along with potential solutions. Useful statistics for the various service elements can be added to the customer flow map and service blueprint to complete the picture, such as average wait times, process capacities and costs, average cycle times, customer arrival patterns, queue lengths, and customer feedback. With this information, decisions can be made to modify design elements such as signage, service system layouts, hiring and training procedures, equipment, hardware and software used, and reports generated.

Demand Variability and Service Capacity Utilization

All customers hate waiting. To successfully manage customer relationships and to keep customers flowing through service processes, it is therefore absolutely essential that service firms know when customer visits are likely to peak, and how these demand variations are going to affect service capacity and customer wait times. Over time, **service capacity bottlenecks** will most likely occur, as unexpected demand exceeds available service capacity, and it is up to management to reduce the likelihood of these occurrences with use of better capacity management and demand management techniques. A number of these techniques are discussed in the following sections.

Capacity Management Techniques for Services

A number of techniques are commonly employed in services to manage capacity, including use of effective employee scheduling, yield/revenue management, capacity sharing, employee cross-training, and self-service. Each of these techniques is discussed next.

Employee Scheduling

Effective scheduling in services occurs when the number of employees scheduled (the service capacity) closely matches customer demand, resulting in minimal customer waits along with minimal idle time for employees. Too little service capacity results in long customer wait times and lost sales, while too much capacity invariably results in idle servers and excessive labor costs. An important consideration is that unused or excess service capacity is lost—it cannot be stored for use at a later time. A trade-off must be considered then by management, namely, the cost of providing additional service capacity versus the cost of making customers wait. Effective employee scheduling can be particularly troublesome when demand varies considerably throughout the day, such as with restaurants, banks, hospital emergency rooms, and customer call centers. However, companies are getting better at scheduling through the use of improved forecasting methods and simulation models such as the one used by Air Canada mentioned earlier.

One approach to the scheduling problem begins with an hourly forecast of demand that can then be converted into staffing requirements for each day of the week. A workforce schedule is developed to match the staffing requirement as closely as possible. Excess staffing can be added based on the customer service level desired. For highly volatile demand situations, firms may opt to use standby part-time workers or floating workers to better match service capacity and demand. Managers must also consider overtime costs, days-off requirements, and other labor contract requirements, further complicating the scheduling problem. Example 8.1 illustrates the use of a simple workforce scheduling heuristic, which allows workers to have two consecutive days off.

In the example, the business owners can use the information provided and modify it to suit their scheduling preferences and customer service goals. For instance, Worker 3, a full-time employee, is not needed on Thursday. She could be given Thursday and Friday off instead, leaving Worker 4 to work only Monday, Wednesday, and Friday, and Worker 5 to work Friday. Alternately, Worker 3 could be given the original schedule

---

Example 8.1   Workforce Scheduling with Consecutive Days Off at Coastal Consulting

Michelle and Steven own a computer consulting business with three full-time and several part-time employees. They desire to develop a weekly schedule that allows all workers to have two consecutive days off per week, given their required staffing levels. After compiling the demand levels for the upcoming week, the worker requirements are as shown below. Assuming that the employees have no preference for which consecutive days they get off, the procedure is as follows:

1. Copy the daily requirements on the line for Worker 1; circle the lowest pair of daily requirements. For ties, choose the pair with the lowest daily requirement on an adjacent day. If a tie still exists, choose the first tied pair of days (for Worker 2 there are three equal pairs, however, the one circled below has lower requirements on adjacent days). Assign the non-circled days to Worker 1.

2. Subtract 1 from each of the non-circled days, then place the new daily requirements on the line for Worker 2. Repeat Step 1 for Worker 2 and then for the remaining workers, until no more workers are required.

	M	T	W	Th	F	S	Su
Requirement	4	3	4	2	3	1	2
Worker 1	4	3	4	2	3	①	②
Worker 2	3	2	3	1	②	1	2
Worker 3	2	1	2	0	2	①	①
Worker 4	1	⓪	①	0	1	1	1
Worker 5	0	0	1	0	0	0	0

SOLUTION:

Schedule: Worker 1 has S/Su off; Worker 2 has F/S off; Worker 3 has S/Su off (and could also have Th off); Worker 4 (a part-timer) has T/W/Th off; and Worker 5 (a part-timer) works on W.

---

and the company would have excess capacity on Thursday (perhaps the historic demand variance is high on Thursdays, making it desirable to have excess capacity).

There are a number of workforce management and scheduling software and web-based applications for hospitals, call centers, retailers, and manufacturers that seek to find optimal workforce schedules given a demand distribution and a number of scheduling and workforce constraints. Covenant Health Systems of Waterloo, Iowa, manager of health and elder care organizations, faced challenges of controlling labor costs, recruitment, maintaining adequate staffing for the required level of patient care, and improving its tracking and reporting capabilities for JCAHO (the Joint Commission on Accreditation of Healthcare Organizations). Recently, it replaced its old system with one from API Software, Inc. of Hartford, Wisconsin called Active Staffer. In 12 months Covenant was able to realize full system payback through labor savings and improved worker productivity. More productive scheduling saved an average of 15 labor hours per month; replacing manual staffing and payroll processes saved more than $14,000 per year; and a bonus-pay internal agency program motivated employees to work extra shifts, saving Covenant over $200,000 annually.[8]

Sam Ash Music Corp., a U.S. retailer of musical instruments, rolled out its automated workforce management solution from Massachusetts-based Kronos Inc. in 2003 because it was rapidly expanding its workforce. Employees clocked-in and sales performances were tracked using finger scans. Payroll was then tabulated automatically, including commissions and hourly wages. Employee schedules were also generated, taking into account Sam Ash's scheduling and overtime policies.[9]

Lincoln-based Nebraska Book Company also used a Kronos software solution called Workforce Central® to automate the collection, storage, and management of vital human resource information. Now the company employees use the system's self-service functions such as time-off requests, change of address, and accrual data. Managers can look at employee histories, compensations, positions held, health information, commendations, employees currently working, employee tardiness, and disciplinary actions, all with one database. "Kronos has given us exactly the tools we needed to address all of our workforce management objectives, and as a result, we're able to focus on more strategic issues," says Brenda McLey, director of human resources for Nebraska Book.[10]

Yield/Revenue Management

Yield management, also called **revenue management**, refers to the objective of trying to sell a limited or fixed capacity to the right customers at the right price, so as to maximize revenues. Industries commonly using yield management systems include airlines, railroads, hotels, cruise lines, and car rental agencies. Texas-based American Airlines, using its Sabre computer reservation system, is typically given credit for developing the field of yield management after the airline industry's deregulation in 1978. The airline's yield management strategy after deregulation was to allow some seats to be sold for low fares, to compete with the new start-up carriers, while using differential pricing for its remaining seats. In 1992, American Airlines reported that use of its revenue management system resulted in an additional $1.4 billion in sales over a three-year period. Likewise, U.S.-based Hertz car rentals reported a 5 percent increase in average revenue per customer in 1995, and Chevys Fresh Mex® restaurants, headquartered in California, reported a similar result using its revenue management systems.[11]

Today, the general yield management strategy consists of a combination of overbooking, allocating capacity among customer segments, and a differential pricing scheme for customer segments. **Overbooking** refers to accepting more reservations for service than can be provided. For an airline, a certain percentage of customers will typically fail to show up for a flight; if the airline does not overbook, then the empty seats can represent millions of dollars in lost revenue per year. The argument for airline, restaurant, and car rental overbooking is the same and straightforward—companies that overbook effectively can make far more revenue than those that do not. The question then becomes not whether to overbook, but *how much* to overbook. Most airlines overbook a certain percentage of seats using automated systems based on available information such as class (first, business, or coach), destination, days prior to departure, current reservations, and cancellations. These systems will develop optimal overbooking policies for different classes for each flight, considering the costs of turning a reserved customer away, alternate flight arrangements, and empty seats. Example 8.2 illustrates the decision regarding how much to overbook at a restaurant.

Allocating fixed capacity to different customer groups is another concern in yield management. This decision regards when to turn away one type of customer with the hope that a higher revenue customer will arrive later. With airlines, for example, high-revenue frequent business travelers tend to make reservations close to the departure date, while low-revenue vacationers make reservations much farther in advance. The airline must therefore decide at what point reservations for low-revenue customers will be shut down in anticipation of incoming high-revenue passenger reservations. A simple approach is to set a number of reservations allowed for high-revenue customers, and a number allowed for low-revenue customers. Continuing with the airline example, the firm may decide to hold 75 percent of its seats for high-revenue customers and

---

Example 8.2   Overbooking at Grebson's Bar-B-Que Restaurant

Phyllis, the reservations manager at Grebson's Bar-B-Que, has compiled information from the recent reservation history of the restaurant to determine the probability of no-shows and to determine the optimal overbooking policy to use. The restaurant's capacity is fixed at 28 tables. The following table shows the historic number of no-shows on a typical evening, along with the probability of occurrence.

NO. NO-SHOWS	PROBABILITY
0	0.10
1	0.25
2	0.30
3	0.20
4	0.15

The question facing Phyllis is how many reservations should she accept, given the probability of a no-show as shown in the table, if the average profitability of one table is $60 and the cost of lost goodwill due to overbooking is $30 per table. Given that the profit is greater than the overbooking cost, it is advisable to overbook.

The next table shows the outcomes for various overbooking policies, using the no-show probabilities. Note that there is no reason to take reservations for more than 32 tables, since the worst case scenario would still fill the restaurant.

PROBABILITY	RESERVATIONS/SHOWING UP				
	28	29	30	31	32
0.10	28	29	30	31	32
0.25	27	28	29	30	31
0.30	26	27	28	29	30
0.20	25	26	27	28	29
0.15	24	25	26	27	28

Using these outcomes and their associated probabilities, Phyllis can calculate the expected profit for each overbooking policy, to determine the most desirable policy. The final tables show these calculations.

SOLUTION:

CUSTOMERS SHOWING UP	EXPECTED PROFIT – 28 RESERVATIONS				
	28	27	26	25	24
Tables Filled	28	27	26	25	24
Profit ($)	1,680	1,620	1,560	1,500	1,440
Turnaways	0	0	0	0	0
Cost ($)	0	0	0	0	0
Net Profit	1,680	1,620	1,560	1,500	1,440
Probability	0.10	0.25	0.30	0.20	0.15
Expected Net	168	405	468	300	216
Total Value ($)	1,557				

CUSTOMERS SHOWING UP	EXPECTED PROFIT – 29 RESERVATIONS				
	29	28	27	26	25
Tables Filled	28	28	27	26	25
Profit ($)	1,680	1,680	1,620	1,560	1,500
Turnaways	1	0	0	0	0
Cost ($)	30	0	0	0	0
Net Profit	1,650	1,680	1,620	1,560	1,500
Probability	0.10	0.25	0.30	0.20	0.15
Expected Net	165	420	486	312	225
Total Value ($)	**1,608**				

CUSTOMERS SHOWING UP	EXPECTED PROFIT – 30 RESERVATIONS				
	30	29	28	27	26
Tables Filled	28	28	28	27	26
Profit ($)	1,680	1,680	1,680	1,620	1,560
Turnaways	2	1	0	0	0
Cost ($)	60	30	0	0	0
Net Profit	1,620	1,650	1,680	1,620	1,560
Probability	0.10	0.25	0.30	0.20	0.15
Expected Net	162	412.5	504	324	234
Total Value ($)	**1,636.5**				

CUSTOMERS SHOWING UP	EXPECTED PROFIT – 31 RESERVATIONS				
	31	30	29	28	27
Tables Filled	28	28	28	28	27
Profit ($)	1,680	1,680	1,680	1,680	1,620
Turnaways	3	2	1	0	0
Cost ($)	90	60	30	0	0
Net Profit	1,590	1,620	1,650	1,680	1,620
Probability	0.10	0.25	0.30	0.20	0.15
Expected Net	159	405	495	336	243
Total Value ($)	**1,638**				

CUSTOMERS SHOWING UP	EXPECTED PROFIT – 32 RESERVATIONS				
	32	31	30	29	28
Tables Filled	28	28	28	28	28
Profit ($)	1,680	1,680	1,680	1,680	1,680
Turnaways	4	3	2	1	0
Cost ($)	120	90	60	30	0
Net Profit	1,560	1,590	1,620	1,650	1,680
Probability	0.10	0.25	0.30	0.20	0.15
Expected Net	156	397.5	486	330	252
Total Value ($)	**1,621.5**				

Based on the profit per table, the cost of turning away customers, and the probability of no-shows, it is concluded that the optimal policy is to overbook by three tables. The expected profit generated is $1,638. If the cost of turning away customers increases, Phyllis should overbook fewer than three tables. She can recalculate the expected profitabilities to determine the optimal overbooking policy.

25 percent for low-revenue customers. To keep from turning away high-revenue customers when seat allocation is full, the airline might also decide to allow the low-revenue passenger seats to be sold to either class of passenger, on a first-come-first-served basis. Providing protection in this way to some seats for a particular class of passenger can also result in unused seats, which explains why customers can frequently find inexpensive travel accommodations at the last minute. Automated yield management systems are dynamic, meaning that as the reservation date approaches, decisions can be made "on the fly" to protect or unprotect capacity for high-revenue customers, based on the actual reservations to date, compared to expected reservations.

The final topic area of yield management is **differential pricing**. The idea is to segment customers into different categories, such that high prices will be charged to customers willing to pay them, and low prices will be charged to customers who would not use the service at a higher price. As mentioned earlier, a typical full-service air carrier offers three classes of passenger service: first class, business class, and economy class, with designated seating. In many cases, economy class tickets for the same flight may cost only 10 percent of a first class ticket, and a third to half as much as a business class ticket. Additionally, as departure dates grow nearer, prices of all three classes will fluctuate based on the automated decisions from the yield management systems. This has resulted in complicated fare structures for many large airline companies, and since September 11, 2001, many of these carriers have had financial problems and declared bankruptcy. Low-cost U.S. air carriers like Dallas, Texas-based Southwest Airlines, with simplified pricing and only one class of ticket, have maintained profitability during this same period.[12]

Firms must be aware, though, that differential pricing and, indeed, yield management in general, can be viewed as unfair by some customers. The idea that customers are told there is no more capacity when in fact there is, can be hard for customers to accept, and in some cases, firms must take this view into account when setting yield management policies. In September 2000, for instance, some of the customers of on-line retailing giant Amazon.com began noticing they were paying different prices for DVD movies, based on their previous purchasing patterns. Customers started flooding chat sites with complaints against the company. Amazon quickly issued statements that it was merely testing consumer response to various prices, cancelled its differential pricing, and refunded the differences charged to those who paid more for their DVDs.[13] Because of the potential unfairness problem, customers are typically kept uninformed of various pricing and capacity protection policies.

Gradually, many industries have seen customer acceptance of yield management practices. For example, about 12 years ago, a study comparing the airline and hotel industries found that yield management practices were seen as fair in the airline industry, but unfair in the hotel industry. A similar study eight years later showed that customers viewed differential pricing equally fair in both industries. Since yield management was relatively new to the hotel industry at the time of the first study, it appears that, with time, customers had come to accept these practices.[14]

Capacity Sharing

Due to the high cost of many service delivery processes, firms are faced with finding other uses for capacity during periods of underutilization. Airlines, for instance, might share gates, baggage-handling equipment, and ground personnel. Small air freight carriers like Switzerland-based Swiss World Cargo and Korean Air Cargo of South Korea, for example, have **capacity sharing** agreements between various destinations to reduce the amount of business turned away.[15] Capacity sharing in the passenger airline indus-try has come to be known as **code sharing**. Code sharing agreements between airlines can fall anywhere between outright mergers to arm's length agreements for sharing reser-vation systems or aircraft capacity, and they can be argued to be either pro-competitive by creating new services at lower costs, or anti-competitive by creating less capacity, higher fares, or foreclosure of the competition from markets. The code sharing agreement between American Airlines and U.K. airline British Airways at London's Heathrow Air-port, for instance, has been argued by Texas-based Continental Airlines to be anti-competitive, because it allows the two airlines to collude on capacity, prices, and reve-nue sharing.[16]

Vacation hotels might lease large blocks of rooms to conventioneers during the off-season, while ski resorts can lease their properties out to concert promoters during the summer. Other forms of capacity sharing allow service providers to make their ca-pacity more flexible, and reduce the costs of overbooking. Hotels, for example, may en-ter into formal agreements to use each others' vacant rooms for customers when one property has no rooms available. Some passenger airlines also have similar arrange-ments. One airline company, Iceland-based Air Atlanta Icelandic, exists for the sole purpose of leasing aircraft and crews to other airlines worldwide for both air cargo and passenger needs.[17]

Cross-Training Employees

For services with multiple operations or service delivery processes, employees in an idle process can be moved temporarily to a busy process, adding additional capacity to the process and reducing overall customer wait times. This necessitates the use of em-ployee cross-training combined with close monitoring of service processes, but the benefits are plainly evident in businesses like department stores and supermarkets. When lines at cash registers become long, for example, floor salespeople or stockers can be moved to idle registers until the customer queues are gone. Care must be taken, though, to avoid the excessive use of temporarily transferring workers, which results in a short-term significant loss of service quality or processing capability, also called the **relearning effect**. This can lead to forcing a choice between cross-training and then tem-porarily moving workers to various processes to reduce the potential for long customer waits and perhaps reduce employee boredom or fatigue, or creating process specialists that remain at one process to potentially maximize service quality. In fact, researchers Pinker and Shumsky referred to service worker transfers as the potential creation of *consistent mediocrity*. They warned that flexible workers may not gain sufficient expe-rience at each process to provide high-quality service to any one customer, and what is gained in efficiency can be lost in service quality.[18]

In the automobile industry, the current use of heavily automated, flexible manufactur-ing systems with a flexible workforce, along with the potential loss of quality from worker transfers, does not seem to be a problem. In fact, Koki Hirashima, CEO of Honda of America, has stated that flexible employees are the new competitive frontier in automobile manufacturing.[19] Jill Dagilis, head of the Department of Health and Human Services (DHHS) in Worcester, Massachusetts, is also using cross-training effectively. Here is how she explains it: "Cooperation, commitment, hard work, mutual respect and a dedicated staff. If something doesn't work, we try to find a way to make it better. The city manager challenges us to be creative. We have a flat budget and ask for very modest ad-justments. That means plugging holes and moving people around." Some of her divi-sions were once small, isolated operations with little clerical support. After reorganization brought these divisions under the DHHS umbrella, they were able to share financial assistance, technology, equipment, and other resources. "We're building a team based on collaboration to maximize what we have. We try to teach and shore up one another," Dagilis said.[20] Thus, in many cases, it can benefit the firm to cross-train employees.

Using Self-Service

Many services can use customers as co-producers, and in some cases customers view this as a positive characteristic. Customers can customize services to fit their needs, potentially saving time as well as money, because firms generally understand that customers should be compensated for their work through lower prices. Since customers use the service exactly when it is needed, service capacity becomes much more flexible. Proper customer training, however, can become a problem for some services—adequate signage and instructions must be available for customers at the self-service process access points. Service providers must also be aware of all the potential mistakes that customers can make, and design contingency plans to adequately deal with customer mistakes when they occur.

Web-based technologies have enabled both customers and employees to obtain company information quickly, while reducing routine and time-consuming tasks for managers and service personnel. Many companies use automated human resource systems that allow employees to track their personnel, payroll, and tax records, for example, as well as to download training and other employment documents. This frees up time for human resource personnel to perform more strategic activities, such as personnel hiring and training.[21] At Texas-based media company Clear Channel Entertainment's Broadway Across America (BAA) division, customers have multiple ways to get the information they need. BAA gives callers the option to either use the interactive voice response (IVR) system or talk to a live representative. Information that customers would normally use the web to locate is now also easily accessible via telephone. "They can pull down directions to a particular venue, how to park, time or day of shows, and ticketing information," says Dan Fisher, Clear Channel Entertainment's national telecommunications manager. "All of the things you could find on our BAA Web site can be, for the most part, accomplished via the text-to-speech, voice recognition, and IVR system."[22]

Demand Management Techniques

The topic of demand management was introduced in Chapter 5, as a tool for managing demand when forecast errors cause potential product stockout or overstock situations. Similarly, when variable demand patterns cause service capacity and customer queuing problems that are only partially aided by the use of capacity management techniques as discussed in the preceding section, the firm can rely on demand management tactics to better manage the available capacity. Any number of techniques may be used in order to manipulate demand, and in services, these include use of reservations, complementary services, demand sorting, and pricing policies or promotions. These discussions follow.

Reservations

When service capacity is likely to be constrained, as on an airline, at a doctor's office, or during peak dining hours at a restaurant, demand can be managed through use of a reservation system. Aside from being used to segment customers and charge variable prices as in yield management (discussed earlier), reservations can act to regulate customer arrivals and more evenly spread demand over a period of time, allowing more accurate employee scheduling and better utilization of available capacity. Use of reservation systems requires earlier planning on the part of customers and cause businesses to incur added expenses for the reservation system and employee training; but in the right applications, reservations are viewed as fair by customers and preferable to long waits for service. Additionally, reservations might be used as a way to guarantee better service for frequent, high-value customers such as a firm's key supply chain trading partners.

Online reservation systems are already commonly used by customers for airline and hotel bookings, and corporate use of these systems is saving companies millions of travel dollars. California-based computer network and routing manufacturer Cisco Systems, for example, began using an online travel provider in the 1990s and estimates it saved $14 million on travel costs in 2004 alone.[23] Recently, online reservation systems have also become popular for making dinner reservations. The e-Commerce Perspective feature presents a general discussion of the growth of online reservation usage for restaurant patrons.

Many services, though, find that reservation systems do not work well. For example, retail and fast-food customers would not accept a reservation system, since most of these purchases tend to be spontaneous. Other businesses are experiencing technical problems regarding their reservation systems, which can be problematic since many of these problems can drive customers away. InterContinental Hotels Group of the United Kingdom found it difficult to add personalization content and capacity to its original online reservation system, and finally had to completely overhaul the system a few years ago. It estimates that the newly designed system has contributed an additional $100 million in revenues for the company since its implementation.[24]

Complementary Services

Service capacity problems may also be reduced through use of **complementary services**. For instance, a lounge area or bar may serve as a way to occupy customers who are waiting for a table at a restaurant. A restaurant, driving range, and pro shop can keep golfers occupied while waiting for their tee times. Movie theatres have video game rooms to entertain moviegoers while waiting for a show to begin. These service diversions not only tend to better occupy the time of waiting customers, but also can be a source of additional revenues—a win-win proposition. Muvico Theaters, headquartered in Coral Springs, Florida, has continued to expand its number of theaters in an industry plagued by dropping attendance by offering the ultimate in complementary services to its moviegoers. Arriving customers can use a valet parking service and, once inside, dine in full-service restaurants and reserve spacious loveseats in the balcony.[25] Seasonal services also develop complementary services to utilize capacity during characteristically slow periods of the year. Examples of this include an air-conditioning repair firm that also offers heater repair services, a snow ski resort that schedules mountain bike tours in the summer, and a ski boat retailer that sells snowmobiles in the winter.

Demand Sorting

Sometimes, an initial "sorting" of customers can be performed as they first enter the service system to better direct them to the appropriate service processes or available servers, resulting in less overall wait time. A municipality's motor vehicle department, for instance, may have a desk just inside the door to direct patrons to the appropriate service area, effectively reducing the occurrence of customers waiting in the wrong line. Automated answering services perform **demand sorting** by directing callers to select numbers for various services or information. And finally, airplane passengers are sorted into groups based on seat assignments in order to board them starting from the rear of the airplane, to reduce total boarding time. Demand sorting systems can also be

e-Commerce Perspective

The Boom in Online Reservation Systems

Online reservation networks and their restaurant clients say they have disproved the naysayers who predicted in the mid-1990s that consumer apathy and lack of operator interest would undermine the potential growth of table bookings via the Internet. But despite becoming a key tool for marketing and table management at tens of thousands of restaurants in less than a decade, some operators still harbor skepticism about the viability and effectiveness of Internet-based reservations. They argue that nothing is better when making reservations than a human, a phone, a pencil, and, if necessary, an email.

At least two dozen popular restaurant reservation sites apparently dominated by OpenTable.com but including RestaurantRow.com, Foodline.com, and more recently, DinnerBroker.com, have become sophisticated, visually enticing, and consumer friendly. Diners who use such websites not only are offered the freedom and confidence of selecting the day and time of their choosing, but also can lock in specific tables in dining rooms around the world. Prospective guests even can view menus, see pictures of the dining room, read the chef's bio, inform the kitchen about allergies, read restaurant reviews, and alert the staff if the dinner is a special occasion.

Those network reservation sites do not include the untold number of independent, restaurant-run websites that take reservations. Nor do they include the vastly more numerous Internet sites of airlines, hotels, credit card companies, consumer magazines, city tourist bureaus, web browsers, and others that allow bookings of restaurant seats or offer links to online partners that do.

Still, many dubious restaurateurs say they are less turned on by potential online reservations sales gains than they are turned off by the technology's removal of the human element.

"We don't accept them at our restaurants," said Tracy Nieporent, director of marketing for Myriad Restaurant Group, the New York-based operator of a string of sizzling-hot dining attractions such as Nobu and TriBeCa Grill, from Manhattan to San Francisco. However, Myriad does use OpenTable.com two times a year: the one-week periods in the winter and summer when New York operators promote themselves during Restaurant Week, Nieporent conceded. During the other 50 weeks, however, the impersonal system is avoided, Nieporent stressed. "We are in the people business, so what is the point of removing the human element?" he asked. "We like to talk to our guests, see what their special needs are, if the dinner is something special. Online reservations can be a neat little excuse for not talking to your guest," Nieporent observed. "The human aspect should not be put on the side."

Even operators who said they are major fans of reservation networks said Internet-accessed bookings fill only a fraction of their seating. "I think when I was general manager at Verbena, we were the first in the city to sign on with OpenTable in '97 or '98, and I've been a big fan ever since," said Todd McMullin, general manager of Off The Menu Corp., operator of the highly popular restaurant Ouest and the new Cesca in Manhattan. "But it is not a huge number of seats OpenTable fills for us, maybe 10 percent at best. These systems will never replace a human and a phone." McMullin said he really appreciates that online systems give guests the freedom to book whenever they want, not just when the restaurant is open. He said the majority of the reservations made through OpenTable.com come in between 10 P.M. and 10 A.M.

Operators who use OpenTable.com pay a one-time installation fee to access a central database, a subscription fee, and a $1 charge for every person in a confirmed party. Twenty-five cents is charged per person if the reservation was made through the restaurant's own website but used OpenTable.com's software engine. OpenTable.com officials stress that their real-time, two-way system taps a restaurant's actual inventory of available tables to prevent overbookings. Moreover, the database provides clients with such hospitality aids as guests' historical ordering habits, seating preferences, and special needs.

Paul Pinnell, general manager of Nana in the Wyndham hotel in Dallas, said OpenTable.com reservations probably account for about 3 to 5 percent of the bookings at his 170-seat restaurant on any given night. But he says the system pays for itself. "Ever since we remodeled in 2001 and adopted OpenTable, our sales have been rising each month, much of it led by online reservations," Pinnell said. "It grows every month. We think it has been very successful for us."

Source: Prewitt, M., "Operators See Pros, Cons in Online-Reservations Boom," *Nation's Restaurant News*, V. 39, No. 9, 2005, p. 1. Reprinted with permission from *Nation's Restaurant News*.

based on such things as customer importance, customer preference, or customer value. In Las Vegas, Nevada, for example, many restaurant buffets and resort shows have VIP lines that allow high-value guests to avoid longer waits.

As the technological ability to analyze and segment customers matures, more applications present themselves to businesses seeking to improve their marketing performance. Ohio-based Dorothy Lane Markets uses MarketEXPERT from customer database product producer VRMS, headquartered in Michigan, to segment its customers using many different variables. For instance, each year CEO Norman Mayne shows up at the homes of his top five customers with gifts for their continued patronage.[26] Ian Dunbar, a founder of U.K.-based consulting firm Market Segmentation Co., recommends that companies start with customer needs. "Find out what are the delights and disappointments that customers experience," he suggests. Professor Roger Palmer of the Cranfield School of Management in the United Kingdom adds, "Keep it in single figures. Don't have too many segments. I'd suggest around half a dozen, the sensible mid-point between selling the same thing to everyone and something different to everyone."[27]

Pricing Policies and Promotions

For many services, lowering prices can increase customer purchases, while raising prices will reduce demand. Lowering prices during slow-demand periods and/or raising prices during periods of high demand can also smooth the demands placed on existing capacity and reduce customer flow problems. Nevada Power, for instance, an electric utility in Nevada, allows customers to participate in a peak-demand reduction program, which pays customers to let their electricity be turned off for a few minutes every hour during peak-usage periods. This allows Nevada Power to better manage its electricity capacity, and avoid having to purchase electricity during these peak periods at high prices on the spot market from other electricity providers. Restaurants also may offer reduced, early-bird dinner prices to encourage patrons to eat prior to 6 P.M. Similarly, movie theatres offer reduced prices for moviegoers willing to watch a movie during daytime hours.

Advertising promotions are commonly used with pricing changes to create even larger changes in demand, for example, during off-seasons, holidays, evenings, and weekends. Hotels and resorts may promote their facilities to conventions or for business meetings during seasonally slow months. Cell phone companies advertise their free weekend minutes, quick-change oil shops send out mailers promoting cheaper mid-day prices, and grocery stores promote double-coupon savings days. All of these promotion and pricing strategies seek to make better use of available capacity while reducing demand during peak usage periods. In turn, the firm is able to serve more customers with less overall capacity, allowing customers to wait shorter periods of time for service, while at the same time improving productivity.

Managing Customer Queues

Even with the most adept management of service capacity and customer demand process, bottlenecks, with the accompanying long queues of customers, will still occur from time to time. The dynamic properties of the service itself are to blame—customers arrive randomly and unexpectedly with varied requirements, while the service system's capacity varies based on the level of staffing and each server's processing capability. With a little luck and some queuing management skills, though, service bottlenecks will occur infrequently and only for short periods of time. Customers will not wait long, however, in most situations before loudly complaining or simply leaving. Thus, it is up to management to address the trade-off in the cost of supplying greater levels of service capacity (more employees, more training, more automation, a larger facility) with the cost of making customers wait (loss of customers' current and future purchases, and negative word-of-mouth advertising).

Since the cost of supplying additional service capacity can be high, it is important for companies to understand and make use of the psychological aspects of customer waiting and "virtual queues." By addressing these issues, customers can become desensitized to the time spent waiting in queues, thus reducing the cost of customer waits. In turn, this will reduce the need for additional or reserve capacity throughout the service system. These topics are addressed next, followed by a discussion of the analysis and design of queuing systems.

The Psychology of Waiting

A number of approaches to dealing with waiting customers are addressed in a classic paper by David Maister, a consultant who studied the psychology of waiting in queues.[28] One approach recommends occupying people while they wait. Examples of this approach include having customers listen to music while they are on hold on the telephone, providing TVs to watch in waiting rooms, and placing mirrors next to elevators. Occupied customers feel more comfortable while waiting, and perceive their wait times to be shorter.

Waiting time uncertainty can produce anxiety and make the wait seem longer to customers in a waiting situation. Consequently, another common queue strategy is for the organization to keep customers informed of the approximate remaining wait time. City bus stops post arrival times for various bus routes; amusement parks post signs declaring the wait time remaining from that specific point in the queue; and city automobile license departments post the time remaining for customers in various queues. In Alaska, for example, people can view real-time web cameras at each of the state's motor vehicle department offices to see how busy an office is, prior to leaving their office or home.[29]

Waits perceived as unfair can also produce customer anxiety, and make the wait time seem even longer. Instead of using separate queues, organizations can use a multiple server "snake line" to increase the perception of fairness. They can also use separate queues for priority customers, out of the line of sight of other customers. Some retailers are using electronic line management systems to move customers through queues more quickly and fairly. These systems feature display units located at each cashier station, along with lights and sound to direct customers to the next available cashier, eliminating congestion at cashier stations and eliminating the need for staff members to direct traffic.[30]

Communicating with other customers can make waiting time seem shorter, so many organizations have made an effort to design waiting areas conducive to conversation. Attention to how chairs, tables, sofas, and coffeepots are situated can help to spark conversations, providing yet another distraction to help pass the time. Managing these customer perceptions is a form of demand management and is equally as important as managing the actual waiting time. If customers perceive the wait to be less than or equal to their initial expectations, their overall service experience will be impacted in a positive way. On the other hand, a customer's perception that the wait time was too long may negatively affect the probability of future visits.

Using Virtual Queues

In spite of all efforts to reduce the actual and perceived waiting time for customers, there may be periods of time when queuing problems persist. This may be particularly true for process capacities that are difficult or expensive to expand. For these situations, the **virtual queue** concept can be employed. Restaurants located in malls, for instance, might provide customers with pagers, allowing the restaurant to track their place in a virtual queue while allowing customers to walk around or even shop while waiting for a table. In Destin, Florida, the Fudpucker's restaurant provides customers with pagers and a shuttle to the nearby Fud's Fun Factory, an indoor carnival attraction, to occupy families facing long waits in the restaurant's queue.[31] Walt Disney World in Florida was the first company to design and use the virtual queue concept in amusement parks. Its system, called FASTPASS™, was installed in five of the park's most popular attractions in 1999. Park-goers used their admission ticket to register at a ride they wanted to attend, and the park's computer system estimated their wait time and notified them when to return. Customers' places were then held in a virtual queue. When guests returned at the designated time, they could immediately proceed to the attraction with no further waiting. Guests were overwhelmingly supportive of the concept, and Disney World found that people spent less overall time in queues, spent more money, and visited more attractions. FASTPASS is now used at all Disney amusement parks worldwide.[32]

The Analysis of Queuing Systems

Once customers are placed in a real queue, businesses must also strive to design the most effective system for serving them. To develop an effective queuing system, managers need to know approximately how long customers must wait for service given a particular queuing system, as well as the impact that additional servers, configurations, and equipment will have on the wait times. Managers must also know how long their customers are willing to wait for service before **reneging** (giving up and leaving the line) and how short the queue must be to avoid **balking** (not joining the queue in the first place, because it is too long). Designing effective queuing systems therefore requires the use of queuing models combined with actual observations. Obviously, managers using queuing system models do not know what actual demand variabilities over time will be, but they can use predictions of demand as the basis for initially designing queuing systems. Once they are in place, managers should collect data based on observations of actual demand and the resulting customer behavior, and then use that data to make periodic adjustments to their queuing system. These adjustments should help reduce actual and perceived waiting time, maximize queuing system performance, and increase customer satisfaction.

Many queuing systems are complex and require computer simulations to adequately analyze and predict system characteristics. For these systems, readers are referred to one of the many detailed treatments of this topic such as Wolff's *Stochastic Modeling and the Theory of Queues.*[33] For basic systems with one queue and one or two servers, though, the analysis is rather straightforward and is discussed here. Given a demand source, a customer arrival rate, and a service process with a certain configuration and speed, queuing theory can estimate the average queue length, the number of people in the system, the average wait time, and the system utilization. Figure 8.3 shows a simple queuing system.

Customers arrive from the **demand source** according to an **arrival process**. If servers are idle, then the customer is processed and leaves. If the servers are busy, then the customer joins a queue, according to a **queuing configuration**. Figure 8.3 shows a one-queue, two-server configuration, or the aforementioned "snake line." Customers may balk prior to entering the queue if it appears too long. Customers are queued into and then selected from the system according to a **queue discipline**. The **service process** might consist of any number of servers and services, in series or parallel. Once the entire service is completed, customers depart the system. A more detailed discussion of these segments follows.

Demand Source

Demand sources can contain a finite number or a very large (infinite) number of customers, and be homogenous or nonhomogenous. For example, the demand source for an office candy machine might consist of ten customers (the employees), whereas the demand source for a restaurant in a large city could be considered infinite. For the candy machine, the probability of additional arrivals diminishes as people join the queue. With the restaurant, the probability of additional arrivals is assumed to stay constant as customers arrive. The demand source for the restaurant can also be considered homogenous (same types of people all in the same queue, with similar expectations), while customers at a hospital, for instance, might be nonhomogenous (emergency patients, outpatients, and patients arriving for surgery with different needs and expectations, requiring different services and queue disciplines). Simple queuing models assume homogenous demand and an infinite population.

Arrival Process

The arrival process describes the time between customer arrivals, or the distribution of interarrival times. Research on this topic has found customer interarrival times in many instances to be exponentially distributed. In these cases, there is a high frequency

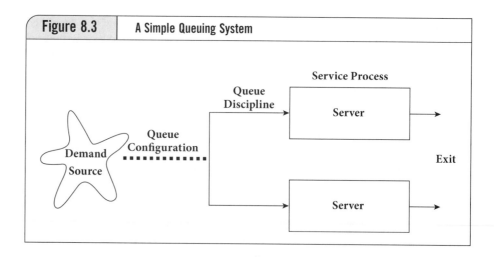

Figure 8.3   A Simple Queuing System

of arrivals with very low or low interarrival times, and a diminishing frequency as in-terarrival times increase. In other words, customers arrive in groups, or one right after another, during specific periods of time. This is when a queuing system's design is most important, as during lunchtime or dinnertime at a restaurant. If we assume that customer interarrival times are exponentially distributed, then this means that the cus-tomer arrivals per hour are Poisson distributed. In other words, if interarrival times are exponentially distributed with a mean of three minutes, then the arrivals per hour are Poisson distributed with a mean of 20 per hour.

If, for example, we wish to find the probability that exactly 30 customers will arrive in one hour assuming a mean arrival rate of 20 customers per hour and exponentially distributed interarrival times, we can use the Poisson probability function to find the probability of n-arrivals during the time period t:

$$f(n) = \frac{(\lambda t)^n e^{-\lambda t}}{n!}$$

where

> λ = average arrival rate per unit time (minute, hour, day, etc.)
> t = number of time periods (usually 1)
> n = number of arrivals of interest
> e = natural log base (2.718...)

So, the probability of exactly 30 customers arriving in one hour would be:

$$f(30) = \frac{20^{30} e^{-20}}{30!} = 0.0083 \text{ (a very small probability)}$$

It would probably be much more useful to find the probability of *fewer than* 30 cus-tomers arriving per hour, then subtract this from 1.0, to find the probability of 30 *or more* customers arriving per hour instead of finding the probability of exactly 30 cus-tomers arriving in one hour (this would require calculating the probabilities of 0 custom-ers arriving per hour, then 1 customer arriving per hour, and so on, up to the probabil-ity of 29 people arriving per hour, summing all 30 of the probabilities, then subtracting this quantity from 1 to arrive at the answer). If, however, a service process was designed to theoretically handle 30 customers per hour, with a reasonable average waiting time in the system, then knowing the probability of exactly 30 customers arriv-ing per hour might be useful information.

Queuing Configuration

The queuing configuration refers to the number and type of queues and the spatial arrangements. A bank's teller window arrangement may have three bank teller agents serving one continuous queue or snake line, for example. This arrangement is often seen as the most fair by customers, since it ensures a first-come-first-served ordering policy, keeps line switching or **jockeying** from occurring, and reduces the average cus-tomer wait time when compared to multiple queue configurations.

A fast-food restaurant like McDonald's, for instance, may have a three-server, three-queue configuration. Entering customers must decide which queue to join; this can cause customer aggravation and jockeying to occur as queues slow down and speed up. Parties of customers may be tempted to split up, with each joining a different queue, to try and reduce waiting time. Advantages of multiple queues, though, include the use of express lanes, the flexibility to select a server, and the appearance of smaller queues, which can reduce balking.

A grocery store meat counter may have a customer-take-a-number queue, where entering customers select a number, guaranteeing them a place in line (another example of the virtual queue concept). This variation of the single queue concept allows customers to sit, wander around, and perhaps purchase other items, or talk to other customers without fear of losing their place in the queue. These are just three of the most common examples of queuing configurations.

Due to their one-server, one-line arrangement for each ride, amusement parks have inherently difficult queuing problems. According to Westlake Technical Products, a Southern California–based company specializing in line management solutions for the entertainment industry, waiting in line is the number one complaint in theme parks. On average, more than 50 percent of a visitor's time is spent waiting. To deal with this problem, amusement parks are filled with diversions to occupy visitors winding their way through a line. California-based media conglomerate Universal Studios uses video clips of everyone from animated cartoon characters Shrek and Spider-Man to actors Charlie Chaplin and Marilyn Monroe in an attempt to occupy customers in a queue. And Buzz Lightyear's Space Ranger Spin ride features an interactive queue with an animated version of its star.[34]

Queue Discipline

The queue discipline refers to the policies used to select the next customer in the queue for service. For people physically standing in a queue, the most popular queuing discipline is the **first-come-first-served** (FCFS) policy. Other examples include the use of queuing segments or partitions. For example, an auto repair garage may have separate queues depending on the work to be performed, such as oil changes, tire repairs, or engine overhauls. Within each queue, though, it is most common to see the FCFS policy used. Hospital emergency rooms use a most-urgent-care-required priority system as a queue discipline, while night clubs might use a most-important-customer-first or VIP type of queuing policy with a secondary FCFS queue of "other" customers for the remaining seats.

Service Process

The service process consists of the servers, the process time distribution, the arrangement of servers, and the server management policies. For relatively easy and short service processes, such as haircuts, fast-food preparation, or making change at a cash register, service times have been shown to be exponentially distributed. Using parallel servers for a service (several bank tellers or cashiers) allows managers to quickly vary capacity as demand fluctuates, which generally requires service employees to be cross-trained, to enable capacity to vary at several service processes while minimizing server costs. At a bank, for instance, loan officers sufficiently trained in teller operations can double as tellers when customer queues at the teller windows become long.

The servers themselves can have a significant impact on queue length. Some servers can make interesting conversation, operate equipment, and serve customers simultaneously with seemingly little effort, while others may exhibit careless attitudes toward customers or be unable to do more than one thing at a time. Susan Ross, owner of restaurant training service Waiter Training of Denver, Colorado, thinks one of the biggest problems among servers is boredom. "There is this old-timer syndrome that says, 'I've been here 13 years; this is how it's always done.' They know they will make X amount of dollars every month, and it's just enough to get by on. I think it's human nature to relax, to feel so comfortable and not want to make it better or improve ourselves. People need to be reminded things can be better," she explains.[35] Other factors include the willingness of customers to stand in the line, and the overall quality of the service. These differences along with variations in customer requirements can cause service times to vary and greatly impact queue length and repeat customer sales.

Queuing System Operating Characteristics

For simple queuing system configurations with a few assumptions, operating characteristics can be determined and then applied by managers seeking to serve customers successfully while minimizing server costs. As stated earlier, managers can use these characteristics to design a potentially effective queuing system, but must also observe actual customer behavior after implementation while employing methods to minimize customers' perceptions of waiting time to maximize the firm's ability to provide adequate levels of customer service. More detailed and complicated services will most likely require use of a system simulation to model the queuing system in any meaningful way.

The simple one-server, one-queue service with the following assumptions leads to some very straightforward queuing characteristics:

- Customers arrive from an infinite population and their arrival rate is Poisson distributed
- Single waiting line with no balking or reneging
- The queue discipline is FCFS
- One server, with negative exponential distribution of service times
- The average service rate is greater than the average arrival rate

The queuing characteristics for this system can be shown as follows:

λ = mean arrival rate

μ = mean service rate

ρ = mean server utilization $= \dfrac{\lambda}{\mu}$

L_q = mean number of customers in the queue $= \dfrac{\rho\lambda}{\mu - \lambda}$

L_s = mean number of customers in the system $= L_q + \rho$

W_q = mean waiting time in the queue $= \dfrac{L_q}{\lambda}$

W_s = mean waiting time in the system $= W_q + \dfrac{1}{\mu}$

P_0 = probability of zero customers in the system $= 1 - \rho$

P_n = probability of n customers in the system $= \rho^n(1 - \rho)$

Example 8.3 provides an application of these characteristics.

The multiple-server, single-queue system is somewhat more complex, and the operating characteristics follow. Aside from the single server assumption, all of the preceding assumptions apply. The queuing system consists of multiple servers, serving one source of customers in separate queues, as in a bank teller setting.

λ = mean arrival rate

$s\mu$ = mean service rate, where s = number of servers

ρ = mean server utilization $= \dfrac{\lambda}{s\mu}$

Example 8.3   Operating Characteristics at Mary Jane's Video Rentals

Mary Jane owns and operates a small video rental store. She is also the only employee. Lately, she has wondered if she could improve her queuing system so that customers would not have to wait so long at times to rent a video. She decides to observe customer arrivals and determine some operating characteristics. She finds that over the course of a typical day she can serve about five customers every 15 minutes, and by the end of an eight-hour day she has served approximately 100 customers. With the standard assumptions, she calculates her store's characteristics as:

$$\lambda = 12.5 \text{ customers per hour}$$
$$\mu = 20 \text{ customers per hour}$$
$$\rho = 0.625 \text{ or } 62.5\% \text{ utilization}$$
$$L_q = \frac{(.625)(12.5)}{20 - 12.5} = 1.04 \text{ customers}$$
$$L_s = 1.04 + 0.625 = 1.67 \text{ customers}$$
$$W_q = \frac{1.04}{12.5} \text{ hours} \times 60 \text{ minutes per hour} = 5 \text{ minutes}$$
$$W_s = 5 \text{ minutes} + \frac{1}{20} \text{ hours} \times 60 \text{ minutes per hour} = 8 \text{ minutes}$$
$$P_{>1} = \text{Probability of more than 1 customer in the system} = 1 - (P_0 + P_1)$$
$$P_0 = 1 - 0.625 = 0.375$$
$$P_1 = (.625)(1 - 0.625) = 0.234$$
$$\text{Thus } P_{>1} = 1 - (.375 + .234) = 0.391 = 39.1\%$$

So, almost 40 percent of the time, customers will have to wait in line, prior to receiving service.

P_0 = probability of zero customers in the system

$$= \frac{1}{\sum\limits_{n=0}^{s-1} \frac{(\lambda/\mu)^n}{n!} + \frac{(\lambda/\mu)^s}{s!}\left[\frac{1}{1 - (\lambda/s\mu)}\right]}, \quad \text{for } s\mu > \lambda$$

L_q = mean number of customers in the queue $= P_0 \dfrac{(\lambda/\mu)^s(\lambda/s\mu)}{s!(1 - \lambda/s\mu)^2}$

L_s = mean number of customers in the system $= L_q + \dfrac{\lambda}{\mu}$

W_q = mean waiting time in the queue $= \dfrac{L_q}{\lambda}$

W_s = mean waiting time in the system $= W_q + \dfrac{1}{\mu}$

P_n = probab. of n customers in the system $= P_0 \dfrac{(\lambda/\mu)^n}{n!}$, for $n \leq s$

$\qquad = P_0 \dfrac{(\lambda/\mu)^n}{s!s^{n-s}}$, for $n > s$

Example 8.4 illustrates these operating characteristics. It is seen that adding a second server significantly improves the queuing system's customer service capability. During busy periods, the added server is a tremendous benefit to the service. Even so, the additional server may not be preferable for the business. The obvious trade-off that must be considered is whether the added cost of an additional server is overcome by the reduced cost of making customers wait.

Example 8.4   Operating Characteristics for the Two-Server Single-Queue System

Mary Jane's friend Sally decided to help serve customers one day at her video rental store, on a second cash register at the check-out counter, just to determine the impact on customer waiting time. Customers still arrived at the same rate as in Example 8.3, and Sally served customers at the same rate as Mary Jane. The new operating characteristics were then:

$\lambda = 12.5$ customers per hour
$s\mu = 40$ customers per hour
$\rho = 0.3125$ or 31.25% utilization

$$P_0 = \frac{1}{\frac{(12.5/20)^0}{0!} + \frac{(12.5/20)^1}{1!} + \frac{(12.5/20)^2}{2!}\left(\frac{1}{1-.3125}\right)}$$

$$= \frac{1}{1 + .625 + .195(1.45)} = 0.524$$

$$L_q = 0.524 \frac{(12.5/20)^2(12.5/40)}{2!(1-(12.5/40))^2} = 0.068 \text{ customers}$$

$$L_s = 0.068 + 0.625 = 0.693 \text{ customers}$$

$$W_q = \frac{.068}{12.5} \text{ hours} \times 60 \text{ minutes per hour} = 0.326 \text{ minutes}$$

$$W_s = 0.326 \text{ minutes} + \frac{1}{20} \text{ hours} \times 60 \text{ minutes per hour} = 3.326 \text{ minutes}$$

$P_{>1}$ = Probability of more than 1 customer in the system = $1 - (P_0 + P_1)$
$P_0 = 0.524$
$P_1 = (.524)(12.5/20) = 0.328$

Thus $P_{>1} = 1 - (.524 + .328) = 0.148 = 14.8\%$

Thus, it is seen that adding a second server greatly reduces customer wait time. About 85 percent of the time, there is no customer wait time.

Managing Work Flows

The topic of work flow management is receiving substantial attention as software solution providers are developing applications to automate work flows. At its most basic level, **work flow** can generally be defined as:

> *The movement or transfer of work from the customer or demand source through the organization according to a set of procedures. Work may include documents, information, or tasks that are passed from one recipient to another for action.*[36]

In other words, work flow is the movement of tasks, information, and paperwork that accompany some service or manufacturing activity, until final delivery to the end recipient or user. Work flow normally comprises a number of logical, understood, or mandated steps that can involve a manual or machine activity. Automating the flow of work can greatly increase organizational productivity, and is thus a hot topic within automated information systems development. As a matter of fact, business process automation and the one-word term, "workflow," as it appears in many business periodicals have become almost synonymous.

Consider, for instance, the automated bank teller machine, or ATM. This concept revolutionized the way banks managed money for bank depositors, greatly impacted the use of bank employees, and substantially changed forever the way bank depositors interacted with their banks. More recently, Internet banking has further changed how depositors interact with their banks and manage their flows of money.

Work Flow Analysis

Managers should analyze work and its flow to determine how it adds value to the organization, and particularly prior to the purchase of any process automation software. A work flow analysis should seek to find answers to the following questions:

1. Who requires the work, and how often is it required?
2. Is this work value-enhancing for the organization?
3. Who is performing the work?
4. What are the steps the work is taking to flow through the organization? And
5. Can the work be automated or redesigned to improve value and productivity?

Work flow analysis can be used to tighten the connection between what the organization does, and what the internal users or external customers want. Delving into these questions can help the firm achieve process performance breakthroughs as a result of rethinking and redesigning various work processes. Further, analyzing work flows can help to identify jobs or processes that can be eliminated or combined with other work to improve company performance. As a result, firms in many cases can achieve improvements in cost, quality, and customer service.

Analyzing work flows in an organization is much easier said than done. Though most people understand how they perform their own tasks, they may not be able to understand or identify the conditions necessary to initiate the next step in a work flow process. Describing how work is currently accomplished and how it *should be* accomplished usually requires input from a number of people in several different departments. "You have to get people thinking about business processes," says Richard Kesner, CIO at Babson College, located in Wellesley, Massachusetts. "And since most people think very narrowly about their work, that's actually not a small task."[37]

One common example is a home loan application and approval process at a lending institution. A simplified map of the flow of work is shown in Figure 8.4. Prior to the automated loan processes now typically in use at banks and other mortgage lenders, an application would be delivered in person or by mail to the lending institution, where it was then distributed to a loan clerk. The clerk checked the loan for completeness and either returned it to the applicant for more information, rejected it based on unsatisfied loan requirements, or keyed the application into the company's loan document database and then forwarded the application to the next required approval clerk or loan officer. The next step in the process was then to confirm the applicant's risk level by reviewing loan and repayment history, debt level, income, and other pertinent information. Verification forms would be mailed to employers and banks for completion. A loan decision would then be made by an underwriter or committee, and if approved, the funds would be made available and the loan would close. This loan process might have taken several days or even weeks to complete.

The use of work flow process mapping has led to the automation of many office work flows. To continue with the home loan example, within the past ten years technologies have made the loan process extremely efficient. For example, loan officers can complete a mortgage application and gain pre-approvals quickly at the point buyers are ready to make an offer on a home. Software systems enable loan officers to pull credit

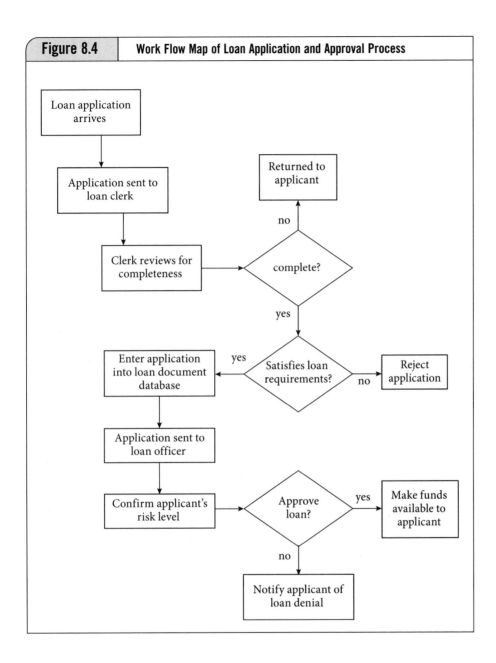

Figure 8.4   **Work Flow Map of Loan Application and Approval Process**

reports, pre-qualify borrowers, submit applications, and receive underwriting decisions within just a few minutes. The mortgage lending process has been transformed from a manual one to a highly automated one, using improved process mapping and technology implementation at critical steps in the approval process to streamline and speed up work flow. U.S. mortgage lenders now originate trillions of dollars in new mortgage loans each year, with automated underwriting systems and credit-scoring tools processing hundreds of thousands of loans per day. What used to be stacks of manually prepared closing papers are now completed by the lender's automated loan origination system and returned to the closing office within minutes. Technologies allow dozens of orders for title reports to be completed in the time it used to take for just one.[38]

Managing Work Flows in the Office

As shown in the previous section, technology has greatly improved work flows for some organizations and processes. But according to David Alien, a U.S. management consultant and described by *Fast Company* magazine as "one of the most influential thinkers on productivity," technology has tended to also increase some work flow problems and can make it harder for office workers to be productive. Sifting through mounds of spam emails each day to find the few important ones is one such example. Some of Alien's suggestions for taking control of daily office work include emptying email inboxes every 24 to 48 hours, doing things immediately if they will take less than two minutes to complete, categorizing to-do lists into various action categories, reviewing calendar and action lists daily, and finally, doing tasks based on the actions required, time and energy available, and the priority of the work.[39] Care must also be taken to not think of office work flow management as simply the automation of current office practices. Rather, the overall objective of work flow management should be to redesign work processes so that they become more simple, adaptive, seamless, or visible. Robert Wah, spokesperson for TRICARE, the U.S. military healthcare system, explains, "Oftentimes we see ... this showroom syndrome—providers go to a big meeting and they come back with the biggest, brightest, shiniest box ... and they think this is going to solve all of their problems, without really thinking about what they need. And then they open the box and find out that it doesn't do what they want it to, because they haven't really thought about what they needed."[40]

Office work flows are often complex, involving multiple parallel process paths with complex dependencies and decision trees or what-if scenarios. Office work flows also typically include use of online resources; desktop and mainframe applications; networks; multiple servers; and email, phone, and FAX communications. Thus, information systems and network managers are usually involved in developing work flow solutions that allow users to take the correct process steps in the correct sequence, with the proper documentation, all in a seamless fashion. For large office environments, these are not typically off-the-shelf solutions, but must be customized to create the types of output required.

In the legal industry, for instance, law firms are interested in managing case documents, court calendars, phone calls, emails, client contact information, invoices, and time sheets, as well as other documents, and are increasingly becoming paperless as new office management software is developed for both small and large law firms. Tools are being quickly developed that allow office workers in these and other environments to use technologies to manage work flows without being overburdened by incompatibilities, training regimens, or security issues. Seattle Washington-based Microsoft's Office franchise, which generates almost $3 billion per quarter in global sales, is busy positioning its software application worldwide as a tool to help employees read, edit, and route documents and information that get stored in business applications. The Global Perspective feature provides a profile of this new form of work tool.[41]

In small office healthcare settings such as doctor and dentist offices, managing work flows can mean higher quality patient care, fewer medication errors, lower costs, better staff interactions, and improved office productivity. San Francisco, California dentist Cynthia Brattesani noticed that use of film X-rays was causing patient bottlenecks to occur in her office because of the time required to develop the films. New digital radiography equipment alleviated this problem by reducing darkroom time to zero. Viewing X-rays immediately also meant that there were no more patient interruptions for

Global Perspective

The New World of Work

Microsoft has been talking up a "new world of work" lately, one that is characterized by intercompany collaboration, heavier business regulation, and more foreign outsourcing. The vendor is developing software for team productivity, company-wide information searching, and managing email from outside the office that could help make employees more productive while shielding them from information overload.

Microsoft is counting on that to help boost sales of its mammoth Office franchise, which generates sales of about $2.7 billion each quarter and enjoys profit margins of 70 percent, but shows little growth. It's positioning Office as a set of tools that can help employees read, edit, and route documents and information that get stored in major business applications. It's also getting ready to release updates to its SQL Server™ database, BizTalk Server® workflow engine, and Visual Studio® development tools that could make it easier to work with documents in the XML format.

Microsoft's belief in a new workplace is influencing the company's product design. For example, the next version of Office will include software that Microsoft acquired when it bought Groove Networks, which will quickly set up team workspaces without the need to reconfigure servers. Microsoft also is pushing hard to get new search software to market. "It's a feature we want to give all Windows users," says Microsoft CEO Steve Ballmer, "when the next version of the operating system, code-named Longhorn, comes out."

"Tying all of these products together for the new workplace will be a challenge," says Paul DeGroot, an analyst at consulting company Directions. Microsoft is a product company. "But the new world of work isn't about products—it's about processes, workflow, and Web services," he says. "It's a bigger and more complicated picture than what people usually associate with Microsoft."

New products such as the updates to SQL Server, BizTalk Server, and Microsoft's development tools could help Microsoft sell more complicated systems. Also, the company plans to release updates to its Exchange Server for email and Windows Mobile® software for PDAs and cell phones that would let users get new emails as they arrive, instead of waiting for the devices to sync.

Source: Ricadela, A., "Microsoft Targets 'New World of Work'," *InformationWeek*, June 13, 2005, No. 1043, p. 24. Used with permission.

retaking and redeveloping additional X-rays. The time savings allowed her to spend more time with her patients and focus more on patient care and education.[42]

E-prescribing is a technology finding use and acceptance among physicians. Dr. Salvatore Volpe, a Staten Island, New York, physician, participated in the initial testing of Texas-based Zix Corp.'s PocketScript®, a handheld wireless device with connectivity to pharmacies. "The 5.52 version of Zix Corp.'s PocketScript improves my office work flow and adds to the services I provide my patients," said Volpe. "Thanks to the alternative medication reminder, I am prompted to prescribe a generic version when available, saving my patients money. Second, the drug interaction and drug allergy alerts are extremely useful for enhancing patient safety and the new ability to submit prescriptions directly to the mail order programs significantly reduces paperwork for my office and my patients."[43]

The following section provides a discussion of work flow management among supply chain trading partners.

Managing Work Flows Along the Supply Chain

Sharing information and communicating quickly and effectively among supply chain partners is becoming a necessity as demand, capacity, supplies, technologies, and the competition undergo frequent and sometimes radical change. Nowhere is this more apparent than in the emergency services industry. Terrorist attacks, severe weather disasters, disease epidemics, and earthquakes tend to dramatically test the ability of various supply chains to manage their work flows. For example, many of the current hospital supply chain management systems allow materials managers to identify products and equipment by department and analyze usage patterns. With this knowledge, they can create a list of supplies necessary for each type of disaster as well as where those supplies are stored and who will deliver them. These systems efficiently process transactions from the purchase order to confirmation of receipt and to billing. Staff time is not consumed by counting and receiving supplies, and clinicians can focus instead on more valuable patient care and emergency response. Supply chain management systems call upon pre-established supplier contracts for emergencies and contain the key contact information for the organization's most critical suppliers. By starting a work flow for a specific disaster, a simple automated email can call into action a standing order for supplies and other activities.[44]

The ability of companies to provide real-time visibility to their trading partners has become a reality with the use of sophisticated ERP systems, allowing firms to respond to exceptions, track partner performance, monitor shipments, and respond to order requests for instance. The result is heightened readiness, lower safety stock levels, better customer service, and easier planning. When transactions occur at the warehouse for Lanier Worldwide, a distributor of copiers and related document management systems headquartered in Atlanta, Georgia, the changes are reflected on its logistics visibility and control system within a matter of seconds. Recently, Lanier's marketing people have begun using its system data to get current snapshots of product being purchased rather than relying on weeks-old billing data.[45] Illinois-based Philips Lighting Electronics used the services of Zuken, a Japanese work flow systems consulting firm, to electronically link its engineering CAD systems with procurement to automate their in-house supply chain. The result will be the automation of its component selection process and data flow from engineering to procurement to manufacturing. Process reports are automatically generated and stored with the new system. Philips says that labor productivity will increase by approximately 7 percent, and the standardized processes will eliminate the need to redesign products if manufacturing is moved to another factory.[46]

Typical global companies have many versions of different inventory control systems in various installations around the world, providing connectivity and visibility in varying degrees to the organization as a whole and its trading partners. Managing the flows of work with these systems is a complex task, and a number of applications are currently available that enable products and information to be shipped out and received throughout a supply chain using the existing, varied systems. **Supply chain event management** (SCEM) software collects real-time data from multiple supply chain sources and converts it into information that gives business managers a good idea of how their supply chains are performing. When a problem is identified, email, FAX, and PDA alerts are issued to relevant personnel and recommendations are made regarding how to improve the situation. SCI Systems, an electronics manufacturer from Alabama, uses Ohio-based

Teradata's SeeChain® software to analyze the performance of its supply chain. "With SeeChain, we can manage supplier performance, react to demand changes, and more efficiently enhance our customers' business performance," says Vincent Melvin, SCI Systems' chief information officer. "This is a new market," explains Chris Stone, CEO of Tilton, a Massachusetts-based provider of SCEM solutions. "This doesn't replace the big ERP and database investments. It takes that data and provides a dashboard of performance. It shows how you're doing on inventory turns, on safety-stock levels, on contract prices versus actual, on logistics costs, and a range of other metrics."[47]

Effective use of technologies is allowing companies and their supply chain trading partners to organize work, to exchange information, to react to market changes, and to make better decisions more quickly than competing supply chains. To be effective, however, firms must also consider the processes themselves and the cultural changes that ultimately accompany significant changes in how work is done.

SUMMARY

This chapter has discussed the topics of customer and work flow management. Customer flows can be analyzed through use of flow maps and service blueprints, which allow managers to visualize how customers interact with, and travel through, the service system. Customer flow is impacted by service capacity, and this topic was presented including discussion of capacity management techniques of employee scheduling, yield management, employee cross-training, and self-service. Demand management interacts with service capacity to affect customer flow; therefore this topic was also discussed. Finally, queuing system design directly affects how customers are serviced, and several queuing systems were analyzed, along with the impact that various queue management tactics have on the psychology of waiting. As services and products make their way through the organization to the customer, work flows are created that must also be managed effectively to maximize firm competitiveness. The concepts of work and work flow were discussed, along with the impact technology has had on managing work flows.

KEY TERMS

arrival process, 296

balking, 295

capacity sharing, 288

code sharing, 289

complementary services, 291

customer contact points, 280

customer flow map, 277

demand sorting, 291

demand source, 296

differential pricing, 288

first-come-first-served, 298

jockeying, 297

overbooking, 285

queue discipline, 296

queuing configuration, 296

relearning effect, 289

reneging, 295

revenue management, 285

service blueprinting, 281

service capacity bottlenecks, 283

service process, 296

supply chain event management, 306

virtual queue, 295

work flow, 301

yield management, 285

DISCUSSION QUESTIONS

1. What is the value in creating a customer flow map?

2. Go to a favorite restaurant or tavern, create a customer flow map, and identify any customer flow problems.

3. What does service blueprinting have to do with customer contact points?

4. Create a service blueprint for the same restaurant or tavern used in Question 2. Critique the service based on the flow map and blueprint.

5. What techniques are used to manage capacity in services?

6. What is the definition and objective of yield management? Give an example.

7. What are three ways that firms can increase capacity utilization and flexibility? Provide some examples.

8. Describe some ways that services can manage or influence demand.

9. Discuss the relearning effect and what it has to do with capacity utilization and customer service.

10. How can service firms manage the psychological aspects of waiting to reduce customers' awareness of waiting in line?

11. Define the term *work* as it is used in the text, and describe what work flow is.

12. Describe how work flow can be analyzed in organizations.

13. How has technology changed the way that work is managed in organizations today?

14. How have automated work flows tended to impact supply chains?

PROBLEMS

1. Determine a consecutive days off schedule for the following daily worker requirement at a service. Use part-time workers if needed.

	M	T	W	TH	F	S	SU
Requirement	6	4	5	4	3	2	2

2. What is the probability that 10 customers will arrive in an hour when the mean arrival rate is 20 customers per hour and interarrival times are exponentially distributed?

3. What is the probability that *more than two customers* will arrive in an hour, when the mean arrival rate is two customers per hour and interarrival times are exponentially distributed?

4. Nik's Hot Dogs is a one-person hot dog stand, serving about ten customers per hour. Assuming that Nik can serve one customer in about three minutes, calculate the stand's queuing characteristics. What is the probability that there is more than one customer in the system at any given time? Does he have an acceptable queuing system?

5. Nik gets a hot dog stand competitor, consisting of a two-person trailer with twice the capacity of Nik's stand in Problem 4. What are the queuing characteristics of this stand assuming the demand is still ten customers per hour? What is the probability of more than one customer in the system at any given time? Do you think this system is preferable to the one in Problem 4?

INTERNET QUESTIONS

1. What are some of the recent developments and products in automated work flows?

2. Find some companies that are dealing with customer queuing problems and describe what they are doing to manage the problem.

INFOTRAC QUESTION

Access http://www.infotrac-thomsonlearning.com to answer the following question:

1. Use InfoTrac to find current articles discussing the following topics:

   a. customer flow analysis

   b. work flow software solutions

REFERENCES

Dickson, D., R. Ford, and B. Laval, "Managing Real and Virtual Waits in Hospitality and Service Organizations," *Cornell Hotel and Restaurant Administration Quarterly*, V. 46, No. 1, 2005, pp. 52–68.

Fischer, L., ed. (2005), *Workflow Handbook 2005,* Future Strategies, Inc., Lighthouse Point, FL (particular use was made of a chapter by R. Allen, "Workflow: An Introduction").

Fitzsimmons, J. A., and M. J. Fitzsimmons (1998), *Service Management,* Irwin/McGraw-Hill, New York, NY.

Meredith, J., and S. Shafer (1999), *Operations Management for MBAs,* John Wiley & Sons, Inc., New York, NY.

Metters, R., K. King-Metters, M. Pullman (2003), *Successful Service Operations Management,* Thomson South-Western, Mason, OH.

Murdick, R., B. Render, and R. Russell (1990), *Service Operations Management,* Allyn and Bacon, Needham Heights, MA.

Schmenner, R. W. (1995), *Service Operations Management,* Prentice-Hall, Englewood Cliffs, NJ.

Waller, D. (2003), *Operations Management: A Supply Chain Approach,* 2nd ed., Thomson, London, UK.

ENDNOTES

1. Brideau, L., "Flow: Why Does It Matter?" *Frontiers of Health Services Management,* V. 20, No. 4, 2004, pp. 47–51.

2. Sheth, J. and R. Sisodia, "High Performance Marketing," *Marketing Management,* V. 10, No. 3, 2001, pp. 18–23.

3. Clarke, N., "High Roller Walks Over Ferrari Fiasco," *Las Vegas Review Journal,* Tuesday, July 12, 2005, p. 3A.

4. Schneider, I., "Here Today … Everywhere Tomorrow," *Bank Systems and Technology,* V. 41, No. 11, 2004, pp. 47–50.

5. Levinson, M., "The Brains Behind the Big, Bad Burger and Other Tales of Business Intelligence," *CIO,* V. 18, No. 11, 2005, p. 1.

6. Chong, K., M. Grewal, J. Loo, and S. Oh, "A Simulation-Enabled DSS for Allocating Check-In Agents," *INFOR,* V. 41, No. 3, 2003, p. 259.

7. Gelsomino, J., "True Tales of Customer-Centric Retailing," *Chain Store Age,* October 2004, p. 44A.

8. Weber, N. and L. Patten, "Shoring Up for Efficiency," *Health Management Technology,* V. 26, No. 1, 2005, pp. 34–35.

9. Scheraga, D., "Sam Ash Tunes in to Biometrics," *Chain Store Age,* May 2005, p. 35A.

10. Anonymous, "Kronos Gives Nebraska Book Company a Single Solution for Its HR and Time and Labor Objectives," Kronos website, http://www.kronos.com/Profiles/NebraskaBook.htm.

11. Wirtz, J., S. Kimes, J. Theng, and P. Patterson, "Revenue Management: Resolving Potential Customer Conflicts," *Journal of Revenue and Pricing Management,* V. 2, No. 3, 2003, pp. 216–223.

12. Flouris, T. and T. Walker, "The Financial Performance of Low-Cost and Full-Service Airlines in Times of Crisis," *Canadian Journal of Administrative Sciences,* V. 22, No. 1, pp. 3–20.

13. Cox, J., "Can Differential Prices Be Fair?" *The Journal of Product and Brand Management,* V. 10, No. 4/5, 2001, pp. 264–275.

14. Kimes, S. and J. Wirtz. "Has Revenue Management Become Acceptable?" *Journal of Service Research,* V. 6, No. 2, 2003, p. 125.

15. Armbruster, W., "With Oliver Evans, Executive VP of Cargo, Swiss International Airlines," *Journal of Commerce,* July 7, 2003, p. 1.

16. Bond, D., "Slow Motion," *Aviation Week & Space Technology,* V. 162, No. 16, 2005, p. 40.

17. See http://www.atlanta.is for more information.

18. Pinker, E. and R. Shumsky, "The Efficiency-Quality Trade-Off of Cross-Trained Workers," *Manufacturing and Service Operations Management,* V. 2, No. 1, 2000, pp. 32–48.

19. Chappell, L., "Worker Training Is Next Honda Frontier," *Automotive News,* V. 79, No. 6111, 2004, p. 43.

20. Nemeth, R., "User-Friendly DHHS Holds Big Umbrella," *Worcester Telegram & Gazette,* September 4, 2005, p. C2.

21. Weatherly, L., "HR Technology: Leveraging the Shift to Self-Service—It's Time to Go Strategic," V. 50, No. 3, 2005, pp. A1–A11.

22. Bailor, C., "It's Showtime!" *Customer Relationship Management,* V. 9, No. 2, 2005, pp. 34–38.

23. Atkinson, W., "Travel Spend Flies onto Procurement Radar," V. 134, No. 10, 2005, pp. 18–19.

24. Bailor, C., "Checking In with E-Commerce," *Customer Relationship Management,* V. 9, No. 7, 2005, p. 57.

25. Chittum, R., "The Show Before the Movie; Themed Megaplexes Entice Shoppers to the Mall, Cinema," *Wall Street Journal,* June 15, 2005, p. B–1.

26. Tarnowski, J., "Touch of Class," *Progressive Grocer,* V. 84, No. 8, 2005, pp. 16–18.

27. Garrett, A., "Crash Course In … Segmenting Your Customers," *Management Today,* July 2005, p. 22.

28. Maister, D., "The Psychology of Waiting Lines," in Czepiel, J., M. Solomon, and C. Suprenant, eds., *The Service Encounter,* D.C. Heath & Co., Lexington, MA, 1985, pp. 113–123.

29. Benoit, T., "OPINION: Maine Learns to Drive," *Knight Ridder Tribune Business News,* August 13, 2005, p. 1.

30. Castro, B., "Line Up Customers and Sales," *Chain Store Age,* V. 80, No. 6, 2004, p. 85.

31. Toole, A., "A Factory of Fun," *Knight Ridder Tribune Business News,* July 7, 2005, p. 1.

32. Dickson, D., R. Ford, and B. Laval, "Managing Real and Virtual Waits in Hospitality and Service Organizations," *Cornell Hotel and Restaurant Administration Quarterly,* V. 46, No. 1, 2005, pp. 52–68.

33. Wolff, R., *Stochastic Modeling and the Theory of Queues,* Englewood Cliffs, NJ: Prentice-Hall, 1989.

34. Koseluk, C., "Are We There Yet?" *Amusement Business,* V. 116, No. 25, 2004, pp. 14–17.

35. Berta, D., "Q&A: Give Your Serving Staff a Step Up," *Nation's Restaurant News,* V. 38, No. 2, 2004, p. 16.

36. Allen, R., "Workflow: An Introduction," Introductory chapter of the "Workflow Handbook 2005" published in association with the Workflow Management Coalition, edited by Layna Fischer, at http://www.wfmc.org.

37. Liebmann, L., "Managing Workflow—Chart Your Gameplan," *Communications Week,* February 5, 1996, p. 43.

38. O'Neill, D., "Electronic Orders—Critical Technology to Fulfill the Mortgage Origination Process," *Mortgage Banking,* V. 63, No. 5, 2003, pp. 83–84.

39. Anonymous, "A Five-Step Process for Managing Workflow and Boosting Your Performance Output," *IOMA's Report on Managing Training & Development,* V. 5, No. 4, 2005, pp. 4–6.

40. Lee, J., C. Crain, S. Young, N. Chockley, and H. Burstin, "The Adoption Gap: Health Information Technology in Small Physician Practices," *Health Affairs,* V. 24, No. 5, 2005, pp. 1364–1366.

41. Ricadela, A., "Microsoft Targets 'New World of Work'," *InformationWeek,* June 13, 2005, p. 24.

42. Brattesani, C., "Improving Office Workflow," *Dental Economics,* V. 95, No. 9, 2005, p. 116.

43. Anonymous, "ZixCorp Brings Out New Version of PocketScript," *Wireless News,* May 23, 2005, p. 1.

44. Wyatt, J., "Code Red: Ready to Roll," *Health Management Technology,* V. 24, No. 11, 2003, p. 26.

45. Michel, R., "Reaching Beyond the Four Walls," *Modern Materials Handling,* V. 60, No. 7, 2005, p. 43.

46. Sullivan, L., "Philips Cuts Costs by Aligning Procurement, Engineering," *EBN,* October 13, 2003, p. 1.

47. Mann, P., "Tweak the Supply Chain," *MSI,* V. 20, No. 2, pp. 57–58.

Chapter 9:

MANAGING INFORMATION FLOWS

"Information sharing is a fundamental approach that underlies both communication and collaboration."[1]

"At the source of every error which is blamed on the computer, you will find at least two human errors, including the error of blaming it on the computer."[2]

Learning Objectives

After completing this chapter, you should be able to:

- Understand the concept of information flow and the need to manage it.
- Audit information flows in an organization, and complete an information flow map.
- Describe the notable historical developments of the ERP system.
- Know how best to select an ERP system.
- Understand the many ERP system implementation requirements and why many implementations fail.
- Describe the many ERP system add-on applications, including the three most popular ones.
- Describe the tools used to integrate ERP within the supply chain.
- Describe the underlying principles and latest trends in automated process management.

Chapter Outline

Process Management in Action

B2B Integration Spells Sweet Success

The California and Hawaiian Sugar Refining Co. set up shop in 1906 in the town of Crockett, California, occupying a 19th-century refinery that would become the headquarters of C&H Sugar. As the company prepares to mark the 100th anniversary of its founding, it has also been working to bring its information technology infrastructure into the 21st century by implementing enterprise resource planning and business-to-business (B2B) integration technology that will ensure another 100 years of sweet success.

The heart of C&H's IT infrastructure, until recently, was a legacy mainframe system, along with an add-on application for electronic data interchange (EDI) with the company's customers through a value-added network (VAN). The mainframe's manufacturer had long since stopped providing maintenance for the system, and C&H relied on a single employee to support the equipment. A second employee supported the company's EDI messaging, doing a considerable amount of manual processing to keep the transactions running because of message failures and other hiccups in the system. In short, the legacy platform was "unsupported, unstable and very difficult to manage," according to Gary Walden, chief information officer at C&H.

The sugar company originally brought in Walden at the end of 2002 to evaluate C&H's options for replacing the mainframe system with an up-to-date enterprise resource planning (ERP) system. C&H wanted not only to gain better visibility into its production and inventory by deploying a new system but also to be better able to collaborate with its trading partners and to be more responsive to its customers. After evaluating various systems, in early 2003 C&H selected a hosted version of mySAP™ ERP system from German enterprise solution provider SAP, and the company asked Walden to stay on to run the project.

With the decision made to go with SAP, C&H also began looking at options to update its EDI network. Electronic data interchange is mission-critical for C&H, particularly on the retail side of the business, where as much as 70 percent of incoming orders are transmitted electronically via EDI. In addition, outside warehouses that receive and ship C&H products on the company's behalf also wanted to begin using EDI to communicate, so the sugar company needed a solution that would allow it to scale up its EDI usage over time.

After evaluating the different vendors offering B2B connectivity solutions and services, C&H ultimately tapped SEEBURGER, a company founded in 1986 and with U.S. headquarters in Atlanta. Walden says that the choice fell to SEEBURGER to an extent based on a side-by-side comparison of features with the one other provider that C&H considered. But what closed the deal in SEEBURGER's favor, Walden says, was the solution provider's close relationship with SAP. SEEBURGER, in fact, has been working with SAP for more than ten years and has more than 1,500 joint customers with SAP as an integration vendor.

C&H wound up implementing SEEBURGER's Business Integration Server (BIS) in conjunction with its SAP implementation. BIS comes with application adapters, a conversion engine for handling various message formats, 60 different communications protocols and, importantly, pre-defined SAP workflows. The SAP implementation initially was to take five months and go live in mid-2003, but about three months into the project C&H decided to extend the scope of the implementation by five months to encompass warehouse management so as to provide better visibility into the company's warehouse facilities and boost inventory control. As a result, the project went live at the start of October 2004.

The changeover to the new ERP system was relatively painless, Walden says, explaining that C&H's approach in implementing the project was to keep the scope as limited as practical and

Continued

focus on moving away from the company's legacy system. "We knew that there were lots of other capabilities we could do, but our philosophy was to define the scope around what it took to get off the mainframe," he says. Not that the deployment was without its challenges. For instance, in the midst of the SAP/SEEBURGER implementation, one of C&H's major retail customers—which include the likes of Wal-Mart and Costco, as well as supermarket chains such as Safeway and Albertsons—requested that the sugar company start using AS2, a protocol for the secure transport of EDI documents over the Internet. C&H was able to jury-rig a solution based on the old mainframe before the new ERP system went live and then switch over to using the new solutions once the implementation was completed. Since then, as various other major customers have expressed interest in moving away from using VANs to communicating via AS2, C&H has been able to buy additional AS2 licenses from SEEBURGER to accommodate those customers.

Moving forward, C&H is considering ways to extend the use of its new EDI capabilities to its supply base, perhaps trading purchase orders and receiving notices with some of its key suppliers. Currently, the sugar company is looking to link with its outside contracted warehouses directly via EDI. To date, C&H has simply provided the warehouses with PCs and printers at their locations, and the warehouse staff provides the "sneaker-ware," entering transactions for receiving and shipping C&H's products in both their own systems and directly into the sugar company's SAP system. C&H currently is in the process of establishing those EDI links with a handful of its larger warehouses so that these facilities systems can send transactions directly into C&H's ERP, and the company is considering additional projects in this regard as it sees the benefits of reduced labor at the warehouses and increased inventory accuracy from the direct, system-to-system transactions.

The return on investment in moving to the SAP/SEEBURGER solution has come in several forms. For instance, the completion of the project has freed up employees previously occupied with supporting the mainframe and EDI traffic, allowing these resources to be devoted to other projects, including implementing EDI with additional customers. This will, of course, result in some cost savings as C&H is able to move more of its business off of fee-based VANs. And the company is seeing improved customer satisfaction just because of the reliability of the transactions, the visibility of the transactions, and the reduction in transaction errors. But Walden says that the most significant payoff has been just moving away from the old mainframe system. "The legacy system was near collapse, so our goal was basically to ensure that we could continue to support our customers as well or better than we were able to before," he says, concluding, "Basically the choice was either we do this or we don't run the business with an ERP system."

Source: Reese, Andrew K., ed., "B2B Integration Spells Sweet Success," *Supply & Demand Chain Executive*, V. 7, No. 1, 2006, pp. 14–15. Used with permission.

Introduction

Information flow and its visibility both within the firm and extending along its supply chains is perhaps *the most crucial process component* for firms proactively managing their supply chains. The value of information flow for the firm and its supply chain trading partners cannot be stressed enough, and the technologies and products available to help supply chains manage this information are immense and growing rapidly. Most firms are literally inundated with all kinds of good and bad information, and a systematic effort to manage these flows of information will lead to more efficient and effective organizational processes. A group of researchers studying automobile supply chains referred to the lack of good information as one of the three "top pains" facing key industry suppliers. They found that information flow among trading partners was commonly withheld, masked, distorted, or just plain missing. And the cost of this lack of good information in terms of the bullwhip effect alone can be very high, perhaps adding as much as 20 percent to a firm's total costs.[3] The development of enterprise resource planning (ERP) systems, along with the emergence of many other information system applications such as customer relationship management (CRM), warehouse management systems (WMSs), and manufacturing execution systems (MESs), have greatly facilitated communication, information sharing, planning, and decision making within the firm and among the firm and its trading partners, helping to reduce costs.

To stay competitive, firms are gradually becoming more global in nature by building foreign manufacturing and retail facilities, creating global distribution networks, and partnering with foreign companies. This has created the need for global information visibility to communicate system inventory levels, reduce system safety stock levels, create more accurate forecasts, and reduce order cycle times, just to mention a few things. These extended enterprises have created a huge volume of information along with the corresponding need to better manage the flows of work that are created from much of this information. The topic of work flow was discussed at the end of Chapter 8. In this chapter, information flows will be discussed in a more general fashion, which in some cases includes the creation or flow of specific tasks or work.

As information technology moves ahead, managers are further tempted to add to the layers of existing information with automated process management software applications such as business process management (BPM) and business process reengineering (BPR). This chapter will review the concept of information flow and the development of information system applications, as well as discuss how managers use these tools to manage the many flows of information constantly bombarding the global firm.

The Concept of Information Flow

Information and its flow can be thought of in the same manner as material flow. In fact, supply chains consist of two equally important substructures—the physical item flow system (which was discussed at length in Chapter 7), and the information flow system. The hub-and-spoke systems operated by some airlines along with centralized computer reservation systems provide a good example of the separate flows of physical

© 1997 Ted Goff http://www.tedgoff.com

items and information. Passengers and cargo are routed through airlines' primary hubs to reach destinations. Computers linked to the airlines' reservation systems mainframe computers are located at travel agents, airlines, and online travel sites, and communicate information regarding passengers and cargo.[4] Information thus has value just as materials do—it can be referred to as an asset or, more appropriately, an **intellectual asset**. Information technologies influence how information coordination takes place—they replace human coordination, reduce uncertainty, improve decision making, promote new coordination structures, and substitute information and knowledge for inventory.

Most organizations have three key informational flows: **corporate information flow**, or the flow of information from the firm to its customers; **environmental information flow**, which is the flow from customers to the firm; and **internal information flow**, or information flow within the firm. In each case, managers must consider how information is captured, transformed, and exchanged, along with the interplay between the three flows, and the existing information capabilities of the local information system hardware and software. A description of the key information flows at a bank is as follows:[5]

> *ATMs, online communication portals, and advertising generate corporate information flows, offering transaction opportunities to customers. In response, customers make deposits at an ATM, triggering a transaction and generating environmental information flows, completing the transaction. To support the transaction, internal information flows such as data processing, customer account updating, and reports creation occur, which are necessary for effective management of the new environmental information. Additionally, banking information technologies have today allowed most of these transactions to occur in real time.*

As with materials, the flow of information can be impeded or made to move faster, depending on the number of internal and external intermediaries and delays involved in the transfer of information. As paperwork is created and the number of information processing locations increases, the flow of information slows and its value tends to decrease. Organizations can thus manage internal and external information flows by reducing paperwork and the number of information processing locations or entities. Texas-based computer manufacturer Dell Inc. redesigned and better integrated its supply chain by reducing non-value-adding information flows within its supply chain. Today Dell's supply chain is leaner and faster, with information flowing very effectively from Dell's end-item sales to raw materials suppliers. The results are higher levels of quality and customization, and faster delivery times.[6]

Inside the firm, the purchasing process represents an area where attention to the reduction of information transfers has reduced order costs as well as delivery times. For small purchases of MRO (maintenance, repair, and operating) items, many buyers are allowed to use corporate credit cards with preset limits to purchase catalogue items covered by a pre-negotiated blanket contract. This process leaves out the various layers of internal approval that used to be required in the typical organization. As a result, the cost of small orders and the order cycle time has been greatly reduced for firms using corporate credit cards.

Information velocity is a term used to describe how fast information flows from one process to another. Systems that handle e-commerce transactions, such as web servers, require capabilities that allow for huge variations in information velocity without adversely impacting performance, such as during the Christmas buying season. In systems characterized by multiple human interactions and decision steps, or in other words, a lack of automation and process integration, information velocity and the information itself can be adversely impacted. Several years ago, for instance, a top manager for one of the major suppliers to the U.S. automobile industry remarked, "It takes two or more weeks for information from the automaker regarding the increase in the sales of a specific type of model that translates into materials requirements for our company, to get to us. This leaves us with about a week to manage our supply chain, leaving our inventory management ad hoc at best."[7]

In some cases, though, information velocity can be so high as to create additional problems. With some processes, it may be preferable to have a manual or slower information system to allow for more time to consider the consequences of certain actions or decisions. Email systems, for instance, tend to reduce personal discussions or negotiations, sometimes resulting in communication errors, leading to things like stockouts and incorrect orders, missed delivery dates, deliveries to the wrong location, or incorrect payment methods.

Information volatility is another common term associated with information flow. Volatility refers to the uncertainty associated with information content, format, or timing. Spikes and lulls in daily web page transactions are associated with information volatility. This volatility can increase during holiday, seasonal, weekday, or even hourly periods, and firms must be able to accommodate this volatility. Use of historical data and forecasting allows firms to plan for these times with extra system capacity.

Relationships with suppliers and customers are thus impacted not only by the accuracy of information but also its availability, velocity, and volatility. The emergence of computers, computer networks, and software applications have given managers the ability to store, retrieve, process, and distribute large amounts of information quickly to users within the organization and among trading partners at a reasonable cost. Consequently, managers must consider how the flow of information impacts and adds value to the supply chain. As with the flow of materials, it becomes important to map information flows to better understand and optimize their use and value.

Information Flow Mapping

Mapping information flows allows managers to identify how information is transmitted from one point to another both within the firm and externally, to suppliers and customers. Flow maps serve as a basis for analyzing information needs and the services necessary to align the firm's information collection and transfer capabilities with the information needs of its internal and external users. Mapping information flows involves the following series of steps:[8]

1. Determine the current internal and external customers, suppliers, and users, and identify their information usage. This is called an **information audit**. The items of interest include knowledge of each constituent's products, services, operating environment, information sources and system architectures, software applications, and other factors that influence the use of information. The audit should uncover current information sources and uses.

2. Map the firm's and constituents' information flows. This will allow the analyst to see where redundancies or overlaps exist, and where information usage and sources can be eliminated or consolidated.

3. Identify information needs that are currently not being satisfied. Discuss these potential needs with all internal and external constituents. Determine common informational needs and rank the needs based on the level of agreement regarding each information requirement. The analyst can then make suggestions for

reallocation of information sources, consolidation of information needs, and more optimal solutions for information flow based on a "greatest common need." The flow map allows the organization to focus on who has what information while uncovering information gaps or needs within the organization and its supply chain trading partners.

4. Add any new information flows to the map as the decision to implement solutions for these requirements is made. These additions will make the design of the information flow map a dynamic process. Periodically revisit the flow map to identify better use of technologies, better flow arrangements, or new information requirements.

A basic information flow map is shown in Figure 9.1, presenting the internal and external informational flows of a manufacturer and its suppliers and customers. The manufacturer communicates corporate information or orders to suppliers through use of supplier websites, traditional purchase orders that are mailed or faxed to suppliers, bid requests, reverse auctions, intermediaries such as foreign agents and shipment consolidators, and through existing supplier contracts. When suppliers act on these orders, they become environmental information flows or transactions. The manufacturer also communicates corporate information or offers to customers through use of the firm's website, media advertisements and promotions, field sales representatives, and distribution centers. Customers act on these offers by purchasing products and services, creating environmental information flows or transactions.

Figure 9.1	A Map of Internal and External Information Flows for a Manufacturer

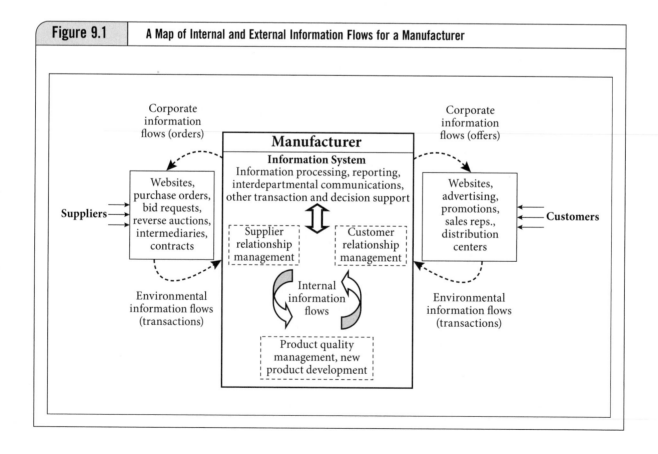

The environmental information created by suppliers and customers is captured and processed using the firm's information system network and software applications. As indicated in the figure, information is transmitted to the manufacturer's supplier relationship management (SRM) and customer relationship management (CRM) applications where it is added to suppliers' and customers' information files. Internal information flows are created when supplier and customer information is analyzed and used to help identify new purchasing and product marketing strategies, to create performance reports, for interdepartmental communications, for product quality assessments and improvement efforts, and for a host of other decision support purposes. As needs for more information are discovered, the firm must then consider implementing other information system modules or applications. While the information flows in Figure 9.1 appear to be fairly comprehensive, an actual map of an organization's information flows may uncover several areas where customers, suppliers, or internal users are not receiving up-to-date information or any information at all. An information flow map can thus serve to highlight a firm's information flow strengths and weaknesses.

Information Flow Among Supply Chain Trading Partners

In supply chains, successful partnerships are highly dependent on effective information flow and support. Supply chain partners require accurate information, for example, on current inventory levels, order and delivery status, production and forecast changes, and the latest product design changes. The difficulty may be in how all this information is brought together, analyzed, and transmitted within the firm and to the relevant trading partners. The integration of information flows along the supply chain is discussed later in this chapter.

Supply chain information flow problems are common, for instance, in the construction industry. A construction project could involve a large number of companies including architectural firms, construction companies, engineering firms, and independent subcontractors working closely in a time-pressured environment for extended periods of time. Large numbers of documents are passed between the companies, from technical drawings, legal contracts, and purchase orders to permits, build schedules, and delivery schedules. These projects tend to be paper intensive and can be slowed significantly by building code problems, labor availability, and late supply deliveries. Initial project bids, for example, can be too low or high, depending on the availability and accuracy of information, leading to construction cost overruns or incomplete work. The timely sharing of information, reduction of errors and waste, and better use of information are all facilitated by use of information technologies in construction project management.[9] The use of information system applications and the compatibility of communication tools as information flows within and between trading partners is thus an extremely important topic when considering supply chain performance, and this is the topic of the next section.

The Emergence and Use of Enterprise Resource Planning Systems

Having information available in real time can reduce uncertainties and lead times, and can improve material and product tracking as wells as planning capabilities. Unfortunately, information is not always easily accessible or reliable, and can become extremely complicated as the number of products, parts, suppliers, customers, and interactions increases. Added to these problems is the existence of arm's length trading relationships and a general lack of trust in many supply chains and even within a single organization, making the idea of information sharing and process integration unrealistic. Slowly, organizations are starting to come to the realization that information sharing among a firm's departments and units and extending to trading partners is beneficial to end customers and all supply chain constituents.

Along with this growing realization has been the growth of integrated material requirements planning systems, as described in Chapter 6. Also termed **manufacturing resource planning** or MRP II systems, these systems were an outgrowth of the older **material requirements planning** or MRP systems, and allowed functional area personnel to interact with the system, obtain real-time information, and perform what-if analyses using a shared database within the corporate unit. While still in widespread use across the globe, many of these MRP and MRP II applications are evolving into corporate-wide **enterprise resource planning** or ERP systems. The term *enterprise resource planning* was actually coined in a 1990 report by Connecticut-based Gartner, Inc., a provider of research, analysis, and consultancy services for the global information technology industry. Deloitte Consulting, headquartered in New York City, provided one of the more comprehensive definitions of ERP in a 1999 news story:[10]

> *ERP is a packaged business software system that lets a company automate and integrate the majority of its business processes, share common data and practices across the enterprise, and produce and access information in a real time environment.*

Figure 9.2 illustrates the ERP system, showing how each of the older planning system approaches fit in with the ERP. The following section describes the historical developments of these systems.

Notable Historical Developments Leading Up to ERP

While there were several MRP-type systems in use dating from the early 1960s, computing power at that time was such that these systems were extremely basic. The first MRP applications were run on the IBM 305 and 650 RAMAC (Random Access Method of Accounting and Control), and could do only the most basic net change material requirement calculations. In 1961, at the J.I. Case tractor manufacturing facility in Racine, Wisconsin, IBM employees Ted Musial and Gene Thomas, Case employees Joe Orlicky and A. R. Brani, and other IBM and Case employees designed and installed the first continuous net change MRP system, using the IBM 305 RAMAC.[11]

The people perhaps most responsible for developing and advancing the concepts of MRP were Joe Orlicky, George Plossl, and Oliver Wight. By 1971, Orlicky, Plossl, and Wight had convinced the American Production and Inventory Control Society (APICS) to officially launch "The MRP Crusade," creating a high degree of interest in MRP among American manufacturers.[12] Joe Orlicky wrote the first definitive book on MRP in 1975, and together these men would eventually author a number of textbooks on MRP and related topics, and become sought-after speakers and consultants.[13]

Starting in 1978, with IBM's MAPICS™ system (which stands for manufacturing, accounting, and production information control system) running on IBM's much improved System 36 mainframe, the concept of MRP as we know it today began to really take off. MAPICS became the most popular MRP system of its time. By 1981, there were a reported 8,000 industry-wide MRP implementations. In 1993, IBM sold MAPICS to the ERP software developer Marcam Corporation, and in 1997, MAPICS was spun

---

Figure 9.2 | **The Enterprise Resource Planning (ERP) Model**

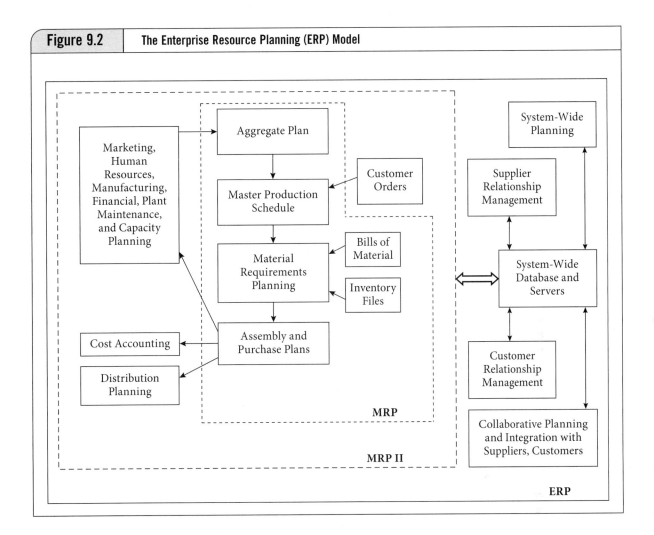

---

off into its own publicly traded company; at the time there were about 15,000 MAPICS applications worldwide.[14] Today, MAPICS is still plugging along and has become an ERP application provider using an IBM platform. It was acquired by Infor International Limited, a subsidiary of Georgia-based enterprise software developer Infor Global Solutions, in 2005.

In 1981, Oliver Wight wrote a book describing manufacturing resource planning, or MRP II (terms he coined), which expanded the original MRP idea to include shop floor and accounting functions along with a financial management system, allowing for "what-if" analyses.[15] Companies could thus have an integrated business system that provided material and capacity requirements along with a financial impact, given a desired production plan, and finally providing suggestions for items or quantities that could not be produced with the given conditions. The MRP logic, along with the what-if analysis capability, allowed various functional planning activities to occur, making MRP II extremely popular. In 1984 alone, 16 companies sold $400 million in MRP II software. And by 1989, sales eclipsed $1.2 billion.[16] The primary breakthrough of MRP II was that it connected all of the departments of a business unit into one computer system, providing a common database that all employees could use. This easy access to information encouraged more planning to occur, contributing to better manufacturing control and investment decisions. The information requirements were very large though, and in the 1980s, these systems still required mainframes or mini computers such as the IBM System 36 or the AS/400.

A few years earlier and across the globe, five former IBM systems analysts founded software developer SAP AG (Systemanalyse und Programmentwicklung, or Systems Analysis and Program Development) in Mannheim, Germany (now headquartered in Walldorf, Germany). Their vision was to develop software that enabled users to process data interactively in real time, using a computer screen as the focal point of data processing. Their first product was financial accounting software in 1973, which later came to be known as the R/1 System ("R" stands for real-time data processing). In 1979, SAP released its R/2 System for mainframes, and in 1992 it introduced the R/3 client/server software system. SAP continued to add packages to its system over the years, including materials management, asset accounting, cost accounting, personnel management, plant maintenance, and production planning and control applications. By 1993, SAP had a global customer base of 3,500 companies, 15 global subsidiary companies, and was selling software in 14 different languages. In 2000, SAP announced the introduction of mySAP.com, linking e-commerce solutions to existing ERP applications, using web technologies. By 2005, 12 million users were working each day with over 25 SAP business software applications in 120 countries. Today SAP is the world's third largest software supplier and the largest ERP application provider, with about 65 percent of the global ERP market. Its latest application, SAP NetWeaver®, is providing end-to-end business process applications that integrate people, information, and processes within the company and to its trading partners.[17]

SAP's largest competitor, California-based enterprise software developer Oracle, has been very busy acquiring its competition. By the end of 2005, Oracle had spent over $19 billion buying out more than a dozen software companies including PeopleSoft, JD Edwards, Siebel Systems, Retek, and Profit Logic. Currently, it is developing an ERP system called Fusion that uses the best applications from the various companies it purchased, due out in 2008. As of the middle of 2006, the global ERP market was estimated to be over $70 billion and still growing rapidly.[18]

Thus, during the 1990s as computer speed and technologies advanced, ERP systems were developed as bundled suites of applications that could be run on client servers, allowing greater scalability, support for more concurrent users, and lower cost hardware. Many of these systems today still use the original MRP-based net requirements and order release capabilities, along with the planning capabilities of the MRP II systems, which is why Figure 9.2 shows ERP to be encompassing both of these earlier systems. In many companies with extensive existing or **legacy systems**, ERP vendors will connect these existing software applications as well as provide other custom applications, allowing the ERP system to become a central information repository and a data distribution facility for all departments and units in an organization. However, as the move towards lower inventories, shorter lead times, and lean manufacturing continues, ERP systems are focusing more on providing real-time information visibility across all of the organization's global business units and ultimately among trading partners, tracking various performance metrics, and facilitating collaboration through customer relationship management, supplier relationship management, and quality management applications.

Actually, the idea of integrating processes with supply chain trading partners in real time using ERP system applications such as supplier relationship management, warehouse management, transportation management, and customer relationship management modules was the topic of a 2000 report by Gartner (recall they coined the original ERP term), wherein they sought to create the next label for planning systems: "**ERP II.**" On the other hand, supply chain management advisory firm AMR Research, headquartered in Massachusetts, favors the new label "**enterprise commerce management**" or "ECM."[19] Whatever the moniker employed, the concept of real-time integration of outward-facing applications such as CRM and SRM into internally focused or back-office ERP applications is the vision that many companies as well as software providers are adopting and promoting. The result is that companies must face the reality that their existing ERP investments are most likely going to require further investments in "add-ons" or other applications, to make real-time supply chain information sharing and collaboration a reality. Add-on applications are discussed later in this chapter. This also means that most enterprise systems are, or soon will be, considered **best-of-breed systems**, with applications purchased from various vendors over time. Consequently, application compatibility has become a big concern for many ERP system owners.

Selecting an ERP System

ERP systems have been described as everything from an absolute business necessity to an utter bird's nest of forever-tangled problems; nevertheless, these systems may still be the largest single information system application investment a firm will make, and like any large investment, careful planning can help firms avoid a time-consuming and costly mistake. In fact, it could be an extremely costly mistake. In 2004, the research firm Meta Group (now part of Gartner) surveyed 63 small, medium, and large companies in various industries to study the total cost of ERP systems, including hardware, software, professional services, and maintenance and upgrade costs over an average two-year ERP implementation period. It found the average total cost to be $15 million (the maximum was $300 million and the minimum was $400,000). Additionally, the average total cost per "heads-down" user over the two-year period was found to be a whopping $53,000![20] To stay on the lower end of this cost range, several steps are recommended when selecting an ERP system:[21]

1. Use an ERP project manager – An ERP project manager should be selected to manage the identification of user needs, vendor evaluations, system evaluation, and selection and purchase processes. The project manager should be an effective liaison between the firm and the potential vendors, and between management and users. This person will also create an ERP selection team, consisting of users within the firm from all relevant functional areas. Even if the firm decides to use a consultant to manage the ERP selection decision, an internal project manager should still be used to ensure that key user needs are addressed.

2. Assess user needs – It is important to identify the features and functions desired by all of the potential users of the system. Firms can start with lists of available features obtained from potential system suppliers and then modify these through surveys and discussions with the users. Features can then be ranked in order of importance so that vendors with strengths in these areas can be identified.

3. Identify ERP system suppliers – The project team can match the list of required features to the features available from potential suppliers. As discussed earlier, a significant degree of consolidation is occurring in the enterprise software industry; SAP and Oracle appear at this time to be the primary system providers. (In a recent survey of 148 ERP users across a number of industries, SAP was being used by 41 percent of the respondents, while Oracle/JD Edwards was used by 15 percent; the remainder were split between 21 smaller providers.[22])

4. Develop a detailed request for proposal (RFP) – When the system requirements have been identified and ranked, and a list of potential suppliers has been developed, an RFP can be created and sent to a list of suppliers.

5. Rank the ERP system suppliers – Once proposals have been received from the suppliers, the proposals can be analyzed by the team, based on the ranked list of user requirements. Higher-ranked requirements should receive higher weights in the analysis. Cost analyses should also be performed. Finally, the firm should include considerations of implementation time, training requirements, supplier reputation, and software customization capabilities. The firm should identify the top three suppliers.

6. Plan supplier demonstrations – The top three suppliers should be asked to provide demonstrations of their systems, involving as many key users as possible. After each visit, the project team can identify the likes and dislikes regarding each supplier by talking to the users present at each of the demonstrations. An assessment of each supplier's system can then be developed.

7. Schedule site visits – If possible, the evaluation team should visit companies using the ERP systems of the three suppliers, to witness real systems in action and discuss the benefits and problems with real users. The overall system evaluation can then be revised to reflect this new information.

8. Make final system selection – When the selection team has completed Step 7, it should be confident that the proper planning has been performed, and consequently be able to make the best, informed purchase decision.

The Advantages and Disadvantages of ERP Systems

For many companies leading up to the end of 1999, ERP implementation was seen as a solution to the Y2K issues that were thought to exist on many information systems at the time. This urgency to beat the new millennium deadline resulted in implementations that were less than ideal, leaving companies and their untrained employees unprepared to properly utilize the various ERP applications purchased. Consequently, many did not realize the full potential of these systems and the systems themselves were blamed for many of the problems. This lack of preparedness also led to a second wave of implementations later, in an attempt to more fully optimize the original (and expensive) ERP investments.

A number of high-profile ERP failures have been noted over the past 15 years. In fact, in a study of 64 Fortune 500 companies, 25 percent responded that they suffered from a drop in performance when their ERP systems went live.[23] In another study that tracked ERP implementations since 1994, more than half exceeded their budgets and did not meet implementation timelines, and nearly one-third had been completely abandoned in progress.[24] Examples include Pennsylvania-based confectionary manufacturer Hershey Foods' decision—after spending $112 million to install ERP modules supplied by SAP, Manugistics, and Siebel—to "go live" with all three systems simultaneously just prior to the busy 1999 Halloween season and 18 months earlier than originally planned. Consequently, Hershey was unable to effectively fill orders for both the Halloween and Christmas seasons that year due to system failures, resulting in a 12 percent decline in 1999 revenues.[25] Also in the fall of 1999, major home appliance manufacturer Whirlpool Corp., headquartered in Michigan, blamed lengthy shipping delays on difficulties associated with its new ERP implementation.

Most experts agree, though, that ERP system failures are most often the result of poor training. "Very rarely are there instances when it's the ERP system itself—the actual software—that fails," says Jim Shepherd of Boston-based AMR Research. "Blaming the failure on a system implementation has become a convenient excuse for companies that have missed their quarter-end [earnings] target."[26] Additional factors leading to ERP implementation failures include lack of management commitment, failure to include key personnel on the project team, poor communication, incomplete needs analysis reports, personnel conflicts, and hidden agendas.[27]

With ERP, customer service representatives become far more active with customers. When customers make an inquiry, their credit ratings, purchase and return histories, and letters received and sent can be quickly identified, along with system inventory levels, on one computer screen. What resources should be assigned to this inquiry? Will the customer likely pay on time? Can we interest them in other products? Will orders be filled and shipped as promised? These are questions that customer service reps must deal with every day while using ERP, and they can affect customer lifetime purchases as well as the firm's reputation. Warehouse workers who used to track inventory levels on scraps of paper must now input accurate inventory levels into the ERP system and keep them updated *all the time.* If they fail to do this, the customer service reps may see zero inventory levels in the system and tell customers the product they want is out of stock. Responsibility, information visibility, communication ease, and the need for adequate training have never existed like this in organizations before.[28]

As alluded to earlier, the implementation requirements for ERP systems can be daunting. To install an ERP system, the very way businesses and their employees operate will likely need to change. ERP's shared database becomes the one source of "truth" for the organization. No longer will the finance department have one set of numbers while purchasing, sales, and marketing have others; and all revenue contributions for the various business units will immediately be known to everyone, since all are using the same system. During the implementation period, which can very easily last up to two years, firms often discover that one or more of their important processes is not supported by the ERP software. At this point, either the firm must change to accommodate the software (which may mean substantial changes to the culture of the firm, its mission, its processes, and/or its people), or the firm must modify the software to fit the processes, which slows down the implementation process considerably, adds significant customization and training costs to the total ERP bill, makes future upgrades more difficult, and may introduce bugs into the system.

Total ERP system costs, as mentioned briefly above, can be enough to make even businesses with very deep pockets nervous. In addition to the initial software price, businesses need to plan on costs for consulting, process reengineering, integration testing, training and retraining, software customization, hardware, data conversion and warehousing, and extra application software to further enhance the original ERP investment. In fact, in a 2001 study by systems integration consultant Computer Sciences Corp., headquartered in California, 1,009 global information system managers replied that further optimizing their enterprise systems was their main priority.[29] Meta Group Inc.'s vice president of application delivery strategies says ERP implementation costs should be in the range of $3 to $10 *for every dollar* spent on the software itself.[30]

While there is certainly no shortage of "hype" from ERP system suppliers concerning the expected benefits from ERP implementations, a number of benefits have been identified by a majority of ERP users. These are listed in Table 9.1. A number of these benefits occur at various time periods during the post-implementation phase. Directly

Table 9.1	ERP Benefits
BENEFITS	
Improved management decision making	
Improved financial management	
Improved customer service and retention	
Ease of expansion/growth	
Improved flexibility	
Faster, more accurate transactions	
Head count reduction	
Cycle time reduction	
Improved inventory/asset management	
Fewer physical resources/better logistics	
Increased revenue	

Source: Hawking, P., A. Stein, and S. Foster, "Revisiting ERP Systems: Benefit Realization," *Proceedings of the 37th Hawaii International Conference on System Sciences*, 2004, pp. 1–8.

after implementation and for a period of perhaps one year, companies familiarize themselves with the ERP system and the process changes that have occurred. This can be referred to as the **stabilize phase**, and it is during this time that many users may develop the opinion that the ERP system was a failure because initial expectations have not yet materialized. For approximately the next two years (the **synthesize phase**), companies seek organizational improvements by improving processes, adding complementary software applications, mastering the ERP system, and gaining additional support for the system. After three years, the ERP system along with its users have reached a level of maturity where system optimization is most likely to occur, also termed the **synergize phase**.[31] As shown in these discussions of ERP, the systems are quite likely to be expensive, time consuming, and require some process and even cultural changes; but with some patience, organizations can expect to see improvements in customer service and retention, inventory deployment and costs, and total revenues.

One final note regarding ERP systems and benefits is worthy of mention: Poorly managed organizations with many deep-rooted problems are unlikely to suddenly rise to the occasion after implementing an ERP system. Long-term firm success lies more in the collective knowledge and experience of the employees, than in the information systems used by the firm.

As with the notable failures, there have been many notable ERP system successes. The New York City-based Colgate Palmolive Company, a multibillion-dollar global consumer products company, implemented SAP's R/3 system in 1993 and eventually was able to reduce finished inventory levels by 50 percent and cut order receipt-to-delivery time for its top 50 customers from 12 to five days.[32] In 2000, Marathon Oil Corp., a multibillion-dollar integrated energy company headquartered in Houston, Texas, wanted to fold its major business processes into one central information system, so it chose SAP to provide the core ERP system. Heeding the warnings from the many high-profile failures of the time, Marathon was able to successfully go live with a global implementation of eight enterprise application modules in a record 13 months. The Marathon ERP implementation team offered several lessons they learned from the implementation process:[33]

- Plan the work and work the plan. Use sound project management techniques.
- It is all about the people. Make sure they are fully involved throughout the entire project.
- Do not scrimp on talent. Pick your third-party integrators carefully.
- Support has to include the CEO's sponsorship and visible involvement.
- Make change management an integral discipline in the project.
- Do not give in to the lure of tweaking this and that. Minimize the customization of code. It will only add time and cost.
- Transfer the full spectrum of ownership. Make sure the users have the knowledge to use the new tools, the responsibility to make them work right, and the vision to capitalize quickly on new capabilities.

Adding Applications to the ERP System

To reduce implementation and familiarization time, organizations are likely to start small, investing in a basic ERP system to combine with, or replace, an existing MRP, MRP II, or some other legacy system. Later, as users gain familiarity with the capabilities of the system, customizations are desired in the form of **application add-ons**. A comment made by Oracle chairman Larry Ellison at a 2001 AppsWorld conference supports this approach. He told the audience his company's e-Business Suite, "… doesn't do everything our customers want. We have an 80 percent or 85 percent solution." If used straight out of the box, though, as Ellison said Connecticut-based global conglomerate General Electric did at 20 manufacturing plants, "… an 85 percent solution in five months is better than a 100 percent solution in three years."[34]

Moreover, as products, markets, and the competition change, businesses look for modules to serve these changing needs, and vendors are likely to have a suitable and compatible add-on application to sell them. As a follow-up to its ERP implementation previously described, Colgate added a vendor-managed inventory application in 1998 and by 1999 had it installed in 70 percent of its customer facilities; it also implemented supply network planning modules in all of its manufacturing and distribution facilities. In late 1999, it added production planning, scheduling, and demand planning modules and integrated them with the SAP applications, along with business information warehouse software. Since then, this system has helped Colgate achieve improved sales revenue and net income growth.[35]

The primary ERP suppliers want their product to become the foundation of firms' planning system infrastructures by making the ERP system a central information repository, with the ability to connect legacy applications, other business systems, and future add-on applications in the areas of production and distribution, finance, sales and marketing, human resources, and a host of other industry-specific applications. "The packaged application gives you a starting point," says Larry Ferrere, vice president of marketing at Virginia-based Vastera Inc., an ERP application supplier. "There's no need to reinvent the wheel," he says. "Users can focus on coding objects specific to their business processes."[36]

The e-Commerce Perspective feature provides a description of just how one of these add-on applications works for Cascade Engineering, a firm that is using its ERP system applications to help implement just-in-time deliveries with its suppliers.

In a 2004 study, a comprehensive survey of ERP issues was distributed to a wide range of companies. The findings revealed 11 different ERP modules that were being used—finance, marketing/sales, human resources/payroll, production, logistics, inven-

---

e-Commerce Perspective

Internet Application Supports Lean Manufacturing

Cascade Engineering, a $200-million-a-year global manufacturer based in Grand Rapids, Michigan, designs and builds durable plastic components that go into automobiles, home and office furniture, and other products. To support its lean manufacturing model—which calls for building only as many products as are needed to fill current orders—Cascade asked its suppliers to deliver smaller amounts of parts at more frequent intervals.

"We have some suppliers delivering four times a day, or more, so that we don't have huge amounts of inventory on hand," says Sandi Ragan, Cascade's materials manager. But, Ragan adds, some suppliers initially had difficulty gauging how much material to bring on each trip. That meant Cascade often found itself holding more inventory than it needed. As Cascade's customers changed their requirements from day to day—lowering or raising order quantities or changing ship dates—Cascade's suppliers continued to deliver according to the prearranged delivery schedules, often leaving Cascade's inventory out of sync with its actual demand.

Ultimately, Cascade tackled that problem by installing an Internet-based software package that gives its suppliers a real-time view of Cascade's current inventory levels and production schedules. This tool, which Cascade calls a supplier visualization portal, is an extension of the ERP package that Cascade purchased from QAD of Carpinteria, California.

Now, Cascade has its QAD inventory management system programmed to send automatic updates on inventory status to the supplier portal every ten minutes. "Our suppliers can look into the portal and see exactly where we stand in terms of consuming the inventory they sent on previous deliveries," says Linda Kelsey, a lean leader in the Cascade business unit that builds products to improve the acoustics inside automobiles. "It has really helped one supplier that was constantly sending too many parts. Instead, shipping in line with a schedule that was created Monday, they can look and see exactly how many parts we need to have each day."

Not to be outdone by the upstart vendors, many established ERP suppliers now have flow functionality in their software suites. QAD's supplier visualization portal is a prime example. It's also clear that companies welcome the software vendors' support, whether it comes from an established ERP supplier or a newer company with a stand-alone package. According to Ragan, Cascade Engineering's material manager and a QAD user, "Since we adopted lean manufacturing, our inventory has gone down considerably. Inventory turns are up, and accuracy has improved. The combination of lean events to streamline processes and eliminate waste, and tools like the QAD software, have helped with that."

Source: Hill, S., "Can Flow Encompass the Supply Chain?" *MSI,* V. 21, No. 4, 2003, p. 38. Used with permission.

tory/purchasing, quality control, plant maintenance, project management, banking, and decision support. The finance, production, and logistics modules were being used the most, and all three were used by 43 percent of the respondents. Approximately 40 percent of the companies had installed more than three modules, and 34 percent had plans to install additional modules later. The ERP add-on modules used by these firms supplied support for a number of techniques and practices including performance measurement, benchmarking, customer profitability analysis, ABC inventory control, quality cost analysis, and target costing.[37]

These add-on modules are providing much of the sales growth in the ERP market, and literally hundreds have been designed for many different industry applications or niche markets that have previously been ignored by the bigger application suppliers. Linda Hecht, marketing director for the Environmental Systems Research Institute in California, started using a marketing resource management ERP application to automate routine actions and improve strategic marketing planning. "Before, we had a system that could do emails, but not campaigns. Now, we are getting our marketing managers to start designing and building campaigns rather than just mailing something out," she says.[38] "Financial applications are back in vogue," says John Van Decker, senior program director at Meta Group, Inc. Implementations are propelled by government mandates to speed reporting and corporate anxiety over financial data accuracy and transparency. "Companies are all asking, 'Is what I know correct?' and they're willing to invest in software that helps them drill down and understand performance," he explains.

Profit management automation (PMA) combines profit planning, activity-based costing, and treasury and audit management into an integrated application suite and has become a big growth area in the ERP module market. "PMA will give controllers and treasurers the same sort of control over capital that traditional ERP provides regarding transactional data," says IDC analyst Dennis Byron. Steve Miranda, vice president of applications development at Oracle, touts his company's Daily Business Intelligence application. This portal-based interface gives users in finance, human resources, sales and other functions the ability to analyze various ERP data in real time.[39]

A product from IDS Scheer, a German consulting and software company, points to a trend away from customization and towards more prebuilt applications. Its Smart-Path™ modules are designed for the chemical and durable goods sectors and include ERP systems from either SAP or Microsoft Business Solutions. Its product reduces ERP implementation time by helping users quickly configure the applications according to industry best practices. Jamaica-based Grace Kennedy's food trading division has implemented the SmartPath solution and expects annual savings of about $2.4 million from the deployment.[40] Descriptions of several of the more popular ERP add-on modules follow.

The Customer Relationship Management Module

As companies grow, acquire other companies, sell off poorly performing units, and enter new markets, their customer base also changes, along with the associated databases and ERP system applications. Firms eventually find they need a customer relationship management (CRM) application to organize customer data and manage it from one central location. Frequently, companies will purchase ERP systems that come prepackaged with a CRM application, but even in these cases companies still find it necessary to expand their system's CRM capabilities as customer databases change. Companies can purchase, customize, and integrate CRM applications or opt to use **on-demand CRM**

services instead, wherein a monthly fee is charged to the user to access application software over the Internet.

California-based Salesforce.com, begun in 1999, offers on-demand CRM services and by 2006 had 300,000 customers and realized a profit of $4.4 million during the first quarter of that year. Oracle and SAP have also begun developing on-demand capabilities.[41] ResortCom International, a small, San Diego-based process outsourcing company for vacation property developers, signed a three-year contract with CRM solution provider RightNow Technologies, headquartered in Montana, for on-demand CRM services when it realized its cost would be $125 per user per month compared to the $300,000 (plus implementation and support costs) for an onsite CRM solution. For small firms like ResortCom that can accept out-of-the-box CRM with few customization requirements, these systems can be very beneficial.[42]

As discussed in Chapter 3, the general idea behind CRM is to identify and segment customers, such that profitable ones are kept satisfied through better mixes of the products and services they want, while unprofitable customers are either converted to profitable ones or fired. The primary benefit of CRM software applications is that they provide the firm with accurate, consolidated, and current information on all customers, such that the firm can do a better job of tracking and managing customer relationships. Customer statistics can be easily generated and functional groups in the firm can look at different views of the customer database. Consequently, field sales and call center personnel can be quickly connected to customer accounts; marketing departments can more easily design promotional campaigns targeting specific groups or customer segments; and engineering personnel can design products that customers are more likely to purchase.

Tarantella, a California-based remote access software provider, uses its CRM application to allow its customers to connect to the firm via a web portal, enabling the firm to gain the customers' views of the business. Their application also allows automated data entry and has automated letter preparation capabilities, allowing the firm to trim 20 percent off of the time normally required to create and ship customer mailings.[43] Barclays Bank PLC of London purchased Ohio-based information technology provider NCR's CRM software to deliver targeted marketing campaigns to individual customers through multiple marketing channels. The application alerts Barclays of any significant changes in customer behavior indicating new financial interests. The information can then be acted on by delivering relevant bank product information to the particular customer using the most appropriate channel, including email, the Internet, ATMs, mail, telephone, or face-to-face contact.[44]

Like other enterprise system applications, the market for CRM applications is huge and growing. According to AMR Research, the global CRM software market will reach $16 billion per year by 2009, up from about $11 billion in 2004. The lucrative market is also causing a take-no-prisoners battle among CRM software competitors. When Oracle president Charles Phillips was asked at a press briefing whether its on-demand CRM application rival Salesforce.com was next on its list of companies to be acquired, he responded, "In this case, it may be more fun to crush them." Salesforce.com countered by advertising a $5,000 signing bonus for any current Siebel (owned by Oracle) employee hired before the end of 2006.[45]

The Supplier Relationship Management Module

As with CRM, supplier relationship management (SRM) is an operating philosophy that is now using automation to make the job cheaper, easier, and more effective. As will be described in Chapter 12, SRM embodies the management of relationships with suppliers, with the goal of increasing suppliers' abilities to provide better service and products for less cost. SRM modules provide users with analytical tools, tracking capabilities, web services, and reverse auction technologies, among other capabilities, to allow for better use of existing ERP systems, faster and more flexible decision making, and better control of strategic sourcing, purchasing contracts, and supplier management activities. In the most general terms, SRM software applications search the supplier and parts databases, select the most appropriate parts and suppliers based on a set of requirements, and then track ongoing quality and supplier performance. SRM systems also give engineers, buyers, and other decision makers the ability to perform what-if analyses, which is valuable if early supplier involvement is desired during the new product development phase.

Spend management is another capability of many SRM modules, giving the user the capability to analyze and hopefully reduce total purchasing costs. Global diversified manufacturer PPG Industries of Pennsylvania uses its spend management software to consolidate spending across the corporation and use fewer vendors, resulting in higher-quality, lower-cost materials. Since implementing California-based spend management software provider Ariba's Visibility Solution in 2003, it has saved over $10 million in purchasing costs. "Once you make the investment and get up and running, it's amazing how much money can be saved. The solution gives us better visibility. We knew we couldn't improve spend management if we couldn't see it," says PPG purchasing director James Polak.[46] ABB, the Swedish maker of power and automation technologies, implemented an SRM software solution in all of its units in 100 countries around the globe in 2001 to better control the billions it spends each year on procurement. All purchase orders are scanned into its system and updated weekly. This way, it can see the purchases piling up among its suppliers, giving it leverage to negotiate better terms as time goes on.[47]

Supplier selection is perhaps the most troublesome and technical aspect of an SRM application, if the selection is based on anything other than purchase price. Systems might employ mathematical programming models, weighted-factor scoring models, artificial intelligence, or case-based models to help with this decision. A model used by Honeywell Consumer Products Limited (Hong Kong), for example, identifies the current sourcing need, finds a previous successful purchasing decision within the database that most closely fits the current need, uses that case to suggest a solution, and then afterwards evaluates the supplier and updates the system. Suppliers are evaluated based on delivery, price, product defects, and user complaints. Honeywell found that its SRM system decreased average delivery delays, improved delivered product quality by 50 percent, and reduced complaints by 7 percent.[48]

In many cases, SRM application vendors resist putting the SRM label on their products because of the catch-all term it has become. "It's a very broad term that doesn't use the obvious lingo," says John Madrid, vice president of sourcing for Georgia-based Procuri, an SRM application provider. "I've been to SRM conferences where none of the speakers define SRM because it is such a complex concept," he adds. Massachusetts-based SupplyWorks (a division of Intuitive, an ERP system provider) doesn't use the term SRM on its supply management solution. Its product, called MAX, enables manufacturers to communicate and collaborate more tightly with suppliers, and helps them optimize the flow of parts and materials, to reduce cycle times and inventory. Its customers report 20 to 30 percent reductions in raw materials inventories, 25 percent reductions in supplier lead times, 10 percent improvements in on-time deliveries, and 5 percent reductions in material costs.[49]

The Financial Management and Accounting Module

The financial management and accounting module is one of the more vital modules in any ERP system, incorporating applications such as general ledger, accounts receivable/payable, fixed assets, cash management, financial statement preparation, cost control, and budgeting. In many cases, ERP financial management capabilities also include activity-based costing, product life cycle costing, stock purchases, continuous internal audit capabilities, financial ratio analysis, profitability analysis, and balanced scorecards for performance-monitoring purposes. Many of these systems also incorporate pattern recognition capabilities that enable the recognition of fraud. With these technologies, accountants and other finance professionals have moved from being the traditional scorekeepers to today's decision makers. In a 2004 study of 26 companies that had implemented ERP, all were found to have a financial/accounting management module. The reasons for implementing these systems were found to be the need for real-time information, information for decision making, the need for cost reductions, and a desire to improve sales.[50]

Globalization, competition, mergers and acquisitions, and outsourcing have all combined to demand efficiency improvements through cost reductions, process performance and quality improvements, and faster delivery times to improve customer service for most organizations. Consequently, enterprises are changing rapidly, requiring financial and other types of decisions to be made quickly and frequently. This means that the finance function must have access to information in real time across all business units and departments to support rapid decision making. Additionally, the right kind of information must be collected and analyzed to avoid making ineffective organizational decisions. For example, a large fast-food company wanted to reduce the food waste in its restaurants, so it began measuring waste at the store level and rewarding managers for reducing their unit's waste. Unfortunately, to maximize their bonuses, managers had their restaurants stop preparing as much food in advance, resulting in longer customer waits and an accompanying drop-off in sales.[51]

The relatively recent accounting scandals at companies like Texas-based Enron, Virginia-based WorldCom, and Illinois-based Arthur Anderson led in part to the 2002 U.S. Sarbanes-Oxley Act (SOA), a public company corporate accountability law, with oversight by the Securities and Exchange Commission. Thus, a host of ERP financial management modules now contain sections that address SOA compliance, drastically cutting the time required to keep up with the SOA financial rules, through automation of accounting processes. For instance, Section 404 of SOA requires a visible, repeatable, and tested financial reporting process, while Section 409 specifies a "significant event" reporting mechanism more timely than the SEC 8-K filing.[52]

The Production Management Module

Also termed **manufacturing execution system** (MES) modules, this ERP system add-on has long been sought as a way to tie management planning to the plant floor. In a rather tongue-in-cheek article written in 2004, it was stated that SAP had finally discovered the plant floor, with the unveiling of several initiatives designed to marry ERP and manufacturing processes. Manufacturers that use a shop floor control system realize the value of these systems in eliminating paperwork, scheduling production, and managing work-in-process inventories. The problem has been in making real-time shop floor data accessible to ERP systems. Taking orders and generating production plans at the global enterprise level cannot be accomplished effectively if the people doing these jobs can't determine in real time what's happening at every facility around the world. "The ERP vendors missed a big market by not integrating with the plant floor," said a systems architect at a large manufacturer of electrical test equipment. "We built our own interface for our MES and MRP systems."[53] When shop floor personnel are forced to manually input manufacturing data into an ERP system, and in some cases when the MES is not adequately integrated into the ERP, shop floor data input errors can cause a whole host of planning and execution problems, as evidenced in the Process Management in Action feature.

MES software communicates the manufacturing plan (consisting of which products to make, how many, and what assembly operations to utilize) from the ERP to the shop floor. Then, as products are manufactured, the MES sends data from the shop floor (what materials and components were used, how many units were actually produced, what orders were shipped) back to the ERP. This feedback is necessary to ensure that the right amount of materials are being purchased, the right amount of product is being produced, and customer due dates are being met. MES applications automate the recording and transmission of this data, reducing errors and the time to transfer information. Electronic records of shop floor activities are created and placed on a database for use in planning and decision making at the ERP level. "Using a standard MES will give us an IT infrastructure that promotes agility by streamlining the process of getting plans to the plant floor, as well as delivering the production information needed to make critical decisions at the corporate level," says Geir Einset, director of operations development at Elcoteq, a Finnish telecommunications manufacturer. "For example, a view of global operations and capacity will enable management to make decisions about whether the company should take certain orders, decide where the work should be done, and at the same time, ensure profitability by making better use of capacity," says Einset.[54]

As with any software implementation, there can be problems associated with implementation time, user training, and customization cost. But when the application must be integrated with an existing ERP system, compatibility and configuration problems must also be overcome. Another consideration is whether or not to implement an entire system-wide MES at once, or in piecemeal fashion (to reduce cost and implementation time). According to Mark Roache, associate director of IT Consulting Services at KMI, an MES consulting company, not fully implementing an MES can mean loss of some essential functions. "MES is one of those things in which if you complete 80 percent of what you said you were going to do, the remaining 20 percent is where all the value was," Roache says. Lack of standardization in the ERP software industry causes yet another problem. "Implementing the MES so that it matches the processes of a particular user, given that those processes change radically from user to user, means that the implementation is different every time," adds Roache.[55]

The Logistics Management Module

Also termed **logistics execution suites, logistics management modules** is a blanket term for a family of logistics-oriented software applications including **transportation management systems, warehouse management systems, yard management systems,** and **returns management systems**. Companies are finding significant benefits from integrating their basic ERP systems with logistics execution systems. In fact, worldwide expenditures on logistics software applications grew to nearly $3 billion in 2006.[56] These systems provide "a networked view of the world" says Tillman Estes, SAP's director of business development for supply chain execution. "It will include everyone from order routing and transportation planning and execution to event management, the consumer and everything in-between," he adds.[57]

Process Management in Action

Lies Your ERP System Tells You

Tens of thousands of large and medium-size companies have installed enterprise resource planning (ERP) software to harmonize business, manufacturing, and supply chain operations. Many have achieved outstanding returns. Others, however, found their systems yield results that are just wrong. They lie.

That seemed to be the case three years ago, when Nick Testa received a panicked call from the managers of a medium-size manufacturer. The parent company had given them 30 days to find and fix millions of dollars of inventory write-offs.

Testa, one of a small army of consultants who help businesses wrestle with ERP systems, had a good idea of where the problem might lie. His firm, Acuity Consulting Inc. of Cypress, California, had helped install the company's ERP system several years earlier. At the time, Testa recommended that the company buy ERP software with a feature called a configurator. It enabled companies to stock subassemblies and configure them into final products at the last possible second.

"They bought the system, then decided the configurator was too complex to implement," Testa said. Instead, they opted for a process that used the ERP system to create pick lists of parts needed for each final product. Workers would then grab the subassemblies from inventory and assemble them. This seemed to work just like the configurator, with one subtle difference: The configurator passed along the labor cost of the subassemblies to the final product. Pick lists did not. "They were entering their labor costs into the system and ignoring them in cost of goods sold," said Testa. In effect, the labor costs were indistinguishable from money invested in inventory. "As a result, each year they were overstating the value of their inventory by millions of dollars," Testa said. "They didn't know what caused the problem and they didn't want to find out, so they just wrote off the difference until the parent company called them on it."

"That's the biggest problem with ERP systems," Testa said. "People muck with them. They try to make them perform the way they want rather than the way that's correct." Testa knows. He has been tackling similar problems since the 1970s, when companies began installing material requirement planning (MRP) systems, the forerunners of today's ERP software, to plan production and track inventory.

ERP systems go much further than MRP. They are the corporate system of record, a single database linking manufacturing with such business processes as new orders, purchasing, credit, accounting, supply chain management, and planning. For many manufacturers, ERP delivers on its promises. Yet ERP has a weakness. Its power depends on recording and tracking thousands of individual transactions, or events, ranging from sales orders to each component on a bill of materials. It then models how those processes interact with one another. Like dominoes in a row, each new transaction sets off a cascade of events. A new sales order, for example, triggers factory work orders, claims inventory, reserves manufacturing capacity, and schedules labor.

ERP models reflect reality only when each transaction registers true. "Yes, it is costly to enter each transaction," Testa said. "But as soon as you go around the system, it begins to degrade. Once that happens, people stop trusting it, and then they have another reason not to use it. It's a death spiral that's inherent in ERP: If you don't trust the system, you validate that the system's data is bad by screwing it up."

That seems to happen most often when ERP systems reach down to the factory floor. There's a disconnect. Sometimes, ERP simply does not provide the answers. Part of the problem is manufacturing complexity. "ERP is great for deploying standardized processes across an enterprise, but it has had a hard time bridging that last mile due to the complexity and disparity of plant operating solutions," said Russ Fadel, vice president of manufacturing applications at SAP Labs LLC in Palo Alto, California.

As CEO of Lighthammer Software Development Corp., which SAP acquired in 2005, Fadel tried to cross that bridge. His company developed software to link factory data with ERP information. He plays a similar role at SAP, whose manufacturing customers can have between 80 and 800 separate factory floor systems. At worst, that means data and process models are scattered everywhere. At best, automated facilities use manufacturing execution systems that harmonize competing models and data, and moderate the flow of manufacturing information to and from the ERP system.

An ERP system that does not capture changes in a bill of materials, for example, may schedule too much production time or too few workers. Supply chains may carry too much or too little inventory. Companies may lose money because they always have to expedite late orders. This leads to a classic ERP problem, said Joshua Greenbaum, a principal at Enterprise Applications Consulting in Berkeley, California. "ERP does materials management and resource planning, but if you don't have accurate shop floor data, ERP forecasts are not much better than putting your finger in the wind," he said.

Yet despite the difficulties inherent in linking ERP to manufacturing, Greenbaum sees an even more pressing issue. "Implementation," he said, "is the number one, two, and three problem in ERP. It's not that the systems are inflexible, but that they're so very flexible." Most ERP systems come with best practices—models of how business processes should be conducted and who should receive information embedded in the software. "The conflict comes when companies try to reconcile what software says they should be doing with the way they've always done things," Greenbaum said. "Companies that spend millions of dollars on ERP software would like to think that the software works for them and not the other way around."

Author and consultant Robert Stein of Cedar Park, Texas, has implemented more than 20 ERP systems. He says inventory balances are the most telling indicator of ERP health in manufacturing. Stein's approach is to run a negative balance report that shows products that have negative amounts of inventory on the shelves. Clearly, such a situation cannot exist, but it happens all the time. "I get page after page of negative balances," said Stein. "The most common mistake I have found is that someone receives parts at the back door and takes them to the shop floor without ever doing the computer transaction." After those parts are used, many ERP systems catch up with them through a process called backflushing. This occurs when workers enter a finished part into the ERP system. The system automatically backflushes all of the components out of inventory. Since no one entered the components into inventory to begin with, backflushing produces a negative tally.

Sometimes analysts estimate rather than measure data, said Nicholas Dewhurst, executive vice president at Boothroyd Dewhurst Inc. in Wakefield, Rhode Island. He recalls a meeting with managers who found a part too expensive to manufacture. "We looked at the details and it was striking," he said. "Each of the part's machining operations took ten minutes. When we dug further, we found they only took two or three minutes. Someone who was not familiar with the operation had estimated the time."

All these data problems and informal shop floor workarounds have something in common. They are all symptoms of a lack of the discipline needed to enter every transaction, ensure it is correct, and do it every time. ERP vendors are making it easier to get that information. Market leader SAP, for example, is collaborating with companies that make manufacturing software.

Continued

One of them is Invensys Systems Inc. in Lake Forest, California, developer of the Wonderware®️ manufacturing execution system.

Wonderware links directly with more than 1,000 different motion controllers, RFID readers, instruments, and other devices, according to Claus Abildgren, production-end performance management program manager at Invensys. It then translates SAP's ERP plans into manufacturing actions and reports plant data to the ERP for use in future plans. "People don't like working in a factory where everything is chaos and you're expediting things all the time," said Mike Frichol, vice president of global industry marketing for discrete manufacturing at Infor Global Solutions, an ERP developer in Alpharetta, Georgia. "A system that enforces discipline creates a calmer, more structured environment with lower labor turnover."

In the end, though, individuals have to take responsibility for entering the right data time and again. They must do it despite ongoing changes in models, specifications, and configurations. That sounds daunting. Yet every company operates at least one system where the data is always perfect. It is a system where everyone takes personal responsibility for accuracy. Where they report mistakes immediately. Where no one accepts any lies from their software. It is, of course, payroll.

Source: Brown, A. S., "Lies Your ERP System Tells You," *Mechanical Engineering*, V. 128, No. 36, 2006, pp. 36–39. Article courtesy of *Mechanical Engineering* magazine; copyright *Mechanical Engineering* magazine (the American Society of Mechanical Engineers International).

Transportation Management Systems

Transportation management system (TMS) applications allow firms, for instance, to select the best mix of transportation service and pricing, to determine the best use of containers or truck trailers, to better manage transportation contracts, to rank transportation options, to clear customs, to track product movements, and to track carrier performance. Rhodes International, a frozen bread dough manufacturer in Utah, uses its TMS to determine its truckload shipments and shipment routings, and track them once they leave the warehouses.[58] With these systems, visibility and security are very important. Shippers, governments, and customers want to know where the goods are, which means that real-time information about an item's location during warehousing and delivery to the final destination is required. Consequently, information may need to be provided by the manufacturer, third-party logistics providers, agents, freight forwarders, and others as products move through global supply chains. Technologies employed to provide this visibility include bar code scanners, RFID tags, GPS devices, and phone/fax. Wal-Mart, for example, mandated its top suppliers to begin implementing use of RFID tags in 2005 to provide them with needed supply chain visibility. It has a very long way to go, however. Wal-Mart has over 61,000 suppliers in the United States alone, and by the end of 2005, less than 1,000 of its suppliers were using RFID. Other major retailers now following suit include Target and Albertsons in the United States, Tesco and Selfridges in the United Kingdom, and Metro Group in Germany.[59]

The desire to secure national borders against unwanted shipments has increased due to terrorist concerns, causing a number of governments to more closely regulate the flow of goods across their borders. This has added further risk of transportation delays as companies deal with an added layer of bureaucracy and reporting at various border entry sites. Thus, many TMS software applications have added capabilities for customs declaration, denied-party screening, calculation and payment of tariffs, duties and duty drawbacks, and advanced filing of shipment manifests.

Warehouse Management Systems

When a TMS is coupled with a warehouse management system (WMS), supply chain effectiveness is further enhanced. For example, a company might use its TMS to forecast throughput volumes based on data provided by the WMS and then report back the most efficient modes of shipping. The WMS could then determine warehouse picks based on TMS shipping requirements. One result might be that one fully loaded truck instead of two partially loaded trucks would be dispatched for a delivery. And, as fuel and shipping costs continue to escalate, these considerations become even more vital to a firm's success. Warehouse management systems track and control the flow of goods from the receiving dock of a warehouse or distribution center until the item is loaded for outbound shipment to the customer. RFID tags placed on products and pallets within the distribution center play a central role in controlling the flow of goods. The goals of a WMS include reducing distribution center labor costs, streamlining the flow of goods, reducing the time products spend in the distribution center, managing distribution center capacity, reducing paperwork, and managing the cross-docking process.

Michigan-based office furniture maker Haworth Inc. completed a $14 million rollout of its TMS and WMS in 2004, resulting in greatly reduced freight costs and greater warehouse worker efficiencies. Its TMS considers customer orders, factory schedules, carrier rates and availabilities, and shipping costs, and then produces an optimum, lowest-cost delivery plan. Plans are updated every 15 minutes, and there is an automated system that lets Haworth negotiate deliveries with its carriers. Its WMS tracks finished goods from Haworth's three distribution centers to the various customer sites. Acting on shipping plans from the TMS, the WMS directs the movement of goods using real-time data on distribution center space, equipment, inventory, and personnel. "You take a standard workstation like this," says Michael Moon of Haworth. "You've got the walls, the desk, the overhead files, and so forth. All these may come from different manufacturing sites, all coming together at a distribution center and then to the customer site in a sequence that allows them to install it. And maybe the customer wants to install his furniture over the weekend. You can't have missing parts off the truck, or he may not be able to move in on Monday."[60]

WMSs are also being used in manufacturing shop floor applications. For example, U.S. computer manufacturer Hewlett-Packard uses a WMS to route incoming materials from the receiving docks to the JIT assembly lines at some of its computer assembly facilities. It then uses the system to manage finished goods from the production lines to the shipping docks for delivery to customers.[61]

As mentioned previously, use of RFID technologies has dramatically increased with use of TMS and WMS applications. Joe Dunlap, supply chain solutions head at Michigan-based material handling systems manufacturer Siemens-Dematic, thinks that RFID has the potential to change the supply chain execution picture from top to bottom. "In a WMS that directs order pickup or delivery by scanning bar codes, there's the possibility of the operator putting the load in the wrong place, but scanning the correct location barcode label, thus producing an out-of-stock situation." The use of RFID would eliminate that potential for error as readers automatically collect the information.[62] In 2006, Wal-Mart began using handheld RFID scanners in back room storage areas to identify products needed to restock shelves. Wal-Mart has since found that stockouts have been reduced by 16 percent with use of RFID-tagged cases and pallets.[63]

Service Perspective

International Paper's RFID Solution

The homegrown system, up and running for about a year at International Paper's (IP) Texarkana, Texas, bleach-board mill, centers around wireless transmission of production-to-warehouse-to-shipping dock instructions that track the stocking and storage of thousands of rolls of paper each day. Since implementing the system, the Texarkana mill has increased inventory turns by 5 percent, improved on-time delivery performance, and leveraged the system's preplanning and tracking capabilities to ship 70,000 tons of paper in March 2004, a new record. "The bottom line to all this is that we turned warehousing into a function that actually helps increase production," says Scott Andersen, RFID product manager for IP's Smart Packaging business unit.

To understand what's produced and stored in the Texarkana mill is to understand why IP picked that location for the implementation of its first RFID solution. The mill converts raw timber into massive rolls of bleach board used in making milk and juice boxes. "Think of huge spools of thread stacked on top of each other, row after row," says Andersen. Forklift trucks outfitted with padded "hands" grip and lift the rolls, which weigh between two and seven tons each. The forklift operators place the rolls on end and stack them three to eight high, depending on their weights.

With the warehouse having to make an average of more than 5,000 moves a day to get one roll out of the way of another, product tracking and placement was becoming costly and ineffective. "That's where every other attempted solution, including painted lines and three generations of bar coding, was failing in terms of inventory accuracy," says Troy Ashmore, Texarkana's production, scheduling, and distribution manager.

Dissatisfied with the results of those efforts, Andersen and the team decided to test RFID applications that IP had developed in-house under the guidance of Steve Van Fleet, director of the Smart Packaging business unit. Van Fleet presented a business plan to IP's chairman and was awarded funding to develop new RFID-based products.

Now that the stage had been set, it was up to the Texarkana team to begin charting a solution for the mill's unique visibility issue. Their vision: A tracking system that would use an RFID tag to give each roll a unique identifier while providing visibility into how it is processed, where and how it's stored, and how it's shipped.

IP decided to run with Matrics, of Rockville, Maryland, for its 900MHz tag as well as its RFID reader, which is mounted on the padded forklift "hands" that pick up and move the rolls. For systems integration and consulting, IP went with Toledo, Ohio-based ESYNC, while Apriso of Long Beach, California, was chosen to provide the middleware that maps out locations and directs forklift drivers via truck-mounted computer screens.

The project was not without its challenges. First, the development team struggled to find the proper frequencies for transmitting information inside the mill. The second challenge was designing new technology that could withstand the harsh surroundings. "We needed to make sure that we had technology that could read through a 75-inch diameter roll and survive in a mill environment," recalls Ashmore. To make that possible, IP and its vendors developed rugged, gripper-mounted readers and placed the tags inside the cores of the paper rolls, a move that significantly reduced the chance of damage to the tags.

When an order first comes in, all of the specs for each roll—the customer's name, date needed, grade, width, and mode of transportation, are entered into the mill's information system. That data is linked to a tag, which receives a unique identifying number and is applied to the roll's core. The core identification number then is married to a unique identifier for each "unit," or bundle of rolls destined for a particular customer. This linking of core identifier and unit identifier sets the foundation for the tracking system.

Once a roll comes out of production, it's picked up by a forklift using grippers equipped with tag readers. As soon as the tag has been read, the driver sees detailed information about that roll, including the next set of instructions, on a forklift-mounted screen. "Let's say a roll needs to move onto a conveyance (an internal conveyor system) to be shipped out by truck that day," says Ashmore. "The screen displays which conveyance it needs to be on, and whether it's going by truck or rail—and we've only touched the product one time." If a roll needs to be stored, drivers are directed to a preplanned storage location.

Because each tag includes detailed information, the mill can better plan its operations. "I can now take that information and preplan the production on that order," Ashmore says. "I know how we need to make that roll, which machine to use, when it needs to be produced. I can also go ahead and preplan if I need to put it into the warehouse or if I need to put it on a conveyance and ship it to a customer at a particular time."

The system is also helping the mill to manage its transportation costs. "We know up front whether or not a roll needs to be shipped by truck or rail," says Ashmore. "And since each mode has a related cost and we can plan shipments far in advance, we can now ship at the lowest cost available."

To maintain efficiency and engage employees in the project, the Texarkana team developed a program that is loosely based on the National Football League's Quarterback Rating. Texarkana's version rates forklift operators on the number of valid, invalid, and efficient moves, as well as average moves per day. An invalid move into the wrong conveyance, for example, would be equivalent to an interception; the successful loading of 30 or 40 rolls into the correct conveyance, leading to a complete and on-time shipment, would be a touchdown. If a driver has taken a roll to the wrong conveyance or truck door, the system immediately issues an alert and the move is noted on the driver's score. A correct move improves the driver's rating. But the program does more than simply motivate employees, Ashmore notes. "This is a real-time, high-level application that gives me a record of everything a driver has done for that particular day," he says.

Andersen stresses that IP's RFID system is achieving its promise not because of what it is, but because of what it can do. "This isn't just a chip on a box or a chip on a product," he says. "The value comes in the information, how you aggregate that information, and how you use it to figure out what it means to your operation. The true test is to ensure that an RFID solution can evolve and be a real solution."

Source: Levans, M., "IP Strikes Gold," *Logistics Management,* V. 43, No. 6, 2004, pp. 30–32. Used with permission.

For an example of a WMS that employs RFID, read the Service Perspective feature on International Paper. A second example of RFID use is described in the NYK Logistics profile of its yard management system, seen in the second Service Perspective feature.

Returns Management Systems

Reverse logistics, discussed at length in Chapter 15 and defined as the process of returning finished products for replacement, repair, or cash, is a necessary and costly part of supply chain management. Some studies have found that about 20 percent of products are returned, and that it adds approximately $1.50 in costs for every $1 of

Service Perspective

NYK Logistics' Automated Yard Management System

NYK Logistics needed to optimize its operations to keep up with one of the highest-volume, most demanding distribution channels in the world: Target Corp. of Minneapolis, Minnesota, which posted annual sales of almost $47 billion in its most recent fiscal year.

The hub of NYK Logistics' activity for Target takes place in Long Beach, California, at a 70-acre facility featuring 1,200 parking slots and 250 dock doors. NYK is responsible for managing more than 50,000 inbound ocean freight containers from the Port of Los Angeles/Long Beach and 30,000 outbound trailers every year. It coordinates shipments to 22 different distribution centers across the United States. NYK Logistics processes more than 1,000 gate transactions daily during peak season, checking in and out containers and trailers from steamship lines and domestic carriers.

Previously, the company had relied on a homegrown yard management system. Personnel, armed with clipboards, pads of paper, and walkie-talkies, manually entered data and scanned bar codes on containers to try to keep up with the yard's current inventory. "No matter how many people we threw at the problem—we even used an old pick-up truck to expedite the data collection process—we were always a day late and a dollar short," says Charles Kerr, equipment control manager of NYK's Long Beach operations. "And in our case, those days and dollars quickly escalate into thousands of dollars when you consider higher inventory, more labor and lengthy yard turns."

With volume steadily increasing and tapping out its facility capacity, NYK Logistics decided to use technology and automate its yard. "In hindsight, we wished that we had made the move sooner," Kerr says. The company installed WhereNet's (Santa Clara, California) wireless active radio frequency identification (RFID) real-time locating system (RTLS) and WhereSoft Yard™ 4.0 yard management software. Deployed in less than 75 days, the WhereNet wireless system provides NYK with accurate location information for every container, trailer, and tractor within NYK's yard. The system has allowed NYK to automate more than 90 percent of its yard operations, which has increased dock door utilization, reduced yard congestion, and increased yard throughput. NYK realized a complete return on investment in less than one year.

"Traditional passive RFID technology just doesn't cut it for our operations. It's not good enough to know that a trailer or container has entered our yard; we must know its exact whereabouts and status at all times," Kerr says. "For example, during our peak pre-holiday season, it's not uncommon that we are required to expedite a container that just arrived at the port, deconsolidate it, and transload its contents onto several different outbound trailers headed for different parts of the country. With WhereNet, we can execute this type of double transaction in less than 20 minutes. We could have never dreamed of doing that with the old system."

Upon arrival at the gate, every container or trailer gets "tagged" with a small, active radio transmitter. From this point forward, NYK Logistics personnel have constant connectivity to their yard assets wherever they are. Yard workers use handheld devices and rugged tablet PC devices mounted in the tractors to transmit data through the WhereNet infrastructure.

WhereSoft Yard 4.0 includes a yard rule manager that controls the movement of trailers and containers to dock doors, assigns parking spots within the yard, and verifies that trailers and containers being checked out are allowed to leave the yard. NYK uses the rules to ensure that the lowest cost carriers are selected first for particular routes and to minimize detention by processing older containers first. The only human intervention in this process takes place when the tractor driver receives the request through his wireless tablet PC device, maps the location of the requested trailer with his touch screen, and pulls the trailer to the designated door.

Gate check-ins and checkouts are performed using mobile handheld devices and software. During the check-in process, a user enters information about the unit and driver, and then attaches an active wireless RF-transmitter tag to the container or trailer that is about to enter the facility. The system automatically attempts to find a matching automatic shipping notice and prints a ticket for the driver with instructions on where to park the unit and which unit (if any) to pick up. The ticket serves as a gate pass for the driver. Driver information is obtained by swiping the driver's license on a magnetic card reader integrated with the mobile printer. This data is transmitted via the wireless local area network and captured in the WhereNet database so that NYK Logistics has accurate, automated records of everyone who enters its facility.

"With WhereNet, we essentially know the DNA of every container. What's in it, when it arrived at the port, its location on our site, and where the contents ultimately need to be shipped," Kerr says.

Source: Kempfer, L., "NYK Logistics Automates Yard Management," *Material Handling Management*, V. 61, No. 2, 2006, pp. 48–49. Used with permission.

merchandise returned.[64] Returns management systems (RMSs) are thus being created to respond effectively to a firm's customer database and provide global visibility, standardization, and documentation of product returns, while minimizing reverse logistics costs. In addition to managing returns, the RMS can also be designed to handle returnable assets such as pallets, platforms, and containers.

In many cases, returns capabilities are built into WMS applications. Some companies use their WMS to facilitate the returns process before the original product is even shipped. "Many direct-to-consumer companies will have the WMS create a return label when they are printing out the initial paper work," says Noah Dixon, industry strategy leader at RedPrairie, a Wisconsin-based logistics system provider. "A residential customer can then go to a shipper like FedEx, UPS, or the post office and use that label to process the return."[65] Product recalls can also be handled using the RMS in combination with the WMS. A WMS with lot and serial number tracking capability, for example, allows a company to bring back only units of product that have been identified with a particular defect.

Seagate Inc., a disk-drive manufacturer in California, found that its returns system became extremely complex and costly as its business grew. "The returns system had been in place for 12 years," said Jay Remley, worldwide sales director. "Sales had grown from 1 million disk-drives per quarter to 25 million per quarter. The business model was becoming much more complex." Seagate was not doing well with its existing returns system, which used a combination of online, phone, fax, and email communications for returns. It ended up using an RMS developed by returns management application provider eBoomerang, Inc. that was easily integrated with its Oracle ERP system. When a return is encountered, the application checks to confirm that the product was shipped, what warranty remains, and the ship date. If the return is validated, the system assigns the product, permits a bar code label to be printed, and provides any credit value for the customer. Next, the shipper is notified to send the product, and the method for shipping is based on predetermined rules. Once the product is delivered, the final transaction is sent to the ERP.[66]

Integrating ERP within the Supply Chain

Returning to the core idea of supply chain management—to share information, to communicate, and to collaborate on internal and external processes such that end users get what they want, when they want it, at the desired levels of quality and price—technology is enabling this to happen more effectively, quicker, and more efficiently than ever before. Here's a simple example: Shifting to shared enterprise applications will eliminate the manual rekeying of data as information passes from one organization to the next; this problem is astonishingly prevalent among many trading partners today. This sort of redundant activity is one of the more obvious areas for cost savings when considering the integration of enterprise applications. More specifically, the term **enterprise application integration** refers to the use of plans, methods, and tools designed to modernize, consolidate, integrate, and coordinate computer applications.[67]

By their very nature, ERP applications are interactive. Many add-on applications require process data and other information to be shared both internally among departments and units, and externally among the firm, its suppliers and/or its customers. This creates the need for internal integration between various applications and the ERP, and for external integration of applications connected to trading partners' ERP systems. To accomplish this in real time would greatly speed up the manufacturing and delivery processes, and reduce errors and redundant activities. Consequently, many organizations are investing in internal and external application integration software, also called **middleware**, along with other integration solutions. Several of these are discussed in the following segments.

Internal Enterprise Application Integration

As companies invest in various enterprise applications, they find they need to share information between these and other legacy applications. If not managed correctly, this can become a time-consuming and expensive process. One way to avoid problems is to purchase a suite of application modules in one package from one supplier, covering a wide range of applications such as CRM, MES, WMS, TMS, and RMS. In this way, the integration capabilities are already designed into the application suite. SAP, for instance, unveiled its single-solution NetWeaver application and integration platform sometime in 2003, and is retooling all of its software to run on this system. It is staking much of its future on this architecture, which so far has cost more than $1 billion and required 250,000 people-days of work to develop.[68] A similar approach is to purchase a set of **composite applications**, potentially at different times, which are compatible applications designed by one supplier that can be mixed and matched, using a centralized data structure. "With composite applications, you can have a yard management system that can access and use pieces of radio frequency identification, labor standard, and event management solutions," says Noah Dixon (formerly of RedPrairie), vice president for product management at Catalyst International, a Wisconsin-based enterprise application provider. "They are all launched from the same point, have the same technology, and share the same data objects."[69]

When applications are purchased from different vendors, the user normally has to tie the applications together using integration middleware. The furniture maker Haworth, discussed earlier, used eGate™ Integrator, an integration tool from SeeBeyond Technology Corp. of California, to tie together its TMS and WMS applications. The software passes customer orders, shipping plans, and shipping notifications between the two applications and Haworth's other systems. Its entire system became more directed with the use of eGate Integrator. "TMS sets up a plan and feeds it to WMS, and WMS says 'Here's what's to be done; here's your task list.' It greatly reduces the amount of time it takes a new employee to get productive," says Jim Rohrer, process manager at Haworth.[70] Oracle developed Fusion Middleware to integrate, for instance, computer-aided design (CAD) system information and the ERP. Even small manufacturers might have 10 or 15 different manufacturing systems, and every time a change is made to a bill of materials, all of the systems have to reflect the change. This middleware application is an open standards-based application specifically developed to be a rich environment for specifying products to meet the data needs of the diverse systems associated with it and all of the government and industry regulatory requirements such as Restriction of Hazardous Substances, and Waste Electrical and Electronic Equipment.[71]

Another way to achieve application integration, particularly when the applications are purchased at different times from different suppliers, is to use **web services**. Web services let applications communicate with one another without the need for custom coding, eliminating barriers caused by incompatible hardware, software, and operating systems. This allows companies to achieve internal integration when best-of-breed applications have been added to ERP systems over time. Web services can also be used to achieve integration with trading partner ERP systems.[72]

External Enterprise Application Integration

In a basic supply chain interaction, information flow is from purchase order to inventory control, to shipping, receiving, and then accounts payable. Prior to the emergence of ERP and the latest data exchange technologies, communications involved phone conversations, faxes, and emails between buyers and suppliers. Today, if a supplier has electronic data interchange (EDI) capabilities, the buyer's XML-based ERP communications can be translated by a middleware application into the supplier's X12-based EDI communication system, and vice-versa. In this way, the buyer's ERP system can generate an order and transmit to the EDI system of the supplier, and then receive order confirmations, shipping notices, and invoices from the supplier's EDI system. Middleware thus acts as an information broker in the integrated supply chain.

Canada-based Mark Anthony Group, owner of Mike's Hard Lemonade®, provides a great example of the use of externally integrated information systems. It owns no facilities—rather, it contracts out the manufacturing, bottling, and distribution processes. It has designed its own integration platform, or middleware, based on Microsoft's BizTalk®, and installed by Canadian integration technology provider Sunaptic Solutions. This gives it the ability to monitor inventory levels, distribution patterns, and product formulas, using a number of information system applications of Mark Anthony and its partners. Sunaptic took a conservative piecemeal approach to the integration project. "We use a divide-and-conquer approach," said Sunaptic president Mike Hilton. "We look for situations where we can measure the business value of the project, and see change by the end of a quarter."[73]

Use of web services also allows for systems integration between trading partners. As long as ERP systems or other applications are web service–oriented, then applications from any trading partner can connect to and interact with a company's internal system via web services. "There are different flavors of the service-oriented architecture, including Microsoft's .NET™, SAP's NetWeaver, and IBM's WebSphere®," says Tom Kozenski, product marketing leader at Wisconsin-based logistics solution provider RedPrairie. "The service-oriented architecture defines how the components are structured and provides a vehicle to communicate from application to application."[74]

Another method for integrating trading partner processes and applications is through use of a **web portal**. This is a website that provides secure access to data, applications, and services to business partners. Portals support multiple languages, platforms, and software content. "A Web-based front end will allow you to enable your suppliers with a tool to give you advance ship notification. It will allow them to drop ship for you, store inventory for you, and ship orders to your warehouses. And that Web-based front end, because it is integrated, can be part of your logistics network now," says Kozenski. "BMW uses portals, and they have upward of 3500 suppliers that are doing vendor managed inventory and exchanging forecasts, production planning, and inventory," he adds.[75]

Care must be taken, however, to avoid overreliance on automated, shared processes. A good relationship with a supplier, for example, can be put at risk if process integration causes less frequent value-enhancing, face-to-face or telephone communications. In other words, software applications cannot replace relationship-building activities. World-class supply chains have built their success on employees who communicate with trading partner employees, not just on software applications with data exchange capabilities. Frequent face-to-face communications will still be warranted from time to time with both suppliers and customers. Good integration middleware companies can help to identify these needs and provide the client with **hybrid integration solutions**, employing both automated and manual components. Selecting the middleware itself, though, can also be a problem. Most middleware is proprietary, and some process applications require specific brands of middleware (recall in the chapter's opening Process Management in Action that C&H chose SEEBURGER as an integration solution provider because of SEEBURGER's association and application compatibility with SAP). The arrival of web services and web portals, though, has allowed companies to bypass this problem to some extent.

Automating Process Management—BPM and BPR

While readers no doubt will be thinking that this entire textbook is written on the topic of process management, and wondering why there is now a section on business process management, this is a point well taken. However, the term **business process management** (BPM) has come to be recognized as automated process management and all of the software applications now available that assist firms in managing and automating business processes. BPM, by many accounts, also includes software applications that assist firms in reengineering processes as well, although here we separate the two and provide a separate section on business process reengineering.

Recall from Chapter 1 that a process is a sequence of activities designed to achieve a specific outcome. The processes of a business define what the business does; they are responsible for making the business successful; they are how the business responds to its customers' requirements. Managers should be interested in carefully designing, assessing, and improving these processes, such that customers get the best quality products and services, when they want them, at the prices they are willing to pay. Without this continuous effort to manage key business processes, the company will eventually be left in the tailwinds of businesses that are more proactive with respect to ever-changing customer requirements. BPM offers a structured, standardized, analytical approach to this effort. The objectives of BPM are to automate processes, reduce paperwork, and make information more accessible, such that employees are more productive and work is accomplished more quickly and efficiently. The underlying principles of BPM include:[76]

- Processes must be adequately mapped and documented;
- Key processes should focus on customers;
- Procedures should be documented to ensure consistency and repeatability of quality performance;

- Measurement activities should assess individual processes;
- Process management should be based on a continuous approach to optimization through problem solving; and
- Process management should be inspired by best practices to ensure that superior competitiveness is achieved.

Specifically, conducting BPM should start with the identification of all core processes and the assignment of processes to process management teams; be followed by the mapping of the processes, performance assessments, identification of performance problems, selection of improvement activities; and end with the implementation of process changes.

To many, this may sound similar to total quality management or W. Edwards Deming's Plan-Do-Check-Act Cycle (discussed in Chapter 13), and in many ways, it is. However, it must be remembered that what sets BPM apart from these approaches is the existence of software applications designed to automate processes. BPM encompasses these quality assessment and improvement elements in an information system format. BPM applications bring real-time visibility, accountability, and reporting capabilities to the management of processes. When integrated with ERP systems and other associated applications, BPM gives managers the power to see how processes are performing across the entire organization. Ultimately, though, BPM applications *will not fix broken processes.* But they will identify process strengths and weaknesses, and allow good process designs to become better.

Today, use of BPM software solutions is becoming widespread across all industries. In fact, in a survey performed by the Meta Group in 2003, 85 percent of the respondents indicated they either already had or would have a BPM implementation underway within 18 months. According to Meta Group vice president John Van Decker, the emergence of new information technologies has rekindled an interest in BPM. "Clearly, the Web-based tools are enabling organizations to get more folks involved in business process performance. Historically, planning and reporting has been an Excel-based process. Companies are trying to get away from that." Van Decker also points out that the U.S. Sarbanes-Oxley Act will require companies to be more diligent about their reporting, and web-based BPM tools will make it easier to share data among business units and to quickly identify any red flags.[77] In fact, companies most often purchase BPM software to automate and improve their regulatory compliance and customer service processes.

BPM applications enable businesses to design and optimize business processes using tools such as modeling and simulation, performance monitoring, and reporting features. In many cases, companies are opting to purchase a **BPM template** that can be used repeatedly and consistently by the firm for numerous process applications, rather than relying on an internally designed BPM solution for each specific process analysis. Additionally, implementation times can be greatly reduced, using an off-the-shelf BPM application, to as little as two or three months. Examples include automatic correspondence-processing templates used by mutual fund companies, enabling them to preconfigure letter text, integrate addresses, and print, fax, mail, or email customer correspondence with little or no employee involvement; healthcare provider templates for scheduling, financial counseling, registration, claims processing, denial management, and payment processing; mortgage lending templates for loan condition fulfillment, appraisals, broker communications, and post-closing verification; and call center applications that enable firms to obtain vital customer information quickly from a number of other applications and integrate with computer telephony, digital call recording, and the Internet.[78]

Utah-based O.C. Tanner, distributor of employee recognition products and services, selected a BPM application from Texas-based Fuego to track and maintain its highly customized employee recognition programs. It was able to reduce the time to get a new customer on-stream from 12 days to 7, as well as make the entire process completely visible. Blue Rhino, distributor of bar-be-que propane tanks headquartered in North Carolina, sought to implement formalized and automated control of its financial transactions. It selected e-Work™ from Maryland-based software provider Metastorm and achieved the level of control it was looking for. Additionally, it was able to reduce the time required during audits.[79] Canadian Cambrian Credit Union installed HandySoft's BizFlow® BPM software in a few months in 2005 to automate its loan processes. During this time, it mapped each of the actual processes for its eight different loan types. This involved determining where information flowed as loans went from initiation through processing and then to closing. BizFlow keeps the loan process moving by alerting the next person in the process that a new loan needs attention. The software also allows underwriters and other employees to add comments, supporting documents, and other materials as needed. The credit union can now process 800 loans per month, compared to 650 prior to BizFlow implementation. "We find this process helps things move much more efficiently," says Rick Male, Cambrian's vice president of retail credit. "We're the fastest growing credit union in Manitoba."[80]

Most recently, companies have been looking to BPM applications as a means for encouraging the sharing of ERP system information. Customers, trading partners, and employees in geographically dispersed units are demanding real-time access to key processes of the organization. BPM solutions that can integrate with ERP systems and other enterprise applications and allow this type of access to key process information create a much more agile organization—one that can react quickly to changes in the firm's external and internal environments. CEOs and other managers can use BPM to view and manipulate hundreds of predefined reports in real time, or create new ones. Michael Beckley, vice president of product strategy at Virginia-based Appian Corp., a provider of BPM applications, says, "BPM is emerging because it fills a need, not because we're so clever to have thought of it. It fills the critical need to distribute and orchestrate work across previously incompatible applications, databases, infrastructures, organizations, countries … all those borders and barriers are breaking down because we can now build and share processes from the underlying technology. We're seeing more enterprise BPM deals, which are typically larger than departmental workflow deployments."[81] GAF Materials, a New Jersey-based roofing and building materials manufacturer, uses its enterprise-wide BPM tool to allow supply chain, sales, distribution, and finance departments to work from the same forecast. "Once we've determined our sales forecast, the BPM solution can give us all the SCM information required to meet that forecast, including capacity, raw materials, expenses, costs to deliver, and budgeting needs. All of it is done with one BPM solution. Our company has 30 sites, and every one of them is using the same numbers. All the SCM calculations roll up into the financial application of BPM to guide our P and L's," says Rick Stevenson, director of supply chain planning and business intelligence.[82] The Global Perspective feature describes Sumitomo Mitsui Banking Corp.'s use of BPM.

Business Process Reengineering

Business process reengineering (BPR) has followed a boom/bust/reborn again life cycle. In the early 1990s, Hammer and Champy's very popular book, *Reengineering the Corporation: A Manifesto for Business Revolution,* along with many statements from notable business experts like Peter Drucker along the lines of "reengineering is new and

Global Perspective

Sumitomo Mitsui's BPM Initiative

Known for its global reach, Sumitomo Mitsui Banking Corp. has branches across the United States, Asia, and Europe. Commercial customers often conduct business with the bank through multiple locations. However, disparate operating systems often created redundant and erroneous customer data. Each region of Sumitomo's operations managed its own processing systems and customer databases. In addition to processing redundant data, these disparate, manual systems exposed the bank to customer identification errors and impeded customer service, according to Rise Zaiser, vice president of business applications.

For example, during the bank's customer intake process, service executives manually completed documents and handled transactions. Besides being subject to errors, the process was not standardized on a global level. "Every application within each country had its own system to identify each customer," explains Zaiser. "If a customer deals with multiple branches, they could end up with a unique code within each location." A lack of standardization also made compliance challenging.

Sumitomo began a search in January 2003 for an automated, web-based business process management (BPM) solution that could integrate with its existing Oracle database platform, centralize customer data, and electronically deliver it to account officers during transactions. "Our ideal solution would capture our customer information, create a unique user code and automate the fact-checking process," Zaiser says.

In March 2003, Sumitomo bought Maryland-based Metastorm's e-Work™ BPM solution. E-Work interfaces with Sumitomo's multiple processing systems and an enterprise customer data warehouse that consolidates all customer information into a single repository. The solution is accessible via Sumitomo's corporate intranet. As an account officer logs onto the system with a secure password, e-Work moves a customer's application through various stages, including verification, customer identification program requirements, and Patriot Act certification requirements. Once the data and regulatory requirements are satisfied, the customer's information is added to the bank's Oracle database with a unique customer ID number.

Since account officers in the international banking division began using the application in October 2003, the bank's manual input operations have decreased, improving efficiency, and Patriot Act screenings became automated, Zaiser reports. "The solution allows us to increase our ability to comply with regulatory requirements and improve our audit and tracking of compliance," Zaiser explains. "That has helped us save a lot of capital."

In 2005, Sumitomo updated the new customer information process and began to apply the BPM solution to other processes, including travel expense reimbursement and the new supplier process. Zaiser says Sumitomo may use e-Work to manage its change management processes in the future. "This would play a role with Sarbanes-Oxley compliance," she explains. It can track changes, how long ago they happened and keep us abreast of any remediations to accounts."

Source: Amato-McCoy, D., "Bringing It All Together," *Bank Systems & Technology*, V. 42, No. 7, 2005, p. 38. Used with permission.

it has to be done," created a fervor at the time among managers seeking another panacea for making businesses successful.[83] Unfortunately like so many other management fads, most of the BPR efforts at the time failed to live up to the hype and expectations, causing many to claim by the later 1990s that reengineering was over.[84] However, other business leaders recognized that the real value behind reengineering—the fundamental rethinking and redesign of business processes to improve efficiency and effectiveness—had significant merit. They realized that if used correctly (instead of as an excuse for downsizing), it required business employees to think creatively and realistically about how to create greater value for customers through process change.

BPR, like its companion BPM, uses simple data-driven methodologies and software applications to provide cost-effective, optimal process reengineering solutions. BPR seeks to create a systematic, automated approach to change management through assessments of current processes, design of better processes using modeling techniques, implementation of the new processes, and continuing performance assessments. Development of software applications for BPR is ongoing, and in some cases products are referred to by other names such as business process improvement, business process redesign, and business process reinvention (perhaps the word "reengineering" still has a negative connotation from the 1990s).

Due to rapidly escalating costs in the U.S. healthcare industry, its extensive use of BPR has been widely documented, and has been shown to increase profitability, reduce patient mortality, and improve patient satisfaction. Further, a study of U.S. healthcare information system experts found BPR to be one of the highest priority research topics.[85] The Memorial Hermann Healthcare System in Texas, for example, utilized an IT-enabled BPR approach to find a more efficient laboratory courier service to meet the needs of its newly designed laboratory system, while maintaining or improving the levels of service. A set-partitioning traveling salesman model was used to determine the most efficient courier routes meeting the desired service requirements and an integer-programming model was used to staff the courier routes to minimize the number of couriers needed. The new courier service was projected to save $117,000 annually while providing a higher level of delivery service.[86]

SUMMARY

This chapter has presented a detailed discussion of an extremely important topic regarding a firm's competitiveness and that of its trading partners—namely information flow management. Not only must firms be aware of the types of information the firm requires and is continuously subjected to (through an information audit), but the firm must also decide how best to manage this information, both inside the firm and with its trading partners. Systems like MRP, MRP II, and ERP have played key roles in managing enterprise information, along with the many system add-ons that now accompany most enterprise applications. Advances in information system technologies have allowed process management to become automated, improving productivity and customer service while reducing costs. A number of automated applications have been developed as a result, including reengineering applications.

KEY TERMS

application add-ons, 327

best-of-breed systems, 323

BPM template, 345

business process management, 344

business process reengineering, 346

composite applications, 342

corporate information flow, 316

enterprise application integration, 342

enterprise commerce management, 323

enterprise resource planning, 320

environmental information flow, 316

ERP II, 323

hybrid integration solutions, 344

information audit, 317

information velocity, 316

information volatility, 317

intellectual asset, 316

internal information flow, 316

legacy systems, 322

logistics execution suites, 333

logistics management modules, 333

manufacturing execution system, 332

manufacturing resource planning, 320

material requirements planning, 320

middleware, 342

on-demand CRM services, 329

profit management automation, 329

returns management systems, 333

reverse logistics, 339

spend management, 331

stabilize phase, 326

synergize phase, 326

synthesize phase, 326

transportation management systems, 333

warehouse management systems, 333

web portal, 343

web services, 343

yard management systems, 333

DISCUSSION QUESTIONS

1. Explain why information is considered an intellectual asset.

2. What are the three key informational flows in most organizations?

3. Describe the key information flows that might occur at an online retailer.

4. Define information velocity and describe its importance to and impact on the firm.

5. Define information volatility and describe its importance to and impact on the firm.

6. What is information flow mapping used for, and what role do information audits play in flow mapping?

7. Design an information flow map for a specific type of firm other than the one shown in Figure 9.1.

8. What is ERP?

9. Describe the historical developments leading up to today's ERP systems.

10. What is ERP II?

11. How much does an ERP system cost?

12. Why have ERP implementations failed so often in the past?

13. Why are ERP systems so expensive?

14. What are the benefits of an ERP system?

15. Describe the three post-implementation phases for ERP system users.

16. What are ERP system application add-ons, and which ones are the most popular?

17. What are CRM and SRM applications used for, and how do they benefit the organization?

18. How important is RFID in WMS and TMS applications?

19. What do logistics management systems consist of, and why are they considered important to firms that use them?

20. Would it be a good idea to combine a TMS and a WMS? Why?

21. What is an RMS used for?

22. What does enterprise application integration refer to, and how is this accomplished?

23. How is internal application integration accomplished?

24. How is external application integration typically accomplished?

25. What is business process management?

26. How is BPM accomplished?

27. Can BPM solutions be integrated with ERP?

28. What is business process reengineering?

INTERNET QUESTIONS

1. Go to Oracle's and SAP's websites and look at the current ERP applications offered by these companies. What is available?

2. Go to one of the many ERP add-on application providers' websites and report on its applications.

3. What are the current applications available for BPR, and who are the suppliers?

 INFOTRAC QUESTION

Access http://www.infotrac-thomsonlearning.com to answer the following question:

1. Use InfoTrac to find current articles discussing the following topics. Use these as topics for a term paper.

a. Information flow mapping

b. Dell Inc.'s supply chain

c. The history of MRP

d. Enterprise commerce management and ERP II

e. Warehouse management systems

f. Business process reengineering

REFERENCES

Krovi, R., A. Chandra, and B. Rajagopalan, "Information Flow Parameters for Managing Organizational Processes," *Communications of the ACM,* V. 46, No. 2, 2003, pp. 77–82.

Lawrence, F., D. Jennings, and B. Reynolds (2005), *ERP in Distribution,* South-Western, Mason, OH.

Raturi, A., and J. Evans (2005), *Principles of Operations Management,* South-Western, Mason, OH.

Meredith, J., and S. Shafer (1999), *Operations Management for MBAs,* John Wiley & Sons, New York, NY.

ENDNOTES

1. Titus, S. and J. Bröchner, "Managing Information Flow in Construction Supply Chains," *Construction Innovation,* V. 5, 2005, pp. 71–82.

2. Unknown author; found on *Computer Sayings,* at http://www.wilk4.com/humor/humorm223.html.

3. Childerhouse, P., R. Hermiz, R. Mason-Jones, A. Popp, and D. Towill, "Information Flow in Automotive Supply Chains—Identifying and Learning to Overcome Barriers to Change," *Industrial Management & Data Systems,* V. 103, No. 7, 2003, pp. 491–502.

4. Lewis, I. and A. Talayevsky, "Improving the Interorganizational Supply Chain Through Optimization of Information Flows," *Journal of Enterprise Information,* V. 17, No. 3, 2004, pp. 229–238.

5. Lejeune, A. and T. Roehl, "Hard and Soft Ways to Create Value from Information Flows: Lessons from the Canadian Financial Services Industry," *Canadian Journal of Administrative Sciences,* V. 20, No. 1, 2003, pp. 35–53.

6. Krovi, R., A. Chandra, and B. Rajagopalan, "Information Flow Parameters for Managing Organizational Processes," *Communications of the ACM,* V. 46, No. 2, 2003, pp. 77–82.

7. See note 6 above.

8. Based in part on Hibberd, B. and A. Evatt, "Mapping Information Flows: A Practical Guide," *Information Management Journal,* V. 38, No. 1, 2004, p. 58.

9. See note 1 above.

10. http://www.computerworld.com/news/1999/story/0,11280,34738,00.html.

11. Orlicky, J., "Net Change Material Requirements Planning," *IBM System Journal,* V. 1, 1973, http://www.ibm.com. The authors are most appreciative of discussions held with Mr. Gene Thomas regarding the history of MRP and his role in its development.

12. http://www.evolvingexcellence.com/MRP, On The Rocks, December 14, 2005; Waddell, B., "MRP R.I.P.," http://www.bestmanufacturingpractices.com.

13. See, for example, Plossl, G. and O. Wight, *Production and Inventory Control: Principles and Techniques,* Englewood Cliffs, NJ: Prentice-Hall, 1967; Orlicky, J., *Material Requirements Planning: The New Way of Life in Production and Inventory Management,* New York, NY: McGraw-Hill, 1975; and Wight, O., *The Executive's Guide to Successful MRPII,* New York, NY: John Wiley & Sons, 1982.

14. Weston, R., "MRP Veteran Mapics Going Strong," http://news.com.com/MRP, January 2, 2002.

15. Wight, O., *Manufacturing Resource Planning: MRP II: Unlocking America's Productivity Potential,* Boston, MA: CBI Publishing Co., 1981.

16. Hopp, W. and M. Spearman, "To Pull or Not to Pull: What Is the Question?" *Manufacturing & Service Operations Management,* V. 6, No. 2, 2004, pp. 133–148.

17. http://www.sap.com/company/history.epx.

18. "SAP Offers Surprisingly Strong Outlook," January 25, 2006, and "Oracle Details Postmerger Plans," January 18, 2006, on *ZDNet News,* http://www.news.zdnet.com.

19. Mello, A., "Battle of the Labels: ERP II vs. ECM," http://www.techupdate.zdnet.com/techupdate/stories/main, September 13, 2001.

20. "Enterprise Resource Planning," *Darwin Magazine Executive Guides,* http://www.darwinmag.com/technology/enterprise/erp/index/htm.

21. http://www.health-infosys-dir.com/how_to_select_an_erp_system.htm.

22. Doran, J. and C. Walsh, "The Effect of Enterprise Resource Planning (ERP) Systems on Accounting Practices in Companies in Ireland," *The Irish Accounting Review,* V. 11, No. 2, 2004, pp. 17–34.

23. See note 20 above.

24. Stapleton, G. and C. Rezak, "Change Management Underpins a Successful ERP Implementation at Marathon Oil," *Journal of Organizational Excellence,* V. 23, No. 4, 2004, pp. 15–22.

25. Koch, C., "Hershey's Bittersweet Lesson," *CIO Magazine,* November 15, 2002, http://www.cio.com.

26. Wheatley, M., "ERP Training Stinks," *CIO Magazine,* June 1, 2000, http://www.cio.com.

27. Hawking, P., A. Stein, and S. Foster, "Revisiting ERP Systems: Benefit Realization," *Proceedings of the 37th Hawaii International Conference on System Sciences,* 2004, pp. 1–8.

28. See note 20 above.

29. See note 27 above.

30. See note 20 above.

31. See note 27 above.

32. Wang, B. and F. Nah, "ERP + E-Business = A New Vision of Enterprise System," in Dasgupta, S., ed., *Managing Internet Technologies in Organizations: Challenges and Opportunities,* Hershey, PA: Idea Group Publishing, 2001.

33. See note 24 above.

34. Hayes, F., "The 85 Percent Solution," *Computerworld,* V. 35, No. 8, 2001, p. 74.

35. See note 32 above.

36. Radding, A., "ERP—More than an Application," *InformationWeek,* April 5, 1999, p. 1A.

37. See note 22 above.

38. Robb, D., "Marketing Gets with the Program," *Computerworld,* V. 38, No. 21, 2004, pp. 21–22.

39. "USA Industry: ERP Shows Few Signs of Slowing Down," *EIU ViewsWire,* February 18, 2003.

40. "Industry Models for Enterprise, Supply Chain Quicken Start-ups, If No Wheels Are Reinvented," *Manufacturing Business Technology,* V. 23, No. 8, 2005, pp. 37–38.

41. Waxer, C., "The Fight Over CRM," *Chief Executive,* January/February 2006, pp. 24–27.

42. Overby, S., "The Truth about On-Demand CRM," *CIO,* V. 19, No. 7, 2006, p. 1.

43. Beasty, C., "Secret of My Success," *Customer Relationship Management,* V. 9, No. 6, 2005, p. 58.

44. "Spotlight—CRM: Barclays Banks on CRM Software," *European Banker,* May 2006, p. 13.

45. See note 41 above.

46. Fulcher, J., "What's in a Name?" *Manufacturing Business Technology,* V. 23, No. 11, 2005, pp. 22–25.

47. See note 46 above.

48. Choy, K., W. Lee, and V. Lo, "An Enterprise Collaborative Management System—A Case Study of Supplier Relationship Management," *Journal of Enterprise Information,* V. 17, No. 3, 2004, pp. 191–204.

49. Fulcher, J., "Global Execution," *Manufacturing Business Technology,* V. 24, No. 3, 2006, p. 38.

50. Spathis, C. and S. Constatinides, "Enterprise Resource Planning Systems' Impact on Accounting Processes," *Business Process Management,* V. 10, No. 2, 2004, pp. 234–241.

51. Cross, M., "Decision Support Systems," *CMA Management,* V. 75, No. 9, 2002, pp. 48–49.

52. Ruderman, G., "Relieve the Burden of Regulatory Compliance," *MSI,* V. 22, No. 6, 2004, pp. 34–37.

53. Bartholomew, D., "SAP Discovers the Plant Floor," *Industry Week,* V. 253, No. 7, 2004, p. 63.

54. See note 49 above.

55. Russell, R., "Manufacturing Execution Systems: Moving to the Next Level," *Pharmaceutical Technology,* V. 28, No. 1, 2004, pp. 38–43.

56. Kerr, J., "3 Key Software Trends," *Logistics Management,* V. 43, No. 3, 2004, pp. 53–55.

57. Zuckerman, A., "What's Working (and What Isn't) in Integrated Supply Chain Technology," *World Trade,* V. 18, No. 6, 2005, pp. 50–54.

58. See note 57 above.

59. Ciuba, G., "Seeking Security in the Supply Chain," *Logistics Today,* V. 45, No. 9, 2004, pp. 42–44.

60. Anthes, G., "Refurnishing the Supply Chain," *Computerworld,* V. 38, No. 23, 2004, pp. 39–40.

61. See note 60 above.

62. Witt, C., "LES Is More (Important)," *Material Handling Management,* V. 59, No. 4, 2004, pp. 28–32.

63. Sullivan, L., "Hey, Wal-Mart, a New Case of Pampers Is on the Way," *InformationWeek,* January 23, 2006, p. 28.

64. Coia, A., "Smoothing Reverse Flow," *Frontline Solutions,* V. 6, No. 5, 2005, pp. 34–36.

65. Trebilcock, B., "Managing Returns with WMS," *Modern Materials Handling,* V. 59, No. 10, 2004, pp. 33–36.

66. See note 64 above.

67. Mendoza, L., M. Perez, and A. Griman, "Critical Success Factors for Managing Systems Integration," *Information Systems Management,* V. 23, No. 2, 2006, pp. 56–75.

68. Bacheldor, B., "Billion-Dollar Bet," *InformationWeek,* June 28, 2004, pp. 34–39.

69. Kevan, T., "Execution Software's Virtual Company," *Frontline Solutions,* V. 6, No. 6, 2005, pp. 26–29.

70. See note 60 above.

71. "Production Engineering—Production Software: The Hub of the Matter," *The Engineer,* January 30, 2006, pp. 36–38.

72. See note 69 above.

73. Stoller, J., "Navigating the Inter-Application Zone," *CMA Management,* V. 78, No. 7, 2004, pp. 32–35.

74. See note 69 above.

75. See note 69 above.

76. Lee, R. and B. Dale, "Business Process Management: A Review and Evaluation," *Business Process Management Journal,* V. 4, No. 3, 1998, pp. 214–223.

77. Surmacz, J., "BPM May Push Excel Aside," *Darwin Magazine,* September 17, 2003, http://www.darwinmag.com.

78. Puccinelli, R., "BPM Templates," *KM World,* V. 14, No. 1, 2005, pp. S4–S5.

79. Lamont, J., "BPM: From the User's Perspective," *KM World,* V. 15, No. 1, 2006, pp. 14–15.

80. Britt, P., "How to Get There from Here," *Bank Systems & Technology,* V. 42, No. 12, 2005, p. 39.

81. Moore, A., "Who's on First?" *KM World,* V. 15, No. 1, 2006, pp. S2–S3.

82. Leahy, T., "Solutions for Supply Chain Woes," *Business Finance,* V. 11, No. 9, 2005, pp. 37–39.

83. See, for example, Burgess, R., "Avoiding Supply Chain Management Failure: Lessons from Business Process Reengineering," *The International Journal of Logistics Management,* V. 9,

No. 1, 1998, pp. 15–23; Hammer, M. and J. Champy, *Reengineering the Corporation: A Manifesto for Business Revolution,* New York, NY: Harper Business, 1993; and Morris, D. and J. Brandon, *Re-engineering Your Business,* New York, NY: McGraw-Hill, 1993.

84. See, for example, Davenport, T., "Why Reengineering Failed: The Fad That Forgot People," *Fast Company,* V. 1, No. 1, 1996.

85. Jansen-Vullers, M. and H. Reijers, "Business Process Redesign in Healthcare: Towards Structured Approach," *INFOR,* V. 43, No. 4, 2005, pp. 321–339.

86. Revere, L., "Re-engineering Proves Effective for Reducing Courier Costs," *Business Process Management Journal,* V. 10, No. 4, 2004, pp. 400–408.

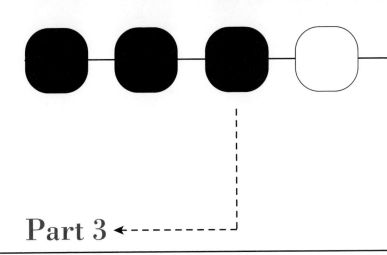

Part 3

Lean Production Systems

Chapter 10:

OPERATING WITH LEAN

"Lean is often equated with the elimination of waste. But in its strict sense, lean is really about gaining a critical understanding of what the customer values—and then tailoring everything in the process to produce, deliver, and service what that customer wants. Without this understanding, you may become very efficient at creating things that are unwanted or unnecessary."[1]

"The power and magic of lean is to continually discover the opportunities existing all around you."[2]

Learning Objectives

After completing this chapter, you should be able to:

- Understand the history of lean production.
- Define the key principles of lean thinking.
- Describe the operational goals of lean thinking.
- Identify the seven forms of waste found in an organization.
- Differentiate between traditional manufacturing and lean manufacturing.
- Understand the characteristics of lean supply chains.
- Use the five value stream mapping tools.

Chapter Outline

Process Management in Action   *Lean Thinking a Winner*

Jacksonville (Florida)-based Medtronic Xomed's manufacturing operations have been deemed one of the best in the nation. *Industry Week* declared Xomed one of the nation's ten best manufacturing operations in its October (2002) issue. Xomed's Southside facilities employ 550—299 of those in manufacturing. Xomed is a developer, manufacturer, and marketer of surgical products for ear, nose, and throat specialists. It joined Medtronic, a leading technology company, in 1999. "These people [in manufacturing] don't get a whole lot of recognition, so this can be very rewarding," said David Drickhamer, who headed the award program for the magazine.

The award recognizes the best-performing plants of North America, Canada, and Mexico. Companies submit the initial information covering 100 performance areas, and then a representative of the publication visits to verify the information. Xomed was selected by the trade publication's staff and outside experts from more than 300 companies that were nominated. Other winners include Boeing's C-17 aircraft production plant in Long Beach, California, and three Collins & Aikman automotive interior parts plants, including one in Americus, Georgia.

Xomed decided to start a massive reorganization to improve its processes. The company said there were no overwhelming problems but a desire to evolve. Since the plan began, the company has made significant gains, such as reducing its production lead time from 253 days to 129 days. It has also significantly freed floor space in the plant and reduced inventory while retaining all jobs.

The company used a model based on Toyota's production system to reform business practices. The premise is that at every step, employees should evaluate whether that decision will create value for the customer. Eliminating decisions that do not bring value reduces waste and improves the flow of the company. So, a plant that used to be rigid has become a flexible operation that thrives under change.

Instead of anticipating what the customer wants and creating a large batch of a product at once, the company now responds to a customer's order, reducing excess inventory, said Jerry Bussell, vice president of global operations for Xomed. It's this "lean thinking" that eliminates waste and drives decisions. "Lean is the way I think American businesses are going to stay competitive; lean is the way you nibble away at costs," said City Councilman Lad Daniels, who is also the president of First Coast Manufacturers Association.

The company created 48 value (stream) maps that document the flow from supplier to production to delivery of products to the doctors, hospitals, and surgery centers. "It's been very empowering," Bussell said. "Traditionally, decisions were made because we always made the product this way ... now, we don't necessarily follow the normal course but think about it and do it if it makes sense." All manufacturing employees were trained in the process so they would be able to step back and think about the overall impact of their decisions. The energy instilled by the program was bolstered by the award, Bussell said.

Inside Xomed, the lean concept is reinforced. The "lean walkway," which connects the plant's distribution center to the main manufacturing building, has inspirational terms relating to lean thinking on each of the pillars and a related glossary at each end of the walkway. Based on this thinking, the company also has reduced the cost of a shipped product, including costs of purchased materials, by 38 percent, according to the company. And on-time delivery, based on a customer's requested dates, is now at 96 percent.

Continued

Introduction

Lean production is arguably the leading way today, to reduce waste. Lean production evolved from the adoption of just-in-time (JIT), which primarily refers to the management of materials, in the 1970s and took hold in the early 1990s. Some refer to lean production as the **Toyota Production System**, world-class manufacturing, big JIT, or JIT/Quality Control, although others use the terms lean production and JIT interchangeably.

The Toyota Production System (TPS), developed in the 1950s by Toyota and later implemented in the United States, first adopted JIT principles, which later evolved into lean thinking—a broader approach to process improvement. The TPS and its variations are distinguished by a focus on continuous learning and keeping things simple. The idea is to make the best use of an organization's time, assets, and people in all processes in order to optimize productivity. Thus, lean principles can be applied to any setting, including services as well as manufacturing. The ultimate goal is to make lean thinking pervasive throughout the supply chain. As Norman Bedeck, consultant and author of several books on lean manufacturing, said, "Lean is an unending journey to be the most innovative, most effective and efficient organization."[3] The opening Process Management in Action feature on Medtronic Xomed, a U.S. manufacturer of surgical products for ear, nose, and throat specialists, provides an illustration of how one company took that journey.

This chapter begins with the history and principles of lean thinking, including a short discussion of the differences between lean and traditional production methods. The elements of a lean production system are then described. The application of lean principles to the supply chain follows, and the chapter concludes with a discussion of value mapping tools.

A History of Lean Production

Lean principles were developed over a period of 90 years and are based on the Toyota Production System.[4] Sakichi Toyoda, an inventor of the power loom in the early 1900s and owner of the Toyoda Automatic Loom Works, founded the Toyoda Group, which built and sold automobiles, beginning in 1937, along with his son Kiichiro. During this time Ford Motor Company and General Motors were the two largest automobile manufacturers in Japan, making and selling more than 90 percent of all cars there. Kiichiro came to the United States to study Ford's production system with the intent of adapting it to smaller production quantities. He learned, for instance, that Henry Ford had developed the process to build a car from ore excavation to product completion in four days. Based on his findings, Kiichiro developed a production process that came to be known as just-in-time by the Toyoda Group. Just-in-time focused on the delivery of small quantities of parts just before they were needed for production. Strong ties were built with parts suppliers who were located nearby and could make frequent deliveries. As a result, lower inventories were kept on hand, reducing Toyoda's holding costs.

Sakichi Toyoda's nephew, Eiji Toyoda, had worked for the Toyoda Automatic Loom Works and also moved over to the auto manufacturing company as managing director. He spent some time in the United States and studied U.S. manufacturing methods. As a result, he implemented Ford Motor Company's suggestion box system, a foundation of the continuous improvement philosophy discussed in Chapter 13. Based on Eiji's recommendations the Toyoda Group was renamed, first to The Toyota Company in 1957 and then to Toyota Motor Corporation in 1983. After Eiji traveled to the United States again in 1986, he realized that Toyota needed a production system of a higher caliber than that used by the U.S. automakers. As a result, he challenged his workforce to be more creative, resourceful, and productive.

Tai'ichi Ohno, a Toyota engineer who was a major contributor to the creation of the Toyota Production System and later considered the Father of the Kanban System, was also inspired by Henry Ford, as well as Frank and Lilleth Galbraith and Frederick Taylor, all Americans. The Galbraiths and Frederick Taylor both studied time and motion in a manufacturing setting to reduce both (also termed **scientific management**). Ohno also incorporated ideas from observing U.S. supermarkets, which successfully operated with a continuous, as-needed flow of product to their store shelves. Working at Toyoda Automatic Loom Works, he used the concepts developed by Kiichiro Toyoda as a base and then created methods that could be used to manufacture the needed parts just when needed for final assembly. Ohno then worked for Toyoda's auto assembly plants, first as an assembly manager in the 1940s and eventually as vice president in 1975. During his early years, Toyota was frequently on the verge of bankruptcy and could not afford to invest heavily in large inventories or new equipment. Ohno discovered inexpensive ways to improve the company by reducing waste and dependency on inventory.

Shigeo Shingo was also a contributor to the Toyota Production System, becoming an expert in productivity improvement, statistical process control, and setup time reduction through his work for several manufacturers in the 1940s and 1950s, and later as a consultant to Toyota and others.

With the advent of the oil crisis in the 1970s, Americans started buying imported Japanese cars with better fuel efficiencies. By 1979, Japanese automakers had cornered approximately 25 percent of the U.S. market. In response, U.S. automakers retooled their factories to build smaller cars. At the same time, they adopted the Toyota Production System. Toyota's lean thinking framework for process improvement has since been adopted by companies around the world and is discussed in more detail next.

Lean Thinking Principles

Businesses in general expect to maximize their competitiveness and profitability by first distinguishing or differentiating themselves from the competition to draw in customers. As a result, revenue is generated primarily through sales. However, firms must also work at minimizing the physical costs of production, distribution, and storage to increase their profits. To reduce costs, an organization has to cut out as much waste—or *muda* as it's known in Japan—as possible while retaining the value-added steps that attract customers. (Value, as described in earlier chapters, is added to products and services when efforts are taken or resources are used to make someone better off than before.)

Adapted from the Toyota Production System, the phrase **lean thinking** was created in the early 1990s to describe the idea of connecting each value-added step in a process, in the best sequence and most effective way possible without interruption, at a point in time when another entity places an order somewhere downstream. That entity might be the customer or another point in the production system. The word *lean* is used because organizations are looking for ways to be more productive by doing more, but with less equipment, human effort, time, and space, while at the same time satisfying customers. Lean thinking thus has roots in the continuous improvement programs adopted by organizations, as discussed in Chapter 13. As a result, lean thinkers argue customers should be more satisfied with lean companies than with competitors that do not practice lean, because they recognize the value in the lean companies' products and services, and thus will spend their money with them.

The operational goals of lean thinking are to improve quality, minimize lead time by speeding up delivery from the time an order is placed until it is delivered, and reduce inventory levels. To accomplish these goals, lean thinkers start with an extensive analysis of their processes. These companies also actively engage the workforce in their lean processes. For example, rather than inspecting for quality, they rely on workers to spot problems and solve them as they occur. Although still in the early stages of implementation, leading-edge organizations are extending lean thinking beyond their immediate organizations to suppliers and customers in the supply chain. For instance, they develop long-term relationships with their suppliers to jointly eliminate waste.

However, to begin the process of lean thinking, companies must first understand the various forms of waste that can occur. Waste is possible in three major areas of the value stream of a product or product family: new product development, which includes concept development through detailed design and engineering to production launch; physical transformation, which covers the conversion of raw materials into a finished product; and customer delivery, which includes order taking through detailed scheduling to delivery and into the hands of the customer.[5] Waste can also be broken down into seven categories, as discussed next.

Seven Forms of Waste

As mentioned previously, the Japanese refer to waste as **muda**, or anything that does not add value to an item or a process. Tai'ichi Ohno, whose contributions to the lean movement have already been discussed, identified seven forms of waste in manufacturing.[6]

Overproduction

Essentially, **overproduction** occurs when companies are building products or creating services they are not selling. In other words, these organizations are producing more products than demanded, or sooner or faster than needed, resulting in excess inventory. For example, Ford Motor Company found itself with high inventories of large sport utility vehicles (SUVs) and full-sized vans in 2006 when gas prices went above $3.00 a gallon.[7] Overproduction can also happen in a restaurant when it prepares too many dinner salads in anticipation of more customer orders than actually materialize on a particular day.

Overproduction results when companies rely on inaccurate forecasts, are overly optimistic in their forecasts, or use the forecast to motivate the sales force. California-based computer manufacturer Apple, Inc. had to write off $388 million in inventory in the second quarter of 1996 because it over-forecasted the demand for its computers.[8] Also, companies are reluctant to let workers and machines sit idle. Ideally, only the amount needed to meet demand should be produced. Not only is there the cost of production, but firms must also consider money that has been invested in warehouses or storage areas to stock unneeded product, additional workers and machines to make products no one wants, additional parts and materials, and interest payments on loans to support production.

Delays Between Processing Steps

Delays occur when workers must wait for material that has not been delivered, when a worker stands at a machine waiting for a part to be processed, or a worker is waiting while a machine is being repaired. These delays can be observed in cafeteria-style restaurants, where workers can be found waiting for the kitchen to prepare more food items before they can refill the line. Customers become dissatisfied as they wait for their favorite food or stand impatiently until the person in front of them moves forward. Delays also occur when defective parts need to be reworked, or a production line stoppage occurs at a manufacturing facility. These types of delays extend the lead time to produce and deliver products, which result in late deliveries and, most likely, customer complaints. Machines and workers also might not be used productively, resulting in money spent needlessly on wages and the fixed costs of lighting, rent, heating or cooling, and insurance.

Unnecessary Transportation of Products, Parts, or Supplies

Anything that needs to be moved on the shop floor incurs a cost, such as employee wages or machine costs. This is often the result of a poorly designed layout, the use of batch production, or even the use of exceptionally large equipment. If batch production is used, for example, these large batches must be moved from process to process. To minimize transportation, lean companies place everything, including the parts necessary for production, indirect materials such as lubricants, and tools, close at hand or adjacent to the work area. Offices are similarly organized, where an employee's workstation consists of all the tools necessary, including computer, telephone, and work-related supplies. Cellular or group technology manufacturing, one of the elements of lean production, make this type of organization possible and will be discussed later in the chapter.

Overprocessing

Overprocessing in manufacturing occurs when parts are processed on equipment that operates too fast or too slow, or even too accurately to meet the customer's definition of value. Too much accuracy might not seem possible, but this form of waste frequently occurs because a company places engineering goals above customer needs. As a result, parts or tooling are "overengineered" to meet all situations and design costs increase. In certain instances, such as the production of airplanes where safety is a concern, overprocessing is justified. However, for many products, overprocessing simply adds cost to the product and doesn't measurably increase safety or generate additional revenue through higher prices, because the customer sees no extra value.

In services, overprocessing as defined by Bill Kastle, author of *What Is Lean Six Sigma?*, is "doing more work than is absolutely necessary to satisfy or delight customers."[9] Kastle suggests overprocessing occurs for two reasons. First, organizations often don't understand the wants of the customer. For example, mortgage lenders may provide return envelopes for their customers, which add value for some but is waste for those who have set up an automatic transfer of funds for their monthly payment from their checking account. Second, there may be too much redundancy within a process, such as the number of approvals required.

Overstocked Inventories

Generally this situation occurs because a firm carries too much unnecessary inventory in the form of raw materials, parts, work-in-process, and finished goods. This is often the case when manufacturers use a material requirements planning (MRP) or manufacturing resource planning (MRP II) system, which pushes production out the door without considering actual demand from the downstream customers (see Chapters 6 and 9 for good discussions of MRP). The mindset is that "we will make extra, just in case." Overstocking also occurs due to the bullwhip effect discussed in other chapters, in which organizations within the supply chain overreact to unexpected demand fluctuations, and buy or make more than immediately necessary. These miscues typically occur because companies are not in direct contact with the consumer and do not receive real-time sales data from the retailer. Unfortunately, too much stock hides a multitude of problems, and has an **opportunity cost** attached to it. In other words, the funds could have been spent elsewhere and generated a higher return.

While it might not seem as intuitive, overstocking also occurs in service organizations. Too much "inventory" comes in the form of too many callers on hold, too much work piling up in the office worker's in-box, people standing in line at a restaurant or bank, or unread email requests, to name a few.

Needless Movements by Employees

Unnecessary reaching or twisting often results in ergonomic injuries due to excessive straining when processing or checking a part, and can adversely affect quality. However, it might be surprising to learn that another form of waste is simply walking. For example, a manufacturing employee is not productive when he or she must walk to the tool room to retrieve components or parts. An administrative assistant is also unproductive when he or she has to walk to another part of the building to make photocopies. An analyst loses productivity as he or she gathers expense data from other employees. As mentioned earlier, lean companies keep parts and materials close to the employee by improving layouts and the replenishment of parts. They are also implementing ERP systems (as discussed Chapter 9), which integrate several databases and improve employee productivity.

Production of Defective Parts

When products or services are made that do not meet the given design specifications, any mistakes must be fixed. Correcting problems uses additional employee time and materials to uncover and fix the source of the problem, and may result in lost customers or, even worse, lawsuits. As the batch size increases in manufacturing, for example, the cost of producing defective parts grows because problems generally go unnoticed until the end of the batch run, resulting in more defective parts having to be reworked or scrapped. The cost of quality problems are even higher if the defect is not caught until the product or service reaches the customer. A pharmacy technician noticed while restocking shelves, for example, that one box of 15-cc bottles of Syrup of Ipecac received from the manufacturer had a much brighter color than the others. Fortunately, he immediately contacted the Food and Drug Administration (FDA) and an investigation was launched within a day. The FDA determined that a labeling mix-up had occurred and the product was not actually Syrup of Ipecac but something else that would not treat a case of poisoning. As a result the product was recalled.[10]

To eliminate as much waste as possible, organizations must begin by adopting the principles of lean thinking, which are discussed in the following section.

Principles of Lean Thinking

There are five key principles of lean thinking. First, **value** is *defined* from the customer's perspective rather than from the producer's, and then it is *created* by the producer, whether a manufacturer, service provider, or a combination of the two.[11] Thus the producer must evaluate the **value stream** for each product or product family, the second principle. The value stream has been defined by authors Womack and Jones in their book *Lean Thinking* as "a set of all actions, both value and non-value added, required to bring a specific product (whether a good, a service, or some combination of the two) through the (critical) main flows."[12] Generally firms will have multiple value streams. A hotel, for example, might have value streams for three products: rest, food and beverages, and recreation. A study of each value stream will uncover some actions that add value, other steps that add no value but cannot be eliminated for some reason, and still other steps that add no value and can be eliminated immediately. The firm must then create an effective uninterrupted flow of the remaining value-added activities for each product or product family along with the non-value-adding steps that cannot be eliminated, the third principle. Once a flow has been created, products should only be produced based on a **pull system**, the fourth principle. Pull systems are in place when synchronized work takes place only upon authorization from another downstream user in the system rather than strictly to a forecast.

U.S. clothing retailer J.C. Penney, for example, is a partner with TAL, Ltd., a Hong Kong shirt maker, using a pull system. When a shirt is sold, sales information is electronically transferred to TAL. Using historical demand data, TAL determines the number of shirts it needs to make. If a retail outlet is out of stock, TAL will air express a given number of shirts and ship the remainder by a slower means. In the past, J.C. Penney would have held six months of inventory at its warehouse and three months in each store. Using a pull system, virtually zero inventory above that placed on the shelves is held by J.C. Penney, resulting in fewer unsold shirts and lower overall costs in the supply chain.[13]

The practice of lean principles assures an organization that no unwanted products are created, and as these first four principles are put into practice the fifth principle is initiated, wherein companies begin to strive for **perfection**. In other words, they discover there is always room for improvement and develop continuous improvement methods to reduce all forms of waste.

Companies that adopt lean principles generally begin with **lean production/service delivery**, or **lean manufacturing**, rethinking the organization of work and the appropriateness of currently operating machines, warehouses, and systems to fit the process flow. The goals are to reduce throughput times and inventory levels, cut purchase order lead times, increase quality, and improve customer responsiveness with fewer people and other assets. As lean production/service delivery is implemented and inventory levels are reduced, layers of previously hidden waste begin to emerge, which can then be identified and removed. Some problems that create waste are listed in Table 10.1. For example, Porsche AG, the famous German sports car manufacturer, implemented

Table 10.1	Problems Hidden by Inventory
Unstable demand	Obsolete product
Poor forecasting	Quality problems
Excess work-in-process	Excess scrap
Machine downtime	Overproduction
Operator error	Late deliveries
Supplier problems	

lean production in 1991. Within five years, Porsche had doubled its productivity in operations while cutting defects in supplier parts by 90 percent and first-time-through errors in-house by more than 55 percent. Two years later, the automaker had shortened product development time significantly, cut its manufacturing space in half, shortened conversion of raw materials to finished vehicle from six weeks to three days, and cut parts inventories by 90 percent.[14]

Service organizations like Jefferson Pilot Financial (JFP) have also applied lean principles to improve performance. The U.S.-based company faced slow growth in its life insurance products due to product proliferation. Competition in the form of niche players was also accelerating because of their lower costs and faster turnaround time in policy processing. JFP started the lean production process by reengineering its New Business Processing and Underwriting Unit operations, creating a "model cell" of the entire process. Testing was then performed to determine if the model cell was feasible. The company placed linked processes next to each other and balanced the employees' workloads. It also started measuring productivity and performance from the customer's perspective. As a result, JFP increased market share and moved to first place over industry competitors in terms of costs and profit margin.[15]

As firms improve production, they generally transition from lean production to a **lean organization** in order to strive for excellence within a business unit. This transition means implementing better methods for order fulfillment, logistics, and after-sales service, among others. Lean organizations view the customer more holistically, incorporating customer relationship management (CRM) techniques as described in Chapter 3. For example, firms will use different approaches and measurements for each distinct market segment. More sophisticated organizations then take the next step and become **lean enterprises**, integrating lean thinking practices across business units. This transition works particularly well when business units share common customers, suppliers, and distribution centers. Planning and coordination are now performed by an inter-business unit and enterprise measurements are applied. For example, lean enterprises will often set up global buying units to achieve consistent quality and lower costs in their purchases. At the same time they often will create global selling units.

However, optimizing each enterprise separately in a supply chain will not necessarily result in a low-cost, optimized solution for the entire supply chain. Rather, companies are beginning to take a **lean supply chain** approach, implementing lean principles cooperatively along the supply chain. Value and target costs for each product or product family for these companies are defined jointly among supply chain members. Together, they work to eliminate waste to meet joint target cost and return-on-investment goals.

Once target costs are met, supply chain members will jointly continue to identify new forms of waste and set new targets. Key processes are aligned along the supply chain, focused on delivering an uninterrupted flow of goods and services and coordinating inventory policies. Operational information also flows in both directions to ensure transparency of all activity within the supply chain. REACH Air Medical Services, an air emergency ambulance operation headquartered in northern California, worked with the hospitals in its supply chain to improve response time and critical patient bedside time. More on how REACH used a lean approach can be found in the Service Perspective feature.

According to Rick Cicconi, director of supply chain operations at Procter & Gamble, the world's largest consumer products company with more than 170 manufacturing facilities and 20 research and development (R&D) centers globally, "we consider that 'the consumer is boss.'" Using a lean supply chain approach, production is based on a combination of actual consumer demand and some forecasting. The company starts by watching demand patterns at the store level to understand consumer behavior and uses a direct delivery system to its network of retailers. Direct delivery allows it to monitor demand closely and adjust quickly to changing customer preferences. It has also developed sophisticated information technology to coordinate product flows, which has significantly reduced inventory levels. Lastly, the company engages in joint business process improvements with its supply chain partners.[16]

A 2004 study revealed that companies that work with supply chain partners to become leaner see the benefit of exchanging data and are more likely than non-lean companies to develop data standards so they can exchange data more easily. They are also more likely to work with their supply chain partners to standardize processes and products. Lean supply chains were found to have significantly higher inventory turns, lower days of sales inventory on hand, lower cost of goods sold, and were more responsive to changes within the supply chain.[17]

To further understand lean thinking, the following sections will first discuss concepts related to lean production and then further discuss aspects of the lean supply chain.

Traditional Versus Lean Production

For many years manufacturers built products, and in many cases still do, in anticipation of finding a market for them. In what is otherwise known as **mass production**, operations traditionally rely on sales forecasts to develop production schedules and then stockpile inventories "just in case" or until they are needed. It is then up to marketing to "push" or create product demand through a variety of means, including national and local advertising, coupons, quantity discounts, and promotions.

Traditional manufacturers operate with **batch and queue production**, in which they make each part that goes into a finished product in large lot sizes (or batches) and then move the batch of items on to the next operation before they are all actually needed there. As illustrated in Figure 10.1, traditional **production lot sizes** are based on the economic order quantity (EOQ) inventory model extension known as the economic production quantity (EPQ), in which manufacturers set up long production runs (sometimes weeks or months), spreading fixed costs over a large number of parts (a fuller discussion of the EPQ can be found in Chapter 6). In other words, parts are made in

Service Perspective

Lean Learning Center Helps REACH Air

REACH Air Medical Services has shaved critical time off its emergency air ambulance operations due to its application of "lean thinking" throughout the company. Headquartered in northern California, REACH serves over 3,000 patients a year with 60 percent of its transports being hospital-to-hospital (interfacility), and 40 percent being 911 scene responses. Working closely with several large receiving hospitals and approximately 200 sending hospitals, the company operates five bases of helicopter operations and one base of airplane operation—all manned 24/7.

REACH's lean endeavors began after its director of program development, Jennifer Hardcastle, attended a week-long course at the Lean Learning Center (Novi, Michigan). Unlike many lean education providers who focus on manufacturing, the center's approach applies to any industry by focusing on lean guiding principles and rules. With a dedicated lean learning facility tailored to develop lean thinkers, concepts are taught through discovery, simulation, case study, peer coaching, personal action planning, role playing, and journaling. "After attending the Lean Experience class, I realized how lean thinking could significantly improve our response time and critical patient bedside time while conducting an interfacility transport. By implementing tools like value stream mapping, we saw how many broken links there were along the chain between REACH and our hospital customers," says Hardcastle.

Prior to working with the Lean Learning Center, REACH had no structured methodology in place for the sending hospitals to convey how urgently a patient needed to be transported. Using lean rules, the first step was to study the process flow between hospitals and REACH. "We worked with the hospitals to define a Level One Acuity patient—someone requiring the most urgent need for care and transport," reports Hardcastle. "We established four patient categories—acute aortic emergencies, unstable trauma, unstable pediatric, and anyone requiring critical lifesaving intervention. We then identified what sending hospital staff members can expect when they encounter each patient category and the processes involved in emergency treatment and transport. For this level of patient minutes can mean the difference of life and death—so process efficiency through lean thinking took on the highest level of importance."

The teams worked on structuring a process flow for each Level One category to eliminate wasted time. Now a facility calls REACH's dispatch center and notifies it that it has a Level One request, activating a plan that launches an aircraft to that facility (Point A) even if a patient's ultimate destination (Point B) is not yet known. Historically, an aircraft wouldn't be launched until Point B was determined. But by launching prior to confirmation of the final destination, the company has eliminated up to 40 minutes of wasted wait time.

Lean also helped REACH reduce time spent collecting bedside information at a given facility prior to transporting a patient to another facility. Before, the verbal report between the bedside nurse and REACH's transport nurse had no structure to it. Hardcastle says, "The bedside nurse-to-nurse report was a series of questions and answers which varied greatly depending on the people involved." A one-page flow sheet was created that contained essential information for each Level One Acuity category, making the transfer of information standardized and quicker—ultimately saving from three to five minutes.

Another action taken by REACH that has probably reduced the most waste involves the medication infusion procedure. The equipment a patient is hooked up to must stay at the sending facility, meaning REACH must transfer all the infusions from the hospital equipment to its own equipment. Replacing established infusion lines and transferring them to new transport tubing is very time-consuming. To combat this, REACH now stocks its own transport infusion pump at the hospital and has trained the hospital staff on how to utilize it. Now when there is a Level One Acuity patient, the hospital transfers the patient to the REACH equipment and the patient is ready for transport when REACH arrives. This shaved off ten critical minutes.

Says Hardcastle, "My own mindset before attending the Lean Learning Center was one of frustration, thinking that little could be done to solve the inefficiencies inherent in our systems ... I now know differently." "Lean transformation starts with a change in the way everyone thinks about what they do, how they do it and why it matters," says Jamie Flinchbaugh of the Lean Learning Center. "REACH grasped this concept early on and has been able to eliminate waste in the form of valuable time. And, using this systematic approach will help them sustain these results." "By viewing problems as individual process flows that can be restructured, dramatic change is possible," says Hardcastle. "If we can do it, so can others in healthcare."

Source: "Lean Learning Center Helps REACH Air Shave Critical Time Off Rescue Missions," *PrimeZone Media Network,* April 6, 2005. Reprinted with permission.

large batches based on shop orders, which are then transferred to the next process. Thus, a large stock of each item waits in a queue or line to be processed and then accumulate after processing, resulting in significant funds tied up in large piles of work-in-process inventories.

Machines that perform one part of the process are physically grouped together into work centers, sometimes referred to as a **job shop** environment. The goal is to optimize the utilization of each work center's capacity. Thus, each work center schedules its own production levels and controls the flow of materials. The order of material flows is determined based on preestablished dispatch rules, such as first-in first-out (FIFO), shortest processing time (SPT), or earliest due date (EDD). Material requirements planning (MRP) or manufacturing resource planning (MRP II) systems are used in mass production environments to track, order, and control the flow of inventory on the shop floor. (More on dispatch rules, MRP, and MRP II can be found in Chapters 6, 7, and 9.)

Unfortunately traditional manufacturing practices can result in a great deal of waste. High levels of inventory can cover up poor forecasting practices, late deliveries, excess work-in-process, and product defects, among others. There is a high probability that quality problems will go undetected until a batch is moved to the next stage of processing. As a result, the cost to scrap and remanufacture a large batch is much greater than if products are made as they are needed. See the Global Perspective feature for an example of how Bourgault Industries, a Canadian manufacturer of farm equipment, switched from traditional batch and queue manufacturing to lean principles and significantly improved quality and productivity.

The three key elements of lean production are (1) an efficient use of resources by eliminating all forms of waste, (2) keeping inventory levels low, and (3) implementing JIT production and delivery practices. By eliminating waste, lean producers are able to create a continuous flow of product that matches customer demand. By lowering inventory levels to a minimum, lean companies uncover and fix problems hidden by large amounts of inventory, and as a result often improve quality, shorten production times, reduce machine downtime, lessen space needs, and reduce lead times, all

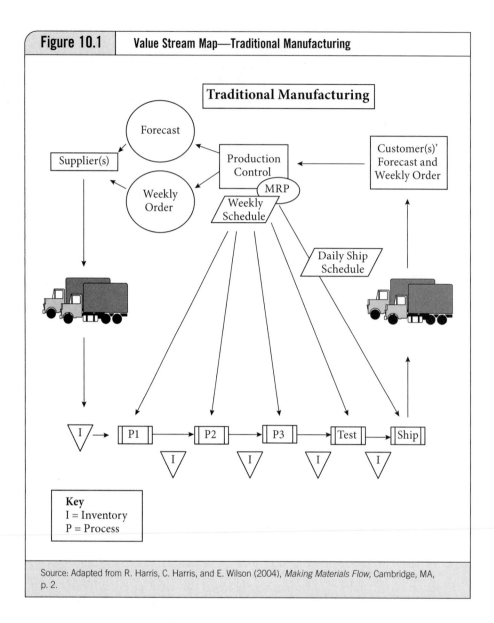

Figure 10.1 | Value Stream Map—Traditional Manufacturing

Source: Adapted from R. Harris, C. Harris, and E. Wilson (2004), *Making Materials Flow*, Cambridge, MA, p. 2.

resulting in an increase in productivity. Lastly, JIT production involves "pulling" a customer order through the facility whereupon products are manufactured to fill customer orders for immediate shipment. A pull system is a production system set up to respond to customer demand created by marketing. Figure 10.2 provides an illustration of a value stream map of lean production. The theory is that organizations should end up with less unwanted inventory and thus less unnecessary costs in the system by implementing lean production. The following sections describe, in more detail, the principles behind lean production.

Cellular Layouts

Cellular layouts are self-contained, physical arrangements of machines and people so that processing steps are placed next to each other in sequential order. Rather than a department style layout used in mass production, lean producers use these manufacturing

Global Perspective

Thinking Lean? Think Gorbel

Bourgault Industries has a two-word motto: "Pursuing Perfection." Looking to broaden its markets in recent years, this Saskatchewan-based company took that pursuit of perfection into international arenas and sought to gain an advantage through a "lean manufacturing" strategy. A Gorbel Easy Arm™ Intelligent Lifting Arm not only helped the strategy succeed, it became a prime example of "lean thinking." The Easy Arm was simple to implement, results were almost immediate, and the cost was easy to rationalize from a value perspective. All one had to do was look at the entire process—and the one most often doing the looking was Garry Kupchinski, Bourgault's lean integration leader. "After evaluating the agriculture machinery market in North America we decided to look at markets in other parts of the world," said Kupchinski. "We identified good opportunities in the Ukraine and the former Soviet Union countries, but we also knew we would have some large companies as competitors." At that point, said Kupchinski, Bourgault embarked on a quest to learn how to manage processes more effectively— how to deliver quality products in the most efficient manner.

As Bourgault's motto suggests, the company is no stranger to quality products. When Frank Bourgault started the business out of a little shop some 30 years ago, he did so to meet a need for more durable cultivators and other farm equipment that could withstand the rough terrain in that area of Canada. Three decades later, 400 Bourgault employees continue to make and sell quality products. It's also true that "pursuing perfection" might well describe the general principles of lean manufacturing—eliminating waste, minimizing inventory and cost, and maximizing overall efficiency.

As Bourgault began to make the transition to lean manufacturing, management decided to start with one of its smaller product families as a test case. It settled on a device called the Mid Row Bander®, which is offered as an option on Bourgault's seeding systems. The Mid Row Bander supplies high rates of fertilizer exactly between the seed rows, providing optimum physical separation between seed and fertilizer. "The Mid Row Bander was growing in popularity and sales," said Kupchinski, but we were experiencing some challenges in effectively manufacturing our newest version of it. We figured that if lean manufacturing would work in this situation, it would work anywhere for us. Yet it was still just a small part of our business, so we weren't taking on a huge risk."

To implement lean manufacturing in this process, Bourgault abandoned its old "batch and queue" methods and designed a continuous flow system that could more efficiently move partially assembled products from one station to the next. A first step was to relocate some parts of the process so that all the major stations required to produce the Mid Row Bander were under one roof. In a continuous flow system, empty racks move to a weld station, pick up welded parts, move along to a paint station, and then take painted parts to a CNC mill where the parts are then fed directly to an assembler as the empty racks circle back to the weld station. The loop continues all day, several times a day.

Bourgault added greatly to the efficiency of the cycle by installing a Gorbel Easy Arm to lift the assembled Mid Row Banders from the assembly bench to a transport rack, which can carry 16 banders at a time. "Each assembled Mid Row Bander weighs about 100 pounds," said Kupchinski. "In the past, we used electric hoists, but they were too slow and constrained the flow. Basically, we had a $350,000 machining center waiting while a $10,000 electric hoist held things up. We knew we had to find a way to alleviate the bottleneck to implement continuous improvement." With the Easy Arm in place, an operator can now move the assembly from the table to

Continued

the transport rack without assistance, unnecessary movement, or effort. Operator fatigue has been greatly reduced and the product now flows to shipping and to the customer with greatly reduced inventory.

Bourgault had been aware of the Gorbel Easy Arm for several years, but, in its "pre-lean manufacturing" mindset, hadn't recognized its value. "In our old thinking we tried to justify the cost of any piece of equipment based strictly on labor-savings in the particular area where it would be placed," said Kupchinski. "So, if we were to look only at the cell where the Easy-Arm operates, I couldn't justify its cost simply to move an unassembled piece of product from one point to another. However," he said, "when we look at the entire flow and the gains that the Easy Arm helps us make in throughput—and the additional sales that we can accommodate—then its cost is very easily justified. It's a matter of considering the value rather than the cost. That's how lean thinking is transforming the way we approach challenges and opportunities." In this specific case using the Gorbel Easy Arm allowed Bourgault to increase productivity of the cell by 80 percent and reduce manpower by 33 percent. In addition, gross profit of the cell more than doubled.

Installing the Easy Arm was a simple procedure. "We just bolted it in place, our electrician wired it in, and we were off and running," said Kupchinski. "And, it was our own employees working in that cell who recommended this solution. Gorbel clearly has been instrumental in the success our lean initiatives so far," said Kupchinski. "As we look at our other processes and value streams, I'm sure we'll be purchasing more of their products."

Source: Anonymous, "Gorbel Inc. Thinking Lean? Think Gorbel," *Material Handling Product News*, September 2005, p. 54. Reprinted from *Material Handling Product News*. Copyright 2005 Material Handling Product News, Reed Business Information a division of Reed Elsevier.

cells to build components that are fed into an assembly line, or an entire product. Methods are used to process parts through each step continuously or in small batches based on customer orders. Ideally, as one part of a product is completed, it moves to the next workstation, and so on, until the product is finished. Thus, no, or very low levels of WIP accumulates. Work cells can vary in size, operating with anywhere from 2 to 10 people performing 3 to 15 operations (these are also sometimes referred to as **group technology cells**). Cell operators are trained to work on several pieces of equipment, rotate jobs, and frequently take on responsibilities previously assigned to supervisors or managers. Cells are frequently used for the manufacture of electronics, plastics, and steel castings. They are organized to exploit the similarities in information processing, product making, and customer service.

La-Z-Boy, a furniture manufacturer located in Ohio, recently started the transformation from traditional mass production using batch manufacturing to lean production. Before the transition, its sewing, poly, metal, wood, and cutting operations were located in separate departments. Now the company has newly created cells that contain all operations except cutting. It currently operates with 3 cells but plans to eventually create 37 cells. As a result, the cycle time to make a chair has been reduced from two and a half days to three hours. Eventually the company plans to add the boxing of furniture for shipment to the cell.[18]

The cell layout is a radical new way of thinking for mass producers. Companies converting to cell manufacturing may have previously processed items with different marketing characteristics and manufacturing requirements on the same equipment

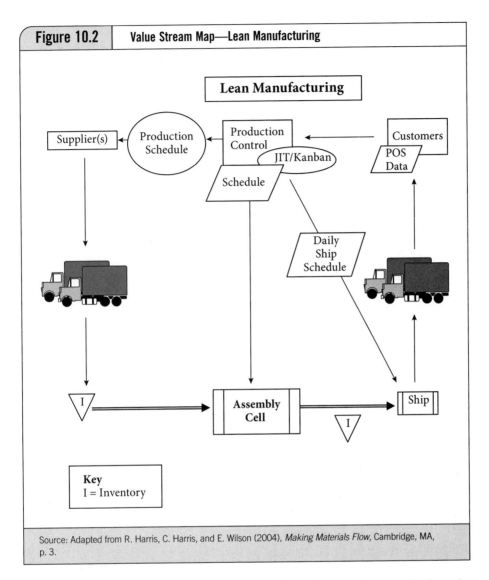

Figure 10.2 | **Value Stream Map—Lean Manufacturing**

Source: Adapted from R. Harris, C. Harris, and E. Wilson (2004), *Making Materials Flow,* Cambridge, MA, p. 3.

using the same labor. Parts and subassemblies may have previously traveled miles to be processed. Now these companies must first analyze their products and the way they service their customers by looking for similarities in processing steps, grouping like products into families, and then assigning the needed resources to produce these product families.

However, using cell layouts has been found to reduce paperwork, materials handling, and inspection. Also, because employees are more highly trained, inspect their own work, and see the process from end to end, they tend to take greater ownership and feel more responsible for making improvements.

Setup Time Reduction

Even before the advent of lean thinking and the Toyota Production System, Henry Ford understood the advantages of reducing wasted production time. As he said in 1926, "One of the most noteworthy accomplishments in keeping the price of (our) products low is the gradual shortening of the production cycle. The longer an article is in the process of manufacture and the more it is moved about, the greater is its ultimate cost."[19]

Production lines are often created to manufacture more than one type or size of a part or product. For example, a paper mill cuts and packages several sizes of paper, each requiring a new equipment setup. A **setup** is the changeover or modification of equipment in preparation for manufacturing a different part or product. It is the amount of time between when the last good part comes off the current production run and when the first good part comes off the next production run, when operating under optimal conditions. An internal setup is a step that has to be performed when the operation or machine is stopped; an external setup is a step that can be done while the operation is still up and running. Thus, setup time reduction is centered on internal times only. Internal setup time usually represents about 5 to 10 percent of total processing time, which appears at first glance to be nominal. However, shortening setup times means batch sizes can be reduced, which can actually reduce total processing time by another 5 to 10 percent, and reduce work-in-process inventories as well. The cost to reduce setup times up to 50 percent generally does not require additional capital expenditures in new equipment, which can be expensive. Rather, modifications can be made to the existing equipment.

When lot sizes and productions runs for each product are decreased, the number of setups can also increase, which allows for more flexibility in production. Organizations that alternate the production of items to more closely meet demand provide greater responsiveness to customers, one of the goals of lean thinking. Automaker Honda of Japan, for example, operates a factory with two production lines and builds six different models—highly unusual for U.S. automakers. Because setup times average only three minutes, Honda can quickly change from production of one model to another.[20] Setup time reduction is also needed to implement the other components of lean production effectively. Thus, companies work to minimize setup times.

To cut setup times, manufacturers should start by monitoring some key measures, such as current work in process, current average lead times, average setup times, and average number of late orders. They should then work on a project that will reduce setup time at the biggest bottleneck with the goal to reduce setup time by 50 percent without spending any money. When that bottleneck's setup time has been reduced by 25 percent, they can then move on to the next biggest bottleneck, and so forth. The next task is then to reduce batch sizes by 25 percent or more so that total lead times and inventories can be reduced.

To shorten setup times, producers will also take other measures. For example, they will use, when possible, multipurpose equipment with attachments that can be used for multiple jobs. **Group technology** may also be used, wherein parts similar in shape and required materials will be processed in the same cell and where setups are very similar. Another tactic is to review the labor involved in a setup and then look for ways to reduce human movement and effort. Whitcraft, a Connecticut-based parts supplier to companies such as General Electric and Rolls-Royce, improved setup times by making a simple change to the height of its dies. "Making all dies used on a punch press the same height eliminated the need to recalibrate and then test the machine before resuming work," Jeffrey Paul said. "A transition that once took 45 minutes to an hour now requires about three minutes. Workers are trained to think in those terms."[21]

In some instances, companies may partner with their equipment suppliers to develop machinery that will meet their needs. Aircraft engine manufacturer Pratt & Whitney, headquartered in Connecticut, worked with one of its suppliers, Progressive

Technologies, to modify its own equipment to meet special ergonomic and cell layout needs. As an added benefit, Bill Barker, sales engineer for Progressive, says, "Lean is finding its way into our factory also. We used to build our equipment in batches, but with customization like we did for Pratt & Whitney we (also) need to work with smaller lot sizes."[22]

Small Lot Sizes

As discussed in the previous section, smaller lot sizes are not possible until setup times have been reduced. Although the "ideal" lean lot size is one unit, most manufacturers have not been able to attain this standard. Some companies, for example, process several parts for one finished product at the same time and then assemble the parts as they come off the production line, or they have machines that require long setup times that cannot be reduced. However, they do work to keep lot sizes to a minimum.

When small quantities, or lot sizes, of each product are manufactured it is easier to adjust to changes in the production schedule. Small lot sizes also help reduce inventory levels, which reduce carrying costs, space requirements, and excessive WIP. An added benefit is that the costs of poor quality are less because there are fewer items to inspect and repair when problems are detected. Lastly, scheduling flexibility is increased when combined with shorter setup times. If, for instance, a company produces three different products using lean manufacturing principles, it will frequently shift from making one product to another based on actual customer demand. Should demand for a particular product suddenly increase, the company can then quickly respond by adding more units to the production schedule. Determining the actual lot size is another matter. Two tools—kanban and level loading with mixed model scheduling—are used to control the lot size and are discussed next.

Kanban

The **kanban** (pronounced "con-bon") is a visual tool—often a card in a rectangular vinyl envelope—used to authorize production (a **production kanban**) of a specified kind and quantity for a downstream customer, or the withdrawal of parts from an upstream supplier (**withdrawal kanban**). However, a kanban can also be an assigned space on the production floor, a storage rack, an empty parts bin, or an electronic message on a computer screen. Parts and products always travel with the kanban. Other information on the card may include the supplier of the part or product, the customer, where the part or product is stored, and instructions on how the part or product should be transported.

The production and withdrawal kanbans are used together, as shown in Figure 10.3. When a workstation needs more parts, a worker will go to the storage area and withdraw one container of parts. The worker then takes the kanban from the container and places it in a predetermined spot where it is visible to everyone else, and takes the container to his or her workstation. Next, a stock person picks up the posted kanban and replaces the withdrawn container with another full container. Parts are resupplied to the storage area based on usage. These withdrawals and replenishments happen upstream and downstream, from suppliers to finished goods inventories. In the event inventories start to build up, otherwise known as being "too loose," the number of kanbans may be reduced. On the other hand, if the reverse happens and the system appears "too tight," more kanbans can be added.

Osborne Wood Products of Georgia, a supplier of wood component parts such as chair and table legs to furniture manufacturers, historically operated using batch production based on forecasts instead of orders. However, its batch sizes were too large and

| Figure 10.3 | Example of Withdrawal and Production Kanbans |

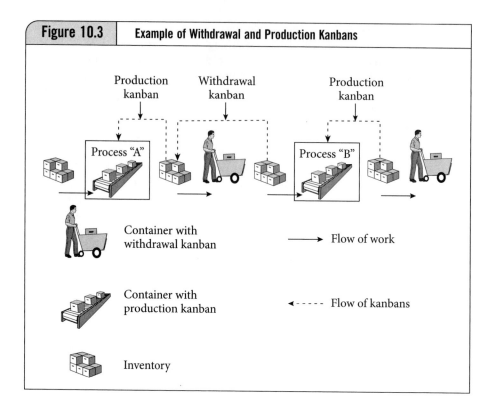

employees were unable to locate materials because the warehouse was so disorganized. It switched to lean manufacturing and started using withdrawal kanban cards to manage inventory more efficiently. Now, as inventory of an item falls below a preset level, a kanban card with a predetermined reorder quantity is withdrawn from an inventory shelf and placed on a yellow board that is visible to all employees and stock is then replenished. In the event the item is not in stock, the card is placed on a red board. Any items on the red board are manufactured within two days and then shipped in three days. As a result, inventory levels are now in sync with parts demand. As a company representative stated, "We used to have a million-dollar inventory in 10 or 15 parts. Now we have a million-dollar inventory in 100 parts."[23]

To calculate the number of kanbans needed for a production period, the following formula can be used:

$$K = \frac{UW(1 + X)}{C}$$

where:

K = Number of containers needed (1 kanban card per container)
U = Planned usage rate of work center, parts per hour
W = Average waiting time for replenishment plus average production time for one container of parts, hours
X = safety factor set by management due to inefficiencies in the system
C = capacity of one standard container (not to exceed 10 percent of daily usage), parts

Example 10.1 illustrates the use of this formula. Notice that rounding up will make the system "looser" while rounding down will make it "tighter."

Pull systems, as mentioned earlier, are used in conjunction with kanban cards to manage the flow of inventory efficiently. There are actually three types of pull systems, based on customer demand and lead time. The **make-to-stock replenishment pull system** is used when lead times are relatively short and customer orders occur frequently. Finished goods or parts are replaced when a customer orders or withdraws them. A store of finished goods is placed at the end of a production line and any parts needed to produce that good are kept within the production area. The quantity of finished goods and work-in-process stored will depend on production and withdrawal rates.

The **make-to-order replenishment pull system** is used when customer demand is relatively low and lead times are long. The pace of production is usually set further upstream than for make-to-stock environments. Work that takes place downstream from the **pacemaker** (the workstation that sets the pace of production) flows in a first-in-first-out (FIFO) sequence. Smaller, less expensive parts are stored next to the assembly line, while the larger, more expensive parts are brought to the line as needed to keep inventory costs down. This second type of pull system keeps very little or no finished goods inventory on hand. Rather, custom orders are delivered to the customer as soon as they are completed.

In the **combination replenishment pull system**, two different replenishment systems run in parallel because the organization produces both make-to-stock and make-to-order items. Orders arrive at each line, with high-frequency, make-to-stock orders funneled

---

Example 10.1   Kanban Card Calculation

Peter, Paul, and Perry supervise a lean operation that uses kanban cards to control production. They have collected the following data to calculate the number of kanban cards needed for one of the parts used in production:

Usage $=$ 100 units/hour
Standard container size $=$ 6 dozen units
Cycle time $=$ 105 minutes
Safety factor $=$ 15%

How many containers are needed?

SOLUTION:

Using the formula,

$$K = \frac{UW(1 + X)}{C}$$

$$K = \frac{(100)(105/60)(1 + .15)}{(6)(12)} = 2.8 \approx 3 \text{ kanbans}$$

In this example, we rounded up, which will make the system "looser." (In practice, rounding up is generally used.)

Note that usage and cycle time must be in the same units, that is, minutes, hours, or days, so you must convert cycle time to hours. In this example, the cycle time must be converted to hours or the usage to minutes. We converted the cycle time by dividing it by 60 minutes to get 1.75 hours (105/60).

through the first system and custom orders put into the second system. Again, kanban cards are used to authorize production.

Level Capacity Loading and Mixed Model Scheduling

How often should each product family be produced? What is the mix going to be for each product family, or in other words, what is the **production interval**? **Level capacity loading** is a technique for balancing production throughput at each workstation to meet expected cycle times. **Mixed model scheduling** involves developing a sequence of products scheduled for assembly while at the same time maintaining a level workload at each workstation which helps production stay within the takt time.

Takt time, also introduced in Chapter 7 as an aid in designing assembly lines, is the rate of expected product demand in the marketplace. Takt time is a calculation of how frequently each unit will be produced (also referred to as **cycle time**) and is used to design manufacturing cells. Takt time lets those on the production floor analyze the production process quickly and determine if there are any problems that require attention. For instance, when takt time has been calculated to be two minutes, a product should be produced every two minutes. If a product is actually produced every three minutes, production should quickly recognize there is a situation that needs to be corrected to get the line moving again at a rate of two minutes per unit. The correction may require more people be added to the production line or some other measure.

Sovereign Showers, a small British manufacturer of shower enclosures, was experiencing productivity, quality, and customer delivery problems. The company had large customer order backlogs. Customers were demanding 1,300 fabricated units per week while Sovereign was only producing 600. The company estimated its needed takt time as 101 seconds based on daily operating time to meet demand and used that as a basis to set performance goals and find ways to reduce waste.[24] Retailers such as Target Stores also use takt time and a flexible workforce, for example, to monitor the checkout lanes. An employee oversees the lines forming in the checkout lanes and if more than a given number of customers are forming a line, the employee calls for additional employees to man unopened lanes.

Takt time should be used for simple manufacturing cell designs where there are very few setups, a single routing, and the same work times for all products manufactured in the cell. The formula to calculate takt time is:

$$\text{Takt Time (TT)} = \frac{\text{Daily Operating Time}}{\text{Average Customer Demand} + \text{Expected Variability in Demand}}$$

The daily operating time is the total time available per day and is typically based on the normal eight-hour shift less any scheduled breaks, lunches, meetings, etc. A realistic estimate should also include an allowance for unscheduled breaks and unexpected downtime. Average customer demand is based on existing customer orders plus some expected amount of variation to account for uncertainty in customer demand. These uncertainties are often due to last-minute changes in the needed quantity or product mix. Thus, if the daily operating time is 445 minutes and average customer demand plus an estimate for variability is 223 units, takt time would be 445/223 = 2 minutes per unit. In other words, a manufacturing cell needs to be designed to process one unit of product every two minutes. Example 10.2 provides the calculation of takt time based on customer orders and expected variability in demand. Note that the variation in demand is estimated based on management experience and judgment, but as a rule of thumb should be no more than 50 percent of average demand. Companies may also use a simple tool, the **Heijunka box**, first developed by Toyota, as a visual scheduling

Example 10.2   Calculation of Takt Time

Bob and Joe, owners of BJ Manufacturing, are changing their operation from the traditional job shop to lean production. As a result, they need to design manufacturing cells for production of their existing product line. They used the following daily orders for one of their products to estimate the takt time:

	MONDAY	TUESDAY	WEDNESDAY	THURSDAY	FRIDAY
Units Ordered	300	380	315	365	345

SOLUTION:
To estimate the takt time for this product, Bob and Joe first calculated the average customer demand per day:

$$(300 + 380 + 315 + 365 + 345) \div 5 \text{ days} = 341 \text{ units}$$

Because their average customer orders are less than the highest expected demand on Tuesday, they calculated a coefficient of variability in the following manner:

$$\text{Variation coefficient} = (380 - 341)/341 = 39/341 = 0.1144 \times 100 = 11.44\%$$

Using the variability coefficient, they estimated the designed daily production rate:

$$\text{Daily production rate} = 341 + (341 \times 11.44\%) = 341 + 39.01 = 380.01$$
$$\approx 381 \text{ units (rounded up to nearest unit)}$$

The owners run one 8-hour shift per day. They estimate daily operating time to be

$$8 \text{ hours} - (\tfrac{1}{2} \text{ lunch break} + \tfrac{1}{2} \text{ hour for two 15-minute breaks})$$
$$= 7 \text{ hours} \times 60 \text{ minutes/hour} = 420 \text{ minutes}$$

Thus,

$$\text{Takt time} = 420 \text{ minutes}/381 \text{ units} = 1.10 \text{ minutes/unit}$$

system that shows the amount of work which needs to be done by each team within a given time frame. The box then allows the operations team to see how well they are performing against takt time during the work shift.

Mixed model scheduling gives operations some flexibility to manufacture a wide range of products, reduce inventories of finished products, and improve customer delivery times. The issues that need to be addressed are (1) sequencing of the models, (2) the number of cycles that should be created, and (3) the number of units to produce in each cycle. Model sequencing should depend heavily on setup time and similarity. If, for example, four models will be produced on an assembly line and three have similar setups that can be performed quickly, it makes sense to sequence those three models first and the model with a longer or more complex setup last. The number of cycles is determined by the demand requirements for each model. Most likely, each model will be produced within a cycle at least once. Thus, the number of cycles will generally be determined by the model with the lowest daily production requirement (although this is not always the case). In Example 10.3, a company is producing four models with given production requirements. Using this simple heuristic, Model 401 has the lowest production requirements and so is the basis for the number of cycles.

In this example, the daily production quantities could easily be divided to a whole number. However, this will not likely be the case. In that event, the production manager

Example 10.3   Mixed Model Scheduling

Ken and Barry produce and sell four models of light aviation aircraft. The setup time for each model is the same. They desire to create a production schedule using mixed model scheduling. The daily production requirements are shown in the following table:

MODEL	DAILY PRODUCTION
101	20
201	15
301	10
401	5

SOLUTION:

Because only five 401s will be built, Ken and Barry use this number to determine the number of cycles. To calculate the number of units built in each cycle, they divide the daily production requirement for each model by 5. The following table shows the calculations:

MODEL	DAILY PRODUCTION	UNITS PRODUCED PER CYCLE
101	20	20/5 = 4
201	15	15/5 = 3
301	10	10/5 = 2
401	5	5/5 = 1

Thus, the production schedule would look like the following table:

CYCLE 1	CYCLE 2	CYCLE 3	CYCLE 4
401 (1); 301 (2); 201 (3); 101 (4)	401 (1); 301 (2); 201 (3); 101 (4)	401 (1); 301 (2); 201 (3); 101 (4)	401 (1); 301 (2); 201 (3); 101 (4)

may produce the odd units throughout the schedule to approach a near-level schedule. Example 10.4 provides an example of this scenario.

The examples provided are fairly simple. In an actual manufacturing environment, production managers deal with numerous models, each made up of many parts. Software is available to help companies adjust to mixed model scheduling practices. Husqvarna, a Swedish manufacturer of power products for forestry and lawn and garden maintenance, had to integrate an additional product line into its Beatrice, Nebraska, lawn and turf care equipment plant. The facility already appeared to be operating at full capacity during peak demand periods and was also experiencing backlogs and losing business because it couldn't manufacture and ship orders on time. Husqvarna decided to use Colorado-based Pelion Systems MPO software, which could analyze the resources needed for a new mixed model production line, including service parts to meet demand. The production team used "what-if" scenario modeling included in the software to create and evaluate several possibilities before changing the flow of production.[25]

Standardized Work

While it might seem counterintuitive, standardizing the tasks of a process actually increases flexibility as long as the workforce is properly trained and has been given the

---

Example 10.4   **Mixed Model Scheduling with Irregular Daily Production Quantities**

Ken and Barry are in week 2 of production scheduling. Daily production requirements and units to be produced per cycle are as follows:

MODEL	DAILY PRODUCTION	UNITS PRODUCED/CYCLE
101	21	$21/4 = 5.25$
201	14	$14/4 = 3.5$
301	6	$6/4 = 1.5$
401	4	$4/4 = 1$

Ken and Barry decide to mix in production of Models 101, 201, and 301 to achieve as close to level production as possible.

SOLUTION:
Following is one potential solution:

CYCLE	1	2	3	4
Pattern	101 (5); 201 (3); 301 (1); 401 (1)	101 (5); 201 (3); 301 (1); 401 (1)	101 (5); 201 (3); 301 (1); 401 (1)	101 (5); 201 (3); 301 (1); 401 (1)
Extra Unit(s)	101	201	201; 301	301

---

responsibility for maintaining the set standards. Operating standards create a safe environment and are the most efficient way of ensuring consistent, repeatable work. In this way, tasks are performed the same way, or with minimal variation, no matter who is doing the work. As a result, the customer should see more consistent quality in products and services.

Standardizing the work, however, does not mean the tasks never change. Rather, operating standards should be seen as a living document. Because the workforce has the authority to stop a production line when a problem occurs and then search for the underlying causes and fix it, a new and better way of performing tasks may be uncovered. Thus, the process may be altered to avoid future problems. However, as processes are improved the standards need to be updated and become the baseline for improvement.

The 5S System

Each company has daily routines in the workplace. However, some employees are better than others at keeping work and routines orderly and organized, which is necessary for a smooth, efficient flow of activities. Periodic, preventive maintenance is an absolute must for every piece of equipment within a lean production system. **5S** is another idea that originated with the Toyota Production System and is one of the means to reduce waste and optimize productivity by maintaining an orderly workplace and using visual cues to achieve more consistent operational results. There are five areas of 5S—Sort (Seiri), Set in Order (Seiton), Shine (Seiso), Standardize (Seiketsu), and Sustain (Shitsuke).

Much like the work area in your kitchen, workers should sort, or keep the required parts, tools, and instructions, at the workstation and remove anything that is not needed. The required parts and tools should then be clearly identified and arranged neatly (set in order). All machinery should be cleaned and maintained (shined) to realize optimal performance. Once the first three areas are accomplished, employees should continue these practices regularly to keep the work area in top condition (standardize). The mindset within each worker should be to continue practicing the first four steps without end (sustain).

In sum, this lean method encourages workers to improve their working conditions and facilitates their efforts to reduce waste, unplanned downtime, and in-process inventory. 5S provides the foundation on which other lean methods, such as total productive maintenance, cellular manufacturing, just-in-time production, and Six Sigma, can be introduced.

Clean Burn Inc., a used-fuel furnace manufacturer located in Pennsylvania, estimates it wasted about 20 percent of its labor costs on things like looking for misplaced tools. The production area was in disarray and employees were often on the line without work because parts were out of stock. It has since implemented lean manufacturing principles, including 5S. Now tools are color-coded and easily located. As a result, the company ships orders more quickly and efficiently while requiring 40 percent less warehouse space. The change was not without its challenges, however. Particularly for companies that operate with a union shop, there may be resistance to these kinds of changes. Thus, innovative ways to motivate employees may be necessary.[26]

Total Productive Maintenance

In a lean environment, machine uptime needs to be predictable or it will be tough to produce in accordance with customer demand. To ensure process capability, equipment must be up and running at all times. Thus, organizations create **total productive maintenance** (TPM) (also known as total preventive maintenance) programs to maximize the effectiveness of production equipment in order to avoid unplanned equipment downtimes. This includes the total elimination of all losses, including breakdowns, equipment setup and adjustment losses, machine idling and minor stoppages, reduced speed, defects and rework, spills and process upset conditions, and startup and yield losses. Why is this important? It only makes sense that as equipment failures and downtime increase, the capacity of the system goes down and repair costs go up. As companies move toward lean thinking, they begin to notice unscheduled equipment downtime, which was previously hidden in the process because everyone assumed it was "a part of doing business."

Traditionally, the maintenance of equipment within an organization is assigned to a maintenance department. The philosophy behind lean production is that everyone in an organization is responsible for quality. Thus, with total productive maintenance, all levels and functions within an organization are actively involved in maintaining production equipment. The workforce is trained and focused on taking care of the equipment and machines with which they work, performing routine maintenance while the equipment is operating normally and then fixing them quickly when breakdowns occur. For example, workers may perform daily maintenance tasks on their own equipment, such as cleaning, inspecting, tightening, and lubricating.

A lean manufacturer begins the total productive maintenance process by building a solid, plant floor–based system to prevent equipment-related accidents, defects, and breakdowns, also known as **poka-yoke** or mistake proofing. To accomplish this, management first looks at the entire production system life cycle and designs and installs equipment, where possible, that requires little or no maintenance. A company may also set certain performance criteria with its supplier to meet its standards. Both customer and supplier then test the equipment to see if they get the same capability results. The supplier may also provide data on the equipment's components so the customer can determine how often the machine will need to be inspected and the required level of planned maintenance.[27] BPL Sanyo, a global joint venture with production facilities in India, manufactures consumer electronics and was experiencing difficulties with an assembly line that packaged speakers into corrugated boxes. If the boxes were not removed in a timely manner, they would fall off the conveyor belt, causing damage to the package. To prevent the problem from recurring, BPL Sanyo installed a stopper with a limit switch attached to it. When a box touched the limit switch, the line was automatically stopped.[28]

A company also looks for ways to make maintenance needs clearly visible and easier to perform. For instance, gauges may be colored to indicate normal and abnormal operating ranges or lubricating points may be color-coded to match the color of the correct dispensing container. Additionally, machine operators may be required to collect daily information on the health of the equipment. Metrics might include the actual downtime of the equipment, whether planned or unplanned; product quality using statistical process control data or reject rates; or maintenance performed.

Close Relationships with Suppliers

Past research has shown that when a company adopts a lean strategy, suppliers typically experience higher logistics costs initially in terms of increased transportation (more trips to the customer), additional inventory carried to meet customer demand, and a greater number of stockouts when customers unexpectedly change their requirements. This often happens because suppliers have not adopted a lean strategy and are simply reacting to new customer demands. Thus, it is important that suppliers also adopt a lean strategy to avoid these additional costs. In the best-case scenario, both the manufacturer, or service provider, and its suppliers simultaneously adopt and operate in a lean environment. To a great extent, larger companies will usually adopt lean principles and then assist their smaller suppliers in converting to lean production. However, companies may also turn around and look for opportunities to improve through lean thinking with their customers. Fujitsu UK, a Japanese-based IT and communications solution company, has applied lean principles to its IT service with customers. For example, it looks for patterns in the change requests received from customers. When Fujitsu detects an unusually high number of requests, it works with the customer to address the issue and streamline the customer's process.[29]

As suggested by previous discussions, lean thinking requires organizations to have closer relationships with their suppliers who have adopted lean practices. Because lot sizes are small, suppliers are expected to make more frequent small deliveries on a regular basis. Thus, it is important for suppliers to know, in advance, the customer's production and delivery schedule as a basis to create their own schedules. Because quality is also a high priority, suppliers are expected to deliver a consistently high level of quality to minimize or even eliminate incoming inspections (inspections are considered a non-value-added activity). Thus, suppliers will most likely need to improve their own quality practices. Manufacturers' supply management teams often work with suppliers to improve quality and delivery through supplier development and supplier certification programs. More on supplier development and supplier certification can be found in Chapter 12.

Because closer relationships take more time, however, supply managers typically cut back the list of suppliers (known as **downsizing** or **optimizing the supply base**) and focus on improving relations with fewer key first-tier suppliers of major subassemblies. They may also search for suppliers that are located closer to them, although this is not a requirement. Supply managers then rely on these first-tier suppliers to manage relationships with second-tier suppliers. This view is the opposite of the traditional U.S. approach and it has been difficult for supply managers to convert to this new form of lean supply chain thinking. In the past, they have typically worked with many suppliers, providing them product specifications, and then used a bidding process to obtain the lowest prices. The results of a 2004 survey indicate that supply managers still like to have at least two suppliers for any purchased item.[30]

Information Technology and Lean

While many of the practices of lean production do not seem to lend themselves to the use of computer software, developers have stepped in and created self-contained "flow manufacturing" versions of enterprise resource planning (ERP) and add-on programs to traditional ERP systems to support lean manufacturing. (Traditional ERP systems are designed to support mass manufacturing using a push system.)

Software in and of itself will not create a lean environment; rather, companies must have lean principles in place first. Ducati, an Italian-based motorcycle manufacturer, purchased software developer Oracle's E-Business Suite to support a lean manufacturing and supply chain environment. Lean practices were in place, however, before the software was installed. More on Ducati's adoption of lean thinking and information technology support can be found in the e-Commerce Perspective feature.

Lean add-ons to existing ERP systems are also being purchased. Some features of the add-ons include:

- Kanban logic to recalculate the size and number of kanban bins required on an ongoing basis with alerts to workers to make changes to existing kanbans if physical kanbans are used; electronic kanbans will automatically change;
- Support for just-in-time procurement through the supply chain to suppliers;
- Flow logic necessary when products are configured to order;
- Conversion of traditional multi-level MRP bills of material to "flat" one-level bills of material necessary for lean production;
- Flow production planning tools needed for scheduling;
- Performance reports for all inventory transactions upon completion of a single unit;
- Immediate transfer of engineering change orders to the production line; and
- Daily and periodic performance reports such as kanban shortages, material use variances, resource utilization, daily planned production, and actual versus planned supplier delivery frequency.[31]

Radio frequency identification (RFID) technology is also used in lean manufacturing environments to track materials in real time. RFID tags are attached to each part, which can then be used to record inventory levels as each part moves from one workstation to the next. The tags hold data that uniquely identify each part. An RFID reader can also add data, such as engineering specifications, to the tag as it passes through the assembly process. This technology is particularly useful for complex assemblies, such as automobiles that contain approximately 25,000 parts.[32]

Disadvantages of Lean Production

Lean production has been proven to be effective. A 2006 study by the Massachusetts-based business research firm Aberdeen Group revealed that 75 percent

e-Commerce Perspective

Ducati Rides Lean

The principle of "lean" has always dominated thinking at Ducati. While other motorcycle brands were busy adding power and weight to their machines, the legendary Italian manufacturer has always believed in keeping weight to a minimum. That has helped deliver Ducati's trademark stability while the bike is leaning hard over into a fast, sweeping bend. Now the company has embraced lean principles throughout its manufacturing process as part of a major turnaround in its operations. And the results are as impressive as Ducati's track record of racing successes: Production costs are down by as much as 25 percent, throughput time has been shortened by 50 percent, and motorcycle build quality before delivery increased by 70 percent. These results are the culmination of a three-year drive toward achieving a lean enterprise, led by Giovanni Contino and Filippo Pellerey, joint managing directors of Ducati Consulting, which was set up to mastermind the project.

Founded in 1926 in Bologna, Northern Italy, as an industrial components manufacturer, Ducati produced its first motorcycle engine in 1946 and went on to build a reputation for off-road bikes. The modern history of Ducati as a superbike maker began in 1972, when its 750 V-twin took first and second place in the Imola 200. Today, Ducati Motor Holding is one of the world's leading motorcycle manufacturers. It is listed on the New York and Milan stock exchanges and has a brand presence in 40 countries worldwide.

The move to lean manufacturing follows the acquisition of Ducati in 1996 by the Texas Pacific Group (TPG). TPG began by changing the international subsidiary structure and revamping the dealer network, and then instigated "Operation Turnaround" in 1999 to improve the return on investment. The new management wanted to fill its newly improved dealer network with motorcycles, so its first goal was to increase production volumes from 12,000 bikes a year to 40,000 within five years. This would have to be achieved in the existing factory space and without increasing the number of employees.

Ducati's solution was to outsource as many noncore activities as possible and focus its efforts on assembly and on research and development. Pellerey, who headed a five-person process improvement team, took up the challenge. "We wanted to eliminate all non-value-adding activity, eliminate waste, and improve quality, all without any major new investment," he says. "We decided that outsourcing and embracing Lean principles were the keys to achieving these targets. We started by adopting the Kaizen philosophy and just-in-time [JIT] methodology, whereby you can achieve major change without big investments by taking it a step at a time. We conducted a careful analysis of our production processes, which revealed all of our problems. For example, in the machining shop, the machines were laid out in such a way that components had to follow a long path to get to the various operations. So we improved the material flow and the factory ergonomics and devised a total productive maintenance approach to improve machine reliability. Some of the most significant results in that department included an increase of up to 12 percent in machine reliability and a reduction of 23 percent in hourly costs."

The Ducati team also changed the flow logic for the production lines, from "push logic" to "pull logic," using assembly kits carrying the materials needed for only one engine or one vehicle. The kits are made in areas, known as "supermarkets," that are themselves supplied via a kanban system. This has reduced inventory, obsolescence, and error rates and has improved flexibility. These changes have reduced defects by 70 percent over the past three years. "As we worked through all these changes, we found that we could cut the cost of our product by 25 percent, which was a great start," Pellerey says. "Because only 8 percent of the cost of our

Continued

product was produced internally, it was necessary to extend, develop, and implement the Kaizen philosophy and the JIT methodology to the supply chain."

Because the greatest potential for improvement lay within the supply chain, Giovanni Contino, who at the time was Ducati's purchasing and logistics director, joined the team. He began the challenging task of exporting the company's new lean manufacturing culture to its suppliers. "We had 380 suppliers, and the Lean philosophy was new to most of them," Contino says. "We had to select only those suppliers that could follow our new approach, so we ended up cutting back from 380 to 175. To get them on board, we introduced an integration program that involved Ducati people and supplier staff working in teams. We considered our suppliers an extension of Ducati, so it has been necessary to connect them via the Web to exchange and accelerate the flow of information such as production planning, parts price lists, invoices, and quality reports."

Sixty percent of Ducati's procurement comes from Italy, because of the rich automotive heritage of Northern Italy. Twenty-five percent comes from other European Union countries and the rest from Japan. Right now, the first 100 suppliers are directly connected to Ducati's IT network. Ducati started this process before selecting the enterprise software that would make the lean approach universal, repeatable, and scalable. "We wanted to test the Lean approach first and then look for the software that could match our vision and make it happen," Contino explains. IBM was engaged to help find the ideal software solution, because the old IT system, based on an IBM AS/400 platform, was not up to the task. Each department was consulted and asked to present its requirements for actual needs and future perspectives. The final recommendation, after a software selection process among all the major software providers, was to implement Oracle's E-Business Suite.

"Today, it is possible to create the conditions to compete effectively in the market only with an IT system that is entirely internet-enabled," says Enrico Pirrone, IT director. "The policy we have pursued involves a complex project that has ambitious implementation objectives, which could be addressed only with a technological partner that is reliable, competent, and a market leader. That is why, after assessing various solutions, we chose Oracle." Ducati deployed Oracle's E-Business Suite in two phases. The first phase was implemented at the Cupertino, California-based Ducati North America in 2004, with the support of Oracle Consulting, and is about to be rolled out to the rest of the Ducati network. When the implementation is complete, more than 1,000 Ducati employees will be connected to the system.

Oracle E-Business Suite is a suite of Internet-based business applications that automate critical business processes, offering customers choice and flexibility in implementing applications. Its back-office systems and supply chain modules will play a critical role in helping Ducati reap the benefits of lean manufacturing. "Oracle gives us the tools to make Lean work," Contino says. "The system is extremely fast. It offers very good integration with our suppliers and delivers excellent business intelligence."

Marcelo Di Rosa, vice president of the Application Sales business unit for Oracle Southern Europe, is proud of the part Oracle is playing in Ducati's lean enterprise. "Ducati has a special place in motorcycling, with a rich heritage, and it has taken radical steps to ensure that it retains its unique position," he says. "We are delighted that it has chosen Oracle E-Business Suite to help deliver a Lean enterprise supply chain. In addition to the obvious benefits, Lean manufacturing also means shorter cycle times, allowing manufacturers to respond more quickly to market shifts, and greater flexibility. This is especially important in industries, such as the motorcycle industry, in which product lifecycles are shrinking."

In the ten years since TPG acquired the company, Ducati's worldwide sales have tripled. The remarkable V-twin motorcycles continue to achieve racing victories, and the brand enjoys stronger-than-ever customer loyalty. Placing lean principles at the company's manufacturing heart has clearly paid dividends. However, Pellerey points out that the lean enterprise is a journey rather than a destination. The next step on Ducati's journey is to move closer to the concept of a demand-driven supply network (DDSN). "Right now, that's something we know we want," he says. "We want anyone who desires a Ducati motorcycle to be able to walk into a dealer and get one in the shortest-possible time, but that will require further development of the information process between our dealer network and the factory. We are working on that now." Pellerey and Contino now are able to run Ducati Consulting as a profit center, helping manufacturers worldwide—inside and outside the automotive sector—benefit from their own experience in implementing lean principles. What started as an internal improvement drive in one motorcycle factory in Bologna has become a remarkable success story on its own terms.

of the best-in-class firms studied exceeded their shareholders' expectations in terms of reducing inventory and assets, and manufacturing and design costs, while improving manufacturing and supply chain flows as well as product quality and customer service.[33] However, lean production is difficult to achieve. Companies need to make the financial commitment to lean operations and also understand that initially there may be some losses in production before any gains are realized.

Signs of problems that need to be addressed during the changeover to lean may include fluctuating levels of inventory between processing steps, intermittent flows of product, an excessive use of batching, varying levels of output over time, and an inefficient use of human effort. Changes in management procedures and policies will be necessary and a company will need the commitment from all employees to be successful. Suppliers must also be cooperative, willing to build and ship parts frequently and in small quantities. As well, customers need to be convinced to take frequent deliveries of small quantities of product.

Lean Versus Agile

The term **agile manufacturing** has also been used and may sometimes be confused with lean manufacturing. Agility is the ability to take advantage of marketplace changes that are unpredictable and variable.[34] Thus, agile businesses attempt to maximize profitability by configuring each order to customer specifications, and the market winner is one that offers the best service level. As shown in Figure 10.4, lean manufacturing is generally for large manufacturers of standardized products and stable demand whereas agile manufacturers build customized, quickly changing products with uncertain demand patterns and short life cycles.

Customer satisfaction is the agile manufacturer's number one measure of success rather than low costs. These companies work to minimize obsolescence and stockout costs, but not at the loss of customer service. They operate with a group of suppliers that have the ability to quickly adjust to changes in the marketplace. They also have a culture that can deal with unpredictable situations. Essentially the traditional roles of competitor, supplier, and customer firms may frequently change to take advantage of opportunities in the marketplace. While lean thinking is designed for the large mass producer, the agile manufacturer is generally smaller with more flexible production facilities.

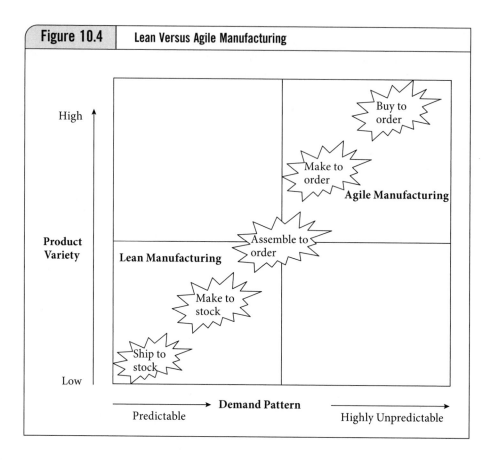

Figure 10.4 | **Lean Versus Agile Manufacturing**

Lean Thinking along the Supply Chain

Lean thinking, as described earlier, is most valuable when applied along the supply chain. For example, lean principles can be used to minimize the bullwhip effect. If you'll recall from earlier in this chapter, the bullwhip effect referred to the fact that small changes in demand become progressively exaggerated or amplified as demand is transferred upstream in the form of forecasts, from one member of the supply chain to another. Exaggerations in demand, along with supply chain safety stocks, increase when senior management insists that it is the supplier's responsibility to meet their demand regardless of how variable it is. Excess inventory is also created because companies continue with the functional silo mentality, where each function optimizes decisions based on its own needs rather than those of the supply chain. Lastly, pricing discounts contribute to the bullwhip effect because supply chain managers generally will take advantage of them, resulting in excess inventory in the system and increased warehousing needs.

Compounding the problem is the way demand and activity data is transferred through the supply chain. Demand data is typically transferred from company to company and function to function, but not always accurately and on a regular basis. Activity data reflects production and product movements within an organization and between supply chain members. Unfortunately, these two types of data are not always accurate nor are they communicated on a regular basis, which compounds the bullwhip effect.

In addition, the bullwhip effect leads to other problems, including:

1. Troubles with scheduling production, particularly responding to demand changes, either up or down;

2. Difficulties estimating and managing labor requirements because of the variability of demand, resulting in overtime and undertime;

3. Problems with inventory control, especially inventory levels and warehousing needs;

4. Poor customer service, such as late deliveries and shorted orders; and

5. Wasted administrative time putting out fires because deliveries are late or incorrect.

There are ways to minimize the bullwhip effect by applying lean thinking principles, which in turn reduces the amount of waste found in the supply chain. Companies can begin by trying to smooth demand by using a set average demand over a given time frame, eventually setting production as close to average demand as possible. Safety stock should initially be used to cover for supply variability, starting with a somewhat generous amount and then gradually reducing it to a minimum. Duplication of safety stock should be avoided, placing it in strategic locations based on a joint decision by supply chain members. Organizations can also set up a standing order size between supply chain partners and not change it without joint approval from the entities involved. Additionally, supply chain members can share actual demand information on a regular basis, say weekly. Significant demand changes should also be shared and the response should be decided, as a supply chain, on how to react. For instance, supply chain partners may change production or stocking levels. Lastly, a demand management team should oversee the supply chain and monitor demand patterns, inventory, and activity rates regularly, probably on a weekly basis and review monthly.

Most of these changes are possible only if cooperation exists among supply chain participants. However, supply managers can make a major impact on the implementation of lean principles by facilitating the integration of key internal processes with those of their suppliers. Intracompany waste, for example, results when suppliers are unable to be more efficient within their own company processes. It is up to the supply manager to use supplier management strategies to eliminate as much waste as possible, which will happen as supply management helps suppliers make gains in productivity. For example, they may work with suppliers to improve their layout or learn lean tools and techniques as discussed earlier in this chapter.

Intercompany waste results when different members of the supply chain value stream are unable or unwilling to share strategies and integrate their internal processes. To eliminate this type of waste, supply managers must coordinate with their suppliers to standardize supplier processes and procedures along the supply chain. For example, quality standards and programs should be the same. Similarly, a cooperative spirit should exist. Supply managers can assist suppliers in learning just-in-time, statistical process control, kanban, and other lean techniques. These will most likely be applied to key suppliers who are a major source of value-added in the supply chain. Postponement and customization strategies can also be effective, where final assembly of completed products is done at the last feasible point in the supply chain.

Computer manufacturer Dell Inc. has significantly reduced intercompany waste by wisely managing demand. It uses a build-to-order model and builds a computer based on customer demand. Dell also works with its suppliers to develop new technologies, improve processes, and keep inventory levels low. These closer relationships have enabled Dell to beat the competition time and again, and eliminate waste in both its components and finished goods.[35]

To identify where waste is occurring in the supply chain and make improvements, value stream mapping tools can be particularly useful. Five tools are available that can help firms identify and then eliminate the various forms of waste described at the beginning of the chapter. The following section describes these tools.

Value Stream Mapping Tools

Five evaluation tools are available to attack the various forms of waste as described in the previous sections. Table 10.2 illustrates the usefulness of each of these tools in reducing a specific form of waste. Four of the tools have been drawn from industrial engineering, logistics research, and system dynamics, while the fifth, quality filter mapping, was created by Peter Hines and Nick Rich of Cardiff University's Business School in the United Kingdom.[36] The following segments describe each tool in more detail.

Process Activity Mapping

Process activity mapping has been discussed in other chapters and is useful in identifying all forms of waste. In general, a team will begin by analyzing a given process from order to delivery, making a record of all steps involved in this process in a visual map. The team considers whether every action taken at each stage of the process is needed. A format used by many organizations is the **5W1H**, or five questions beginning with *W* and one *how* to analyze each process activity—*why* is this activity occurring, *when* is it

Table 10.2	Value Stream Mapping Tools						
	FORMS OF WASTE						
MAPPING TOOL	**OVER PRODUCTION**	**DELAYS BETWEEN PROCESSING STEPS**	**UNNECESSARY TRANSPORTATION**	**OVERPROCES-SING PARTS**	**OVERSTOCKING INVENTORIES**	**NEEDLESS EMPLOYEE MOVEMENT**	**DEFECTIVE PARTS**
Process activity mapping	*	‡	‡	‡	†	‡	*
Supply chain response matrix	†	‡	–	–	‡	*	–
Production variety funnel	–	*	–	†	†	–	–
Quality filter mapping	*	–	–	*	–	–	‡
Demand amplification mapping	†	†	–	–	‡	–	–

Key
–No correlation/usefulness
*Low correlation/usefulness
†Medium correlation/usefulness
‡High correlation/usefulness

occurring, *where* is it occurring, *who* performs this task and on *which* machine, and lastly *how* is it performed? The team will identify all forms of waste and determine whether the process can be changed in some way to make it more efficient. This may involve rearranging the flow pattern, changing the layout or transportation routes, moving materials to different staging points, or eliminating non-value-adding steps.

Supply Chain Response Matrix

The supply chain response matrix shown in Figure 10.5, also referred to as a time-based process map, has been used in the automotive, food, and clothing industries. Particularly useful in identifying problems with lengthy lead times, large lot sizes, and overstocks of inventory, the matrix is a mapping technique illustrating the ability of a company and its supply chain trading partners to respond to customer demand. The horizontal axis represents the lead times associated with obtaining each type of inventory. The vertical axis represents the amount of inventory, equivalent to days of demand at each stage, held in the system. The total supply chain response time is the sum of the two time periods. Once the response matrix has been determined, supply chain

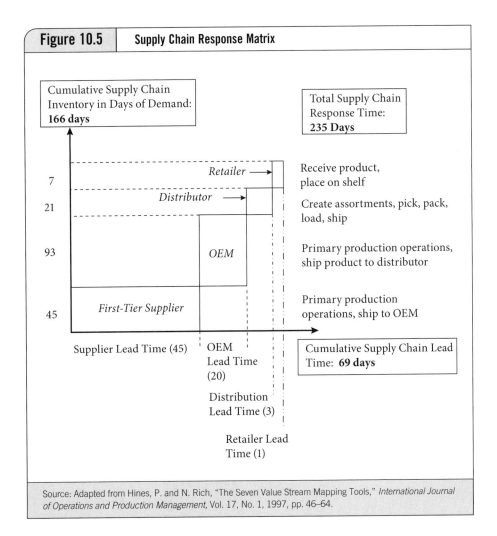

Figure 10.5   Supply Chain Response Matrix

Cumulative Supply Chain Inventory in Days of Demand: **166 days**

Total Supply Chain Response Time: **235 Days**

7 — Retailer → Receive product, place on shelf

21 — Distributor → Create assortments, pick, pack, load, ship

93 — OEM — Primary production operations, ship product to distributor

45 — First-Tier Supplier — Primary production operations, ship to OEM

Supplier Lead Time (45)   OEM Lead Time (20)   Distribution Lead Time (3)   Retailer Lead Time (1)

Cumulative Supply Chain Lead Time: **69 days**

Source: Adapted from Hines, P. and N. Rich, "The Seven Value Stream Mapping Tools," *International Journal of Operations and Production Management,* Vol. 17, No. 1, 1997, pp. 46–64.

organizations can target specific inventories or lead times (starting with the largest contributors) for improvement in overall response time.

Production Variety Funnels

A production variety funnel is a visual representation of the complexity of the supply chain that helps organizations to create a strategy to improve the management of their product lines. Managers can compare their types of firms with the funnels to identify where inventory reductions may be needed or how products might be processed differently to achieve lower inventory levels. As shown in Figure 10.6, production activities typically fall into four general shapes. An "I" plant has one directional, continuous production of several similar items, such as chemicals or beer. A "V" plant uses a small number of raw materials and turns them into a wide variety of finished goods, such as textiles or metal fabrication. An "A" plant, on the other hand, uses

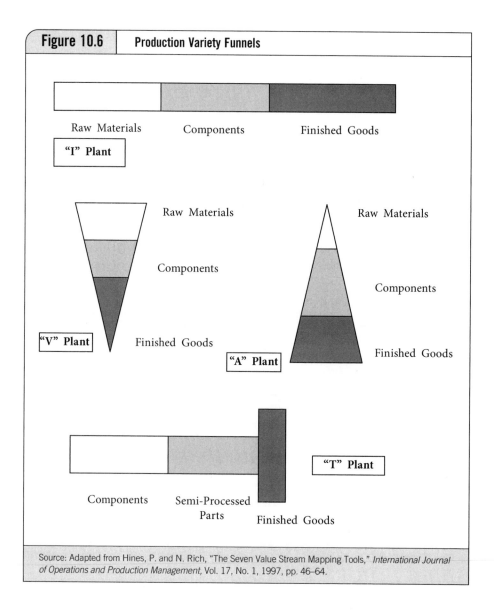

Figure 10.6 | **Production Variety Funnels**

Source: Adapted from Hines, P. and N. Rich, "The Seven Value Stream Mapping Tools," *International Journal of Operations and Production Management,* Vol. 17, No. 1, 1997, pp. 46–64.

many types of raw materials to produce a limited number of finished products, such as the aerospace and automotive industries. Lastly, "T" plants process a limited number of components into semi-finished parts, which can be turned into a large number of finished products based on customer demand, such as household appliances.

Quality Filter Mapping

Quality filter mapping helps organizations determine where quality problems are occurring in the supply chain, which can be used to improve quality. Quality problems are broken down into product defects that are discovered by the customer rather than internal inspection, service defects such as late deliveries or incorrect billing, and internal scrap discovered during inspections. For example, Carys Hutcheson and David Simons, researchers at the Cardiff Business School, used quality filter mapping to evaluate the agri-food supply chain for lambs, from breeding through distribution to the retailer. They measured quality conformance based on total losses due to sheep mortality, partial losses from poor butchering, and rework because the meat did not conform to consumer expectations or the fat content was too high.

Each category of defect is plotted for each member of the supply chain, as shown in Figure 10.7. Note in the figure, for example, that the distributor has the greatest problem

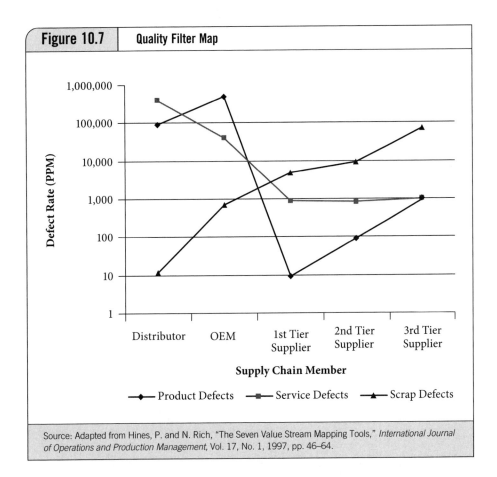

Figure 10.7 | Quality Filter Map

Source: Adapted from Hines, P. and N. Rich, "The Seven Value Stream Mapping Tools," *International Journal of Operations and Production Management*, Vol. 17, No. 1, 1997, pp. 46–64.

with service, while the third-tier supplier is experiencing the greatest problems with scrap. In this instance, the original equipment manufacturer (OEM),[37] who is also experiencing severe product defects, needs to work with its supplier to minimize scrap and the distributor to improve service, as well as improve internally, to lower the overall costs of the supply chain and improve customer satisfaction.

Demand Amplification Mapping

Demand amplification mapping is used to illustrate changes in demand and supplier orders in the supply chain across a period of time, or the bullwhip effect. Essentially, as product demand is communicated upstream through a series of supply chain partners, amplification of demand variation increases at each point, although end-item demand may be relatively stable. As a result, excess inventory tends to build up in the supply chain in an effort to meet demand. Figure 10.8 illustrates this point. Professors often use "The Beer Game," first developed by MIT in the 1960s, to illustrate to their students how the bullwhip effect works. The map in Figure 10.8 can be used to help organizations manage demand fluctuations better, reduce safety stocks, improve visibility in the supply chain, improve forecasts, and create separate solutions for regular demand versus promotional sales.

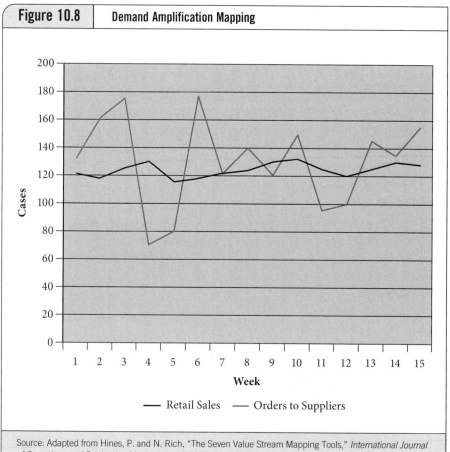

| Figure 10.8 | Demand Amplification Mapping |

Source: Adapted from Hines, P. and N. Rich, "The Seven Value Stream Mapping Tools," *International Journal of Operations and Production Management,* Vol. 17, No. 1, 1997, pp. 46–64.

SUMMARY

Today more than ever organizations are looking for ways to remain competitive. While many firms focus on revenue generation, improving the flow of production and minimizing waste will reduce production costs and improve profitability. Lean principles are being adopted by manufacturers and service providers alike to cut costs and improve productivity. Because lean thinking is so important, this chapter begins with the concepts of lean thinking and provides an in-depth discussion of the elements of lean production and lean supply chain management. If firms can extend the principles of lean thinking to their supply chain partners, the positive effects are even more powerful. Thus, this chapter contains a discussion of the lean supply chain. However, firms must also have the tools to analyze the existing organization. Several value stream mapping tools are discussed at the end of the chapter as aids to production managers.

KEY TERMS

5S, 379

5W1H, 388

agile manufacturing, 385

batch and queue production, 365

cellular layouts, 368

combination replenishment pull system, 375

cycle time, 376

downsizing, 381

group technology, 372

group technology cells, 370

Heijunka box, 376

job shop, 367

kanban, 373

lean enterprises, 364

lean manufacturing, 363

lean organization, 364

lean production/service delivery, 363

lean supply chain, 364

lean thinking, 360

level capacity loading, 376

make-to-order replenishment pull system, 375

make-to-stock replenishment pull system, 375

mass production, 365

mixed model scheduling, 376

muda, 360

opportunity cost, 362

optimizing the supply base, 381

overprocessing, 361

overproduction, 360

pacemaker, 375

perfection, 363

poka-yoke, 380

production interval, 376

production kanban, 373

production lot sizes, 365

pull system, 363

scientific management, 359

setup, 372

takt time, 376

total productive maintenance, 380

Toyota Production System, 358

value, 363

value stream, 363

withdrawal kanban, 373

DISCUSSION QUESTIONS

1. What is the Toyota Production System? Find and describe two companies that have applied TPS to their organization.

2. Define lean thinking. What are the operational goals of lean thinking?

3. What are the three major areas of an organization where waste occurs?

4. The following are the seven forms of waste that occur in an organization. Provide an example of each form of waste from your own experience or from a trade journal you have read.
   a. Overproduction
   b. Delays between processing steps

    c. Unnecessary transportation of products or parts

    d. Overprocessing of parts

    e. Overstocked inventories

    f. Needless movements by employees

    g. Production of defective parts

5. What is the difference between lean production, a lean organization, a lean enterprise, and a lean supply chain?

6. What are the characteristics of companies that work with supply chain partners to become leaner?

7. What are the characteristics of traditional production? What are the disadvantages of traditional manufacturing?

8. Compare and contrast traditional versus lean production.

9. Describe the characteristics of cellular layouts. What are the advantages of a cellular layout?

10. Why do lean producers work to reduce setup times?

11. What are the advantages of producing in smaller lot sizes?

12. What is level capacity loading? Why is this practice important to lean producers?

13. What is mixed model scheduling? Why do lean producers practice mixed model scheduling?

14. What is the 5S system? Why is this practice important in a lean environment?

15. What is total productive maintenance, and why is it important in a lean environment?

16. What types of technology are available to support a lean environment?

17. What are the drawbacks to operating in a lean environment?

18. Describe the difference between lean and agile manufacturing.

19. What can lean organizations do to overcome the bullwhip effect?

20. Why is it important for organizations to expand beyond lean production to a lean supply chain?

21. Describe five value stream mapping tools.

PROBLEMS

1. Hobbs Bakery produces a variety of cakes that are shipped to grocery stores. The owner, Ken Hobbs, wants to try to reduce inventory by changing to a kanban system. He has developed the following data for the chocolate cake with white frosting and asked you to finish the project by telling him the number of kanbans (containers) needed:

Daily demand	500 cakes
Production lead time	2 days
Safety stock	.25
Kanban size	250 cakes

How many kanbans are needed?

2. Fergie's Electronics, Inc. (FEI) produces custom microwave radios for railroads and other industrial clients. The production manager has been asked to reduce its inventory by introducing a kanban system. After several hours of analysis, you develop the following data for one of the parts, the connectors, used in one of FEI's work cells:

Daily demand	325 radios
Production lead time	1 day
Safety stock	.30
Kanban size	50 radios

How many kanbans do you need for this connector?

3. The Gumbo Company makes and sells safes and other security equipment for larger corporations. The production manager is under the gun because there has been an increasing number of backorders for its safes. The current production line makes one safe every 252 seconds.

a. Estimate the takt time in seconds using the following information:

# of shifts/day: 1
hours/shift: 8
lunch break: ½ hour
other breaks: 2 @ 15 minutes
average customer demand: 160/day

b. Does the production manager need to make any changes? What should be the next steps?

4. 3K Manufacturing makes and sells four different products using lean production and mixed model scheduling. Following is this week's production schedule based on customer demand:

PRODUCT	DAILY PRODUCTION
A1	24
A2	4
A3	12
A4	16

Calculate the number of cycles per day and a production quantity per cycle.

5. 3K Manufacturing's production schedule for the following week is as follows:

PRODUCT	DAILY PRODUCTION
A1	25
A2	4
A3	14
A4	18

Calculate the number of cycles per day and a production quantity per cycle to approach as close to level production as possible. Assume the production sequence is A1, A2, A3, A4.

INTERNET QUESTIONS

1. See if you can find different examples of companies that apply lean thinking to their supply chains.

2. Find an example of a company that gets help using a software application to become more lean.

INFOTRAC QUESTIONS

Access http://www.infotrac-thomsonlearning.com to answer the following questions:

1. Use InfoTrac to search for the term *Toyota Production System*. Write a paper on the history of the Toyota Production System and the contributions of Shigeo Shingo and Tai'ichi Ohno using your findings. Include a bibliography.

2. Use InfoTrac to search for the terms *lean thinking* and *supply chain*. Write a paper on the application of lean thinking to the supply chain. Include a bibliography.

REFERENCES

Feld, W. M. (2001), *Lean Manufacturing,* St. Luckie Press and APICS, Boca Raton, FL.

Nicholas, J. M. (1998), *Competitive Manufacturing Management,* Irwin/McGraw-Hill, New York, NY.

Stevenson, W. J. (2002), *Operations Management,* 7th edition, Irwin/McGraw-Hill, New York, NY.

Taylor, D., and D Brunt, eds. (2001), *Manufacturing Operations and Supply Chain Management: The Lean Approach,* London, England: Thomson Business Press, London, UK.

Womack, J. P. (2003), *Lean Thinking,* Free Press, New York, NY.

ENDNOTES

1. Simon Pollard, vice president of the industrial sector for Oracle in Europe, the Middle East, and Africa, quoted in Baum, D., "Creating the Lean Enterprise," *Profit, the Business of Technology,* November 2004, available at http://www.oracle.com/oramag/profit/04-nov/p44lean.html.

2. Quote from an interview with Norman Bodek, author, speaker, and consultant on manufacturing productivity and quality, in "The Essence of Lean Manufacturing and the Toyota Production System: An Interview with Norman Bodek," *Strategos Lean Briefing,* April 27, 2004, available at http://www.strategosinc.com/nbodek.html.

3. See note 2 above.

4. For a history of lean production, see Becker, R. M., "Learning to Think Lean: Lean Manufacturing and the Toyota Production System," *Automotive Manufacturing & Production,* June 2001, pp. 64–65.

5. Womack, J. and D. Jones, *Lean Thinking,* New York, NY: Free Press, 2003, p. 19.

6. Ohno, T., *Toyota Production System: Beyond Large-Scale Production,* New York, NY: Productivity Press, 1988.

7. "Struggling Ford Announces 2007 Product Lineup," June 21, 2006, available at http://www.msnbc.msn.com/id/13458418/.

8. Hanssens, D. M., "Order Forecasts, Retail Sales, and the Marketing Mix for Consumer Durables," *Journal of Forecasting,* V. 17, p. 327.

9. Kastle, B., "Learning to Recognize Process Waste in Financial Services," available at http://www.finance.isixsigma.com/library/content/c040324a.asp, accessed October 10, 2006.

10. "What Is a Product Problem," available at http://www.fda.gov/medwatch/report/DESK/prodprob.htm.

11. See note 5 above, pp. 16–26.

12. See note 5 above.

13. Kahn, G., "Made to Measure," *Wall Street Journal,* September 11, 2003, p. A.1.

14. See http://www.ebizq.net/topics/scm/features/5443.html?&pp=1.

15. Swank, C. K., "The Lean Service Machine," *Harvard Business Review,* October 2003, pp. 123–129.

16. "Lean Supply Chain," *The Manufacturer US,* May 18, 2006, available at http://www.themanufacturer.com/us/content/4248/Lean_supply_chain; Copacino, W. C. and J. L. S. Byrnes, "How to Become a Supply Chain Master," *Supply Chain Management Review Yearbook,* 2002, pp. 37–42.

17. Vitassek, K., K. B. Monrodt, and J. Abbott, "What Makes a Lean Supply Chain?" *Supply Chain Management Review,* October 2005, p. 42.

18. "La-Z-Boy Is Not Lazy about Implementing Lean," *Lean Directions,* March 9, 2006, available at http://www.sme.org/cgi-bin/get-newsletter.pl?LEAN&20060309&7&.

19. Ford, H., *Today and Tomorrow: Commemorative Edition of Ford's 1926 Classic,* New York, NY: Productivity Press, reprinted 2002.

20. Information based on "Quality Circles and Lean Production at Honda," available at http://www.hutchins.co.uk/NW_Toyota.aspx.

21. Marks, P., "Going Lean," Lean Sigma Institute, April 2, 2006, available at http://www.sixsigmainstitute.com/news/lean/2006/04/going-lean.html.

22. "Single Piece Flow," *The Manufacturer US,* February 8, 2006, available at http://www.themanufacturer.com/us/detail.html?contents_id=4018.

23. Forth, K. D., "Becoming a World-Class Manufacturer," *Cabinet Maker,* April 2006, p. 70.

24. DTI Manufacturing Advisory Services Case Study on Sovereign Showers, available at http://www.mas.dti.gov.uk/pluto-resources/2672.pdf.

25. Navas, D., "Manufacturing Shifts from Push to Pull," *Supply Chain Manufacturing & Logistics,* 2005, available at http://www.scs-mag.com/index.php?option=com_content&task=view&id=694&Itemid=87.

26. Doody, A., "Lean Manufacturing Not a Simple Switch," *Central Penn Business Journal,* May 5, 2006, p.1.

27. Hamacher, E. C., "A Methodology for Implementing Total Productive Maintenance in the Commercial Aircraft Industry," dissertation, M.I.T. Sloan School of Management and Department of Electrical Engineering and Computer Science, 2006, p. 51.

28. This example of poka-yoke was found at http://www.tpmclubindia.org/tpmbook.htm.

29. Womack, J. and D. Jones, "Lean Consumption," *Harvard Business Review,* March 2005, pp. 1–11.

30. Morgan, J., "A Profession Turns the Corner: Why So Many Buyers Are in Love with Their Jobs," *Purchasing,* September 16, 2004, available at http://www.purchasing.com.

31. Berger, D. and B. Nakashina, "Can Lean and ERP Work Together?" *Advanced Manufacturing,* September 2000, available at http://www.advancedmanufacturing.com/index.php?option=com_staticxt&staticfile=informationtech.htm&itemid=44.

32. Walter, J., "See how the automotive industry leverages emerging technologies to manage product life-cycle management, product recalls," *PA Manufacturing,* available in 2006 at http://www.catalystconnection.org/news/PaManufacturing/PAM_integration.aspx.

33. The Aberdeen Group, "The Lean Benchmark Report: Closing the Reality Gap," 2006, available at http://www.aberdeen.com/summary/report/benchmark/RA_Lean_JB_2845.asp.

34. http://www.maskell.com/AgileArticle.htm.

35. See note 17 above.

36. Hines, P. and N. Rich, "The Seven Value Stream Mapping Tools," *International Journal of Operations and Production Management,* January 1997, pp. 46–64.

37. An original equipment manufacturer (OEM) is a company that supplies products to other companies, who then resell or incorporate those products using the reseller's brand name. Maytag, for example, manufactures and sells refrigerators to Sears, who then resells them to consumers using the Sears brand name.

Chapter 11:

LOGISTICS AND ORDER FULFILLMENT

Forget logistics, you lose.[1]

We're on the tip of the iceberg. Most people think that Dell has reached the ultimate goal in supply chain management—an inventory of three days. We disagree; everyday we work to bring that number down.[2]

Learning Objectives

After completing this chapter, you should be able to:

- Describe the elements of customer service from a logistics standpoint.
- Explain the role of transportation in the logistics and order fulfillment process.
- Identify the key activities in the order fulfillment process.
- Understand the importance of order cycle time to the customer.
- Define the storage and handling activities that take place in a warehouse.
- Recognize the attributes of an effective logistics network.
- Describe the strategic planning process for logistics.
- Understand some of the concerns logistics managers face today.

Chapter Outline

Introduction

Setting Logistics Customer Service Goals

Transportation Planning and Selection

The Order Fulfillment Process

Warehouse Management

Planning the Logistics Network

Developing a Logistics Strategy

Order Fulfillment and Logistics Concerns

Process Management in Action   *Logistics at Dell*

Dell Inc. was founded in 1984 by Michael Dell. Dell builds and sells computers directly to its customers based on their specifications. The goal is to build and ship computers with short turnaround times, generally less than one week. To achieve this goal, Dell does whatever it can to keep inventory moving from its suppliers, to assembly, and on to the final customer. Every supplier receives a report card that tracks its performance against a certain number of metrics developed by Dell. Suppliers are also expected to keep low levels of inventory—about eight to ten days worth—in locations close to Dell. If a supplier's inventory begins to exceed that level, Dell helps it find ways to lower it. Dell's philosophy is that excessive or obsolete inventory only contributes to a supplier's higher cost structure, which will then be passed on to Dell in the form of higher priced parts.

Today, Dell is more dependent than ever on imports of foreign-made parts to build its computers. At the same time, the company keeps on hand a maximum of three days worth of inventory, operating in a just-in-time environment. To ensure a continuous flow of parts from Asian suppliers and reduce delivery problems, Dell logisticians, together with its transportation specialists located in Long Beach, California, developed a contingency plan in 2002.

Six months later union dockworkers, in a ten-day labor lockout, shut down all West Coast ports, costing U.S. companies billions of dollars in lost revenue. Because of its contingency plan, however, Dell was one of the few companies able to respond quickly to the crisis. As a result, it was ready to charter 18 Boeing 747s from several carriers to airship parts until the strike was over. Dell also negotiated with its freight forwarders to load its parts last on each cargo ship so that these parts would be the first to be unloaded when the West Coast ports were operational again.

Sources: http://www.dell.com; Barlas, S., "10 Best Supply Chains," *Logistics Today,* April 2004, retrieved on April 14, 2005, from http://www.logisticstoday.com; and Breen, B., "Living in Dell Time," *Fast Computers,* Vol. 88, November 2004, pp. 86–94.

Introduction

If you have purchased a product over the Internet, via the telephone, or at a store, you expect the retailer to deliver the product as promised. The delivery process is one of the biggest opportunities for a company to create goodwill with the customer or risk losing that customer's business. To meet the delivery expectation, companies in the past would use inventory as a type of security blanket. Even if forecasts of future demand were totally wrong, warehouses and distribution centers packed with inventory meant there would always be a big enough supply to meet demand. This approach has changed, however, since the 1980s as companies have adopted the lean manufacturing practices first developed by Toyota (more on lean practices can be found in Chapter 10). Companies are also starting to plan collaboratively, as discussed in Chapter 5, to improve the accuracy of their forecasts. As a result, organizations have worked to eliminate as much waste from their supply chains as possible by cutting order lead times, inventory, and excess capacity to the bone to achieve the lowest overall costs. Computer software has also made the movement and tracking of shipments visible to everyone in the supply chain. In other words, companies have developed **lean logistics** strategies to support their lean operations. All this demonstrates the need to manage the logistics side of the organization better than ever, as shown by Dell in the opening Process Management in Action feature.

Logistics has been defined by the Council of Supply Chain Management Professionals (formerly the Council of Logistics Management) as "that part of supply chain management that plans, implements, and controls the efficient, effective forward and reverse flow and storage of goods, services and related information between the point of origin and the point of consumption in order to meet customers' requirements."[3] From a company's standpoint, this means that every hour of every day the people working in logistics are making sure materials, products, supplies, and services reach the point where they're needed exactly when the customer wants. The customer may be a manufacturer, distributor, retailer, service provider, or consumer. Thus, logistics creates value through the order fulfillment process—the placement of inventory where and when it is needed to meet customer requirements. Logistics managers are responsible for seeing that purchased items arrive at the right moment to start a manufacturing process, for managing temporary incoming material storage, for managing finished goods storage at customer-facing warehouses and distribution centers until delivery at a later date, and for meeting the wants and needs of consumers when they shop at their favorite retail store.

The logistics process combines order management, inventory management, transportation management, and warehouse management, as illustrated in Figure 11.1. **Transportation management** includes overseeing the movement of raw materials and parts to a warehouse or storage facility within a manufacturing site as well as movement

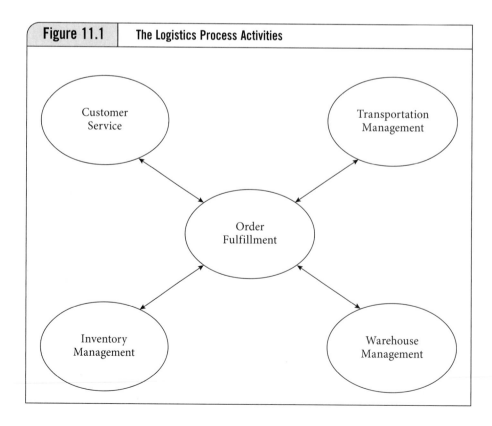

Figure 11.1	The Logistics Process Activities

of finished goods and supplies to distribution centers and retail sites. **Order management** includes the procurement of stock-keeping units (SKUs), which will be sold to the customer, and processing customer orders. **Warehouse management** entails running the operations related to proper storage and movement of inventory and minor manufacturing such as assembly or labeling activities within the warehouse, and movement of shipments onto the transportation carrier. Lastly, **inventory management** includes the control of all inventories—raw materials, work-in-process, and finished goods—when not in use (an in-depth discussion of inventory management is found in Chapter 6). To accomplish these activities effectively, companies must have an effective logistics strategy, which supports the organizational strategy, and a good network of facilities and information flows.

This chapter begins with a discussion of logistics customer service followed by a description of the transportation management process. The next sections will then discuss the activities involved in the order fulfillment process, followed by warehouse management and the attributes of an effective logistics network. The chapter concludes with the mechanics of developing a logistics strategy to effectively coordinate the logistics process and a discussion of concerns for the future.

Setting Logistics Customer Service Goals

Customer service, a fairly broad term, was described in Chapter 3 as a set of intangible activities, some specific and some vague, designed to take care of customer needs before, during, and after the sale. However, **logistics customer service** is more specific and has been defined by logistics expert Dr. James Heskett at the Harvard Business School as "the speed and dependability with which items ordered can be made available."[4]

Two research studies concluded that logistics customer service *does* have an effect on customer satisfaction and future sales.[5] Thus, while often neglected, businesses need to pay closer attention to the logistics side of their operation. As stated in the introduction, logistics adds value for the seller when customers' needs are met while minimizing costs. Ultimately, the goal should be to get all aspects of the order right the first time. Customers usually consider several factors when placing orders. First, they want an adequate selection to choose from. Second, once they place an order, they expect the order to be filled to their satisfaction—accurately, in the promised time frame, and without damage upon arrival.

When orders can't be completely filled because a company is out of stock, or believes it is out of stock due to computer glitches, part of the order is usually filled and the rest is shipped later *or* held until it can be shipped completely. In either scenario, a **backorder** results, in which case the customer is kept from receiving at least part of the order. This is exactly what happened in 1999 when Pennsylvania-based confectioner Hershey Foods Inc. found it couldn't get its Halloween candy to the retailers in time for purchase during the month of October. The candy giant had installed new inventory management software purchased from SAP, but hadn't entered the information on temporary warehouse storage sites into the system, which were filled with inventories of candy. When orders were placed, the software would search for the locations of inventory, but because these warehouses weren't "in the system" the software recorded the order as a backorder and no candy was shipped. As a result, Hershey found itself in the position of having ample inventory but being unable to fill customers' orders![6]

Backorders require additional tracking, either manually or by computer, to maintain the current status of the backorder, as well as additional time spent contacting the supplier to find ways to expedite a shipment so customer orders can be filled. There are also the additional transportation costs incurred when an order is delivered in two shipments. The company may also ship via a more expensive method to expedite the shipment and keep customers happy. All this can add costs to the logistics process and, in the worst case scenario, dissatisfied customers take their business elsewhere.

In essence, logistics completes the promises of marketing. Thus, any customer service initiative should identify the logistical activities important to meeting customers' needs and then set performance goals for each of these activities. The overarching consideration should address whether the cost of each activity involved in the order fulfillment process is justified. If not, the process should be adjusted to ensure a cost-effective fulfillment process. While customer service was discussed from a broader perspective in Chapter 4, the following sections focus on the basic dimensions of customer service from a logistical perspective.

Availability

Suppliers must have enough capacity to meet their customers' order requirements, by stocking enough inventory of each stock-keeping unit. As discussed in Chapter 5, companies generally begin by formulating the demand forecast to predict their customers' future needs. The forecast is then adjusted for things such as expected increases or decreases in the popularity of items, upcoming promotions that will affect sales, and market trends. As you can see, a great deal of planning is required to ensure enough inventory is available to meet customer requirements.

Firms look at three interconnected measures of inventory management performance—**order fill rates, stockouts**, and **orders shipped complete**. In total, these three measures determine the ability of a firm to meet customer demand. The order fill rate measures the percentage of units available to fill a specific order. For example, if a customer orders 200 units but only 175 are in stock, the fill rate is 87.5 percent (or 175/200). The **line order fill rate** refers to the number of line orders filled on the initial order versus the amount of lines ordered. For instance, XYZ Company orders 300 products (300 lines) on purchase order #1234. Its supplier initially ships 280 products (280 lines) and the remaining 20 products five days later. The line order fill rate for the supplier is 280/300, or 93.3 percent.

The number of stockouts across product lines is an indicator of a firm's customer service level. Stockouts occur when a company can't fill a customer's order, either partially or at all. Thus, stockouts and fill rates are directly tied together. Even if a supplier fills 99.9 percent of an order, a stockout situation is still in effect. To manage stockouts, companies set a **service level** for each SKU. In others words, they estimate the amount of safety stock, or extra inventory, required to minimize the probability of running out during the order fulfillment cycle. For example, the owner of a hardware store might keep on hand enough extra inventory or safety stock of a particular brand of chain saw to ensure supply meets demand 95 percent of the time. Firms also look at the impact of stockouts over a period of time to determine the effectiveness of their forecasting methods and inventory policies.

Organizations also monitor the number of orders shipped complete compared to the total number of orders shipped. If one SKU is missing from an order, the order is considered an incomplete shipment. Thus, if a logistics department shipped 150 orders during one particular week, but 25 were shipped with at least one SKU missing from the initial shipment, the performance measure is 125/150, or 83.3 percent of orders shipped complete. In this case, the logistics department manager would likely investigate the possible reason for poor performance, assess current inventory management practices, and make some changes. It is also a good practice to graph weekly (or daily or monthly) performance to note any improvements (or deterioration) in performance based on changes made to the operation.

Order Lead Time

Another dimension of logistical performance is the time needed to process and deliver each customer's order. Customers are most interested in the reliability of the promised order completion date. From the customer's viewpoint, this cycle begins with the order placement and ends when the customer receives the order, or **order lead time**. As the order cycle becomes more inconsistent, the customer will be forced to carry additional inventory to maintain its own customer service levels. There are several points where the timing of activities can vary considerably, making it difficult to guarantee delivery times with certainty. Companies often compensate for this by offering various customer service levels, with premiums charged for more reliable delivery methods. Global Internet retailer Amazon.com, for instance, offers free shipping if customers purchase at least $25 of merchandise. However, delivery times are much longer than when the customer pays for shipping. The company also offers expedited shipping for an additional fee. In a supply chain setting, business customers may charge late penalties for deliveries that do not meet certain promised dates or time windows, and these penalties are typically incorporated into the terms of the purchase contract.

Today, more firms than ever before are operating in a lean or just-in-time environment. As discussed in Chapter 10, the idea behind lean is the elimination of waste, part of which is carrying excess inventory. Inventory should arrive at an organization just in time for production, distribution, or resale. Dell, for example, receives parts and assembles computer parts just as they are needed to build a computer for a customer. This process eliminates additional warehouse space to store parts and computers, reduces the opportunity for loss or theft, and diminishes the probability of obsolescent parts, all of which result in lower inventory carrying costs. This also means companies such as Dell usually have close relationships with their suppliers because parts may need to be delivered several times a day. Shipments must consist of high-quality parts and materials delivered more frequently with short lead times, and arrive according to a precise schedule to make just-in-time work effectively.[7]

Customers are also looking for suppliers who are flexible in meeting emergency, unexpected, or unusual requests. A customer, experiencing unforeseen demand for an item, may request expedited shipping. It is then up to the logistics department to have backup plans to meet unusual or infrequent requests. It's also important to be able to fill an order from an alternate location when the original location is out of stock. Industry courses are even offered to help suppliers create alternative plans. The Automotive Industry Action Group (AIAG), a global nonprofit organization promoting cooperative solutions for the automobile supply chain, for example, provides a one-day seminar on crisis management to automotive suppliers, based on a process created by the three top U.S. automakers—DaimlerChrysler, General Motors, and Ford. These three companies created the procedures to protect their own inbound supply chains and require their suppliers to adopt these procedures.[8]

Reliability

Companies should also be able to provide all aspects of the order fulfillment process reliably and accurately, including status and location information for any outstanding orders. When a supplier accepts an order, this is an implicit promise that the complete order will be filled on time and damage free. FedEx Corporation, a U.S.-based provider of transportation and information services worldwide, improved its reliability by offering "transparent" tracing of packages through the use of a combination of tracking numbers and bar codes, along with utilization of the Internet. Today the company offers connectivity services that improve communications with all trading partners, shipment tracking and tracing to monitor and manage shipments online, and data management services to increase the accuracy and timeliness of shipment information.[9]

Transportation Planning and Selection

Most consumers don't think much about how a product arrives on the shelves. They just know they're unhappy if the shelf is empty. This illustrates one of the elements of logistics customer service and why it's so important for companies to have an effective transportation planning and selection process. Transportation planning begins with the selection of the preferred transportation modes to move freight. The following section begins with a description of the advantages and disadvantages of the most common modes of transportation.

Modes of Transportation

The five basic modes of transportation are air, rail, truck, pipeline, and water carriers. **Intermodal transportation** is also common, where two modes of transportation are combined. For example, **piggyback** refers to loading shipping containers or truck trailers on a rail flatbed car (also known as container-on-flat-car (COFC) and trailer-on-flat-car (TOFC)). The railroad carries the shipment to its destination at the rail depot and a then a truck loads the trailer or container onto the axles and delivers it to the customer. In international shipments, many shippers contract for container ships to move freight. Some cargo airplanes, such as those owned by FedEx, are equipped to carry specially designed containers between airports, sometimes known as **birdyback**. Pipelines provide a special form of transportation—typically oil, natural gas, water, and sometimes coal are transported this way (coal can be pulverized and suspended in water for pipeline transport).

The type of freight generally dictates the mode of transportation used. For example, train cars are used to move coal because of its weight and bulkiness. There is no need to worry about damage to the coal and slower transit times are not a problem. On the other hand, valuables such as paintings and jewelry are usually moved on airplanes because they are lightweight, the chance of damage is a major concern, and speed of delivery can be a priority. However, well-packaged products, such as television sets and refrigerators, may be moved by truck or train.

Access to the carrier may also determine the mode chosen. In other words, not all forms of transportation are available for every origination and destination point. For example, while water transportation is the cheapest form of transportation, not many points in the United States are accessible by water. Trucks have the easiest access to most places and are probably the reason that about 80 percent of all goods in the United States (based on value) are moved in this manner. Therefore, transportation managers need to consider the best mode or combination of modes given any access or customer requirement constraints. The United Kingdom's Royal Mail service, for example, was faced with competition due to deregulation and it reevaluated its modes of transportation, resulting in a redesign of its distribution network. The mail carrier found that, due to the unreliability of the U.K. rail system, trucking would be more efficient and effective. More on Royal Mail's changes can be found in the Service Perspective feature.

Most shippers are concerned about **transit time**, which accounts for a significant part of the order lead time. Transit time is measured from the point where an order leaves the shipper's dock until the time it arrives at its destination. The fastest mode of transportation is air, and the most expensive per ounce or gram, while rail and water transportation are the slowest and cheapest. Because of the trends toward lean production and rapid replenishment, many firms have moved toward faster modes of transportation. However, some manufacturers also use dedicated rail service to meet their just-in-time needs. For example, major U.S. freight carrier Norfolk Southern Railroad offers single-stack COFC service from the Norfolk, Virginia, seaport directly to Chicago, a distance of 1,000 miles, in just three days.[10]

Shippers are also concerned about theft and damage. While a shipment is moving, there is less chance for something to happen. Thus, whenever a shipment is stopped during transit there is always the opportunity for theft or damage. Most damage occurs because the shipment has been poorly packaged. Other than air, trucks have the best record for keeping shipments safe and secure.

Freight Rates

Last but certainly not least, freight rates are of primary concern to the shipper. Cost is generally related to time, distance, and density—the faster the delivery speed and the longer the distance, the higher the cost. Density, or weight per volume, becomes less expensive per pound to transport as density increases. Air transportation is the most expensive, followed by trucking, rail, water, and pipeline in most cases. Unless the shipment is moved by truck, however, two or more modes of transportation will generally be used. As a result, shippers consider the total cost of transportation, which includes both the shipment time and freight rates of all modes used. Freight rates in the United States, in most cases, are now negotiable due to transportation deregulation that began in the 1970s.

Carrier Selection

Once the transportation or logistics manager selects the preferred modes of transportation, either private carriers or specific public transportation providers that will move shipments from the point of origin to the final destination can be used. **Private carriers** refer to the use of the firm's own carriers such as a company truck fleet. **Public carriers** refer to the use of public, for-profit transportation companies, such as Kansas-based global transportation provider Yellow Transportation. With the dramatic increase in globalization, a common occurrence today is also the use of **third-party logistics providers** (3PLs), which provide not only transportation but other services as well. Some of these services include warehousing, document preparation, customs clearance, packaging, labeling, and freight bill auditing. Georgia-based UPS Supply Chain Solutions, a subsidiary of delivery giant United Parcel Service for instance, offers a menu of services, including help in locating and designing facilities, developing transportation solutions, managing inventory and returns, and implementing information systems.[11] Based on management expertise and the desire to provide high levels of delivery service at the lowest cost, firms may decide to use a mix of private carriage, for-hire carriers, and 3PLs.

Service Perspective

Moving Her Majesty's Mail

The stakes for managing asset movement in the distribution center (DC) yard rose significantly for the U.K.'s Royal Mail (http://www.royalmail.com) on January 1, 2006. That's the day that full liberalization of the entire country's mail market began and Royal Mail faced full competition. Under terms of the country's Postal Services Act of 2000, Royal Mail became wholly owned by the U.K. government in March 2001. Between the time its strategic relationship with the government changed and the day on which other companies would be allowed to collect and deliver commercial mail, Royal Mail's most pressing need was to increase efficiency.

"We are restricted by the price we can charge," explains John Szwec, Royal Mail's technology director. "A regulator indicates what prices we can charge using a formula that reflects the retail price index minus 'x' percent. The only way we are going to survive is by driving costs within the organization. That's one of the reasons we went through a huge reorganization—to get more efficiency and reliability and to drive costs out of the network." The postal service provides delivery to each of the 27 million addresses in the United Kingdom at a uniform price, no matter the distance traveled. Daily mail volume is 82 million items, and that volume continues to grow.

Faced with the challenge of increasing its efficiency in the face of such volumes, Royal Mail changed its operational paradigm. Previously it relied on a combination of trains, planes, and trucks to move the mail. Over the recent past, train service and reliability has been deteriorating. Now the postal service puts trucks at the center of its mail distribution activities. "We still use planes because of the nature of our contract as a universal service obligation," explains Szwec. "The service will pick up its First Class mail as late as 7:00 pm and deliver the next morning before 9:00 am. The geography of the U.K. indicates it's impossible to deliver from the very south to the very north without using planes."

Not only did mail handling move more to truck, but also a hub-and-spoke system was put in place in a strategically located facility. The new DC is located in the middle of the country at Daventry. "There are several overlays," Szwec notes, "but the logistics network comprises one large DC at Daventry and ten quite large facilities distributed around the U.K. that feed mail centers. Shipments go from mail centers—of which we have about 66—to one of the regional DCs and then typically, depending on the nature of the mail, a great deal of it ends up getting trucked down to Daventry."

Daventry is a pure cross-dock operation with mail presorted when it reaches the facility. There are some 1,600 gate transactions each day, with arrivals spaced every 26 seconds at peak. Within the Daventry yard, in addition to trucks coming and going, there are 20 shunting vehicles, 110 docks, and 200 parking slots. A single delayed trailer can cause the quality of service to slip at as many as 40 mail centers.

Royal Mail understood the need for a yard management system because of service pressures, time scales, and the sheer number of vehicles using the DC. Too, the supplier that won the job, Montreal-based C3 Solutions Inc. (http://www.C3tools.com), did so through a unique product demonstration. Szwec explains that previous to hiring C3, the mail center conducted its yard management with what it called "a penny exercise." In a huge room was a map of the Daventry yard. To simulate arrivals and departures, penny coins were used to identify vehicles coming in and out. The aim was to simulate where points of congestion were going to occur and other traffic issues might come up. To complete the entire cycle of activities took almost a week.

After narrowing the list of potential suppliers to three, Royal Mail showed its penny exercise to each. C3 wondered why the staff was going to such lengths. The supplier suggested it could get its software, Yard Smart™, to simulate the process. "We gave them our schedules," says Szwec, "and they entered them into their software and got it to simulate our yard. They did in ten minutes what had been taking us a week." Using the C3 simulator it was possible to identify and eliminate congestion areas in the yard. Some congestion points were located at doors close to the gate, and through different scenarios it was determined that by changing the location of originally planned inbound and outbound locations, the problems would be solved. With congestion relieved, by analyzing Royal Mail's service contracts it was possible to rearrange some runs and not affect service levels. The software was able to determine that reducing the number of drops and increasing the number of live operations would help site flow.

The change from old delivery systems to the new happened on January 1, 2005. Instead of gradual movement, it all took place with one Big Bang. "For the Christmas before we were running to various regional hubs and doing some cross-docking there," explains Szwec. "Then on the first week of January, everyone was told not to go to their local hubs, and to drive instead to a new place called Daventry. Some drivers couldn't even find Daventry." From the moment C3 was given the go-ahead for the yard management implementation until the Big Bang was just two months. Deployment went smoothly and other elements of the yard management solution have been incorporated to operations.

People are part of the smooth running of the Daventry yard. As trucks arrive at the gate, they pass a gatehouse keeper, who records the name of the duty and the trailer number. The gate-in process takes about 30 seconds. Szwec foresees greater future efficiency as Royal Mail integrates global positioning system (GPS) vehicle-tracking technology so that logging will happen automatically.

Nearly a dozen people sit in Daventry's control room. They have a complete overview of the yard, including what vehicles are in and at which docks. "The software then does some very clever things, but what it can't do is tell you when the vehicle is on an inbound door," notes Szwec. "For that we use yard marshals with handheld devices, who indicate that a vehicle is now on at a door. When the vehicle moves off, there are dock controllers who inform the control room about the status change. So we have people indoors and outdoors, reporting status changes. It's important because we don't want an empty vehicle sitting on a door for extra two or three minutes during peak time, since that could cause us to miss connections."

As experience grew, Royal Mail began connecting C3 systems to LED boards positioned across the top of each of the doors. The displays provide all information on trailers at the doors, including content, route, destination, and status of incoming trailers. Next, inbound and outbound "agents"—part of the program—were turned on. These agents automate some tasks previously handled by control room personnel. "The inbound agent can prioritize vehicle movement by schedule requirements, who should be parked further off, and how far from a door for greatest efficiencies in the yard," Szwec notes. "There is an outbound agent with the same intelligence, but for the final outbound leg."

Royal Mail achieved its return on investment in less than a year. There have been some further benefits. There has been a 53 percent reduction in the number of shunting vehicles needed. DC control room personnel requirements have dropped. Initial planning called for 20 people on an around-the-clock basis. Only 11 are needed with the yard management system in place. There has also been a 5 percent reduction in fleet size. "Yard management may be pretty bland to talk about, but it's an additional way of driving efficiency in the supply chain," concludes Szwec. "It might not be as sexy as some other programs, but people need to start looking at it."

Source: Morton, R., "Moving Her Majesty's Mail," *Logistics Today*, April 2006, available online at http://www.logisticstoday.com. Reprinted with permission.

While firms certainly consider freight rates important when choosing a transportation carrier, several other factors are important from a service aspect. Customers will have a specific time frame in which they would like to receive their shipment, which results in shippers leaning toward the use of certain modes. Linked to time is the reliability of the carrier. Customers like to have assurances that their shipments will arrive within the time promised. Customers may even promise more business if a supplier reduces its delivery time, so the supplier will consider the additional costs to speed the shipment along versus the opportunity for more business and thus more revenue. In addition, transportation department managers are looking for carriers with good records of minimal losses in terms of damaged or lost shipments en route to customers. If a claim has to be processed, the transportation manager wants that process to be timely and fair. The ability of customers to track their shipments is also important and, as mentioned earlier, is possible today with the Internet and available tracking system software. Overall, managers will select carriers that provide the lowest cost service while at the same time providing the desired levels of customer service.

Maintaining a competitive advantage may also overshadow transportation cost as an important factor, resulting in the selection of certain carriers. Snack-food manufacturer Frito-Lay, headquartered in Texas, for example, has set the bar for delivery reliability at 100 percent to distinguish itself from the competition. The company chose to monitor its 14 core carriers to ensure this promise of perfection to its retail customers. An annual award is made to one of its select carriers to encourage them to maintain the highest possible service level. Virginia-based logistics provider Excel Transportation Services, the three-time winner of Frito-Lay's "Transportation Supplier of the Year" award, maintains an excellent service record by operating in a just-in-time environment and using tracking and tracing tools to monitor shipments.[12]

Today, selection of carriers can involve negotiations between the shipper and carrier. During negotiations, the shipper will most likely be focused on cost, delivery times, and any special handling requirements. The carrier will be more interested in the size of its profit margin, the shipper's delivery schedule requirements, the amount of labor needed to meet the shipper's needs, and balancing the flows of its transportation equipment. Carriers are particularly interested in keeping expenses down throughout their operations. Ultimately, the negotiation process should address anything that is important to either the shipper or the carrier, including volume, performance standards, length of the contract, loss and damage claims, special services, and, of course, rates.

Many firms are moving toward a **core carrier strategy**, which means they focus their efforts on developing good working relationships with a smaller number of transportation carriers. The idea behind this strategy is that better working relationships are possible when using fewer carriers, and should result in improved scheduling, standardized and better delivery schedules, flexibility when unusual situations arise, and more customized services. Additionally, concentrating more shipping business on fewer carriers generally means lower transportation pricing. The Hard Rock Cafe, with headquarters in Orlando Florida, chose U.S. freight hauler Roadway Express for the majority of its deliveries to its 100 plus restaurants. Roadway Express uses an online tracking system so clients can check on delivery status. Hard Rock Cafe has also eliminated virtually all expediting of shipments because Roadway Express provides such reliable delivery.[13]

Transportation Routing and Scheduling

Logistics managers are always looking for ways to keep transportation costs down while at the same time meeting customer demands for reliable, on-time delivery. By improving the routes that vehicles travel between the network of facilities, the logistics manager can actually accomplish both objectives. Managers analyze and develop the route structure by answering the following questions:

- How should deliveries be grouped together to form the routes?
- How should the deliveries be sequenced to best serve customers?
- Are there points on the routes where freight should be consolidated to lower costs?
- Which vehicle type should be assigned to each route?
- What are the capacity limitations of each vehicle type in the fleet?
- Is there a vehicle type better suited to particular customers?
- Are there any time restrictions imposed by the customer that will affect the vehicle type and route chosen, such as delivery windows?
- What are the safety restrictions imposed by the Department of Transportation, such as required rest periods for drivers?

A number of techniques are available to analyze this problem, including heuristic approaches, simulation, linear programming, or a combination of approaches. Heuristic approaches are iterative in nature, meaning that an initial routing solution is developed and then costs and time are considered as additional stops are added or deleted. They can result in good, but not necessarily optimal, solutions. Simulation involves creating possible routing and scheduling scenarios using a software program that mimics reality and then testing the routes to determine the effect on time and cost. Linear programming involves developing a list of constraints and variables of the routing problem to come up with an optimal route structure. In general, a combination of these techniques has been found to result in the most effective routing solution. Today vehicle routing and scheduling software is often used to improve efficiencies and meet customer requirements. Recall that vehicle routing and scheduling algorithms were covered in detail in Chapter 7.

Day-to-Day Management

Once the negotiations are over, the carriers have been selected, and routing/scheduling decisions are made, transportation managers must oversee the transportation movements and monitor the performance of their carriers. In most contracts, customers stipulate certain standards of performance with penalties for not meeting those expectations. As a result, logistics managers generally track several performance measures to determine if carriers are meeting their customer service goals. They will usually focus their biggest efforts on those shipments to customers that generate the most revenue. Some measures of customer service include percent of on-time deliveries, transit time consistency from origin to destination, and percentage of claims for loss or damage. A table of typical measures can be found in Table 11.1.

The Order Fulfillment Process

It is also important to understand the path a customer order might take once it is placed because of its impact on logistics customer service. Any interruptions during the transmittal of an order or miscommunication will increase order fulfillment time and negatively affect logistics customer service.

Table 11.1	Transportation Carrier Performance Metrics
PERFORMANCE METRIC	**MEASUREMENT**
Rates	Carrier comparisons
Billing accuracy	Invoice errors/total invoices
Reliable pickup/delivery	% on-time deliveries
Consistent service	% compliance with posted service standards
Carrier reliability	Available on short notice
Damages/loss	Number of claims/number of shipments
Carrier flexibility	Ability to assist in unusual situations
Equipment availability	Equipment available when needed
Safety	Safety record
Special services	Other value-added services available

Source: Hannon, D., "Getting Serious about Carrier Performance," *Purchasing Magazine Online,* November 6, 2003, retrieved from http://www.purchasing.com on April 28, 2005.

Figure 11.2 provides an example of the typical order fulfillment process. First, a customer order for products or services is transmitted to the supplier. Most orders today are entered into a computer system, which checks to see if the requested product or service is available in the necessary quantity, or if not, whether production has been scheduled to replenish the stock of that item. The customer's credit is also checked to see if it is acceptable to continue processing the order. If the order can be filled and the customer's credit history is acceptable, the order is processed and the shipping documents are created. If the desired product is not available, the customer is given the option to cancel the order or wait until stock is replenished. If the customer agrees to wait, the order is then considered a backorder. Once the order is processed, it is forwarded along with the shipping documents to the supplier's warehouse or distribution center, where it is picked from the warehouse shelves and processed for delivery. At the same time transportation is scheduled to deliver the order. The warehouse informs accounting of the shipment so it can invoice the customer for payment. A transportation provider then picks up the order and delivers it to the customer.

The ordering system provides information that is used in the demand forecasting process. It also generates information for (1) accounting, in the invoicing process; (2) the warehouse, in the form of picking/packing instructions; (3) the transportation manager, in the form of shipping documents such as the bill of lading;[14] (4) the customer, in the form of acknowledging shipment of the order and an invoice; (5) finance, for use in cash-flow planning; and (6) production, for future production scheduling, among others.

Order Cycle Time

The time it takes to fill orders and the reliability of the process are important components in meeting the customer's needs. **Order cycle time** has been defined as "the elapsed time between when a customer places a purchase order or a service request,

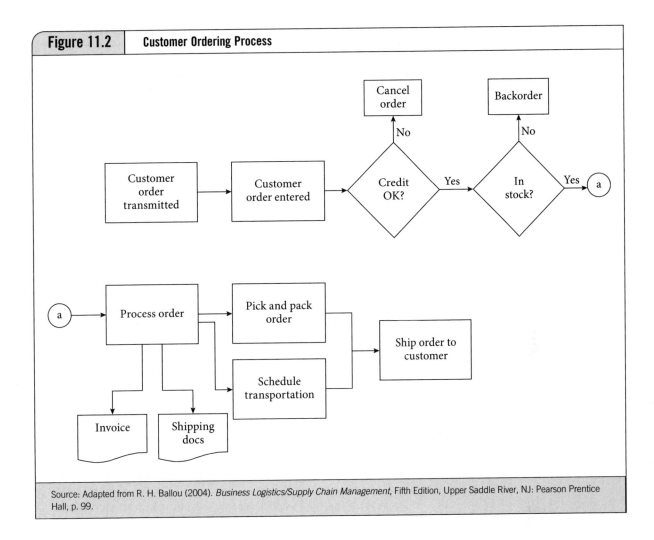

Figure 11.2 | Customer Ordering Process

Source: Adapted from R. H. Ballou (2004). *Business Logistics/Supply Chain Management,* Fifth Edition, Upper Saddle River, NJ: Pearson Prentice Hall, p. 99.

and when the product or service is received by the customer."[15] Late orders are generally not considered acceptable and may result in contract disputes or lawsuits if a pattern becomes apparent, particularly for companies that run lean operations. Manufacturers, for example, lose valuable production time when suppliers do not deliver materials on time, and as a result they compensate by carrying excess inventory and expediting orders. These delays could take place at any point of the order fulfillment process but transportation times are usually the most variable. In one extreme example, U.S. seasonal product manufacturer Paper Magic Group Inc., hired Arkansas-based logistics company J.B. Hunt to deliver an order of Christmas cards to the Target Corporation in 1998. The order arrived four months late and after December 25th! After several years of litigation, the courts determined that J.B. Hunt was liable to Paper Magic for the value of the Christmas cards.[16]

Table 11.2 provides an example of order fulfillment in an international setting. While the process may seem simple, note that there is quite a bit of variability in each step. While not unusual, this variability makes it more difficult to promise specific delivery dates.

Table 11.2	Example of Variability in Order Fulfillment Process Times		
PROCESS ACTIVITY	**MINIMUM TIME (DAYS)**	**MAXIMUM TIME (DAYS)**	**AVERAGE TIME (DAYS)**
Order entry and warehouse processing	5.7	14.8	6.9
Shipment consolidation	0	5	.3
Transport to U.S. port of entry	1.5	1.5	1.5
Customs clearance	2	21	8
Transport to U.S. distribution center	1	3	1.2
Packing/ship to customer	1	2	1.9
Total Time	11.2	47.3	19.8

Source: Adapted from Nichols, E. L. Jr., D. Retzlaff-Roberts, and M. N. Frolick, "Reducing Order Fulfillment Cycle Time in an International Supply Chain," *Issues in Supply Chain Management,* Vol. 2, No. 1, 1996.

In a nutshell, variabilities in the order cycle time are caused by one or more of the following:

- The choice and design of the order transmittal system – phone, fax, email, Internet, or EDI;

- Inventory management policies – stocking levels, ordering points, safety stock, and alternative options when stock is not available;

- Procedures to process orders – customer credit reviews, warehouse management procedures to pick and pack orders, preparation of the bill of lading; and

- Selection of transportation modes – air, truck, train, water, pipeline, or some combination from the factory and/or warehouse to the customer.

U.S. telecommunications company Nextel, for instance, experienced problems with its ordering process as demand for its products increased. Orders were taking more than one week to process and were often inaccurate, resulting in customer dissatisfaction. Many dealers were faxing in their orders, which were hard to read and often lost. With the help of a consultant, Nextel changed to an automated order system using a secure website. Dealers were then able to quickly place orders and check the status of an order or their current inventory levels. During the first year alone, Nextel experienced a cost savings of $24 million.[17]

The length of the order cycle time for individual customers may also vary, depending on the **priority rules** established by a company. In other words, companies may create rules to determine the sequence in which customer orders are processed and shipped. For example, if a backlog of orders occurs because of a lack of stock in the warehouse, companies may decide to ship first to their more valued customers, resulting in longer order replenishment cycles for smaller "less important" customers.

Other priority rules include, but are not limited to:

- Process smaller, simpler orders first;

- Process largest orders (volume or dollar amount are two measures of size) first; or

- Process orders on a first-come-first-served basis.

Perhaps surprising, order replenishment time may also vary because of packaging standards. For example, a supplier may not want to spend additional money on packaging to avoid the chance of damage during shipment. As a result, the customer may have to order replacement units, resulting in a lengthier wait for the replenishment of damage-free goods. However, additional packaging can result in lower overall logistics costs. An outdoor power equipment company, for instance, actually added $5 in packaging costs to a product so it could ship with UPS and FedEx at better rates and on specific delivery dates. The change resulted in 50 percent fewer returns because product damage and delivery failures were reduced. Most importantly, overall logistics costs were reduced by 40 percent.[18]

While businesses often work closely with their suppliers, making their needs fairly predictable, the actual desires of consumers are an unknown quantity; they order based on a combination of price, convenience, seasonality of the item, and impulse. Fortunately, e-commerce has changed the face of traditional order fulfillment for both businesses and consumers, allowing companies to operate within an agile, fast-paced supply chain. Suppliers, manufacturers, and online merchants can now fill individual orders, ship them all over the world, keep track of the location of each shipment, respond to customer questions, and develop a system for customer returns at many times the speed and at a much lower cost than traditional order fulfillment options. As a result, firms have to consider whether to develop processes to handle order fulfillment in-house, outsource the functions to a third party, or use a drop-ship process. **Drop shipping** occurs when companies (primarily manufacturers) sell products to customers and then ship the product directly to the customer. Drop shipping delegates most of the order fulfillment process to the supplier. This is a common practice for mail-order and Internet companies.

Some companies have an existing ordering process that operates within their own network of warehouses and customer service areas. With the aid of company teams or outside consultants, they have made the changes necessary to move toward e-fulfillment and e-logistics processes.

Other firms may choose, however, to contract with third-party logistics providers to perform these services for cost or quality reasons. **Non-asset-based 3PLs** are supply chain intermediaries that link shippers together with available logistics services. They do not own any transportation equipment but may be subsidiaries of companies that do own assets. Menlo Worldwide, for example, headquartered in San Mateo, California, is owned by Con-way Inc., a large North American freight transportation provider. Menlo Worldwide provides a full range of logistics services including strategic planning; system design, coordinating and hiring the right mix of transportation, and distribution companies; and handling customer returns.[19] **Asset-based 3PLs** may also be contracted to design the e-fulfillment and e-logistics processes. These companies use their own vehicles, facilities, and employees to perform the promised service. Some asset-based logistics providers include FedEx, UPS, and DHL.

Warehouse Management

As introduced in Chapter 7 and mentioned at the beginning of this chapter, firms traditionally bought more than enough inventory to meet customer expectations and then stored excess inventory in warehouses or distribution centers until it was needed. However, warehouses still play an important role in linking suppliers, manufacturers, distributors, and consumers as well as providing other services. Today, warehousing is much more strategic and is an important part of lean production and replenishment. Because of the sheer geographic size of the United States, warehouses must be located strategically to serve as support for manufacturing sites operating in a lean environment. Materials and parts coming into the warehouse are sorted, sequenced, and then shipped to the manufacturer just as needed for production by integrating transportation planning.

Warehouses also serve as a point to form outbound specific product assortments, which are then shipped to the customer. In this situation, inventories are stored in the warehouse for only very short periods of time, and the warehouses are more appropriately called **distribution centers** (DCs). This strategy improves customer service while at the same time consolidates products with various demand patterns, resulting in more efficient use of transportation. Some companies have even incorporated **cross-docking**, a continuous replenishment process of creating outbound product order assortments from incoming truckload quantities of goods, which are then quickly shipped to retail and other customers. Cross-docking generally takes place within 24 hours, sometimes less than an hour, after shipment arrivals and is used to replenish high-demand inventories. Wal-Mart, for example, might receive 20 pallets of Tide® detergent into one of its DCs where workers allocate and load 3 pallets in another truck to Store 25, 5 pallets to Store 13, and so on. The idea is to reduce handling and storage of product within the DC, which reduces opportunities for damage and obsolescence, reduces the need for space and equipment, and ultimately reduces excess inventory carrying costs.

Warehouses are also used by some companies to postpone the final manufacturing, labeling, or packaging of product until it is needed by the customer, also known as a **postponement strategy**. A joint study sponsored by software developer Oracle Corporation, information technology consultant Cap Gemini Ernst & Young U.S. LLC, and the operations management association APICS, entitled *The Adaptive Supply Chain: Postponement for Profitability,* found the majority of companies that have implemented postponement strategies are realizing significant improvements in customer satisfaction, lower inventory costs, and more accurate demand forecasting. However, almost half of the participants in the study were not using this strategy because they did not understand the benefits.[20]

A postponement strategy is particularly useful for companies operating in multiple global markets where needs are diverse. Computer manufacturer Hewlett-Packard (HP) sells its printers in Europe, but each country has specific customer requirements. The company redesigned its printers to have modules so each product could be built for a specific market. HP then set up several DCs in Europe where the generic printers are configured for incoming orders by installing the proper power supply and inserting the correct printed materials before shipment to the customer. This approach eliminated the problems of building to forecast and ending up with too much inventory in one market and not enough in another market.[21] Compal Electronics, a Taiwanese producer of notebook computers for Dell Inc. and Taiwanese company Spectec Computers, makes virtually identical machines for the two companies with different brand names and model numbers. As Compal receives the orders, it labels the computers based on the customer and then ships the product with the appropriate manuals.[22]

Lastly, warehouses can be used to perform the **reverse logistics** function. In other words, warehouses may be responsible for getting rid of damaged inventory and goods that don't sell, performing light remanufacturing of recalled products, and refurbishing returned items. There are also times when warehouses must reclaim **controlled inventory**, which comprises hazardous materials and recalled items that may be hazardous to the consumer's health.

Warehouse Planning

Typically a warehouse will have a mission or purpose. For example, while the terms *warehouse* and *distribution center* are sometimes used interchangeably, there is a difference in purpose. The purpose of a warehouse is storage of inventory until needed; the purpose of a distribution center is to keep finished product moving toward its destination. Warehouses may store raw materials, parts, or finished products; distribution centers contain only finished products. Thus, activities at a distribution center include breaking down large shipments into smaller ones and getting them ready for transport. Distribution centers typically serve a larger territory than warehouses. For the purposes of this textbook, however, we have been using the term warehouse generically to describe both forms.

A firm must also determine the ideal number and location of warehouses to serve its customer base most effectively. If a firm could ignore cost, it would have warehouses located close to customers in all of its markets. Of course, the fixed and variable expenses of this number of warehouses would far outweigh the benefits. Going back to the idea of trade-offs, as the number of warehouses increases, customer service levels increase, but warehouse operating costs, inventory carrying costs, and possibly total transportation costs also increase. Thus, this decision is driven by a company's strategic plan and the needs of its customers. Management first looks at how many customers they have, in which locations, and the forecasts of their buying habits. They also determine the service levels needed to satisfy their customers.

Today, many customers are not satisfied unless service levels are close to 100 percent. For example, original equipment manufacturers (OEMs) can have exceedingly high standards and operate in a lean environment. They expect their suppliers to have a distribution network that can deliver parts in short time frames, often within a few hours, so warehouses are often located next to each of these customer's sites. Another important consideration is the expected growth in new markets, so companies often develop a distribution network that will meet its needs a few years out into the future. Seven important criteria in warehouse and DC site selection are:

1. Inbound and outbound freight transportation costs,
2. Site costs,
3. Access to major shipping nodes and arteries,
4. Facility and operating costs,
5. Availability of workforce and labor rates,
6. Potential tax incentives, and
7. Impact on the environment and local community.[23]

New York–based Oneida Ltd., maker of stainless steel and silver flatware, moved one of its DCs from Oneida, New York, to Savannah, Georgia, in 2007. A major consideration was a reduction in freight costs because the new DC would be located near a major port, which was important for deliveries from worldwide supply chain partners. The company also expects improvements in efficiency and customer service levels. The new facility is also double the size of the old one (it went from 205,000 to 500,000 square feet).[24]

Management must also determine the size and design of each warehouse, which is dependent on the expected volume of inventory that will move through the warehouse during a given time frame. Expected volumes will determine the stocking levels and safety stock for each stock-keeping unit held in the warehouse. Designers must also consider room for receiving and shipping, storage and handling equipment, special handling needs, loading docks, areas for light manufacturing such as assembly or labeling and creating assortments, computer equipment, and office space. Figure 11.3 provides a simple example of warehouse design.

Today, much of the inventory located in a warehouse can be moved with **automated storage and retrieval systems** (AS/AR), which use robotics, conveyor belts, bar code and radio frequency scanning systems, stock-picking equipment, and carousels. AS/AR can result in reduced labor cost, floor space, and inventory in the warehouse, thus improving productivity. Global hair care and skincare products manufacturer Matrix uses an AS/AR system to serve its 200,000-square-foot DC located in Solon, Ohio. This facility receives 15 to 30 trailer loads of product daily, which are scanned into its computer inventory software program upon arrival. The software then directs each case or pallet to the proper location. Radio frequency (RF) terminals mounted on forklift trucks are used to record any stock picked from the shelves. Matrix also uses a three-aisle robotics system to manage the salon-only personal care products.[25]

Management also needs to design the information system to be transparent. In other words, are sales, stocking levels, and inventory movements clearly visible to those involved in the replenishment process? Improved technologies that integrate communication between the warehouse, manufacturer, and the customer increase visibility and improve customer service. Warehouse technologies also reduce the need for more warehouses. Computer software specifically designed for warehousing, known as a **warehouse management system** (WMS), has improved many activities, including order requisitioning, stock location, order picking, and the handling of open and back orders. Procter & Gamble, headquartered in Ohio, for instance, has streamlined many of its business processes through the implementation of a new warehouse management system for its Chinese market.[26] More on warehouse layouts and information systems can be found in Chapters 7 and 9.

Warehousing Activities

Once planning is complete, managers must determine the location of inventory, stock the shelves, hire staff to work in the warehouse, set up work procedures, and implement a warehouse management system. Pallets of each SKU are assigned to slot locations that may be variable or fixed. As the name implies, variable assignment means that the location of an SKU will vary each time a shipment is received into the warehouse. However, the warehouse manager may also decide to fix the location of each SKU. This type of assignment makes it easier for employees to remember the location of each SKU.

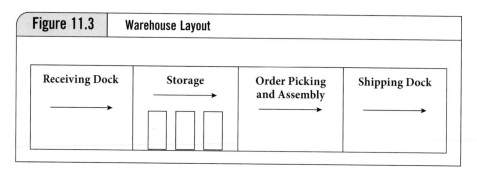

| **Figure 11.3** | **Warehouse Layout** |

| Receiving Dock | Storage | Order Picking and Assembly | Shipping Dock |

Warehouse employees must also be trained for their specific assignments, learn to operate any special equipment, understand the hazards of working in this type of environment, and have a good idea of their role in the supply chain. Once the warehouse is open, these activities continue as needed. The goal is to operate each facility efficiently through a possible combination of storage and handling activities.

The three stages of warehouse material handling are (1) receiving incoming shipments, (2) handling while in storage, and (3) shipping. Initially, the receiving department interacts with the suppliers' transportation carriers to ensure proper and timely delivery of the shipment, so communication is critical. The receiving department, for example, attempts to influence the supplier in the timing and size of the delivery based on preset delivery specifications and employee work schedules, as well as space constraints. An important consideration is installing an information system to improve the communication exchanges among the three parties. The goal is to create a predetermined process flow of materials from the supplier to the carrier, to the receiving dock, and finally to the storage areas without too much congestion or idle time. To minimize this problem, the warehouse manager should create a schedule of inbound shipments that is available to all involved parties.

Once the shipment is received and moved into a staging area, it could be moved into a storage slot or into an area for immediate order selection. If an SKU is placed into storage, it will eventually be selected for shipment once a purchase order is received. Either way, it will eventually be moved into the shipping area. There are times when one or more pallets must be broken down into smaller quantities and used to create assortments for multiple customers, also called **break-bulk**. This work is usually done in a staging area of the DC known as "order selection" or "picking."

The warehouse manager also wants the handling of shipments to be efficient and avoid too much material handling, which can cause damage or loss. These problems have been reduced through the use of bar coding to verify the accuracy of the shipping documents and automatically enter the shipment into the warehouse management system. Bar codes are also scanned during the in-storage handling process as product is removed from its slot and scanned to verify it matches the order request. Radio frequency identification (RFID) tags are also used in warehouses to track the movement of inventory and provide information on the product itself, such as price, color, and model number. Tennessee-based International Paper, the largest paper and forest products company in the world, uses RFID to track the location of its rolls of paper at its warehouses. Forklift drivers deliver large paper rolls to their proper location using information tracked by forklift-mounted readers.[27]

Once an order is assembled for a customer, the order is again verified for accuracy and then moved from the staging area into the transportation vehicle for shipment. Again, communication is important between shipping personnel, the transportation provider, and the customer. Similar to receiving, the shipping department wants all parties to have a clear understanding of the process flow and avoid congestion in the shipping area. At the same time it's important to run a safe operation and avoid damage to the shipment.

Planning the Logistics Network

The order fulfillment process requires a network of parties to make it work, including internal departments and external supply chain partners. The design of this network needs, at a minimum, an integration of the facilities that support the various needs of marketing, production, and supply management for a particular firm. However, today there is more pressure than ever to go beyond the firm's boundaries and integrate all supply chain partners in order to meet the exacting performance standards desired by customers. Transportation, for instance, is an important link between suppliers, manufacturers, warehouses, and retail markets and should be considered a partner in meeting each of the supply chain participant's needs.

Transportation managers must schedule their vehicles for use, incorporating load planning of equipment and scheduling of drivers, in order to maintain an economical utilization level. Poor vehicle scheduling is most evident when shipments are late. This situation often occurs because vehicles are waiting to be loaded or unloaded. Logistics managers must also revise the routing structure for shipments to attain efficient use of their equipment and people.

Technological solutions are being used more than ever before to improve collaborative logistics efforts. Siemens Medical Solutions, headquartered in Germany, uses a web-based collaboration system to share logistics information with its customers and business partners. More can be found on Siemens in the e-Commerce Perspective feature.

To develop a logistics network that adds value to the order fulfillment process, some common questions companies must answer are:

- How many production facilities, warehouses, and/or distribution centers are needed, and where should they be located?
- What are the most effective inventory policies that will satisfy our customers at the lowest cost?
- Which transportation modes and carrier services will provide the required service at the lowest cost?
- What materials handling equipment should be used in the facilities to improve service and reduce loss and damage to inventories?

In other words, companies must have a good understanding of their supply chains to design a logistics network that will meet their customer service goals. However, due to the very nature of business, logistical needs can change fairly regularly, thus requiring network adjustments at times. South Korean automaker Hyundai, for example, operates a parts distribution network to support its dealers' warranty and customer-paid repair needs. Delivery speed and on-time delivery were both important to Hyundai, but it found it was experiencing high stockout levels and transportation costs. Part of the problem was the cost of individual shipments from its four regional DCs to the dealers, when needed parts were located in more than one place. Hyundai decided to reduce the number of regional DCs from four to two. As a result, inventory costs and stockouts were reduced and the dealers' orders were more visible because Hyundai started using one order number to track each consolidated order.[28]

It may also take time, perhaps years, for a new production facility to become fully operational. The logistics network should be planned with that consideration in mind. Another factor is that warehousing needs may vary depending on the time of year, requiring firms to consider the use of **public warehouses** (space rented for short periods of time from for-profit warehousing companies) during peak times to minimize costs. Companies often own their own warehouses, also known as **private warehouses**, but may still choose to rent additional space from time to time. Knowing the location(s) of available public warehouses can enable the company to design the most effective logistics network.

e-Commerce Perspective

Collaboration System Cuts Unexpected Costs

Collaboration technology typically is used for internal company communications, but Siemens Medical Solutions has given it a new role. Siemens recently installed a web-based collaboration system for sharing information with its business partners and customers, and it expects the system to reduce costs associated with the sale of large, complex medical equipment to hospitals.

The sale and installation of equipment such as CT scanners, radiology information systems, and ultrasound machines is often complicated, involving collaboration among salespeople, project managers, freight companies, subcontractors, and customers.

Siemens' new E-Logistics Virtual Information System, based on technology from Groove Networks, gives all parties involved in a sale online access to information. Siemens expects that the system, which cost less than $1 million, will pay for itself within six to nine months, says Doug LaVigne, vice president of logistics.

In the past, communication breakdowns often resulted in delays and extra costs for the company and its customers. For example, technicians attempting to deliver equipment sometimes found it too big to fit through a hospital room's doors. Now, when a salesperson submits a proposal into Siemens' Siebel CRM system, it triggers the creation of a job folder and alerts all involved parties. That folder collects and holds even the most basic information such as door measurements. "We have a total understanding of the project," LaVigne says.

The new system also aids sales forecasting and related functions. The data that's collected in job folders is automatically routed to a data warehouse, where it's analyzed for sales reports.

Providing a common communication platform for business partners is a step ahead of how most companies have used collaboration technology, says Frost & Sullivan analyst David Alexander. He expects that next year, collaboration vendors will try to show how their products can go beyond improving internal communications to solving specific business problems.

Source: Kontzer, T., "Collaboration System Cuts Unexpected Costs," *Information Week*, January 5, 2004, p. 28. Reprinted with permission.

Companies today are also facing a continuously changing landscape of new competition, new suppliers, and new technologies, all of which impact logistics network capabilities. Global competitors are moving into new markets with very efficient supply chain networks, requiring decisions on the part of other organizations on how to compete logistically. New suppliers come and go, requiring organizations to consider whether to develop new relationships, stay with existing suppliers, or do some of both. Lastly, suppliers with newly available technologies are constantly bombarding the firm with promises of improved information flows and product visibility. These factors require companies to evaluate the alternatives and either change the existing network or develop an entirely new network to handle customer requirements. As these issues suggest, logistics network planning requires a great deal of careful thought initially, with organizational needs being revisited as environmental conditions warrant.

More specifically, logistics network planning involves a process of decision making in three areas: location planning, product flow planning, and transportation service planning.

Location Planning

Location planning means making decisions with regards to the size, location, and number of **fixed facilities** that will be used in a company's supply chain. The term *facility* is used here to include manufacturing plants, warehouses, retail outlets, and service centers, and also includes shipping ports and supplier facilities. For service providers, fixed facilities might include retail store locations, automatic teller machines, a collection center for a charity, or a maintenance facility for a city parks department.

Texas-based storage and organization product retailer The Container Store, for example, uses one DC outside Dallas, Texas, to receive merchandise from Asian suppliers, and to then serve 30+ stores across the United States. The retailer also has a website that generates about 5 percent of its revenues. Internet orders are filled through the DC and shipped directly to the customer.[29] The Container Store ships about 35 percent of its inventory with its private fleet of trucks and the rest through a third-party logistics provider. Figure 11.4 provides a visual representation of its supply chain network.

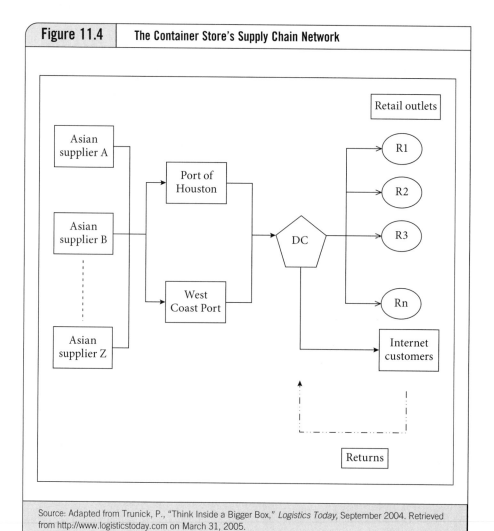

| **Figure 11.4** | **The Container Store's Supply Chain Network** |

Source: Adapted from Trunick, P., "Think Inside a Bigger Box," *Logistics Today*, September 2004. Retrieved from http://www.logisticstoday.com on March 31, 2005.

In locating retail sites, these service providers are most concerned with attracting customers and generating demand for their services. Thus, some important factors that retailers and other service providers consider are things like the demographics of the local population, characteristics of the proposed site itself (the square footage, existing floor plan, and drive-by traffic, for instance), accessibility to the site, proximity to major highways or intersections, and specific legal or cost factors that might be important. Table 11.3 provides a more comprehensive list of location factors considered important to service providers.

On the other hand, manufacturers consider factors such as the location of their suppliers, the cost of inbound transportation of materials, the location of their customers, and the cost of outbound transportation of finished products when locating production facilities and warehouses or distribution centers. Other factors may include:

- Quality of life for the employees, such as schools, recreation, and weather;
- Land and construction costs;
- Labor availability and labor costs;
- Regulatory environment; and
- Tax incentives.

Table 11.3	Site Selection Factors for Service Providers
Population Demographics • Local population base and trends • Income of population and trends	**Traffic Flow** • Number of pedestrians • Types of pedestrians • Number of vehicles • Types of vehicles • Access to major arteries • Street congestion • Road quality • Mass-transit options

Retail Structure
• Types of stores in area
  • Number of competitors in area
  • Number of complementary stores in area
• Vacancy rates
• Closeness to other commercial areas
• Joint promotions with other retailers
	Site Characteristics
	• Available parking
	  • Free parking
	  • Pay lots and rates
	• Visibility to street
	• Lot size
	• Condition of building (if existing)
	• Zoning restrictions

Legal/Cost Issues • Lease costs • Taxes • Maintenance costs • Local merchant regulations	

Sources: Adapted from Ghosh, A. and S. L. McLafferty, *Location Strategies for Retail and Service Firms*, D.C. Health and Company, Lexington, MA, 1987, p. 49; Krajewski, L. J. and L. P. Ritzman, *Operations Management: Strategy and Analysis*. Prentice Hall, Upper Saddle River, NJ, 2002, pp. 408–411.

Of course, the greater the number of facilities in the supply chain network, the more complex the problem of location planning becomes. To create a supply chain network, a firm must collect a significant amount of data, as shown in Table 11.4.

As the reader should notice, there will be trade-offs in every decision made. Because of the large volume of data needed, companies generally rely on consultants and network design software programs to create a network or make adjustments to an existing network. Redesigned logistics networks have been known to reduce costs by as much as 15 percent of the total cost of logistics. Some companies use the **balanced scorecard**, a management system developed in the early 1990s by Robert Kaplan and David Norton, which helps companies to continually refine their vision and strategy. The balanced scorecard uses a set of measures to provide feedback on internal business performance in order to continually improve strategic performance. As shown in Figure 11.5, companies maintain the use of traditional financial measures but also collect feedback from the customer, measure their own learning and growth, and evaluate internal business processes.

Illinois-based International Truck and Engine Corporation's Parts Group, for example, uses a combination of performance metrics to periodically evaluate its supply chain network. A balanced scorecard is prepared for each of its parts suppliers and transportation providers. As shown in Table 11.5, each area of logistics is evaluated on a number of measures. Based on performance, the company considers the trade-offs between service and cost to improve performance of its supply chain and make adjustments to the network.[30]

How do companies select the site for a facility? The general process for location planning is:

1. Identify the general region to locate a facility. Today, a region may be located in a foreign country. This decision is usually based on a number of cost factors,

Table 11.4	Logistics Network Data Examples

Inputs
- Customer service goals
- All products within each product line
- Demand for each product based on customer location
- Customer ordering patterns, such as frequency, size, and content of orders
- Current location of all customers and source points of product
- Capacity limitations of facilities and equipment
- Current inventory policies by location
- Available transportation carriers and rates
- Order-filling policies
- Order cycle times for each activity, including order transmittal rates, order fill rates, and transit times
- Costs to warehouse products
- Purchase costs
- Production costs

Source: Adapted from R. H. Ballou (2004), *Business Logistics/Supply Chain Management*, Fifth Edition, Upper Saddle River, NJ: Pearson Prentice Hall, p. 521.

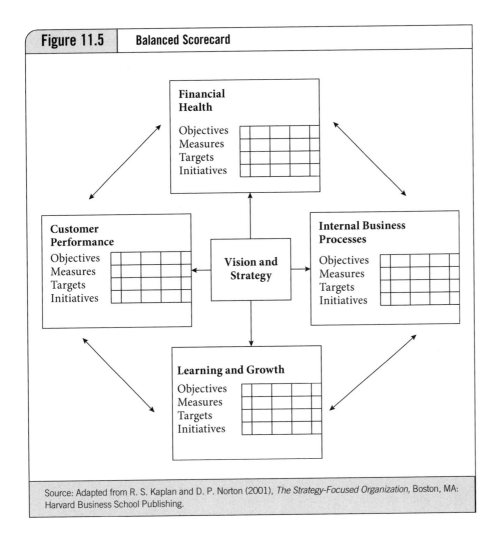

Figure 11.5 Balanced Scorecard

Source: Adapted from R. S. Kaplan and D. P. Norton (2001), *The Strategy-Focused Organization*, Boston, MA: Harvard Business School Publishing.

including the costs of transportation to and from the site, construction costs, taxes, labor costs, and energy costs. A number of methods can be used to determine a first approximation based on the existing network of facilities and expected shipment volumes between facilities and to customers.

2. Identify good candidate cities or metro areas within the selected region. Chosen cities will provide good transportation access, an available workforce, and low land and facility costs.

3. Select candidate properties within the selected metro areas and make the final selection. This decision is most frequently based on the specific purchase cost of the land and building, or lease costs, and the access to highways, airports, and railroad facilities.

Location of a Single Facility

One common method used to locate a single facility is the **center-of-gravity method**. The goal is to find a location that minimizes the total transportation costs between the proposed facility and existing facilities given the volume, distance, and transportation rates of shipments between locations. For example, an organization's logistics department

Table 11.5	Balanced Scorecard Metrics at International Truck and Engine
SUPPLY CHAIN PARTNER	**SAMPLE METRICS**
Parts suppliers	Days late Order fill rates (from suppliers) Shipping quality Backorder volume
Transportation carriers	Transit times Delivery times Delivery cost
Warehouse management	Distribution expenses/shipments Transportation costs/shipments Cycle time dock-to-stock Frequency and lost time due to safety accidents Errors/10,000 lines shipped Accuracy of inventory counts Orders shipped complete to customers
Inventory management	Order fill rates (from on-hand inventory) Frequency of stockouts Cost of safety stock

Source: Richardson, H., "Building a Better Supply Chain," *Logistics Today,* April 2005, retrieved from http://www.logistics.com on April 2, 2005.

may be interested in determining the most cost-effective place to locate a new DC. They might evaluate several sites, based on the location of their existing manufacturing plants.

The center-of-gravity total cost formula is:

$$\text{Minimize TC} = \sum_i L_n R_n d_n$$

Where:

$\text{TC} = $ total cost of transportation
$L_n = $ volume of shipments to location n
$R_n = $ transportation rate to location n
$d_n = $ distance between proposed facility and location n in the network of existing facilities

Transportation rates can be obtained from the transportation provider that will move the freight. The load should be estimated based on company records, and equals the volume of shipments between the firm's manufacturing facility or other existing network facility and each market or warehouse location. Points for each existing and proposed site are then assigned grid coordinates on a map, which represent distance, d_i. To estimate d_i, first find the coordinates of the center-of-gravity location using the following two equations:

$$X^* = \frac{\sum L_n R_n X_n}{\sum L_n R_n}$$

and

$$Y^* = \frac{\sum L_n R_n Y_n}{\sum L_n R_n}$$

Where:

X^* and Y^* = coordinate points of the central facility

X_n and Y_n = coordinate points for the existing facilities in the network

These coordinates are then used to solve for d_n using the following formula:

$$d_n = K\sqrt{(X_i - X^*)^2 + (Y_i - Y^*)^2}$$

Where:

K = a scaling factor that converts a unit on the grid map to
a common distance measure such as miles or kilometers

Example 11.1 provides an example problem and solution for the proposed location coordinates and total transportation costs.

The value of the center-of-gravity method is that it is relatively easy to use and can be set up on a spreadsheet. However, only a rough approximation is possible when

Example 11.1   The Center-of-Gravity Method

XYZ Company has two manufacturing plants that supply two markets. Management is looking for a place to locate a single distribution center that will minimize total transportation costs. Following is a grid map that was overlaid on a map of a portion of Illinois to determine relative point locations:

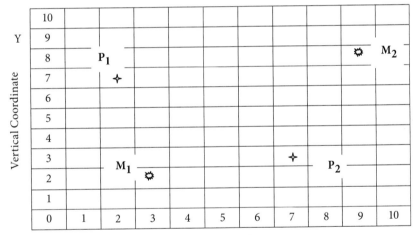

Scale: 1 coordinate unit = 10 miles (the value of "K")

Each plant and market is shown as a coordinate point on the grid map. Product Q is manufactured at P_1 and sold to M_1 and M_2; Product T is manufactured at P_2 and also sold to M_1 and M_2. The coordinate points, volumes shipped, and transportation rates are as follows:

POINT	PRODUCT	TOTAL VOLUME MOVED (CTW)	TRANSPORTATION RATE ($/CTW/MI)	X_n	Y_n
P_1	Q	3,000	$0.040	2	7
P_2	T	2,500	$0.050	7	3
M_1	Q&T	2,800	$0.080	3	2
M_2	Q&T	2,700	$0.070	9	8

Find the initial location and costs for the proposed distribution center.

Continued

SOLUTION:

The best approach to find the grid coordinates is to design two tables in Excel as shown below.

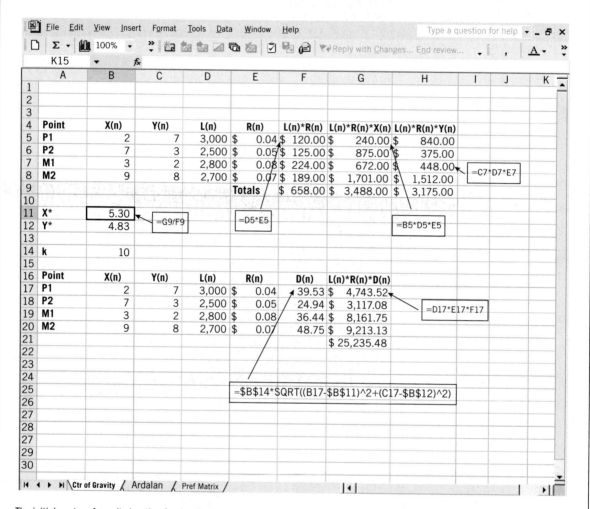

The initial center-of-gravity location for the distribution center was found to be at the coordinates (5.3, 4.8). Once the grid coordinates for the selected location have been calculated, the total cost for the coordinates can be calculated. In this example, the total transportation cost is $25,235.48.

making the site location decision, since the initial calculated location may be infeasible. For example, it may be that the initial site selected, based on the calculations, is not located in or near a major metropolitan area, and this is an important criterion for a company. The selection might also not be served by the company's preferred modes of transportation or carriers. The next step, then, is to find the closest feasible location that provides easy access to the other facilities in the network with easy access to transportation. The final site can usually be moved from the first rough-cut solution with little impact on cost.

Location of Multiple Facilities

Firms are often required to make a location decision for two or more facilities at the same time. This may occur, for instance, if a firm is considering contracting with a new supplier and adding a warehouse simultaneously, or adding several warehouses to the network at the same time. The **Ardalan heuristic** method is one way to estimate facility locations given the (1) distances (a surrogate measure for cost, since transportation cost varies somewhat with distance) from each customer location to every other location, (2) expected demand at each location, and (3) a weighting system where more important customers are weighted more heavily. The goal is to locate only where the customers are, so the idea is to find the one best place to locate and then add a second location, a third, and so on, to minimize transportation costs. Example 11.2 provides a sample problem that explains the method further.

Note that a weighted answer is determined for each location pair and summed. Each row is adjusted: If the value in any row is higher than the selected site, it is lowered to the site value. Otherwise, the value remains the same. The columns are then summed again. Lastly, the highest weighted score for a given location is selected. The score represents the total "cost" to the firm to choose that site. If more than one facility is needed, the first site is removed from the table and the process is repeated to find the second location. Note that in the sample problem, the total cost for selecting a second site is lower than that site's original cost because as more sites are added, the transportation cost to customers becomes lower (goods are traveling shorter distances). The downside is that this method does not consider the trade-off in inventory purchases and carrying costs.

The center-of-gravity approach can also be used to find more than one location, but with some modification. The points of product origin and destination are assigned to arbitrary locations, which are then formed into clusters. An exact center-of-gravity is then determined for each cluster. Once the center-of-gravity locations are determined, the points are reassigned to these locations. The center-of-gravity locations are then found for the revised clusters. The process can be repeated if management wants to consider a different number of facilities.

Generally, transportation costs from distribution centers to customers will go down as the number of facilities is increased (assuming that the new facilities are closer to the customers they serve), although transportation costs from production facilities to many of these distribution centers may rise (due to the greater number of shipments). However, the fixed costs of the facilities, as well as inventory carrying costs, will increase as the number of facilities is increased. Thus, managers should search for a solution that minimizes the total network costs, given the customer service requirements.

For service providers and some manufacturing facilities, accessibility, visibility, and convenience for the customer to their retail locations is a high priority. For example, gas stations are generally located at major street intersections and near highway off-ramps. Restaurant owners like to locate their stores close to the more heavily traveled streets but wish to avoid major intersections where it may be difficult to drive into and out of the parking lot. Auto dealers have always chosen locations on major city streets, but now also build "auto malls" that offer multiple car brands for customer convenience. Thus, service providers, such as retailers and service centers, often use a weighted checklist, also called a **factor rating system**, to determine the best locations for new sites. A combination of diverse quantitative and qualitative factors can be considered for site location comparisons. (Some common site selection factors were noted earlier in the chapter in Table 11.3.)

As shown in Example 11.3, the business owner, manager, or site selection team chooses factors that are considered most important to the site selection decision. Any quantitative factors, such as leasing costs, labor costs, or tax incentives, should be researched thoroughly and can be included in the location decision. Qualitative aspects (things that aren't usually evaluated numerically or in monetary terms) can also be evaluated and added to the analysis. The performance of each factor is then determined, using a common scale. Often, the site selection team will measure the factors on a scale

Example 11.2   Ardalan Method

Abacus Inc. must find a location of a distribution center for a new market where it expects to have four major customers. Management has estimated the expected demand for its products from each customer, and the distance between the customers. They have also weighted the importance of serving each location (the larger the weight, the more important the location). A grid of management's initial data is as follows:

FROM/TO	A	B	C	D	DEMAND	WEIGHT
A	0	11	8	12	10	1.1
B	11	0	10	7	9	1.4
C	8	10	0	9	20	0.7
D	10	7	9	0	12	1.0

Using the Ardalan method, which location should be chosen and why?

SOLUTION:

First, calculate the expected cost for each location pair by multiplying distance × demand × weight. Then add the values in each column. Choose the smallest value as the preferred site. In this case, Location C has the lowest total cost.

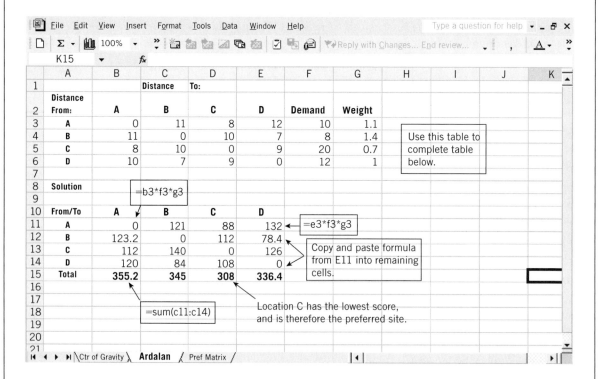

If a second site is desired, the rows are adjusted based on the first selected site's pair. If the value for any other site pair is higher, it is adjusted down to the selected site pair value. Otherwise, it remains the same. For example, for row A, A–C = 88. Therefore, A–B and A–D are adjusted downward to 88. Once this process is complete, the columns are summed again.

FROM/TO	A	B	C	D
A	0	88	88	88
B	112	0	112	78.4
C	0	0	0	0
D	108	84	108	0
Total	220	172	308*	166.4

Next remove C because it has already been chosen and choose the next site with the lowest cost, which is D. Adjust the rows again based on D's lowest score for each row:

FROM/TO	A	B	D
A	0	88	88
B	78.4	0	78.4
D	0	0	0
Total	78.4	88	166.4*

D is the second most preferable site based on score or cost. Note that the total cost to choose D as the second site is less than site D's original cost of 336.4. To choose another site, eliminate D.

FROM/TO	A	B
A	0	88
B	78.4	0
D	0	0
Total	78.4*	88

Based on the A and B totals, site A should be chosen.

of 1 to 5 or 1 to 100. A **preference matrix** is then developed. Each factor can also be weighted based on its perceived relative importance to the location decision. A total weighted score for each location is then calculated, and the location with the highest weighted score is the preferred site.

Other methods used to select a location include linear programming, simulation, the P-median method, and the maximum covering method. These methods are best used with computer software applications and are beyond the scope of this text.[31]

Product Flow Planning

Integral to location planning is **product flow planning**, which is the determination of how products will be moved from the points of origination to demand points. Product flow planning should be used to determine the size, location, and number of fixed facilities in the logistics network. Software often helps companies manage product flows. Branded apparel maker Liz Claiborne, for example, uses trade management software from California-based TradeBeam, Inc. to monitor the flow of product in more than 35 countries. More on Liz Claiborne's solution to product flow planning can be found in the Global Perspective feature.

Example 11.3   Designing a Preference Matrix

Tasteful Creations, a boutique for women, is looking to expand to another location. The owner has narrowed the choice to two locations. The owner and her team develop a list of factors they consider most important to the decision and develop the following preference matrix. Using Excel, which site should they select, based on the weighted scores?

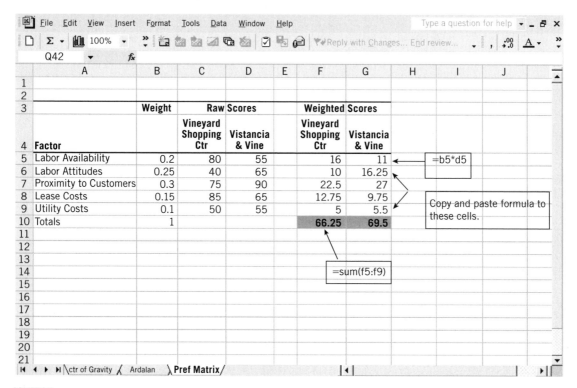

SOLUTION:

Based on the table, the location at Vistancia and Vine is preferable. The sensitivity of the decision can also be analyzed by changing the scores or weights. For example, raising the score for Labor Attitudes by 13 points for Vineyard would make both locations equally desirable.

Product flow planning also includes reverse logistics, or managing the backward flow of materials and products to the original source. For example, Ricoh, a Japanese producer of copiers, leases its machines to organizations and must have a process in place to take them back at the end of the lease period. Companies such as New York-based Eastman Kodak also produce "one-use" products such as cameras, which are returned to be remanufactured and then resold. More on reverse logistics can be found in Chapter 15.

Logistics managers generally analyze product or service flows by developing a flowchart. The flowchart should provide detailed steps involved in the movement of product from origin to destination. In the case of reverse logistics, the flowchart should show the steps from customers back to the company and the products' final disposal or reclamation. The flowchart can then be used to simplify and improve the process. More on product flow planning can be found in Chapter 7.

Global Perspective

Dressed for Success

A recent poll of corporate executives in the United States and Europe reveals that while 80 percent see China as an important part of their growth plans over the next three years, only 16 percent believe their supply chains in China are highly effective. There's little doubt that many American companies are increasingly sourcing and producing offshore, but "offshore" doesn't always mean China.

While competitive and even survival goals are cited as motivators in moving to offshore sources, problems are occurring that can sink efforts in unanticipated legal and financial quagmires. The poll, conducted by Harris Interactive (http://www.harrisinteractive.com), indicates that while 66 percent of executives are trying to manage their supply chains in-house, 33 percent are suffering from "unclear lines of authority" for supply chain management. Some have outsourced all of their offshore activities to third-party suppliers with varying degrees of success. Others have sought to avoid missteps while smoothing longer length supply chain activities by maintaining control through technological solutions.

Strict adherence to governmental rules, meeting appropriate quotas and having all legal matters met is one way Liz Claiborne Inc. (http://www.lizclaiborneinc.com), a $4 billion fashion apparel maker, ensures smooth product movement throughout its global supply chain. Making use of available technological tools is a key for Lois Davis, vice president of global logistics, in gaining visibility and control of the company's moves of more than 250 million units of product sourced in more than 35 countries. Davis is responsible for moving the goods once they come out of a factory through their arrival at final destination, whether a distribution center (DC) or a customer. Although there are a number of solutions available, Davis finds that all they aren't necessary since Claiborne has internal applications to fill needs. Its core purchase order system, for example, works well. However, to monitor actual movement of goods once they leave the factory, Claiborne uses TradeBeam Inc.'s (http://www.tradebeam.com) global trade management solution.

"Depending on final customer requirements and parameters put into the application," explains Davis, "determination is made as to the best mode. With TradeBeam we get the monitoring of the product. We can see whether the movement is by air, ocean, truck or a combination, and we're able to see movement from any origination to final destination."

Claiborne also monitors specific events that must take place for importation. "In the U.S. we have to make an entry to Customs and be released and can't finalize delivery until the shipment is released from Customs," Davis says. "There are specific events like these that we also monitor, even if they're not a physical move. If there are exceptions, they are easy to see and manage." In terms of monitoring events, TradeBeam provides most of the information about the movement of goods from the factory: shipment departure, estimated arrival dates, notification of arrival, arrival at Customs, Customs clearance, release for pick up, and scheduled for final delivery, among other data.

Claiborne is in the process of enhancing its operations by availing itself of other TradeBeam functionality, such as a Product Catalog feature, which will allow the apparel company to maintain line reviews on all of its products, Davis notes. For that, TradeBeam will carry all classifications, categories, fiber content, and all requirements for the Harmonized Tariff Schedule. Product Catalog will interface with Claiborne's enterprise resource planning (ERP) system.

Since the ultimate responsibility for compliance rests with the importer, Claiborne finds it easier to handle Customs compliance internally rather than having to create an additional monitoring

Continued

program. Once Product Catalog is in place Davis expects to incorporate its data into the way it currently handles compliance, simplifying many present processes. The ability to manage by exception has proven invaluable at Liz Claiborne. "Not having to look at every single shipment and being able to focus on those that need to have something happen automatically provides efficiency," Davis says.

Source: Morton, R., "Dressed for Success," *Logistics Today,* June 2005, available at http://www. logisticstoday.com. Reprinted with permission.

Transportation Service Planning

Lastly, transportation service planning is critical because planners must know the modes and carriers available at each potential location. For example, while the costs to build a warehouse and hire labor in a rural area of Montana might be low, transportation services may not be readily available or higher freight rates may offset the original cost savings.

As shown in the Process Management in Action feature, International Truck and Engine Corporation went through the location planning process for its parts distribution facilities. It now uses a combination of strategies: a centralized location for slow-moving parts and several regional DCs to ship most orders that are located within 300 miles of a dealer. Transportation requirements were also an important consideration in the planning process. This example illustrates the need for a logistics strategy, discussed further in the following section.

Developing a Logistics Strategy

A strategy involves companies making plans and decisions for the long term, usually longer than one year, to meet their performance goals. Businesses generally develop an overall strategy and then functional areas, such as logistics, develop strategies that support the overall business strategy. Many firms, however, do not go through this type of planning process. A recent survey indicated that slightly over half of all logistics organizations have a formalized **logistics strategy** development process.[32] In addition, few logistics professionals have direct contact with the customer. Integrating logistics with marketing into the strategic planning process, however, can be a means to improve customer service and increase sales. Smart companies combine great products, a good promotional campaign, and competitive prices with a sound logistics strategy—finding ways to fill orders in a timely manner and meeting the needs of the customer. A strong marketing strategy will win customers the first time but a good logistics strategy will keep those customers for the long term.[33]

Based on their research, Professors Bowersox and Daugherty identified two other strategic orientations and their impact on logistics strategy. The first is a **process orientation**. The focus is on creating a system of only value-adding logistics activities with a result of reduced logistics costs. The second is known as the **information orientation** or **channel orientation**. Management stresses the importance of coordination and control within the supply chain by synchronizing logistics activities with related information.[34] In a separate research paper, Professor McGinnis found that most companies use some

Process Management in Action

International Truck and Engine Corporation

Blending legacy and innovation yields results in manufacturing and logistics for truck manufacturer International Truck and Engine Corporation.

Parts are a small but profitable portion of a manufacturer's business. But more than that, parts represent after-sale contact that helps build and reinforce a bond with the end customer.

International's service parts goal is to provide reliable next-day deliveries to dealers. With 1,000 dealer points to serve, this requires a hybrid central/regional approach. Slow-moving parts are shipped from a central distribution center (DC), while the majority of orders are filled from a regional DC, typically within 300 miles of the dealer.

While International will ship individual items as well as pallet loads, it tends to receive goods and materials by truckload. Intermodal ramps and rail connections are, therefore, important in the DC location and operation.

International also operates a private fleet to handle some of the manufacturing-to-distribution moves. Outbound tends to be less-than-truckload (LTL) and parcel, so proximity to those services and air parcel hubs are important.

One of International's constraints on siting distribution operations is the more capital-intensive manufacturing real estate investment. Maximizing its network opportunities using existing manufacturing facilities places International in some legacy DCs that are over 50 years old.

International has also updated its legacy transportation management methods on inbound shipments. The company had negotiated transportation pricing centrally and provided a routing guide, but plants operated largely autonomously. Those plants are widely dispersed throughout North America.

International also participates in a joint third-party logistics (3PL) venture with Ford Motor Company. This relationship brought systems and software International could not afford to invest in on its own, including transportation management. The combination of efforts provides better visibility up the supply chain and has helped reduce inventories while providing better delivery consistency to the plants, a total supply chain effect.

Source: Staff, "10 Best Supply Chains of 2004," *Logistics Today,* accessed from http://www. logisticstoday.com on March 31, 2005. Used with permission.

combination of these two strategies when making decisions about the complexities of their business environments.[35]

To begin the strategic planning process, logistics managers should ask some important questions, including the following:

1. *Who are our customers, and how do we segment our customers?* As a general rule, different products require different levels of customer service, so there may be many different distribution strategies within a single product line. Often managers will categorize products based on sales volume—high, medium, or low. They will then determine the stocking level, shipping strategy, and warehouse location for each category. For example, a high-volume product category might be shipped directly to the customer, with lower-volume product categories being managed through several warehouse sites.

2. *What do our customers need/want in terms of service?* Generally customers are looking for consistent on-time and damage-free delivery of their order. Again, firms may decide to "differentiate" their customers based on volume requirements.

3. *What are our customer service goals for the upcoming year?* For example, what consistency is wanted in terms of meeting the customer's product requirements? What are the firm's goals for delivery times and on-time deliveries? What types of services will be offered to customers and at what level?

4. *What are our current capabilities?* If the firm's capabilities do not match their customers' needs, what should be done to improve their capabilities?

Once these questions are answered, logistics managers can begin to develop a **logistics vision** for their organization. This vision should include what the organization hopes to accomplish in the future, including some goals that go beyond the company's current capabilities. Once a vision statement has been developed, the logistics organization should carefully develop a list of options or alternatives to accomplish its vision. Each alternative should be carefully weighed and compared using a **cost/benefit analysis**. In other words, a quantitative and subjective assessment of the risks and rewards for each option would be prepared. Based on the analysis, one or more options might be selected and plans for implementation would then take place.

Developing a cost/benefit analysis should be done in light of some guiding principles related to logistics. First, as mentioned earlier, there are multiple activities involved in logistics, including order processing, transportation, inventory management, and warehouse management. Generally, lowering costs in one area increases costs in another. For example, choosing a cheaper transportation method generally results in longer delivery times and, as a result, worse customer service. In addition, because delivery times are longer, firms tend to hold higher levels of inventories to protect themselves from stockouts, thus increasing inventory holding costs. This is what is known as a **cost/benefit trade-off**.

Logisticians also need to look at the total cost of their decisions and choose the alternatives that achieve the required customer service levels at the lowest total cost. These decisions should be based on the customer's needs and expectations, or the **logistics value proposition**. In general, companies will attain some middle ground between lowest costs and highest levels of customer service. Global Gillette, a personal care business unit of Procter & Gamble, for example, took a look at its retailers' needs for easy display of products and increased inventory turns. It found that its packaging was designed to make transportation more efficient rather than to meet its retailers' needs. As a result, Gillette changed the packaging so retailers would have an easier time managing its displays. The changes resulted in higher transportation costs but even higher revenues.[36] With a good strategy, companies can address the logistics needs of their customers. However, the day-to-day operations—transportation, order fulfillment, and warehousing—must be structured to support this strategy.

Order Fulfillment and Logistics Concerns

The role of logistics and order fulfillment within an organization has continued to expand and is more critical than ever before. Firms are integrating logistics into their corporate planning processes and including this function in their supply chain objectives. As logistics moves to the planning forefront and becomes more strategic, some of the more basic transportation and warehousing functions are being outsourced to third parties.

The results of a recent survey by East Carolina University's Department of Industrial Technology indicated several challenges facing logistics managers today. Two of the concerns are legal and physical security.[37] For instance, most developing countries do not have the legal frameworks in place to ensure electronic transactions are binding and enforceable. There are also few policies or technical provisions that protect the privacy and use of personal data online, which has slowed the development of e-commerce and e-logistics in many nations.[38] In terms of physical security, executives see a threat to goods while they are in transit. Thus, more needs to be done to secure the supply chain, including more employee background checks, cargo inspections, government inspections, and patrols.[39]

There are also concerns in the United States that companies won't be able to meet increasing customer service requirements due to infrastructure problems. Road traffic congestion is increasing and considered a problem in approximately 56 percent of urban areas. The airways are heavily congested, with on-time arrival rates deteriorating annually, while the railroads are running at close to capacity and improvements are needed along many corridors to reduce bottlenecks. Finally, cargo volume, measured in tons, is expected to increase 70 percent between 2005 and 2020.[40]

As firms continue to outsource materials and goods globally, more stress has been placed on U.S. ports, which are operating at or near capacity. Much of the freight originating from Asia is shipped by container and continuing growth is expected. As a result, backups at U.S. ports are occurring due to customs requirements, delayed off-loading, and security initiatives. The increase in imports has resulted because manufacturers and their suppliers are importing materials from cheaper sources of supply overseas. The Port of Tacoma, Washington, for example, handled 1.74 million 20-foot-equivalent units in 2003, which was at full capacity at the time.[41]

SUMMARY

The logistics and order fulfillment process involves making some of the most important decisions for a firm. It has an impact on both the relationship with the customer and on transportation and inventory costs, which can account for 10 to 15 percent of product cost. Proper planning results in better use of resources and, as a result, a more competitive organization. As with most other processes, the coordination of order fulfillment with transportation and warehousing should be most effective when a collaborative effort occurs both within the organization and among supply chain partners.

The logistics process for the customer begins with the placement of an order. However, much advance planning must be done to ensure the order fulfillment process is a success—the customer receives the order on time, complete, and damage free. As described in this chapter, some of these activities include designing a network of facilities, determining transportation and warehousing needs, developing a plan for vehicle routing and scheduling, and setting performance standards. Once all this is in place, revisions take place as the customer base changes and technology changes.

With the increase in globalization, the logistics and order fulfillment process has become even more complex. As a result, more companies are turning to third-party logistics providers to provide their expertise and services at a lower cost. What was once done in-house has, in many instances, been outsourced, as demonstrated by some of the company profiles provided in this chapter. Firms are also relying on computer software to make the customer's order visible throughout the organization. However, there are concerns as firms continue to source more goods and materials overseas.

KEY TERMS

Ardalan heuristic, 427

asset-based 3PLs, 413

automated storage and retrieval systems, 416

backorder, 401

balanced scorecard, 422

birdyback, 404

break-bulk, 417

center-of-gravity method, 423

channel orientation, 432

controlled inventory, 414

core carrier strategy, 408

cost/benefit analysis, 434

cost/benefit trade-off, 434

cross-docking, 414

distribution centers, 414

drop shipping, 413

factor rating system, 427

fixed facilities, 420

information orientation, 432

Intermodal transportation, 404

inventory management, 401

lean logistics, 399

line order fill rate, 402

location planning, 420

logistics customer service, 401

logistics strategy, 432

logistics value proposition, 434

logistics vision, 434

non-asset-based 3PLs, 413

order cycle time, 410

order fill rates, 402

order lead time, 403

order management, 401

orders shipped complete, 402

piggyback, 404

postponement strategy, 414

preference matrix, 429

priority rules, 412

private carriers, 405

private warehouses, 418

process orientation, 432

product flow planning, 429

public carriers, 405

public warehouses, 418

reverse logistics, 414

service level, 402

stockouts, 402

third-party logistics providers, 405

transit time, 405

transportation management, 400

warehouse management, 401

warehouse management system, 416

DISCUSSION QUESTIONS

1. What is logistics?

2. How has logistics changed since the 1980s?

3. Why is it important to integrate a logistics strategy with a marketing strategy?

4. What is the difference between a process orientation and an information or channel strategy?

5. What is the process managers should use to develop a logistics strategy?

6. What are the general steps in the order fulfillment process?

7. What are priority rules, and why do companies use them?

8. What are some factors that can affect the variability of order cycle time?

9. What are the three general dimensions of customer service from a logistics standpoint?

10. When logistics managers are developing a network of facilities to serve their customers, what are some questions they should ask first?

11. What are the three areas of decision making in network planning?

12. How is the balanced scorecard used in logistics?

13. What factors play a role in determining the mode of transportation chosen?

14. What is a core carrier strategy, and what is its advantage?

15. What is the goal of transportation vehicle routing and scheduling?

16. What is the role of warehousing in the logistics and order fulfillment process?

17. What is the difference between a warehouse and a distribution center?

SPREADSHEET PROBLEMS

1. Vic owns The Vinery, a four-location wine bar chain in the Phoenix, Arizona, area and is looking for a single central distribution center location to store cases for his four locations. Vic has collected the following data from internal sources and his transportation carrier:

LOCATION	TOTAL VOLUME MOVED PER WEEK (CASES)	TRANSPORTATION RATE ($/CASE)	X_n	Y_n
Phoenix	300	$0.35	3.0	5.2
Glendale	250	$0.55	5.5	7.8
Mesa	150	$0.80	2.5	1.2
Tempe	100	$0.75	1.3	2.7

Find the desired location and the total transportation costs for the proposed distribution center using the center-of-gravity method.

2. Timberline Inc. manufactures rustic furniture made from logs for its customers in the Northwest USA. Management has estimated the expected demand for its products from each customer, and the distance between the customers. They have also

weighted the importance of serving each location (the larger the weight, the more important the location). Following is a grid of management's initial data:

	DISTANCE TO:					
DISTANCE FROM:	A	B	C	D	DEMAND	WEIGHT
A	0	8	29	3	25	2.2
B	15	0	19	5	16	2.8
C	9	11	0	13	40	1.4
D	10	7	9	0	18	2.0

Using the Ardalan method, which location should be chosen for a distribution center and why?

3. Jane has decided to open her own clothing boutique and has narrowed the selection to three possible sites. She has developed a list of criteria she feels are most important to the location decision and weighted the importance of each criterion. She has asked her husband and children to assign a score to each criteria based on the expected performance on a scale of 1 to 5 (5=best). The results are as follows:

		LOCATIONS		
LOCATION FACTOR	FACTOR WEIGHT	TULIP STREET	ROSE AVENUE	GARDENIA LANE
Proximity to markets	0.30	5	4	3
Lease rate	0.15	2	3	5
Parking space	0.15	3	4	3
Traffic congestion	0.20	5	3	4
Easy access	0.10	3	2	3
Visibility to street	0.10	2	5	5

Which location should Jane use, based on the preference matrix? What are other quantitative factors Jane should research?

INFOTRAC QUESTIONS

Access http://www.infotrac-thomsonlearning.com to answer the following questions:

1. Use InfoTrac to search for the term *logistics tracking software*. Write a term paper on the types of software available today that have helped improve the visibility of an order for the customer. Include a bibliography.

2. Use InfoTrac to search for the term *warehouse management system*. Write a paper on how CPFR software improves the warehouse management process and provide company examples. Include a bibliography.

3. Use InfoTrac to search for the term *3PL* (third-party logistics provider). Write a paper on the activities 3PLs use to improve the logistics process for companies today. Include a bibliography.

REFERENCES

Ballou, R. H. (2004), *Business Logistics/Supply Chain Management,* Fifth Edition, Pearson Education Inc., Upper Saddle River, NJ.

Bloombert, D. J., S. LeMay, and J. B. Hanna (2002), *Logistics,* 2002, Prentice Hall Inc., Upper Saddle River, NJ.

Bowersox, D. J., D. J. Closs, and M. B. Cooper (2002), *Supply Chain Logistics Management,* Irwin/McGraw-Hill, New York, NY.

Lambert, D. M., J. R. Stock, and L. M. Ellram (1998), *Fundamentals of Logistics Management,* Irwin/McGraw-Hill, Boston, MA.

ENDNOTES

1. Quote by Lt. General, USA, 7th Corps Commander Desert Storm, found in "Logistics Quotes," *Navy Supply Corp.* Newsletter, May–June 2003, retrieved from http://www.findarticles.com on April 19, 2005.

2. Quote by Dick Hunter, vice president, America's Manufacturing Operation at Dell Inc., in Barlas, S., "10 Best Supply Chains," *Logistics Today,* April 2004. Retrieved from http://www.logisticstoday.com on April 14, 2005.

3. This definition and others can be found at http://www.cscmp.org.

4. Heskett, J. L., "Controlling Customer Logistics Service," *International Journal of Physical Distribution & Logistics Management,* Vol. 24, No. 4, 1994, p. 4.

5. Sterline, J. U. and D. M. Lambert, "Customer Service Research: Past, Present, and Future," *International Journal of Physical Distribution and Materials Management,* Vol. 19, No. 2, 1989, p. 17; Krenn, J. M. and H. N. Shycon, "Modeling Sales Response to Customer Service for More Effective Distribution," *Proceedings of the National Council of Physical Distribution Management,* Vol. I, New Orleans, LA, October 2–5, 1983, p. 593.

6. Carr, D., "Hershey's Sweet Victory," *Baseline Magazine,* December 16, 2002, retrieved online April 21, 2005, from http://www.baselinemag.com.

7. Breen, B., "Living in Dell Time," *Fast Company,* November 2004, pp. 86–94.

8. Douglas, M., "Business Continuity: Ready, Set, Prepare," *Inbound Logistics,* January 2005. Retrieved October 30, 2006, from http://www.inboundlogistics.com.

9. "FedEx Enhances Transportation Management Service," *Logistics Today,* October 8, 2003. Retrieved April 19, 2005, from http://www.logisticstoday.com.

10. "Port Plans to Double Rail Capacity at Cargo Terminal," *Virginia Pilot,* February 20, 2005. Retrieved April 19, 2005, from http://www.manufacturing.net.

11. Information on UPS Supply Chain Solutions was found at http://www.ups-scs.com/transportation/ on April 30, 2005.

12. "Frito-Lay Commends Exel Transport Services," *JOC Online,* April 22, 2004, retrieved April 12, 2005, from http://www.joc.com.

13. "Supply Chain B. Goode," a white paper retrieved on April 12, 2005, from http://www.logisticstoday.com.

14. A bill of lading is the legal contract between the shipper and transportation carrier, specifying the moving of designated freight damage-free to a given location within a certain time frame.

15. Ballou, R. H. (2003), *Business Logistics Management,* Fifth Edition, Upper Saddle River, NJ: Pearson Prentice Hall, p. 98.

16. Calderwood, J. A., "The Case of the Late Christmas Cards," *Logistics Today,* October 2003, retrieved April 18, 2005, from http://www.logisticstoday.com.

17. "Automated Internet Entry Order System Reduces Cycle Time and Saves Money," a white paper, retrieved April 13, 2005, from http://www.integro.com/clients/nextel.icm.

18. Bley, D., "Improving Logistics," *Strategic Finance,* October 2004, pp. 38–41.

19. See http://www.menloworldwide.com for more information on the company.

20. "New Supply Chain Study Finds Postponement Strategies Critical for Reducing Demand Uncertainty and Improving Customer Satisfaction," *Supply Chain Planet,* September 10, 2003, retrieved on April 14, 2005, from http://www.supplychainplanet.com.

21. Harrington, L. H., "The New Warehousing," *Industry Week,* Vol. 247, No. 14, July 20, 1998, pp. 52–58.

22. Chiou, J–S., L–Y Wu, and J. C. Hsu, "The Adoption of Form Postponement Strategy in a Global Logistics System: The Case of Taiwanese Information Technology Industry," *Journal of Business Logistics,* Vol. 23, No. 1, 2002, pp. 107–124.

23. Foster, T. A., "A Process for DC Site Selection," *Global Logistics & Supply Chain Strategies,* December 2002, retrieved April 16, 2005, from http://www.glscs.com.

24. Drickhamer, D., "Lower Freight Costs Prompted Oneida Move to Savannah," *Logistics Today,* August 8, 2006, retrieved November 2, 2006, from http://www.logisticstoday.com.

25. Hartman, L. R., "Pick/Sort Management System Runs More than Skin Deep," *Packaging Digest,* May 1998, retrieved April 30, 2005, from http://www.packagingdigest.com/articles.

26. Case Study on Procter & Gamble Warehouse Management System by Solutions Manufacturing, retrieved April 21, 2005, from http://www.symbol.com/manufacturing/cs_p_and_g.html.

27. "IP Unveils RFID-Enabled Warehouse," *RFID Journal,* August 14, 2003, retrieved April 28, 2005, from http://www.rfidjournal.com.

28. Trunick, P. A., "Sum of Many Parts," *Logistics Today,* March 2004, retrieved April 5, 2006, from http://www.logisticstoday.com.

29. Trunick, P. A., "Think Inside a Bigger Box," *Logistics Today,* September 2004, retrieved March 31, 2005, from http://www.logisticstoday.com.

30. Richardson, H., "Building a Better Supply Chain," *Logistics Today,* April 2005, retrieved April 2, 2005, from http://www.logisticstoday.com.

31. A more in-depth analysis of location models can be found in Ballou, R. H., *Business Logistics Management,* Fourth Edition, 2003, Pearson Prentice Hall, Upper Saddle River, NJ.

32. Retrieved April 19, 2005, from http://logistics.about.com/library/blsupplychainsurveys.htm.

33. Craig, T., "Marketing Strategy: Create Competitive Advantage with Logistics," *Worldwide Shipping,* October/November 1998, retrieved April 19, 2005, from http://www.ltdmgmt.com/mag/april98II.htm.

34. Bowersox, D. J. and P. J. Daugherty, "Emerging Patterns of Logistical Organization," *Journal of Business Logistics,* Vol. 8, No. 1, 1987, pp. 46–60.

35. McGinnis, M. A. and J. A. Kohn (2002), "Logistics Strategy—Revisited," *Journal of Business Logistics,* Vol. 23, No. 2, 2002, pp. 1–16.

36. Field, A. M., "Think it Through," *Journal of Commerce,* January 24, 2005, p. 1.

37. Pagliari, L. R., "Developing a Global Logistics Course," *Journal of Commerce,* April 4, 2005, p. 1.

38. Bayles, D. L., "E-Logistics & E-Fulfillment: Beyond the 'Buy' Button," UNCTAD Workshop, June 25–27, 2002, p. 10.

39. Page, Paul, "High Priorities," *Traffic World,* September 6, 2004, p. 1.

40. Panchak, P., "Transportation: Stuck in the Slow Lane," *SupplyChainEdge,* retrieved April 30, 2005, from http://www.tompkinsinc.com.

41. Trunick, P. A., "Running to Stay in Place," *Logistics Today,* October 2004, pp. 44–45.

Chapter 12:

PURCHASING AND SUPPLY MANAGEMENT

"Supply management exists to explore business opportunities and implement supply strategies that deliver the most value possible to the organization, its suppliers and customers."[1]

"The earlier you can bring suppliers into a project, the better the product you're going to end up with."[2]

Learning Objectives

After completing this chapter, you should be able to:

- Define the role of purchasing and supply management in an organization and the supply chain.
- Describe the strategic sourcing process.
- Discuss supplier evaluation techniques.
- Apply cost management practices to supplier selection.
- Discuss the continuum of relationships between purchasing and its suppliers.
- Describe the supplier monitoring process.
- Describe the types of electronic purchasing.
- Discuss ways purchasing can monitor supplier relationships beyond the first tier.
- Understand some of the challenges purchasing and supply management professionals face today.

Chapter Outline

Process Management in Action

The Bullwhip Rider

Teradyne Inc. occupies an unenviable position. Perched at the very end of an uncertain semiconductor supply chain, the automated test equipment provider is hostage to the last-minute decisions of those who make chips and the eleventh-hour needs of those who test them.

Of course, Teradyne's chip industry customers—half of which today are Asian subcontractors that handle testing for semiconductor suppliers—occupy just a marginally better position than the equipment maker. Often they won't know until late in the game whether the contract to handle a semiconductor supplier's testing will be theirs. Given that unsettled climate, the subcontractors have little visibility into their own requirements.

That's been a jarring adjustment for 43-year-old, Boston-based Teradyne, whose systems have as many as 5,000 parts and sell for anywhere from $100,000 to $3 million each. Some machines can be configured with as many as 150 different options. At the same time, the company maintains a broad footprint in testing: It sells into the data processing, consumer, communications, industrial, automotive, and aerospace/defense markets. Companies across all of those sectors are turning to subcontractors, forcing Teradyne to remain nimble.

As customers pressure Teradyne to be more responsive, the company has acted on a number of fronts. It has trimmed its supply base—from the 80 suppliers that once accounted for 80 percent of its total purchases down to 50 suppliers—and formed deeper relationships with the suppliers it has retained. It has outsourced manufacturing but maintains control over design and procurement for critical components. Teradyne is sourcing parts from China and is developing software in India.

It currently outsources about 58 percent of the manufacturing in its semiconductor- and board-test businesses, which account for about 75 percent of its revenue, according to Credit Suisse First Boston. In the late 1990s, Teradyne made most of its own machines and printed-circuit boards; now, contractors make nearly 90 percent of its products. Outsourcing will increase to 96 percent over the next 12 to 16 months, and will include final assembly and equipment test.

By investing more in raw materials, in particular bare dice, the company has cut lead times for delivery of components from its suppliers by 25 percent. On one product, Kenney said, the company zeroed in on nine suppliers that collectively delivered 45 components that accounted for more than half its purchases. By getting them to focus on responsiveness, Teradyne cut lead time by 16 percent.

Teradyne can now ask its suppliers to create inventory buffers where it believes it needs them for scarce parts, and to eliminate the buffers where it doesn't need them. Teradyne can also more accurately determine the inventory it owns. Thus, ironically, the new system of assuming liability for inventory has helped reduce Teradyne's overall liability 30 percent, Wood said.

Wood cited one critical part—an ASIC that cost $100,000 per unit—that the company generally ordered once a week but sometimes had to order twice a week. By working with the chip supplier, Teradyne set up a pipeline of parts in process and created an inventory buffer that reduced the lead time from 12 weeks to 4.

Teradyne calls this value mapping. The company looks at the manufacturing process at its top 30 suppliers and determines where they can speed their internal processes for delivering parts. Teradyne also looks at the suppliers' inventory and authorizes them to put unique-parts pipelines in place. And it delays its investment in parts that are not unique to Teradyne. The strategy includes key partnerships with ASIC foundries, such as Phoenix Pin Electronics and Tempe ASIC.

Source: Takahashi, D., "The Bullwhip Rider," *Electronics Supply & Manufacturing*, April 4, 2005, available at http://www.my-esm.com. Copyright © 2004 by **CMP Media LLC,** 6000 Community Drive, Manhasset, NY 11030, USA. Reprinted from *Information Week* with permission.

Introduction

At first glance, purchasing materials, services, and other inventory items for a business might seem simple because students are familiar with buying for their own personal needs. As we can see by the opening Process Management in Action feature on Teradyne, however, purchasing and supplying goods for business purposes, also referred to as commercial buying, is far from simple and is an important business process.

Organizations use multiple terms to describe the process of purchasing and supply management. The Institute for Supply Management (ISM), a global, non-profit organization dedicated to the education of purchasing professionals, defines **purchasing** as "a major function of an organization that is responsible for acquisition of required materials, services, and equipment," and **supply management** as "the identification, acquisition, access, positioning and management of resources the organization needs or potentially needs in the attainment of its strategic objectives."[3] These definitions suggest that the term *purchasing* simply describes the act of buying materials and services, while *supply management* is more strategic, extending the definition of purchasing to include the process of finding the most appropriate suppliers and then ensuring that these suppliers perform effectively for the organization. Thus, building and managing supplier relationships are important aspects of supply management. Companies also vary in the level of responsibility placed on purchasing, and departments may simply be known as purchasing, supply management, or purchasing and supply management. People within a purchasing department may be known as buyers, purchasing agents, supply managers, or directors of purchasing, among other titles. Because there is no universal standard, for the purposes of this chapter we will these terms interchangeably to describe the function and the people that work within this area.

Due to the complexities of purchasing in a business environment and the role it can play in multiple supply chains, it is important to take a look at the supply management process more closely. The following sections will cover some of the basics of purchasing and supply management, the general process of buying services and materials from suppliers, and also how information technology is influencing the buying process. The process of analyzing price will also be described, including a discussion on target costing and total cost of ownership. The more strategic process of managing relationships with suppliers in the supply chain is extremely important and will also be discussed.

The Role of Purchasing and Supply Management

As mentioned in the introduction, commercial buying differs on several levels from shopping for personal needs. First, purchasing and supply personnel meet the specialized needs of an organization by buying specific items, sometimes in very large quantities, to be delivered on required dates. U.S. manufacturers spend, for example, an average of half of each sales dollar on materials.[4] Purchasing and supply management personnel also buy services including maintenance, healthcare, travel, and transportation. Thus, a company's costs and profitability can be significantly impacted if purchasing departments effectively and efficiently buy and manage these materials and services.

Because of the sheer volume of purchases made with outside suppliers, an important part of the purchasing and supply management process is developing relationships with suppliers. In many instances, working with a supplier means much more than talking price. A supplier's technology development plans, its production process, as well as new product development information are often shared with the purchasing department. And, purchasing departments view their companies as members of multiple supply chains. Beyond the relationships with immediate or first-tier suppliers, some firms manage several tiers of suppliers. Thus, a purchasing department is seen as the "driver," coaxing its suppliers in the supply chain to improve quality, make deliveries more reliable, and drive down costs, which will hopefully encourage suppliers to coax and manage *their* suppliers in the same way.

A great deal of planning is involved in the purchasing process, and good purchasing and supply managers spend time trying to understand the future needs of their organizations. Forecasting, inventory management, and new product development are among some of the areas that influence purchasing decisions. As a result, in the last 15 years, top-level purchasing professionals have been elevated in position to the extent that, in many instances, they report directly to a top-level executive (president/CEO, executive vice president, chief operating officer, or chief financial officer, among others) and are involved in senior-level decision making.[5] Rick Jacobs, vice president of supply chain at Eaton Corporation, U.S. producer of electrical equipment and hydraulic fluid power components, for example, feels "buyer roles continue to evolve from transactional to strategic. I believe, however, the biggest changes are still ahead of us. These new challenges will include digitization of transactions, making globally leveraged purchasing decisions, and providing business intelligence to each buyer."[6]

Purchasing and supply management professionals identify opportunities to create and improve a company's products and services, whether through discovery and acquisition of new materials or technologies, finding new suppliers, developing existing suppliers, or developing new purchasing methods. Purchasing also identifies and creates strategies to find and use its sources of supply to its best advantage. Those strategies include plans for developing suitable relationships with suppliers, determining the appropriate buying methods, and improving supply chain processes to support the organization's overall business strategy as well as other functional strategies. Purchasing then implements those chosen strategies by managing the buying process and the ongoing relationships with the firm's suppliers.

In a nutshell, the goals of purchasing and supply management are to:

1. Maintain the flow of goods and services to serve the organization and its supply chains, at the desired customer service levels on a continuous basis;
2. Minimize the investment in inventory to free up capital for other projects;
3. Maintain the required quality levels of purchased goods and services;
4. Search for and develop capable suppliers;
5. Standardize goods and services purchased whenever possible to reduce costs;
6. Achieve good working relationships with other functional areas of the organization;

7. Operate the purchasing and supply management department at the lowest administrative cost possible; and

8. Seek ways to improve the organization's and supply chains' competitive positions.[7]

More on the actual process of sourcing services and materials is covered in the following section.

The Strategic Sourcing Process

Strategic sourcing can be broken down into a six-step process. The first three steps involve preparing for the acquisition of materials, supplies, and services, and are generally done together to assess the current situation. The next three steps involve the actual process of purchasing the goods and services. Figure 12.1 provides a flowchart of the process, and each step is described in more detail next.

Conduct an Internal Assessment

Purchases are commonly divided into general **spend categories**, each with common characteristics such as raw materials, customized items, standardized items, and services, and then each of these general categories may be further divided. For example, a specialty sourcing team may buy one type of raw material, such as copper or steel, for an auto manufacturer. Walgreens, a U.S. drug store chain, has five spend categories: sundries and seasonal products, beauty and fashion, franchise cosmetics, pharmacy, and photo and electronics.[8] A specialty sourcing team should have a full understanding of the spend category, such as how the category is defined, the demand history of the category, and the specifications of each product in the category.

The team also needs to identify the users or consumers of the category, any existing relationships with current suppliers used in the spend category, as well as any other potential or known suppliers. Other interested parties, or **stakeholders**, should also be identified, such as marketing personnel, who need to understand the impact purchases might have on product completion dates or advertising possibilities; logistics personnel, who need to understand the product specifications, such as size and weight, for shipping purposes; and finance personnel, who need to know the magnitude of the cost or spend. It's important to clarify the purchasing process to all stakeholders and keep them informed of any changes in the process that might take place in the future.

Assess the Market

The five competitive forces model developed by Michael Porter is a good starting point to understand the current market situation.[9] As shown in Figure 12.2, purchasing specialists make an assessment of external forces in their particular industry to further determine risks and opportunities. First, they need to assess the bargaining power of their organization in relation to their suppliers, based on their size and the volume of purchases. They also should estimate the bargaining power of the current pool of suppliers by identifying the number of current and potential suppliers. Are there many suppliers that will keep the marketplace competitive, a few large suppliers that dominate the market, or one supplier that holds a monopoly on this spend category?

Another key factor purchasing should examine is the opportunity for new suppliers to enter into the market, as well as the risk of new buyer firms purchasing the same items, which will reduce their bargaining power. They should also determine if new

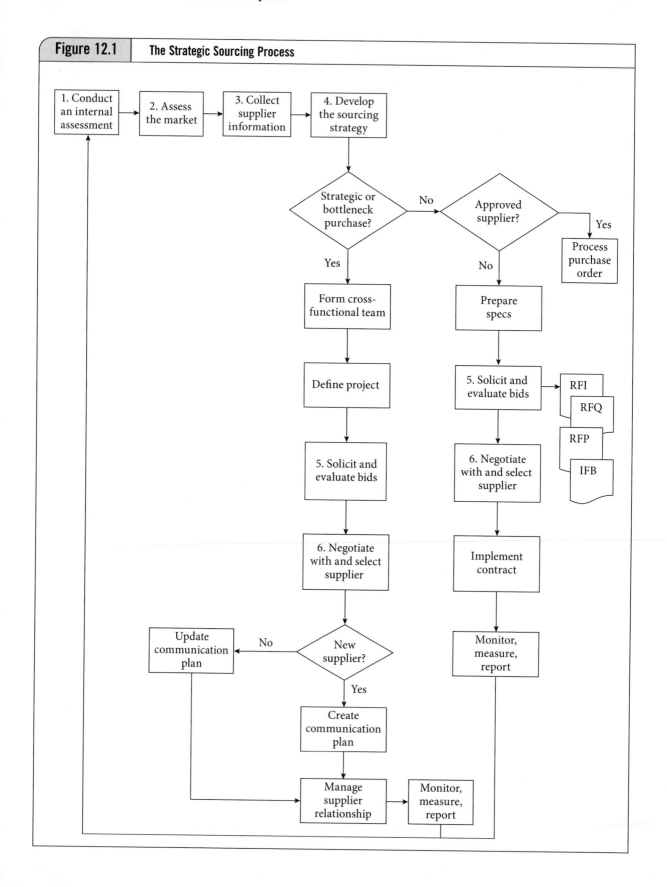

Figure 12.1   The Strategic Sourcing Process

Figure 12.2	Porter's Five Competitive Forces Model

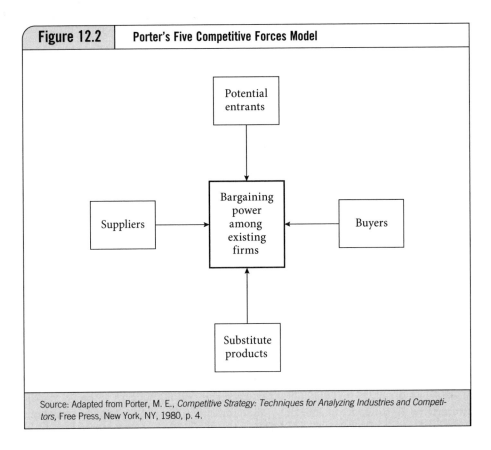

Source: Adapted from Porter, M. E., *Competitive Strategy: Techniques for Analyzing Industries and Competitors,* Free Press, New York, NY, 1980, p. 4.

substitute products are or will become available, which will increase their bargaining power with suppliers.

Kraljic created a two-by-two portfolio matrix to help purchasing and supply personnel develop an appropriate sourcing strategy for items purchased, based on profit impact and supply risk (low and high).[10] As shown in Figure 12.3, items under review are classified into one of four risk categories—non-critical items, leveraged items, bottleneck items, or strategic items. **Non-critical items**, such as office supplies, are thought of more as commodities—highly standardized, easily substituted, and thus purchased with simple contracts or **procurement cards** or **p-cards** (multipurpose bank cards designed to streamline the purchasing and payment processes). Unit cost is important for **leveraged items** because the profit potential is higher, but substitution is possible. For these items, purchasing and supply management personnel seek to exploit their purchasing power to the full extent to obtain the lowest possible prices. **Bottleneck items** have unique, customized specifications, where the supplier's technology is important and thus are considered high risk to the buying firm. Buying firms should purchase bottleneck items in larger quantities to avoid interruptions to supply, monitor inventory levels more closely, and seek out other suppliers to reduce the risk of supply interruptions. **Strategic items** are simply that—strategic to production or service delivery because of their unique characteristics. These items are generally managed through closer, win-win, partnership-type relationships with the supplier.

Volvo do Brasil, for example, buys many of the components and parts that go into the manufacture of its trucks. The Swedish automaker's manufacturing site in Brazil has specialized technology it views as critical to its competitive advantage. It works

Figure 12.3	Applying Kraljic's Model to Semiconductor Industry

Quadrant 1 – Non-critical Items
(Low Profit Impact, Low Supply Risk)
- Commodities
- Easy-to-find substitute products
- Many suppliers available

Quadrant 2 – Leverage Items
(High Profit Impact, Low Supply Risk)
- Large volume purchases
- Unit cost important
- Can find substitutes
- Many suppliers available

Quadrant 3 – Bottleneck Items
(Low Profit Impact, High Supply Risk)
- Unique requirements
- Supplier's technology critical
- Scarce sources of supply
- Difficult to substitute
- Difficult to forecast usage

Quadrant 4 – Strategic Items
(High Profit Impact, High Supply Risk)
- Continuous usage
- Unique specifications
- Supplier technology critical
- Few suppliers available
- Difficult to substitute

Sources: Table adapted from Kraljic, P., "Purchasing Must Become Supply Management," *Harvard Business Review,* September–October 1983; McGovern, S. and S. Costello, "The Challenges of Alternate Sourcing Tool Spares and Consumables," *Future Fab International,* Vol. 13, July 8, 2002, available online at http://www.future-fab.com.

closely with one supplier for each technology, beginning with the product development stage. However, it also has suppliers that make the castings for each technology part, which have the potential to shut down the production line if not available. These are considered the bottleneck items and Volvo purchases additional inventory or safety stock to avoid disruptions in supply.[11] In the semiconductor industry, companies buy different types of tooling used in manufacturing their products. Eventually these companies must buy replacement parts. Considered bottleneck items, these parts are usually purchased from **original equipment manufacturers** (OEMs), which sell them the original tooling. OEMs, as a rule, buy the replacement parts in large volumes from the **original parts manufacturers** (OPMs) and then resell them at a profit.[12]

Collect Supplier Information

Once purchasing and supply has analyzed the market and type of buy, they must make an assessment of the current and potential suppliers. Data collection is an important step in the planning process. This information will be used in designing the competitive bidding process (for non-critical or leveraged items) or the negotiation process (for bottleneck or critical items). Supply managers may use a number of sources of information in their assessment including:

- On-file records of suppliers used in the past,
- Commodity and supplier directories,
- Online and printed catalogs,
- Purchasing and supply management colleagues,
- Trade magazines,
- Suppliers' websites,
- Trade shows and conventions, and
- Sales presentations.

Purchasing will use this information to narrow the list of all available suppliers to the ones who are most likely to meet the organization's preset criteria. It only makes sense that less time will be spent finding suppliers for the non-critical or leveraged items, while a great deal of time and energy will be used searching for the supplier(s) of the more strategic or bottleneck items. For example, if an organization is developing a new product, it wants to ensure all parts, components, and materials purchased will meet design specifications at a reasonable cost from reliable suppliers. In the case of critical parts, purchasing personnel may also be responsible for learning who the second-tier suppliers are that furnish parts to the first-tier suppliers, because they understand that the quality and delivery capability of a supplier are, in turn, affected by the performance of their suppliers. A buying specialist from the purchasing and supply management department will mostly likely be a member of a larger cross-functional team, as discussed in Chapter 2.

Develop the Sourcing Strategy

Using Kraljic's model shown in Figure 12.3 and their knowledge of the supply market, supply management personnel should have a full understanding of the type of purchase they are making. Purchasing and supply personnel should also have evaluated the extent they can motivate suppliers to seek their business based on an analysis using Michael Porter's competitive forces model. If the supply market is competitive, the purchasing and supply management department is in a position to extract better prices and terms. If, on the other hand, the market is not competitive, the purchasing or sourcing strategy will more likely seek ways to collaborate with their suppliers to obtain some service benefits, in lieu of negotiating better prices. For example, the buying firm and a supplier may negotiate to work together to simplify and improve the delivery process, or the buying firm may even invest in the supplier's operations to ensure continued access to supply, technology, or process improvements.

Purchasing can then proceed to develop their **sourcing strategy**—a long-range plan for managing the supply of purchased items, linked to their analysis and goals, and tied to the corporate and supply chain strategies. Purchasing and supply management executives may decide it is necessary to reduce the size of the firm's supply base, devise a program to further develop some of their suppliers, and implement a **supplier certification program** for those suppliers that provide strategic items. Supplier certification often takes place before a supplier is allowed to quote prices or is awarded an order. A cross-functional team from the buying firm will make a visit to the supplier's facilities, observing the supplier's equipment, personnel, facilities, and systems that monitor quality, in order to ensure they meet the buying firm's specifications and quality standards. If those standards have been met, the supplier will be certified.

Ohio-based Owens Corning, a leader in fiberglass technology, spends approximately $3.4 billion annually on building materials. Its four-pronged sourcing strategy is to:

1. Align and standardize global purchasing procedures and systems.
2. Link sourcing and strategic business unit initiatives and incentives through a matrix organization.
3. Make spending visible to all parts of the organization.
4. Make use of online sourcing tools.[13]

Personal care product manufacturer The Gillette Company (now Global Gillette, a unit of Procter & Gamble) launched its Strategic Sourcing Initiative in 2001 to realize cost savings, and then used that money to fund more research and development and invest in company brands. Teams were created to analyze spending on direct and indirect materials using a formal strategic sourcing methodology. Suppliers were evaluated based on cost, quality, and services provided.[14]

Purchasing and supply management personnel, in particular, need to have a good understanding of any internal dynamics within their own organizations before implementing new sourcing strategies, especially if they are planning to integrate their supply chains more fully. If, for example, a purchasing team is considering a new, unproven supplier for a spend category, and the users (such as manufacturing) already have a good working relationship with another supplier, they may not want to make any changes that would damage that relationship. The finance manager (a stakeholder), on the other hand, might consider the move to a new supplier a good one if purchasing costs will go down. Thus, it is up to purchasing personnel to communicate the benefits of their sourcing strategy to both the users (such as manufacturing personnel) and other stakeholders (like the finance manager) when necessary, and potentially make compromises as needed.

Solicit and Evaluate Bids

The sourcing strategy will set the tone for Step 5 of the purchasing process. Purchasing may obtain pricing from its suppliers through a number of means, including verbal quotes, a request for information, a request for quote, a request for proposal, an invitation to bid, or a reverse auction.[15]

Verbal quotes are usually requested for lower cost, non-critical purchases. The buyer will then select one or more suppliers for the purchase, and a verbal agreement with the supplier will be reached on price, the number of items that will be purchased, when and where the purchase should be delivered, the transportation terms, and any other charges. The verbal agreement should be followed up with a fax, email, or mailed written acknowledgement.

Purchasing may also use a **request for information** (RFI) to informally collect general information on price, design, timing, and/or other terms the firm is interested in obtaining. The supplier's estimate is non-binding but provides a means to prepare budgets for the following year, approximate the total cost of purchasing and using a new item or service, or help the firm decide how to prepare a more detailed request for quote.

A **request for quote** (RFQ) is commonly used when the purchasing requirements are clear and are also used in practice for non-critical or leverage buys. Purchasing and supply management personnel send a standardized inquiry form to one or more potential suppliers. The suppliers submit price quotes based on specified quantities or services and promised delivery dates, including a time limit wherein the quote will be honored. The purchaser does not have to buy from any of the suppliers but it must respond to all quotes within the specified time period.

A **request for proposal** (RFP), on the other hand, is a formal, binding request for pricing and is used for the more complex critical and bottleneck purchases. It allows the supplier to develop part specifications based on its own knowledge of the materials and technology needed. A **statement of work** should be attached when specific services are required from the supplier or contractor. Statements of work are just what the name implies—they tell the buyer exactly what will be done and how. Some common services requiring a statement of work include construction, publications, advertising, janitorial services, and laboratory services. Supply specialists may also use an RFP when additional services are required for the purchase of off-the-shelf products, catalog items, or mass-produced software. For example, a company may buy off-the-shelf computers but require a complex network of geographically dispersed computing systems. An RFP is most commonly used as a starting point to negotiate a contract.

An **invitation for bid** (IFB) is similar to the RFP and is used for more costly purchases. The number of suppliers who will be asked to bid, the opening and closing dates of the bid, and the basis for award of a contract are all preset and at that point are binding. Generally, the contract is awarded to the lowest bid meeting all of the requirements; however, bidders might be told instead that bids will be used as a starting point for further negotiations.

Select the Supplier and Implement the Contract

Based on their evaluations and negotiations, purchasing and supply management awards the contract to the winning supplier(s) and then implements the contract. If the supplier is new to the firm, purchasing representatives develop a communication plan that transitions the firm at every contact point between the buyer and the supplier. For example, workers at the receiving dock, accounts payable, customer service, as well as users in the firm must be made aware of the new supplier so they can make the proper changes in their receiving, storing, and usage processes. A new supplier's performance should also be monitored closely during the first several weeks to ensure expectations are met and if not, that corrections are made quickly.

The sourcing process is continuous, with multiple buys occurring at the same time. Due to its complexity, feedback loops are needed to ensure the sourcing process is efficient and effective. Purchasing personnel should track the benefits and/or drawbacks of the buy throughout the life cycle of the contract. This information should then be reported back to the user groups and senior executives on a periodic basis. Additionally, some suppliers may have been acquired or liquidated, contact information for a supplier may have changed, or new suppliers may have entered the market since the last purchase. Lessons learned from each sourcing project should also be discussed and then recorded to avoid making the same mistakes in the future.

Generally, purchasing personnel, along with users, will develop a set of performance standards to which the supplier is compared. With critical suppliers, **performance-based contracts** are often used, which address issues such as (1) customer satisfaction, (2) product/service quality, (3) end-user satisfaction, (4) process performance, and (5) and other unique aspects of the relationship.[16] More on measuring supplier performance can also be found at the end of the chapter.

Cost Management

One of the primary responsibilities of purchasing and supply management is to monitor and control the cost of purchased materials. Thus, the buying firm will often use **cost management** tools in order to evaluate a supplier's pricing structure. Cost management is the process of identifying all the costs associated with company investments by making informed choices about the options that will deliver the best value for the money and managing those costs throughout the life of the investment. A description of two of the most commonly used tools, target costing and total cost of ownership analysis, follows.

Target Costing

The **target costing** process, which is growing in practice, is a good way for a firm to set and communicate cost objectives and performance metrics to the internal organization and its external suppliers. Companies also use target costing to increase cooperation with their suppliers, get the supplier involved earlier in the product development process, and improve their competitive position.[17]

When buying materials for a new product, the purchasing and supply management department begins by collecting historical data and user- and supplier-provided cost data, and establishing a target cost. The target cost for a finished product or service is based on the following formula:

$$\text{Target Cost} = \text{Estimated Selling Price} - \text{Desired Profit}$$

The estimated selling price is usually determined based on input from customers, a company's market research, data on similar product prices, a survey of current market conditions, and the firm's desired profit margin. This information allows the firm to "back into" the target cost and prepare a **cost analysis** (cost breakdown). The cost analysis can then be used as a basis to perform **value engineering**, which ensures that the necessary functions of the newly designed product or service are included at the targeted cost. Purchasing personnel, design engineers, and cost management specialists normally are involved in the value engineering process. The goal of value engineering is to determine, for instance, if less costly or fewer parts can be used without impacting the desired product performance.

Example 12.1 provides an example of target costing. Notice that additional activities may have to take place in order to reach the target cost, such as additional value engineering or further negotiation with suppliers.

Firms also use target costing as a way to reduce costs on existing products. Purchasing personnel may approach their suppliers, for example, and ask them for ways they can reduce their costs. Perhaps the supplier has overhead or non-value-adding activities that can be eliminated. The supplier may also have developed or sourced less expensive materials that can serve the same function. Other activities that could result in cost reductions include design or process changes. With existing products, these cost reduction efforts are referred to as **value analysis**.

Total Cost of Ownership Analysis

Purchasing managers realize that there are costs, other than price, incurred with the purchase of an item, which add to the **total life cycle cost** of the item. **Total cost of ownership** (TCO) determinations can help to guide the supplier selection process through a better understanding of the life cycle costs of the good or service, including sourcing, payment, repair, and operating costs, and eventually salvage revenue. TCO is used most often for capital goods (machinery and equipment) and manufactured parts.[18] However, services can benefit from TCO as well. Saks Inc., the New York–based retailer, develops total cost models to buy its private label clothing and goods in Southeast Asia with the help of e-purchasing tools. To select a supplier, the company includes factors such as (1) country of origin, (2) delivery charges, (3) any agents' fees and tariffs, and (4) design alternatives that can affect the weight and size of apparel in their model.[19] Carglass, a European vehicle glass repair and replacement provider, was using only price

Example 12.1   Target Costing

The Gynoble Company sells an electronic component for $90.00/unit and expects a 15 percent profit, or $13.50/unit. The cost management team, made up of members from finance, purchasing, and engineering, has collected cost information from historical prices, users, other functional areas, and suppliers and has come up with the following cost estimate for the component.

PRICE COMPONENT	COST
Materials	$23.00
Labor	$ 6.50
Overhead	$25.75
Sales, general, and administrative	$12.50
Technical support	$ 3.50
Research, development, and engineering	$ 8.30
Cost estimate	$79.55
Target price	$90.00
Profit margin	$10.45

The expected profit margin falls short by $3.05 ($13.50−$10.45), and senior management asks the team to reduce component costs. Engineering performs value engineering activities to reduce defect rates and scrap during the production process and determines improved processes can reduce these costs by $2.00/unit. Purchasing then goes into lengthy negotiations with its suppliers and is able to reduce material costs by $1.00/unit. As a result, the team is able to closely meet its target costs.

as a basis for purchase decisions, but developed a TCO analysis when the company faced serious quality and delivery problems. It now uses TCO to improve its suppliers' quality, reduce time-to-market for its products, and reduce inventories.[20]

As with target costing, total cost modeling may also be used to analyze the cost of previously purchased parts. Delphi Automotive Systems, for example, a Michigan-based supplier to automotive companies including General Motors, Ford, DaimlerChrysler, and Toyota, works to reduce the total life cycle cost of each product. Commodity teams determine the cost drivers for a part and then look for ways to lower those costs.[21]

To begin the total cost modeling process, a cross-functional team is formed that typically includes purchasing personnel, any technical experts, finance specialists, and end users. The team develops a set of ground rules for any assumptions made and creates the modeling process that will take place. At this point, the team can develop a list of relevant costs based on predetermined cost categories such as pretransaction costs (before purchase), transaction costs (during purchase), and posttransaction costs (after purchase). Lastly, an acceptable method for calculating these costs is developed and applied to determine the total cost of ownership of the item. Table 12.1 provides an example of the relevant costs for the purchase of desktop personal computers.

Any cost risks or opportunities are also evaluated at this time, which could include things such as supply shortages, new processes, or new technologies. For example, in 2004 the United States experienced cement shortages due to increasing demand from Chinese companies, resulting in delayed completion of home construction and road projects, as well as increased cement prices. As a result, purchasing managers had to factor in price increases as well as delivery issues in their planning process.[22]

Table 12.1	Examples of Total Cost of Ownership Components for PC Purchase	
COST COMPONENT	**PROCESS**	**EXAMPLES**
Pretransaction	1. Identify need 2. Investigate sources 3. Qualify sources 4. Add supplier to computer system 5. Educate supplier on firm's operations 6. Educate firm on supplier operations	Sourcing: Two full-time equivalent employees for two months Supplier quotes for software licenses and equipment Administration: One full-time equivalent for one week to set up computer invoicing system
Transaction	1. Delivery/transportation 2. Tariffs, duties 3. Billing/payment 4. Inspection 5. Parts returns 6. Follow-up/correction	Purchase price Labor cost to place one purchase order, and ten invoices Labor costs to receive and inspect personal computers
Posttransaction	1. Repair/replacement 2. Technical support	Cost of repairs Equipment support Network support Downtime during transition period Warranty Salvage value

Beyond cost factors, however, other criteria are important in the selection of suppliers, including quality and delivery. The following section discusses the supplier selection process with particular attention to these issues.

Factors in Supplier Selection

Purchasing personnel always use some type of evaluation process when selecting suppliers. Potential suppliers will go through a screening process to evaluate their potential for meeting product design and supplier service requirements, while current suppliers will be evaluated periodically on their past cost, quality, delivery, and service performance. Purchasing personnel may also assess current suppliers in terms of those who have been with the company for some time and are considered reliable, and those newer to the organization with little or no established track record. Both groups will be evaluated intermittently, on a formal and informal basis, but new suppliers will typically be watched more closely to determine if further business will be awarded. As organizations and their purchases increase in size, they tend to rely more on formal written evaluations and less on informal verbal assessments of suppliers.

Use of Evaluation Forms

Generally, an evaluation form should be used to assess a prospective supplier's strengths and weaknesses, although the results from a recent study suggest that slightly less than half of all firms use a formal evaluation process.[23] Questionnaires are also sent to the prospective supplier for completion. Of those firms with formal written evaluations in place, the factors found to be included most often were:

1. All aspects of quality (including the specifications, production processes, outgoing product quality, and quality planning),

2. Continuous quality and process improvement activities,

3. Supplier certification,

4. Capability of supplier's facilities,

5. Physical distribution capabilities, and

6. Supply chain relationship capabilities.[24]

A sample supplier evaluation questionnaire can be found in Example 12.2.

Once the evaluation forms are received, purchasing should summarize the responses received and make an assessment of each supplier. Based on this assessment, a short list is created and the remaining suppliers may be brought in for additional evaluation. Good business practice dictates that the purchasing and supply management department must also provide reasons for rejecting any suppliers and issue a notification to each one.

In making their assessments, purchasing representatives review all the information collected; if more information is needed from any of the suppliers under consideration, it is requested at this time. For example, a supplier may have submitted an RFP with unclear technical specifications. For more complex purchases, the user group may also be asked to help evaluate suppliers. A formal process to evaluate each supplier should be used to make the process as equitable as possible. As shown in Table 12.2, a simple

---

Example 12.2   Sample Supplier Evaluation Questions

Jane, the supply manager, and her sourcing team have developed a survey to help evaluate suppliers during the supplier selection process. The survey is mailed to each potential supplier for completion and used for initial screening purposes.

SUPPLIER NAME: _____

QUESTION	YES	NO	UNDER DEVELOPMENT	N/A
1. Has your company developed and communicated a Quality Policy Statement to its employees?				
2. Does your company have a Quality System in place, with a quality manual, procedures, and work instructions?				
3. Does your management team have regularly scheduled Quality System meetings?				
4. Do you document quality planning objectives for new projects prior to production?				
5. Do you document your efforts and results from continuous improvement projects?				
6. In case of nonconforming product, what remedies do you provide?				
7. Do you inspect customer-supplied materials to your operation(s)? If no, provide separate explanation.				
8. Is your company ISO-9000 or QS-9000 certified?				
9. Is your company ISO-14000 certified?				
10. Can you provide customer references?				

Table 12.2	Supplier Selection Matrix			
EVALUATION FACTOR	ACME CO.	BETA CO.	CEPHUS CO.	DELTA CO.
Price quote	A	B	B	B
Financial stability	Good	Good	Good	Good
Inventory turnover	A	B	C	A
Delivery promises (%)	95	90	85	95
Information technology	Strong	Good	Fair	Good
Technical capability	Strong	Good	Good	Strong
Management quality	Best	OK	OK	OK
Training & development	Yes	No	No	Yes
Special services	Yes	Yes	No	Yes
Ranking of Combined Factors	**1**	**3**	**4**	**2**

Source: Adapted from Estrada, M. U. and M. Harding, "Understanding and Using a Traditional Process," *NAPM InfoEdge*, Vol. 1, No. 12, 1996.

matrix can be designed that contains the factors most important to the selection decision. Purchasing and supply management then ranks each supplier prior to making its final selection. Purchasing representatives should also notify senior executives of their decision when the contract is relatively large, in case disappointed suppliers who weren't selected happen to call them to complain.

General Performance Criteria

The purchasing and supply management department must decide whether a supplier's product or service design will meet specific performance criteria. This is generally determined through a review of the design specifications. In some instances, for example, the design may include parts with features that are hard to manufacture because of unusually tight tolerances. Or, some parts may be extremely fragile and subject to corrosion or contamination. Additionally, the design may contain a large number of parts, increasing the chance that the finished product will be improperly assembled. Problems with poor design can result in waste, damage, and operational failures, which affect quality for both the supplier and the buying firm.

Purchasing personnel must also look at the supplier's processes for making the product, and inspect for quality performance during manufacture and once the product is finished. For example, purchasing and supply may determine a supplier's past track record by examining some of its product quality data, including defect rates, mean time between failures, statistical quality control performance results, and maintenance records. They may also review service performance data, which may include such things as timeliness, dependability, responsiveness, and technical support.

Quality Criteria

As previously mentioned, purchasing personnel may assess the quality plan the supplier has in place. More and more companies are setting quality goals during their strategic planning process, such as improving customer satisfaction or reducing defect rates. Operational quality plans are then developed as a means to meet strategic goals.

As a result, the purchasing and supply management department may require suppliers to submit their quality plans for approval when parts are complex, expensive, and/or critical to the operation. These plans should address important issues such as:

- Where in the production process will quality be checked?
- What procedures will be used to assess quality?
- When will the quality checks take place?
- Who will be involved in the quality checks?
- What quality tools, such as checklists or quality control charts, will be used?

Beyond a quality plan, purchasing representatives will be interested in the activities the supplier has in place to continually improve its products, services, processes, employees, suppliers, and managerial practices. Some best practices a supply manager may be looking for include employee training in flowcharting and methods analysis to improve work procedures, use of employee suggestion systems, use of statistical process control techniques, use of problem-solving teams and supplier development programs, and incorporating reward systems to encourage employees to work more proactively and productively. (More on quality management and continuous improvement can be found in Chapter 13.)

For critical components, the supplier is often a member of the buyer's new product development team, and regularly interacts with other team members and presents ideas to improve product designs or quality. Thus, as part of a key supplier's evaluation, the purchasing and supply management department may even request records from second-tier suppliers to ensure a high level of quality and service will be achieved.

Delivery Criteria

As discussed in Chapter 11, getting the product or service from the supplier to the customer is just about as important as meeting predetermined quality standards. In other words, a product may be manufactured according to quality specifications, but if it is labeled incorrectly or arrives late or damaged due to poor packaging, loading, or using an improper transportation mode the customer will still be unhappy. Or, a service may look good on paper but delivery may be performed poorly due to poor personnel training, an incomplete process, or poor support materials or technology, resulting in customer dissatisfaction. Thus, purchasing representatives must consider the supplier's logistics capabilities during the screening process as well.

Relationship Criteria

Lastly, supply chain relationship quality or capability needs to be considered and refers to the expected value of the buyer–supplier relationship based on past experiences, if any, and similar organizational cultures and values. Essentially, purchasing and supply management tries to determine if the firm will have a good and trusting working relationship with the supplier, once the contract or purchase order is signed.

Negotiating the Contract

When the buy is for a strategic or bottleneck item and there is only one supplier or a few available suppliers, purchasing and supply management personnel will generally negotiate the terms of the contract face to face with a supplier representative or team.

Purchasing may also use negotiations when (1) changes need to be made to the initial specifications or drawings, after the original purchase order is issued; (2) changes occur in the marketplace that affect the quantities needed or prices agreed upon; (3) no acceptable bids are received; or (4) other problems have arisen during the contracted period. Negotiations are expensive and time-consuming and thus need strong justifications for their use.

Larger firms generally employ cost analysts who help purchasing personnel analyze the supplier's cost elements and profit margin before the negotiation even begins. However, for specialized or non-core spend categories, companies may hire a third party with specific knowledge of the category that has a better handle on developing a cost model and strategy.

It is best to collect as much cost information from the supplier as possible in order to be in a good position during the negotiation process. Some knowledge of the supplier's costs also helps the buyer better understand the supplier's pricing structure. The purchasing professional must, however, examine the supplier's costs using good judgment and remember that the ultimate goal is to obtain the best price given the required quantity, level of specified quality, and delivery needs. When an RFP is issued, for example, the buyer usually asks the supplier for a cost breakdown of the item that will be purchased.

However, the supplier may choose not to provide cost data for a number of reasons. Suppliers may not track their costs by individual product if they don't practice **activity-based cost accounting**, which tracks both direct and indirect costs to each specific product sold. Even if suppliers do know their costs for each product or service, they may not be willing to share that data with their customers. In this case, purchasing personnel may have to look at other sources of data, such as prices paid in the past for similar items, pricing provided by other suppliers with similar products, or catalogs.

The negotiation process begins when an RFP is issued to potential suppliers, which is then used as a basis to reach an agreement regarding the terms of the contract. A team, in most cases, will sit down with a supplier and come to some agreement on numerous issues, including product or service specifications, delivery requirements and terms, product support, and price. For example, the buying and supplying firms must agree to what is known as the **FOB terms** and responsibilities for delivery during the transit of an order. The FOB (free on board) terms define when ownership transfers to the buyer and which party will pay for transportation and insurance costs. Table 12.3 provides a more extensive list of issues that may arise during negotiations.

According to Leenders et al., successful negotiation depends on proper planning. Each party most likely will have spent a great deal of time preparing for the negotiation in order to protect their interests. The most successful negotiators develop a written negotiation plan that includes any background information, key strategic issues, organizational objectives, cost parameters, and contingencies. The negotiator should also assess the strengths of both parties. For example, what is the supplier's capacity, ability to meet quality requirements, and past delivery performance? What is the confidence and experience level of the negotiators? Are there other suppliers available in the event this negotiation fails to result in a contract? There may also be time constraints on the negotiation process that will negatively affect the buying firm's position of strength. During the planning process the negotiation strategy should also be determined, including the negotiation team members, target cost objectives and ranges, a course of action, and possible resolutions to deadlock situations.[25]

Table 12.3	Negotiation Issues
GENERAL ISSUE	**SPECIFIC ISSUES**
Quality	• Testing criteria • Compliance with product/service specifications • Compliance with product/service performance • Liability for failure to perform • Product/service reliability • Conditions for design changes • Procedures in the event product/service is rejected
Delivery	• Scheduled times • FOB terms • Designated carrier(s) • Delivery point(s)
Support	• Product/service design • Product/service development • Research • Warranties • Training • Tooling • Spare parts • Packaging • Information technology • Technical assistance
Price	• Price/unit • Any discounts • Provision for price escalations during contract • Taxes • International issues such as exchange rates, import tariffs

Managing Supplier Relationships

Due to the increasing number of items that are purchased in lieu of making them in-house, also known as **outsourcing**, the performance of those items has a growing impact on the buying firm's product quality and reputation. Thus, supply management professionals now spend more time than ever before creating and managing relationships with their suppliers, rather than simply making one-time purchases of goods and services. To achieve the high levels of quality, price, and service demanded by customers, cooperation between the purchasing department and key supplier representatives becomes paramount.

Based on the relative dollar volume of purchases made by supply chain trading partners, the balance of power in supply chain relationships can vary greatly. For example, a purchasing firm may represent a large percentage of a supplier's total sales volume and thus wield a great deal of power in the relationship. Wal-Mart, a worldwide leader in supply chain management, is a good example of a buyer holding tremendous power in the buyer–supplier relationship. In these types of situations, suppliers will often do whatever they can to secure the deal and make the purchasing firm happy.

However, not all suppliers are considered critical or key suppliers, and thus not much time is required building relationships with these suppliers. Relationship depth with suppliers actually runs along a continuum, as shown in Figure 12.4, from arm's length, "adversarial" relationships at one end, to ongoing or informal relationships somewhere in the middle, to strategic alliances/partnerships on the other end. The following sections describe the common characteristics of these three relationship types.

Arm's Length Relationships

In an **arm's length relationship**, buying and supplying firms bargain from certain strengths for control of the resources. This type of relationship is relatively short term and relates to the one-time purchase of a particular product or service. Little information is shared among the two parties other than exchanges regarding the conditions of the purchase. An arm's length relationship works well when the purchase is an "off-the-shelf" commodity-type product or service where quality is consistent among suppliers. The terms of the buy are usually straightforward and no customized services are required. Today the process has been automated by many firms to make it more efficient.

Ongoing Relationships

The arm's length relationship may develop into an **ongoing relationship** when the same purchase is made on a regular basis. Although there are many suppliers available,

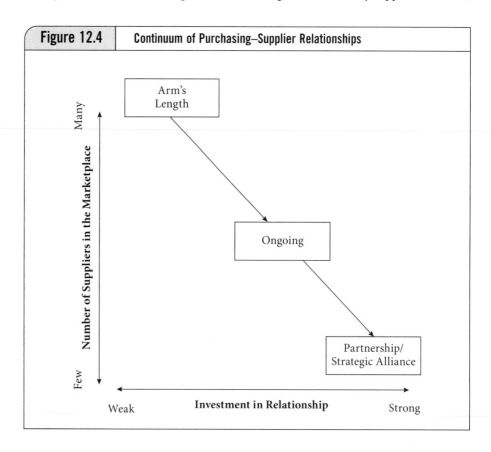

| **Figure 12.4** | **Continuum of Purchasing–Supplier Relationships** |

purchasing professionals may choose to continue buying from a desired supplier on a regular but informal basis. Little information is exchanged between the two parties, though, beyond the day-to-day mechanics of the purchase. Some steps may be taken to make the purchase more routine by setting up certain mechanisms in the buying and supplying firms' information support systems to automate the buying process.

Purchasing personnel may also revert to a competitive bidding process if they are not satisfied with a supplier's performance, substitute products are available at lower prices, or because new suppliers have entered the market.

Partnerships/Strategic Alliances

An ongoing relationship may lead to a **supplier partnership**—also called a **strategic alliance**, **preferred supplier**, or **key supplier**—if the relationship has been more than satisfactory and the two parties see a reason to work together more often and share more information. The reasons for strengthening the buyer–supplier relationship are many but may include (1) a shared desire to improve quality, (2) a greater possibility for price reductions and profit improvements, (3) the purchasing firm's desire to integrate new processes, (4) the supplier's desire to share new proprietary technologies, (5) a mutual desire to integrate the supply chain more fully, or (6) the purchasing firm's desire to ensure against supply disruptions. It's important to remember, though, that relatively few purchases are considered strategic in nature and critical to a firm's success, so partnerships should be used sparingly to save valuable time and effort.

Strategic alliances are seen as a means to build stronger, extensive ties between customers and suppliers, with the overall objectives of lowering costs and improving quality and customer service. The theory is that as quality improves, waste in the form of scrap materials, rework, and warranty repairs will decrease, increasing output and productivity and decreasing cycle time, thus reducing overall cost and improving service capability. Initiatives are designed to create greater integration and true "win-win" relationships that can add value for their respective companies. For example, in a partnership the buying firm would pay the supplier promptly, include the supplier on problem-solving teams, and guarantee a certain percent of its business to that supplier. In return, the supplier delivers its product as promised, responds promptly to concerns on the part of the customer, and offers input to improve the customer's business. Use of this type of relationship is common among trading partners in actively managed supply chains.

Strategic alliances can also vary on a continuum. Professor Lisa Ellram, who has done extensive research on supplier partnering and strategic alliances, identifies four levels of partnerships/alliances, discussed next.[26]

The Basic Alliance

First, the **basic alliance** is the "entry level" of partnering. Partners focus on keeping communication lines open and positive, and sharing information when needed. However, the buying firm still has other sources of supply available (and the supplier has other customers) in the event the alliance doesn't work out, so the risk is low and overall the relationship adds minor value to either organization.

The Operational Alliance

An alliance moves to the second stage, the **operational alliance**, when it becomes operational in nature. The working relationship between the two parties is closer in the form of longer-term contracts—generally one to three years. There may be some joint problem-solving and the supplier keeps the buyer informed about potential changes including future supply levels or pricing.

The Business Alliance

In the third stage, the **business alliance**, the purchasing department is looking for the supplier to add unique value in the form of a customized product or service. Each party has more invested in the relationship in terms of assets, human resources, or special technology and thus mutual dependency has increased to a new level. Both parties clearly define how the risks and benefits of the alliance will be shared. Based on supplier performance, purchasing will devote more of its business to its partner over a longer period of time. The two firms may use cross-organizational teams to solve problems or develop new technologies or processes.

The Strategic Alliance

In the final stage, firms move to a strategic alliance when a service or good is strategically important to a firm's success. The partners share information on their long-term strategies and frequently work together as a team to seek out problems and solve them, both from the buyer's and the supplier's perspective. There is a general understanding that process improvements will ultimately benefit both parties. More elaborate mechanisms are put in place to facilitate the alliance, including **early supplier involvement** in the development of new products and services as a member of the buyer's **concurrent engineering team**. As discussed in Chapter 2, concurrent engineering is the simultaneous design of products and processes using a cross-functional team-based approach. Early supplier involvement entails involving key suppliers early in the new product/service design phase in order to take advantage of any new proprietary technologies owned by the supplier and to help shorten the design cycle, which can give the buying firm a competitive advantage. Through early involvement, the supplier has a better understanding of the buyer's needs, which should result in shorter product development times and higher quality. As part of the new product development team, the supplier should also have a greater incentive to improve the performance of the product or service due to the cooperative nature of the relationship.

Toyota is at the forefront of involving its best suppliers in new product design and development of its automobiles. The Japanese company's suppliers independently perform research and development on their components and then regularly present these findings to Toyota. The automaker sets improvement targets for each supplier based on its capabilities, such as a 5 percent reduction in weight or a 5 percent reduction in cost. Based on joint discussions, Toyota and its suppliers then agree to the use of components, design specifications, and the cost for each component.[27]

Supplier development involves the efforts of a buying firm to improve the capabilities and performance of specific suppliers to better meet its needs.[28] In many cases, purchasing personnel monitor and work together with their strategic suppliers for a number of years and thus have an ongoing relationship with them. Purchasing and supply management finds ways to further develop the capabilities of these suppliers because they sell a fairly important product or service and can provide other value-adding benefits as well. Supplier development activities include supplier evaluation and feedback, site visits, investments in the supplier's operations, and training of supplier personnel.[29] ABB, a Swiss company that designs and manufactures power technologies for power plants, substations, and power lines, has implemented a supplier development policy because it sees suppliers as valued contributors to its competitive advantage. Thus it assists suppliers in continuous improvement activities, lean manufacturing, and quality management. ABB helps customize a supplier's development plan, shares its resources and technologies, exchanges best practices, and monitors the supplier's performance.[30]

Prerequisites for Strategic Alliances

As indicated by the description, strategic alliances are resource intensive, involving the participation and support of top management and cross-organizational teams. Once an investment in time and resources is made, it will be costly to exit the relationship. Thus it is important to consider several factors before pursuing a partnership, according to Professor Ellram,[31] including:

- Cultural compatibility between the two firms,
- Financial stability of the supplier,
- The supplier's long-term plans for expansion, contraction, or a change in mission,
- Design and/or technology capabilities and a willingness to share among both parties,
- Location of supplier's facilities and willingness to expand or relocate, if necessary,
- Local content laws, tariffs, quotas, and other issues for foreign partners, and
- Condition of the supplier's facilities.

A strategic alliance is generally considered successful when both parties feel that the relationship is adding value, and the performance is up to expectations. Often, partnerships break down when communication is not open, one party is not informed of changes made, information sharing isn't occurring, and commitment to the relationship begins to wane.

Ultimately, the level of partnership will vary depending on the degree that (1) purchasing and the supplier communicate effectively, (2) best practices are shared, (3) joint business planning takes place, and (4) performance is reviewed and used to improve practices. The Clorox Company, headquartered in California, for example, constantly looks for ways to keep costs down. In one instance, the manufacturer of household goods found that a supplier of trigger sprayers was packing too few to a box to efficiently feed its production line. The sheer number of boxes had increased Clorox's disposal costs. The purchasing department went to the supplier, a long-time partner, and asked it to ship in bulk containers of 5,000 sprayers each, rather than the 500-count corrugated boxes, emphasizing that both sides would save money. Before implementation, both parties collaborated and tested the idea. The supplier found that pallet-sized bulk boxes, or "gaylords," were large enough to ship the required quantities, could be reused up to ten times, and also protected the sprayers. Clorox evaluated the new shipping boxes and determined it could change its production loading system to accommodate the new packaging successfully. Both sides experienced cost benefits due to lower labor costs and disposal fees for Clorox, and distribution cost savings for the supplier.[32]

Two Examples of Partnerships

Vendor-managed inventory (VMI) as discussed in Chapter 6, is a progressive partner-based approach to controlling inventory and reducing supply chain costs. Customers provide information to the key supplier, including historical usage, current inventory levels, minimum and maximum stock levels, sales forecasts, and upcoming promotions, who then takes on the responsibility and risk for planning, managing, and monitoring the replenishment of inventory. The supplier may even own the inventory until the product is sold. VMI is commonly used in industries that are sensitive to errors such as pharmaceuticals; the grocery business; industries where the good is valuable and demand is unpredictable, such as PC manufacturing; and industries where profit margins are small, such as the automotive parts industry.

Global health and hygiene company Kimberly-Clark, for instance, provides VMI services to some of its largest retailers, including Costco. However, the U.S.-based consumer packaged-goods company carefully selects retailers where it feels there is a "win-win" relationship. Kimberly-Clark analyzes shipment patterns, looking for opportunities to ship more cost effectively, while at the same time maintaining high service levels. It also studies volumes shipped on a weekly basis, and between its manufacturing sites and customer locations, to better understand its customer's profile. This has helped it position its inventory more efficiently.[33]

A number of benefits have been attributed to VMI, including faster order processing time, better fill rates and fewer stockouts, and lower planning and ordering costs. However, the success of the partnership depends on the strength of the buyer–supplier relationship. Increased costs are also attached to switching to another supplier, as well as costs to purchase and implant the required technology as well as make the changeover. Lastly, extensive data and information system support are required to run an effective program.

Just-in-time II (JIT II), an extension of VMI and also referred to as **supplier co-location**, is another form of buyer–supplier partnership with a number of variations. A full-time representative of the supplier resides in the buying firm's purchasing department, holding a dual position as both buyer and supplier representative. This person may also contribute to the buying firm's new product development and value engineering/value analysis teams by suggesting modifications or alternate components during the product design phase that customers would not otherwise be aware of. JIT II results in higher service levels and fewer inventory management problems for the buying firm. The supplier benefits from continued sales, and more opportunities to participate in new project designs and to supply new products to the buyer. More on JIT II can be found in Chapter 6.

Once the purchasing specialist establishes a relationship with each supplier, performance must be monitored to assess whether that relationship should continue, or if some actions can be taken to improve the relationship. The following section takes a closer look at how purchasing departments examine and evaluate supplier performance.

Monitoring Supplier Performance

Measuring and tracking each supplier's performance is an important and ongoing component of the purchasing–supplier relationship. Both informal and formal means are used to evaluate suppliers, although informal evaluations are the common practice in many small organizations. Informally, purchasing personnel may approach product users and others inside the firm in regular contact with the supplier and its products to gather their performance assessments. Supply managers may also talk to others outside their organization at conferences or professional meetings to see if their impressions of the supplier are on target. Some examples of formal performance measurement and supplier reward systems are outlined in the following paragraphs.

Supplier Performance Surveys

Purchasing may develop an internal survey to evaluate the supplier's performance in key areas using a rating system. For example, a supplier may be rated on:

- Product and service quality,
- Delivery and order lead time performance,
- Total cost performance,
- Customer service and support management, and
- Product and technology contribution.

Different techniques can be used to evaluate suppliers. Some firms may choose to simply note whether or not expectations were met for each key area. Other companies may develop more detailed evaluation forms where each area has specific items that are rated using a scale. The type of scale used may vary, but one example is scoring key areas using a numbering system and then assigning a letter grade or description. Purchasing predetermines a desired minimum overall grade to continue working with the supplier. Purchasing may also weight each item based on importance and then tabulate an overall weighted score. U.S.-based aerospace and defense systems integrator Northrop Grumman Integrated Systems, for example, uses a **supplier scorecard** with ratings in four categories to calculate an overall score, as shown in Example 12.3. If there are performance gaps in any area, the purchasing department asks the supplier to provide an action plan to prevent future occurrences. Purchasing professionals also use these evaluations to determine whether additional business should be awarded to the supplier.

Annual Supplier Meetings

Purchasing and supplier representatives may meet annually to discuss the supplier's performance. These meetings are mostly used for suppliers of critical or strategic materials or services and are usually the culmination of a series of other less formal meetings held throughout the year. The annual performance meeting is used as a vehicle to provide the supplier a report of its performance, exchange experiences and results, address ways to improve performance, and develop an action plan for the following year. Suppliers that have not met performance expectations may be placed on a probationary status, with specific goals and a plan for improvement. Probationary suppliers that have not performed well may be told they are no longer going to be used.

Supplier Recognition and Awards

The buying organization may also give awards to suppliers with a demonstrated high level of performance, to serve as motivation to continue performing well and to seek further improvements. A meeting with suppliers can be used to give the awards, which may include a certificate for "best-in-class" or "most improved." Minnesota-based Honeywell Sensing and Control, a manufacturer of switching and sensor technology, rewards suppliers that provide world-class performance with more business. At an annual meeting with its suppliers, the Supply Management Division at Honeywell also presents awards for the most improved supplier and the top-performing supplier in each area of performance, including quality, service responsiveness, competitive value, service value, and supplier assisted value enhancement. One award is given for the overall supplier of the year with the best overall performance.[34]

Electronic Purchasing

Due to the paper-intensive nature of the purchasing process, document preparation and handling has, in the past, been time-consuming. Thus, firms today are looking for ways to streamline paper-based purchasing activities where possible through use of

Example 12.3   Supplier Scorecard Method at Northrop Grumman*

The scorecard is prepared quarterly and posted at the Northrop Grumman OASIS website. A team, composed of members from Quality and Procurement, review each supplier and prepare the scorecard. The supplier is rated on quality, delivery, customer satisfaction, and process health/lean/Six Sigma using the following format:

QUALITY PROFILE RATING		LATE DELIVERY (LAST 6 MONTHS)		CUSTOMER SATISFACTION	PROCESS HEALTH/ LEAN/SIX SIGMA
ACTUAL RATING	POINTS ASSIGNED	ACTUAL PERFORMANCE	EARNED POINTS	AVAILABLE POINTS	AVAILABLE POINTS
100	50	0%	30	10	10
90	45	1%	27	9	9
80	40	2%	24	8	8
77	39	3%	21	7	7
70	35	4%	18	6	6
67	34	5%	15	5	5
57	29	6%	12	4	4
54	27	7%	9	3	3
47	24	8%	6	2	2
44	22	9%	3	1	1
34	17	>9%	0	0	0
30	15		0	0	0
20	10		0	0	0
10	5		0	0	0
0	0		0	0	0

Note: No points were assigned if late delivery performance was >9%. Overall Score = (Quality Score) + (Late Delivery Score) + (Customer Satisfaction Score) + (Process Health Score)

Following is a sample scorecard:

2nd Qtr, 2007

Supplier #	345678
Supplier Name	ABC Company
Supplier Address	222 S. Main St.
	Anytown, USA

Buyer Name	Process Manager	IS Programs
ACS: Smith, G	Black, B	E-2C
AEW: Wren, M		BQM-34
AGS: Brown, A		JSTARS

Scorecard Ratings

	Available Pts.	Earned Pts.
Quality	50	27
Late Delivery	30	30
Customer Satisfaction	10	10
Process Health	10	10
Total		77

Notes:

IS	Integrated Systems
ACS	Air Combat Systems
AEW	Airborne Early Warning
AGS	Airborne Ground Surveillance

Blue = 91-100;   Yellow = 51-74;
Green = 75-90;   Red = 0-50

*The scorecard method was adapted from Northrop Grumman Integrated Systems "Supplier Scorecard Guidelines," September 1, 2004.

e-purchasing tools or **e-procurement tools**. As we have discussed throughout this chapter, purchasing has evolved from simply purchasing goods to strategically managing suppliers and the buying process. In many firms, supply management professionals assess, select, and manage suppliers from all over the world. Software companies have responded by developing **supplier relationship management** (SRM) software. As described in Chapter 9, SRM is part of an organization's ERP system and provides users with analytical tools, tracking capabilities, web services, and reverse auction technologies, among other capabilities, to improve decision making and control of strategic sourcing, purchasing contracts, and supplier management activities. SRM software applications search the firm's supplier and parts databases, select the most appropriate parts and suppliers based on a set of requirements, and then track ongoing quality and supplier performance.

In many cases, purchasing personnel begin with simpler tools and make advances as their knowledge and comfort level with purchasing software increases. As shown in the e-Commerce Perspective feature, Ohio-based Owens Corning started with a full-service e-auction solution, then moved to a self-service solution, and has since adopted supplemental tools to manage costs and improve productivity.

E-procurement tools so far are mostly used for indirect purchases—those items used by an organization to support the business but not used directly in finished products sold to customers—or for direct materials that are easily substituted. Examples of indirect purchases include maintenance, repair, and operating (MRO) supplies used in manufacturing, or office supplies. Ametek, an electronic instrument and electro-mechanical device manufacturer headquartered in Pennsylvania, sources 12 categories of indirect materials, including machine tooling, electrical supplies, and computer hardware through its e-procurement portal.[35]

A number of benefits have been associated with e-purchasing, including:

- Elimination of most paperwork,
- Reduced time between recognition of need and receipt of an order,
- Reduced errors in ordering and order fulfillment,
- Reduced overhead costs, and
- More free time to strategically manage the supply base.[36]

Reverse Auctions

More recently, firms have become more involved in using **reverse auctions**, a form of electronic purchasing or e-sourcing. Reverse auctions work best for leveraged part or catalog item purchases, where specifications are well defined. U.S. heavy equipment manufacturer John Deere, for example, saved money on vehicle signs, forged steel tools, and corrugated packaging through the use of reverse auctions.[37] In reverse auctions, the buying firm controls the bidding process either through proprietary software developed in-house or through a third party. All potential bidders (suppliers) are prequalified before the purchase requirements are released and the bidding begins. Suppliers may then log on to a designated website and place their offers, while watching the bids as they come in, and may reduce their own bids until the close of the auction. If the buyer is not satisfied with the bids by the deadline, the firm can extend the auction.

The supplier submitting the lowest bid meeting the specifications is generally selected. Aside from the benefit of getting low prices, when using a large, full service third-party reverse auction provider such as California-based Ariba, Inc., the buyer can utilize a vast pool of qualified domestic and foreign suppliers, further improving the potential for low prices and even better product quality.

e-Commerce Perspective   *Reverse Auctions at Owens Corning*

Owens Corning, a $5 billion manufacturer of building materials and systems, developed a strategic sourcing plan in 1999 to improve its supply operations and control spending. It spends an estimated $3 billion per year on purchases. At the time, the new home and commercial real estate markets were in a slump. Owens Corning also faced increasing pressure from lower-cost competitors and legal problems related to asbestos. To leverage its sourcing capabilities through e-sourcing, Owens Corning initially adopted a full-service reverse auction solution developed by FreeMarkets (now owned by Ariba) and ran 14 auctions at a cost savings.

The company then moved to an affordable self-service auction tool provided by Perfect Commerce that was easy to use and incorporated supplier support capabilities. The motive was to make the process repeatable and visible to the entire organization. The auctioning process was used for products or services with clear specifications and in markets with multiple suppliers competing for Owens Corning's business. In the first year, purchasing ran 180 successful auctions and has since sourced more than 10 percent of its spending, or $400 + million, online, with an average cost savings of 13.5 percent. Their traditional negotiation process has been reduced from one to three months to one day, freeing up purchasing to identify suppliers, prepare the request for quote (RFQ) documents, and implement the results.

However, to ensure the continuing success of the e-sourcing initiative, several steps were taken. First, the e-process leaders secured buy-in from upper management and plant managers through presentations and demonstrations of the money saved from past auctions. All parts of Owens Corning were continuously kept informed of the initiative through company news articles and internal memos. As the program continued, purchasing's sourcing team looked for new savings opportunities. The company purchased an automated tool that aggregated, classified, and analyzed spending data gathered from its enterprise resource planning (ERP) system, procurement card system, and J.D. Edwards.

In 2004, Owens Corning adopted additional spend management software solutions to negotiate better pricing and terms and improve productivity, including Ariba's Enterprise Sourcing, Category Management, and Analysis tools.

Sources: Aberdeen Group Best Practices Case Study, "Owens Corning Makes Sourcing a Foundation for Success, 2004, available at http://www.aberdeen.com; "Owens Corning Eyes Spend Management," February 10, 2004, available at http://www.sdcexec.com and Corning 2005 Annual report, http://www.corning.com.

Owens Corning, profiled in the e-Commerce Perspective feature, started using reverse auctions in 1999. The supply management group identifies potential suppliers, prepares and communicates the RFQ electronically, and then conducts a one-day bidding event. The process for each purchase used to take from one to three months. Owens Corning ran more than 150 reverse auctions worth $170 million in 2001 and estimates it saved several million dollars in labor and purchased material costs.[38]

Electronic Data Interchange

Electronic data interchange (EDI) has been a common form of information sharing since the 1960s. EDI is a computer-to-computer exchange of business documents such as purchase orders, order status inquiries and reports, promotion announcements, and shipping and billing notices. When computer documents are incompatible with trading partner computers, **value-added networks** (VANs), providers of private networks that allow for secure transmission of documents, have commonly been used but are expensive. Today, more companies are moving away from traditional EDI applications and VAN providers in favor of Internet-provided EDI, which is simpler and cheaper, allowing smaller trading partners without sophisticated information technology structures to participate. Coty, a French cosmetics and fragrance manufacturer, moved from a VAN to Internet EDI to process its 1.5 million purchase orders annually with Wal-Mart and other retailers. Coty paid the EDI provider a one-time fee, eliminating costly ongoing monthly and individual transaction fees associated with a VAN.[39]

Web-Based Marketplaces

To buy goods and services, purchasing and supply management departments may also access supplier websites that are usually free to buyers. At the simplest level, these sites provide information on the company, descriptions of the product offerings, and a set list of prices. Some sites are used as a marketing tool only and the buyer must still use traditional means to make the purchase. In other cases where stronger relationships exist in the supply chain, a supplier may have a dedicated portal for specific buyers to access. For example, Pratt & Whitney, a U.S. manufacturer of engines for commercial and military aircraft, uses an Internet portal to provide important customers such as Airbus and Boeing with customized information on spare part availabilities, service expectations, and delivery status for engine repair and replacement parts. Customers can also use the portal for online collaborative discussions and have access to the entire database of Pratt & Whitney technical documents.[40]

Some catalog companies, including U.S.-based Thomas Corporation and Grainger, help sellers reach industrial buyers by offering one-stop shopping in the form of online catalogs (ThomasNet® and Grainger.com) with a searchable directory of products and services. Photos, detailed specifications, and price comparisons are often provided.

There are also **e-marketplaces**, which are online forums or digital marketplaces that serve as a virtual meeting place for buyers and suppliers. **Vertical e-marketplaces** serve the same industry while **functional e-marketplaces** provide specific functions or automate a process across different industries. Band-X, headquartered in the United Kingdom, provides a range of specialist voice services for the telecommunications industry.[41] California-based Citadon, on the other hand, provides on-demand documentation, business process management, and collaboration solutions to a variety of industries.[42]

Online Purchasing Systems

A firm may also decide to purchase and install a purchasing system developed by an outside provider. The purchasing organization hosts the site, sets up and enforces the rules for buying, and generally buys from preferred suppliers. It automates the administrative tasks, integrating them with other systems. Purchasing departments can also develop additional negotiating leverage by concentrating purchases with fewer suppliers, while reducing cycle times. A self-managed application, however, can be expensive to implement and more difficult to manage. If the buying organization is smaller or doesn't feel it has the expertise to host and manage its own site, it may decide to contract with a third-party service, which hosts the e-procurement application. However, there are a limited number of suppliers that provide this service. Ariba, mentioned earlier, provides a number of e-procurement services.[43] Auction hubs are another alternative where an item is sold to the highest bidder. Commodity auctions for oil, electricity, or gas are common, as well as independent auctions for new and surplus manufactured goods and private auctions for resellers and dealers.

The need for more electronic support has increased as the process of supply management has become more complex. The result is that several software vendors have developed various applications to support the purchasing–supplier relationship ranging from spend analysis, risk analysis, procurement activities, shipment tracking, change order management, and supplier scorecarding to information sharing with warehousing and inventory functions. These applications are commonly adopted as one package by firms seeking to reduce the expense and time that would be needed to transfer the SRM information between all of the individually purchased modules.

Spiegel, for example, a large U.S. catalogue retailer with $2 billion in annual sales, purchased a system from California-based business software maker Epiqtech that allows suppliers to review RFQs, make offers, and participate in competitive bidding events.[44] We Energies, a Midwestern U.S. utilities company that serves 1.1 million electric customers, also decided to adopt SRM software to standardize its seven-step sourcing process. The various modules will track the utility company's portfolio of savings opportunities, improve efficiencies through automation, and increase visibility of monies spent.[45]

Advantages of Electronic Purchasing

The biggest benefits of electronic purchasing tools and SRM usually result when the value of the spend category is high, the product is highly substitutable, a highly competitive market exists, and the company is looking to make its internal processes more efficient. Before buying and implementing the use of one or more of these tools, purchasing departments should conduct a needs analysis and be sure to consider any existing legacy systems and whether integration with new applications is possible. Purchasing personnel should work with users to identify performance expectations and success factors and set some realistic implementation goals. An important part of the process is assessing the organization's willingness to adopt this new technology and what will be needed to get buy-in from the company's stakeholders. For expensive systems, executive support will be needed to keep the project moving to completion. If the project appears feasible, purchasing should then determine the criteria for evaluating the proposed systems.

Once the e-procurement system is purchased and installed, the purchasing department must then incorporate the system into its newly designed purchasing process. Those affected by the changes, such as finance and accounting managers, must also be notified and trained. The system should then be monitored to ensure it continues to meet everyone's expectations.[46] In 2001, Saks Inc. started an ambitious e-sourcing initiative aimed to save money and make the process more uniform and efficient. More on Saks Inc. can be found in the Service Perspective feature.

The sourcing process, whether manual or electronic, requires a good working relationship with suppliers. Automation of the process has in many instances enabled purchasing to spend more time developing and managing suppliers. Thus, the following section goes into greater detail on buyer–supplier relationships.

Beyond First-Tier Supplier Relationships

The fact that firms outsource an ever greater percentage of the goods and services they require, combined with an accelerated pace in global sourcing, has made supply

Imagine buying all the goods needed to stock acres of retail space, plus the supplies and equipment to run more than 300 stores. Saks Inc., with more than $6 billion in annual sales, is just such a company, searching international fashion markets for branded and private-label clothing and accessories, as well as $100 million on nonmerchandise such as cash registers, shopping bags, gift boxes, computers, and janitorial supplies. Saks Inc. owns and operates 358 stores in 39 states such as Saks Fifth Avenue, Saks Off 5th, Berners, Boston Store, Younkers, and others.

The company was using a fairly complicated process to buy the private-label goods that stocked its shelves, which involved many phone calls, letters, faxing, and email. On the other hand, it had no formal process in place to buy nonmerchandise (supplies, furniture, lighting, etc.). As a result, in 2001 it decided to reengineer multiple areas of the organization, including procurement, looking for ways to automate where possible to improve efficiencies.

Because e-sourcing was relatively new, purchasing sent out a request for information (RFI) to potential e-software solutions providers and eventually chose Ariba because of its financial strength, the fact that its products had been on the market and tested, the software's functionality and ease of use, and its market penetration into Fortune 500 companies.

Saks has 200 to 250 private-brand suppliers in the system and works actively with 150 to 200 of them, buying about $200 million of goods annually. Approximately 25–35 of these suppliers have electronic catalogs that can be accessed by store buyers, while the others are used on an ad-hoc basis. Saks hopes to eventually increase the amount of annual spend electronically to $600 million.

For nonmerchandise, Saks has two activities to manage spending. First, corporate contracts are in place where prices are negotiated based on the planned spending volume. Second, it uses "bid events" with prequalified suppliers either through timed e-auctions, sealed bids, or a negotiation-based bid event. The online software helps facilitate document exchanges, has eliminated faxing and mailings, and ensures that all suppliers bidding for its business promptly receive the same information.

Through these initiatives Saks Inc. has improved the spending process, improving efficiency and saving millions of dollars annually. The sourcing cycle time has been reduced, freeing up resources to source more categories of goods. It is also working to reduce the number of suppliers and then direct its spending to the remaining select group.

Sources: Saks Inc. 2003 Annual Report, available at http://www.saksincorporated.com; "Building Value Chains," *Internet World Magazine*, July 1, 2002, available at http://www.iw.com; and "Customer Spotlight: Saks Incorporated," available at http://www.ariba.com.

management more critical and at the same time more challenging. While it is important to develop a strategic sourcing plan for the firm's **first-tier suppliers**, it is also necessary to consider the impacts from parts sold by **second-tier suppliers** and even **third-tier suppliers** on the firm's quality, costs, service capabilities, and competitiveness. This realization has evolved because of an increasing focus on supply chain management in most industries. The challenge, however, has been to bring some kind of discipline to the global network of suppliers. Since the importance of a supply chain approach to process management has been emphasized throughout this textbook, this section will go into more detail on managing supplier relationships beyond the firm's first or immediate tier of suppliers.

U.S. food producer General Mills, for example, examines every stage and all supplier tiers of its food production supply chain, beginning with its raw materials—cereal grains such as wheat and corn—through the distribution of finished products to the retailer. The company then develops innovative solutions to reduce costs. More on some examples of cost savings for General Mills can be found in the Global Perspective feature.

A study prepared for the Center for Strategic Supply Research (known as CAPS), a non-profit supply chain management research organization based in Tempe, Arizona, coined the phrase **tiered supply management** to refer to the integration of a firm's supply management process with its first-, second-, and third-tier suppliers. Professor Anna Flynn, author of the research report, cites a number of benefits to improved process integration between all tiers, including:

- Economic competitiveness,
- Cost savings and cost reductions,
- Reduced lead times for necessary product changes,
- Greater responsiveness to demand and supply changes,
- Greater production efficiency,
- Better forecasting capability, and
- Improved customer response time.[47]

To begin managing second- and third-tier suppliers, the purchasing department should have already implemented a strategic sourcing process, as described earlier in this chapter. The supply base should also be reduced, or *rationalized,* until it is possible to collaborate effectively, maintain strong levels of trust, and gain a high degree of commitment with the remaining suppliers. Additionally, the firm should have a fully developed cost management program in place. Another important factor is to implement lean practices (more on lean thinking can be found in Chapter 10). Lastly, the firm should be able to roll out new products or services at target cost levels. Once the organization is at this level of performance, it is ready to make an impact on the second and then third tiers of suppliers. Managing beyond the first tier of suppliers may take a number of years to accomplish. The CAPS study described three options for managing second- and third-tier suppliers, which are described in the following sections.

Delegation

One option is for the buying firm to design a supplier development program for its first tier of suppliers, which may include training in quality improvement methods, strategic sourcing, technology applications, or other tools specifically needed by each supplier. The first-tier suppliers are then responsible for setting similar priorities and creating supplier development programs for their direct suppliers. In this way, the buying firm is indirectly impacting its second-tier suppliers. Progress in the area of supplier development or supplier management can be discussed during meetings with supplier representatives during the year. Once the first-tier suppliers become adept at these supplier relationship management techniques, they should start to experience benefits in the areas of improved quality, reduced cost, and better supplier service, and these benefits will be what drives them to pass these practices along to their suppliers. This transition process may be lengthy and all parties will have to commit to the program.

Global Perspective

Smart Buying Saves $1 Billion at General Mills

It's one thing for a company to say it is wary of total costs, but purchasing at General Mills, the international food and consumer products giant based in Minneapolis, Minnesota, backed up its statement with a cold, hard goal. Starting in 1991, the company ambitiously set out to keep its total production costs—not adjusted for inflation—constant for a decade. By 2000, the company had reduced total costs by 9 percent, no small accomplishment considering the company's annual revenues exceed $7.5 billion.

Through a cross-functional, corporate-wide effort with purchasing's goals at the forefront, the company cut more than $1 billion from its total production cost bill without compromising quality. Some of the savings came from traditional cost-cutting procedures, but most came from innovations put into place with suppliers.

The company started out by looking closely at every step in food production, from grain merchandising to distribution of finished product to retail shelves, including purchasing, manufacturing, and engineering. What the company identified through its analysis were some great relationships with raw materials suppliers, suppliers' suppliers, and distribution partners nested throughout the supply chain.

One innovative solution came from the analysis of raw materials. "We buy a large volume of egg whites for use in angel food cake and other food products," says Kevin Fitzpatrick, director of Strategic E-Business Alliances in General Mills' Supply Chain Operations division. "But there is an inherent supply chain problem because chickens don't lay egg whites," he says. To the General Mills purchasing staff, egg yolks are considered a by-product of egg whites. But for a pasta and noodle manufacturer, the reverse is true.

So, General Mills partnered with an egg noodle manufacturer to buy whites and yolks collaboratively. Both companies approached the egg supplier with a question: "If we take our tonnage of egg whites and the egg noodle manufacturer's tonnage of yolks," Fitzpatrick recounts, "can you set up your system to run complementary product specifications and save us more money?" The collaboration greatly simplified product specifications, resulting in cost savings for the egg supplier which was, in turn, passed on to General Mills and the egg noodle manufacturer.

"Then we took it a step further," Fitzpatrick says. "By dealing closely with the egg supplier, we discovered that their biggest cost driver in producing egg whites and yolks was the cost of chicken feed, which is mostly corn." We are, first and foremost, a grain milling company, so we're very familiar with futures and options and other risk-management tools associated with buying agricultural commodities effectively. So, we actually started buying the inputs (corn grain) for the chickens that make the egg whites that we buy collaboratively with the egg noodle company." Now that General Mills has aligned its supply chain and taken advantage of purchasing and risk-management tools, the company is saving more than a million annually on its egg whites buy.

Source: Reilly, C., "Smart Buying Saves $1 Billion at General Mills," *Purchasing*, June 7, 2001, available at http://www.purchasing.com/article/CA84438.html. Reprinted with permission.

Direct Management of All Tiers

Purchasing and supply management personnel may also opt to manage their firm's more distant suppliers directly in addition to the delegation process previously described.

While purchasing representatives may have already rationalized the first tier to a manageable size, taking on the responsibility of trying to influence these indirect suppliers may actually reduce the effectiveness of the supplier relationship management process.

It may be possible for the buying organization to require that some of its first-tier suppliers use a specific supplier, for example, and require that this second-tier supplier make use of various quality, cost, or service strategies. If the buying firm has enough purchasing power, this may be a feasible alternative. This sort of forced approach to supply chain management may be good from a time perspective, but it may also be counterproductive in terms of developing long-term, trusting strategic alliances.

Cross-Organizational Teams

A third option is creating a team made up of members from the purchasing organization, along with direct and indirect suppliers. Some of the issues that will naturally arise involve team representation, time requirements from each team member, team leadership, and the decision-making process. Selecting this option will depend on the resources available in each organization, the level of existing working relationships among the organizations, the skill levels of the team members, and the perceived level of importance attached to supply chain management. Due to the time requirements, there will be costs attached to this option that will have to be allocated.

If this approach is taken, the buying organization must determine how decisions will be made within the team. One possibility is to use the team to consider alternatives for improving supply chain effectiveness and make recommendations to the upper management of the firms represented by the teams. Another possibility might be to allow the team to reach a consensus and then implement the decision.

The difficulties with each of these approaches, as Professors Stanley Fawcett and Gregory Magnan point out, lie in the time commitments, resources, and management support required. As a result, supply chain management efforts rarely go beyond the first tier. They see these and other supply chain management activities in their "infancy" with many opportunities for improvement.[48]

Supply Management Challenges

While influencing a second- or third-tier supplier is difficult, there are other challenges as well. One of the big challenges for purchasing is aligning its objectives with organizational objectives. Senior executives look at the "big picture"—growth, financial goals, increased market share, or simply survival. Purchasing and supply management, as mentioned early in this chapter, seeks to ensure a continuing supply of materials and services at a prescribed level of quality, within lead time constraints, and at the lowest possible price. Purchasing professionals must then develop an action plan that transforms corporate objectives into purchasing objectives, leading to a combination of activities such as supply base "rightsizing" or rationalization, strategic sourcing, cost management, supplier development, quality improvement, and supply chain management. Throughout the process, the purchasing department monitors and evaluates supplier performance as well as its own performance to determine if corporate objectives have been met.

There are also a number of risks that purchasing personnel must be aware of and control by designing and implementing risk strategies. For example, the flow of supplies and services may be delayed or interrupted because of weather, strikes, supplier bankruptcy, terrorism, or transportation problems. The terrorist attacks in the United States in 2001, for example, caused major supply disruptions for many U.S. manufacturers operating in a just-in-time environment. While some things are beyond the buying firm's control, suppliers should be carefully evaluated to minimize some of these risk factors.

There is also the risk of price increases. In 2005, for example, steep worldwide increases in the price of oil affected both the cost to manufacture products using oil-based parts and to transport goods. Currency exchange rate fluctuations also impact prices, particularly given today's global economy. The buyer may want to use a **forward purchase contract**, which is a contract to purchase goods at some future date, priced in today's currency value. If a U.S. buyer thinks the value of the dollar is decreasing relative to the value of the foreign currency, this would be a good strategy. If the buyer thinks the value of the dollar is increasing relative to the value of the supplier's currency, it would be best to wait and purchase the goods when they are needed. These and other types of **hedging strategies** can be useful in decreasing price risk.

There are a number of ways a firm can reduce its risk exposure and meet corporate objectives which have been woven into this chapter, including:

- Value analysis/value engineering of products,
- Careful supplier selection,
- Use of a cost management program,
- Use of long-term contracts,
- Developing strategic alliances, and
- Use of ongoing supplier performance assessment.

The risks will never be eliminated but can be minimized through proactive management of the sourcing process with the tools available today.

SUMMARY

This chapter has addressed many of the issues involved in purchasing the goods and services necessary to run an organization's day-to-day operations. Because of the degree of outsourcing today, and in order to remain competitive, the process of purchasing and supply management has become increasingly strategic. Firms spend upwards of 50 percent or more of their sales dollars on direct and indirect materials, services, and capital equipment. For new product development, purchasing personnel often serve as members of a cross-functional team that includes members from finance, engineering, and marketing, and their input is highly valued in terms of minimizing costs or improving quality. Additionally, with the help of automation, supply professionals today are able to spend more time managing suppliers than paperwork.

Supply base reduction, strategic sourcing, supplier development and certification programs, and supplier partnering are some of the initiatives implemented by organizations to manage the supply base more effectively. Supply management is also beginning to reach out across the supply chain to manage second- and third-tier suppliers in order to improve quality and lead times, and cut costs. Supply management must also be aware of new trends and opportunities to improve supply chain effectiveness, as well as detect threats that could potentially disrupt supply. As discussed in the last section of this chapter, worldwide events play a bigger role than ever in the complexity of the supply management process.

KEY TERMS

activity-based cost accounting, 458

arm's length relationship, 460

basic alliance, 461

bottleneck items, 447

business alliance, 462

concurrent engineering team, 462

cost analysis, 452

cost management, 451

e-marketplaces, 469

e-procurement tools, 467

e-purchasing tools, 467

early supplier involvement, 462

electronic data interchange, 468

first-tier suppliers, 471

FOB terms, 458

forward purchase contract, 475

functional e-marketplaces, 469

hedging strategies, 475

invitation for bid, 451

just-in-time II, 464

key supplier, 461

leveraged items, 447

non-critical items, 447

ongoing relationship, 460

operational alliance, 461

original equipment manufacturers, 448

original parts manufacturers, 448

outsourcing, 459

p-cards, 447

performance-based contracts, 451

preferred supplier, 461

procurement cards, 447

purchasing, 443

request for information, 450

request for proposal, 450

request for quote, 450

reverse auctions, 467

second-tier suppliers, 471

sourcing strategy, 449

spend categories, 445

stakeholders, 445

statement of work, 450

strategic alliance, 461

strategic items, 447

supplier certification program, 449

supplier co-location, 464

supplier development, 462

supplier partnership, 461

supplier relationship management, 467

supplier scorecard, 465

supply management, 443

target costing, 452

third-tier suppliers, 471

tiered supply management, 472

total cost of ownership, 452

total life cycle cost, 452

value analysis, 452

value engineering, 452   vendor-managed   verbal quotes, 450

value-added networks, 469   inventory, 463   vertical e-marketplaces, 469

DISCUSSION QUESTIONS

1. Define purchasing and supply management.

2. What are the goals of purchasing and supply management?

3. Briefly describe the strategic sourcing process.

4. Choose a spend category in your company and analyze the marketplace using Porter's competitive forces model.

5. Using Kraljic's model, categorize the spend category chosen in Question 4.

6. Define target costing and total cost of ownership. How are these two cost management techniques used in supplier selection?

7. Discuss the different ways purchasing personnel obtain pricing from suppliers.

8. How have e-procurement tools and supplier relationship management software changed the sourcing process?

9. Why is purchasing and supply management concerned about supplier quality? What are some steps buyers can take to ensure a given level of quality from its suppliers?

10. Why does purchasing and supply management have different types of relationships with different suppliers? Briefly describe instances where each type of relationship would be appropriate.

11. Describe four ways purchasing and supply management monitors supplier performance.

12. Why are firms looking beyond their relationships with immediate suppliers, towards managing additional tiers of suppliers?

13. What are some of the challenges and risks facing purchasing departments today?

14. What are some ways buyers can reduce their firm's risk exposure?

 ## INFOTRAC QUESTIONS

Access http://www.infotrac-thomsonlearning.com to answer the following questions:

1. Find three articles that describe sourcing strategies companies have developed. Compare and contrast the similarities and differences between each strategy. Include a bibliography.

2. Find articles that discuss cost management tools and write a paper comparing and contrasting each tool. Include a bibliography.

3. Find articles that address supplier performance measurement and write a paper. Include a bibliography.

REFERENCES

Evans, J. R., and W. M. Lindsay (1996), *The Management and Control of Quality,* West Publishing Company, New York, NY.

Leenders, M. R., H. E. Fearon, A. E. Flynn, and P. F. Johnson (2002), *Purchasing & Supply Management,* McGraw-Hill Irwin, Boston, MA.

Slaight, T. H. "Strategic Sourcing," *Inside Supply Management,* June 2004, pp. 24–31.

ENDNOTES

1. ISM Information Sheet, available at http://www.ism.ws/AboutISM/MediaRoom/WhatIsSupplyMgmt.cfm.

2. Quote by John Haydon, Vice President of Global Supply Management at Nortel, in Carbone, J., "The Changing Face of Nortel," *Purchasing Magazine,* May 19, 2005, available at http://www.purchasing.com.

3. Flynn, A. E., "Defining Supply Management," *Inside Supply Management,* March 2005, pp. 22–26.

4. U.S. Census Bureau, *Annual Survey of Manufactures,* December 20, 2002, Table 2.

5. Johnson, P. F. and M. R. Leenders, *Supply's Organizational Roles and Responsibilities,* Tempe AZ: CAPS Research, 2004.

6. Interview with Rick Jacobs, Vice President of Supply Chain at Eaton Corp., in *Purchasing,* November 2, 2006, accessed November 17, 2006, at http://www.purchasing.com/article/CA6384870.html?industryid=23509.

7. Leenders, M. R., H. E. Fearon, A. E. Flynn, and P. F. Johnson, *Purchasing and Supply Management,* 12th Edition, Boston, MA: McGraw-Hill Irwin, 2002, pp. 40–43.

8. Frederick, J. ,"Walgreens Adds Staff in Purchasing Revamp," *Drug Store News,* June 2, 2000, accessed November 19, 2006, at http://findarticles.com/p/articles/mi_m3374/is_9_22/ai_63609723.

9. Porter, M. E., *Competitive Strategy: Techniques for Analyzing Industries and Competitors,* New York, NY: Free Press, 1980.

10. Kraljic, P., "Purchasing Must Become Supply Management," *Harvard Business Review,* September–October 1983, pp. 109–117.

11. Linder, A. and U. M. Majander, "Transfer of Export Process from Customer to Supplier: The Case of Volvo do Brasil," college master thesis, Goteborg University, 2004.

12. McGovern, S. and S. Costello, "The Challenges of Alternate Sourcing Tool Spares and Consumables," *Future Fab International,* July 8, 2002, accessed July 21, 2005, at http://www.future-fab.com/documents.asp?grID=384&d_ID=1303.

13. Aberdeen Group, "Owens Corning Makes Sourcing a Foundation for Success," *Best Practices in E-Sourcing 2004,* 2004, available at http://www.aberdeen.com.

14. Dolan, T. and K. M. Fedele, "Strategic Sourcing: Reducing Cost and Supporting Diversity Goals," presentation made at the 89th Annual International Supply Management Conference, April 2004, accessed November 19, 2006, at http://www.ism.ws/files/Pubs/Proceedings/GFDolanFedele.pdf.

15. Whittington, E., "You Paid How Much?—Writing a Good RFP/RFQ," *ISM's 88th Annual International Supply Management Conference Proceedings,* May 2003, available at http://www.ism.ws.

16. "Critical Supplier Relationships," *Purchasing Today,* February 1999, accessed July 4, 2005, at http://www.ism.ws.

17. Ellram, L. M., *The Role of Supply Management in Target Costing,* Tempe, AZ: CAPS, 1999.

18. Ferrin, B. G. and R. E. Plank, "Total Cost of Ownership Models: An Exploratory Study," *Journal of Supply Chain Management,* Vol. 38, No. 3, Summer 2002, pp. 12–19.

19. "Seven Habits of Effective Sourcing Organizations," available at http://www.ariba.com.

20. Hurkens, K., W. van der Valk, and F. Wynstra, "Total Cost of Ownership in the Service Sector: A Case Study," *Journal of Supply Chain Management,* Winter 2006, pp. 27–37.

21. Carbone, J., "Delphi Demands Lowest Total Cost from Suppliers," *Purchasing,* September 18, 2003, pp. 15–19.

22. Sigmund, P., "Cement Shortage Puts Crunch on Contractors," June 15, 2004, available at http://www.constructionequipmentguide.com.

23. Simpson, P. M., J. A. Siguaw, and S. C. White, "Measuring the Performance of Suppliers: An Analysis of Evaluation Processes," *The Journal of Supply Chain Management,* Vol. 38, No. 1, 2002, pp. 29–41.

24. See Note 23.

25. Leenders, M. R., H. E. Fearon, A. E. Flynn, and P. F. Johnson, *Purchasing and Supply Management,* 12th Edition, Boston, MA: McGraw-Hill Irwin, 2001.

26. Ellram, L. M., "The Supplier Alliance Continuum," *Purchasing Today,* February 2000, p. 8.

27. Sobek, D. K. II and A. C. Ward, "Principles from Toyota's Set-Based Concurrent Engineering Process," ASME Design Engineering Technical Conferences and Computers in Engineering Conference, Irvine, CA, August 18–22, 1996, pp. 1–9.

28. Krause, D. R., "Supplier Development: Current Practices and Outcomes," *International Journal of Purchasing and Materials Management,* Spring 1997, pp. 12–19.

29. See Note 28.

30. See ABB's website at http://www.abb.com for details on its supplier development statement.

31. Ellram, L. M., "A Managerial Guideline for the Development and Implementation of Purchasing Partnerships," *The Journal of Supply Chain Management,* Vol. 31, No. 2, 1995, pp. 10–16.

32. "Clorox's Efforts Trigger Comprehensive Savings," *WasteWise Update, EPA530-N-98-003,* April 2003, p. 10.

33. Interview with Bill Lee, Supply Chain Director for Kimberly-Clark, January 2001, available at http://www.supplychainbrain.com/archives/1.01.lee.htm?adcode=30.

34. Honeywell Sensing and Control Supply Management's Customer Delight Program.

35. "Choosing the E-Procurement that Works for You," *CIO,* June 15, 2003, available at http://www.cio.com/archive/061503/eproc.html.

36. Adapted from Leenders, M. R., H. E. Fearon, A. E. Flynn, and F. P. Johnson, *Purchasing and Supply Management,* 12th Edition, New York, NY: McGraw-Hill Irwin, 2002, p. 140.

37. Smock, D., "Deere Takes a Giant Leap," *Purchasing,* September 6, 2001, available at http://www.purchasing.com.

38. Mendoza, M., "Strategic Sourcing and Reverse Auctions Mean Success for Owens Corning," presentation made at the Supply Management 360° Conference, November 2001.

39. Bednarz, A., "Internet EDI: Blending Old and New," *Network World,* February 23, 2004, available at http://www.networkworld.com.

40. Foster, T. A., "Opening a Portal to Supply-Chain Collaboration," *Global Logistics & Supply Chain Strategies,* April 2003, available at http://www.supplychainbrain.com.

41. See http://www.band-x.com for more information on Band-X.

42. See http://www.citadon.com for more information on Citadon.

43. See http://www.ariba.com for more information on Ariba.

44. Information on Spiegel is available at http://www.epiqtech.com/supplier-SRM-System.htm.

45. "We Energies Tackles Supplier Relationship Management," *Supply & Demand Chain Executive,* July 13, 2005, available at http://www.isourceonline.com.

46. "Doing Business Electronically: Selection the Best Options," an ISM Seminar Series, Program No. SSS-01-0029, April 11, 2002, available at http://www.ism.ws/Seminars/SatSems/files/DoBusnElect.pdf.

47. Flynn, A. E., *Tiered Supply Management, Critical Issues Report,* September 2004, Tempe, AZ: CAPS, p. 3.

48. Fawcett, S. E. and G. M. Magnan, *Achieving World-Class Supply Chain Alignment: Benefits, Barriers, and Bridges,* Tempe, AZ: CAPS, 2001.

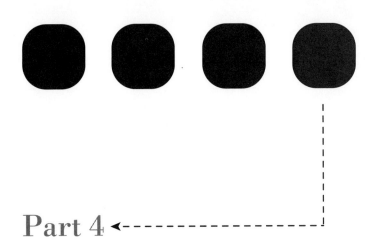

Part 4

Quality Issues and Process Performance

Chapter 13:

MANAGING QUALITY FOR CONTINUOUS IMPROVEMENT

"Most human error is caused by lack of attention rather than lack of knowledge. Lack of attention is created when we assume that error is inevitable." [1]

"Almost all quality improvement comes via simplification of design, manufacturing (or service delivery), layout, processes, and procedures." [2]

Learning Objectives

After completing this chapter, you should be able to:

- Understand the meaning of quality and continuous improvement.
- Explain the process companies follow to improve quality.
- Describe process capability and its relationship to quality.
- Define the costs of poorly performing processes.
- Explain how companies move from quality planning to quality implementation.
- Identify problems and their underlying causes.
- Describe the quality control process.
- Construct quality control charts.
- Explain the role of quality management in the supply chain.

Chapter Outline

Introduction

Continuous Improvement

Processes and Quality

The Quality Improvement Process

Quality Management along the Supply Chain

Process Management in Action   *Boeing Aerospace Support*

Boeing Aerospace Support (AS) is part of the Boeing Company, the largest aerospace company in the world. Boeing AS provides products and services, including aircraft maintenance, modification, and repair, and training for aircrews and maintenance staff, to reduce life cycle costs and increase the effectiveness of aircraft. Ninety-seven percent of Boeing AS's business comes from military customers.

Key factors to the success of Boeing AS are its commitment to customer satisfaction, performance to plan, and on-time delivery of quality products and services. Since 1998, the "exceptional" and "very good" responses from government customers regarding Boeing AS's performance have gone up 23 percent. In 2003, the exceptional responses nearly doubled those in 2002.

Since 1999, on-time delivery of maintenance and modification products and services, significant hardware, and other products has been between 95 and 99 percent. Quality rating for the C-17 aircraft has been near 100 percent since 1998 compared to its competitors, which trailed at 70 percent in 2002 and 90 percent in 2003.

A key element of Boeing AS's successful on-time delivery rate is its partnership with its suppliers to ensure high-quality services and products. As a result, the Supplier On-Time Delivery Rate improved from about 68 percent in 1999 to about 95 percent in 2003, matching best-in-Boeing results.

PROCESSES ARE KEY TO SUCCESS

Carefully planned and well-managed processes combined with a culture that encourages knowledge sharing and working together have been essential to Boeing AS's ability to deliver high-quality products and services. Boeing AS has developed a seven-step approach for defining, managing, stabilizing, and improving processes. This process-based management, or PBM, methodology also is used to set goals and performance metrics and requires interaction and agreement among process owners, users, suppliers, and customers.

Developing a sound, long-term strategy and then turning that strategic intent into meaningful action is another of Boeing AS's strengths and competitive advantages. It uses an enterprise planning process (EPP) comprised of four process elements: key data factors, strategy, plans, and executions, and ten defined steps, including lessons learned and process improvements, to plan and execute key strategies. Senior leaders and business, strategic planning, and functional councils each have a role in developing and executing the EPP to ensure that all business functions and sites are integrated and aligned to the overall strategic plan.

To improve performance, a five-step system helps Boeing AS select, analyze, and align data and information. The system begins by gathering requirements and expectations from stakeholders and results in a set of action plans and performance goals and metrics. A "Goal Flow-down" process communicates goals and directions not only throughout the organization but also to customers and suppliers. Measurement, analysis, and knowledge management systems provide performance status and other information needed to make decisions. Finally, performance analyses and reviews are conducted regularly, resulting in recommendations or actions needed to improve performance at all levels.

Source: NIST, Boeing Aerospace Support Profile, available at http://www.quality.nist.gov.

Introduction

Collectively companies spend billions of dollars per year working to attract new customers through advertising, new products and services, or the addition of new stores. Yet it's been shown that it is six to ten times more expensive to attract a new customer than it is to retain an existing one. But how do companies retain customers? Probably the most important way is by offering high-quality service experiences and products.

Another key point is that it only takes a customer about 30 seconds to form an opinion about a company or its products. Thus, that first impression is very important and companies need to be sure that customers have a positive experience from the moment they open the box of a newly purchased item or walk through the door of a service organization. A negative experience of buying a product or service can have a lasting impression, potentially resulting in lost customers and therefore lost future revenues. It has generally been found that satisfied customers tell 5 other people about their experiences, while unhappy customers tell 20 others. Thus, the quality of a product as well as the entire service experience is critical to customer retention. A fundamental way products and services can be improved is through use of better performing processes. Boeing Aerospace Support, as described in the opening Process Management in Action feature, has improved its processes through a seven-step approach, involving process owners, suppliers, users, and customers.

Any step taken within a process that can help satisfy or delight customers is considered an element of quality. Thus, the scope of quality management today includes just about any organizational improvement, including employee task performance and skill levels, optimizing processes and procedures, and extending beyond the organizational boundaries to supplier performance in the supply chain. However, it's important to remember that any changes in these areas should ultimately result in higher levels of customer satisfaction, or in other words, added value. Many organizations tend to focus on activities that are thought to provide benefits important to the customer but ultimately don't result in adding value. For example, while there are numerous features available in computer software applications today, the average consumer uses only a small fraction of them.

There are also times when companies should primarily focus on their core competencies, while outsourcing other non-core processes rather than attempting to make internal improvements in them. For example, ThreeCore, a supply chain management consulting firm headquartered in Massachusetts, specializes in creating competitive bidding events using the reverse auction concept as discussed in Chapter 12. Manufacturers outsource the job of supplier selection to ThreeCore, because it will visit, monitor, and evaluate potential suppliers, eliminating the legwork commonly done by internal purchasing professionals.[3]

Two important developments in the past 30 years have redefined the role of quality management according to David Watkins, executive vice president and director of international operations for Omnex Inc., a Michigan-based consulting firm. Companies began by moving from assigning product quality control to a quality assurance department, to today's much broader companywide responsibility. A more recent development has been globalization, which Watkins says "redefined the role of quality management in supplier relationships, necessitating a quantum leap from dealing with supplier quality problems to supply chain management."[4] Manufacturers, under intense pressure to keep prices down, aggressively began sourcing from foreign markets with significantly lower labor costs. At the same time, global quality standards such as

ISO 9000 have been established, and companies have developed ways to assess quality and certify suppliers to meet their requirements.

These changes indicate a need to study quality management in more depth. This chapter will begin with a discussion of quality management and continuous improvement from the customer's standpoint. The quality planning and implementation process will then be covered along with a discussion of quality control. Lastly, the chapter will cover managing quality along the supply chain.

Continuous Improvement

What is really meant by the term **continuous improvement**? A number of definitions of continuous improvement exist, including:

1. The review, analysis, and rework directed at improving practices and processes.
2. The constant efforts to eliminate waste, reduce response time, simplify the design of both products and processes, and improve quality and customer service.
3. A quality philosophy that assumes further improvements are always possible and that processes should be continuously reevaluated and improvements implemented.
4. A never-ending effort to expose and eliminate root causes of problems; small step improvement as opposed to big step improvement.[5]

Inherent in these definitions is the idea that continuous improvement is a process-oriented way of thinking and a proactive management approach to problem solving within an organization. Rather than waiting until a problem occurs or the competition is threatening their business and *then* reacting or "firefighting," companies should be organized at all levels to make incremental improvements continuously, always with the external customer in mind. The philosophy of continuous improvement, often referred to as **kaizen** because of the Japanese influence, also assumes that the improvements in product and service quality can be more readily achieved when the quality of a firm's employees is improved. In other words, when managers give employees the tools, support, and encouragement to help them identify problems, evaluate alternatives, and make the appropriate decisions, products and processes will improve.

Companies tend to focus more on quality improvement when processes are performing poorly and as a last resort to avoid further financial losses. They may alter the flows of inventory, customers, or work; eliminate certain activities; or relocate employees. To accomplish these activities more effectively, organizations should have programs in place that enable them to continually plan, implement, and review their quality efforts. Technology has helped, in many respects, as demonstrated by Georgia-based UPS, the global provider of specialized transportation and logistics services. Through its quality management efforts, UPS has streamlined its package delivery process and provides value-adding services through its website. More on UPS can be found in the e-Commerce Perspective feature.

There are four major areas where quality improvement efforts are important. Joseph Juran, a well-known quality guru, identified the four areas of manufacturing (although they can also be applied to service design) where companies can initiate improvement activities and, as a result, lower costs:

1. *Designing the product/service.* For example, in the 1990s, U.S. car manufacturers revamped the new product design process from an "over-the-wall approach" to concurrent engineering. (Recall from Chapter 2 that concurrent engineering

e-Commerce Perspective   *UPS Online*

UPS is the largest package delivery company in the world, delivering about 3.6 billion packages in 200 countries and territories. The company invests more than $1 billion annually in technology to support solutions that positively impact its customers, its internal operating systems, and its processes. Its ultimate goal? *All* customers will communicate with UPS online.

Is UPS really getting the bang for its buck? Jos du Jardin, European director of e-commerce at UPS, thinks so. "A customer may ring the call centre to find out who signed for a package or how long delivery is likely to take. If this process is not efficient, the cost of the enquiry can actually be more than getting the package to its destination," says du Jardin. He believes that the information provided regarding the shipment's progress will optimize the customer's business processes and add value that is far beyond simply getting the goods from point A to point B.

To cut costs and improve quality, UPS took a number of steps. To increase visibility, the UPS.com website was transformed from a simple "bulletin board" of information to an interactive engine allowing customers to easily determine the location of each shipment. Secondly, it incorporated a server-based application known as UPS WorldShip, which lets companies track UPS shipments and deliveries on in-house computers. Lastly, it created application programming interfaces (APIs) using XML language, which lets the customer create and manage UPS transactions directly with partners and other customers without contacting UPS.

UPS also uses electronic tagging and smart labels. Smart labels can be read by both machines and humans so that all employees know things such as the address of origin, zip code, and weight. At the same time, each label has a unique number and bar code that is machine readable, speeding up package processing. In less than a second, the location of a package can be determined through machine scanning.

Today businesses can manage multiple sites through one shipping system; billing, customer inquiries, and cost allocation processes have been streamlined; and the costs and complexity of shipping across borders have been reduced. More than 90 percent of U.S. and 70 percent of European customers send at least some package-level data to UPS online. And as a result of its efforts, UPS has an integrated, global network that is difficult to beat in terms of visibility and reliability.

Source: UPS Annual Report 2004; "In Practice: UPS," 2004, available at http://www.infoconomy.com; and "The Information Age Interview," available at http://www.infoconomy.com.

---

uses a cross-functional team approach, which results in shorter design times and thus faster product introductions.)

2. *Making a prototype product/service and testing it.* At this stage, new products or services are designed, built, and tried out in test markets.

3. *Distributing and placing the product or service on the market.*

4. *Continuing to test the product or service while in use; finding out what the user thinks of it and why the nonuser has not bought it.* Control charts, surveys, checklists, fishbone diagrams, and process maps are just some of the tools used to ensure customer satisfaction (these tools are discussed later in this chapter and in Chapter 14).[6]

For example, something as simple as a measuring tape has been improved by Chinese manufacturers with the addition of more user-friendly features. Beijing Guangpu Measures Co. Ltd manufactures a measuring tape with a solar-powered calculator, and Jianghua Measure sells measuring tapes that feature memo pads or calculators. These companies use more durable materials such as high-carbon steel and special coatings for the measuring tape, and have also improved their manufacturing processes.[7]

At the same time, organizations need to understand their suppliers' capabilities and leverage them where possible. As discussed in Chapters 2 and 12, companies have moved from vertically to horizontally integrated organizations as members of multiple supply chains. As a result, products are created and manufactured based on the inputs of several parties, and maintaining quality has become more complex. Companies work to improve quality through customer–supplier partnerships, supplier site visits, supplier certification programs, formal performance evaluations, and supplier development programs, among others.

Why Continuous Improvement Efforts Fail

Despite their proven value,[8] continuous improvement efforts often fail for a number of reasons.[9] A major reason is the lack of management commitment. Senior executives, for instance, tend to focus on "winning" at something, be it the low-cost leader, market leader, or the fastest, forgetting that continuous improvement efforts complement rather than conflict with these goals. If the expected results aren't seen quickly enough, management might turn to other methods to reach their goals. A related problem is that the firm's leaders may simply tire of current quality initiatives and move on to something else, hoping for more dramatic performance gains.

Problems during implementation can also lead to failure of quality improvement initiatives. For instance, the importance of continuous improvement initiatives may not be meaningfully conveyed to the workforce. As a result, employees see the program as "just another fad" and do not put forth their best efforts. This attitude is reinforced if senior management delegates the initiatives to a staff group without the power to make the necessary organizational changes. The staff group may also tend to hide any implementation problems and challenges from senior management that keep the program from moving forward. Lack of adequate training during the program implementation period can also lead to employee frustration, lack of personnel buy-in, and lack of tangible results, which can also lead to program failure.

Mergers, acquisitions, leadership changes, and corporate strategy changes may also occur, which can postpone or derail current improvement efforts. Necessary funding may be diverted or cut completely. World events also often lead to new initiatives to deal with the changing environment. For example, in the most recent decade the economy has slowed down, the terrorist bombings occurred in New York, and financial misappropriation of funds at the highest corporate levels occurred in some organizations. These occurrences caused concern in many organizations that costs, markets, and customer service elements would be impacted. Consequently, in some cases management found it necessary to revisit their business models, strategies, and cost or quality initiative efforts.

Thus, while organizations will always recognize the need to improve quality, they may eventually transition to new quality initiatives based on changing circumstances or emerging best practices. The following sections provide a general framework for developing and maintaining quality programs, beginning with a discussion on the relationship between process management and quality management.

Processes and Quality

As discussed in Chapter 1, process outputs are the goods, services, and information that embody both product features—the characteristics that meet the needs of the customer and result in customer satisfaction, and deficiencies—and the things that go wrong and result in customer dissatisfaction. A process should operate seamlessly, but this doesn't always appear to be the case because processes usually cross over multiple departments, each with its own manager and set of rules. When individual departmental rules don't match up, customers may perceive a problem with the company, resulting in customer dissatisfaction. For example, a U.K. study of public water utilities found that 10 percent of customers failed to pay their water bill, not because they couldn't afford to pay but because of problems due to the functional silo effect. For example, the customer service department might be seeking payment on a delinquent account, while the administrative services department was busy updating the same customer's address or revisions to a service plan, which prevented payment.[10]

The Costs of Quality

All quality problems cost organizations money and these **poor-quality costs** can be classified in one of three ways: (1) appraisal costs, (2) internal failure costs, and (3) external failure costs.[11] Alternately, firms can invest money to prevent poor quality, and in most cases, this investment more than pays for itself by reducing the costs of poor quality. Several examples of prevention costs and the costs of poorly performing processes are provided in Table 13.1.

Appraisal Costs

Appraisal costs are the costs associated with discovering defects before the customer is affected, such as inspecting products to make sure design specifications are met, and checking processes to make sure they are running as expected. Appraisal activities take place every day in all organizations. Insurance companies, for example, assign employ-

Table 13.1   Costs of Quality

COSTS OF CONTROL		COSTS OF FAILURE	
PREVENTION	**APPRAISAL**	**INTERNAL FAILURE**	**EXTERNAL FAILURE**
• Quality planning and administration • Process analysis and improvement • Design and development of quality information equipment • Recruitment and training • Quality training and workforce development • Product design verification • Systems development and management	• Test and inspect purchased materials • Laboratory acceptance testing and other measurement services • Periodic inspection and testing • Checking quality of direct labor • Test and inspect equipment and material; setup; maintenance • Quality audits • Field testing	• Scrap (labor+material) • Scrapped forms and reports • Rework (labor+material) • Additional material+ procurement costs • Disposal costs • Product and production engineering time spent on quality problems • Production interruption, downtime, and rescheduling	• Warranty costs • Complaints out of warranty • Service cost to correct defects • Product liability • Product recall • Product returns • Loss of reputation, future sales, and profits • Payment of interest penalties • Legal judgments

ees to inspect policies before mailing them to the client. A manager asks an assistant to proofread a report before making copies for an executive meeting. Firms may also perform quality audits and lab tests, and inspect any purchased materials before they are used in production. Appraisals take place because companies expect to find poor quality and try to fix the problems before they reach the customer.

Internal Failure Costs

Internal failure costs are incurred when companies spend money to repair, replace, or discard poor-quality work prior to a customer's purchase. Some common examples include paying overtime to maintain a production schedule, repeating a test for quality assurance because incorrect procedures were followed the first time, discarding parts because they didn't perform correctly, repainting a house due to poor workmanship, and time spent to correct errors in software programs.

External Failure Costs

External failure costs are the costs of poor quality once the product or service is purchased. When the customer is aware of the failure, the company may experience a loss of goodwill and have to devote extended efforts and money to retain disgruntled customers or recapture lost customers. External failures cause companies to spend money on warranty claims, customer complaint resolutions, correction of billing errors, "freebies" to make up for poor products or services, and liability litigation losses. In some cases, external failure costs can be quite expensive, ranging up to 20 to 30 percent of sales.[12] It's important to remember, however, that these costs are not just borne by the company. Customers and suppliers, too, experience the costs of poor product quality. For example, as shown in Table 13.2, when a business customer buys a poorly performing software package for its operation, the problems can range from time spent dealing with the problems to lost customers when errors occur as the result of the software. Because organizations operate as part of a supply chain, many of the product components are purchased from outside suppliers. As a result, costs of external failures extend to all those involved in the product's manufacture or service delivery.

Prevention Costs

Companies also spend, in varying amounts, money to prevent quality problems, also known as **prevention costs**. Some examples include the up-front efforts to ensure that a predetermined level of quality is designed into products and processes, the use of

Table 13.2	Software Purchase: Examples of External Failure Costs

- Employees' and customers' wasted time fixing the failure
- Lost future business when products fail, resulting in lost revenues
- Frustrated employees quit, resulting in new hiring and training costs
- Demos or presentations to potential customers fail because of the software, resulting in lost business
- Failure costs when attempting other tasks that can only be done once
- Cost of replacing product
- Cost of reconfiguring the system
- Cost of recovery software
- Cost of tech support

quality improvement programs, investments in employee quality training, and supplier quality certifications. For instance, manufacturing engineers might test the capability of a process during the design phase of a new product to make sure design specifications can be met before full production starts.

Philip Crosby, author of *Quality Is Free*, argued that as companies spend more on preventing poor quality from occurring in the first place, less money will be spent on appraisal, and internal and external quality problems will diminish or even disappear. When these poor-quality costs decrease, revenues should increase at least sufficiently to cover the costs of prevention, making the cost to maintain a high level of quality "free."[13]

To improve performance and drive waste out of existing processes, companies today such as global technology and services conglomerate General Electric, headquartered in New York, are implementing the Six Sigma methodology. As described more completely in Chapter 14, the Six Sigma methodology is a data-driven quality improvement initiative used to measure and significantly improve a company's organizational performance by identifying and minimizing defects in its processes and products. In order for Six Sigma initiatives to be successful, investments are made in employee training to help them become "expert" problem solvers.

Tracking the Costs of Poorly Performing Processes

While external failure costs are easier to track, most of the costs of quality are not specifically found in traditional accounting reports, so many managers see them as "just the cost of doing business" or may not even be aware they exist. There are ways, however, to uncover these costs.

Management can begin by identifying all of the activities existing only because of poor quality by creating a team of people who have firsthand knowledge of the process in question. Brainstorming can be used to reveal all tasks that exist expressly to fix problems caused by poorly performing processes. Organizations should also determine where the cost of each of these activities takes place in the organization. These costs may actually be contained in one or multiple areas of various accounting reports.

Once these activities and costs are identified, management can then calculate the cost of its poorly performing processes by one of two methods. The **total resources method** identifies the total resources used within a category and the percentage of those resources used for activities associated with fixing the effects of poor quality. The data needed for the total resources method is relatively easy to collect but requires some expertise in allocating the resource percentages. The **unit cost method** is another option, wherein the numbers of times deficiencies occur are identified along with the average cost to fix each deficiency. Data collection for the unit cost method is more difficult but, if done properly, should result in a more accurate cost allocation. The data is then collected and costs are estimated. Once this process is complete, management can begin to tackle quality problems in order to reduce these costs, resulting in increased profitability. Example 13.1 illustrates the use of each of these methods.

Process Capability

Product designers and manufacturing engineers are particularly interested in **process capability** and develop process capability studies to help them predict how well a process will meet the required specifications or tolerances and to specify the amount of

Example 13.1   Costs of Poorly Performing Processes

Total Resources Method

ACTIVITY	COST LOCATION 1	COST LOCATION 2	COST LOCATION 3	TOTAL COST OF RESOURCES	% OF RESOURCES USED TO COUNTERACT POOR QUALITY	TOTAL COST OF ACTIVITY
Final Inspection	Wages & Benefits	Training		$147,000	× 75%	$110,250
Rework	Wages & Benefits			$ 97,500	× 15%	$ 14,625
Customer Complaint Resolution	Wages & Benefits	Training	System Maintenance (phone and computer)	$ 73,850	× 100%	$ 73,850
					Total Annual Cost	$198,725

Unit Cost Method

ACTIVITY	COST LOCATION 1	COST LOCATION 2	COST LOCATION 3	ACTIVITY FREQUENCY (# TIMES/YR)	AVERAGE COST	TOTAL COST OF ACTIVITY
Final Inspection	Wages & Benefits	Training		12	× $9,250	$111,000
Rework	Wages & Benefits			8	× $2,800	$ 22,400
Customer Complaint Resolution	Wages & Benefits	Training	System Maintenance (phone and computer)	45	× $1,950	$ 87,750
					Total Annual Cost	$221,150

control necessary as well as the equipment requirements. Process capability is a measure of the uniformity of a process, or in other words, a measure of the ability of the combination of inputs and resources—employees and other people, machines, methods, and materials—to consistently produce a product or service *within design specifications* or tolerances. For example, a quart container of milk could be designed to weigh 32 ounces with a tolerance of +/− 0.5 ounce. Thus, the design tolerances are between 31.5 ounces and 32.5 ounces.

The process is then tested to see if it is capable of performing within the design specifications. Continuing with the milk example, if the design specification requires the weight of a milk carton to be within 0.5 ounce, a process requiring a worker to manually fill cartons using a bathroom scale will probably result in a lot of nonconforming product! In this case, the process is not capable of meeting the design specifications. This process would result in too much scrap, rework, and lost time. In other words, too many cartons will be rejected, or some will have to be refilled to the proper weight, resulting in wasted material and labor time.

If a process is not capable of meeting design specifications, management has some options. On the one hand, management could leave the process as-is and use inspection to catch any errors; however, some mistakes would not be caught, inspection costs would increase, and this option could result in customer complaints. On the other hand, design specifications could be relaxed, but result in higher internal and external failure costs, and a poorer quality product. A third option is to design a new error-proof process using better technology, training, or tools (prevention costs). While expenses would initially be incurred, internal and external failure costs would diminish.

In 2001, Ford Motor Company tackled a problem with the rear liftgate glass in its Explorer and Mercury Mountaineer. Several brackets would become loose as the gate was repeatedly opened and closed, resulting in the glass detaching and eventually shattering. According to Anne Stevens, vice president of manufacturing, the problems were attributed to a process "that we thought was error proofed, but it wasn't."[14] This example clearly demonstrates the need to consider process capability at the design stage, resulting in higher prevention costs but much lower internal and external failure costs.

Figure 13.1 shows five possible process capability situations that can occur. The first situation shows that the process is easily capable of meeting the design specifications because the natural process variation is much less than design specifications. In the second situation, the process conforms comfortably to design specifications because the natural process variation is less than the design specifications. In the third situation, the process variation is equal to the design specifications so most of the time the process will be capable of meeting requirements. The fourth situation shows that the process is not capable of meeting the design specifications (natural process variation is greater than the design specifications). If the process is left as is, there will be some defective output, resulting in scrap and rework. In the fifth situation, the process is capable of meeting the specifications but some of the output will not meet the lower specification because the process is out of control (the specifications are greater than the natural process variation but the process mean is off-center). If the process can be adjusted so that the process mean is equal to the design target, then most of the output will meet the design specifications. Thus, process capability is important because it aids in the understanding of process variation by comparing the actual process to the way it was intended to work (i.e., the design specifications).

Up to this point, this section has looked at process capability theoretically. However, estimations can be calculated showing whether a process is capable of meeting design specifications. The **process capability ratio** (C_p) can be estimated using the following equation:

$$C_p = \frac{\text{Upper specification limit} - \text{Lower specification limit}}{6\sigma}$$

where

6σ = the actual range of process variation, which for most firms is $+/- 3\sigma$, or 6σ

(Recall that σ is the standard deviation of the actual process measures.)

If the process capability is less than 1.0, the process range (the denominator) is greater than the desired tolerance range (the numerator), which means the process is *not capable* of producing within the required design specifications [in Figure 13.1, this is shown in part (d)]. When the process capability is equal to 1.0, the process is capable of producing within the design specifications most of the time [a small percent of the time, the process variation will cause the process to be incapable; refer to part (c) in

Figure 13.1	**Examples of Process Capability**

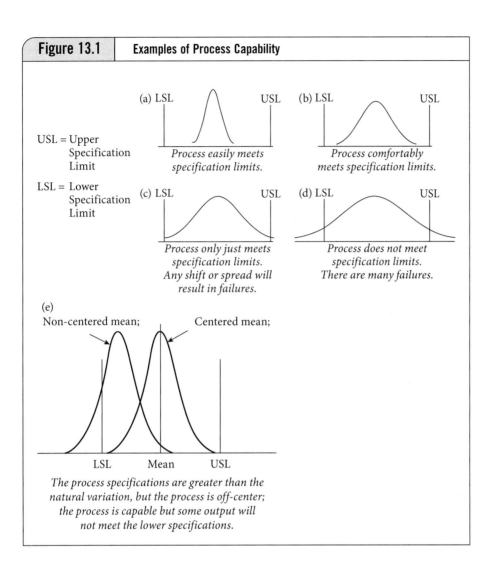

USL = Upper Specification Limit

LSL = Lower Specification Limit

(a) LSL ... USL
Process easily meets specification limits.

(b) LSL ... USL
Process comfortably meets specification limits.

(c) LSL ... USL
Process only just meets specification limits. Any shift or spread will result in failures.

(d) LSL ... USL
Process does not meet specification limits. There are many failures.

(e) Non-centered mean;   Centered mean;

LSL   Mean   USL

The process specifications are greater than the natural variation, but the process is off-center; the process is capable but some output will not meet the lower specifications.

Figure 13.1]. Lastly, if the process capability is greater than 1.0, then the process is capable of producing within the design specifications all the time [this is shown in parts (a) and (b) of Figure 13.1]. Example 13.2 illustrates the use of the capability ratio.

The **process capability index** (C_{pk}) shows whether the process mean has shifted away from the design target and is off-center. The equation for the process capability index is:

$$C_{pk} = \min\left[\frac{\text{Overall mean} - \text{Lower specification}}{3\sigma}, \frac{\text{Upper specification} - \text{Overall mean}}{3\sigma}\right]$$

If the process capability index is greater than 1.0, then both parts of the equation are greater than 1.0, and the process is deemed capable of meeting the design specifications. Design and manufacturing engineers are concerned when the C_{pk} is less than 1.0, because this indicates the process mean has moved closer to either the upper or lower design specifications and, as a result, will result in product defects [refer to part (e) of Figure 13.1]. When the C_{pk} is equal to 1.0, the process mean is equal to the design target and should meet the design specifications most of the time (again, because of process variation, the process will not meet design specifications in a small number of instances). Example 13.3 provides an example using the process capability index.

Example 13.2   Process Capability Ratio

Krebs Corporation makes 100-watt light bulbs that are designed to have a life of 1,225 hours, +/− 220 hours. The manufacturing process can make light bulbs with a mean life of 1,150 hours and a standard deviation of 45 hours. Calculate the process capability ratio. Is the process capable of meeting the design specifications? Why/why not?

SOLUTION:

$$C_p = \frac{(1,225 + 220) - (1,225 - 220)}{6(45)} = \frac{1,445 - 1,005}{270} = 1.63$$

Based on the process capability ratio of 1.63, the process is capable of meeting the design specifications.

Example 13.3   Process Capability Index

Recall from Example 13.2 that Krebs Corporation produced light bulbs designed to have a life of 1,225 hours with a tolerance of +/− 220 hours. The manufacturing process was capable of producing light bulbs with a mean life of 1,150 hours and a standard deviation of 45 hours. Calculate the process capability index. Is the process mean on- or off-center? Why/why not?

SOLUTION:

$$C_{pk} = \text{minimum} \left[\frac{1,150 - 1,005}{3(45)}, \frac{1,445 - 1,150}{3(45)} \right]$$
$$= \text{minimum} \left[\frac{145}{135}, \frac{295}{135} \right]$$
$$= \text{minimum} (1.07, 2.19)$$
$$= 1.07$$

A process capability index of 1.07 indicates that the process is not off-center because the calculated index is greater than 1.

Process capability calculations will help organizations identify process problems such that solutions can be implemented which will ultimately reduce the costs of poorly performing processes. Companies should also develop an attitude of continuous improvement which requires the creation and implementation of an ongoing plan to meet quality goals. Control methods should also be developed and implemented to ensure that products and services are performing according to the standards set and then to allow corrective actions to be taken when necessary. More on the planning process is found in the next section.

The Quality Improvement Process

W. Edwards Deming, an important and world renowned quality expert, wrote that product and service design today is a "helix of continual improvement of satisfaction of the consumer, at a lower and lower cost."[15] As stated here, organizations first and foremost need to understand their customers when planning and implementing quality improvement initiatives. To accomplish this, a three-step process is recommended to successfully plan for and realize quality improvement goals: (1) strategic quality planning, or the process of planning for meeting quality goals; (2) implementation of the quality plan; and (3) quality control, or the process of meeting quality goals during the day-to-day operations of an organization. This discussion of each of these steps in the quality improvement process follows.

Strategic Quality Planning

Strategic quality planning should take place with a company's overall strategic goals and objectives in mind. An organization can begin by identifying its customers—both external and internal—and then determine how it will create value for its customers through its core or key processes, while keeping in mind the firm's mission and vision. If a company hasn't done this before, it should begin the planning process by developing definitions of "quality" for each key process. While this may seem intuitive, many companies struggle with what quality really means to their organization and their supply chain trading partners. Also, although quality can mean many different things, it should always come down to the fact that quality needs to begin and end with the customer. In other words, workers, departments, and companies need to have a good understanding of how they will consistently meet or exceed their internal and external customers' expectations.

Each company will most likely define quality differently based on its customer base, product line, mission statement, and competitive strategy. A good place to start is to identify product or service features that will meet the customers' most important needs and "wants." Once an organization has established what is important to its various customer segments, it is then time to translate these customer desires into product or service specifications that, when implemented, will result in customer satisfaction. An important point to remember is that customers generally buy products because they will solve some "problem" for them. For example, in 1904 Thomas Sullivan, a seller of loose-leaf tea, was looking for a way to meet customers' requests to sample teas. At the time, many customers bought their tea at restaurants. He started shipping samples in small silk bags with instructions to slit open the bag and pour the tea leaves into the cup for brewing. Instead of following the instructions, however, customers simply placed the bag into a cup of boiling water, eliminating the problems of messy leaves floating in their tea, the more complex brewing process, and tea leaf disposal. As a result, the tea bag was born.[16] In this instance, quality in the eyes of the consumer was a good cup of tea without the fuss.

David Garvin, a Harvard Business School professor and author of *Managing Quality*, also suggests considering eight dimensions of quality, as shown in Table 13.3, to help identify customers' needs and wants.[17] In the healthcare field, for example, a hospital's patient base might say it expects a high level of quality and be referring to performance, reliability, features, or conformance. As to performance, patients could be referring to the need for properly performed surgeries that correct the problem, to be up and around quickly following the procedure, and/or to have no complications or infections after the surgery. Conformance could mean that patients expect to receive the correct procedure at the expected price. Patients could also be talking about features—how well they will be treated by the staff, whether the hospital room has satellite television with multiple free channels, or whether a chaplain visits them on a regular basis during their

Table 13.3	Garvin's Eight Dimensions of Quality	
QUALITY DIMENSION	**HOSPITAL**	**DVD PLAYER**
Performance	Surgery performed correctly; problem corrected; no complications	Operates as promised
Features	Free satellite TV	Has surround sound, MP3 playback, and 5-speed scanning capabilities
Reliability	Good probability surgery will be effective	Player operates as expected each time it is used
Conformance	Patients get exactly what they expected at the expected price	Player operates according to manual
Durability	Surgery results will last	Player will last past the warranty period
Aesthetics	Cheerful room	Sleek design; controls easy to read
Serviceability	Easy to schedule follow-up care	Easy to return for service under the warranty period
Perceived Quality	Hospital has a world-renowned doctor and has an excellent reputation	Known brand name

Source: Adapted from D. Garvin, "Competing on the Eight Dimensions of Quality," *Harvard Business Review*, Nov./Dec. 1987, pp. 101–109.

stay. On the other hand, they might be concerned about the reliability of a given procedure, or in other words, the statistics on success rates.

Organizations do not have to excel on all dimensions according to Garvin. Rather, firms should determine which dimensions are most important to their customers, and possibly which dimensions are not currently being provided by competitors, and market those to customers as areas of emphases. These dimensions become a company's **quality niche strategy** or positioning strategy. For example, one hospital may place an emphasis on features—expensive room furnishings, the latest equipment, and extra nurses—while another may position itself based on perceived quality because it is a teaching hospital with world-renowned doctors on staff. The quality niche and associated quality dimensions also need to be shared with suppliers so they have a truer understanding of the end consumers' expectations as well as the needs of their immediate business customer. A recent trend in healthcare, for example, has been for U.S. and Canadian citizens to travel to India for required or elective surgeries. The appeal is substantially lower costs with surgeries performed in state-of-the-art hospitals by doctors trained at the best medical schools. Known as medical tourism, the patients pay for a package that includes airfare, hotels, surgery, and a post-operative vacation.[18]

One way to determine a quality niche is through a point allocation exercise. To begin, managers develop a list of all the "wants" of their customers. They will then ask customers to allocate 100 points to each of these "wants" based on perceived importance. Generally one or two dimensions will stand out. Once the customers' overall definition of quality has been determined, the company should measure itself against these expectations. For example, if features are important, management should measure their performance with respect to the important features and see how they compare to their competition. Companies can also use **benchmarking** to determine best practices in a particular area. Benchmarking involves making a comparable study of best practices or products (either internally or at another organization) and then implementing improvements based on the findings of the study. These steps are often performed using quality function deployment (QFD), a tool described earlier in Chapter 2.

Along with developing a quality niche, companies should also consider any long-term economic, technological, and demographic forecasts or studies that may have an impact on their products and customers in the future. Hospitals, for instance, face decisions regarding the purchase of new technology. They can now purchase full-screen, expensive digital mammography machines, which were FDA approved for use in 2002. These machines take pictures similar to a digital camera and have been found to result in better readings, particularly in younger women, than the traditional film-screen machines.[19] As a result, hospitals must decide whether the additional equipment expense will result in a higher level of satisfaction and attract new patients to their facility.

Because customers and their needs are constantly evolving, companies often respond by periodically analyzing their existing customer base and making some changes. They might also consider looking for additional customers to expand their market presence. The firm may also decide to fire some unprofitable customers and develop strategies to increase revenues from existing low-profit customers through new products and services (more on firing customers can be found in Chapter 3).

If a company finds that customer complaints are high for an existing product or service, efforts to improve the situation may be undertaken or the product might be eliminated while new, higher quality products or services are developed. For instance, Bell Canada had always focused on the quality of a good connection, be it telephone, broadband, IP, or wireless. However, recognizing that business customers had become more sophisticated and wanted more control and influence over the service, the communications network company brainstormed and put several new ideas into practice. For example, it created several multimedia products and services to increase the simplicity and value of its offerings. It also developed secure information services with redundant capabilities to meet the storage needs of its clients.[20]

Once a customer assessment is made, the planning team should then compare these assessments to the company's mission and desired goals, and develop a course of action if inconsistencies are found. In other words, comprehensive strategic quality planning should steer all of the firm's products and services towards its overall mission. Often a company's quality plan is limited or ill-defined, which leads to less than optimal results. For example, a company may focus on identifying problems and then solving them while ignoring the customer relationship management process as discussed in Chapter 3. Other companies may focus on using quality improvement tools in one area, such as production or new product design, while failing to use them in other areas of the organization.

The best quality plans consider all of the elements impacting the firm and its customers, including the firm's processes, employees, training, culture, mission, goals, competitors, equipment, and finally customers. For example, The Bama Companies, Inc., Oklahoma-based manufacturer of frozen, ready-to-serve food products, developed a ten-year vision during their strategic planning process in 1999. It envisioned $1 billion in annual sales, recognition of the company's world-class quality, being the supplier of choice in all markets, and providing employees and other stakeholders with unequalled personal and financial opportunities. With these goals in mind, it focused on five strategic outcomes: (1) creating and delivering loyalty, prosperity, and fun for its employees, (2) learning and innovation, (3) continuous improvement, (4) the first choice for customers, and (5) value-added growth. Short-term action plans were then developed and the company used the balanced scorecard (discussed in Chapter 11) to assess its progress.[21]

Once a strategic quality plan has been developed, implementing it becomes the next critical step. The method of implementation may vary, but there are some general guidelines that can help organizations. These are covered in the following section.

Implementing the Quality Plan

Several key ingredients are required to successfully implement a strategic quality plan. First, top management must support and be actively involved in implementing the plan. Sporadic quality improvements may occur due to the industrious nature of a few individuals, but the company will not move forward in a significant way without the active involvement of its leadership.

Another important factor is that all employees must participate in carrying out the quality plan. Most employees will be willing to participate in the process if they see management supporting the plan, and if they witness a visible outcome or return. It may take some time to instill confidence in employees if past attempts have failed. But, in the words of actor Mickey Rooney, "You always pass failure on the way to success."[22] To improve their acceptance rate, workers must be properly trained and motivated. Generally employees will respond to encouragement, recognition, rewards, and support. Lastly, workers are more likely to participate when their suggestions for improvement are taken seriously and considered for inclusion in a process or product improvement activity.

Organizations also should tailor the implementation to their unique strengths and culture. In other words, there is no "one size fits all" in quality improvement. Some companies may find existing plans from trading partners that adapt well; others may hire consultants; still others may develop their own quality plans in-house. Tennessee-based Caterpillar Financial Services, for example, emphasizes both customer and employee satisfaction as critical success factors. It keeps its efforts constantly focused on process improvement and develops its own quality improvement plans using leading-edge technology, employee training, and employee recognition programs. Ninety-seven percent of its employees are trained in Six Sigma procedures for designing new processes and improving existing ones. It also uses the Malcolm Baldrige Award criteria to assess its organization and guide improvement efforts.[23]

The quality plan should be consistent with both customer and supplier quality plans. Many large companies, for example, are requiring their suppliers to have a quality plan in place, often providing direction on design and implementation. Georgia-based Newell Rubbermaid, a global manufacturer and marketer of branded consumer products, provides online documentation for its suppliers, including a Supplier Quality Assurance Manual that discusses the required components of a supplier's quality plan. Their expectation is that "suppliers must meet or exceed defined requirements."[24] Organizations should also strive to understand their customers' requirements and proactively seek ways to develop a quality plan that meets these requirements.

World-class organizations tie their quality action plans to performance and financial returns. Quality initiatives will require some financial investment so companies should pay close attention to the return on each of these investments. Comparing the quality investment to savings in the costs of poor quality will enable the firm to justify further quality improvement projects. Any well-planned quality investment, given a reasonable time lag, should add value for the organization and the customer. Companies that have adopted Six Sigma, for example, consider the cost and projected return on each project before implementation. The Bama Companies, Inc., mentioned earlier, have implemented Six Sigma and measure quality program performance using the balanced scorecard.

Upper management may not always be aware of the current state of development and implementation with regard to their quality plans. To assist in this effort, international accounting and consulting firm PriceWaterhouseCoopers (formerly Coopers and Lybrand) developed a quality maturity matrix, as shown in Table 13.4, to describe the current state or "maturity" of a firm's quality endeavors. The stages are briefly described here:

- *The innocence stage* – The organization has not become aware of the need to improve product or service quality. It accepts everything but the worst quality from suppliers and responds to only the worst complaints from customers. Companies at this stage view quality efforts as an additional expense to be avoided if possible.

Table 13.4	Quality Maturity Matrix				
	INNOCENCE	**AWARENESS**	**UNDERSTANDING**	**COMPETENCE**	**EXCELLENCE**
APPROACH	Reactive; fire fighters	Quality improvement	Defect prevention	Design in quality	Innovate for quality improvement
Top management's role	No involvement	Takes responsibility	Believes in a process focus	Measures all aspects of performance	Nurtures creativeness
Quality responsibility	Quality department	Management	Transferred top to bottom	Quality at the source	Shared companywide
Quality process	Inspect, correct	Develop new procedures	Process control	Ask for real-time market feedback	Improve innovatively
Customer relations	React to worst complaints	Recognize employee as internal customer	Plan for customer requirements	Develop improvement plans tied to the customer	Customer-supported innovation
Supplier relations	React to worst defects	Educate suppliers; reduce amount of inspection	Implement joint quality programs	Develop long-term strategic partnerships	Work mutually to adapt to market trends
Quality cost (% of sales)	>20%	15%–20%	8%–15%	3%–8%	<3%
Training	Little	Focus on techniques	Develop training plans	Continuous; all employees	Research

Source: Coopers & Lybrand, *Integrated Quality*, New York, 1988.

- *The awareness stage* – Companies begin to undertake some quality efforts because they are losing sales due to quality problems. Customer relations begin to improve, and the firm recognizes the needs of its internal customers. It also spends time educating its suppliers in quality management.
- *The understanding stage* – Companies believe in the benefits of a quality program and involve employees in quality training classes. Products and services are designed to meet the requirements of major customers. They have begun some quality initiatives and developed a basic quality improvement system. Suppliers have become involved in efforts to jointly improve quality.
- *The competence stage* – A company works within an integrated quality system, uses advanced quality techniques, measures the effects of its quality efforts, and gives feedback to employees regarding their quality efforts. Key suppliers become strategic partners.
- *The excellence stage* – The firm provides in-demand products and services based on customer feedback in a timely fashion. As partners, suppliers work in conjunction with the firm to develop quality products and services based on forecasts of market trends.

Once companies understand the maturity of their quality efforts, they can begin to develop more effective implementation strategies. After surveying 580 companies on 945 business practices, international accounting and consulting firm Ernst & Young and the American Quality Foundation recommended companies use two measures of performance to supplement their self-assessment. First, they can measure their **return on assets** (ROA), which is calculated as:

$$ROA = \text{After-tax income/Total assets}$$

And **value added per employee** (VAE), which is:

$$VAE = \frac{\text{Sales} - \text{Costs (materials, supplies, outsourcing costs)}}{\text{Number of employees}}$$

As shown in Table 13.5, low performers, or those in the innocence stage as described by PriceWaterhouseCoopers in Table 13.4, will benefit the most if they can move to a higher level of quality program maturity. This might include looking for processes with significant value-added potential, and then improving them to meet customer and market demands more effectively. Providing quality training, forming quality improvement teams, and benchmarking competitors with high-quality products and services are also important. Medium performers, those in the "awareness" and "understanding" stages, will gain the most by further refining practices that improve VAE, customer satisfaction, and time to market, and then documenting the improvements made. They should also benchmark world-class companies; develop new products and services based on customer feedback, internal ideas, and formal market research; implement a supplier certification process; and develop compensation programs for employees based on teamwork and quality performance. Lastly, high performers, those in the competence and excellence stages, should develop self-managed, cross-functional, and cross-organizational teams. These teams need to focus on improving processes that cross boundaries, such as new product development and logistics.

At the operational level, employees are responsible for monitoring day-to-day processes to control quality, or in other words, ensuring products and services meet company-set standards. The following sections provide additional information on this topic beginning with a discussion on the process of problem solving.

Table 13.5	Quality Management Implementation Categories		
CHARACTERISTIC	**LOW PERFORMERS**	**MEDIUM PERFORMERS**	**HIGH PERFORMERS**
ROA **VAE**	<2% <$47,000	2%–6.9% $47,000–$73,999	>7% >$74,000
Best practices	• Focus on fundamentals • Identify value-adding processes and simplify • Benchmark competitors • Listen to the customer • Select suppliers on price and reliability • Buy turnkey technology • Reward frontline employees for teamwork and quality	• Refine processes and practices further • Document results • Benchmark world-class leaders • Gather customer feedback, formal market research, and employee ideas for new products and services • Develop supplier certification process • Use facilities more flexibly • Compensate employees based on teamwork, quality	• Self-managed teams • Cross-functional teams • Focus on horizontal processes • Benchmark processes against world-class firms • Use customer input, formal market research, and employees to generate new product/service ideas • Select suppliers primarily for quality and technology • Develop strategic partnerships • Refine practices • Develop senior management compensation tied to quality and teamwork

Source: Adapted from Ernst & Young and American Quality Foundation, *International Quality Study,* 1992.

Controlling Quality

Once a strategic quality plan has been developed and implemented, quality control processes must be in place to ensure products and processes continuously operate according to the standards set by the organization. Firms should implement activities to detect and improve poor-quality products and processes, and then to monitor the improvements to ensure that the problems have been adequately corrected. The idea is to keep control of the process inputs and outputs by monitoring **process variation**.

Process Variation

Variation in the way inputs are converted into finished products and services is everywhere. Generally more variation is found in service organizations because of the differences found among frontline servers. For example, two employees providing the same service will have different mannerisms, backgrounds, and training, leading to variations in the service provided. Thus, a customer will perceive a different experience because of the variation between the two employees. A single employee's delivery may also vary from day to day, creating daily variations in service performance. For instance, a store cashier may satisfy customer needs most days but on one particular day, because he doesn't feel well, makes a customer unhappy because he doesn't initially offer a smile and friendly greeting. Service providers may try to minimize variations in performance through extensive training, use of technology, and scripted work rules. For example, customer service representatives in the insurance industry generally answer customer calls using a computer screen with question/answer protocols.

Variations can also be attributed to other sources, including materials, tools, employees, customers, and measurement gauges. For example, the same materials received from different suppliers may vary considerably in thickness, strength, color, and weight. Tools may also vary in their composition, strength, and calibration, resulting in different levels of output and wear. Natural vibrations from equipment can alter machine settings, while electrical surges can create variations in power. Employees also increase the chance for variation because repetitive tasks will not be performed exactly the same way each time. Customers can cause variations due to their changing perceptions and also their inputs in self-serve processes.

When taken together, most of these "random" variations are an expected part of process performance and can account for a significant portion of the disparity in output, also known as **common causes of variation**. In many cases, organizations cannot do much to reduce common causes of variation. On the other hand, variations can also come from things that are not a natural or expected part of the process, such as a poorly trained or motivated employee, a poor batch of materials received from a supplier, or miscalibrated equipment. These are known as **assignable causes of variation** and they can be identified and eliminated or controlled. Statistical methods are primarily used to detect assignable causes of variation.

Organizations can thus focus on identifying and reducing the assignable causes of variation in any work done across the functional areas so that completed tasks will have a positive impact on quality. With time, a continued emphasis on identifying and eliminating these assignable causes will pay off in terms of reducing the costs of poor quality— less inspection, scrap, rework, warranty repairs, and customer complaints. Ultimately, customers will benefit because they will receive a more consistent level of quality.

A Framework for Solving Quality Problems

To begin solving quality problems, organizations should separate the problem from the "mess" according to Professors James Evans and William Lindsay, who have done extensive research on quality management.[25] A mess, according to Russell Ackoff, is a "system of external conditions that produces dissatisfaction."[26] Evidence of a mess includes high defect rates, low customer satisfaction, or excessive rework. When one or more of these signs of a mess is evident, it becomes critical to determine the underlying causes. Some of the common reasons a quality problem occurs is because employees do not understand how a process works or should work, mistakes are made in the process steps, unnecessary process steps are taken which create waste, or there is too much variation in the way the process is performed.

Organizations need to create a structure for finding problems and correcting them. In the 1950s, W. Edwards Deming developed a model of problem solving by adapting Walter Shewhart's cycle of plan-do-see into a four-stage cycle known as the **Deming Plan-Do-Study-Act (PDSA) Cycle**, also referred to as the Plan-Do-Check-Act (PDCA) Cycle.[27] Using the PDSA Cycle, process improvement decisions are based on actual data rather than opinion and speculation. In other words, a plan for improvement is formulated, put into use, checked through measurement and observation, and the improvement is then either standardized if it has actually improved the problem, or modified if not enough improvement is evident. As a result, there is a better chance that improvement initiatives will actually result in improved product or service quality. Since Deming's time, others including Kaoru Ishikawa, a Japanese management leader and colleague of Deming, have expanded the definition or understanding of each stage. The following discussion incorporates the Deming Plan-Do-Study-Act Cycle with the ideas of others as a good way to approach problem identification and solution.

As shown in Figure 13.2, the graphic of the Deming PDSA Cycle is round, to depict a never-ending cycle of process improvement. Following is a summary of the four

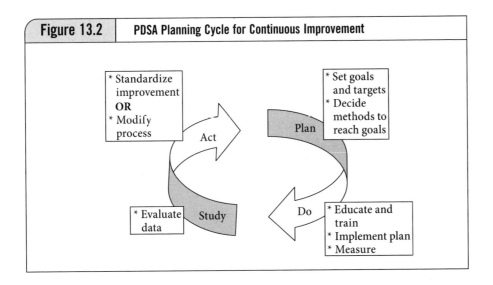

Figure 13.2   PDSA Planning Cycle for Continuous Improvement

stages using the example of PQ Systems, an Ohio-based software and training company. At the time the case was written, PQ Systems was looking for ways to improve response times to customer support calls.[28]

Applying the PDSA Cycle

The *planning phase* in the PDSA Cycle is usually triggered by some need for change or evidence of a problem. An improvement team is formed, and the team establishes its goals and targets and then determines the methods that will be used to reach its goals. Essentially the team is deciding which change or changes should be implemented and tested. They analyze the current process with the help of flowcharting and the use of performance measures. Based on the team's analysis, the company formulates a proposal for improvement and predicts the improvement outcome or results.

During the planning phase, PQ Systems formed an inbound telephone inquiry team of support call analysts, a sales representative, and a software development person. The team discovered that while phone calls were answered within one or two rings, the analyst with the most expertise in helping a particular customer wasn't always available. Customers would leave a message to be called back, but the elapsed time until the return phone call averaged 50 minutes. The team thought callback times could be improved, so they created a flowchart of the telephone callback process and a communication board to visually show each step of the improvement project and the team's progress. Based on their research, they set a goal to reduce the time required for call completion and developed an action plan to collect and analyze callback data.

During this stage, improvement teams should ask some important questions, such as:

1. Will the proposed change(s) directly address the problem?
2. Will the effect of the change(s) be seen in a reasonable amount of time?
3. Can the change(s) be tested on a small scale?
4. Will the effect of the change(s) be easy to measure?
5. Will the cost of change(s) be feasible for the company?

If the answer is "yes" to all these questions, the change or changes should most likely be implemented and tested as soon as possible to determine their effectiveness.

Most teams are seldom so lucky to answer all questions with a "yes," but the number of "yes" answers gives a rough order of priority among different possible solutions.

There is another guiding principle that might be overlooked. In the long run, a change that reduces process variation without making the average performance measure worse is more desirable than one that improves the average performance while leaving the process variations as great as before. For example, if PQ Systems were to find a way to reduce the average number of rings before the phone is answered, while leaving the variation in the number of rings high, the solution will still potentially leave the same number of customers dissatisfied.

The *do phase* of the PDSA Cycle involves executing the plan. Documented steps are taken in a controlled environment. The team observes and records what happens as the changes are implemented, notes what went well and what didn't, and collects supporting data. PQ Systems implemented its action plan and collected new callback data by recording times on a **control chart**, which is a graph used to visually track the performance of a process against calculated control or warning limits. (More on control chart design can be found later in this chapter.)

In the *study stage* of the PDSA Cycle the team reviews the performance data and information, determining the effect of the changes on the process. They should note any changes from the initial baseline measures that were taken, comparing the outcomes with the predictions by collecting both objective and subjective feedback. One method is to observe internal or external customer behavior to see if the newly improved process is meeting their needs. Observations may be direct, or may include use of surveys or the monitoring of customer complaints, sales trends, or the amount of warranty work.

Certain tests may also be performed as necessary to analyze the effect of any changes. In general, any testing should be as least disruptive as possible. The tests should be fairly simple, easy to administer, and the results should be straightforward in terms of interpretation. As tests become more complex, it becomes increasingly difficult to interpret the results of the changes. Lastly, the reliability of the tests is critical. In other words, the results should be interpreted in the same manner no matter how many times they are run. Control charts are generally used when analyzing the impact of process improvements.

Once testing is complete, the team should analyze the results along with other feedback. If the team concludes that the process changes were successful and resulted in positive outcomes (increased customer satisfaction and reduced variance), the organization should incorporate those practices into the daily work routine. If not, then adjustments should be made and the outcomes studied further until an acceptable level of quality has been achieved and variations have been reduced. The PQ Systems team analyzed their control charts and found that their recommendations had reduced callback times an average of 36 percent. While studying this problem, however, they uncovered another more serious area for improvement and created a second team to collect data related to these problems. As a result, another PDSA cycle was initiated.

In the *act stage* of the PDSA Cycle, the team takes action to standardize or further improve the process using what they have learned. They also create "fail-safe" practices where possible that will prevent similar process failures from occurring again, and revisit the plan as necessary. In the case of PQ Systems, the team standardized the callback process into the call center's daily routine.

Detecting Problems and Assignable Causes

The PDSA framework provides a system for diagnosing and treating problems in processes as they occur. To specifically identify problems and their potential causes, several tools are used that can lead improvement teams to design the most appropriate plan for process improvement. These tools are discussed in the following section.

Check Sheets

To detect problems, some formal process of data collection is needed. A process improvement team will first need to determine what type of data will help them in their analysis, the source of that data, and how the data will be collected in a cost-effective manner. A **check sheet** is often used, which is a very simple data collection form. Example 13.4 illustrates the use of a check sheet to classify problems at a customer call center for a large telephone company. Four problems were thus identified.

Pareto Charts

When used in quality improvement efforts, a **Pareto chart** visually shows the relative magnitude of each problem identified using a check sheet and is used to identify which problem to work on first. Pareto analysis is based on the 80/20 rule, or the idea that only a few processes are causing the biggest percentage of the problems. Joseph Juran, a quality expert mentioned earlier in this chapter, analyzed 200 types of field failures for automobile engines, for instance, and found that less than 3 percent accounted for a third of all failures.[29] The data in a Pareto chart is transformed into a bar chart or **histogram**, with each bar representing the frequency of a particular defect or problem. The bars are ordered by frequency from high to low. A Pareto chart will also include a line representing the cumulative frequency of the defects. Example 13.5 provides an illustration in the use of Pareto charts, using the data gathered from the check sheet in Example 13.4.

Example 13.4   Use of a Check Sheet

WTT, a large regional telephone company, has experienced an increase in customer complaints on its Customer Care Hot Line. Management assigns a quality team to investigate the problem and develop some solutions. The team reviews the complaints from the past two weeks to better understand the reasons for the complaints. The team tallies each type of complaint on a check sheet, as follows:

TYPE OF COMPLAINT	COMPLAINTS	SUBTOTAL
Too many rings before answering	///// ////	9
On hold too long	///// ///// ///// ///// //	22
Answering system too complicated	///// ///// ///// ///// ///// ///// ///// ///// ///// ///	48
Could never talk to a "real person"	///// ///// ///// ///// ///// ///// ///// ///// ///// ///// ///// ///// ///// ///// ///// ///// ///// //	87
	Grand Total	**166**

Example 13.5   Use of a Pareto Chart

WTT uses the check sheet found in Example 13.4 to create a Pareto chart. The quality team re-orders the types of defects by their relative magnitude and percentage, from high to low:

TYPE OF COMPLAINT	NUMBER	PERCENT OF TOTAL
Could never talk to a "real person"	87	87/166 = 52.41%
Answering system too complicated	48	48/166 = 28.92%
On hold too long	22	22/166 = 13.25%
Too many rings before answering	9	9/166 = 5.42%
Total	**166**	**100%**

The team then creates a Pareto chart using Microsoft Excel:

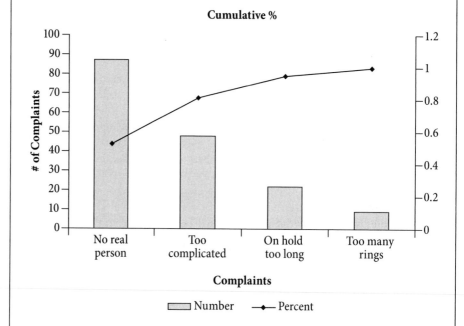

The team finds that the first two complaints, inability to talk to a real person and a complicated answering system, account for approximately 80 percent of all complaints. Solving these problems first would allow for the greatest improvements in the number of complaints.

Cause-and-Effect Diagram

The **cause-and-effect diagram**, developed by Kaoru Ishikawa, and also known as a **fishbone diagram** or **Ishikawa diagram**, is a graphical tool that represents the quality team's current understanding of a given quality problem. The quality team brainstorms, identifies, and then categorizes possible causes of the quality problem (the effect), using a blank cause-and-effect diagram. The four possible categories of problem causes are also referred to as the **4-Ms,** which stand for manpower, materials, methods, and machinery. It is generally assumed that the vast majority of problem causes are in one or more of these categories. Sometimes, an "other" category is also added to the cause-and-effect diagram for causes

Example 13.6   Use of a Cause-and-Effect Diagram

WTT's quality team reviews the Pareto chart created in Example 13.5 and decides to brainstorm using a cause-and-effect or fishbone diagram to try and improve the biggest problem first—that customers cannot reach a live person with the present answering system. Following is a partially completed diagram using the 4-M categories.

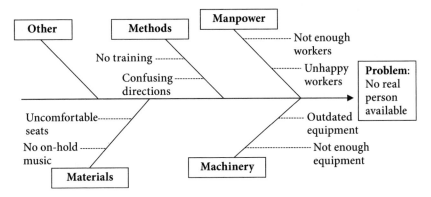

Based on their diagramming and brainstorming exercise, the quality team identifies several potential causes that need to be studied further to hopefully reduce the "no real person available" complaints.

that cannot be categorized in one of the other four areas. The cause-and-effect diagram thus gives structure to the brainstorming process.

Once the diagram has been created and potential causes brainstormed, the improvement team must then become detectives, studying the process to observe if the potential causes are actually responsible for the original problem. Here, more detailed check sheets can again be used to gather specific causal data. Example 13.6 illustrates the use of a cause-and-effect diagram for solving the "no real person available" problem identified in Examples 13.4 and 13.5. The most likely causes then become the basis for implementing improvement ideas.

Once processes are performing smoothly (few internal and external customer complaints), firms can monitor process variations in an ongoing fashion, using statistical process control charts. The following section provides a discussion of the statistical approach to process control.

Statistical Process Control

Responsible firms have control or monitoring processes in place to ensure the desired level of quality is achieved on a daily basis. In general, the current performance of a product feature or a process is regularly compared to some preset goal or measure. This evaluation process may be done automatically through the use of computers, human observation, or other physical and chemical tests. For example, many manufacturers use software to generate quality control charts used to monitor production processes. On the other hand, some processes require visual inspection to assess performance. For instance, in the wood products industry, inspectors determine the grade of lumber by a visual check for the size, number, and location of knots in the wood. In banking, tellers count the cash in their drawer at the end of the day to make sure they are in balance.

A number of instruments are also available to measure product and process features. Clocks, tape measures, weight scales, and thermometers are just a few examples. Michigan-based pizza delivery company Domino's Pizza, for example, has measured the time it takes for each stage of the pizza delivery process using a stopwatch and computer software that "time-stamps" each stage. The pizza-making stage, for instance, takes 2 minutes and 14 seconds. Each retail outlet tracks its own process times and then reports them to Domino's headquarters. Action is subsequently taken at underperforming stores to improve processing times.[30]

Companies may also outsource some of the process-monitoring work. As seen in the Service Perspective feature, Taco Bell uses secret shoppers, employed by an outside firm, to monitor customer service and food quality.

Performance evaluations are usually reported to an evaluator. The evaluator may be the person who takes the measurements, a supervisor, or someone located in a separate quality assurance department. There are a number of means to report the results, including verbally, with the use of computer spreadsheets such as Excel, or by creating control charts. The evaluator then reviews the results, comparing process performance to the preset standard. Standards should be based on the initial design specifications, unless changes have been made to the product, service, or process since then. If this is the case, any changes to the initial specifications should be recorded and provided to the evaluator so they can be considered during the control process.

In most cases, process variations will occur randomly over time, requiring workers to continually monitor process performance. When the difference between actual performance and the standard or goal is too great, assignable causes of variation are assumed to be present, triggering a PDSA Cycle. As mentioned earlier, the cycle begins with an investigation of the underlying causes, starting with the problem, and using the tools discussed earlier. Once the investigation is complete, a plan to improve the process or product is devised to bring performance in line with the goal or standard. For instance, the organization may decide that an employee needs more training, or a

"Deploy the Quality Control!"

Service Perspective

Mystery Shopping at Taco Bell

Taco Bell has used a mystery shopping program since 1996 to support its quality program known as CHAMPS. The acronym stands for cleanliness, hospitality, accuracy, maintenance, and speed. Mystery shoppers visit approximately 9,000 company-owned stores and franchise restaurants once or twice during a four-week period, asking about 35 questions covering areas including the cleanliness of the facility, hospitality of the employees, the accuracy of a filled order, the ingredients used, speed of service, and product quality.

These mystery shoppers place orders, observe the service provided, and then take their meals out to their cars for a closer inspection. Once back inside their cars, they take measurements such as the temperature of the food and the proportions of an item.

Their goal is to make sure that customers receive a consistent level of quality no matter which restaurant they visit. These ratings are used as a basis to pay out bonuses to store leaders and above-store leaders, as well employee recognition. Mystery shopping also reinforces the sales and service skills taught to frontline employees during training and measures whether the training methods used are actually effective.

Timely feedback has helped managers improve their customers' experience. Since starting the program, Taco Bell has cut almost a minute off the average drive-through wait time. The quality of its products and services has also gone up.

Sources: Steindorf, S., "Shoppers Spy on Those Who Serve," *Christian Science Monitor,* May 28, 2002, available at http://www.csmonitor.com; Moozakis, C., "App Solves Taco Bell Mystery," *Internet Week,* November 27, 2000, available at http://www.internetweek.com; and Pavilkey, S., "Good Service No Mystery with Proper Test Shoppers," *Business First,* June 8, 2001, available at http://www.bizjournals.com/columbus/stories/2001/06/11/focus2.html?page=1.

supplier may have to ship new parts to replace defective ones and then improve its own quality management program. Once corrections are implemented and problem causes eliminated, workers will continue to monitor the product, service, or process using process control charts to ensure that the process remains problem free.

Designing and Using Control Charts

Control charts have been mentioned throughout this chapter and are diagrams used to visually evaluate whether a sample of observations is abnormal. Workers use them to monitor output measures of a process and to identify when assignable or special causes of variation are likely to be present. As assignable causes of variation are removed, scrap, rework, and other poor-quality costs are reduced, resulting in higher levels of productivity, customer satisfaction, and profits. Within the supply chain, buyers often require suppliers to provide evidence that their processes are being monitored using statistical process control.

Type I and Type II Errors

Control charts are used to help employees decide when to actually take action and make adjustments to a process. As stated earlier, there will always be some natural variation in the process, requiring evaluators to understand when a process is exhibiting natural process variations, and when it is exhibiting assignable, out-of-control process variations. Interpretation of control charts is subject to some set guidelines, helping an evaluator determine when a process is likely out of control and in need of improvement. Mistakes can be made, however, in interpreting control charts when errors are made in understanding the data or because mistakes are made during the sampling process (also known as sampling error). A **Type I error** occurs when a process is mistakenly thought to be out of control and an improvement initiative is undertaken unnecessarily. Conversely, a **Type II error** occurs when a process is thought to be exhibiting only natural variations and no improvement is undertaken, even though the process is actually out of control. Both types of errors are costly to the firm and can be avoided by properly training the employees who are reading and interpreting the control charts.

Variable Data and Attribute Data

There are several types of control charts and workers need to know when one is more appropriate than another. An organization, for example, may be measuring **variable data** such as weight, distance, or length. These are data that can be measured on a continuous scale. Control charts to measure variable data are primarily used in manufacturing settings; however, they can sometimes also be used in services. Measuring customer waiting time at a doctor's office, for instance, is variable data. On the other hand, **attribute data** assumes two values such as pass/fail, yes/no, good/bad, or acceptable/unacceptable. The data are usually collected based on either visual inspection or answers to survey questionnaires and are also used in manufacturing and service settings. For example, an insurance company may decide that an insurance form is unacceptable when two or more errors have been made in its completion. A restaurant manager might be interested in tracking whether customers enjoyed the service. An auto manufacturer might also visually inspect a paint job or a seat assembly installation for acceptable or unacceptable quality.

Once it has been determined which type of data is being monitored, data collection and creation of the control charts can proceed. The next section begins with a description of control chart design.

Sampling Plans and Control Chart Design

Sampling is done to calculate the value of a variable or attribute for a quality characteristic that is important to the quality of a product, service, or process. For example, the weight of a box of Cheerios® is important to the consumer (and cereal maker General Mills can be fined by the U.S. Department of Weights and Measures if its cereal boxes don't consistently weigh the stated amount). So, a sample is collected and the average value of the measurement for the sample is calculated and used as an indicator of the performance of the process, product, or service (generally speaking, an average of several observations or measurements taken at different times is a better indicator of true process performance than one single measurement at one instant in time). Thus, General Mills quality inspectors would use the weight of a sample of Cheerios cereal boxes to periodically calculate the mean process performance and to determine if its cereal box filling equipment is operating properly.

Before actual sampling is done, a **sampling plan** to collect and analyze the samples must be designed. As briefly described above, a sample is a quantity of randomly selected observations that represent the population, or all observations. Continuing with the Cheerios example, if General Mills is monitoring the weight of boxes of Cheerios, each box in a given sample should weigh the same as all the cereal boxes manufactured on the production line. In a process that is in control, each sample's mean should exhibit very close to the same value. If assignable causes are present, the probability of seeing differences between samples or within the samples collected should be high. Thus, if the sample mean is significantly different from other samples, or if the range of measures within a sample is high, the control chart reader can quickly identify a potentially out-of-control process and investigate further.

The sampling plan will also include a decision about the **sample size**, or how many units will be randomly selected and measured each time a sample is collected. Designers want to be able to determine whether special causes of variation are present based on the smallest possible sample size to reduce the time spent monitoring a process. However, with larger sample sizes, the sample average will more closely describe the true process performance. As a rule of thumb, when measuring variable data, a sample size of 5 has been found to work well in detecting process shifts of two standard deviations or larger. Larger sample sizes of perhaps 15 to 25 are necessary if a company is trying to detect smaller shifts in the process mean. When measuring attribute data, the sample size should be based on the premise that it needs to be large enough to detect at least one nonconformance.

Another aspect of the sampling plan is **sampling frequency**, or in other words, the time interval between sample collections. There are no exact rules for sampling frequency but the goal is to detect shifts in the process as quickly as possible to avoid producing a large number of defective items. However, as the frequency increases, the chance of making both Type I and Type II errors is reduced. Past experience is probably the best indicator of how frequently one should sample and how large the sample should be.

Lastly, the control limits must be calculated to determine when improvement actions should be initiated. A control chart has a central line or nominal value, which can be the company's target or goal for the process, the design specification, or simply the average of a large number of sample means. Using the General Mills cereal box example, the nominal value or central line is 16 ounces. There also needs to be an **upper control limit**, or the maximum acceptable value for the sample measure, and a **lower control limit**, or the minimum acceptable value. Employees collect, measure, and plot the samples, and then determine whether the process is in control (no action is taken) or out of control. If the process is deemed to be out of control, an investigation is made to find the assignable causes of variation, and corrective actions are implemented. Generally, a process is considered out of control when sample plots fall outside the control limits or when the plots do not fall randomly around and close to the center line.

Generally, the control limits may be set anywhere from one to six standard deviations from the control chart center line. (Recall that a standard deviation is a statistic used as a measure of the dispersion or variation in a distribution.) The upper and lower control limits should be set to minimize the chance of a Type I or Type II error. The tighter the control limits (the fewer the standard deviations) around the center line, the greater the chance of making a Type I error, which then results in wasted time and money looking for nonexistent causes of variation. A more detailed discussion on sampling is outside the scope of this text but can be found in *Sampling Techniques* by William G. Cochran.[31] Also, further discussion of control chart design can be found in *Understanding Statistical Process Control* by Wheeler and Chambers.[32]

While the previous discussion has been about control charts in general, several types are used depending on the quality characteristic that will be measured. The following sections will describe three types of charts that are used, based on whether the sample represents variable data or attribute data.

Variable Data Control Charts ($\overline{X}$ Charts and R Charts)

Variable data requires the use of two charts, the sample means or $\overline{X}$ chart, and the sample range or R chart, which are interpreted together. The $\overline{X}$ chart is used to monitor the centering or mean performance of the process, while the R chart is used to monitor the variation of the measures within each sample. Both charts must be monitored simultaneously for variable data measurements, since it is possible to have a perfect sample mean with the sample measures widely dispersed (an unacceptably high range), or a very low sample dispersion (which is good) with a sample mean that is unacceptable. In both cases, the process would be deemed to be out of control. Example 13.7 provides sample data that will be used to describe the creation of the two charts.

In this example, the diameter of an engine shaft is the variable data gathered. Three diameter measurements were taken from the process for each of 25 samples collected over a 25-hour period. For each sample, the mean, $\overline{X}$, and the range, R, is calculated. The target or center-line value of the $\overline{X}$ chart, if not already predetermined, is calculated as the overall mean of the sample means, also referred to as $\overline{\overline{X}}$ (note that when constructing control charts, we assume the process is already under control, otherwise the control charts will not be valid). The average range of the sample ranges, $\overline{R}$, is also calculated and is used as the target value or center-line of the R chart. Calculations for the two measures are:

$$\overline{\overline{X}} = \frac{\overline{X}_1 + \overline{X}_2 + \overline{X}_3 + \ldots + \overline{X}_k}{k}$$

where:

$\overline{\overline{X}}$ = overall mean
$\overline{X}$ = sample mean
k = number of samples

and:

$$\overline{R} = \frac{R_1 + R_2 + R_3 + \ldots + R_k}{k}$$

where:

R_i = range for the ith sample (or the largest value minus the smallest
  value for each sample)
$\overline{R}$ = mean of all sample ranges

The control limits are then calculated for the two control charts using the overall range and overall mean. The control limits for the R chart are:

$$UCL_R = D_4\overline{R}$$
$$LCL_R = D_3\overline{R}$$

where:

UCL_R = the upper control limit
LCL_R = the lower control limit

D_3 and D_4 are factors used for estimating three standard deviation limits, and are dependent on the sample size.

The control limits for the $\overline{X}$ chart are:

$$UCL_{\overline{X}} = \overline{\overline{X}} + A_2\overline{R}$$
$$LCL_{\overline{X}} = \overline{\overline{X}} - A_2\overline{R}$$

where:

$$UCL_{\overline{X}} = \text{the upper control limit}$$
$$LCL_{\overline{X}} = \text{the lower control limit}$$

A_2 is a constant used for estimating three standard deviation limits and is dependent on the sample size.

A table for the constants D_3, D_4, and A_2 can be found in Table 13.6. Note that the term sample size as used in Table 13.6 refers to the number of observations in one sample, not the number of total samples.

Example 13.7   Control Chart Construction Using Variable Data

Following is the sample data collected to measure the diameter of a machine shaft.

SAMPLE #	OBS. 1	OBS. 2	OBS. 3	R	$\overline{X}$
1	2	1.9998	2.0002	0.0004	2.0000
2	1.9998	2.0003	2.0002	0.0005	2.0001
3	1.9998	2.0001	2.0005	0.0007	2.0001
4	1.9997	2	2.0004	0.0007	2.0000
5	2.0003	2.0003	2.0002	0.0001	2.0003
6	2.0004	2.0003	2	0.0004	2.0002
7	1.9998	1.9998	1.9998	0.0000	1.9998
8	2	2.0001	2.0001	0.0001	2.0001
9	2.0005	2	1.9999	0.0006	2.0001
10	1.9995	1.9998	2.0001	0.0006	1.9998
11	2.0002	1.9999	2.0001	0.0003	2.0001
12	2.0002	1.9998	2.0005	0.0007	2.0002
13	2.0002	2.0001	1.99998	0.0002	2.0001
14	2	2.0002	2.0004	0.0004	2.0002
15	2	2.0001	1.9996	0.0005	1.9999
16	1.9994	2.0003	1.9993	0.0010	1.9997
17	1.9999	1.9998	2.0004	0.0006	2.0000
18	2.0002	2.0001	2.0001	0.0001	2.0001
19	2	1.9994	1.9998	0.0006	1.9997
20	1.9997	2.0007	1.99999	0.0010	2.0001
21	2.0003	2.0003	2.0001	0.0002	2.0002
22	2	1.9998	1.9997	0.0003	1.9998
23	1.9997	2.0001	2	0.0004	1.9999
24	2.0004	1.9998	1.9997	0.0007	2.0000
25	2.0003	1.9999	2.0001	0.0004	2.0001
			Averages	0.0005	2.0000

Using the average range and overall mean, and factors from Table 13.6, the control chart limits can be calculated as follows:

$$LCL_R = 0(0.0005) = 0$$
$$UCL_R = 2.575(0.0005) = 0.0013$$
$$LCL_{\overline{X}} = 2.000 - 1.023(0.0005) = 1.9995$$
$$UCL_{\overline{X}} = 2.000 + 1.023(0.0005) = 2.0005$$

The R chart and $\overline{X}$ chart can now be created using the calculated control limits, and the sample means can be plotted. These charts confirm that the process is in control.

Continued

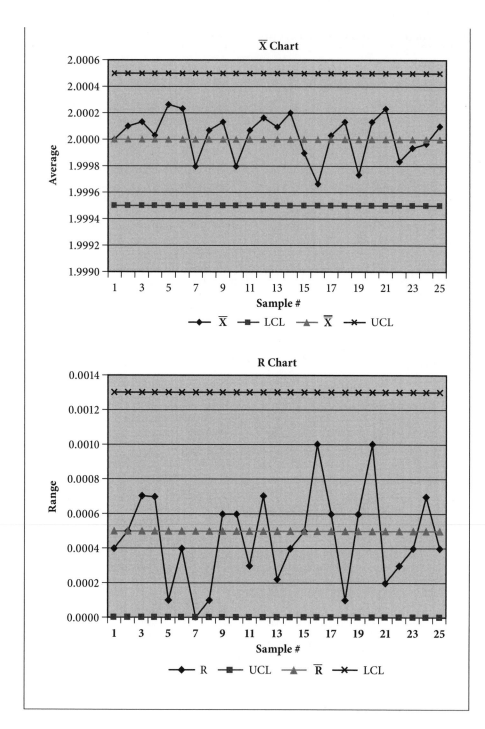

When the control charts are developed as described, they can then be placed next to the process where the data was gathered and used to monitor ongoing performance. The assumptions we make here are that the users are trained in how to gather sample data, measure it, plot it, and then interpret the plots; and that most importantly, the process is in control to begin with (as mentioned earlier, the firm would not want to design control charts using a process that is already out of control). As a check, the original 25 sample means and ranges can be plotted on their respective control charts to see if the process appears to be in control.

Table 13.6	Factors Used to Calculate 3-Sigma Limits for the $\overline{X}$ Chart and the R Chart		
SIZE OF SAMPLE	FACTOR FOR LCL AND UCL FOR $\overline{X}$ CHARTS (A_2)	FACTOR FOR LCL FOR R CHARTS (D_3)	FACTOR FOR UCL FOR R CHARTS (D_4)
2	1.880	0	3.267
3	1.023	0	2.575
4	0.729	0	2.282
5	0.577	0	2.115
6	0.483	0	2.004
7	0.419	0.076	1.924
8	0.373	0.136	1.864
9	0.337	0.184	1816
10	0.308	0.223	1.777

For both charts, an in-control process will exhibit plots that (1) fall randomly around the center line, (2) are mostly close to the center line with no plots outside the control limits, and (3) have no visual data patterns. If either chart fails to exhibit any of the three stipulations, then assignable causes of variation are likely to be present and evaluators should investigate the process further, either by gathering more sample data to plot or by going through the PDSA framework steps.

Some of the specific data patterns that might trigger an investigation for assignable causes include:

1. One or more data points falling outside of the control limits;
2. A run of eight points on one side of the center line;
3. Two of three consecutive points falling outside a 2-sigma limit, but still inside the control limits;
4. Four of five consecutive points that are beyond a 1-sigma limit; and
5. An unusual or nonrandom pattern in the data such as:
   a. A trend of seven points in a row upward or downward, or
   b. Cycles in the data.

If assignable causes of variation are suspected when plotting the original data used to design the control charts, the process needs to be first improved prior to gathering another set of data that would then be used to design more accurate control charts.

Attribute Data Control Charts (P Charts)

As stated earlier, P charts are used to study attribute or pass/fail data. The P chart is used to monitor the percentage of nonconforming or defective items produced in one lot. For example, a hotel manager might review customer feedback surveys for the past week, calculate the percentage reporting a negative experience, and compare it to a goal the hotel has set for customer satisfaction. While the data for P charts are relatively easy to collect, a large sample size (large enough to discover a defect) is required to make the results statistically valid. Thus, each sample collected may have up to 100 or even more observations. After collecting a number of samples over a period of time, the mean percent defective, or $\overline{P}$, is calculated and used as the center line of the P chart. The sample standard deviation is then calculated and used to construct the control limits. The formulas for $\overline{P}$, the sample standard deviation, and the 3-standard deviation control limits are:

$$\overline{P} = \frac{P_1 + P_2 + P_3 + \ldots + P_k}{k}$$

$$S_P = \sqrt{\frac{\overline{P}(1 - \overline{P})}{n}}$$

$$UCL_{\overline{p}} = \overline{P} + 3S_P$$

$$LCL_{\overline{p}} = \overline{P} - 3S_P$$

where:

P_i = the percent defective in the ith sample (or the number of sample defects divided by the sample size)
$\overline{P}$ = average percent defective for all samples
k = number of samples
S_p = sample standard deviation
n = number of items *in one sample*

(Note that if the calculated lower control limit is less than zero, a value of zero is used since a negative percent defective cannot occur.) The P chart can then be used to

Example 13.8   Control Chart Construction Using Attribute Data

Arizona Federal Savings Bank monitored its customers' credit card statements for 30 days in order to construct a process control chart for customer service. Each day the billing department selected a random sample of 200 bills and reviewed them for accuracy. Any mistakes were viewed as a customer service failure. The following table shows the results for the 30-day period:

SAMPLE #	NUMBER OF BILLS WITH ONE OR MORE MISTAKES	P	SAMPLE #	NUMBER OF BILLS WITH ONE OR MORE MISTAKES	P
1	10	.05	16	7	.035
2	12	.06	17	9	.045
3	7	.035	18	8	.04
4	8	.04	19	14	.07
5	5	.025	20	3	.015
6	14	.07	21	1	.005
7	6	.03	22	5	.025
8	9	.045	23	10	.05
9	3	.015	24	8	.04
10	2	.01	25	3	.015
11	12	.06	26	8	.04
12	14	.07	27	7	.035
13	16	.08	28	4	.02
14	14	.07	29	1	.005
15	12	.06	30	10	.05
			Total Bills with Mistakes	242	

The billing department prepared a P chart based on the following calculations:

$$\overline{P} = 242/[(30)(200)] = 0.0403$$

$$S_p = \sqrt{\frac{(0.0403)(1 - 0.0403)}{200}} = 0.0139$$

$$LCL_{\overline{p}} = 0.0403 - 3(0.0139) = -0.0014 = 0$$

$$UCL_{\overline{p}} = 0.0403 + 3(0.0139) = 0.082$$

The P chart with plots looks like:

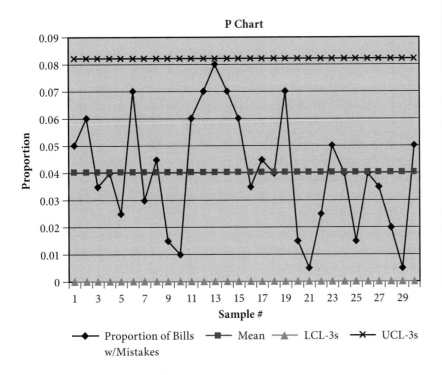

Based on the control chart, the process does not appear to be out of control.

monitor percent defectives in the process, again assuming that the process was in control to begin with when the control chart was designed. The original data collected can be analyzed to ensure the process was indeed in control. Interpreting the data plots can proceed similar to the variable data charts. If any plotted points fall outside the upper control limits or there are any unusual trends, an investigation to identify and eliminate assignable causes of variation is warranted. Note that for attribute data only one type of control chart is needed. Also be aware that the evaluator should not be very concerned if a plot falls below the lower control limit, since this indicates a smaller percent defective (which is most often viewed as a good thing). An example using attribute data is presented in Example 13.8.

While it would be ideal for each sample size to be the same, there are times when the sample size may vary because the number of units produced in a period may vary, or because of the difficulty in collecting equal-sized samples. For example, a hotel may randomly survey hotel guests each day and analyze the results weekly, but the number of guests each day may vary. To compensate for a variable sample size, the average sample size, $\overline{n}$, can be used to calculate approximate control limits and to plot data. The formula for the sample standard deviation in this case would be:

$$S_P = \sqrt{\frac{\overline{P}(1-\overline{P})}{\overline{n}}}, \text{ and}$$

$\overline{P}$ would simply be calculated using the actual number in each sample.

Example 13.9 provides an example using this method. In this example, there is one plotted value above the upper control limit, which should be investigated. The control chart itself should also be redesigned when the guest complaint problem has been reduced.

Quality Management along the Supply Chain

While internal process quality management and control are important, many companies also develop performance standards for their suppliers. These standards are part of a **supplier quality assurance program**, which helps instill confidence that a supplier's product or service will fulfill the buyer's needs. Collaborative relationships between the buyer and supplier are created to ensure products will be fit for use with minimal corrective action and inspection.

For example, California-based router and switch manufacturer Cisco Systems makes switching equipment that connects to the Internet. Its network of suppliers, distributors, and contract manufacturers are connected through Cisco's extranet, forming a virtual supply chain. As customer orders come in, messages are instantly posted to con-

---

Example 13.9   Creating a P Chart When the Sample Size Varies

Our Lady of Perpetuity Hospital has patients complete a satisfaction questionnaire before they are released. Following is the data collected on satisfaction with the hospital room for a recent 15-week period.

WEEK	NUMBER OF RESPONDENTS	NUMBER DISSATISFIED	P
1	45	2	.044
2	48	3	.063
3	42	2	.048
4	51	2	.039
5	49	3	.061
6	43	3	.07
7	52	5	.096
8	44	3	.068
9	49	1	.02
10	48	4	.083
11	42	3	.043
12	47	2	.043
13	55	4	.073
14	46	1	.022
15	47	3	.064
Total	**708**	**41**	

Because the number of surveys collected each week varied, a P chart was prepared using the following calculations:

$$\bar{n} = 708/15 = 47.2$$

$$\bar{P} = 41/708 = 0.0579$$

$$S_p = \sqrt{\frac{(0.0579)(1 - 0.0579)}{47.2}} = 0.034$$

$$UCL_{\bar{p}} = 0.0579 + 0.034 = 0.0919$$

$$LCL_{\bar{p}} = 0.0579 - 0.034 = 0.0239$$

And the P chart with plots would look like:

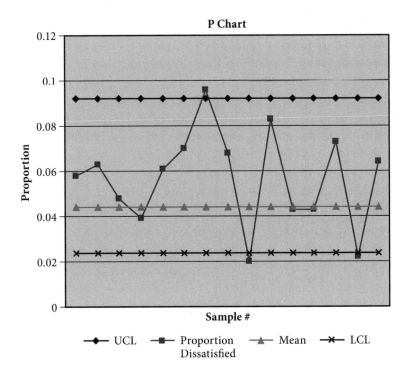

One data point is above the upper control limit and most of the data points are above the center line, which are causes for concern. The two plots below the lower control limit are not of any concern.

tract manufacturers through the extranet. Distributors also receive a message to ship any generic components such as the power supply. As time progresses, Cisco uses the extranet to monitor each contractor's assembly line to ensure the order will be completed on time. This is possible because factory assemblers place a printed bar code on each part as it comes off the assembly line, then scan it and "plug" the part into Cisco's online testing software. Cisco can then look up the bar code, match it to the customer's order, and make sure it meets the customer's requirements. If the part meets the customer's specifications, Cisco releases the customer's name and address to the contractor so the part can be shipped.[33] Intel, the leading semiconductor manufacturer headquartered in California, also knows the importance of supplier quality and implemented a supplier continuous quality improvement initiative several years ago to raise the bar of quality performance. More on Intel can be found in the Global Perspective feature.

To create this kind of collaborative environment, product or service quality performance should be a major factor in the selection of suppliers whenever possible. In fact, total quality performance generally ranks as one of the three most important elements of supplier evaluation and selection in a number of studies on this topic.[34] Other important factors considered include the state of the supplier's facilities, safety programs, equipment maintenance, use of statistical process control, and commitment to quality. For critical parts, purchasing and supply departments may base their selection criteria on the **Malcolm Baldrige Award** criteria or one of the **International Organization for Standardization** (ISO) certification sets of requirements. More on these topics follows.

Global Perspective

Intel Looks for World's Best

When you consider what impact a quality problem could have on Intel's bottom line, it's no wonder that the largest global semiconductor manufacturer strives to have the best suppliers in the world. The cornerstone of Intel's quality system is its Supplier Continuous Quality Improvement (scqi) program that was initially instituted in 1987. To win Intel's coveted scqi award, suppliers have to meet and adhere to rigorous quality standards set forth by three high-level requirements—a supplier report card score, a Standard Supplier Quality Assessment (ssqa), and a scqi plan that measures how well the supplier has met its improvement goals.

How well a supplier performs to these requirements determines its eligibility for either Intel's Preferred Quality Supplier (PQS) or scqi award. In both cases, suppliers are expected to meet a high level of performance in key areas of cost, technology, quality, on-time delivery, and responsiveness. The differentiation comes about in terms of how high the scores are. "These programs drive improvements among all of our suppliers and recognize that suppliers meet certain performance goals," says Dave Martinich, materials quality systems manager for Intel Corp., Chandler, Arizona.

Intel began the scqi program primarily because of the impact that suppliers have on its business results, Martinich says. "If you take a look at what Intel's revenues are, any kind of problem from a supplier such as a delivery problem or quality issue has an enormous potential revenue impact on Intel. It's much more than any other semiconductor company in the world," Martinich says. "If we have a problem with a supplier it could mean a billion dollars to us. There aren't too many other semiconductor manufacturers that face a billion-dollar jeopardy if there is a supplier problem."

The result is a set of extremely high standards for its supply base. "We've decided to take a leadership role with the scqi program and drive improvements among our supply base. The fundamental goal of scqi is to help our suppliers become better companies," Martinich says.

And the winners of Intel's coveted scqi award agree that the company has driven them to become quality suppliers on a road to continuous improvement. Earlier this year, Intel announced the three winners of Intel's scqi award that include Kester Solder, Pulse, and Racal Instruments. Kester provides solder flux and pastes, Pulse supplies magnetic components for data networking and power, and Racal provides systems testers.

Stephen Santangelo, vice president of quality assurance for Kester Solder Division, Litton Systems Inc., Des Plaines, Illinois, says: "In terms of customer requirements, Intel's quality systems and other special requirements are more stringent and a higher level of requirements than the typical customer we have. Intel has been a driver for change within Kester because they forced us to make improvements which have been helpful. It has given us a better ability to support other customers of the same caliber of Intel," Santangelo adds.

Martinich explains that when Intel talks about total quality, it goes beyond just the technical elements such as how many defective units were sent to Intel. It translates into all issues that impact Intel or Intel's customers. "For instance, when we look at the availability of materials," Martinich says. "Do we get the materials at the right factory, in the right amount, at the right time when we need it. We also look at the supplier's readiness to jump to the next level of technology when Intel needs it."

Intel's scqi program is centered on the weak link in the chain theory. The quality of Intel's product is only as good as the poorest-quality supplier that goes into that product, Martinich says. "If we can make our supply base a stronger link that will make Intel a stronger link in its supply chain to its own customers. We look at a program like scqi to try to drive improved performance among our suppliers."

Source: Roos, G., "Intel Looks for World's Best," *Purchasing,* November 16, 2000, available at http://www.purchasing.com/article/CA139654.html?text=iso+9000. Reprinted with permission.

The Malcolm Baldrige Award

The Malcolm Baldrige Award was created in 1987 to motivate U.S. companies to improve the quality of their products. Only U.S. organizations are eligible, and winners of the award are profiled at the National Institute of Standards and Technology (NIST) website (http://www.quality.nist.gov/) and in various press releases, so others can learn how to manage quality through their example. Criteria were set up and have been periodically revised to help non-profit and for-profit organizations evaluate their efforts to improve quality, to facilitate communication on best practices, and to serve as a working tool to help them manage performance. These are shown in Figure 13.3. The seven criteria are leadership, information and analysis, strategic planning, human resource focus, process management, business results, and customer and market focus.

Leadership, strategic planning, and customer and market focus represent the leadership triad, and are grouped together to emphasize the importance of leadership in developing a good strategy and to achieve high levels of customer satisfaction. Human resource focus, process management, and business results represent the second triad, focusing on results. All of these criteria point toward business results, which is a composite of the organization's performance in terms of product and service quality, customers and the market, and operational performance. Ongoing through the process is measurement and analysis of all facets of the model.

Companies often look to see if suppliers are modeling their quality program based on the Malcolm Baldrige Award. Organizations like Caterpillar Financial Services, mentioned earlier in this chapter, also use the Baldrige Award criteria to assess their own organization and guide their continual improvement efforts.

ISO 9000 Standards

Companies may also require suppliers to have certification in one or more ISO standards. For many U.S. suppliers, this is a cost of doing business, particularly in Europe. The International Organization for Standardization (ISO), a non-government organization headquartered in Geneva, Switzerland, includes members from national standards organizations in over 130 countries. Its goal is to assist countries in developing some agreement on global quality standards through formal agreements. For example, the standards for the physical attributes of credit cards, such as thickness, were developed by the ISO. These standards ensure that credit cards can be used worldwide. ISO has a family of ten standards and guidelines but ISO 9000, 9001, and 9004 are the most broadly used. ISO 9000 covers quality management systems vocabulary and fundamentals; ISO 9001 addresses quality management systems requirements to attain customer satisfaction; and ISO 9004 provides guidelines for performance improvements in a company's quality management system.

| Figure 13.3 | Malcolm Baldrige Criteria |

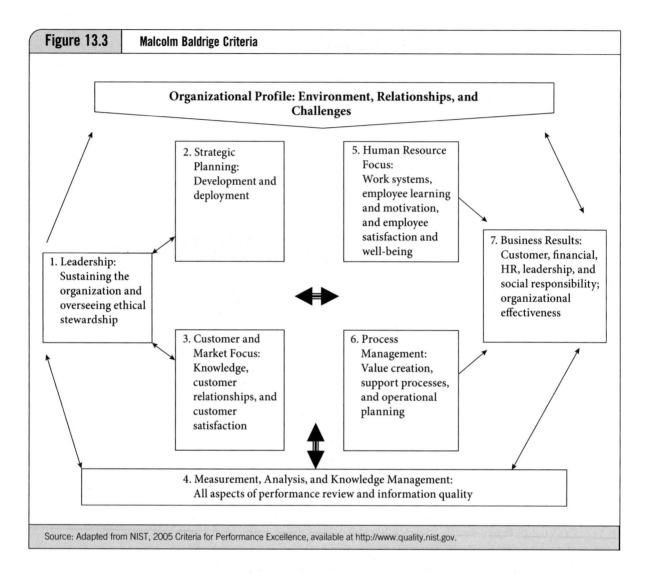

Organizational Profile: Environment, Relationships, and Challenges

2. Strategic Planning: Development and deployment

5. Human Resource Focus: Work systems, employee learning and motivation, and employee satisfaction and well-being

1. Leadership: Sustaining the organization and overseeing ethical stewardship

7. Business Results: Customer, financial, HR, leadership, and social responsibility; organizational effectiveness

3. Customer and Market Focus: Knowledge, customer relationships, and customer satisfaction

6. Process Management: Value creation, support processes, and operational planning

4. Measurement, Analysis, and Knowledge Management: All aspects of performance review and information quality

Source: Adapted from NIST, 2005 Criteria for Performance Excellence, available at http://www.quality.nist.gov.

To be certified using ISO 9001, a company must meet all the requirements laid out (unless there are activities or functions not performed by that company). For example, a company must know and periodically review its customer requirements, make sure those requirements are attained, and measure and monitor customer satisfaction. A company must also show how it takes preventive and corrective actions to continuously improve customer satisfaction.

Collaborative Planning Activities

Once suppliers are selected, joint or collaborative quality planning activities should take place, according to J. M. Juran, a noted quality expert mentioned earlier in this chapter. Customers will often expect suppliers to develop quality plans in line with their own if they have not already done so. Suppliers may also be asked to develop a plan in line with certain certification standards, such as ISO 9000. Customers may specify second- and third-tier suppliers that the supplier may use, evaluate and certify second- and third-tier suppliers and their quality systems, or assist their direct suppliers in managing these suppliers.

Customers also may cooperate with their suppliers during the execution of the purchase contract to help them attain set quality standards. Illinois-based telecommunications company Motorola, for example, developed in-house statistical process control software and distributed it to their first- and second-tier suppliers so they could uniformly submit material to incoming inspection areas. [35]

Quality Assurance

During the purchase contract period, the customer may also require proof of conformance to its quality requirements. For example, quality control charts or other reports are often required. Companies may also send teams to audit their suppliers' facilities.

As discussed in Chapter 12, certification of key suppliers is often done to ensure high levels of quality. Certification means that the supplier's processes and methods are in full control and shipped parts and components do not have to be inspected by the customer upon receipt. To attain certification, a supplier may need to allow its customer's inspection team to perform a detailed audit of its manufacturing site. Of course, the risk for the supplier is a loss of the customer's business, or demands for improvement before further business is awarded. To maintain the desired level of quality, the customer may also periodically reevaluate the supplier.

Lastly, customers will create and use supplier quality ratings to ensure continued quality. Kansas-based light aircraft manufacturer Cessna, for example, uses a supplier rating system known as STARS 2000, which rates supplier performance based on recently collected data. Four areas are measured—quality, reliability, cost performance, and adherence to schedule—on a scale of 1 (outstanding) to 5 (unacceptable). Should a supplier receive a 5 in any area, Cessna will make a formal request for corrective action, requiring a documented response. The supplier must respond in a timely manner, or experience a negative impact on future business.

Measuring Quality along the Supply Chain

As pointed out earlier, processes often cross over multiple organizations. Quality is reflected in any materials purchased from suppliers and subcontractors, internally in the production process, during outbound shipments to customers, and after the purchase.

Some metrics used to measure process capability along the supply chain include **total supply chain material costs**, **average supply chain delivery performance**, and **average supply chain perfect order performance**. Total supply chain material costs is a measure of the monies spent for purchase and use of materials, including any additional funds spent due to defective materials along the supply chain. Organizations need to know not only the amount of total waste but where it's happening in the supply chain, so a process of continuous improvement can begin to take place. Average supply chain delivery performance represents the average percentage of orders filled and delivered on time to each receiving member in the supply chain. Tracking delivery performance will help determine why the final customer may or may not receive their order as specified and when to begin the process of improvement. Lastly, average supply chain perfect order performance is a measure of the average percent of orders received not only on time, but complete and damage free. As pointed out earlier, Cisco uses this measure and has increased its performance through the use of the Internet. [36]

SUMMARY

This chapter has focused on methods to gain continuous improvements in quality of organizational processes across the supply chain. To improve, organizations must first have a good understanding of what quality means to their customer base. Thus, they must establish a basis to determine whether or not they are offering a quality product or service. A planning process to set quality goals needs to be established. However, the greatest challenge lies in implementing the quality plan and maintaining a high level of motivation and commitment among employees.

Controlling quality is also important and this chapter has introduced some quality tools that help this process. Beyond quality within the organization, however, it's more important than ever to monitor and improve quality across the supply chain. Some guidelines for meeting this challenge have been included at the end of the chapter.

KEY TERMS

4-Ms, 506

appraisal costs, 488

assignable causes of variation, 502

attribute data, 510

average supply chain delivery performance, 523

average supply chain perfect order performance, 523

benchmarking, 497

cause-and-effect diagram, 506

check sheet, 505

common causes of variation, 502

continuous improvement, 485

control chart, 504

Deming Plan-Do-Study-Act (PDSA) Cycle, 502

external failure costs, 489

fishbone diagram, 506

histogram, 505

internal failure costs, 489

International Organization for Standardization, 519

Ishikawa diagram, 506

kaizen, 485

lower control limit, 511

Malcolm Baldrige Award, 519

Pareto chart, 505

poor-quality costs, 488

prevention costs, 489

process capability, 490

process capability index, 493

process capability ratio, 492

process variation, 501

quality niche strategy, 496

return on assets, 500

sample size, 511

sampling frequency, 511

sampling plan, 510

strategic quality planning, 495

supplier quality assurance program, 518

total resources method, 490

total supply chain material costs, 523

Type I error, 510

Type II error, 510

unit cost method, 490

upper control limit, 511

value added per employee, 500

variable data, 510

DISCUSSION QUESTIONS

1. Describe continuous improvement and find an example of one company that practices continuous improvement. What are some ways that a company motivates its employees to improve?

2. What are four areas of a manufacturing or service organization where improvement efforts can be focused?

3. What are the three costs of poorly performing processes? Give at least two examples of each cost.

4. What are Garvin's eight dimensions of quality? Select a company and give an example of each dimension.

5. What are prevention costs of quality? Why are they important to an organization?

6. What is process capability? How do organizations use process capability measures to improve quality?

7. Briefly describe the quality planning process. Why should companies go through this process periodically?

8. What is a quality niche strategy? Find a company you are familiar with and describe their quality niche strategy.

9. List at least three factors that help ensure companies are successful in implementing their quality plan.

10. Using the quality maturity matrix, identify companies that are at each stage of maturity.

11. Companies often find themselves in a quality "mess." What is some evidence of a "mess"?

12. Describe the Plan-Do-Study-Act Cycle developed by Deming.

13. What is process variability? How is it used to control quality?

14. What is the difference between common causes and assignable causes of variation?

15. How are control charts used to control quality?

16. Why are companies spending more time monitoring their supplier's quality? What are some ways companies are working to improve the quality of their suppliers?

17. Visit a bank, fast-food restaurant, dry cleaners, or grocery store. What are the processes where control charts could be used?

18. Investigate a quality problem where you work or at school. Develop a checklist based on the data you have collected. What was the single biggest cause of the quality problem? Based on this chapter, what would be your next steps to find possible solutions to the problem?

PROBLEMS

1. Two Buck Chuck's sells fine wines and cheeses online and has experienced a number of problems with its customer ordering process, resulting in customer complaints and lost sales. Senior management has assembled a quality team and assigned it the task of determining what projects will result in the biggest improvement in its operations based on the cost of complaints and lost sales. The team decides to look at the costs of ordering, and comes up with seven categories of problems, shown in the following table.

COST CATEGORY	COST ($000s)	CUMULATIVE Cost ($000s)	CUMULATIVE PERCENT
Spoilage: Spoiled cheeses/broken wine bottles received from supplier	$ 20		
Returns: Customer returns/price reduction	110		
Short Orders: Losses from short orders	75		
Downtime: Website downtime	40		
Breakdowns: Equipment breakdowns in the warehouse	10		
Turnover: Employee turnover	15		

Complete the table and create a Pareto chart. Based on your results, where should Two Buck Chuck's focus its improvement efforts (and why)? State your justification.

2. Penny's Party Clothing is a small mail-order company that contracts with Upscale Postal Service (UPS) to deliver orders to its customers. Because Penny's customers often plan to wear their purchases within a few days, Penny's goal is to process orders and get them to the customer within three days. Thus, Penny's also expects Upscale Postal Service to pick orders from its warehouse and deliver them quickly. Penny's promises its customers that orders will be delivered within three days, +/− one day.

Penny's distribution manager, Chuck, has developed a quality control plan and tracked UPS's delivery times by randomly selecting five orders each day. The data collected is as follows:

	OBSERVATIONS				
SAMPLE	D1	D2	D3	D4	D5
1	5	4	6	3	1
2	6	4	3	3	3
3	3	3	1	5	4
4	2	1	5	5	3
5	4	4	3	4	1
6	5	1	3	2	3
7	2	3	5	1	6
8	1	3	1	4	2
9	5	3	3	6	4
10	6	8	3	1	3
11	6	1	3	3	2
12	5	3	4	4	5
13	6	2	2	2	4
14	4	5	3	3	2

a. Construct an $\overline{X}$ chart and an R chart using three standard deviations. Are assignable causes of variation present? Why/why not?

b. The standard deviation for the process is 0.1914. Use the process standard deviation given to calculate the process capability ratio and index. Is the process capable of meeting Penny's delivery promises?

3. As part of its quality control plan, Penny's Party Clothing has an 800 phone number where customers can call with problems, complaints, or questions. Penny's customer service manager, Pauline, reviews the records for 200 calls received each week and keeps a tally of those she considers complaints. Following are her records for the past 20 weeks:

WEEK	COMPLAINT CALLS	WEEK	COMPLAINT CALLS
1	25	11	21
2	13	12	10
3	35	13	15
4	38	14	16
5	17	15	24
6	21	16	29
7	19	17	13
8	15	18	16
9	31	19	24
10	33	20	31

Construct a P chart for this process using two standard deviation control limits. Are assignable causes of variation present?

4. Just Juice packages small boxes of juice. The weight specification for each box is 4.75 ounce, +/− 0.1 ounce. The operations manager monitors the process using an R chart and $\overline{X}$ chart. Four boxes are randomly selected every three hours and weighed. Data collected for the last ten samples is as follows:

SAMPLE	OBSERVATIONS (OUNCES)			
	1	2	3	4
1	4.80	4.86	4.75	4.85
2	4.68	4.89	4.77	4.75
3	4.65	4.75	4.89	4.77
4	4.81	4.70	4.75	4.76
5	4.75	4.88	4.89	4.80
6	4.77	4.85	4.75	4.82
7	4.80	4.82	4.88	4.80
8	4.82	4.81	4.72	4.75
9	4.75	4.77	4.80	4.76
10	4.73	4.70	4.75	4.80

a. Construct an R chart and $\overline{X}$ chart using the sample data. Are assignable causes present?

b. The operations manager has calculated the standard deviation of the process to be 0.009. Calculate the process capability ratio and index using the sample data. Is the process capable of filling boxes of juice to 4.75 ounces?

5. Just Juice (Problem 4) also visually inspects boxes of juice before shipment to make sure there are no defects. The number of boxes a quality assurance employee inspects varies, but any defective boxes are pulled off the production line. Following is the data on defective boxes for the past 12 hours:

HOUR	DEFECTIVE BOXES	# OF BOXES INSPECTED
8 a.m.	19	900
9 a.m.	25	1000
10 a.m.	55	950
11 a.m.	28	975
12 noon	35	1000
1 p.m.	12	990
2 p.m.	40	980
3 p.m.	29	950
4 p.m.	63	980
5 p.m.	39	1000
6 p.m.	44	960
7 p.m.	27	975

Construct a P chart using the sample data and three standard deviation control limits. Are assignable causes of variation present? Why/why not?

 ## INFOTRAC QUESTIONS

Access http://www.infotrac-thomsonlearning.com to answer the following questions:

1. Find three articles that describe quality management planning developed by companies. Compare and contrast the similarities and differences between each strategy. Include a bibliography.

2. Find articles that discuss quality management tools and write a paper comparing and contrasting each tool. Include a bibliography.

3. Find articles that address quality measurement in the supply chain and write a paper. Include a bibliography.

REFERENCES

DeFeo, J. A., and W. W. Barnard (2004), *Juran Institute's Six Sigma: Breakthrough and Beyond,* McGraw-Hill, New York, NY.

Evans, J. R., and W. M. Lindsay (1996), *The Management and Control of Quality,* West Publishing Company, New York, NY.

Russell, R. S., and B. W. Taylor III (2003), *Operations Management,* 4th Edition, Prentice Hall Inc., Upper Saddle River, NJ.

ENDNOTES

1. Crosby, P. B., *Quality Is Free,* New York: New American Library, 1980.

2. Tom Peters.

3. http://www.threecore.com.

4. Watkins, D. K., "Quality Management's Role in Global Sourcing," *Quality Progress,* V. 38, April 2005, p. 24.

5. These definitions and others of continuous improvement were found at http://www.google.com/search?hl=en&hs=NFL&lr=&client=firefox-a&rls=org.mozilla:en-US:official_s&oi=defmore&q=define:Continuous+Improvement.

6. DeFeo, J. A. and W. W. Barnard, *Juran Institute's Six Sigma: Breakthrough and Beyond,* New York, NY: McGraw-Hill, 2004.

7. *Global Sources,* http://www.hardware.globalsources.com.

8. See Hendricks, K. B. and V. Singhal, "Does Implementing an Effective TQM Program Actually Improve Operating Performance? Empirical Evidence from Firms That Have Won Quality Awards," *Management Science,* V. 43, 1997, pp. 1258–1274; Hendricks, K. B. and V. Singhal,

"The Long-Run Stock Performance of Firms with Effective TQM Programs," *Management Science,* V. 47, 2001, pp. 359–368.

9. See note 6 above.

10. Bielenberg, D., "The Financial Impact of Bad Customer Service," *Credit Control Journal,* V. 27, No. 4/5, 2006.

11. See note 6 above.

12. Krajewski, L. J. and L. P. Ritzman, *Operations Management: Strategy and Analysis,* Upper Saddle River, NJ: Pearson Education Inc., 2002, p. 146.

13. Crosby, P. B., *Quality Is Free: The Art of Making Quality Certain,* New York: New American Library, 1980.

14. McCormick, J., "Making it Right—Ford Motor Co. VP of Manufacturing Anne Stevens," *Automotive Industries,* June 2001, available at http://www.findarticles.com.

15. Deming, W. E., *Out of the Crisis,* Cambridge, MA: Massachusetts Institute of Technology, 1986, p. 180.

16. Alwattari, A., "Innovation Strategy: Does Your New Product Idea Really Solve a Customer Problem?" available at http://www.innovationtools.com/Articles/EnterpriseDetails.asp?a=149.

17. Flower, J., "Managing Quality: A Discussion with David Garvin," *Healthcare Forum,* V. 33, No. 5, 1990, available at http://www.well.com/user/bbear/garvin.html.

18. Cravit, C. R., "Sun, Sea, and — Surgery?" *50-Plus.com,* 2006, accessed October 6, 2006 at http://en.50plus.com/display.cfm?libraryID=105&cabinetID=323&documentID=13852.

19. "Digital versus Film-Screen Mammography," *Detroit Free Press,* September 17, 2005, available at http://www.freep.com.

20. Remarks by Michael J. Sabia, President and CEO of Bell Canada Enterprises, at the Canadian Telecom Summit, Toronto, Ontario, on June 17, 2004.

21. A profile of The Bama Companies, Inc. is available at http://www.nist.gov/public_affairs/releases/2004baldrigewinners.htm.

22. http://www.quotesandpoem.com/quotes/listquotes/subject/failure.

23. More information on Caterpillar can be found at http://www.nist.gov/public_affairs/baldrige2003/Catrpllar_3.3.04.pdf.

24. Documentation for suppliers can be found at http://www.newellrubbermaid.com/newellco/aboutus/business.jhtml?id=id2&frag=qualityAssurance.

25. Evans, J. R. and W. M. Lindsay, *The Management and Control of Quality,* 3rd Edition, New York: West Publishing Company, 1996, p. 351.

26. Ackoff, R., *The Art of Problem Solving,* New York: Wiley, 1978.

27. Deming, W. E., *Out of the Crisis,* Cambridge, MA: MIT Center for Advanced Engineering, 1986.

28. Cleary, B. A., "Supporting Empowerment with Deming's PDSA Cycle," *Empowerment in Organizations,* Vol. 3 (Issue 2), 1995, pp. 34–39.

29. Evans, J. R. and W. M. Lindsay, *The Management and Control of Quality,* 3rd Edition, Minneapolis, MN: West Publishing Co., 1996, p. 365.

30. Data was included in a class project for Operations Management, Fall 2004.

31. Cochran, W. G., *Sampling Techniques,* 3rd Edition, Hoboken, NJ: John Wiley & Sons, 1977.

32. Wheeler, D. J. and D. S. Chambers, *Understanding Statistical Process Control,* 2nd Edition, Knoxville, TN: SPC Press Inc., 1992.

33. Koch, C., "The ABCs of Supply Chain Management," *CIO Magazine,* June 22, 2002, available at http://www.cio.com.

34. See, for example, Carr, A. S. and J. N. Pearson, "Strategically Managed Buyer-Supplier Relationships and Performance Outcomes," *Journal of Operations Management,* V. 17, No. 5, 1999, pp. 497–519; Kannan, V. R. and K. C. Tan, "Supplier Selection and Assessment: Their Impact on Business Performance," *Journal of Supply Chain Management,* Fall 2002, pp. 11–20; Verma, R. and M. E. Pullman, "An Analysis of the Supplier Selection Processes," *OMEGA: International Journal of Management,* V. 26, No. 6, 1998, pp. 739–750.

35. "Motorola Offers Innovative Manufacturing Process Software for Improved Profitability," June 4, 2001, available at http://news.thomasnet.com/fullstory/5054.

36. Wisner, J. D., G. K. Leong, and K. C. Tan, *Principles of Supply Chain Management: A Balanced Approach,* Mason, OH: South-Western, 2005 pp. 442–443.

Chapter 14:

SIX SIGMA—TAKING QUALITY IMPROVEMENT TO THE NEXT LEVEL

"We (now) use Six Sigma as our breakthrough improvement methodology for our most significant and complex projects, where we need a team-based, structured approach that lends itself to using statistical/analytical tools."[1]

"I look at Six Sigma as a foundation on which you can build more innovation."[2]

Learning Objectives

After completing this chapter, you should be able to:

- Describe the role of Six Sigma initiatives in breakthrough process improvement.
- Understand the various roles of employees in implementing Six Sigma.
- Describe the DMAIC cycle.
- Understand the documentation needed to implement a successful Six Sigma project.
- Apply analysis tools to Six Sigma projects.
- Describe the organizational requirements to make breakthrough process improvements.
- Understand the role of Six Sigma in the supply chain.
- Discuss some of the challenges in implementing Six Sigma initiatives.

Chapter Outline

Process Management in Action

Dow's Innovative Use of Six Sigma

Reducing moving vehicle accidents (MVAs) is just one facet of Dow's overall commitment to safety and health. Dow is a science and technology company that develops, manufactures, and provides chemical, plastic, and agricultural products and services to customers in over 180 countries. In 1994, Dow adopted a set of voluntary ten-year environmental, health, and safety (EH&S) goals designed to dramatically improve its performance by 2005, one of which called for a reduction in the number of MVAs per million miles by 50 percent (from a 1994 base). As part of this initiative, Dow's Hydrocarbon and Energy (HC&E) business unit launched a project in 2002 to reduce MVAs by its employees. HC&E procures the fuels and crude oil–based raw materials and supplies, and the power that Dow uses in its global operations.

From September 1, 2001, to August 31, 2002, there were 25 work-related MVAs among HC&E employees. The drivers involved in the accidents were the sales and marketing personnel who drive to client sites, and the employees who drive vehicles on-site at HC&E facilities. In addition to personal injuries, the MVAs contributed to lost sales and productivity while the HC&E employees were away from work recovering from their injuries. To reduce these negative consequences, HC&E management decided to launch an effort using the Six Sigma methodology to understand the causes of MVAs and implement permanent improvements that would allow HC&E to meet its goal of a 50 percent reduction in MVAs.

THE MEASURE PHASE

HC&E created an MVA project team that established an initial goal of reducing MVAs by 20 percent over a 12-month period to be followed by continued reductions until the 2005 goal was achieved. After creating a project charter, which defined the project's timelines and objectives, the team began to collect information on the variables associated with MVAs. These variables included factors related to the accident, the driver, and the vehicle driven, along with details of the accident itself.

THE ANALYZE PHASE

After identifying the variables associated with MVAs, the team divided them into three categories of possible risk factors: methods, people, and environment. Variables in the methods category were related to driving skills; risk factors in the people category were largely behavioral; and variables in the environment category were related to both the driver and the condition of the environment. The team next performed a root-cause evaluation that analyzed the probability of each risk factor occurring and determined whether it was measurable. The actual MVAs were then classified according to (1) site (i.e., off-site, on-site, business sites, plant within site), (2) environmental conditions (e.g., weather, light), (3) vehicle (i.e., Dow-owned or leased), and (4) moving backward or not.

Next, the team studied the police and accident reports of the MVAs and surveyed the drivers involved to determine which factors played key roles in the accidents. The analysis confirmed that the following three variables were the root causes of most of the company's MVAs: not focusing on driving tasks in general, not having a clear picture of surroundings (e.g., not properly evaluating road conditions or other drivers), and not checking behind the vehicle before backing. Through its analysis, the team determined that all of the accidents involving backing up were avoidable as were 81 percent of the other accidents.

Continued

THE IMPROVE PHASE

After determining the most significant root causes of the MVAs through the analysis and validation steps, the team developed a series of driver procedures or steps to address the risk factors. For example, all drivers involved in MVAs were required to complete a course on defensive driving and have their driving observed by a supervisor in an "in-car" driver improvement course. These drivers develop a "Learning Experience Report," which is shared with other HC&E employees. In addition, topics pertaining to driving are discussed at monthly environmental, health, and safety meetings. Every employee must also review a ten-step "Arrive Alive" checklist before driving a Dow-owned or leased vehicle, and suggested procedures for backing up and guidelines for using cell phones are provided.

To ensure that all Dow HC&E employees understood the root causes of MVAs, the team published the findings of the Six Sigma project in *Drive to Zero,* the HC&E business unit's monthly EH&S improvement newsletter.

THE CONTROL PHASE

The final phase of the project required that controls be established to sustain the project's immediate MVA reduction and to develop further improvements in line with Dow's 2005 goals. The project team developed and held a series of specific presentations, some with general information geared to all drivers, and others with more in-depth information for drivers involved in MVAs and/or who drive over 30,000 miles per year in an assigned vehicle.

The project team also established new criteria for investigating future MVAs that provided for the continuing collection of relevant data. All MVAs became the subject of root-cause investigations, and the findings are reviewed and tracked by an MVA reduction team. As new risk behaviors are identified, this team is responsible for developing appropriate corrective measures and employee education programs.

THE RESULTS

The project was conducted during the third quarter of 2002, and the improvements and control plan put into place beginning January 2003. From 2001 to 2004, HC&E experienced a 30 percent reduction in MVAs. This number exceeded the 20 percent reduction established as the immediate goal by the project charter and placed the Dow HC&E business unit even closer than anticipated to its 2005 goal of 50 percent fewer MVAs. Following this success, many of the training materials developed by the project team (such as the Vehicle Pre-Startup Checklist) have been adopted for use at other Dow business units. The project team believes that the Six Sigma methodology was a key factor in the project's success.

Source: Adapted from U.S. Department of Labor, Occupational Safety & Health Organization, "Motor Vehicle Accident Case Study: The Dow Chemical Company's Use of 'Six Sigma' Methodology," December 2005, available at http://www.osha.gov/dcsp/success_stories/alliances/dow/motor_vehicle_case_study.html.

Introduction

W. Edwards Deming and Joseph M. Juran, two well-known quality experts, have argued that most of the quality problems experienced by companies are associated with the processes currently in place. As they have discussed over the past 50 years, and as it remains to this day, many companies don't have a good understanding of their customer requirements or their key processes. Often, cumbersome, costly processes have developed over time in response to company growth or downsizing, recent changes in technology, or new environmental and tax laws. In many instances, processes have never been formally assessed or documented. However, the results of a study by Professor Michael McGinnis indicate that well-designed processes do indeed contribute to a firm's competitive advantage.[3]

Thus, companies must first understand how their processes work and create value and then, as Deming and Juran stressed, continuously improve them in order to gain the organization the competitive advantage generally found in companies with high-quality, low-benefit products and great customer service. Organizations have adopted a number of assessment and improvement programs over the years as discussed in Chapters 9 and 13, including reengineering, total quality management, and ISO 9000. They have also used national awards such as the Malcolm Baldrige Award and the Deming Prize as roadmaps for improving quality. Currently, implementation of what is termed the **Six Sigma methodology** for quality improvement is experiencing an upward trend among organizations worldwide.

This chapter takes a deeper look at breakthrough process analysis and improvement using the Six Sigma methodology, and continues the discussion on quality management from Chapter 13. The next section provides a discussion of the term Six Sigma as it relates to process improvement, followed by sections describing in detail the Six Sigma methodology. The chapter continues with a discussion on the activities needed to make breakthrough improvements of business processes using Six Sigma and concludes with a discussion of implementing Six Sigma initiatives along the supply chain.

Defining Six Sigma

The Six Sigma methodology, known simply as Six Sigma, was pioneered by global communications leader Motorola, and is a data-driven framework designed to make *breakthrough* or very significant quality improvements in value-adding processes. It is loosely based on the quality concepts first developed by Deming, Juran, and others beginning in the 1920s. Six Sigma (with the capital S's) is actually a registered trademark of Motorola. During the mid-1980s, Illinois-based Motorola was facing stiff competition from foreign companies that were able to produce higher-quality products at a much lower cost. To better compete, the company designed the Six Sigma methodology to help it focus on attaining virtually error-free business performance.

Quality perfection is represented by the term Six Sigma, which refers to the statistical likelihood that 99.99966 percent of the time, a process sample average will fall below a control limit placed 4.5 standard deviations (or sigmas) above the true process mean, assuming the process is in control and the process sample measurements are normally distributed around the process mean. More importantly, this represents the goal of having a defect occur in a process only 0.00034 percent of the time, or 3.4 times out of every million measurement opportunities—a lofty goal.

But the Six Sigma concept is not only about statistics. The statistical description actually makes it sound like the methodology should be called 4.5 Sigma. The 1.5 sigma difference is rather arbitrary, and refers to a somewhat confusing term called **sigma drift**.[4] Sigma drift refers to an idea that process variations will grow over time, as process measurements drift off target. In truth, any process exhibiting a change in process variation of 1.5 sigma would be detected using quality control charts, instigating an improvement effort to get the process back on target.

Regardless of the origin and underpinnings of the name, Six Sigma is meant to embody more of a philosophy or organizational quality culture wherein everyone from the CEO to frontline service employees is involved (thus the use of capital letters to distinguish Six Sigma from the statistical meaning of six sigma). Today, many organizations practice Six Sigma, including early adopters Honeywell, General Electric, and Dow Chemical. These large, global U.S.-based firms and others focus on significantly improving the bottom line through benefit savings or increased sales as a result of breakthrough process improvements, not simply small incremental improvements. In fact, Motorola has stated that its savings to date from the use of Six Sigma has exceeded $17 billion.[5] This type of outcome is possible as firms uncover their customers' key requirements, review performance against Six Sigma performance standards, and then take the actions necessary to achieve those standards. The most successful projects meet strategic business objectives, reduce product and service variations to optimal levels, and produce a product or service that satisfies the customer.

A **defect** can be defined as any instance or event where a process, product, or service does not meet the customer's requirements, while an **opportunity** is a chance that a defect could occur, such as when process sample measurements are taken or when products are being used. Measuring and tracking defects and opportunities are part of the Six Sigma methodology. For example, if a manufacturing process exhibits performance of Three Sigma, it means that 93.3 percent of the time the output will be defect free, and 6.7 percent of the time a defect will occur. While this may sound pretty good, the manufacturer would actually produce defective output about 67,000 times per million units of output. Table 14.1 translates each value of Sigma into defects per million opportunities. Remember that the table values include the 1.5 sigma drift mentioned earlier, and the percentages of defect-free output refers to the portion of the normal curve that is below an upper control limit placed at the given number of standard deviations above the true process mean.

Example 14.1 provides the Sigma calculations for a mythical cable TV company. At a quality standard of Three Sigma, for instance, customers would be without cable TV the equivalent of 11.256 hours or approximately 675 minutes per week, which would be unacceptable to most customers. However, if the cable company can improve the quality

Table 14.1	Six Sigma Metrics	
NUMBER OF STANDARD DEVIATIONS ABOVE THE MEAN	**PERCENT OF OUTPUT THAT IS DEFECT FREE**	**DEFECTS PER MILLION OPPORTUNITIES**
2	69.15	308,537
2.5	84.13	158,686
3	93.32	66,807
3.5	97.73	22,750
4	99.38	6,210
4.5	99.865	1,350
5	99.977	233
5.5	99.9968	32
6	99.99966	3.4

Note: Standard deviations include 1.5 sigma "drift."

Example 14.1   Six Sigma at Surefire Cable Company

Surefire Cable Company provides cable TV service to the suburbs of a mid-sized Midwestern city. The company's customers currently experience cable outages averaging 11.256 hours/week, resulting in numerous complaints. What is the cable company's current quality standard in terms of Six Sigma? If Surefire Cable operated at Four Sigma, how many hours/week would cable customers experience outages? At Six Sigma?

SOLUTION:

Surefire Cable Company operates 24 hours/day, 7 days per week. This is the equivalent of 168 hours/week. Computing the defect rate:

11.256 hours/168 hours = 0.067 or 6.7 percent defect rate or
1 − 0.067 = 0.933 or 93.3 percent defect-free quality level.

Using the chart in Table 14.1, it is seen that the Surefire Cable Company is operating at the equivalent of Three Sigma.

At Four Sigma, the cable outages would be:
168 hours × (1 − 99.4%) = 1.01 non-operating hours per week

And at Six Sigma quality levels, the outages would be:
168 hours × (1 − 99.9997%) = 0.000504 non-operating hours, or 1.81 seconds per week.

---

standard to Four Sigma, cable outages would be reduced to about one hour per week, and if it can operate at Six Sigma, cable would be out less than two seconds per week.

As mentioned earlier, most processes embody multiple activities. Candy production, for instance, involves several activities, including purchasing the ingredients, inspecting them, mixing them, forming them, and then packaging the final product. If we assume that each of the five activities operates at Three Sigma, with the same loss of quality at every stage, this means that only 70.7 percent of the finished candy will be defect free based on the following calculation:

$$93.3\% \times 93.3\% \times 93.3\% \times 93.3\% \times 93.3\% = 70.7\%$$

In other words, there will be almost 30 percent of product losses due to quality problems within the five activities. Overall then, the process performs much worse than Three Sigma. This is a simple example but serves to illustrate how each activity of a process will probably have multiple steps with varying defect rates, acting collectively to drag down quality. To improve quality then, firms must analyze a process by analyzing each of its activities, and focus on the individual activities causing the greatest problems.

Mikel Harry and Richard Schroeder, authors of *Six Sigma: The Breakthrough Management Strategy,* state that most companies today operate at about the Three Sigma level, while a few have reached Four Sigma.[6] The difficulty for most companies is in finding ways to make changes that will result in significant overall process improvements. Improving from Four Sigma to Five Sigma requires a 27-fold performance improvement and improvement from Five Sigma to Six Sigma requires approximately another 60-fold improvement. While nearly impossible to achieve, many companies are still striving for Six Sigma by implementing the Six Sigma methodology to identify and minimize defects in their processes. The following sections provide a framework companies can use to design Six Sigma improvement programs, beginning with the roles people play in deploying Six Sigma projects.

Organizational Roles in Six Sigma Initiatives

The Six Sigma methodology operates best within a team environment. Thus, organizations need to understand the roles and responsibilities of each Six Sigma team, beginning with the leadership group.

Leadership Group

This group consists of executives who will be in charge of setting up the infrastructure for Six Sigma projects, selecting the projects and determining resource allocations, and reviewing project progress and assessing each project's impact on the firm's benefits and profitability. To successfully lead an organization through Six Sigma and achieve significant improvements, the leadership group must set clear performance goals and mobilize the workforce to pursue these goals in light of the company's mission and vision. As with any other organization-wide initiative, Six Sigma must have the full support and commitment from senior management.

Team Sponsor

The **team sponsor** or **project champion** is typically a **process owner**, a member of the **leadership group**, and someone who helps select the Six Sigma project. The term process owner describes a person who is accountable for the performance of a process and should have a good enough understanding of the process to be considered an expert. Whether the person's title is team sponsor, project champion, or process owner, he or she aids in the selection of the Six Sigma team, provides the team with the direction and rationale as to why the team was formed, and furnishes the team the scope of the project along with their goals and objectives. The team sponsor should be a facilitator, removing any obstacles to the team's progress and ultimate success in completing the project. Lastly, the team sponsor will be involved in making any major decisions on solutions that will be implemented.

Team Leader

A **team leader** helps guide the team through the Six Sigma project and is responsible for its completion. Thus, this person will work closely with the team sponsor, reviewing the project's progress and clarifying issues as they arise. The team leader will also select or aid in the selection of team members, manage the team by keeping the project on schedule, and motivate the team through virtual or face-to-face meetings and other forms of communication such as email and phone calls. He or she will also work with functional managers to transfer new solutions and processes to the operations level and document the final results.

Team Members

Team members work for the team leader and are chosen because of their particular expertise for the given project. Typically they will come from different functional areas of the organization, such as engineering, marketing, purchasing, and finance. They are responsible for implementing the project and report to the team leader. Teams should include people who (1) are from that part of the organization where the problem has been occurring, (2) are from area(s) where the *source* of the problem is likely to be found, (3) have good diagnostic skills, and (4) could be helpful in coming up with a solution. Each team member should have some direct knowledge of the problem and be readily available to serve on the team. Once the team has been formed, a kick-off meeting is often held to give team members an opportunity to meet, understand the project further, and develop a sense of purpose. The meeting also provides the process owner and project leader a chance to generate excitement for the project and set performance goals.

Six Sigma Coach

Some organizations use a **Six Sigma coach** or outside consultant who is primarily responsible for providing any required technical expertise to the process owner and team, but who may also be an expert in change management or process design strategies. A coach or consultant may be needed when the company is experiencing less than full cooperation from employees, when teams are experiencing dysfunctional behavior, or when teams are having difficulty sticking to the project schedule.

Six Sigma Specialists

The terms **Master Black Belt**, **Black Belt**, **Green Belt**, and **White Belt** are used in many Six Sigma organizations to describe employees with various levels of specialized skills in statistics and the technical aspects of process or product improvement. These are briefly reviewed next.

Black Belt

Motorola originated the use of the term Black Belt in conjunction with Six Sigma, drawing from the martial arts field. In general, Black Belts have at least 160 hours of Six Sigma training covering fairly sophisticated statistical techniques and other tools. The designation Master Black Belt is awarded as an employee gains experience, manages successful projects, and becomes an "expert" in statistics. Black Belts oversee the larger problems that may cross over functional and geographical boundaries and product lines. They may also oversee and approve the selection of Six Sigma projects.

Green Belt

Green Belts have received approximately 80 hours of Six Sigma training and are qualified to serve as team members on a Six Sigma project or oversee a medium-sized project that relates directly to their own position in the company. Honeywell, for example, used Green Belts to improve web development in its marketing program, resulting in a savings of $3.4 million. More on this project can be found in the e-Commerce Perspective feature.

White Belt

More recently, the designation White Belt has come into use for employees who lead Six Sigma projects that are considered too small for a Black Belt or a Green Belt. These projects are usually contained within a work cell or department and are completed within a month. White Belts receive about 40 hours of training in Six Sigma principles. Table 14.2 gives two possible structures using these designations.

Administrative Support Team

Larger organizations may also utilize an **administrative support team** or person to support the leadership group on issues related to project implementation. For example, this team may help in project selection or project reviews. They may also be called on to help in making personnel recommendations for key roles, develop training procedures, or document processes.

e-Commerce Perspective

Six Sigma Improves Design, Saves Money

Six Sigma, a quality improvement methodology that began as a manufacturing process, is helping business-to-business (B2B) companies save time and money on specific marketing tasks such as producing marketing collateral and improving website design. In an October 2004 article, *BtoB* examined how large industrial companies such as General Electric Co. and Dow Chemical Co. have begun using Six Sigma in marketing areas such as new product development and customer support to reduce benefits, improve performance, and boost the bottom line.

Other B2B companies, such as Honeywell and Cummins Engine Co., are realizing returns with Six Sigma by applying the process to specific marketing-related functions. Honeywell was an early adopter of Six Sigma, first implementing it in the early 1990s to improve its manufacturing processes. In 1999, following its merger with Allied-Signal—another Six Sigma company—Honeywell established an improved methodology called Six Sigma Plus. "Now, Six Sigma permeates everything we do," said Reid Walker, vice president of communications for Honeywell Specialty Materials, which manufactures chemicals, electronics materials, fibers, and other materials used in manufacturing.

GREEN BELT–CERTIFIED IN SIX SIGMA

Walker came to Honeywell from GE, where he was green belt–certified in Six Sigma. He is responsible for marketing communications, internal communications, media relations, advertising, and web development for Honeywell Specialty Materials. Recently, Walker spearheaded a project within the communications department to redesign the division's website, which previously had more than 50 separate sites for specialty materials.

"We wanted to develop a unified Web strategy and present a single face to the market," Walker said. He led a small team of Six Sigma–trained employees on the project, from communications, marketing, and IT. Using the standard DMAIC (define, measure, analyze, improve, and control) Six Sigma process, the team identified areas of improvement based on customer feedback.

CRITICAL TO QUALITY ISSUES

In interviews with customers, Honeywell defined critical to quality (CTQ) issues that should be addressed in the website redesign, from the readability of the font size to navigation paths on the site. "These issues formed the basis of the metrics that would define what is successful," Walker said. "We 'rescoped' it and built it from scratch on customer requirements."

Honeywell initially had about eight different design groups working on the site, each with its own style of writing, graphics, and design. "Every product line and group was recreating the site, and there was no consistency," Walker said. As part of the redesign, Honeywell consolidated its web design with Agency.com, although it still uses other outside web design firms for minor projects.

Using the Six Sigma process to implement and measure the changes identified as critical to quality, Honeywell Specialty Materials relaunched its site in March. "We have seen huge results," Walker said, pointing to projected benefit savings of $3.4 million for the first half of 2005 for the Specialty Materials site alone. The site has achieved a 104 percent increase in repeat visitors and has reduced its development costs by 84 percent. Now, Honeywell is using Six Sigma for its overall site design and has a project team of 50 to 60 people working on the project globally.

Source: Maddox, K., "Six Sigma Helps Marketing Improve Design, Save Money," *BtoB,* Vol. 89, No. 13, 2004, pp. 3–4. Reprinted with permission.

Table 14.2	Six Sigma Structures and Roles	
ROLE	**COMPANY A**	**COMPANY B**
Oversees and guides the project	Sponsor/Champion	Master Black Belt and Sponsor/Champion
Coaches or supports project leader	Master Black Belt	Black Belt
Leads the project to successful completion	Black Belt or Green Belt	Green Belt or Team Leader
Performs analysis and implements the solution	Improvement Team (White Belts)	Improvement Team (White Belts)

Source: Adapted from Pande, P. S., R. P. Neuman, and R. R. Cavanagh, *The Six Sigma Way,* New York, NY: McGraw-Hill, 2000.

Once the structure for a Six Sigma organization has been established and everyone understands the organization's strategic objectives, management can begin the process of selecting and then deploying improvement projects using the DMAIC cycle, discussed next.

The DMAIC Cycle

The **DMAIC cycle**, which stands for the stages Define, Measure, Analyze, Improve, and Control, is an integral part of the Six Sigma methodology developed by Motorola, and is utilized by Six Sigma teams to identify and improve any existing processes not meeting Six Sigma quality standards. The following sections provide a discussion of each phase of the DMAIC cycle as illustrated in Figure 14.1, along with descriptions of tools teams may use in Six Sigma projects to increase productivity and improve results.

The DMAIC Cycle Stages

The Define Stage

In this stage, organizations define who the relevant customers are, and what their requirements are for products and services. Processes are also identified and the process flows are mapped. Potential improvement projects are also identified when gaps between process outputs and customer requirements are found. These potential projects are then ranked and selected. A generic depiction of the project selection process is provided in Figure 14.2. The projects should also be tied to an organization's strategic goals. Once projects have been identified, organizations use a systematic review process to evaluate the Six Sigma proposals and then select the most promising ones to pursue. The formal review process is typically led by the firm's Master Black Belt or senior management team.

The Measure Stage

During this stage, the improvement teams for the selected Six Sigma projects create a data collection plan. Baseline performance measurements of the processes are taken and recorded. Measurements taken at this phase are tied to the inputs to the process that make an impact on process performance, and the outputs that affect customer satisfaction. Relevant data is collected, some of which may have been gathered during the

| Figure 14.1 | The DMAIC Cycle |

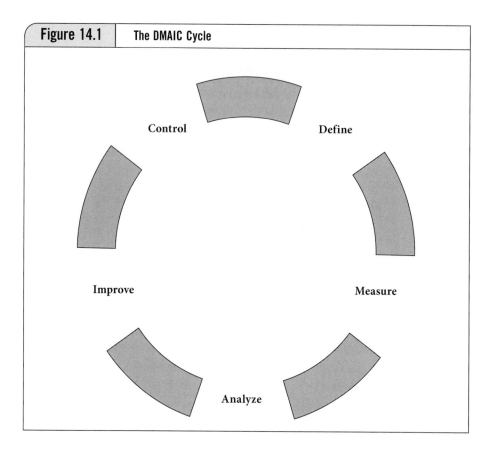

project selection phase. Check sheets such as those described in Chapter 13 might be used. A more detailed process flow map is also prepared, including all of the associated process activities, to provide an accurate picture of the current process to further understand what is currently taking place and where problems and assignable causes may be occurring. The process map should include all key inputs, each process step, all outputs, and value-added assessments. The process map details should be supported by documented information gathered from those involved in the process, including employees, process users, information systems, suppliers, and customers.

At this point, a more accurate and detailed comparison of customer requirements and process capabilities can be performed to determine if the firm can realize an improvement significant enough to justify continuing on with the improvement project. If the expected benefits do not appear to offset improvement costs it may be necessary to either abandon the project or reduce its scope. This detailed assessment may also lead the team toward other, more urgent problems that need to be addressed, resulting in the birth of other Six Sigma projects. If the project is pursued further, it will move to the Analyze stage, a phase of deeper analysis, wherein the team works to identify the key assignable causes most likely to be creating process variations.

The Analyze Stage

For projects in this stage, there has already been a considerable amount of measurement and analysis performed. The team should have a good understanding of the critical process inputs and activities that significantly impact the process outputs. Generating ideas for identification of assignable causes involves a review of the collected data and

Figure 14.2	Project Development Process

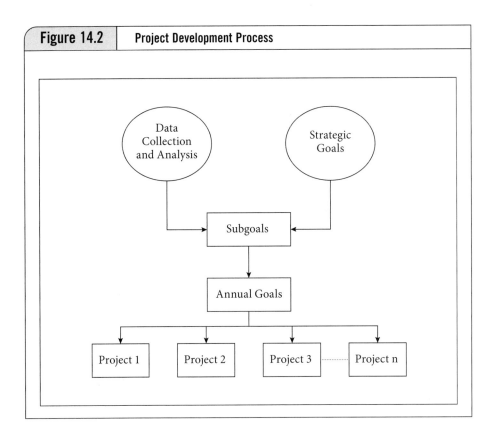

some brainstorming among the team members, using tools such as the fishbone diagram discussed in Chapter 13. The team should also test their list of potential causes by observing process activities again, searching for evidence of problem causes. Check sheets can be designed to collect more specific data. Evidence should also include feedback from experts such as process users, customers, suppliers, and management. Pareto charts can be employed to help the team identify the cause contributing most to the specific process problem. When the largest contributing cause(s) have been identified, the project can move on to the Improve stage.

The Improve Stage

For projects in this stage, team members look to develop innovative solutions to fix problems and prevent further occurrences. Multiple solutions will most likely be generated so the team will have to narrow down the list to the few most promising options that meet the team's goals, fit the organizational culture and budget, and that are most likely to be successful. With potential guidance from a Master Black Belt, the process owner, and the leadership group, the team will then select the solution(s) that will be implemented. In many cases other recommendations originally considered but not chosen are, in fact, feasible and may be selected at a later date for implementation.

The next step is to develop an implementation plan. A **pilot test**, which is a preliminary small-scale test or study, is recommended before full-scale implementation takes place to eliminate any bugs in the revised process, and to minimize implementation costs, if the pilot test does not produce the expected results. In the event the pilot test has not met its goals, further analysis of the process may be needed, or the team may move on to implement one of the other more promising solutions. Example 14.2 provides some questions a good Six Sigma team might answer as it develops a set of recommendations to improve the process under consideration. On the condition that a solution has been implemented and the results are satisfactory, the Six Sigma team will move on to the Control stage.

The Control Stage

The purpose of this stage is to keep the improved process performing well and prevent any future similar process failures. A plan is developed that generally includes when, where, and how the process will be monitored; how the measurements will be documented and who will receive performance reports; a description of any new operating procedures; and any required training of the workforce. Process employees will then be trained on any new technology, equipment, or procedures incorporated into the process and control will subsequently be released back to them. Statistical process control techniques such as those discussed in Chapter 13 are typically applied at this stage, and modifications to structures and employee incentives may also be included to institutionalize the process improvements. Dow Chemical's implementation of the DMAIC cycle is illustrated in the chapter opening Process Management in Action feature.

Selecting Six Sigma Projects

All processes in an organization are not equally important or do not operate at the same level of quality. Valuable time can be wasted working on less critical processes, resulting in only negligibly improved business results. Thus, Six Sigma projects should be selected based on their greatest potential to improve overall customer satisfaction while at the same time having the largest positive impact on the firm's costs and profits.

Honeywell's Aerospace Electronics unit in Singapore, for example, used Six Sigma to reduce waste in its key business processes. In the past, all of Honeywell's products had been 100 percent inspected by a U.S. inspection team. Based on the Aerospace Electronics unit's Six Sigma effort, it eliminated this form of inspection and now relies on the U.S. Federal Aviation Agency (FAA) for certification of any products manufactured in Singapore. Products are then shipped directly to storage at its plant in Kansas, saving about $1 million annually with no loss in quality.[7] Providence Hospital's Six

---

Example 14.2   Key Factors in Selecting a Six Sigma Solution

- What are some solutions that will help the team eliminate the root cause of the problem and help the team achieve its goals?
- Which of these solutions is actually feasible in terms of cost, resources, and time?
- Which of these solutions will likely achieve the team's goals and cause a minimum of disruption and expense to the organization?
- How should the team test the selected solution(s) to help guarantee those solutions will be effective?
- What are the next steps the team must take to implement the solution(s) permanently?

Source: Adapted from Pande, P. S., R. P. Neuman, and R. R. Cavanagh, *The Six Sigma Way,* New York, NY: McGraw-Hill, 2000, p. 276.

Sigma project focused on the extreme variation in service times in its care for emergency room patients, which had resulted in high levels of patient dissatisfaction. More on the Michigan hospital's improvement process can be found in the Service Perspective feature.

Critical to Quality Trees

Companies generally begin the process of identifying and selecting Six Sigma projects by looking at those important customer-related issues that are currently confronting the organization, otherwise known as **critical to quality**, or CTQs. The Six Sigma team determines the drivers of each CTQ and then develops at least one representative measure for each driver. This activity will require some data collection through customer surveys or other company documentation to determine the current situation.

To understand the process of identifying CTQs further, let's use a hypothetical new home construction company that has been experiencing a dramatic downturn in customer satisfaction in the past two years. A Six Sigma team analyzes the results of completed customer satisfaction surveys, which are sent to homeowners following one year of ownership, and finds that resolving warranty issues is the number one complaint. The team then mails out a second survey to gather more specific reasons for homeowner dissatisfaction with the builder's warranty. Using the results, the team creates a **CTQ tree** as shown in Figure 14.3, which breaks the complaints into the four main drivers of dissatisfaction. A list of CTQs is then created that details those specific activities that should improve customer satisfaction. The results of the CTQ tree can then be used to improve the warranty process.

Key Selection Criteria

Using the CTQs as a basis, companies then use other key criteria to evaluate potential projects, as listed in Table 14.3. As mentioned at the beginning of the chapter, some of these factors include whether the project has clearly defined goals, aligns with the organization's strategic initiatives, ties in to other Six Sigma projects, is feasible (does the company have the resources and data necessary to implement the project), and will result in measurable improvements and cost savings.

Companies also need to consider the size, complexity, and costliness of the problem. In 2001 auto manufacturer Ford Motor Co.'s Six Sigma Group tackled the serious and costly problem of excessive exterior surface defects found on cars imported from its global manufacturing sites to U.S. dealers. A protective transit film would lift away from the vehicle, trapping dirt and debris between the film and the vehicle's finish. A Six Sigma team created a process map of the vehicle transit process and then examined it for possible points of failure. Within the production areas, for example, they analyzed the installation of the film, the differences among operators and shifts, the training of operators, the type of transit film used, and the surface cleaning methods. Using quality tools, they pinpointed the problems as quality issues with the transit film, and operator training and supervision. By using an alternative coating method and increasing operator training and supervision they were able to decrease defect rates from three defects per vehicle to one, saving the company more than $500,000.[8]

Projects Outside the Scope of Six Sigma

Problems that are more easily solved and that do not affect the basic structure of work generally do not become Six Sigma projects but may instead be targeted for smaller

Service Perspective

Six Sigma at Providence Hospital

If you had reduced the mean door-to-doctor time in your emergency department (ED) from 64.3 minutes to 39.8 minutes (a 38.1 percent improvement) in seven months, you'd probably be pretty happy. But for Maureen Kelly-Nichols, RN, MSA, the ED nurse director at Providence Hospital in Southfield, Michigan, that was not the key measure of success in her recent Six Sigma project.

Six Sigma is a disciplined, data-driven approach and methodology for eliminating defects in any process. In the most recent project, the most meaningful statistic for Kelly-Nichols was the standard deviation in wait time, which was reduced from 44.7 minutes to 27.7 minutes—a 38 percent improvement.

Standard deviation, she explains, illustrates the variability around the process you are seeking to improve. "Averages are not a good way to assess your performance," she asserts. "If you have [a good average wait time and] a patient who waits 10 minutes, [that person is] happy, but the one who waits 90 minutes is not."

In terms of wait times, it's important to identify the "upper spectrum"—how long a wait patients are willing to tolerate—and then strive to keep all patients below that spectrum, Kelly-Nichols says. "We did a 'voice of the customer' survey and found they were willing to accept 60 minutes to see a physician," she adds.

When they started, 70 percent of the patients were seen between 20 minutes and 110 minutes, says Ben Miles, MBA, Six Sigma Master Black Belt at St. John Health, the system to which Providence belongs. Master Black Belts are quality leaders responsible for Six Sigma strategy, training, mentoring, deployment, and results. "Once we got done, for 70% of the patients, it was between 20 minutes and just over one hour," he says.

They let the data drive their decision making, says Kelly-Nichols, noting that is an important lesson for ED managers to learn. "What you think is the problem isn't necessarily correct," she says.

Six Sigma helps keep ED managers on the right track because of its core DMAIC (define, measure, analyze, improve, control) method. "It does take a lot of discipline, because you want to move right to the solution," Miles notes. "We wanted to go on our intuition and say we didn't need to measure the process, but when we did, we had a few 'Aha!' moments. Some of the things we did not think would be critical were the chief drivers of variability." Those drivers turned out to be:

- whether the patient was a fast-track patient;
- whether there was a bed available; and
- whether the patient had an X-ray performed.

Miles advised that the first process to bring under control (and the subject of this seven-month project) should be the fast-track patients, as they almost exclusively were the purview of the ED.

The problem with express care is that it wasn't, Kelly-Nichols says. "The patients were waiting two to three times longer than the average patient, because they were less acute. We tend to treat the sickest patients first." Clearly, no one was going to treat the acute patients more slowly, so the express process had to be sped up. The area used to open at 11 a.m., but there was no formal physician coverage until 1 p.m.; until that time, it was staffed by a nurse and floating physicians from other departments. Now when the area opens at 11 a.m., there is a board-certified ED physician, a nurse, and a physician extender—usually a nurse practitioner.

"At times, we will also float a nurse in there, which is almost a shifting, not an added [full-time equivalent]," she says.

"One thing that precluded getting the patients to express care as quickly as we would like was registration," Miles notes. The registrar has been moved, and registration is now done at the bedside. "When you walk in the door, we do a quick assessment of vitals, but full registration is done at the bedside," Kelly-Nichols adds.

A final factor was improving ergonomics to aid work flow. "We moved a computer [to make it more accessible] and a refrigerator to make flow smoother," she says. "We've moved our meds to where we have more counter space and gone to automatic medication dispensing." As a result of the project, the ED has reduced its left-without-being-seen rate to less than 1 percent, even though volume is higher than it ever has been. Kelly-Nichols says volume is up 5 percent this year, to 63,000 annual visits. "What we've done is change the whole philosophy in express care. The staff strives for quick, efficient care and quality care."

Source: "Six Sigma success story: Reducing variations is key," *ED Management,* July 1, 2005. Reprinted with permission.

Figure 14.3	CTQ Tree Example

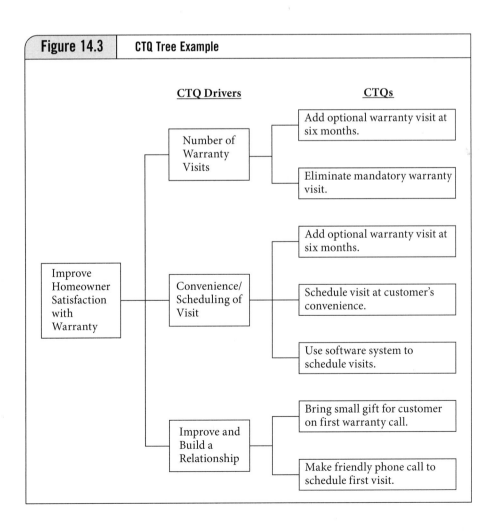

Table 14.3	Project Criteria

CRITERIA	QUESTIONS TO ASK
Seriousness of problem	Is this a chronic problem? Will the project correct an ongoing problem, not just a single incident?
Importance of results	Will the results significantly improve the situation? Will the results be worth the time and effort?
Size/scope of project	Is the project a manageable size (no longer than six months to a year)?
Financial measures	Will costs of poor quality be reduced? Will ROI improve? Will market share increase?
Qualitative measures	Will customer retention increase? Will we find new customers? Will customer or employee satisfaction improve?
Urgency	Does this problem affect quality in our core services? Does this problem make us susceptible to competitive forces? Does this problem affect key customers?
Risk	What is the certainty of a positive outcome? How long will this project take to complete (longer time to complete implies greater risk)?
Resistance from employees	To what extent do we think our employees will resist recommended improvements from this project?

Source: Adapted from Defeo, J. A. and W. W. Barnard, *Juran Institute's Six Sigma: Breakthrough and Beyond*, New York, NY: McGraw-Hill, 2004, p. 231.

continuous improvement activities. On the other hand, larger problems may require scrapping the old process completely and creating an entirely new process. These projects generally require the direct involvement of senior management and are beyond the scope of a Six Sigma project. For example, insurance companies are replacing their old manual system of claims processing with automated ones provided by service solutions providers such as New York-based IBM. Automation has resulted in faster turn-around times for claims processing and allows patients direct online access to the system to check on the status of their claims. However, this type of project has far-reaching repercussions throughout the organization and would not normally be considered a Six Sigma project.[9]

Once a Six Sigma project has been selected, organizations want to make every effort to ensure its successful completion. Documentation of the project's progress, while considered a necessary evil for many within an organization, helps hold the team members accountable and provides a paper trail. Some examples of the documents typically used in these projects are described in the next section.

Six Sigma Project Documents

Once a Six Sigma project has been approved the project team is formed and the team sponsor and/or a Black Belt prepare a **project plan**, which includes a **project problem statement**, a **project mission statement**, and a **team charter**. These documents are used to formalize and clarify the project in writing. These documents can also be used as templates for future Six Sigma projects.

Project Problem Statement

A project problem statement is a short description of the problem that will be solved. A good problem statement specifically states what is wrong with the process and makes a distinction between this problem and other similar problems. There should be observable evidence of this problem, and the team should be able to assess current and expected performance quantitatively. For example, the team may plan to reduce costs, cut cycle times, or reduce the frequency of defects by a stated amount.

Project Mission Statement

The mission statement briefly describes what the team plans to accomplish in relationship to the problem being addressed. The mission statement should not lay blame on anyone in the organization or try to state the causes of the problem, which is not always easy. Certain team members may want to share their preconceived ideas about the root causes of the problem, which may be outright wrong, inaccurate, or misleading to the rest of the team. The team should also avoid any attempts to design a solution at this stage because they haven't studied the process enough to be able to identify the assignable cause(es) of the problem. Example 14.3 provides an example of a problem statement and mission statement developed by Mount Carmel HealthProviders, an Ohio-based company for one of its accounts receivables projects. Note that the quantitative measures included in Mount Carmel's problem statement include days late, the average collection rate, the number of late charges, and the amount of lost revenue.

Team Charter

While not mandatory, a team charter is often developed, identifying the team's responsibilities and giving the team authority to pursue its mission. Team charters are often used in larger, more formal organizations as a green light to begin the project. If a charter is used, it should initially be drawn up by the team sponsor and then refined as necessary by both the team sponsor and a Black Belt, with final approval given by

---

Example 14.3   Project Problem Statement and Mission Statement

Mount Carmel HealthProviders, an Ohio-based company, developed the following problem statement for its accounts receivable improvement project:

> "Baseline analysis charges billed to insurance companies show that the average collection rate on charges that have not been paid by 90 days past the date of service is about 34.5 percent compared to the overall average collection rate of 76 percent. This has been a long-standing problem. A review of the aging balance summary of March 7th revealed 10,404 charges over 90 days not paid, totaling $413,811 in gross revenue."

The team also created the following mission statement:

> "To reduce insurance claims with no activity at 90 days by 70 percent from a baseline of 4.77 percent of gross revenue to 1.43 percent by December 1, 2001."

Source: Schutte, P., "Using the Six Sigma Management System to Increase Primary Care Office Efficiency," *Group Practice Journal,* July/August 2002, p. 8.

the leadership team. In most organizations the charter will be revised as the team gains a better understanding of the problem and more data is analyzed. The key elements of a charter are provided in Table 14.4.

A team charter is considered a living document, meaning that it will not necessarily be complete by the end of the Define stage of the DMAIC cycle and may undergo changes as the project progresses. For example, by the end of the Measure stage, the team sponsor and/or Black Belt should be able to include in the charter the scope of work for each subsequent project phase and the date when the team expects to complete that portion of the project (known as **project milestones**). This step is important because it creates team commitment and a sense of urgency to keep the project on track and meet expectations.

The Scheduling System

More often than not, Six Sigma teams will be given a deadline to complete the project. To estimate the feasibility of completing the project within the expected timeframe a **work breakdown structure** will first be developed, which is an account of all work tasks that need to be completed for the project. These tasks are then usually categorized into major work components. The work breakdown structure is then used to create a **Gantt chart** or **critical path network** (recall that Gantt charts were also discussed in Chapter 7). Both tools provide a graphical representation of the activities required for implementation and the expected completion times for each activity.

A Gantt chart is a type of bar chart used for obtaining a rough estimate of the project's completion time, while the critical path network is a more exact tool, showing the link between project activities through a series of interconnecting arrows and highlighting the activities critical to timely project completion (i.e., the critical path). Both charts identify all preceding and subsequent tasks, but the critical path network more closely

Table 14.4	Six Sigma Project Charter			
ITEM	**DESCRIPTION**			
Process	*Process description*			
Project description	*Problem and goal statement*			
Project scope	*Dimensions of project*			
Benefits to external customer	*Benefit #1* *Benefit #2* *Benefit #3* *Benefit #4*			
Objective	*Key process metrics affected by project*	Process Metric: Metric 1 Metric 2 Metric 3	Baseline	Goal
Baseline case	*Expected financial improvement or other gain/justification*			
Team members	*Name, current job description, team responsibility*			
Other needed support	*Description of support and resources required*			
Project schedule	Key Completion Milestones: Measurement Analysis Improvement Control	Date Completed:		

Source: Adapted from Z. Swinney, "Project Charter and Templates," available at http://www.isixsigma.com/library/content/c010218b.asp.

illustrates the interdependencies between each task. The time duration and function of each task is also typically included.

The two most commonly used critical path networks are the **critical path method** (CPM), which uses deterministic time estimates and the **program evaluation and review technique** (PERT), which uses probabilistic time estimates. Figures 14.4 and 14.5 provide graphical representations of a Gantt chart and a critical path network. There are several software programs available today to help Six Sigma teams create Gantt charts and critical path networks, including Microsoft's Project®, Pennsylvania-based Primavera Systems' Primavera®, and SmartDraw.com's SmartDraw®.

It is important to remember that as the project progresses, the time line may change for any number of reasons. For example, a particular activity may take a different

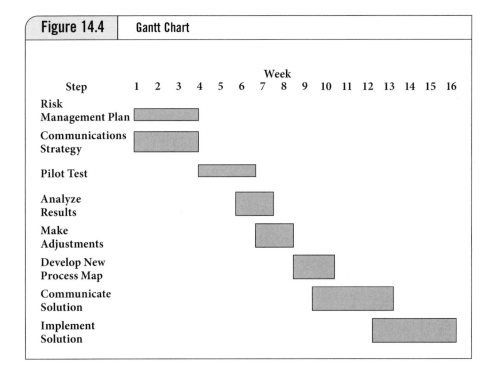

Figure 14.4 | **Gantt Chart**

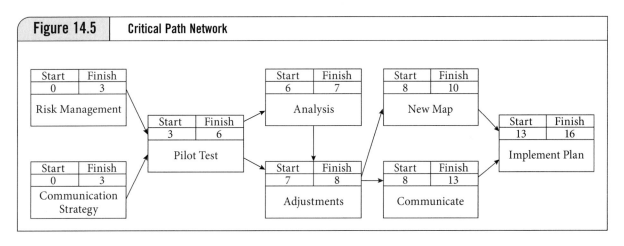

Figure 14.5 | **Critical Path Network**

amount of time than what was originally estimated. Additional work, not previously identified, may also be needed to complete the project. Certain team members may also not have as much experience as the team leader initially thought, resulting in longer activity completion times. Additionally, the project may take longer because the team may have little or no experience working on teams or on Six Sigma projects, thus experiencing a steeper learning curve.

Thus, as delays in the project occur, the Gantt chart or critical path network should be updated to reflect any changes in activity times. If the project is taking longer than expected, activities not yet started should also be reviewed to see if they can be shortened or done simultaneously to keep the project operating within the planned completion time. Once the project is over, these graphs can then be used as a basis for estimating the time needed to complete similar activities for subsequent projects. A more in-depth discussion on the creation of Gantt charts and critical path networks can be found in a good project management textbook such as *Project Management in Practice* by Mantel et al.[10]

Sharing Project Information

Frequent monitoring of a Six Sigma project is important to prevent problems from occurring, and project reports are prepared to disseminate the results. These reports generally contain the aggregation and analysis of any data collected for the project. Project reports will be prepared periodically but the content and frequency will vary from company to company, depending on the target audience and the purpose of the report.

With the advent of the Internet, the status of a project can easily be communicated regardless of where the team members are located. Secure web pages are being used to gather, store, and disburse project information to all team members, senior management, and other stakeholders. Project progress, resources that have been assigned to a project activity, the current status of an activity, or project expenditures can all be shared.

Software also aids in managing project data and information. Microsoft Project®, for example, includes a tool known as Project Central® which, when linked to a firm's computer network, allows anyone with the proper access to update and send their portion of the project plan to the project manager.[11]

Risk Management Plan

Some of the early activities during the Improve stage of the project include developing a **risk management strategy**. Risk management is a proactive approach and begins by identifying all the major sources of risk and the probability each risk will occur during implementation of the problem solution. Some of the more common sources of risk, according to Mantel et al. include a poorly planned implementation, changes in the senior management mandate, lack of team skills or character, changes in user requirements, or underestimating the cost of implementing the solution.[12] The team may use a combination of statistical analysis, scenario analysis, and documentation from prior project experiences to address these risks. A **risk management plan** is then developed, which details any backup plans, actions, or measures that will be taken should any of the risks materialize.

Communication Plan

Developing a **communication plan** is also important to gain buy-in from the workforce and involves, first of all, deciding what types of communication will be most important to a successful Six Sigma implementation. Deciding on what forms of communication will be used naturally depends on the culture of the organization. Face-to-face meetings, conference calls, video-conferencing or Internet meetings if the team members are in different locations, emails, and newsletters are some of the tools available.

Regular productive meetings are an important component of any Six Sigma project. They can help keep the team members motivated in moving toward the completion of project goals. Meetings also provide the project leader an opportunity to hold each team member accountable for their progress in meeting deadlines. Conflicts within the project team can be a cause of trouble in moving a Six Sigma project forward and regular meetings can help mitigate these problems. Table 14.5 provides some potential sources of conflicts in projects and ways to resolve these issues.

It is equally important that the team decide the frequency of each type of communication used and which stakeholders should be included. Xerox leaders, for example, communicate to the workforce frequently through speeches, meetings, and newsletters. The New York–based technology and communications giant has also set up an intranet site that offers extensive deployment details, project successes, reference information, and answers to frequently asked questions.[13]

Control Plan

The team should also develop a **control plan** that describes the methods and tools the organization will use to keep the improved process in statistical control and at optimal performance. Control charts, check sheets, fishbone diagrams, and Pareto charts, described in detail in Chapter 13, are some of the more commonly used control tools. The plan should also include any additional systems or activities needed to reduce the chances of future errors occurring, such as using information technology to control and measure the process precisely or increasing the amount of self-inspection for errors. How performance will be measured and any actions that will subsequently take place when standards are not met should also be included in the control plan. Finally, a training program should be developed and included in the plan to ensure that anyone interacting with the improved process is capable of maintaining the new operating conditions of the process.

Table 14.5	Sources of Project Conflict
CONFLICT SOURCE	**RECOMMENDATIONS**
Schedules	Continually monitor work in progress. Communicate results to affected parties. Forecast problems and consider alternatives. Identify potential trouble spots needing closer surveillance.
Technical Issues	Early resolution of technical problems. Communication of schedule and budget constraints to technical personnel. Emphasize adequate, early technical testing. Facilitate early agreement on final designs.
Labor	Forecast and communicate staffing requirements early. Establish staffing requirements and priorities with functional and staff groups.

Six Sigma Project Tools and Measures

Some level of data collection and quantitative analysis will likely be performed at each stage of the DMAIC cycle. A number of tools and measures, some of which have been described in earlier chapters, are available that are valuable to a Six Sigma team throughout the project. They are briefly described in the following sections.

Project Characteristics

During the Define stage, a Six Sigma team will need to measure relevant characteristics of the process under consideration for a Six Sigma project, some of which are described next.

The Costs of Poorly Performing Processes

Information on calculating the costs of poorly performing processes was found in Chapter 13, but this can be applied to Six Sigma projects as well as continuous improvement initiatives. Recall that these costs fall into three categories: appraisal, internal failure costs, and external failure costs. Those processes where excessive monies are being spent to fix poor quality are a good fit for Six Sigma projects.

Cycle Time Analysis

An analysis of process cycle time may help the team uncover any problems causing time lags within the process activities, such as waiting on parts, machine breakdowns, or excessive rework activities. The average process cycle time performance and variation from the mean should be calculated and compared against a cycle time standard for each key process.

Variations can be analyzed by calculating the standard deviation of the cycle times. For example, assume a catalog company promises that all orders will be filled and shipped within five business days to its customers, but the number of customer complaints regarding delivery times has increased significantly over the past few months. A review of order cycle times over the given time frame reveals that the average time is four days, but a calculation of the standard deviation indicates that the variation is +/− two days. In other words, order fulfillment may take as long as six days, beyond the promise date and a likely cause of customer complaints. Thus, a Six Sigma project to review and improve the process may be called for.

Defect Types and Number/Location of Defects

The number and type of defects is also important to understanding a process and can be collected using a check sheet, a simple data collection tool discussed in detail in Chapter 13. For example, if a company assigns a Six Sigma team to investigate and resolve the issue of an unusually high level of IT requests, the team might begin with a review of all the IT tickets used to make requests over the past three months and create a check sheet of all of the listed issues. The check sheet could then be used as a basis to categorize those issues and determine which category contributed the highest percentage of IT requests.

Defect Trends and Cycles

The team may also want to look at **defect trends**—the number of defects from a process going up or down over time, and **defect cycles**—or predictable periods when the number of defects increases. An upward trend in defects indicates a need for further investigation and potentially a Six Sigma project. Trend line analysis using Microsoft

Excel® can be useful in developing trend lines, and time-based line charts can be used to identify cycles.

Defects per Unit (DPU) and Defects per Million Opportunities (DPMO)

Both **defects per unit** (DPU) and **defects per million opportunities** (DPMO) are indicators of the quality capabilities of a process. In other words, DPU and DPMO are measures that reflect the amount of wasted materials and time spent on reworks. DPU is the ratio of the total number of defects found in a given number of inspected units divided by the total number of units inspected, or:

$$DPU = \frac{\text{Total number of defects}}{\text{Total number of units checked}}$$

If the team finds the DPU to be too high, they may initiate a Six Sigma project to look at each process step to determine where the defect problems are occurring.

DPMO, on the other hand, normalizes the reject rate based on opportunities for a defect to occur, and is measured using the following formula:

$$DPMO = \frac{\text{Total number of defects}}{\text{Total number of units checked}} \times 1,000,000$$

An example using DPMO is found in Example 14.4.

Both DPMO and DPU measures can be used to analyze the current performance of an organization and also be used as a baseline for improvement. For example, researchers analyzed the performance data from three medical laboratories and determined sample sizes and the number of defects or errors. The data were then converted into DPMO, which were then converted to Sigma values.[14] The results are presented in Table 14.6, which shows that measures can be applied to just about any process to make improvements.

Cost/Benefit Analysis

Often several Six Sigma proposals must be evaluated at the same time, and resources typically are constrained within an organization. Thus, management will likely prioritize the value of each project using a **cost/benefit analysis**. The analysis should include an

---

Example 14.4   Calculations of DPU and DPMO

A tire manufacturer produced 6,000,000 tires for one brand of sports utility vehicle. Its goal is Six Sigma quality. Since production began, there have been 2,000 accidents reported due to the subsequent failure of the tires. How is the tire production process performing? Calculate the DPU and DPMO and convert the measures to a Six Sigma metric. Assume a defect is defined as a tire that causes an accident.

SOLUTION:

$$DPU = 2,000/6,000,000 = 0.000333$$
$$DPMO = 0.000333 \times 1,000,000 = 333$$

Using Table 14.1, the production process performance is slightly lower than Five Sigma but still falls short of a Six Sigma goal. When quality problems such as this could result in huge liability losses and customer injury or death, Five Sigma quality may not be good enough.

Table 14.6	Performance Indicators and Six Sigma at Three Medical Laboratories	
QUALITY INDICATOR	**DPMO**	**SIGMA VALUE**
Order accuracy	18,000	3.60
Duplicate test orders	15,200	3.65
Patients did not receive wristband	6,500	4.00
Laboratory proficiency testing	9,000	3.85
PAP smear rescreening due to false negatives	24,000	3.45
Reporting errors	477	4.80

Source: Nevalainen, D., L. Berte, C. Kraft, E. Leigh, and T. Morgan, "Evaluating laboratory performance on quality indicators with the six sigma scale," *Arch Pathol Lab Med,* 124, 2000, pp. 516–519.

evaluation of the costs to improve each poorly performing process under consideration, each project's expected return on investment (ROI), as well as a consideration of other key factors identified by the project's stakeholders. Using an extreme example, if it is possible for an existing process to produce 500 units per day but the current performance averages 250 units per day, there is certainly a lot of room for improvement and this project will probably be given a high priority, even if the improvement cost is significant. On the other hand, if current performance averages 480 units per day with little variation, there is probably little room for improvement and, unless the improvement cost is very low, the project will receive a very low priority. The European Building Products Division of Pilkington, a premier glass products manufacturer with headquarters in Austria, uses ROI and Pareto chart analysis to select Six Sigma projects. More about Pilkington can be found in the Global Perspective feature.

The cost/benefit analysis may also be reviewed again later during the Improve stage of the DMAIC cycle to determine if a Six Sigma team's recommended solution to a problem is likely to result in a breakthrough improvement—significantly lower costs and increased customer satisfaction. Because a team will often devise multiple solutions, the one(s) that will result in the greatest bottom-line savings for the lowest costs should be selected.

Pareto Analysis

Pareto analysis, also discussed in Chapter 13, is another tool that helps the senior management team decide which of several potential projects should be selected, based on a ranking system. Pareto analysis will result in selecting the few Six Sigma projects with the greatest number of defects. Improving these process problems will potentially improve the company the most. There are two ways to use Pareto analysis, either by creating a chart or calculating an index. The chart, for example, can be used to look at the costs of a poorly performing process and then select the one or two categories of costs that account for the highest percentage of costs. Example 14.5, on page 557, illustrates the use of a Pareto chart at a paper mill.

A **Pareto Priority Index** (PPI) can be calculated for each potential project as follows:

$$PPI = \frac{\text{Savings} \times \text{Probability of success}}{\text{Cost} \times \text{Time to completion}}$$

The PPI represents a ratio of benefits to costs. If, for example, a company is considering three Six Sigma projects for deployment, the one with the highest PPI should be given first consideration. Example 14.6, on page 558, illustrates the use of the PPI to evalu-

Global Perspective

Improving World Glass

The European Building Products Division of Pilkington, already a world-class operation, makes big improvements in performance by applying Six Sigma training to its glass production sites. Pilkington is renowned for its revolutionary float glass process. In Europe alone the company's building products division has twelve float-glassmaking plants, each producing some 2,000 to 6,000 tons of glass a week. Here even small improvements can make a big difference. It is no surprise, therefore, that worldwide the Pilkington Group has a well-established operating excellence program. It includes adopting Six Sigma methodology supplied by Six Sigma Qualtec. This offered the 14-strong European manufacturing improvement team, based in St. Helens, a structure and objective methodology for training and developing the team and individuals. Additionally, people from the manufacturing sites across Europe have been trained and now Six Sigma is seen as an important part of their training.

The European Building Products Division has also found the return on investment (ROI) to be rapid and profitable. The first wave of 11 Black Belt projects saved some £2 million from a one-time incremental investment of £250,000. That gave an overall ROI of 8:1 in less than a year.

Investment per Black Belt averaged £23,000. All achieved valued payback. In one example, within months, a Black Belt candidate reduced excess edge loss due to on-the-line product change from eight hours to two hours. That saved £50,000 to £100,000 a year, a project ROI of between 2:1 and 4:1. In another example, a Six Sigma Black Belt and his team traced the cause of losses from glass sheets breaking during stacking to edge damage caused by variation in the earlier edge trimming stage. In only a few months that saved £50,000 a year, a project ROI of 2:1. In other projects, Black Belts trained by Six Sigma Qualtec achieved even more dramatic results, including improved profitability and real competitive advantage. Understandably, Pilkington is keeping those details to itself.

Pilkington Building Products in Europe has applied its Six Sigma training to continuous-process glassmaking sites. These plants can run nonstop for 13 to 15 years with a continuous ribbon of glass traveling at speeds approaching one mile an hour 24 hours a day, 365 days a year. Clearly, although this is not part production, it responds just as well and maybe better to Six Sigma methodology. With production on a large industrial scale, small savings can mount up quickly and the payback is immediate. This is where project selection is so important.

Tim Jenkinson has strong views on project selection. It must be very focused to achieve deliverables and payback, especially with lines that run nonstop for 13 to 15 years regardless of demand. If demand is high so is profitability, but if demand is depressed the line keeps running, but at reduced output that can be far from profitable. This affects ROI calculation. A second consideration comes from Pareto chart analysis. According to Jenkinson, often the first two bars need to be tackled in a Six Sigma project, not just the leading problem.

In-house reactions to Six Sigma are positive. It has the support of Bill Pardoe, manufacturing director for Europe, and Don Wilkinson, vice president of Technology, Building Products. The first-wave Black Belts were presented with their certificates at a meeting of Pilkington senior managers from across Europe.

According to Tim Jenkinson, who has been spearheading Six Sigma in St. Helens, the manufacturing improvement management was attracted by the promise of Six Sigma as reported from U.S. plants. Indeed, Jenkinson went to the United States for his Black Belt training with Six Sigma Qualtec, organized by Pilkington North America in Toledo. "The training was superb," he said. "It

Continued

gave us so many skills we just did not have." In his view, Black Belt training takes some well-known and some not well-known techniques and, with Six Sigma disciplines and objectivity, combines them in a remarkably powerful and usable package. "Six Sigma black belt training gives you an excellent tool bag and, very importantly, a very focused and structured approach to the way you do your work. It forces you to question the way you have done it before and what people say. I can see that I have changed the way I work," he said.

The same is true for the first wave of Black Belts. They too have changed remarkably. Now they look for and ensure that they collect the data. As a world-class glass maker it is important that the last remnants of glassmaking as a black art and its shaky solutions are being replaced by the predictably dependable and durable solutions, based on logic, which we now create from Six Sigma methodologies. "One project has been particularly significant in proving the error in some in-house formulation folk law," said Tim Jenkinson.

Source: Heath, M., "Improving World Glass," October 22, 2006. Researched and written by Mike Heath at M&MS, for Six Sigma Qualtec Inc. courtesy of Pilkington Glass.

ate a number of hypothetical projects. Once some type of ranking system has been created, typically senior management and/or a Master Black Belt will select the project(s).

House of Quality Matrix and Failure Mode Effects Analysis

Two quality tools that can enhance the value of a process map include the **house of quality matrix** and **failure mode and effects analysis** (FMEA). The house of quality matrix, discussed in more detail in Chapter 2, can be used to identify the inputs and outputs that make the greatest impact on key customer requirements. Customer requirements can then be translated into design specifications, which will ultimately be translated into the right processes, parts, and production requirements.

A failure mode and effect analysis may also be used in conjunction with the process map and the house of quality matrix. The FMEA is a chart that shows the possible process defects, the effects and severity of those defects (SEV), and their possible causes. Scales are used to represent the likelihood that each process defect effect will occur (OCC), and the probability the defect will be detected should it occur (DET). The measures are then multiplied together to determine the overall impact of the defect, also known as the reported priority number (RPN). Example 14.7 provides an illustration of how a FMEA might be used.

Affinity Diagrams

An **affinity diagram** is one brainstorming tool commonly used to narrow the search for a feasible solution. The affinity diagram organizes ideas based on their similarities into some meaningful categories using Post-it® notes. Using an affinity diagram, a solution is selected, which lays the groundwork to implement and test its feasibility. Affinity diagrams are often put together using results from previous analyses and brainstorming, as well as other data collected from internal memos, employee surveys and interviews, and customer letters. Figure 14.6, on page 560, provides an example of an affinity diagram for comments collected from internal users of a copy machine. The statements were written on individual Post-it notes of one color and then grouped together. A few category headings (using Post-it notes of a second color) emerged based on statement content and then even broader headings were created using a third color of Post-it note.

Example 14.5   Pareto Diagram

Pop's Paper Mill has experienced a number of problems, resulting in a high rate of returns in the last six months. Pop assembles a Six Sigma team and assigns it the task of determining what projects will result in the biggest returns. The team decides to look at the costs of their milling process, and comes up with seven categories, shown in the following table:

COST CATEGORY	COST ($000s)	CUMULATIVE COST ($000s)	CUMULATIVE PERCENT
Rework: Returned for processing	$550	$550	59.5%
Returns: Customer returns/price reduction	120	670	72.4%
Short Orders: Losses from short orders	85	755	81.6%
Materials: Avoidable premium prices/material waste	80	835	90.3%
Equipment: Equipment downtime	50	885	95.7%
Inspection: Excess inspection	20	905	97.8%
Testing: Avoidable testing	20	925	100%

A graph of the costs and cumulative percent of costs was created using Excel, as follows:

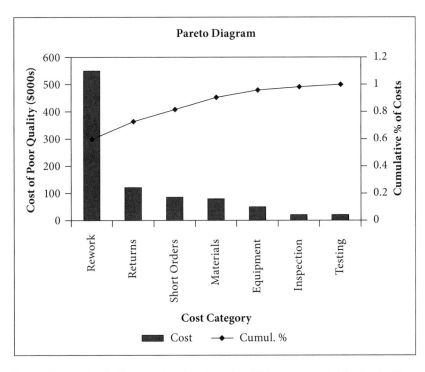

The team learned that the first two categories—Rework and Returns—accounted for close to 75 percent of unnecessary quality costs. Rework was the most significant cost, accounting for almost 60 percent of unnecessary costs. As a result, the team recommended that a project to address Rework was clearly needed.

Example 14.6   Pareto Priority Index

QTC, a manufacturer of ski equipment, has three Six Sigma projects under review. The team has gathered some data for each potential project and calculated the Pareto Priority Index, as shown in the following table:

PROJECT	SAVINGS ($000s)	PROBABILITY OF SUCCESS	COST ($000s)	TIME TO COMPLETE (YEARS)	PPI*
Eliminate customer delivery complaints	$300	0.6	$100	1	1.80
Reduce material defects by 50%	$ 90	0.7	$ 25	1.25	2.02
Improve assembly process quality by 50%	$ 70	0.7	$ 30	0.5	3.27

$$PPI = \frac{\text{Savings \$} \times \text{Probability of success}}{\text{Cost \$} \times \text{Time to complete}}$$

The PPI calculations indicate that the company's resources should first be used to improve assembly process quality, then reduce material defects, and lastly eliminate customer delivery complaints.

Example 14.7   FMEA Example

The U.S. military uses a particular type of rifle in combat. A team has been assigned to review the performance of this rifle because of recent problems with weapons failure in the field. The team first creates the following process map to graphically depict the use of the rifle:

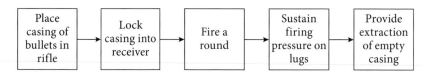

The team then reviews the process map to identify possible failure points in the process. They determine that fracturing and jamming are possible during the five steps of the process, which can result in catastrophic failure of the weapon (the weapon is destroyed and personnel are injured) or jamming, which results in the weapon failing to function properly. The team creates a FMEA table to calculate a risk priority number, or in other words, the chance that one of these failures is certain, hazardous, and can be detected. A sample table is as follows:

PART/FUNCTION	POTENTIAL FAILURE MODE	POTENTIAL EFFECTS OF FAILURE	DELTA	SEV	POTENTIAL CAUSE(S) OF FAILURE	OCC	CURRENT DETECTION METHODS AND QUALITY CONTROLS	DET	RPN
Rifle Bolt • Chambering • Locking • Firing • Sustain firing pressure • Extraction	Fracture	Catastrophic failure— destruction of weapon, injury to personnel	Yes	10	- Shrinkage - Porosity caused by improper feed	6	- Incoming part inspection - Dye penetrate testing	5	300
	Jamming	Failure of weapon to function	Yes	8	- Out of specification - Change in shell refractory	5	- Measure patterns - Confirm finished casting dimensions	3	120

Key: RPN = SEV × OCC × DET   Delta = Critical characteristic that could affect quality

Severity (SEV) - Potential Effects of Failure:

	DELTA	SEV (SEVERITY)
Catastrophic failure with destruction of weapon and injury to personnel	YES	10
Failure of weapon to function	NO	1

Likelihood of Occurrence (OCC) – Estimated Potential Occurrence of Failure:

RANKING	PROBABILITY OF FAILURE
1	Nearly impossible
2	Remote
3	Low
4	Relatively low
5	Moderate
6	Moderately high
7	High
8	Repeated failures
9	Very high
10	Extremely high: failure almost inevitable

Probability of Detection (DET):

RANKING	DETECTION PROBABILITY
1	Almost certain detection
2	Very high chance of detection
3	High probability of detection
4	Moderately high chance of detection
5	Moderate chance of detection
6	Low probability of detection
7	Very low probability of detection
8	Remote chance of detection
9	Very remote chance of detection
10	Absolute uncertainty – no control

Based on the FMEA table, the team took specific actions and recalculated the RPN based on testing the results. Additional columns were added to the original FMEA table to record the results and could be set up as follows:

RECOMMENDED ACTIONS	RESPONSIBLE PARTY AND TARGET COMPLETION	ACTIONS TAKEN	SEV	OCC	DET	RPN

Statistical Tools

A number of statistical tools may also be used to test the cause/effect relationships through hypothesis testing. Some of these tools are described in Table 14.7. A **histogram**, for example, gives the team a graphical representation of the data set, showing the frequency of occurrence for each identified problem within a given range of activity. Histograms can be used to compare a process to actual requirements, or to look at the differences between specific machines, operators, suppliers, or time periods.

| **Figure 14.6** | **Affinity Diagram Example for a Copier Machine** |

Right physical dimensions

Small and compact

"Not enough space to operate copier properly."

"We never have enough space in the office."

"The copier is too big for the room."

Machine is user friendly

"The toner cartridge is messy."

"I bang my knee on the cabinet doors."

"I had trouble finding paper jams."

"I couldn't understand the directions."

Provides fast and reliable results

High volume important

"If it takes more than five minutes for a print job, I'm in trouble."

"I have a backlog of print orders and that just won't work."

Machine is 100% reliable

"The machine is always jamming."

"I went to another copier because this one was too unreliable."

"We have learned how to fix it ourselves."

Copier never causes stops in the workflow

"Any jams will stop the work flow."

"It's a critical bottleneck at certain times of the day."

Source: Adapted from model developed by Baxter International and discussed in Buchanan, J., B. Smith, and A. Williamson, "Baxter International Wins Team Excellence Award Competition," *The Journal for Quality and Participation,* Summer 2005, pp. 32–36.

Regression analysis and **correlation analysis**, discussed in Chapter 5, are generally used together to determine the relationship between one or more input variables and a specific output, while **analysis of variance** (ANOVA) can be used to test hypotheses about differences between two or more means. For example, a Six Sigma team may want to test the effect of noise levels on productivity in the workplace using ANOVA. A more in-depth discussion of these tools can be found in *The Six Sigma Handbook* by Thomas Pyzdek.[15]

Table 14.7	Statistical Analysis Tools
STATISTICAL TOOL	**DESCRIPTION**
Histograms	Graph of a data set; shows frequency of occurrence of identified problems within a given range of activity.
Box plots	Graphical summary of the distribution of given data, showing 25th, 50th, and 75th percentiles plus outliers.
Analysis of variance (ANOVA)	Used to test hypotheses regarding differences between two or more means.
Regression analysis	Tests relationship between one or more input variables and a specific output.
Multivariate analysis	Used to determine dominant sources of variation in a process. Appropriate when output variables (y) are continuous and inputs (x) are discrete.
Correlation analysis	Used to test whether a change in an input relates to a change in output.

Larger organizations may decide to use a **design of experiments** (DOE) to plan and carry out any experiments that will improve the process. Simply stated by George Eckes, author of *The Six Sigma Revolution* and a Six Sigma consultant, "Designed experiments are ways to *create* significant events and be there to observe the results."[16] In other words, the inputs or factors expected to affect the process output are tested, using analysis of variance (ANOVA), to find the best solution. The advantage of DOE is that, through a controlled environment, the effect of multiple factors and interactions among factors can be uncovered.

A U.S. cell phone design and prototype manufacturing facility, for example, wanted to reduce assembly throughput time and was experiencing some difficulties adhering a plastic viewing lens to its cell phones. The machine's pressure setting to attach the lens had been 30 pounds per square inch (psi) for nine seconds. Using design of experiments a team ran a series of tests, using eight combinations of bonding times and pressure settings on one batch of 40 phones, by dropping each phone from a height of five feet. The team found that while pressure setting was not a significant factor, bonding time was. They then used two additional batches, keeping the pressure setting constant to vary the bonding times. As a result, the team recommended a pressure setting of 30 psi for six seconds to meet quality requirements and was able to decrease assembly time by 33 percent.[17]

Balanced Scorecard

Once all improvements have been implemented, the team should periodically audit the process using a **balanced scorecard** to be sure that initial gains continue to be realized. Recall from Chapter 11 that a balanced scorecard is a set of measures used to monitor business performance. If performance results are positive, the team can then turn over the control and monitoring process to the process operating personnel.

The results of any quantitative analysis should help the team uncover the root causes of the problem under review. However, the team can't be absolutely certain their conclusions are correct based only on a statistical analysis, so teams should apply some commonsense logic to their findings. The explanation for the problem should fit both what the team sees happening as well as what's *not* happening. This can be done by actually viewing the process while it is actually taking place. Observation will help the team either validate or question their statistical findings. The team should also visit with those involved in the process, be it customers, suppliers, internal users, or other stakeholders to confirm, refine, or reject their hypothesis. Lastly, the team should be sure they have reached some kind of consensus, and they all understand and agree that the documentation regarding the process, problem, and root cause(s) match the actual situation.

The Keys to Breakthrough Process Improvement

In order to successfully make significant, value-enhancing or **breakthrough improvements** using Six Sigma projects, an organization needs to possess some key characteristics, as discussed next.

Knowledge of Customer Requirements

A Six Sigma project will not be as successful unless companies have a clear understanding of their customers' current and ongoing requirements. While it sounds simple, this step is often easier said than done. The Westin Hotel, part of the Starwood Hotels & Resorts Worldwide hotel family, for example, *thought* it understood customer requirements. However, as the hotel worked through the adoption of Six Sigma practices, it discovered that clearly understanding its customers' needs wasn't always the case. With respect to room service, it was accurate in believing that fast delivery and food quality were the top two factors. However, customers also identified menu variety as the third most important factor, which was not on Westin's radar.[18]

Stretch Goals

Companies will also need to create some **stretch goals** (goals that are not easily attainable) to achieve breakthrough improvements. Stretch goals help push employees to think "outside the box," leading to more innovative improvements and bigger performance gains. Typically, improvement breakthroughs will occur when companies focus on improving those value-adding activities that are critical to the achievement of existing organizational strategies and that have a significant impact on customer satisfaction and product quality.

Figure 14.7 provides a general approach for attaining breakthrough improvements that can be adapted to most organizations. Companies can start by reviewing and agreeing on a set of strategic business objectives. These objectives should be tied to the company's mission, vision, and values, and identify what type of business it is in, what types of customers it serves, and how and where it generates revenues. Some generic examples of strategic business objectives include:

- Claiming a larger market share,
- Providing better customer service than key competitors,
- Possessing a stronger reputation than key competitors,
- Attaining lower costs than key competitors,
- Providing higher-quality products and services than key competitors, and
- Being a leader in technology or product innovation.

Figure 14.7	Breakthrough Improvement Process Map

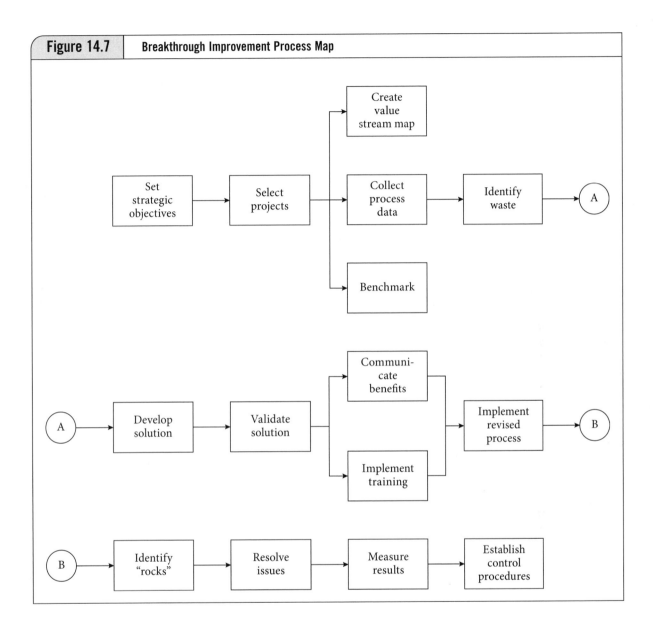

A Process View

Employees should also view the organization as a series of processes rather than functions or departments. In an environment of breakthrough improvement, they need to be given the authority to identify and correct process problems immediately, with the help of other knowledgeable employees. They will also be responsible for systematically and continuously improving value-adding processes to attain higher levels of quality, cycle time, and overall operational performance. This view goes beyond incremental continuous improvement, wherein the focus is on monitoring and controlling processes, and making improvements in more of a reactive manner.

Organizations also need to be transparent, where the flows of material, employees, customers, and work are clearly visible. Transparency is possible with process-oriented information systems, such as enterprise resource planning as described in Chapter 9, and by assigning job responsibilities so that cross-functional management of processes exists.

As well, firms need a good understanding of how their internal processes interact with each other and with the processes of external constituents, including customers, suppliers, distributors, and competitors. With that firm understanding, companies can then begin to integrate their processes internally and with customers and suppliers.

Six Sigma along the Supply Chain

It's highly unlikely that organizations can truly approach Six Sigma performance without including key suppliers in the process and developing closer relationships with them. Suppliers also experience variation in the quality of their products and services, which are then passed on to customers. With the complexity of global supply chain networks, variation in lead times, for instance, can result in a greater chance for supply disruptions. Significant process variation can also result in lost productivity, customer dissatisfaction at best and lost customers at worst, and ultimately a negative impact on the bottom line. Supply chain lead times can be affected by factors such as inventory pick rates in the warehouse and delivery time variations of supply chain trading partners. Thus, the goal for many companies is to use Six Sigma initiatives to reduce variabilities along the supply chain, resulting in more reliable lead times, bullwhip effect and safety stock reductions, and greater responsiveness to sudden shifts in the inputs within a reasonable time frame.[19]

Six Sigma initiatives will most likely make relationships with customers easier and more profitable as well. Ford, for example, created and applied a Six Sigma program to all areas of the material flow process to make its supply chains more robust and improve customer service. At the Wayne, Michigan, Assembly Plant, for instance, Ford employees found that inventory levels of incoming materials to production of the Ford Focus varied by 20 percent within a one-month period and traced the problem to the unloading procedures at the plant's receiving dock. Workers needed to unload 212 trailers per day to support two eight-hour shifts, but the current process was capable of unloading only 180 trailers, resulting in production interruptions. As a result, dealers were unable to deliver new cars to their customers as promised. Using the DMAIC cycle, the Six Sigma team concluded that the receiving dock was underutilized due to inefficient and inconsistent unloading of parts. Improvements were made, including reallocation of material handling workers, reassignment of some trailers, and prestaging of equipment, resulting in a savings of more than $3.7 million annually.[20]

Thus, companies need to better understand their business customers' requirements, which usually happens when strategic alliances are in place. Supply managers also need to have a good understanding of their suppliers' performance using the balanced scorecard or other supplier relationship management tools. Companies such as Kansas-based light aircraft manufacturer Cessna Aircraft Company and Minnesota-based landscape equipment manufacturer The Toro Company, have created dedicated supplier improvement teams that incorporate Six Sigma into their supplier relationships. The results have been positive, with more standardized, automated processes and transactions, the elimination of duplicate processes and testing, and vendor-managed inventory programs.[21]

Companies can also help their suppliers develop appropriate balanced scorecards to assess their own performance. Supply managers in world-class organizations have worked to standardize metrics and procedures across all sites, track a larger proportion of the total supplier base, and then share performance scores with their suppliers. Auto manufacturer Daimler-Chrysler, for instance, has developed "formal channels to receive, evaluate, implement, and measure results of cost-reduction or improvement suggestions from suppliers," according to a 2005 article in *Supply Chain Management Review*.[22] As a result, the automaker has saved more than $1 billion from supplier suggestions.

Companies need to maintain a good understanding of their customers over time, whether business or consumer. As noted in Chapter 3, customer relationship management programs can be an effective way to know and manage customers. Building customer communities is one way to develop exchanges of ideas between the customer and company personnel. Lastly, focus groups, telephone surveys, and mail surveys are also tools to help companies measure their performance in the eyes of the customer.

Supply Chain Management and Six Sigma in Action

Johnson Controls headquartered in Wisconsin, a global market leader in automotive systems and facility management and control, started Six Sigma initiatives in 2000, beginning with projects to improve customer satisfaction and then finding ways to encourage its suppliers to also adopt Six Sigma. The company has Six Sigma projects in more than 24 countries. Its business unit in Malaysia, for example, was facing a significant loss in planned service agreements (PSAs) for building equipment because customers felt they could get better service elsewhere. A Six Sigma project team surveyed those customers who had not renewed PSA contracts and identified the service processes that needed improvement. The team developed a program to significantly improve the management of scheduled service. Once the new process was deployed, they were able to win back 80 percent of the discontinued PSAs, while at the same time improve service productivity by 60 percent.[23]

From a service perspective, New York-based Citibank, a global financial services provider, also uses the Six Sigma methodology to improve its supply chain. One of its divisions, Worldwide Securities Services (WWSS), clears and settles cross-border securities for major broker dealers, custodian banks, and institutional investors. The WWSS team set a goal to reduce the securities fail rate by 60 percent for eight large customers in six emerging markets. The team was able to meet that goal, and three team members went on to start other programs to implement solutions in their areas. Staff with expertise in different parts of the organization were then brought together to analyze and improve supply chain problems end to end.[24]

Six Sigma Challenges

While Six Sigma is a firm-wide improvement methodology, not all firms will benefit from its use. Many companies already have good process improvement efforts in place that aid problem solving and improve costs, quality, customer service, and the bottom line. The cost to implement Six Sigma projects can be significant in terms of training and the time required, so companies also need to consider the necessary investment up front. Some of the costs of implementing Six Sigma may include but are not limited to direct and indirect payroll costs, training and consulting costs, and the expenses related to implementation of new process designs and/or new solutions.

Lastly, there are instances where an organization is already in a state of disarray due to mergers, acquisitions, and a barrage of program, market, or technology changes. In those instances it may be best to wait until structural changes have slowed and new leadership has been established because Six Sigma projects will need management and staff support. Two U.S. technology giants, Honeywell and AlliedSignal, were able to successfully integrate the best of their Six Sigma programs together following their merger in 1999. This was because they both believed in applying new methodologies to meeting customer needs.[25]

In 1999, Xerox Corporation, a U.S. technology and services enterprise with more than $15 billion in annual revenues, decided to consolidate 36 administrative centers into 3, potentially saving millions of dollars in fixed and variable costs. However, the company was in the middle of reorganizing its sales division and unfortunately the result was chaos across Xerox's billing system. Customers were receiving invoices listing equipment they had never ordered or showing price quotes they had never agreed to. These mistakes took several months to sort out, and some longtime customers took their business elsewhere.[26]

Working with employees to accept the changes to an existing process is also a challenge. While the team may be enthusiastic about the proposed solution, employee resistance can easily undermine any possible gains. This may happen for a number of reasons, including:

- Fear of the unknown,
- Contentment with the status quo,
- New skills that have to be learned,
- The "not invented here" syndrome,
- No agreement that a problem exists, and
- Previous solutions that have failed.

Thus, an improvement team will need to develop a plan in advance of implementation addressing how to deal with potential worker acceptance problems. It's important to give employees adequate time to adjust to the changes. Including them in various stages of the DMAIC cycle will also make them feel included and valued in the process. The team, too, may decide to perform the new job functions for a short period to develop a better understanding of the employee's new work life based on these changes. A solid communication strategy tailored to the organizational culture should ease the process. The organization should deal with any resistance head-on and take employee concerns seriously. The improvement team should also be able to provide evidence that the altered process is more effective than the old process and no new or troublesome issues were created as a side effect when the process was changed.

These circumstances should not mitigate the value of Six Sigma, however, nor preclude organizations from adopting the methodology sometime in the future. Each company should weigh the costs and benefits, given their current situation. A U.S. study of business executives found that Six Sigma initiatives were the most important priority in 2005 for large companies (> $1 billion in sales), second for telecommunications and healthcare companies, and third for consumer goods manufacturers.[27]

SUMMARY

This chapter extended the discussion of quality found in Chapter 13 by focusing in more detail on process analysis using the Six Sigma methodology. Six Sigma is a means to make breakthrough improvements within an organization and beyond to supply chain trading partners. The chapter began with a discussion on improving processes and defined the attributes of organizations that operate within a process environment.

This chapter also provided an in-depth discussion of Six Sigma with examples of how to apply each stage of the DMAIC cycle. While many organizations have analyzed their internal processes for breakthrough improvement opportunities, some have gone beyond to search for improvements in their supply chains. The last section of this chapter explored some ways to apply Six Sigma initiatives to improving supply chains.

Successful Six Sigma projects first require visible commitment from management. Secondly, a company must have a clear definition of its customers' requirements. As discussed in this chapter, companies can further understand their customers through a variety of ways, including direct interviews and surveys. A project environment is also important, with employees trained in project management skills. Once projects are complete, communicating the success stories, rewarding those involved in these projects, and institutionalizing the approach will reinforce the importance of Six Sigma.

KEY TERMS

administrative support team, 537

affinity diagram, 556

analysis of variance, 560

balanced scorecard, 561

Black Belt, 537

breakthrough improvements, 562

communication plan, 550

control plan, 551

correlation analysis, 560

cost/benefit analysis, 553

critical path method, 549

critical path network, 548

critical to quality, 543

CTQ tree, 543

defect, 534

defect cycles, 552

defect trends, 552

defects per million opportunities, 553

defects per unit, 553

design of experiments, 561

DMAIC cycle, 539

failure mode and effects analysis, 556

Gantt chart, 548

Green Belt, 537

histogram, 559

house of quality matrix, 556

leadership group, 536

Master Black Belt, 537

opportunity, 534

Pareto Priority Index, 554

pilot test, 541

process owner, 536

program evaluation and review technique, 549

project champion, 536

project milestones, 548

project mission statement, 546

project plan, 546

project problem statement, 546

regression analysis, 560

risk management plan, 550

risk management strategy, 550

sigma drift, 533

Six Sigma coach, 537

Six Sigma methodology, 533

stretch goals, 562

team charter, 546

team leader, 536

team members, 536

team sponsor, 536

White Belt, 537

work breakdown structure, 548

DISCUSSION QUESTIONS

1. What is the Six Sigma methodology? What are four reasons organizations deploy Six Sigma projects?

2. What roles does the workforce play in a Six Sigma organization?

3. What is a process owner? What are the qualities of an effective process owner?

4. Briefly describe the DMAIC cycle.

5. Identify a process in an organization with which you are familiar that needs a breakthrough improvement. Create some measures that will help you identify the current state of the process.

6. What are two forms of analysis a company can use to evaluate and select Six Sigma projects?

7. What are a Six Sigma project (a) problem statement, (b) mission statement, and (c) charter? What is the purpose of these documents?

8. What is the purpose of the Measure stage in the DMAIC cycle? Choose three measures and use them to evaluate a process in your organization or one for which you are familiar.

9. Describe failure mode and effect analysis.

10. As a Six Sigma team moves to the Improve stage, what types of questions should it be able to answer? What are two tools that can be useful in finding a solution to problems identified in the process?

11. What is the purpose of design of experiments?

12. Describe why a risk management strategy is important to a Six Sigma project.

13. Define and describe the purpose of a communications strategy in a Six Sigma project.

14. What activities should take place during the Control stage of the DMAIC cycle?

15. Why should Six Sigma initiatives include other members of the supply chain?

16. What are three ways companies can address problems with their processes?

17. What are the characteristics of an organization that is ready to tackle breakthrough process improvements?

18. How do strategic business objectives tied to the mission, vision, and values help an organization begin the process of breakthrough process improvement?

PROBLEMS

1. Two Buck Chuck's sells fine wines and cheese through its website. During the month of December, customers had trouble placing and receiving online orders, resulting in complaints and lost sales. Website downtime averaged two hours per day as the information technology (IT) group tried to find and fix the problems. The website is open 24 hours/day. Calculate Two Buck Chuck's current quality standard. (Hint: Use Table 14.1.) How much does Two Buck Chuck's need to reduce downtime to improve to Six Sigma?

2. Two Buck Chuck's sells fine wines and cheeses online and has experienced problems with its ordering process for customers due to excessive downtime at its website, problems in the warehouse, and variation in delivery times. Senior management has three Six Sigma projects under review to correct the problem. The team has gathered some data for each potential project. Calculate the Pareto Priority Index for each project. Which project should be done first?

PROJECT	INCREASED REVENUE ($000s)	PROBABILITY OF SUCCESS	COST ($000s)	TIME TO COMPLETE (MONTHS)	PPI
Reduce delivery time by 50%	$70	0.3	$50	8	
Reduce website downtime by 60%	$60	0.7	$70	4	
Improve distribution process by 70%	$80	0.8	$20	5	

3. The operations manager at Best Value Bank's check processing plant believes her process is working very well. Out of 20,000 checks processed per hour, 306 checks are read incorrectly by the scanning equipment, on average. The bank's goal is Six Sigma quality. How is the check processing operation performing? Calculate the DPU and DPMO and convert the measures to a Six Sigma metric using Table 14.1.

INTERNET QUESTIONS

1. Go to Motorola's website and search for its Six Sigma methodology page. Report on four items it lists as Six Sigma tools or techniques.

2. Search on the term *six sigma drift* and report on your findings on this topic. Who came up with this concept?

3. See if you can find evidence of any Six Sigma failures, and what the reasons for the failures were.

INFOTRAC QUESTIONS

Access http://www.infotrac-thomsonlearning.com to answer the following questions:

1. Find three articles that discuss process analysis and Six Sigma. Write a term paper using your findings. Include a bibliography.

2. Find five articles and write a paper on companies that use the DMAIC cycle to analyze and improve processes. Include a bibliography.

REFERENCES

DeFeo, J. A., and W. W. Barnard (2004), *Juran Institute's Six Sigma: Breakthrough and Beyond,* McGraw-Hill, New York, NY.

Eckes, G. (2001), *The Six Sigma Revolution,* John Wiley & Sons, Inc., New York, NY.

Krajewski, L. J., and L. P. Ritzman (2001), *Operations Management: Strategy and Analysis,* Prentice Hall, Upper Saddle River, NJ.

Pande, P. S., R. P. Neuman, and R. R. Cavanagh (2000), *The Six Sigma Way,* McGraw-Hill, New York, NY.

ENDNOTES

1. Quote from Randal Powell, vice-president of Eastman Chemical Co., in "How Six Sigma Adds Value in an Existing Culture," available at http://europe.isixsigma.com/library/content/c040616b.asp.

2. Jeff Immelt, CEO of GE. Quote found in "Bringing Innovation to the Home of Six Sigma," *Business Week, Special Report,* August 1, 2005, available at http://www.businessweek.com/magazine/content/05_31/b3945409.htm.

3. McGinnis, M. and R. M. Vallopra, "Purchasing and Supplier Involvement in Process Improvement: A Source of Competitive Advantage," *The Journal of Supply Chain Management,* Fall 1999, pp. 42–50.

4. Information about Six Sigma and sigma drift can be found at http://www.wikipedia.org/Six_Sigma.

5. See note 4 above.

6. Harry, M. and R. Schroeder, *Six Sigma: The Breakthrough Management Strategy,* New York NY: Doubleday, 2000.

7. Yoke, M. M., "Honeywell Aerospace Electronics System, Singapore—Implementing Six Sigma Quality," *Productivity Digest,* May 2001, available at http://www.spring.gov.sg/portal/newsroom/epublications/pd/2001_03/index3.html.

8. "Ford Motor Company—Driving Defect Rates Down," available at http://www.onesixsigma.com/minitab/Ford-Motor-Company-Driving-Down-Defect-Rates-01102006.

9. http://www-03.ibm.com/industries/healthcare/doc/content/solution/190859105.html.

10. Mantel Jr., S. J., J. R. Meredith, S. M. Shafer, and M. M. Sutton, *Project Management in Practice,* New York, NY: John Wiley & Sons, Inc., 2001.

11. http://www.microsoft.com.

12. Mantel Jr., S. J., J. R. Meredith, S. M. Shafer, and M. M. Sutton, *Project Management in Practice,* New York, NY: John Wiley & Sons, Inc., 2001, pp. 98–101.

13. Fornari, A., "Lean Six Sigma Leaders Xerox," *ASQ Six Sigma Forum,* August 2004, p. 14.

14. Nevalainen, D., L. Berte, C. Kraft, E. Leigh, and T. Morgan, "Evaluating laboratory performance on quality indicators with the six sigma scale," *Arch Pathol Lab Med,* 124, 2000, pp. 516–519.

15. Pyzdek, T., *The Six Sigma Handbook,* New York, NY: McGraw-Hill, 2001.

16. Eckes, G., *The Six Sigma Revolution,* New York: John Wiley & Sons Inc, 200, p. 149.

17. Phojanamongkolkij, N., "Using Design of Experiments to Trim Plastic Bonding Times," *Adhesives & Sealants Industry,* September 2005, pp. 38–39.

18. Eckes, G., *The Six Sigma Revolution,* New York: John Wiley & Sons Inc, 2001, pp. 21–24.

19. Christopher, M., and C. Rutherford, "Creating Supply Chain Resilience through Agile Six Sigma," *CriticalEYE,* June–August 2004, pp. 24–28.

20. Moore, K. G., "6 Sigma: Driving Supply at Ford," *Supply Chain Management Review,* July/August 2002, pp. 38–43.

21. Minahan, T. A., "5 Strategies for High-Performance Procurement," *Supply Chain Management Review,* September 2005, p. 48.

22. See note 21 above.

23. Found at http://www.johnsoncontrols.com.

24. Rucker, R., "Six Sigma at Citibank," December 1999, available at http://www.qualitydigest.com.

25. http://www.honeywell.com.

26. "How Xerox Got up to Speed," *Business Week,* May 3, 2004, available at http://www.businessweek.com/magazine/content/04_18/b3881605.htm.

27. "Study Finds More Companies May Undertake Six Sigma This Year," *Consultant News,* 2005.

Chapter 15:

RETURNS MANAGEMENT

"A company that currently doesn't monitor its returns (process) can cut between 15% and 30% in credit issuance by correcting this process."[1]

"Returns play an important role because real costs are tied to them, which affect the profitability of the enterprise."[2]

Learning Objectives

After completing this chapter, you should be able to:

- Explain why returns management is important to process management and supply chain management.
- Describe the elements of returns management.
- Understand the role of the returns management team at each stage of the product life cycle.
- Develop a returns management strategy.
- Understand the role of other functions in developing a returns management strategy.
- Explain the operational processes of returns management.
- Define green logistics and green supply chain management.
- Describe alternatives to the disposal of used products and materials.
- Explain the laws that govern the transportation and disposal of hazardous materials in the United States and Europe.

Chapter Outline

Process Management in Action

Dealing with Dealer Returns

Reverse logistics in the automotive sector has its own unique challenges given the oversized nature of the freight and the cost of moving parts back upstream in the supply chain. For Hyundai Motor America, headquartered in Fountain Valley, California, one of its greatest pains has been properly managing returns from dealers. "In general, reverse logistics in the automobile industry applies to dealer returns," says George Kurth, director of supply chain and logistics for Hyundai Motor America. "Every automotive company has a policy that allows dealers to return products they no longer need. Typically, they are allowed to return a certain percentage of orders."

Hyundai cars and sport utility vehicles are distributed throughout the United States and are sold and serviced by more than 640 Hyundai dealerships nationwide. In the past, dealers would mostly send returns to core brokers. When they did send them back to Hyundai, the returns usually arrived sight unseen, and the corporate office gave credit without knowing what they were crediting for. "This created a major bleed to the bottom line," says Joan Starkowsky, president of Roadway Reverse Logistics, Akron, Ohio.

To better account for return credits and streamline its transportation costs, Hyundai Motor America partnered with Roadway Reverse Logistics to manage the returns of automatic transmissions for remanufacturing. Now, once a transmission has been removed from a vehicle at the dealership and a new or remanufactured one put in, Roadway picks up the core or defective unit, inspects it at its facility, and issues credit to the dealer for sending the core back. Roadway then batches the cores on pallets, ships them via rail to San Diego, then on to Tijuana, Mexico, where they are remanufactured.

"We get the remanufactured transmissions back into our inventory and can ship them to dealers to use again," says Kurth. "Roadway's service also allows us to cut shipping costs by using intermodal. And dealers get their credits much faster." Batching returns and shipping via intermodal reduces Hyundai's freight costs by about $250,000 a year, according to Kurth. Currently, Roadway only handles Hyundai returns for automatic transmissions. For other units and parts, the auto manufacturer relies on dedicated carriers. Moving forward, Kurth sees more opportunities to improve its returns management, and is working with Roadway on a possible alternative to using dedicated fleets.

"Roadway has access to a huge fleet of trucks. Dealers can call in their returns, and Roadway will pick them up, take the shipments to its sort center, throw away the junk, and debit the dealers for damage," explains Kurth. "Then it ships a clean return back to our warehouse where we can restock it. That's our primary option versus dedicated delivery." With transportation accounting for 60 to 75 percent of total return costs, the ability to partner with a reverse logistics provider that also has access to an extensive multimodal transportation network is compelling.

"As a subsidiary of Roadway Express, we don't make a margin on transportation as 3PLs do—transportation is another revenue stream for them. Because we're asset-based, we provide value-added services to our customers," says Starkowsky. "Having a major national and international transportation network at our fingertips makes it easy for us to pool return products from a national retailer or dealer group in a time-sensitive circumstance—whether it's a recall or a merchandise change-out."

Another benefit is the convenience of outsourcing returns to one core provider, rather than trying to control myriad independent contractors with different systems and processes. Aside from the clear-cut cost differences, Kurth sees Roadway Reverse Logistics' true value within the four walls of its enterprise. "Roadway's proposition is attractive because it takes work out of our warehouses. We hate nothing more than processing dealer returns at our facilities. It is unproductive work that takes up space," concludes Kurth. Outsourcing the dealer returns process allows Hyundai to give all the grunt work to Roadway, and just wait for the "smooth, clean" returns receipts to come back to them.

Source: O'Reilly, J., "Rethinking Reverse Logistics," *Inbound Logistics,* July 2005, available at http://www.inboundlogistics.com. Reprinted with permission.

Introduction

Supply chain management was defined in Chapter 1 as "the integration of key business processes related to the flow of materials from raw material suppliers *to* the final customer." However, goods also flow backwards *from* customers in the supply chain when they are returned, either by the end-product consumer or an organization within the supply chain. In an ideal world, organizations would have zero returns to manage. Unfortunately, returns are increasing, and the number of mistakes made in the returns process has risen as the number of marketing channels increases. This phenomenon is due to the growth of online shopping, direct-to-store shipments, direct-to-home shipments, and the complexities of global sourcing. Those in operations also face several challenges in the **remanufacturing** of returned items (products are disassembled and all parts are examined for their condition, cleaned, repaired as necessary, tested, and reassembled to attain optimal performance). These challenges include (1) the difficulty in forecasting the number of returns, (2) the problems matching the demand for remanufactured items with supply, (3) the variability that can occur in disassembly and reprocessing times because of the condition of the returned item, and (4) the uncertainty in yields.[3]

Beyond the fact that returns are increasing and have become increasingly complex, the study of returns management is important for a number of reasons. As mentioned in Chapter 1, returns management is one of the eight key supply chain processes, and requires a combination of effective planning, communication, and execution at all stages of the supply chain to minimize the potential enormous cost of returns. Retail customer returns, on average, account for approximately 6 percent of sales and can sometimes be as high as 40 percent. Catalog retailers, for example, experience up to 35 percent of sales revenues in returns for soft goods such as clothes and shoes.[4] The logistical costs to process returns can be very high and run into the billions of dollars each year in the United States. In 2001, just the logistics costs related to returns amounted to $40 billion in the United States. Thus, organizations need to look for ways to improve the returns management process.

The majority of logistics systems are set up to move products towards customers, and returns have traditionally been handled more on an ad hoc basis once they arrive back at the firm or warehouse for handling. These days, for economic reasons or because of government legislation, more firms are incorporating the returns management process into their customer service strategies. South Korean-based Hyundai Motor Company is one of many companies that has placed a priority on its returns management process, as shown in the opening Process Management in Action feature, resulting in greater efficiencies and bottom-line savings. Besides the significant impact on costs, returns also can have a direct negative impact on customer service, future sales, the firm's reputation, and its return on investment if not managed properly.

It is thus important to understand the fundamentals of the returns management process in order to reduce these potential negative impacts on the firm. If an organization has not already done so, it should develop a formal structure to provide strategic, long-range direction for the operational process of returns management. A macro view, as shown in Figure 15.1, highlights six returns management activities that typically occur based on the research of Professor Dale Rogers and others.[5]

This chapter will review each of these areas encompassing returns management for both business customers and consumers. The first section will define some of the terms related to the returns management process. The chapter will continue with a discussion of the importance of returns management at each stage of the product life cycle. Next, the value of developing a returns management strategy and some guidelines to the effective management of returns will be described. The importance of using the returns process to improve the environment and the disposal of hazardous materials are also important topics and will be discussed. Lastly, the complexities of integrating returns management along the supply chain will be addressed.

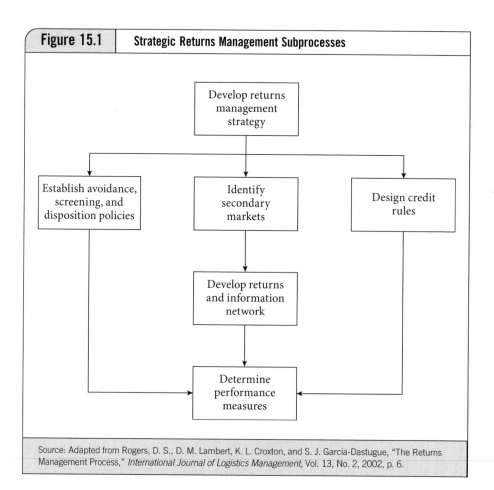

| **Figure 15.1** | **Strategic Returns Management Subprocesses** |

Source: Adapted from Rogers, D. S., D. M. Lambert, K. L. Croxton, and S. J. Garcia-Dastugue, "The Returns Management Process," *International Journal of Logistics Management,* Vol. 13, No. 2, 2002, p. 6.

Defining Returns Management

Returns, closed-loop supply chain management, and **reverse logistics** are terms often used to describe the various activities encompassing the field of returns management. Returns simply refers to the process of receiving and processing merchandise returned for any reason and includes after-sales customer support. Closed-loop supply chain management is a broader term, encompassing both forward and reverse flows of products, including product returns processing, contract service calls, product recalls, re-sales, and refurbishment of used products.

Two other key definitions offer a fairly complete picture of reverse logistics. Professor Stock defined reverse logistics as "the role of logistics in product return, source reduction, recycling, materials substitution, reuse of materials, waste disposal and refurbishing, repair, and remanufacturing,"[6] and another comprehensive definition has been developed by Dr. Moritz Fleischman:

> *"Reverse logistics is the process of planning, implementing, and controlling the efficient, effective inbound flow and storage of secondary goods and related information opposite to the traditional supply chain direction for the purpose of recovering value or proper disposal."*[7]

Dr. Fleischman's definition incorporates the belief that the supply chain is a network of organizations, where materials flow in multiple directions rather than simply towards the customer. Both definitions include the idea that manufactured goods had some previously intended use, and the goal of reverse logistics is to dispose of those goods or attempt to recover some of their original value. Also implied in both definitions is an organization's environmental responsibility in the *proper* disposal, refurbishment, repair, or remanufacturing of returned product. Lastly, both definitions suggest that reverse logistics is a unique form of inbound logistics, in contrast to the traditional inbound delivery of purchased materials for use in manufacturing or other activities. Many of the common reverse logistics activities are listed in Table 15.1.

Returns management incorporates the definitions of returns, closed-loop supply chain management, and reverse logistics. Firms must develop efficient methods for transporting and storing returns, and they must also seek to recover value, if possible, from the returned item. The definition provided by Rogers et al., " ... that part of supply

Table 15.1	Common Disposition Categories for Returned Products

1. Recycling
2. Repair
3. Refurbishing
4. Remanufacturing
5. Cannibalization
6. Landfill
7. Return to supplier
8. Sell as new
9. Sell through outlet or discount store
10. Sell to secondary market
11. Donate to charity

chain management that includes returns (and) reverse logistics …"[8] will be used as a basis to further define the returns management process in this chapter, beginning with a discussion of its importance during each stage of the product life cycle.

Returns Management and the Product Life Cycle

While it might seem surprising, the returns management process is an important factor to consider throughout each product's **life cycle**, not just at the time a product is returned. The idea that a product has a life cycle was introduced in the 1950s. The most commonly cited stages of a life cycle are **introduction stage**, **growth stage**, **maturity stage**, and **decline stage**. However, two other stages are also relevant to this discussion, and they are **development stage** and **cancellation stage**. These six stages are depicted in Figure 15.2.

Each product goes through at least one of these stages in its lifetime, with some products repeating stages, some remaining in a certain stage, and still others skipping stages. For example, it has been estimated that at least 80 percent of new grocery products fail, never leaving the introduction phase. Bread, a staple in our lives, has remained in the maturity stage. New Jersey-based consumer and specialty products manufacturer Church & Dwight Co. Inc. has reinvented Arm & Hammer® baking soda many times since 1846 when it was first introduced to the marketplace, by including it in other products such as laundry detergent and carpet deodorizer, updating the packaging, and using ad campaigns to suggest multiple new uses.[9] Based on the research of Professor Tibben-Lembke, the following sections discuss returns management factors that are important at each of the six stages of the product life cycle.[10]

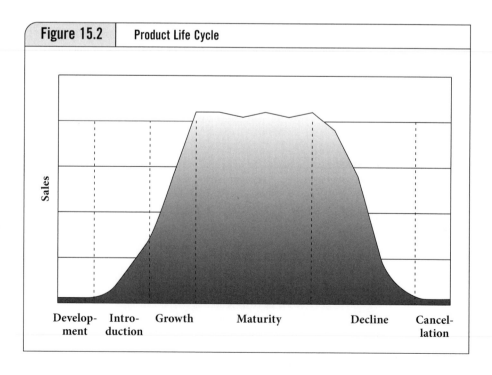

Figure 15.2 **Product Life Cycle**

Product Development

It is important for firms to consider upfront the environmental impact as well as other returns characteristics for a product at the product development stage. Careful consideration of the components that will be used and the design of the production process will make for easier, safer, and less costly disposition whenever a product is returned in its life cycle. Thus, it is important that the employees involved in the returns process, along with designers, operations managers, and purchasing and supply managers, be involved at this stage. If the organization has created any new products, the returns management personnel will have to learn about these products and explore possible avenues for eventual disposition. The product development team may also be able to advise returns management personnel of possible problems customers might experience that could result in an early product return. Hewlett-Packard, a global manufacturer of computer equipment, looks at returns management issues at each stage of its products' life cycles. The California-based company was able to increase recycling of its inkjet supplies, for example, by making some design changes. See more on Hewlett-Packard's approach in the Global Perspective feature.

Returns management personnel can develop some alternatives for disposition of a product based on each potential life cycle problem. Supply managers, based on their evaluations of a new product's component parts, can advise product design engineers of any environmental concerns and recommend alternative, environmentally "safe" parts. Additionally, operations managers can evaluate the expected amount of scrap and waste from the production process and recommend process improvements. If an old product is being "improved" in some way, the returns management team will also need to understand how the company plans to dispose of the old product, the impact of customer return policies on the returns system, and potential **secondary market brokers** in the event the old product will be resold. (Secondary market brokers buy returned product and then resell it for a profit.)

Product Introduction

Once a product is introduced into the marketplace, sales will vary based on customer anticipation, the amount of advertising done, and the company's pricing strategy. It will be difficult to predict the number of returns other than what was forecasted during the product's initial development. If the product is a derivation of an old product that has been tried and tested, the expected return rate may be fairly low. However, a new class of products may initially experience high return rates due to quality issues, poor instructions on product use, or simply that the product did not meet customer expectations. Returns management personnel can provide valuable feedback to the company's product designers by collecting data on the reasons for product returns, and identifying commonalities and trends. This information can then be used to find product design solutions for these issues.

At the product introduction stage, employees must also handle actual returns. The returns process for products that have been modified should be relatively easy and disposition should be relatively similar to that of the original product.

Growth Stage

During the growth stage the manufacturer or service provider often experiences some growing pains as it ramps up production to meet increasing demand. New types of defects may become evident, and as a result the returns will also likely increase as the

Global Perspective

Hewlett-Packard's Design for Supply Chain Program

For more than ten years, Hewlett-Packard has evaluated supply chain impacts on design decisions. Now, design for supply chain (DfSC) is a systematic, repeatable process for product development teams and engineers across the company. DfSC allows HP to consider the impact of decisions:

- On supply chain partners, including suppliers, manufacturing and logistics service providers, resellers, retailers, and end customers, and
- Over time, including during the pre-launch, production, and end-of-life phases of the product life cycle.

With DfSC, HP avoids decisions that improve inventory efficiency by pushing risks onto suppliers or that reduce material costs but cause warranty costs to skyrocket. DfSC has allowed HP to introduce a greater variety of new products more rapidly, while simultaneously lowering costs, increasing revenues, and enhancing the customer experience. To implement DfSC, the program established four questions as a roadmap for development:

1. What is it about a product that makes it a good or a bad fit for a particular supply chain?
2. Which design decisions result in products with those characteristics? For example, if lack of common parts causes excess inventory and lost sales, which design decisions result in unique parts?
3. How and why are these decisions being made? More specifically, when in the product life cycle, who is involved, which performance metrics are important, and what information is available and being used?
4. How do we continue to deliver great products, but at higher end-to-end margins?

In practice, HP uses a portfolio of six DfSC techniques to reduce supply chain costs, enhance customer experiences, and increase profits:

1. Variety control: Trade off supply chain costs and lost sales to determine which product variants are justified in terms of margins, brand equity, and/or channel requirements. Marketing, sales, and retailers usually want more SKUs. But design, manufacturing, and distribution usually want fewer SKUs. The business PC organization reduced inventory by 42 percent while increasing product availability by moving from 107 modules and 95 options to 55 modules and 49 options.
2. Logistics enhancement: Compare distribution costs with design and material costs. A smaller and lighter product may enable economical airfreight, reducing inventory costs and increasing responsiveness. A more rugged product requires less packaging material and experiences fewer returns due to damage. Reducing the physical size of an inkjet printer by 45 percent saved more than $1 per unit.
3. Commonality and reuse: Evaluate the use of unique parts versus common, reused, or industry standard parts. Unique parts often have lower material costs and enable product distinctiveness. Common parts often reduce inventory costs. Reused and industry standard parts frequently accelerate time-to-market. For example, the server business saved $32 million in annual material costs by moving from 12 to 5 kits for mounting servers on racks.
4. Postponement: Determine whether it is worthwhile to design products and manufacturing processes to delay the point of differentiation/customization until end-customer demand is better known. For example, a new product customization process for LaserJet printers in Europe achieves more than a 98 percent fill rate with less than two weeks of supply.

5. Tax and duty reduction: Decide where to source parts and assemble products. Taxes and duties for components, subassemblies, and products will be different based on the country of origin. For example, the network printing capability of a printer is moved to a removable card built in a low-tax location, saving more than $10 million.

6. Take-back facilitation: Consider product and packaging changes to reduce reverse supply chain and environmental costs. Depending on warranty terms, corporate policies, and government regulations, HP will experience costs and benefits of taking back products. For example, design change increases the recycling of inkjet supplies by 25 percent.

Over the past three years, DfSC has been broadly adopted by all HP's business groups and regions. In addition, there have been over 50 individual projects undertaken in collaboration with engineering.

Source: "Hewlett-Packard's Design for Supply Chain Program," *Global Logistics and Supply Chain Management Strategies,* December 2005, available at http://www.supplychainbrain.com/archives. Reprinted with permission.

company attempts to correct these problems. At this point, the returns management team may also need to find alternatives for repairing, reusing, recycling, salvaging, or disposal, subject to any company or legal restrictions. If there have been a serious number of defects and this knowledge has been made public, it may be difficult to find secondary markets until the product has been proven. In other instances, a company may allow some products to *only* be returned to the supplier and then destroyed to retain a competitive advantage.

Maturity Stage

At the maturity stage, product sales typically reach a plateau. Because the product is readily available, and in most instances other competitors have stepped in and introduced similar versions, firms are generally cutting prices or offering sales incentives. As a result, they are focused on ways to reduce costs to maintain desired profit margins. Thus, the goal for returns management at this stage is cost reduction and revenue generation. The firm should be looking for opportunities to speed up the returns process and make it more efficient, negotiate better contracts with secondary markets, or reduce the costs of transportation or recycling, among others. Some companies might also use this as an opportunity to gain public goodwill and take a tax donation by giving returned products to charity.

Decline Stage

As the demand for a product declines, its value to the retailer and any possible secondary outlets also declines. For some product lines, the decline may not be as severe in comparison to others. For example, as manufacturers introduce newer generations of DVD players, the changes may not be so great as to make customers notice. In that event, the manufacturer can command better prices for returned products in their negotiations with secondary market brokers than for products perceived as outdated. In other instances, firms are able to rejuvenate sales through distribution to foreign markets, or through devising new uses as in the Arm & Hammer example mentioned earlier. New designs in ski apparel, for example, are first sold in Europe and then in the United States.

Cancellation Stage

At this stage, returns will slow until they stop completely. If the entire class of products has been eliminated from the company's product line, management may be more open to alternative avenues for product disposition, providing a greater opportunity for returns management to increase returns revenues. However, secondary markets will more than likely lose interest in buying these products and it may even become difficult to donate them. If newer versions of the product are on the market, the cancelled product will still be attractive to secondary markets, or it may be sold as "new" in other countries. First-run U.S. television shows, for instance, are later sold to markets in other parts of the world and packaged as reruns for distribution on cable networks.

Developing a Returns Management Strategy

As evidenced by the brief discussion of product life cycles, beginning with new product development and continuing on through the remainder of a product's life cycle, organizations work to design and sell products and services that are less likely to be returned. They implement company-wide initiatives, such as quality management and Six Sigma programs, business process management, business process reengineering, as well as others discussed in previous chapters, all designed to reduce quality problems and improve customer service.

A returns management strategy plays an important supporting role in these efforts. As previously mentioned, manufacturers often include input from their returns management personnel for product development and to help them improve product quality and ease of use. A returns management strategy is also an integral part of any company's customer service strategy, which is intended to improve its image to the public. For instance, companies often implement and publicize recycling programs to show they are environmentally responsible corporate citizens. Staples Inc., the world's largest office supply products retailer operating in 21 countries, created the "Staples Recycle for Education" program in 2003. The Massachusetts-based company donates $3 to public schools, for instance, for each inkjet or toner cartridge that students collect and return.[11] Trader Joe's, a specialty retail grocery store chain headquartered in California with locations in 15 states, has a food donation program. Its Southeast Portland store, for example, donates 30 to 60 gallons of food daily to local charities.[12]

Return strategies are also typically designed to increase the loyalty of a firm's customers. Consumers and business customers, for instance, are always looking for ways to reduce their purchase risk. As a result, consumers will shop for retailers that not only offer the best prices but also have favorable return policies. Companies further back in the supply chain are also looking to maintain loyalty from retailers and smaller wholesalers through favorable inventory policies. For example, a supplier may make it easier for a retailer to return merchandise that is not selling well. H-E-B, for instance, a regional grocery chain headquartered in Texas, tracks the weekly inventory turnover of each of its products. Slower turning items are quickly replaced with new items to increase profitability. H-E-B and its suppliers also have negotiated a liberal return policy whereby suppliers sell their products on consignment and H-E-B does not pay for the product until it sells. The company also has the option to return the product to the supplier if sales are slow.[13]

Companies may also use these return strategies to increase profitability by protecting certain marketing channels and/or the value of their brand labels. For example, manufacturers sometimes pull slow-moving product from retailers' shelves to avoid it being sold off to less desirable markets. At that point, the product may be repackaged or relabeled and placed back on the shelves. They may also actually destroy the product to protect brand value.

To successfully implement a returns strategy, an organization needs to consider its current returns management capabilities in terms of the current processes, facilities, and personnel. Those involved in order fulfillment and manufacturing also influence the returns management process and should be consulted. Comprehending the order fulfillment process can help returns management personnel understand the physical flows of product, information technology limitations, and any constraints within the logistics system. Those in manufacturing can provide insight on the firm's capabilities in **refurbishing**, repair, and remanufacturing to help them determine the best avenue(s) for recapturing value and **asset recovery**. Refurbishing a product means to restore it to like-new condition. Asset recovery is the process of classifying and disposing of any returned goods, scrap, waste, obsolete materials, surplus, or other assets in a manner that will maximize a return to the owner while, at the same time, minimize the cost and liability associated with disposition.[14]

Organizations should develop a returns management strategy in light of (1) the role of returns in their customer service strategy, (2) the way returns can improve their profitability, and (3) their current capabilities. The returns management process, therefore, should be aligned with the customer relationship management process as discussed in Chapter 3.

Establishing Returns Policies

Once an organization has developed an overall returns management strategy, it should develop a set of policies or guidelines to minimize returns in the first place, screen or gatekeep returns that do come in to be sure they are legitimate, and propose a disposal protocol for those returns. Effective policies will help minimize the expense of returning items through the supply chain. The following sections explain the concepts of **gatekeeping**, **avoidance**, and **disposition** in more detail.

Gatekeeping

Gatekeeping, as applied to returns, is the process of screening all returned goods at the point of entry into the reverse logistics system. The objective of gatekeeping is to balance the value of satisfying customers with the cost and complexity of taking back returned merchandise. While some merchandise can be returned to the retail floor for resale, other returns are not resalable because of defects or damaged packaging. This type of merchandise must be returned to the manufacturer or sold at a discount to a third party, resulting in additional administrative and transportation costs. When gatekeeping is effectively applied, the reverse flow of goods becomes more manageable and less costly.[15]

Customers are aware of the gatekeeping process in the form of company return policies, which can vary from liberal to conservative. Mail order clothing and outdoor equipment company L.L. Bean, for example, headquartered in Maine, has a very liberal policy and states clearly at its website:

> *"Our products are 100% guaranteed to give satisfaction in every way. Return anything purchased from us at any time if it proves otherwise. We do not want you to have anything from L.L. Bean that is not completely satisfactory."*

Large U.S. discount retailer Target Stores has a more conservative return policy, and lists multiple criteria for returns, as shown in Example 15.1.

Avoidance

Companies try to avoid or minimize return requests through a number of means. For example, a woman might shop for an expensive dress at an upscale department store, wear it once to a social event, and then return it. To combat this type of problem and others, information systems can track returned merchandise histories of customers, eventually making it impossible for customers to receive cash if they return items too often. Other stores may simply adopt a return-for-store-credit-only policy for some items.

Example 15.1   Target's Return Policy

We will issue a full refund for most items returned **within 90 days** in new condition, with the original receipt or packing slip, packaging and accessories.

Also, please note:

- Music, movies, video games, software and collectibles must be returned unopened.
- Camcorders, digital cameras, portable DVD players and portable electronics are subject to a 15% restocking fee.
- Holiday and Seasonal merchandise on clearance at the time of the return will be refunded at the current clearance price.
- Any purchase made by check may be refunded as a merchandise voucher.
- Refund value for each item returned will be reduced to reflect value of free gift or discount.
- Other restrictions may apply.

All other returns or exchanges—including those without a receipt—will be offered manufacturers' warranty and repair assistance at 1-800-303-0308.

DON'T HAVE YOUR RECEIPT?
In most instances, Target stores can verify purchases made within the last 90 days on a store account, third-party charge account, check or GiftCard using our unique Receipt Look-up system.

TO RETURN AN ITEM PURCHASED ON TARGET.COM:
You can return most items purchased on Target.com to a Target store. If you choose to return your item to a store, shipping and handling and gift-wrap charges cannot be refunded.

To return a Target.com item to a store, you must have an in-store receipt from our Web site. To print a receipt, visit our Online Returns Center.

The following items **cannot** be returned to a Target store, and must be returned by mail:

- Items listed as "Web only" on their product description page.
- Items purchased from the Amazon.com store at Target.com.
- Items that have been replaced because they were defective, damaged or incorrect.

To find out if your item can be returned to a Target store, visit our Online Returns Center. The "Method of return" drop-down box will let you know if the item can be returned to a store.

Learn more about the Target.com Return Policy.

Source: http://www.target.com/gp/browse.html/ref=br_bx_1/601-9927309-5024139?ie=UTF8&node=1368549.

One specific activity that results in fewer consumer returns is clearly written instructions and illustrations to operate a product. Companies also may review and change internal policies and implement reward systems to reduce the number of returns. For example, paying bonuses to sales people based on quarterly sales quotas has been found to result in **end-of-quarter loading**. Suppliers may use a variety of tools including promotions and discounted prices to sell more product to retailers, for instance. The downside is that the retailer often ends up returning the unsold product in the following quarter. Thus, some suppliers have gone to **everyday low pricing**, consistently selling product at their lowest, profit-generating price and eliminating other sales tactics, to reduce the returns problem.

Suppliers also provide product support to manufacturers and service companies to avoid returns. Texas-based Dell Inc., for instance, requires a customer to talk with a technical customer service representative before any computer can be returned. By walking the customer through the setup process, the representative often talks the consumer out of returning the computer.[16] Companies will also use this opportunity to let the customer return a product in exchange for an upscale model, known as **upselling**, or **cross-sell** complementary products that will enhance the original product's capability.

Some catalog retailers offer free shipping when a consumer purchases a minimum dollar size order and free return shipping, although this approach should be used with some caution. Some customers might use this policy to order with the intention of over-ordering and then returning some of the items. At the strategic level, companies may have to review and revise their policies, and develop metrics to identify return trends. The e-Commerce Perspective feature provides a good example of how online retailer Ashford.com uses gatekeeping and avoidance to manage its returns process more effectively.

Disposition

While gatekeeping and avoidance activities will help reduce the number of returns, some product will inevitably have to be taken back by the supplier. Thus, policies for product disposition are needed. Some returned items may simply be restocked and resold if they are still in new condition. If an item is no longer resalable to regular customers, it may be sold to other parties outside the original supply chain, known as **secondary markets**. For these cases, returns management personnel should evaluate potential secondary markets and determine the ones most suitable, including outlet mall stores, online auctions, and retailers whose specialty is returned merchandise, closeouts, and "seconds."

Saks Fifth Avenue, for example, a New York-based upscale department store, sells merchandise that has been returned or is no longer in season at Off Fifth, its own chain of outlet stores.[17] Big Lots, a popular chain of stores specializing in the sale of closeouts, with headquarters in Ohio, is another secondary market and has been in business since 1985. It purchases closeout merchandise from more than 3,000 manufacturers around the world, including consumables, seasonal products, furniture, housewares, toys, and gifts, and sells them at discounted prices.[18] Online retailer eBay is a well-known website that provides online auctioning of goods, including closeouts,[19] and Auctionindia.com is one example of a business website that uses online auctioning to sell industrial parts.

Returns management policies regarding disposition should also be designed given the current environmental and legal requirements affecting the supply chain. Restrictions on disposal, for example, may be a factor not only in handling returns but also for initial

e-Commerce Perspective

Online Retailer Gets Handle on Returns

Surf through the Ashford.com website and it's easy to see why the company stands as the largest online retailer of luxury goods. Solid gold Rolex watches, diamond-encrusted rings and necklaces, and expensive fragrances adorn the pages. Overnight delivery via FedEx is standard with purchases of $100 or more. But with an average order value in the neighborhood of $530, the issue of product returns is as important as initial delivery. Accordingly, Ashford.com capitalized on its partnership with FedEx and incorporated the FedEx NetReturn application program, in conjunction with tailored customer-service policies. "With NetReturn, we've been able to take a step or two out of the returns process, we've shortened our cycle times and reduced the number of errors," explains Bill Hensler, chief operating officer for Ashford.com.

"Our policy is to cheerfully handle returns, though our primary focus is to not have returns," says Hensler. "To that end, we do several things to ensure that the customer isn't disappointed with the item they ordered online. The images on our web site of products for sale are completely clear, and the descriptions are absolutely plain and accurate and include dimensions. We inspect every single product before it ships. If the purchase is a watch, we set it to the customer's time zone, adjust the date, and ensure that it is operating. And the delivered presentation of the product is outstanding." Product returns are a part of e-tail life, however, despite the best customer service efforts. When they do occur, Hensler calls on FedEx.

Though customers have the option of selecting United Parcel Service or the U.S. Postal Service for delivery, FedEx is the company's standard fulfillment method. "We prefer FedEx because we have in place very favorable rates, we have excellent results on next-day delivery, and we've been able to negotiate insurance protection up to some fairly high levels, which is critical to the shipment of luxury goods." Now, when a customer calls with a return, the customer service agent can log onto NetReturn, take the information, and advise the customer of a time window when the package will be picked up. The FedEx truck arrives, prints out the return label, applies it to the box, and goes. If the customer wants to leave the package in a concealed location for the driver, that information can be provided with the pick-up information. "And again, very important to us, we've been able to arrange to insure the packages on the return trip," says Hensler. Returned merchandise that arrives at the Ashford.com distribution center is opened under camera surveillance. Unworn and unused products in original undamaged packaging material generally are placed back into inventory; malfunctioning items generally are returned to manufacturers; and worn or used items are made available for sale at reduced prices to Ashford.com employees or are otherwise disposed of in secondary sales channels. The company's commitment to customers is to process all returns within five days, though metrics maintained by Ashford.com routinely show the bulk of returns processed in less than two.

However, says Hensler, that initial telephone call from the customer is only a starting point in a process that manages to eliminate a large chunk of potential returns. "Now, when we ship a product out, we include in the package a pre-printed label and all the instructions for the returns process," he says. "One of those instructions requires the customer to place a phone call to us to get a RMA [return merchandise authorization]. That's an inconvenience to the customer, but we've found that many of the customers that call to make arrangements for a return don't end up making the return." Approximately half of potential product returns are thus thwarted, says Hensler. Since Ashford.com's fulfillment team goes to extremes to ensure that they ship the right product and that the product is functional, it's rare that either one of those issues is the basis for a return.

In many cases, returns end up being processed as exchanges, again thanks to intervention by the customer service agents. "In most cases, we're able to resolve the reason for the return or to convert the return to an exchange." But, Hensler points out, some conflicts are beyond the control of mere mortals. "One returns challenge that we have not been able to overcome, and it's our number one reason for diamond returns, is that the lady says 'no.' In those cases, we simply say 'send it back.'"

Source: Hoffman, K. C., "Online Luxury-Goods Retailer Gets Handle on Returns," *Global Logistics & Supply Chain Management Strategies,* February 17, 2001, available at http://www.supplychainbrain. com/archives. Reprinted with permission.

design of the product and packaging. Larger firms are obtaining **ISO 14000 certification**, an international set of standards that helps organizations focus on developing and integrating environmental responsibility into their operations. A lengthier discussion of the environment will be addressed later in this chapter.

Key Factors in Returns Policy and Guideline Development

Customer credit policies and guidelines to help employees determine the value of returned products are an important part of returns management. For example, retailers typically take back merchandise and refund the full purchase price with a receipt. However, consumers returning a product without a receipt might receive a credit for the current sales price, which can be lower than what the consumer originally paid. Some stores require merchandise to be returned within a certain time frame to receive a refund. Florida-based Stein Mart, a discount department and specialty store, offers a full refund if the customer has a valid receipt and the purchase was made within the last 30 days. Refunds may be made through a Stein Mart electronic merchandise credit card (e-credit) or a credit to the customer's charge account, depending on the method of payment. After 30 days, a customer can receive an exchange, credit, or refund, depending on payment method, for the current selling price with a valid receipt. The company requires a ten-day waiting period for any refund on purchases made with a check. If the customer does not have a receipt but a valid ID, Stein Mart will issue an electronic credit (e-credit) for the current selling price.[20] The customer can then buy other merchandise with the e-credit.

In the case of business-to-business returns, the value of a return for business customers and suppliers is often determined through a loose bargaining process, particularly when the product cannot be resold. Often one party is at a disadvantage; thus, organizations often use either in-house specialists or they contract with a third party to negotiate the value of a return. Ohio-based Procter & Gamble Pharmaceuticals Inc. gives credit to wholesalers and retail customers for the return of new product that has not satisfactorily met the customer's expectations within the first six months of purchase, and for expired product gives full or partial credit based on the wholesale acquisition cost less 10 percent. However, the transportation cost for sending returned merchandise back to Procter & Gamble must be prepaid by the customer unless Procter & Gamble made an error in the original shipment.[21]

Another form of credit is a **chargeback**, which means the supplier allows straight deductions or discounts for returns to be taken from the supplier's invoice. A business customer may also be allowed to make **short payments** (pay less than the invoice amount) to the supplier under certain circumstances. In some cases, manufacturers and distributors use a **zero returns policy**, in which they do not accept returns. Instead, they provide rules for acceptable disposition of product and provide a **return allowance** to the retailer or other customer in return for the customer having to deal with the problem. While not particularly successful in actual practice, the advantage of a zero returns policy is the reduced returns costs. However, customers must then attempt to minimize their associated costs for non-returned products. It is also difficult for some manufacturers to enforce this policy. Additionally, downstream partners can dispose of the stock in whatever way they see fit, thus encouraging cannibalization of existing supply and possibly damaging the brand.

To create the most effective policies, representatives from both suppliers and customers should be involved in the returns decision process. The participation of customers is important because they can provide valuable feedback regarding their expectations and desires. Supplier personnel responsible for demand management should also be involved because they can provide long-term demand forecast information, which will help returns management personnel structure guidelines for product return or disposal. Further, order fulfillment personnel can help in the development of disposition and return policies through their understanding of the distribution system. Lastly, purchasing and supply managers can help coordinate with suppliers to decide appropriate avoidance and gatekeeping procedures. In this way a coordinated supply chain effort results, allowing all parties to buy into the process.

Design of the Returns Network

Successful returns management is also impacted by the design of the returns and related information networks. The supplier's customer relationship management team needs to be involved at this stage to ensure their customers' needs are met. Including order fulfillment personnel in the returns network design process is also important because they understand the possible effects of reverse material flows on the existing logistics network and forward material flows. The returns network must also be able to accommodate all of the various types of returns that are possible. Figure 15.3 illustrates a hypothetical returns network.

Companies should consider whether to keep all or part of the returns management process in-house or to outsource it to a third-party logistics (3PL) provider. 3PL providers may offer multiple services, including the coordination of various modes of transportation for shipment from supplier to buyer, creation of logistics information networks, and reverse logistics activities. New York-based copier manufacturer Xerox, for example, offers a "no questions asked" guarantee for its leased equipment—business customers may return or exchange equipment for any reason. Because Xerox replaces or upgrades hundreds of office printing machines every month, it uses a 3PL provider that sends a team of support technicians on-site to uninstall and replace equipment. Xerox provides the training on the correct way to uninstall and replace old equipment so no damage results. The old equipment is then transported to Xerox's "triage center" in California, where its condition is determined and then either scrapped, stripped for parts, held for resale, or shipped out to Xerox's southern California spare parts and refurbishing facilities. Xerox benefits from using a 3PL because it reduces fixed overhead.

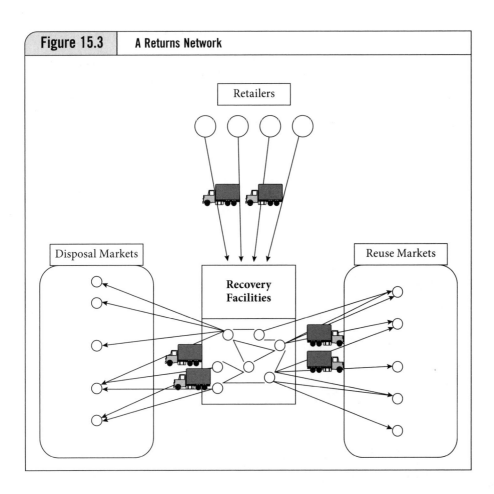

Figure 15.3 | A Returns Network

In-house technicians are reserved for more critical needs. Outsourcing also provides Xerox with flexibility during economic cycles of high and low demand. As a result of this decision, it has significantly increased its equipment recovery rate.[22]

The transportation methods and modes that will be the most effective for the returns are also decided at this stage. Often organizations will choose the least expensive mode for returns regardless of service levels because delivery time is less important compared to original product distribution. Companies may often choose rail service over motor carriers for returns because it is less costly, the concern over shipment damage is less, fewer shipments are required (trains can pull additional cars as needed), and returns can be moved using containers. Another option in certain instances is domestic water or ocean shipping, which offers the same cost advantages as trains. However, the original point of transport must be near a port or the shipment will first have to be moved by some other means, such as motor carrier or train.

As part of the returns network design process, companies also need to consider the movement of recalled products, which can complicate the reverse logistics system even further. In 2004 the Georgia-based soft drink manufacturer Coca-Cola Company immediately recalled more than 500,000 bottles of its Dasani® bottled water in the United Kingdom after discovering it contained higher than acceptable levels of bromate. This quick response was possible because Coca-Cola had integrated business systems in place to trace products through its supply chain. As a matter of fact, beginning in

2005, all food manufacturers within the European Union must be able to trace all products through their food chains.[23] An effective communication network to allay consumer fears in this type of situation should also be a necessary component of the returns process.

Returns Management Information Systems

A well-designed returns management information system is important to an effective returns management process and should be an integral part of a company's supply chain information system. These systems should be able to link every return to a specific customer and the date of original purchase, along with the manufacturing location and the date of manufacture. This data can then be used to assess the extent of manufacturing problems and provide a basis to make process improvements or re-design products or packaging to avoid future damage. Changes in the product or packaging can help eliminate costly damages that occur during transit.

Retailers should also be able to track returns through the reverse logistics pipeline, reconcile inventory levels, communicate with suppliers to charge back the sale, reorder replacement product, and route the product back for processing or temporary storage. In some cases the returned items are defective and need to be shipped back to the manufacturer. The manufacturer will need a system that can generate **return authorizations** (RAs), which are numbered authorization forms used to permit the return of a product, and have screens in place to assure that the return should be accepted. A good system can also generate automated pickup requests to the transportation provider with an **advanced shipping notification** (ASN). An ASN is an electronic version of the shipping notice that is transmitted by the retailer to the manufacturer once the returned product is released to the transportation provider. As returns are received, manufacturers will also need a database to reconcile the returns. The information system should also include the ability to track the performance of the returns process so improvements can be made where necessary.

An effective returns information system, whether for retailer or manufacturer, should also enable a business to analyze the costs to serve each customer by profiling each customer's returns history and looking for trends of abuse. It should also be able to forecast returns so that information can be used to reduce orders for new items. Finally, the information system needs to allow the company to quickly process credits for returns in order to maintain good relationships with its customers. All these attributes suggest that a good information system needs to be flexible, responding to exceptions as they occur, and operating across organizational boundaries.

The development of comprehensive software applications that help companies manage their returns is still in its relative infancy, and developing a system in-house for returns can be very expensive. Some organizations are implementing a warehouse management system (WMS) that includes a module to track and control the flow of returns. Bar Control, a North Carolina provider of software products and consulting services, designed iBEM, an advanced WMS that tracks returns for repackaging, transport to a disposal center, or staging for liquidation.[24] Enterprise resource planning (ERP) systems can also be tailored to include a returns management system but are still quite costly.

Companies with a small number of returns or those that do not consider returns management a core competency are relying on 3PLs that specialize in reverse logistics to handle their returns. 3PLs typically have high enough volumes of returns and have invested in their own proprietary systems to adequately support company returns. Unyson

Logistics, an Illinois-based 3PL, assists companies in managing their returns activities to help them save money. Unyson essentially takes control of managing a customer's returned, damaged, or obsolete products through its customized web-based communication and transportation networks. Clients gain full visibility of each return shipment while it is in transit, enroute to a distribution center or return center for disposal or reconstitution.[25]

Pennsylvania-based Genco Distribution System, a privately-held U.S. third-party logistics provider, works with its supply chain partners Target Stores and Thomson Consumer Electronics, a French manufacturer, to improve their returns management processes. Traditionally, returned products from Target were sent to Thomson's centralized returns center, where the bar code was scanned to determine if it was an acceptable return based on preset conditions. Any damaged items were scrapped and others were sent on to an inspection process. Costly time was spent sorting through the returned items. Genco, using its Value Inspection Process (VIP) software system and its own employees, inspects and determines a return's eligibility for credit before it is sent on to the manufacturer. The process has reduced the number of times a return is handled and reduced the time required for reconciliation and credit to Target.[26]

The Returns Management Process in Practice

Once a company has developed an overall returns strategy, a set of returns policies, and a network to manage its returns, it can develop operational tactics to handle issues related to returns as shown in Figure 15.4. The following sections provide a general template of the returns process in practice.

Customer Initiates Return Request

The returns process begins when a consumer or business customer makes a request to return a product and receive credit. For example, consumers may physically return items to a store, mail them back with a return form in the case of catalog sales, or initiate the process through the Internet, fax, or phone. Business customers generally use a return materials authorization to initiate the process, which is enclosed with the returned product.

Consumer goods are frequently returned to retailers for a number of reasons, as shown in Table 15.2. The top two reasons consumers return items are due to buyer's remorse or because the consumer found the product to be defective in some way. Consumers also return products voluntarily once they have been used, through recycling programs. However, customers may return a product because they receive a recall notice or hear about a recall through television or other publications, unaware previously that a problem existed. In February 2006, for instance, Connecticut-based Unilever recalled more than 400,000 Dove™ SkinVitalizer—Facial Cleansing Massagers because the cleansing pillows on the device were found to loosen or dislodge during use, resulting in scratches to the skin.[27]

Returns from supply chain members other than the end user can be categorized in three ways—**market returns**, **asset returns**, and **environmental returns**. Market returns refer to products returned by an organization somewhere within the supply chain other than the end user for any number of reasons, including slow sales, quality issues, a need to reposition inventory, or product closeouts. Another form of market return is where one manufacturer buys out a retailer's supply of a competitor's product to gain access to

Figure 15.4	The Returns Management Process in Practice

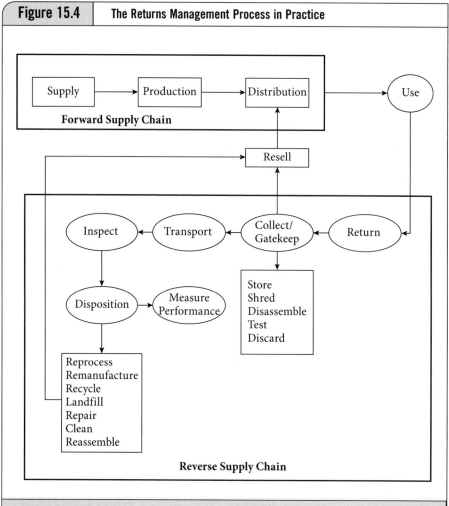

Source: Adapted from Rogers, D., and R. Tibben-Lembke (1999), *Going Backwards: Reverse Logistics Trends and Practices,* Center for Logistics Management, Reno, NV, Chapter 1.

that shelf space, also known as a **buy-out** or **lift. Job-outs** occur when seasonal merchandise is returned at the end of the season. When a supplier sells goods on consignment to a retailer and sales to the consumer do not subsequently materialize, unsold stock may be returned to the supplier for a credit toward future purchases. This practice is common in the grocery business. Figure 15.5 provides an example of a materials return authorization used by a grocery chain to return merchandise to the manufacturer.

Organizations may also *want* certain items returned to reposition that asset, such as equipment and reusable containers, known as asset returns. Fast-food outlet In-N-Out Burger, headquartered in California, for example, uses reusable plastic totes to ship meat patties and bags of dressing from its centralized processing facility to its restaurant locations in and near California.[28] New York-based Xerox Corporation uses nine types of standardized, reusable, corrugated shipping containers for its worldwide distribution network of facilities and suppliers. Xerox has an agreement with a third-party handler to collect, sort, and resell the empty containers where they are needed rather

Table 15.2	Types of Reverse Logistics Returns	
	PRODUCTS	**PACKAGING**
Consumers/Retailers	**Defective product** Buyer's remorse Warranty returns Product recalls Cash for disposal	**Reusable** Recyclable External/internal restrictions on disposal
Supply Chain Partners	**Marketing returns** **Asset returns** End of product life cycle Seasonal returns **Environmental returns**	**Reusable totes/containers** Multi-use packaging External/internal requirements for disposal

Sources: Adapted from Rogers, D. S., and R. Tibben-Lembke, "An Examination of Reverse Logistics Practices," *Journal of Business Logistics*, Vol. 22, No. 2, 2001, p. 134; and Rogers, D. S., D. M. Lambert, K. L. Croxton, and S. J. Garcia-Dastugue, "The Returns Management Process," *International Journal of Logistics Management*, V. 13, No. 2, 2002, pp. 1–18.

than requiring each supply chain member to return them to their point of origin. This system has saved the company packaging, disposal, and other costs.[29]

Firms may also be responsible for following environmental regulations to dispose of hazardous materials, known as environmental returns. Hazardous materials include explosives, gases, flammable liquids and solids, poisons, and corrosive metals. More than 3.1 billion tons of hazardous materials are transported annually within the United States alone.[30] The U.S. Environmental Protection Agency (EPA), for example, has strict regulations, including documentation and audit requirements for the transportation and disposal of hazardous materials. The European Union (EU) has adopted similar regulations for supply chain members. The EU, for example, ratified the Waste Electrical and Electronic Equipment Directive, which legislates that electronic equipment and appliance manufacturers must be accountable for the end-of-life disposal of their products—including refrigerators, computers, TVs, and cell phones. More on disposal of hazardous materials can be found toward the end of this chapter.

In the event the consumer initiates the returns management process, gatekeeping, as discussed earlier, is important to screen out product that should not be accepted back by the supplier. Some ways to reduce return abuse in brick and mortar stores is first to have the return policy clearly posted at the cash register and on the back of the receipt. Sales staff should be trained to explain the return policy to the consumer. Policies can also vary product-by-product. Davis, Hagerty and Gerstner, a team of researchers, found that a retailer is more likely to offer a low-hassle return policy when (1) its product benefits cannot be consumed in a short period of time, (2) its product line offers opportunities for cross-selling, and (3) it can obtain a high salvage value for returned merchandise.[31] Salespeople also need to watch for trends in unnecessary returns, create internal procedures to avoid them, and report any trends back to management.

Once a product has been returned, it enters into the returns network where items are routed to their proper destination, received into a warehouse or centralized returns center, and processed. These reverse logistics activities are described in the following sections.

Figure 15.5	Retailer – Return Form

MANUFACTURER RETURN   Page _____   Of   _____

The following merchandise was shipped from Warehouse number: _____

DATE: _____   CONTROL#: _____   DATE ISSUED: _____

Status: _____

SHIP TO: BILL TO: Bicep # _____
NAME: _____   A/P VENDOR #: _____
ADDRESS: _____   VENDOR NAME: _____
_____   ADDRESS: _____
_____   _____
_____   _____

WHO IS PAYING THE FREIGHT CHARGES TO RETURN THIS PRODUCT TO THE VENDOR? CHECK ONE.

[ ]   VENDOR WILL PAY ALL FREIGHT CHARGES. CHECK ONE.

[ ]   Vendor will make all pickup arrangements. Warehouse to hold product until contacted
by vendor representative.

[ ]   HEB to ship product freight collect via
_____
(Carrier Name)

(Warehouse – If blank, please call Corporate Traffic @ 938-6833)

[ ]   HEB TO PAY ALL FREIGHT CHARGES. SIGNATURE AND ACCOUNT NUMBER REQUIRED.
Director's Signature   _____
Account Number   _____

DESTROY: _____   Signature of Person Destroying: _____

WAREHOUSE SIGNATURE: _____   Date: _____

Reference PO#(s)   RETURN AUTHORIZATION#: _____

(Attach copy of return auth. and/or special instructions)

(If no return authorization then not applicable)

H-E-B CODE	H-E-B PACK	DESCRIPTION	COST PER HEB PACK	QTY IN HEB UNITS	A/R USE COST EXTENSION	WHSE USE ONLY	
						EACHES RETURNED	TOTAL CS, BXS,CRTNS
					$ -		
					$ -		
					$ -		
					$ -		
					$ -		
					$ -		
					$ -		
(ATTACH ADDITIONAL PAGES IF NECESSARY)				A/R INV $	$ -		

REASON FOR MANUFACTURER RETURN: _____

CATEGORY MANAGER SIGNATURE   _____   DATE: _____

VENDOR/BROKER SIGNATURE: _____   DATE: _____

VENDOR BROKER: Please confirm all information is correct.

All returns must be picked up in 10 days or product will be returned freight collect.

A 10% handling fee will be added to all Manufacturer Return Invoices:

CATEGORY MANAGERS: PROCUREMENT RECEIVABLES: WAREHOUSE
SEND ORIGINAL TO A/R   ISSUE CONTROL# /DATE   MINUS FROM INVENTORY
                             FAX: 1 COPY TO WHSE   SEND TO AR:
                             SEND: 1 COPY TO TRAFFIC   SIGNED M.R. W/COUNTS
REVISED   08/07/01   1 COPY TO CATEGORY MGR   BILL OF LADING
                                                        INVENTORY ADJ. REPORT

Initial Routing

After a return is received, employees determine the product's routing and any transportation requirements, if needed, based on preestablished guidelines. When a consumer returns a product, the supplier has a number of options, depending on the type of product, the condition of the product, and the supplier's returns program. If the product is in good condition and the consumer has returned it simply due to a change of mind, the product most likely is placed back on the shelf for resale. If the product is defective, it will be sent back to the manufacturer for inspection and put through quality control checks. Should the product be a seasonal item, such as clothing, it may be transported and sold to a retail outlet for later resale; some items, however, are stored until they are "in season" again or donated to other parties. Many Phoenix, Arizona-area grocery stores and distribution centers, for example, donate recently expired food products to the charity St. Mary's/Westside Food Bank.

In the event a product is being sent back in the supply chain to the manufacturer, a **centralized returns center**, or a warehouse, the receiving location is notified of the incoming shipment. In the case of a centralized return center, returns generally come from retailers and the center sorts them for processing, deciding disposition of each item based on guidelines from retailer and manufacturer.

As outlined in Table 15.3, the advantages of a centralized returns center are many, including:

1. Economies of scale in the center and during transportation occur because returns are shipped and processed in larger quantities, resulting in higher returns on their original value.

2. Specialization of the workforce is possible, where employees can develop an expertise in the returns process.

3. More consistent decision making regarding the disposition of product occurs.

4. Employees can identify errors in the return process and correct them more easily.

5. A centralized process moves returns out of retail locations, reducing the retailer's need for additional space to hold return product. It also shifts labor needs from the retailer to the return center.

6. Customer service often improves because the reconciliation process is quicker (the customer receives credit for their return more quickly) and consolidated information can help the manufacturer determine trends.

7. Retailers find that if they are doing a good job of gatekeeping and have a system in place that allows them to match returned merchandise with the supplier's inventory records, they have an easier time spotting problems with suppliers and products.[32]

There are some disadvantages associated with a centralized returns center, however. Additional transportation costs can be incurred because product that would normally be disposed of at the retail site is automatically transported to a returns center. Firms have also found it difficult to use the same distribution center to operate both forward and reverse logistics systems because forward logistics is typically the distribution center manager's first priority. But, additional sites for managing returns increase disposal costs. Some companies have found they can perform both forward and reverse logistics effectively if they separate the operations, in terms of flow and employees, within the same facility.

Table 15.3	Advantages and Disadvantages of Centralized Returns Centers

ADVANTAGES	DISADVANTAGES
• Store processes simplified • Relationships with suppliers improve • Inventory control easier • Inventory turns improve • Administrative costs decrease • Shrinkage is reduced • Landfill costs decrease • Retailer can focus on core competencies • Transportation costs less due to consolidation of returns	• Transportation of scrap product offsets lower transportation costs • Initial capital investment required: • Need separate returns facility or segregation of returns operations from forward logistics operations

Source: Rogers, D. S., and R. S. Tibben-Lembke, *Going Backwards: Reverse Logistics Trends and Practices*, Reno, NV: Center for Logistics Management, 1999, p. 66.

It is also important to emphasize that transporting returned goods is not a simple process. Labels are frequently inadequate or missing altogether. There are also many more transactions required to process a return than to distribute and sell a new product, thus requiring a greater amount of labor input. For example, an outbound truckload shipment of goods for sale only involves picking up the goods from a warehouse and delivering them to one or a small number of locations. However, returning just ten items could mean transporting them from several locations, with a different disposition for each item.

Determine Disposition

Once returns are delivered to a warehouse or centralized processing center, they will have to be inspected, verified against the returns authorization, and processed. Each return is then assigned a code based on the reason for its return. The codes can also be used when the returns management process is evaluated for its performance. The appropriate disposition must subsequently be determined based on preset guidelines. Returned product is often sold off to secondary markets outside the original supply chain, including liquidators, wholesalers, brokers, other retailers, and exporters.

Some products have been "used" and the consumer is returning them for a number of reasons; this activity is broadly termed **recycling**. Recycling covers the process of returning products for reuse in either the same form, or something completely different through repair remanufacturing or refurbishment. Such is the case for items such as aluminum soda cans, polyethylene terephthalate (plastic) bottles, glass jars, inkjet cartridges, and one-use cameras.

Shoe repair shops, for example, refurbish worn shoes to extend their useful life by replacing the soles of the shoes. As described in the Service Perspective feature, BellSouth understands the importance of the repair process to its customers. The U.S. telecommunications company partners with Florida-based Ryder Logistics, a 3PL, to ensure a smooth movement of parts to its repair sites. New York-based camera and film maker Kodak produces one-use cameras, for example, that are returned, remanufactured, and then resold again and again. Manufacturers also refurbish used products

Service Perspective
BellSouth: Service Quality Trumps Hardware

The most important part of a phone company's operation isn't the hardware and cables that travel throughout its distribution network. It's making sure those materials are available to customers when they're needed. "Our core competency is service performance," says Bill Hightower, assistant vice president of supply chain services with Atlanta-based BellSouth. "We are a service company."

Say what you will about deregulation of the telephone industry, but there's no question that it has forced the players to be more competitive. And the best way to lose a customer is to react slowly when systems go down. So BellSouth promises four-hour turnaround time on parts shipments in an emergency. It provides a constant flow of parts and equipment to more than 20,000 service technicians throughout the U.S. Southeast.

Outsourcing is at the heart of BellSouth's logistics strategy. Both warehousing and transportation are managed entirely by outsiders. In the case of transportation and parts-center management in the nine-state southeastern region, that's Ryder System, Inc.

In the repair business, nearly everything can be considered an emergency of some kind. Yet BellSouth doesn't rely on large caches of parts to guarantee availability. Utilizing a "near just-in-time" strategy, it tries to keep no more than two days of stock on hand at any location, says Hightower. For the most part, inventory is managed on a "pull" basis, geared toward actual demand rather than buffer stock.

The service is specialized, too. Except for the cable, nearly all deliveries are made at night, often unattended, putting parts into the hands of technicians by 7:00 the next morning. Many shipments come from a network of "plug-in" distribution centers (PDCs), operated by Ryder, which deliver critical circuit boards that can be quickly swapped for defective components. "They're the brains of the telephone network," Hubach says.

The system is further supported by a pair of larger, centralized warehouses—one in Suwanee, Georgia, for general merchandise, the other in Bessemer, Alabama, for plug-in units. Ryder's first job for BellSouth was providing linehaul service from those facilities. Now, in addition to the PDCs, it has taken over management of parts storerooms at the local level, usually in remote areas. There, it's the drivers who put away parts and monitor inventory, triggering orders when levels fall below preset minimums.

Ryder's current menu of services for BellSouth extends to the management of reverse logistics. That includes the return of empty cable spools, as well as parts for repair, recycling, redeployment, or disposal. Less than 3 percent of BellSouth's returned parts end up in a landfill, Hightower says with understandable pride.

BellSouth expects to ask Ryder for some enhancements in the carrier's tracking of returns, a capability that currently exists only in the outbound direction. For those shipments, Ryder's online tracking and tracing system follows shipments from the time they're received at the distribution centers to final delivery. Status reports are issued every two to four hours.

Source: Bowman, R. J., "BellSouth: Service Quality Trumps Hardware in Satisfying the Customer" *Global Logistics & Supply Chain Management Strategies,* July 2002, available at http://www.supplychainbrain.com/archives. Reprinted with permission.

to restore them to like-new condition. ReCellular, a cell phone reseller, collects, refurbishes, and resells used wireless phones. It operates a refurbishing and service facility in Fort Worth, Texas, processing up to 50,000 phones per month. Refurbishing includes painting, programming, replacing flashing, and other repairs necessary to bring the phones to near-new quality.[33]

The use of reclaimed materials to create new products is also a form of recycling. Massachusetts-based boat builder Walden Paddlers, for example, makes its kayaks from 100 percent recycled plastics.[34] Some types of plastic can be made into plastic lumber. The automotive industry also uses "shredded" metal from older vehicles to make new parts. More than 85 percent of the aluminum used in a car is **reclaimed**, or collected, and then recycled.[35]

Table 15.4 lists just some of the many products manufacturers create from recycled materials. For example, the freeways of metropolitan Phoenix, Sacramento, and Los Angeles are being resurfaced with rubberized asphalt—a mixture of crumb rubber (granulated rubber particles from scrap tires) and asphalt. Freeway noise has been substantially reduced and the material is guaranteed for several years.[36] Recycling and reuse of materials is one way manufacturers strive to reduce purchasing, transportation, and disposal costs as much as possible.

Defective products are typically returned to the original manufacturer for evaluation. The manufacturer will run tests to determine the reason for product failure, and the information can then be used to make changes to the original design, switch to suppliers that offer more reliable parts, or run additional tests at critical points in the manufacturing process and make changes to improve the production process.

Collect and Analyze Performance Metrics

The last step in the returns management process is to periodically review and measure returns management performance. The returns management process will only be effective in the long term if an organization develops a relevant set of measures to monitor the success of the process and then acts to address any problems that have been identified. Table 15.5 provides some examples of commonly used performance metrics. For example, a firm might collect operational information on return rates, the reasons for returns, and the time to process returns. Financially, a firm could be

Table 15.4	Examples of Products with Recycled Content
PRODUCTS	
Paper and paperboard	Road building materials
Retread tires	Erasable boards
Re-refined motor oil	Mulch
Carpeting	Plastic pipe
Binders	Writing paper, note pads, greeting cards,
Cereal, cookie, and cracker packages	and other stationery supplies
Canned foods and beverages	Plastic flower pots, trash cans, and recycling bins
Detergent and cleaning agents	Packing boxes
Supply containers	Insulation in ski jackets, gloves, and sleeping
Glass containers	bags made from recycled PET bottles
Household paper products, such as	
paper towels and bathroom tissue	
Fencing	

Table 15.5	Returns Management Performance Metrics

OPERATIONAL MEASURES	FINANCIAL MEASURES

• Returns inventory status
• Return cycle times
  • Cycle time to process product returns for resale (days)
  • Cycle time to process obsolete and end-of-life product returns for disposal (days)
  • Cycle time to repair or refurbish returns for use (days)
  • Cycle time to remanufacture items for resale
• Warranties
  • Percent actual cycle time versus published service agreement cycle time
  • Number of repairs performed as a percentage of total number of units shipped annually
• Number of repairs performed internally as a percentage of total number of repairs performed
• Number of repairs performed externally (by third party) as a percentage of total number of repairs performed
	• Returns processing cost
	  • Returns processing cost as percentage of product revenue
	• Cost of units repaired/refurbished internally
	  • Cost of units repaired/refurbished internally as a percentage of total costs
	• Cost of units repaired/refurbished externally
	  • Cost of units repaired/refurbished externally as a percentage of total costs
	• Cost to dispose of obsolete items to landfill
	• Asset recovery ($) as a percentage of original cost

Source: Adapted from P. Rupnow, "Maximizing Performance at Your Reverse Logistics Association," *Reverse Logistics Association Newsletter*, April 2006; http://www.reverselogisticstrends.com/newsletter/2006.

interested in tracking the average cost to process a return and the average recovery rate. Companies may also be interested in measuring the impact of their return policies on customer satisfaction or loyalty. These measures should all be used to improve the returns process, and as a result reduce expenses.

Returns management performance can be analyzed to determine, for example, if there are ways returns can be avoided and how well gatekeeping procedures are being followed. These metrics can also be used as feedback to other stakeholders. A supplier's product design team may review returns information to determine if improvements need to be made to current products. Metrics should also be used to evaluate a firm's financial performance and, to the extent possible, a product return's effect on future sales. Once an analysis has been performed, the team can set goals to improve the returns management process and communicate them to other members of the supply chain.

Drs. Markus Klausner and Chris Hendrickson examined a take-back system for power tools in Germany, a voluntary program for manufacturers. Customers return used power tools to dealers, who then collect the tools in boxes that hold a maximum of 200. Once a box is filled, the dealer calls a third-party logistics provider to arrange for pick-up. The 3PL then transports the filled box(es) to a recycling facility that specializes in remanufacturing power tools. Upon arrival, each tool is weighed, disassembled, and recycled. High-grade plastics are reused and any reclaimed materials are sold to secondary markets. An analysis of the process revealed low return rates, resulting in a $2.30 loss in revenue per power tool. Klausner and Hendrickson ascertained that the take-back system would be profitable if customers returned more power tools, thus increasing the amount of remanufacturing and sale of reclaimed materials. To increase the number of take-backs, they recommended buy-back plans with discounts toward the purchase of new tools, easier access to collection sites for consumers, and cash payments.[37]

Environmental Issues in the Returns Process

The returns management process can also help the environment through activities such as recycling, reusing materials and products, or refurbishing used products, which have been mentioned throughout this chapter. Some refer to this environmental approach as **green logistics** or **green supply chain management**.[38]

Green logistics has been defined as understanding and reducing the ecological impact of logistics in both the forward and reverse supply chain. Programs include customer-supplier partnerships to (1) reduce the environmental impact of certain modes of transportation, (2) achieve ISO 14000 certification, (3) increase energy efficiencies in supply chain logistics activities, (4) reduce the amount of materials used by redesigning products and processes, and (5) make use of reusable totes.

Green supply chain management extends the concept of green logistics to include activities related to environmentally responsible product design, acquisition, production, distribution, use, reuse, and disposal by partners within the supply chain. Companies learn about their suppliers' business practices as they develop closer relationships and, as a result, strive to jointly make cost-effective improvements to their environmental practices and increase innovation in products and process technologies. Paint production, for instance, is one of the worst sources of emissions of regulated chemicals. Paint suppliers, in conjunction with automakers, have recently developed innovative ideas, incorporating or substituting new environmentally safer materials and chemical designs into their paint products. Hazardous waste materials also result from the chemicals used to clean the production equipment. Paint suppliers have found ways to reduce the negative impact to the environment from these chemicals and solvents, a benefit to trading partners and the environment.[39]

Larger organizations are also discovering ways to further develop their suppliers through environmental training and certification programs. Automaker Toyota Motor Manufacturing North America, an environmental leader since 1992 and employer to 30,000 in the United States and Canada, released its publication, "Green Supplier Guidelines: Leadership in Environmental Performance," in 2000. All suppliers of direct and indirect materials must participate in this environmental plan. Suppliers are expected to apply for and receive the ISO 14001 certification, which means their environmental management system meets the ISO standard, and suppliers must also develop policies and procedures that comply with all government regulations, whether local, national, or international.[40]

Figure 15.6 illustrates some of the strategies companies have adopted to dispose of used products and materials. Traditionally, organizations have used landfills for routine product and material disposal but they have become more expensive and some are even closing. Local, state, and federal governments are also imposing stricter rules regarding landfills. For example, most U.S. states ban the disposal of phone books into landfills and about one-third of all U.S. landfills either do not accept pallets or charge an extra fee to dispose of them.

In some cases, these bans have led to innovative methods in dealing with used products. For example the Campbell Soup Company, headquartered in New Jersey, produces V-8®, Prego® spaghetti sauce, Open Pit® barbeque sauce, and several vegetable soups at one of its U.S. plants. Campbell was disposing of approximately 3,800 tons of damaged products annually into the local landfill until a ban was imposed by the local government. In response, Campbell bought and installed a can/liquid separation system. The

Figure 15.6	Reverse Logistics: Strategic Options

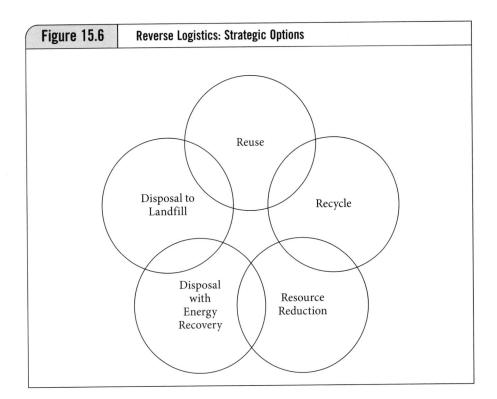

machine tears cans into small strips, washing and magnetically separating the metal. It also crushes glass containers, separating glass from food matter, and washes the glass fragments. The remaining vegetable matter is dried and sold as feed to local farmers.[41]

Integrated circuit manufacturer Advanced Micro Devices, headquartered in California, works with its suppliers to find ways to decrease packaging waste and handling activities. In one instance the company had traditionally used 55-gallon drums to store some of its bulk chemicals, but changed to 300-gallon totes and eventually to bulk tankers to reduce packaging waste that would eventually be delivered to a landfill. Advanced Micro Devices also saved money on both packaging costs and purchasing costs by buying in larger quantities.[42]

An improvement over simple disposal to a landfill is disposal with some form of energy recovery. **Pyrolysis** and **gasification** are two related forms of thermal treatment where materials are incinerated with limited oxygen. The process typically occurs in a sealed vessel, under high temperature and pressure. Converting material to energy this way is more efficient than direct incineration, with better recovery and use of energy. Pyrolysis of solid waste converts the material into solid, liquid, and gas products. The liquid oil and gas can be burned to produce energy or refined into other products. The solid residue, known as char, can be further refined into products such as activated carbon. Gasification is used to convert organic materials directly into a synthetic gas composed of carbon monoxide and hydrogen. The gas is then burned to produce electricity and steam. Gasification is used in biomass power stations to produce renewable energy and heat.[43]

The best way to take advantage of green logistics and green supply chain management, however, is in finding ways to reduce the use of resources. Coors Brewing

Company of Colorado, for example, was able to redesign its 16-ounce beer can, eliminating 12 percent of the aluminum content. The company also saves more than $1 million annually in aluminum costs.[44] Texas-based Chaparral Steel and TXI Cement Division also provide an excellent example of resource reduction. The two divisions operate a steel mill, cement plant, and automobile shredding facility. Their goal is to create enough linkages among the two divisions such that everything the steel mill produces will be a useful product. They use Chaparral's steel slag (a waste product from the smelting process) in TXI Cement's kiln to produce high-quality Portland cement, allowing TXI Cement to skip two energy-intensive steps in cement production. As a result, cement production jumped 10 percent and energy consumption dropped 10 percent, accompanied by a comparable reduction in greenhouse gas emissions. The Chaparral–TXI partnership also spurred the creation of a new company, Applied Sustainability LLC, which assists businesses in identifying by-product sharing opportunities.[45]

Note that there may be some overlap in environmental activities. For example, Illinois-based Schumacher Electric Corporation, a designer and manufacturer of electrical transformers, combines recycling and remanufacturing efforts. The company first bales and recycles corrugated cartons that arrive daily into its manufacturing sites. It then uses these recycled cartons to manufacture its own corrugated packaging parts including cushions, shelves, and partitions that fit inside cartons that contain outgoing freight. Its own packing materials are also reused.[46]

Disposal of Hazardous Materials in the United States

By law, U.S. companies must handle any hazardous waste that they produce in a responsible manner. The U.S. Resource Conservation and Recovery Act of 1976 (RCRA) was passed to create a "cradle to grave" mentality for organizations by requiring them to track all of the hazardous wastes they generate. The act sets up strict, technology-based standards for any hazardous waste deposited into landfills.[47] The 1984 Hazardous and Solid Wastes Amendments to the RCRA have since been added to the original act, which also requires companies producing hazardous materials to establish a waste minimization program.[48]

Most hazardous waste occurs as a by-product of a manufacturing process, but materials in used products may also be classified as such. For example, most computer monitors containing cathode ray tubes must be managed as a hazardous waste. The U.S. Department of Transportation estimates there are approximately 300 million shipments per year of hazardous materials in the United States alone and the total tonnage is expected to increase by 2 percent each year. And intermodal movements of hazardous materials are expected to increase three to four times faster than movements with single modes. While most inspections of hazardous materials are completed by the recipient, shippers play the largest role in the safe transportation of hazardous materials to their destination.[49]

The U.S. government also developed the United States Code of Federal Regulations (CFR), which governs the handling, packaging, and transportation of hazardous materials. The Environmental Protection Agency (EPA) and the Department of Transportation (DOT) have joint responsibility in regulating hazardous substances, defined as "severe pollutants to the environment," with various agencies enforcing the sections of the Code.[50] CFR Title 29 was adopted to protect the health and safety of employees that work with hazardous materials. CFR Title 40, enforced by the EPA, includes a lengthy set of standards for the safe disposal of hazardous waste. For example, hazardous materials may never be disposed of into septic tanks and can only be burned in hazardous waste incinerators that have been issued a permit.

CFR Title 49 regulates the transportation of hazardous materials and is jointly enforced by the Research and Special Program Administration, the Department of Transportation's individual agencies governing air, rail, highways, and the Coast Guard. The following sections provide a brief description of the five areas covered under CFR Title 49.

Definition and Classification of Hazardous Materials

CFR Title 49 provides a listing of several thousand of the most commonly transported hazardous materials. Materials are divided into several classifications, including explosives, radioactive materials, gases, liquid and solid flammables, oxidizing materials, organic peroxides, corrosive materials, poisons, and miscellaneous. Some hazardous materials are designated as "forbidden" and may not be transported at all. Other materials may be not be transported by certain modes such as air transportation.

Communication Issues

Specific warnings regarding each shipped hazardous material must be communicated on shipping documents, package markings and labels, placards that appear on transportation vehicles, and written emergency response information including telephone numbers to be used in case of emergencies. Properly prepared shipping documents must contain an identification of the hazardous material and hazard class or division number, identification number, packing group if applicable, and total quantity shipped.

Packaging Requirements

Markings and labels should contain similar warnings that are provided on the shipping documents. CFR Title 49 also includes specifications as to the size and color of warning labels. For instance, packaging labels should be designed such that anyone can easily recognize that the shipment contains hazardous materials through use of durable and readily visible markings.

Operating Rules

Title 49 also specifies operating rules for companies that ship hazardous materials, including procedures for incident reporting. Transportation carriers must report all incidents and keep them in an automated Hazardous Materials Information System database. Incidents involving aircraft shipments must be reported to the closest FAA Civil Aviation Security Office.

Training

Any employee performing functions in connection with hazardous materials must receive initial training and then again at least once every three years. If new regulations are adopted, employees must receive training on these requirements before they perform their function again. The employer is responsible for providing the training and must keep records.

Guidelines

Regardless of an organization's size, several steps should be taken to manage the safe transportation of hazardous materials. A company should begin by developing a written compliance program with goals and desired outcomes, organization of the agency, and a training plan. To be most effective, the plan should be endorsed at the highest level possible. Ownership and accountability for handling hazardous materials should also be set throughout the organization. To ensure safe movements of hazardous materials and compliance with federal, state, and local laws, employees need systematic and recurrent training as well. All provisions of the written compliance program should be enforced, with strict maintenance of the program and related records.[51] Sufficient resources in terms of money, information, and personnel will ensure that the program is successful.

Disposal of Hazardous Materials in Europe

For the most part, European governments have stricter laws regarding environmental protection than does the United States. The European Union (EU) requires manufacturers to recycle their own products through country-by-country compliance laws. The EU Parliament also has passed the ROHS (reduction-of-hazardous-substances) Directive 2002/95/EC, which has strict rules regarding the use of hazardous substances for electrical and electronic equipment within the EU as of July 1, 2006. All manufacturers selling products within the EU must comply with this directive. Member countries can impose their own penalties for any company that fails to comply with the directive.

Beyond restricting the use of hazardous materials in manufacturing, the EU also has several directives related to the disposal of hazardous materials. Council Directive 91/689/EEC, passed in 1991, governs the management, recovery, and disposal of hazardous waste. The directive provides a list of all hazardous wastes, requires that all hazardous materials must be recorded and identified, and states that an identified hazardous material cannot be mixed with non-hazardous waste or other categories of hazardous waste. Subsequent decisions have resulted in an amendment expanding the list of hazardous materials and outlining the format to be used for information reports.

Council Decision 93/98/EEC, passed in 1993, governs the transportation and disposal of hazardous materials across national boundaries. Some of the provision's requirements include:

- Both parties involved in the movement must consent, in writing, to the transportation of hazardous waste.
- Transboundary movements of wastes are only authorized in those situations where there is no danger attached to their movement and disposal.
- Hazardous materials must be packaged, labeled, and transported in conformance to international rules, and must be accompanied by a movement document from the point at which a movement commences to the point of disposal.
- Either party involved in the movement of hazardous materials may add requirements that are consistent with the provisions of the Basel Convention.[52]

The United Nations passed the Basel Convention on the Control of Transboundary Movements of Hazardous Waste and Their Disposal in 1989. The Basel Convention is an international treaty designed to reduce the transportation of hazardous wastes be-tween nations, and specifically movements from developed to undeveloped countries. In the original document, developed nations were not allowed to ship hazardous waste to undeveloped countries without their prior consent. The goal of the Convention was also to reduce the amount and toxicity of wastes generated. The Convention was signed by 166 nations and it has been in force since 1992, although the United States, Haiti, and Afghanistan have not ratified it to-date. In 1995 the Basel Ban Amendment was passed, which absolutely prohibits the export of hazardous waste to undeveloped countries. The EU made this amendment binding to all member nations through pas-sage of the European Waste Shipment Regulation.[53]

Returns Management along the Supply Chain

As suggested throughout this chapter, companies cannot maximize their returns management capabilities without the help of other supply chain members. Some compa-nies are developing special programs with key customers and suppliers that are more heavily involved in their returns efforts. Anheuser-Busch Inc., for example, manufac-turer of alcoholic and non-alcoholic beverages, includes both key customers and suppli-ers in its efforts to help protect the environment and increase profitability at the same time. The Missouri-based company works with its supply partners in materials recovery to improve the quality of the aluminum cans collected and to increase recycling rates. As a result, Anheuser-Busch recycles more than 100 percent of what it actually ships out. The company also has worked with key suppliers to cut the amount of aluminum used. Together, they have also reduced the amount of solid waste deposited to landfills by al-most 70 percent. Additionally, Anheuser-Busch created a supplier certification program for packaging suppliers. The company sets up requirements that address the environ-ment and continuous improvement. On the customer side, Anheuser-Busch works with its wholesalers to increase recycling of stretchwrap.[54]

Mattel, one of the world's premier toymakers with headquarters in California, has implemented a returns management program to monitor, manage, and prevent returns from occurring by working more closely with a select group of high-volume retailers and its own design and manufacturing teams. Low-volume retailers that are not audited receive a return allowance to manage their returns. However, high-volume partners must ship back all returned Mattel toys for analysis. Mattel then audits each returned item and analyzes collected data on defective versus non-defective returns, using the information to determine if anything related to packaging, instructions, or the product itself can be improved to reduce the rate of returns. It also provides additional training to retailing partners on the setup of displays and warehouse product handling. If the product is defective, the company's manufacturing facility that made a particular item is noted, and sample defective items are sent to product design groups for additional analysis.[55]

SUMMARY

This chapter has discussed the process of returns management, which closes the supply chain process loop. As mentioned early in this chapter, the returns management process should be considered and factored into each product's life cycle to make the disposition of returned goods easier and as environmentally friendly as possible.

Returns management should be closely tied to an organization's customer service process. Thus, as companies develop their customer service strategy, they should also be developing their returns management strategy. A returns management strategy sets the stage for the development of guidelines to design return and credit policies as well as disposal practices.

Companies should also evaluate and find ways to be more environmentally responsible using their returns management process. Examples of green logistics and green supply chain management activities were provided. Companies are legally and morally bound to dispose of hazardous materials to protect the environment, and this topic was also discussed.

KEY TERMS

advanced shipping notification, 588

asset recovery, 581

asset returns, 589

avoidance, 581

buy-out, 590

cancellation stage, 576

centralized returns center, 593

chargeback, 586

closed-loop supply chain management, 575

cross-sell, 583

decline stage, 576

development stage, 576

disposition, 581

end-of-quarter loading, 583

environmental returns, 589

everyday low pricing, 583

gasification, 599

gatekeeping, 581

green logistics, 598

green supply chain management, 598

growth stage, 576

introduction stage, 576

ISO 14000 certification, 585

job-outs, 590

life cycle, 576

lift, 590

market returns, 589

maturity stage, 576

pyrolysis, 599

reclaimed, 596

recycling, 594

refurbishing, 581

remanufacturing, 573

return allowance, 586

return authorizations, 588

returns, 575

reverse logistics, 575

secondary market brokers, 577

secondary markets, 583

short payments, 586

upselling, 583

zero returns policy, 586

DISCUSSION QUESTIONS

1. Why is returns management important to organizations today?

2. What is returns management? How does the definition of returns management differ from the definitions "returns," "reverse logistics," and "closed-loop supply chain management"?

3. Identify the role of returns management at each stage of the product life cycle.

4. What three factors are important in developing a returns management strategy?

5. Define avoidance and gatekeeping. Share a past experience, where a company either avoided taking back a returned product or used gatekeeping.

6. Who should be involved in setting policies and procedures for returns, and what role should they play?

7. What are secondary markets? Provide three examples.

8. Read the opening Process Management in Action feature on Hyundai Motor America. What was the role of Roadway, a third-party logistics provider, in Hyundai's returns management process?

9. Collect the credit policies of three retail stores, restaurants, or other service providers. Compare and contrast their policies. Which company has the most liberal policy? The strictest policy?

10. Describe three types of credit policies offered by manufacturers to their business customers.

11. What are the top two reasons consumers return products?

12. What is the difference between market returns, asset returns, and environmental returns?

13. What are some possible options for the disposition of returned products?

14. What are the advantages and disadvantages companies should consider in setting up a centralized returns center?

15. Define each of the following terms and identify a product example for each term.
    a. Repaired
    b. Refurbished
    c. Remanufactured
    d. Recycled
    e. Rebuilt

16. Why is the collection of performance measures or metrics important to the returns management process?

17. What are the attributes of a good returns management information system?

18. What is the difference between reverse logistics and "green" logistics? What is an example of an activity considered "green" logistics but not reverse logistics?

19. What is the least environmentally friendly form of product disposal? What is the most environmentally friendly form of product disposal?

20. Describe the three "titles" of the United States Code of Federal Regulations that apply to the disposal of hazardous materials.

INTERNET QUESTIONS

1. Go to the International Organization for Standardization's website and report on the ISO 14000 "family" of standards. How do they differ?

2. Find a website of a firm that specializes in the purchase of remanufactured products and report on the company and its activities.

INFOTRAC QUESTIONS

Access http://www.infotrac-thomsonlearning.com to answer the following questions:

1. Find three articles that describe returns management strategic planning developed by companies. Compare and contrast the similarities and differences between each strategy. Include a bibliography.

2. Find articles that discuss centralized returns centers at three different companies and identify the commonalities and differences. Include a bibliography.

3. Find articles that address the use of third-party logistics providers (3PLs) in the returns management process and write a paper. Include a bibliography.

REFERENCES

Rogers, D. S., D. M. Lambert, K. L. Croxton, and S. J. Garcia-Dastugue, "The Returns Management Process," *International Journal of Logistics Management,* V. 13, No. 2, 2002, pp. 1–18.

Rogers, D. S., and R. S. Tibben-Lembke (1999), *Going Backwards: Reverse Logistics Trends and Practices,* Center for Logistics Management, Reno, NV.

Tibben-Lembke, R. S., "Life after Death: Reverse Logistics and the Product Life Cycle," *International Journal of Physical Distribution and Logistics Management,* V. 32, No. 3/4, 2002, pp. 223–244.

ENDNOTES

1. Joan Starkowsky, president of Roadway Reverse Logistics, quoted in Malone, R., "Reverse Side of Logistics: The Business Side of Returns," *Forbes.com,* November 3, 2005.

2. Quote by Bill Wascher, president and CEO of SEKO Worldwide, found in Malone, R., "Closing the Supply Chain Loop: Reverse Logistics and the SCOR Model," *Inboundlogistics.com,* January 2004.

3. Guide Jr., V., "Production Planning and Control for Remanufacturing: Industry Practice and Research Needs," *Journal of Operations Management,* V. 18, 2000, pp. 467–483.

4. Trebilcock, B., "The Seven Deadly Sins of Reverse Logistics: You may think your company is doing an adequate job of managing returned goods, but can you be sure you haven't been snared by one of these pitfalls?" *Logistics Management,* June 2002, p. 31.

5. Rogers, D. S., D. M. Lambert, K. L. Croxton, and S. J. Garcia-Dastugue, "The Returns Process," *International Journal of Logistics Management,* V. 13, No. 2, 2002, pp. 1–18.

6. Stock, J. R., *Development and Implementation of Reverse Logistics Programs,* Oak Park, IL: Council of Logistics Management, 1998, p. 20.

7. Fleischman, M., *Quantitative Models for Reverse Logistics,* Berlin: Spring-Verlag, 2001, p. 6.

8. Rogers, D. S., D. M. Lambert, K. L. Croxton, and S. J. Garcia-Dastugue, "The Returns Management Process," *International Journal of Logistics Management,* V. 13, No. 2, 2002, p.1.

9. A timeline on the history of Arm & Hammer baking soda can be found at http://www.armhammer.com.

10. Tibben-Lembke, R. S., "Life After Death: Reverse Logistics and the Product Life Cycle," *International Journal of Physical Distribution and Logistics Management,* V. 32, No. 3/4, 2002, pp. 223–244.

11. See http://www.staples.com for program guidelines.

12. See http://www.metro-region.org/article.cfm?articleid=854 for more information on the Trader Joe's food donation program.

13. Interview with Curt Mowen, H-E-B category manager, September 5, 2000.

14. Rogers, D. S., and R. S. Tibben-Lembke, *Going Backwards: Reverse Logistics Trends and Practices,* Reno, NV: Center for Logistics Management, 1999, p. 66.

15. See note 14 above, p. 38.

16. UPS Supply Chain Solutions, "Reverse Logistics – The Least Used Differentiator," 2005, p. 3.

17. More information on Saks and Off Fifth can be found at http://www.saksincorporated.com.

18. More information on Big Lots can be found at http://www.biglots.com.

19. See http://www.ebay.com.

20. Stein Mart's return policy can be found at http://www.steinmart.com.

21. Procter & Gamble Pharmaceuticals, Inc., Returned Goods Policy, Form PGP 1002 05/05.

22. Coletto, T., "When Do It Yourself Is a Waste of Money," accessed March 3, 2006, at http://www.fita.org/aotm/0101.html.

23. "Coke Recall Highlights Need for Traceability," *BeverageDaily.com,* March 25, 2004, available at http://www.beveragedaily.com.

24. http://www.barcontrol.com/reverselogistics.htm.

25. Malone, R., "Reverse Side of Logistics: The Business of Returns," November 2, 2005, available at http://www.forbes.com.

26. "Target, Thomson Treat Returns as V.I.P.s," *Chain Store Age,* November 1998, p. 102.

27. U.S. Office of Consumer Product Safety Commission, "Unilever Recalls Dove™ Facial Cleansing Massager after Nine Reports of Minor Injuries," February 28, 2006, available at http://www.cpsc.gov/cpscpub/prerel/prhtml06/06098.html.

28. Saphire, D., *Delivering the Goods: Benefits from Using Reusable Containers,* New York, NY: Inform Inc., 1994.

29. Case study No. 9607, Xerox Corporation, available at http://web.indstate.edu/recycle/9607.html.

30. Office of Hazardous Materials Safety, *Hazardous Materials Shipments,* Washington, DC: U.S. Department of Transportation, 1998, p. 1.

31. Davis, S., M. Hagerty, and E. Gerstner, "Return Policies and the Optimal Level of 'Hassle'," *Journal of Economics and Business,* September–October 1998.

32. See note 14 above, p. 56.

33. "ReCellular Inc. Opens 50,000 Sq. Ft. Cell Phone Refurbishing/Repair Facility in Fort Worth," July 2004 news release available at http://www.recellular.net.

34. Larson, A. L., "Paddling to a Network Solution Through Recycling," *Strategic Direction,* March 2001, pp. 18–20.

35. Statistics found at North American Die-Casting Association website, *Environmental Newsletter,* http://www.diecasting.org/environment/.

36. See http://www.rubberizedasphalt.org/products.htm for more information.

37. Klausner, M., and C. T. Hendrickson, "Reverse-Logistics Strategy for Product Take-Back," *Interfaces,* May/June 2000, pp. 156–165.

38. Rogers, D. S., and R. Tibben-Lembke, "An Examination of Reverse Logistics Practices," *Journal of Business Logistics,* V. 22, No. 2, 2001, p. 130; Zsidisin, G. A. and S. P. Sifer, "Environmental Purchasing: A Framework for Theory Development," *European Journal of Purchasing and Supply Management,* March 2001, p. 69.

39. Geffen, C. A., and S. Rothenberg, "Suppliers and Environmental Innovation: The Automotive Paint Process," *International Journal of Operations and Production,* V. 20, No. 2, 2000, p. 166.

40. "Toyota Leaders Suppliers into Green Parade," August 29, 2000, available at http://www.socialfunds.com.

41. More information on this case can be found at http://web.indstate.edu/recycle/9505.html.

42. Trowbridge, P., "A Case Study of Green Supply-Chain Management," *Greener Management International,* Autumn 2001, pp. 121–135.

43. Information was found at http://en.wikipedia.org.

44. Further case details can be found at http://web.indstate.edu/recycle/9605.html.

45. See http://www.epa.gov/jtr/topics/eipex.htm.

46. See http://web.indstate.edu/recycle/9503.html.

47. Kellogg, M., "After Environmentalism: Three Approaches to Managing Environmental Regulation," *Regulation,* V. 17, No. 1, 1994, pp. 25–34.

48. Gupta, M. C., "Environmental Management and Its Impact on the Operations Function," *International Journal of Operations and Production Management,* V. 15, No. 8, 1995, pp. 34–51.

49. NE Department of Transportation, *Departmentwide program evaluation of the hazardous materials transportation programs, executive summary,* March 2000, available at http://hazmat.dot.gov/.

50. United States Code Annotated, Title 40, St. Paul, MN: West Publishing Company, 1993, p. 239.

51. Currie, J. V., "Hazmat Safety Is No Accident," *Logistics Management and Distribution Report,* V. 38, No. 10, 1999, p. 65, retrieved from Business & Company Resource Center Database.

52. See http://europa.eu.int/scadplus/leg/en/s15002.htm for more information on EU Directives.

53. http://www.basel.int/pub/pub.html.

54. "Anheuser-Busch 'Greens' Its Supply Chain for Cost Savings," *Purchasing,* May 17, 2001, p. 22.

55. Rupnow, P., "Why Mattel's Reverse Logistics Team Gets All the Resources They Need," a Reverse Logistics Association Report, available at http://www.reverselogisticstrends.com.

Appendix 1
Areas Under the Normal Curve

This table gives the area under the curve to the left of x, for various Z scores, or number of standard deviations from the mean. For example, in the figure, if Z = 1.96, the value .97500 found in the body of the table is the total shaded area to the left of x.

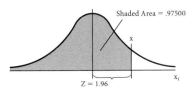

Z	.00	.01	.02	.03	.04	.05	.06	.07	.08	.09
.0	.50000	.50399	.50798	.51197	.51595	.51994	.52392	.52790	.53188	.53586
.1	.53983	.54380	.54776	.55172	.55567	.55962	.56356	.56749	.57142	.57535
.2	.57926	.58317	.58706	.59095	.59483	.59871	.60257	.60642	.61026	.61409
.3	.61791	.62172	.62552	.62930	.63307	.63683	.64058	.64431	.64803	.65173
.4	.65542	.65910	.66276	.66640	.67003	.67364	.67724	.68082	.68439	.68793
.5	.69146	.69497	.69847	.70194	.70540	.70884	.71226	.71566	.71904	.72240
.6	.72575	.72907	.73237	.73536	.73891	.74215	.74537	.74857	.75175	.75490
.7	.75804	.76115	.76424	.76730	.77035	.77337	.77637	.77935	.78230	.78524
.8	.78814	.79103	.79389	.79673	.79955	.80234	.80511	.80785	.81057	.81327
.9	.81594	.81859	.82121	.82381	.82639	.82894	.83147	.83398	.83646	.83891
1.0	.84134	.84375	.84614	.84849	.85083	.85314	.85543	.85769	.85993	.86241
1.1	.86433	.86650	.86864	.87076	.87286	.87493	.87698	.87900	.88100	.88298
1.2	.88493	.88686	.88877	.89065	.89251	.89435	.89617	.89796	.89973	.90147
1.3	.90320	.90490	.90658	.90824	.90988	.91149	.91309	.91466	.91621	.91774
1.4	.91924	.92073	.92220	.92364	.92507	.92647	.92785	.92922	.93056	.93189
1.5	.93319	.93448	.93574	.93699	.93822	.93943	.94062	.94179	.94295	.94408
1.6	.94520	.94630	.94738	.94845	.94950	.95053	.95154	.95254	.95352	.95449
1.7	.95543	.95637	.95728	.95818	.95907	.95994	.96080	.96164	.96246	.96327
1.8	.96407	.96485	.96562	.96638	.96712	.96784	.96856	.96926	.96995	.97062
1.9	.97128	.97193	.97257	.97320	.97381	.97441	.97500	.97558	.97615	.97670
2.0	.97725	.97784	.97831	.97882	.97932	.97982	.98030	.98077	.98124	.98169
2.1	.98214	.98257	.98300	.98341	.98382	.98422	.98461	.98500	.98537	.98574
2.2	.98610	.98645	.98679	.98713	.98745	.98778	.98809	.98840	.98870	.98899
2.3	.98928	.98956	.98983	.99010	.99036	.99061	.99086	.99111	.99134	.99158
2.4	.99180	.99202	.99224	.99245	.99266	.99286	.99305	.99324	.99343	.99361
2.5	.99379	.99396	.99413	.99430	.99446	.99461	.99477	.99492	.99506	.99520
2.6	.99534	.99547	.99560	.99573	.99585	.99598	.99606	.99621	.99632	.99643
2.7	.99653	.99664	.99674	.99683	.99693	.99702	.99711	.99720	.99728	.99736
2.8	.99744	.99752	.99760	.99767	.99774	.99781	.99788	.99795	.99801	.99807
2.9	.99813	.99819	.99825	.99831	.99836	.99841	.99846	.99851	.99856	.99861
3.0	.99865	.99869	.99874	.99878	.99882	.99886	.99889	.99893	.99896	.99900
3.1	.99903	.99906	.99910	.99913	.99916	.99918	.99921	.99924	.99926	.99929
3.2	.99931	.99934	.99936	.99938	.99940	.99942	.99944	.99946	.99948	.99950
3.3	.99952	.99953	.99955	.99957	.99958	.99960	.99961	.99962	.99964	.99965
3.4	.99966	.99968	.99969	.99970	.99971	.99972	.99973	.99974	.99975	.99976
3.5	.99977	.99978	.99978	.99979	.99980	.99981	.99981	.99982	.99983	.99983
3.6	.99984	.99985	.99985	.99986	.99986	.99987	.99987	.99988	.99988	.99989
3.7	.99989	.99990	.99990	.99990	.99991	.99991	.99992	.99992	.99992	.99992
3.8	.99993	.99993	.99993	.99994	.99994	.99994	.99994	.99995	.99995	.99995
3.9	.99995	.99995	.99996	.99996	.99996	.99996	.99996	.99996	.99997	.99997

Appendix 2
Answers to Even-Numbered End-of-Chapter Problems

Chapter 2

2. manufacture in house: <2,667,
outsource: >2,667

Chapter 5

2. a. $F_1 = 33$, $F_2 = 35.4$, $F_3 = 32.68$, $F_4 = 36.94$, $F_5 = 38.59$
b. $F_1 = 33$, $F_2 = 33.6$, $F_3 = 33.28$, $F_4 = 34.22$, $F_5 = 35.18$
c. MAD ($\alpha = .80$) = 3.67, MAD ($\alpha = .20$) = 3.06

4. a. $1,102,306.60
b. Yes; correlation coefficient = 0.9407,
Coefficient of determination = 0.8849

Chapter 6

2. a. $\text{EPQ} = \sqrt{\dfrac{2DS}{\left(1-\frac{d}{p}\right)iC}} = \sqrt{\dfrac{2(3,500,000)(100)}{\left(1-\frac{14,000}{22,000}\right)(.25)(.08)}}$

$= \sqrt{\dfrac{700,000,000}{(.364)(.02)}} = 310,242 \text{ tees.}$

b. It will take about 14 days to produce that many tees
(or 310,242/22,000).

c. The maximum inventory level will be $310,242 - 14,000(14)$,
or about 114,242 assuming that each day they ship or sell
14,000 premium tees. This is about 8 days of inventory.

4. $\text{ROP}_{DT} = d(L) + Z\sigma = \dfrac{2,300}{365}(12) + 2.33(6) = 75.6 + 14 \approx 90 \text{ rolls}$

$\text{ROP}_{SG} = \dfrac{1,800}{365}(6) + 1.28(4) = 29.6 + 5.1 \approx 35 \text{ bottles}$

$\text{ROP}_{H} = \dfrac{650}{365}(21) + 0.84(3) = 37.4 + 2.5 \approx 40 \text{ hammers}$

The safety stocks for the three items are shown above, as the
2nd term in the equation.

6. Place the items in order from largest cost/yr to smallest.

Item	Cost/Unit ($)	Forecasted Annual Demand	Annual Cost	Classif.
3	$ 17.49	6,240	$109,138	A
6	345.00	300	103,500	A
2	7.80	7,500	58,500	B
5	105.99	150	15,898	C
4	44.00	260	11,440	C
1	6.40	1,700	10,880	C

Note: With only 6 items, it is unlikely the ABC classes will conform to the 70/25/5 rule. You have to compare the total costs.
Items 3 and 6 will require the closest monitoring and highest
safety stock levels, and items 5, 4, and 1 will require the lowest
safety stocks and monitoring effort. Item 2 will require a "medium" level of monitoring and safety stock.

Chapter 7

2. $C = (960 \text{ min/day})/(80 \text{ units/day}) = 12 \text{ minutes/unit.}$
Note: The other information is not needed.

4. Min. takt time = 7 min. (D is the bottleneck.)
Output = 480/7 = 68 units/day;
Efficiency = 28/(6)(7) = 67%;
Idle time = 42 − 28 or 14 min./unit or 14(68)
= 952 min./day or 15.87 labor hrs./day

6.

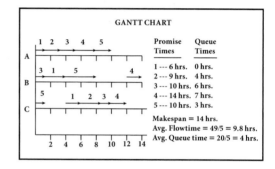

8.

Jobs	Time	Time	Late	Tardy
1	6	0	2	0
2	10	5	5	0
3	7	3	0	0
4	14	7	6	0
5	10	3	6	0

Makespan = 14
Avg. flowtime = 9.4
Avg. queue time = 3.6
Avg. lateness = 3.8
Avg. tardiness = 0

At time = 0, there are 3 jobs waiting at Machine A, 1 at B,
and 1 at C. Using the CR rule at A, we get Job 1 (CR=8/6),
Job 2 (CR=3), Job 4 (CR=20/7), so Job 1 has priority.

At time = 1, there are queues at A (Jobs 2, 3, 4) and at B
(Jobs 1, 5). At A, using the CR rule, we get Job 2 (CR=14/5),
Job 3 (CR=2), Job 4 (CR=19/7), so Job 3 has priority.
At B, using the CR rule, we get Job 1 (CR=7/5) and
Job 5 (CR=15/6), so Job 1 has priority.

At time = 3, there is a queue at A (Jobs 2, 4). Using the CR rule,
we get Job 2 (CR=12/5) and Job 4 (CR=17/7), so Job 2
has priority.

At time = 4, Job 5 is alone at B, so it is processed, and there is a
queue at C (Jobs 1, 3). Using the CR rule, we get Job 1 (CR=2)
and Job 3 (CR=3), so Job 1 has priority.

At time = 5, Job 4 is processed at A. At time=6, there is a queue at
C (Jobs 2, 3). Using the CR rule, we get Job 2 (CR=3) and
Job 3 (CR=1), so Job 3 has priority.

At time = 7, Job 2 is processed at C.

At time = 8, Job 5 is processed at A.

At time = 10, Job 4 is processed at C. All jobs are now complete.
The CR rule appears to work fairly well.

Chapter 7 (continued)

10.

Delivery	Promised Arrival Time	Estimated Completion Time	Vehicle Number
1	9:00 AM	9:20 AM	1
2	9:45 AM	10:15 AM	1
3	10:00 AM	10:45 AM	2
4	10:30 AM	11:00 AM	1
5	10:45 AM	12:15 PM	3
6	11:00 AM	11:45 AM	2
7	11:30 AM	12:00 PM	1
8	12:30 PM	2:00 PM	1 (Veh. 1 is closest)
9	1:00 PM	1:45 PM	2 (Veh. 2 is closer)
10	1:30 PM	2:30 PM	3
11	2:30 PM	3:15 PM	2 (Veh. 2 is closer)
12	3:00 PM	4:00 PM	3 (Veh. 3 is closer)
13	3:30 PM	4:30 PM	2 (Veh. 2 is closer)

Vehicle	Schedule	Start / End Times
1	1-2-4-7-8	9:00 AM/2:00 PM
2	3-6-9-11-13	10:00 AM/4:30 PM
3	5-10-12	10:45 AM/4:00 PM

Chapter 8

2. Use the formula: $f(n) = \dfrac{(\lambda t)^n e^{-\lambda t}}{n!}$.

So, the probability of exactly 10 customers arriving in one hour would be:

$$f(10) = \frac{20^{10} e^{-20}}{10!} = 0.00582 \text{ or } 0.58\%, \text{ a small probability.}$$

4. $\lambda = 10$ customers per hour

$\mu = 20$ customers per hour

$\rho = 50\%$ utilization

$L_q = \dfrac{(.5)(10)}{20 - 10} = 0.5$ customer

$L_s = 0.5 + 0.5 = 1.0$ customer

$W_q = \dfrac{0.5}{10}$ hour $= 3$ minutes

$W_s = 3$ minutes $+ \dfrac{1}{20}$ hour $= 6$ minutes

$P_{>1} =$ Probability of more than 1 customer in the system $= 1 - (P_0 + P_1)$

$P_0 = 1 - 0.5 = 0.5$

$P_1 = (.5)(.5) = 0.25$

Thus, $P_{>1} = 1 - 0.75 = 0.25 = 25\%$

So, 25 percent of the time, customers will have to wait in line prior to receiving service. Based on this, he appears to have a good system.

Chapter 10

2. $8.45 \approx 9$

4. $A1 = 6$

$A2 = 1$

$A3 = 3$

$A4 = 4$

Chapter 11

2. D, because score is lowest.

Chapter 13

2. a. $UCL_R = 8.31$;

$LCL_R = 0$;

$UCL_X = 5.68$;

$LCL_X = 1.15$;

no assignable causes present.

b. $C_P = 3.95$;

$C_{PK} = 3.95$;

yes process is capable.

4. a. $UCL_R = 0.27$;

$LCL_R = 0$;

$UCL_X = 4.69$;

$LCL_X = 4.87$;

no assignable causes present.

b. $C_P = 3.18$;

$C_{PK} = 3.16$;

yes process is capable.

Chapter 14

2. Improve distribution process

PPI (reduce delivery time)=0.0525;

PPI (reduce Website down time) = 0.15;

PPI (improve distribution) = 0.64.

Appendix 3
URL List

http://www.donotcall.gov

http://www.privacyalliance.org

http://www.the-dma.org

http://www.w3c.org

http://www.theacsi.org

http://www.albertsons.com

http://www.mysteryshop.org

http://www.ibf.org/

http://www.vics.org

http://www.quality.nist.gov/

http://www.inventoryops.com

http://www.e-z-mrp.com

http://www.purchasingnetwork.com

http://www.royalmail.com

http://www.C3tools.com

http://www.harrisinteractive.com

http://www.lizclaiborneinc.com

http://www.tradebeam.com

Glossary

A

ABC inventory classification An approach used to help companies manage their independent demand inventories. The idea is to pay closer attention to items accounting for a larger percentage of the firm's annual sales. Typically, the Class A items (the most important) represent approximately 75 to 80 percent of annual sales and about 20 percent of inventory SKUs, the Class B items account for approximately 15 to 20 percent of annual sales and represent 25 to 30 percent of inventory SKUs, and the Class C items are the least important to the firm, representing about 50 to 60 percent of the inventory SKUs while accounting for only about 5 percent of sales.

active external integration phase The most advanced stage of the integration model; the firm's abilities to integrate internally have matured, creating successful process collaborations between personnel throughout the firm. As the firm witnesses these successes and realizes the value inherent in process integration, the desire to collaborate and integrate processes with supply chain trading partners also grows.

active internal integration phase When firms reach a stage of development wherein internal process integration is a normal operating condition.

activity-based cost accounting An accounting system that tracks both direct and indirect costs to each specific product sold.

administrative support A person or team who supports the leadership group on issues related to Six Sigma project implementation.

advanced shipping notification (ASN) An electronic version of a shipping notice that is transmitted by the retailer to the manufacturer once the returned product is released to the transportation provider.

affinity diagram A graphic used in Six Sigma projects that organizes ideas based on their similarities into some meaningful categories using Post-it® notes.

aggregate plan Annual production plans and human resource plans.

aggregation forecasting approach See **bottom-up forecasting approach.**

agile manufacturing The process of building customized, quickly changing products with uncertain demand patterns and short life cycles to maximize customer satisfaction.

American customer satisfaction index (ACSI) Produced by the Ross Business School at the University of Michigan; developed in 1995; an annual index of customer satisfaction in the United States.

analysis of variance (ANOVA) A statistical calculation used to test hypotheses about differences between two or more means.

anticipation inventories Inventories held with the intent of fulfilling demand during periods of expected high demand, such as holidays like Christmas or Valentines Day, or the period following an advertising campaign.

application add-ons Software applications that are added after the firm has purchased an ERP system.

appraisal costs The costs associated with discovering defects before the customer is affected, such as inspecting products to make sure design specifications are met, and checking processes to make sure they are running as expected.

approach to analytics When firms develop capabilities to work with the customer information floating around the organization to create marketing or customer service opportunities.

Ardalan heuristic A mathematical method used to estimate facility locations given the (1) distances (a surrogate measure for cost, since transportation cost varies somewhat with distance) from each customer location to every other location, (2) expected demand at each location, and (3) a weighting system where more important customers are weighted more heavily. The assumption is that a firm will only consider locating where the customers are, so the idea is to find the one best place to locate, then add a second location, then a third, and so on, to reduce transportation costs.

arm's length relationship A buyer–supplier relationship in which buying and supplying firms bargain from certain strengths for control of the resources. This type of relationship is relatively short-term and relates to the one-time purchase of a particular product or service. Little information is shared among the two parties other than exchanges regarding the conditions of the purchase.

arrival process Describes the time between customer arrivals, or the distribution of interarrival times.

assembly line High-volume production with little flexibility; equipment is dedicated to one or two tasks with a high degree of precision.

asset-based 3PLs Companies that use their own vehicles, facilities, and employees to provide logistics services.

asset recovery The process of classifying and disposing of any returned goods, scrap, waste, obsolete materials, surplus, or other assets in a manner that will maximize a return to the owner while at the same time minimize the cost and liability associated with disposition.

asset return Items returned for repositioning in the supply chain, such as business equipment and reusable containers.

assignable causes of variation Variation in a process that can be observed and eliminated or controlled.

attribute data Data that assumes two values such as pass/fail, yes/no, good/bad, or acceptable/unacceptable.

automated customer service agent Automated systems such as interactive voice response, speech recognition, and call routing systems.

automated decision systems Systems that combine artificial intelligence and decision support systems. These systems typically make actual decisions in real time, often without any human intervention, after analyzing other data inputs for a particular customer or situation. Also see **smart BPM systems.**

automated storage and retrieval systems (AS/AR) Computer-controlled systems used in warehouses to store and retrieve items. May include a combination of robotics, conveyor belts, bar code and radio frequency scanning systems, stock-picking equipment, and carousels.

average supply chain delivery performance A measure representing the average percentage of orders filled and delivered on time to each receiving member in the supply chain.

average supply chain perfect order performance A measure of the average percent of orders received not only on time, but complete and damage free.

avoidance The process of minimizing return requests through a number of means such as providing clearly written instructions for product use.

B

backorder A case where the customer is kept from receiving at least part of the order, usually due to a stockout.

balanced scorecard A management system developed in the early 1990s by Robert Kaplan and David Norton that helps companies to continually refine their vision and strategy. The balanced scorecard uses a set of measures to provide feedback on internal business performance in order to continually improve strategic performance.

balancing the line Used when laying out assembly lines; achieves a number of positive outcomes by dividing the processing work equally, achieving an equitable work assignment for employees.

balking Not joining a queue after seeing how long it is.

base demand The average sales demand for an item before considering other factors.

basic alliance Known as the "entry level" of strategic alliances. Partners focus on keeping communication lines open and positive, and sharing information when needed.

basic research Discovering ways to increase the number of product innovations and then converting that research into commercial applications.

batch and queue production Each part that goes into a finished product is made in large lot sizes (or batches). The batch of items is then moved on to the next operation before actually needed there.

batch process Each part that goes into a finished product is produced in large lot sizes (or batches), and then the batch is moved to the next operation before the parts are all actually needed there. Production has some flexibility; equipment is more specialized and automated than in a job shop.0

benchmarking Studying how things are done well in other firms to potentially make use of the same methods.

best-of-breed systems When the most effective software applications are purchased from various vendors over time.

bill of materials (BOM) A recipe for a product, indicating all of the raw materials, parts, components, subassemblies, and assemblies required for manufacturing. It also indicates how many of each part are required, the parts that go into each subassembly or assembly, and the order of assembly. The simplest form of a BOM is a **product structure diagram.**

birdyback A transportation term referring to the shipment of containers using airplanes.

black belt A person that oversees large Six Sigma projects that may cross over functional and geographical boundaries and product lines, with at least 160 hours of Six Sigma training covering fairly sophisticated statistical techniques and other tools.

bottleneck A type of constraint that acts to restrict material flow, reduce overall capacity and product output capability, increase process cycle time, and hence, negatively impact customer service capabilities of the organization and its supply chain trading partners.

bottleneck item A purchased item that has unique, customized specifications, where the supplier's technology is important and thus is considered high risk to the buying firm. Buying firms should purchase a bottleneck item in larger quantities to avoid interruptions to supply, monitor inventory levels more closely, and seek out other suppliers to reduce the risk of supply interruptions.

bottom-up branding See **viral marketing.**

bottom-up forecasting approach Managers develop forecasts for each regional location and then roll them up into one national-level forecast.

break-bulk A warehouse activity where one or more pallets of goods are disassembled into smaller quantities, which are then used to create assortments for multiple customers.

break-even analysis Computing the cost-effectiveness of make-or-buy sourcing decisions or process choice decisions.

breakthrough improvement An organizational change that will significantly lower costs and improve customer satisfaction.

bullwhip effect A term referring to ineffective communication between buyers and suppliers and infrequent delivery of materials, combined with production based on poor forecasts along a supply chain that results in either too little or too much inventory at various points of storage and consumption.

business alliance The second level of strategic alliance, where the purchasing department is looking for the supplier to add unique value in the form of a customized product or service. Each party is heavily invested in the relationship in terms of assets, human resources, or special technology and thus mutual dependency is high.

business case A written justification for approving a new product or service idea.

business performance management The "other" BPM; refers to a formal set of process analytic activities supported by information technologies that address financial and operational performance.

business process The collection of activities and operations involved in transforming inputs, which are the physical facilities, materials, capital, equipment, people, and energy, into outputs, or the products and services.

business process integration The sharing of ideas and information, coordination of process activities, and collaboration on process design and implementation between supply chain members such that products and services are provided at the desired levels of quality, speed, and cost along the supply chain—from raw material suppliers to end-product consumers. Allows each participant within the supply chain to learn the actual purchase plans of their customers, to share new product design and development plans with suppliers, and to jointly develop better ways to purchase, build, and deliver products.

business process management (BPM) A term used to describe a structured approach to process assessment and organizational improvement, typically involving the use of commercial software applications.

business process management template Allows the firm to repeatedly and consistently use numerous process applications rather than relying on an internally designed BPM solution for each specific process analysis.

business process outsourcing The outsourcing of processes that could be deemed strategic in nature, or core activities, such as in information systems management, purchasing, or human resources management.

business process re-engineering (BPR) Seeks to create a systematic, automated approach to change management through assessments of current processes, design of better processes using modeling techniques, implementation of the new processes, and continuing performance assessments.

buy-out When a manufacturer purchases a retailer's supply of a competitor's product to gain access to that shelf space. Also known as **lift.**

C

capacity The maximum rate of output that is possible within a facility.

capacity requirements planning A software application typically included with MRP, MRP II, and ERP systems. Given MPS quantities, the planned order releases from the MRP, the current shop load, the part routing information, and the processing and purchasing lead times, the short-range capacity requirements can be developed for the entire production facility. Initially, the MPS may be found to be infeasible given the shop's current workload and the capacity of each work center. If this is the case, the choices are either to increase capacity or reduce the MPS. The MRP II system generates load reports for each work center for a series of time periods. These load reports compare the required capacity for the given MPS with the projected available capacity. Given this information, production managers can determine if workloads need to be shifted to later periods, overtime needs to be scheduled, or work needs to be contracted out. Ultimately, a feasible production schedule and capacity plan is decided upon.

capacity sharing agreements Due to the high cost of many service delivery processes, firms are faced with finding other uses for capacity during periods of under-utilization. Airlines, for instance, might agree to share gates, baggage-handling equipment, and ground personnel. Also see **code sharing.**

cause-and-effect diagram A graphical tool used to categorize the possible causes of a quality problem.

cellular layout A self-contained, physical arrangement of machines and people so that processing steps are placed next to each other in sequential order. Lean producers use these manufacturing cells to build components that are fed into an assembly line or to build an entire product.

center-of-gravity method A mathematical technique used to find a location that minimizes the total transportation costs between the proposed facility and existing facilities given the volume, distance, and transportation rates of shipments between locations.

centralized return center A processing location for returns from retailers. The center sorts the returns for processing, deciding the disposition of each item based on guidelines from retailer and manufacturer.

channel orientation A philosophy where management stresses the importance of coordination and control within the supply chain by synchronizing logistics activities with related information.

charge-back A supplier allows straight deductions or discounts to be taken from the supplier's invoice for returns.

check sheet A very simple data collection form used to track quality defects.

Clark and Wright savings heuristic A well-known heuristic method for solving the traveling salesman problem.

clickstream tracking software Software that enables the storage of each request for information made by a visitor to the firm's website.

closed-loop supply chain management A broad term, encompassing both forward and reverse flows of products, including product returns processing, contract service calls, product recalls, resales, and refurbishment of used products.

cluster-first-route-second heuristic A heuristic method for solving a general vehicle routing problem.

code sharing Capacity sharing in the passenger airline industry.

cold calls Telemarketing calls from salespeople who know nothing about the customer or their needs.

collaborative environments Allow two or more participants to communicate and coordinate processes to accomplish a shared objective. These environments use a com-bination of communication technologies such as instant messaging, email, chat rooms, mobile communicators, whiteboards, and web conferencing capabilities. Also see **open source communities.**

collaborative new product and process development (NPPD) Encourages representatives from all key trading partners to act as full partners on design-build-support teams. Collaboration spans all disciplines, functions, divisions, projects, and target markets to gather and use expert knowledge and make effective business plans.

collaborative planning, forecasting and replenishment (CPFR) Collaborating with customers and suppliers to optimize the supply chain by improving demand forecast accuracy, delivering the right product at the right time to the right location, and consequently reducing inventories across the supply chain, and avoiding stockouts, while improving customer service.

combination replenishment pull system Two different replenishment systems run in parallel, using kanbans, because the organization produces both make-to-stock and make-to-order items.

common causes of variation Random changes in a process that cannot be identified.

communication plan A written document that outlines the types and frequency of communication that will be used during a Six Sigma implementation.

complementary services Additional services aside from the primary service. For instance, a lounge area or bar is used as a complementary service for customers who are waiting for a table at a restaurant.

composite applications Compatible applications designed by one supplier that can be mixed and matched, using a centralized data structure.

composite processes Technology-enabled, cross-organizational process flows designed to share and act on changes in demand.

computer-aided design (CAD) A software program that uses computer graphics to design component parts with great precision.

computer integrated manufacturing (CIM) A system for managing the interconnecting processes of computer-aided design (CAD) systems, computer assisted manufacturing (CAM) systems, and group technology (GT) cells, using central integrated computer control for planning, scheduling, and decision-making purposes.

computer numerically controlled machines (CNC) Manufacturing facility machines that are controlled by computer programs in order to perform the processing steps exactly the same way each time they are performed.

concurrent engineering Designing the manufacturing process or service delivery system simultaneously with the design of the product.

concurrent scheduler approach A heuristic method for solving a vehicle scheduling problem.

consumer surveys A qualitative forecasting method using a survey of consumer opinions of existing products, their expected future buying habits, or new product ideas.

continuous inventory review The use of bar codes, scanners, and computer systems that allow the firm to know instantly when a reorder point is reached, causing an order to be generated exactly when desired, not when someone notices that inventory levels are getting low. This further reduces the likelihood of stockouts as well as the required safety stock.

continuous production Production with virtually no variety in output; equipment is dedicated to one task.

continuous replenishment See **efficient consumer response.**

control chart A graph used for quality control to visually track the performance of a process against calculated control or warning limits, or a graph used in forecasting to track the tracking signal against preset limits.

control matrix A house of quality matrix that converts characteristics of the manufacturing process into more specific operational tasks and control procedures.

control plan A written document that describes the methods and tools an organization will use to keep an improved process in statistical control and at optimal performance.

controlled inventory Hazardous materials and recalled items that may be hazardous to the consumer's health.

cookie files Files that store clickstream information captured on a website as users interact with the site.

core carrier strategy A transportation strategy that entails companies focusing their efforts on developing good working relationships with a smaller number of transportation carriers.

corporate information flow The flow of information from the firm to its customers.

cost analysis A cost breakdown.

cost/benefit analysis A quantitative and subjective assessment of the risks and rewards for each option under consideration.

cost management The process of identifying all the costs associated with company investments by making informed choices about the options that will deliver the best value for the money, and then managing those costs throughout the life of the investment.

critical path method (CPM) One form of the critical path network that uses deterministic time estimates to determine the completion time for a project.

critical path network A graphic showing the link between project activities through a series of interconnecting arrows and highlighting the activities critical to timely project completion (i.e., the critical path). The time duration and function of each task is also typically included.

critical to quality (CTQ) An important customer-related issue that is currently confronting an organization.

cross-docking A continuous replenishment logistics process of creating outbound product order assortments from incoming truckload quantities of goods, which are then quickly shipped to retail and other customers. Cross-docking generally takes place within 24 hours, sometimes less than an hour, after shipment arrivals and is used to replenish high-demand inventories.

cross selling Offering complementary products that will enhance the original product's capability in order to avoid a full product return.

CTQ tree A Six Sigma tool used to break down customer complaints into the main drivers of dissatisfaction.

customer behavior The mental and physical activities that result in decisions to purchase and use products and services.

customer call centers See **customer contact centers.**

customer churn When customers no longer visit a firm or buy its products or services; when firms lose customers.

customer communities Using the web to build a network of customers to facilitate communication or the exchange of ideas between customer members and also with company personnel.

customer contact centers Customer service departments that integrate all of the methods customers can use to contact a business, including telephone, mail, comment cards, email, and website messages and chat rooms.

customer contact points Any time customers interact with company employees, both intentionally and unintentionally.

customer flow map Allows the analyst to visualize the flow of customers through the service delivery system, with the objective of identifying potential problem areas related to the processing of customers.

customer focus A belief that the customer should drive all strategic marketing decisions.

customer lifetime value (CLV) Assigning a profit figure to each customer by summing the margins of all the products and services purchased over time, less the cost of marketing to and maintaining that customer, such as the costs of direct mail and sales calls and the service costs for each customer. Additionally, the firm forecasts future purchased quantities, profit margins, and marketing costs for each customer, discounts these back to the current date, and then adds this projected profit quantity to the current profit amount.

customer loyalty programs See **frequency programs.**

customer managed interactions See **personal knowledge banks.**

customer participation approach See **self-service.**

customer relationship management (CRM) To manage the firm's customer base so that customers remain satisfied and continue to purchase goods and services.

customer satisfaction A person's feelings of pleasure or disappointment resulting from comparing a product's perceived performance or outcome, relative to expectations.

customer segmentation Grouping customers within a firm's existing customer database to allow the company to design specific CRM initiatives that will satisfy these segments of customers; provide personalized services to the most profitable customers; and allow marketing efforts to be targeted to specific sets of customers.

customer service The provision of information, help, and/or technical support to customers in a way that meets or exceeds customer expectations.

customer service departments A focal point for service assessment and improvement; can be the drivers for creating a service culture in the organization.

customer service failure When any of the customer service activities are neglected or performed poorly; can lead to additional costs and possibly loss of goodwill, customer defections, and reduced future sales revenues.

customer service management Provides the structure for delivering products and services to customers and attending to customer needs.

customer service teams Consist of a temporary grouping of executives, department managers, design engineers, and other personnel to react to a significant customer service problem.

customer wants Characterized by the desire to make an already-satisfactory condition better, such as wanting a bigger house or a more fuel-efficient car. Customer wants

are influenced by factors like financial resources; the groups they belong to; their cultural influences; and their environmental surroundings. Thus, as personal wealth increases, consumers are likely to want more expensive goods and services.

cycle inventories Created when the firm purchases or produces a quantity or lotsize large enough to last until the next purchase or production period.

cycle time See **takt time.**

cyclical patterns Wavelike movements in demand that are longer than a year and influenced by macroeconomic and political factors.

D

dampen Smooth out fluctuations in demand.

data mining Using software to identify hidden patterns of behavior or common interests among customer groups.

data warehouses Information system structures used to store data that was collected from the various divisions of the firm.

decomposition forecasting approach See **top-down forecasting approach.**

defect Any instance or event where a process, product, or service does not meet the customer's requirements.

defect cycles Predictable periods of time when the number of defects increases.

defect trends The number of defects from a process are going up or down over a given time horizon.

defects per million opportunities (DPMO) A normalized ratio of the reject rates; a calculation of the number of defects per million opportunities for a defect to occur, multiplied by 1,000,000.

defects per unit (DPU) A ratio of the total number of defects found in a given number of inspected units divided by the total number of units inspected.

delivery system The method service providers use to deliver their services to customers.

Delphi method A qualitative forecasting method in which a group of experts are surveyed during several rounds to gain consensus on future events.

demand amplification mapping A mapping technique used to illustrate changes in demand along the supply chain across a period of time.

demand management A set of activities that range from determining or estimating the demand from customers through converting specific customer orders into promised delivery dates to help balance demand with supply.

demand sorting When customers are "sorted" as they first enter a service system to better direct them to the appropriate service processes or available servers, resulting in less overall wait time.

demand source The population that might enter a queue to use a service. It can contain a finite number or a very large (infinite) number of customers and be homogenous or non-homogenous.

Deming Plan-Do-Study-Act Cycle (PDSA) A quality model where a plan for improvement is formulated, put into use, checked through measurement and observation, and then either standardized if the changes have actually minimized or eliminated the problem, or modified if not enough improvement is evident.

dependent demand The internal demand for raw materials, parts, and components that are necessary for building finished products and supplying services.

dependent variable A measurable factor that is observed and quantified in response to one or more independent variables.

design-build-test A process where design engineers make up detailed drawings of the new product and develop prototypes, either with actual physical models or by using computer-aided design. Tests then are done to simulate the actual use of the product.

design for manufacturing and assembly (DFMA) Simplification of parts, products, and processes to improve quality and reduce costs.

design matrix A house of quality matrix that converts a new product's technical requirements into the features of key product parts.

design of experiments The inputs or factors expected to affect the process output are tested, using analysis of variance (ANOVA), to find the best solution.

differential pricing Segmenting customers into different categories, such that high prices will be charged to customers willing to pay them and low prices will be charged to customers who would not use the service at a higher price.

differentiation strategy A method for making products and services that are unique in some way, or that differentiates them from similar competitor offerings.

direct mail An announcement, offer, or some other type of hard-copy communication that is sent to a customer's or potential customer's address.

dispatch rules Rules established to allow machine operators to determine which job to process next from a queue of jobs waiting to be processed at various work centers.

distribution center A warehouse that forms outbound specific product assortments which are then shipped to the customer.

distribution requirements planning (DRP) A software planning application that allows the firm's regional distribution centers and local warehouses (and indirectly, customers) to communicate actual orders to the MRP and to allow the firm to look ahead and anticipate when orders will need to be placed, just as with the MRP.

DMAIC Cycle A Six Sigma methodology utilized to identify and improve any existing processes not meeting Six Sigma quality standards.

downsizing the supply base See **optimizing the supply base.**

drop ship Companies (primarily manufacturers) sell products to customers and then ship the product directly to the customer.

DRP record A table very similar to the MRP part record. The demand profile at each warehouse is translated into a demand forecast for each period, and this replaces the gross requirements used in the MRP. The forecast requirements are subtracted from the warehouse's on-hand inventories and planned receipts. Net requirements are generated as safety stock levels are reached, and planned shipping quantities are generated based on the delivery lead times (similar to the planned order releases in the MRP). The planned shipping quantities for all warehouses are then aggregated into one set of time-phased requirements for a central distribution center or the manufacturing facility.

drum, buffer, rope concept (DBR) A popular terminology for explaining the Theory of Constraints. A bottleneck machine is the capacity-constrained resource and determines the processing rate of the entire facility. This machine represents the drum that sets the pace (the beat of the drum) for the facility. The buffer is the inventory placed or extra work time incorporated into the schedule at the bottleneck. The rope refers to the control or scheduling of work releases to the facility, which is derived according to the drum and the buffers.

E

earliest due date dispatching rule The job with the earliest due date is selected first.

early supplier involvement Suppliers provide product and process technology and knowledge to support the design process. Customer firms hope to take advantage of any new proprietary technologies owned by the supplier and to help shorten the design cycle, which can give them a competitive advantage.

economic order quantity model (EOQ) A model that determines the order quantity that will minimize the sum of the annual inventory holding cost and the annual order cost, given a number of assumptions.

economic production quantity model (EPQ) A model that determines a production quantity that will allow inventory to gradually build up over time at a rate equal to the daily production rate less the daily demand rate. Then when the full manufacturing lot size is produced, inventory will gradually decline at the daily demand rate, until a production order is placed and the production cycle once again commences.

e-CRM Targeting customers for CRM purposes using email; also includes other forms of electronic communication with customers.

efficient consumer response Methods used to increase inventory speed as it flows from supplier to buyer; the impetus behind supply chain management. It is also sometimes referred to as continuous replenishment or quick response. The most common strategy to increase speed or reduce delivery lead times is to utilize the Internet.

electronic data interchange (EDI) A computer-to-computer exchange of business documents such as purchase orders, order status inquiries and reports, promotion announcements, and shipping and billing notices.

e-marketplace Online forum or digital marketplace that serves as a virtual meeting place for buyers and suppliers.

end-of-quarter loading Using a variety of tools including promotions and discounted prices to sell more product to retailers at the end of a financial quarter.

enterprise application integration The use of plans, methods, and tools designed to modernize, consolidate, integrate, and coordinate computer applications.

enterprise commerce management system Also termed ERP II or ECM, it refers to the concept of real-time integration of outward-facing applications such as CRM and SRM into internally-focused or back-office ERP applications.

enterprise resource planning system (ERP) A packaged business software system that lets a company automate and integrate the majority of its business processes, share common data and practices across the enterprise, and produce and access information in a real-time environment.

environmental, health, and safety (EHS) excellence More than achieving a "green" supply chain. EHS professionals are collaborating on cross-functional supply chain management teams to improve customer retention, revenue generation, cost reduction, and asset utilization along the supply chain.

environmental information flow The flow of information from customers to the firm.

environmental return Material returned for disposal in compliance with environmental regulations.

e-procurement tools See **e-purchasing tools.**

e-purchasing tools The use of electronic purchasing software and the web for making business-related purchases.

everyday-low-pricing Consistently selling products at their lowest, profit-generating price and eliminating other sales tactics to reduce the returns problem.

expedite To identify incoming material purchases and jobs on the shop floor that are behind schedule, and then do what is necessary to get materials delivered and jobs completed by their due dates.

exponential smoothing forecasting A quantitative forecasting method in which the forecast for the next period's demand is the current period's forecast, adjusted by a fraction of the difference between the current period's actual demand and its forecast.

external customer service audit Identifying changes in the service requirements of customers, and determining current customer service performance of the firm and, ideally, its competitors.

external failure costs The money spent to fix poor-quality problems once the product or service is purchased.

external inventory control The collaborative inventory management activities occurring between the focal firm and its supply chain trading partners as purchased parts and materials make their way to the firm and as finished products are delivered to customers.

F

facility A bricks-and-mortar location such as a manufacturing plant, warehouse, retail outlet, or service center; also includes shipping ports and supplier facilities. For service providers, facilities might include retail store locations, automatic teller machines, a collection center for a charity, or a maintenance facility for a city parks department.

factor rating system A weighted checklist that is used to determine the best locations for new sites. A combination of diverse quantitative and qualitative factors can be considered for site location comparisons.

failure mode and effects analysis (FMEA) A chart that shows the possible process defects, the effects and severity of those defects, and their possible causes. Scales are used to represent the likelihood that each process defect effect will occur, and the probability the defect will be detected should it occur. The measures are then multiplied together to determine the overall impact of the defect, also known as the reported priority number.

false positive blocking When email messages are incorrectly identified as spam and blocked.

finished goods inventories Completed products ready for delivery to business customers or consumers.

firing customers When firms encourage low-value, high-cost customers to stop buying their products or services through either raising product prices or reducing the availability of the products and services these customers purchase.

first-come-first-served queuing discipline The most popular queuing discipline when people are in the queue.

first-tier supplier A manufacturer's direct supplier.

5S System A system of preventative maintenance developed in Japan that includes sorting, setting in order, shining, standardizing, and sustaining.

flexibility The ability of a supplier to meet a customer's emergency, unexpected, or unusual requests.

flexible manufacturing system (FMS) Uses a central host computer, computer numerically controlled (CNC) machines, and a plant-wide, automated material handling system equipped with automated conveyors, automated guided vehicles (AGVs), and automated storage and retrieval systems (AS/RS) to schedule small batches of products, route and store parts, and control machining operations among carefully laid-out assembly areas for a number of similar products.

flow management Designing the manufacturing or service processes to achieve the desired flexibility to meet ever-changing customer requirements.

flow time Begins when a job arrives at the shop, and ends when it leaves.

FOB origination/destination Taking ownership of purchased products at the seller's location (origination) or buyer's location (destination).

focus groups An assembled group of customers giving their opinions to company personnel regarding various product, service, or proposed CRM initiatives.

forecast bias Occurs when a forecast has a tendency to be either consistently higher or lower than actual demand.

forecasting A process of estimating resource requirements by identifying and quantifying all sources of demand.

forward buying Purchasing more than what is immediately necessary because of unexpected promotions or incentives offered by a vendor.

forward purchase contract A contract used to buy goods at some future date from a foreign supplier, with pricing in today's currency value.

forward scheduling A tactic used to control shop loading, to estimate a completion date, and to determine when a job can be released or started in the shop. Forward scheduling means to schedule jobs forward from their arrival date at the facility.

4-Ms Four possible categories of quality problems used in cause-and-effect diagrams, which stand for manpower, materials, methods, and machinery.

frequency programs When repeat customers are rewarded with discounts, credits, cash, or prizes, depending on the value and frequency of the repeat purchases.

frozen time period See **time fence.**

functional e-marketplace An online marketplace that provides specific functions or automates a process across different industries.

G

Gantt chart A timeline used for planning purposes, and for obtaining a rough estimate of a project's completion time. Can be used in tandem with forward scheduling (or any other scheduling technique) to monitor and adjust job loadings at each work center, and to schedule downtime for maintenance activities, shift changes, operator days off, or other shop floor activities.

gasification See **pyrolosis.**

gatekeeping The process of screening all returned goods at the point of entry into the reverse logistics system.

global data synchronization (GDS) A term that refers to automated direct product data exchange between supply chain partners.

globally optimizing the supply chain Taking actions to minimize total supply chain inventory costs while satisfying the service requirements of supply chain members.

green belt An experienced member of a large Six Sigma project or someone who oversees a medium-sized project that relates directly to their own position in the company. Have at least 80 hours of Six Sigma training.

green logistics A philosophy of understanding and working to reduce the ecological impact of logistics in both the forward and reverse supply chain.

green supply chain management Extends the concept of green logistics to include activities related to environmentally responsible product design, acquisition, production, distribution, use, reuse, and disposal by partners within the supply chain.

group technology cells See **cellular layout.**

H

happy-productive worker hypothesis The idea that overall job satisfaction leads to high levels of employee service performance.

hedge inventories Created when the firm desires to hold inventory as a protection from some potential future event such as a sudden upsurge in purchase prices or an unforeseen shortage of some commodity or part.

hedging strategy A plan to minimize the chance of price increases.

Heijunka box A visual scheduling system developed by the Japanese. The schedule allows the operations team to see how well they are performing against takt time during the work shift.

heuristic A solution method that yields a reasonable estimate or solution in a relatively short period of time, but does not necessarily guarantee the best solution.

high-quality customer service When the firm achieves excellent customer service through attention to four basic service principles—reliability, recovery, fairness, and the "wow factor."

histogram A bar chart used to uncover quality problems; each bar represents the frequency of a particular defect or problem.

house of quality A series of tables assembled together that show the translation of customer requirements into the product attributes, the technical specifications (how the product will be built), an evaluation of how competitive the product will be, and a technical evaluation of the product against its competitors.

hybrid integration solutions Customized integration middleware employing both automated and manual components.

I

income segmentation A type of niche segmentation; identifying and catering to customers with large disposable incomes.

independent demand The external demand for finished products and replacement parts created by market conditions.

independent variable A predictor of a dependent variable.

individual marketing See **one-to-one marketing.**

individual segmentation Segmenting customers individually, and then marketing to each one separately.

information audit Determining the current internal and external customers, suppliers, and users, and identifying their information usage.

information orientation See **channel orientation.**

information velocity A term used to describe how fast information flows from one process to another.

information visibility The degree that information is communicated and made available to various constituents.

information volatility The uncertainty associated with information content, format, or timing.

input-output control Using input levels and output levels to control work-in-process levels. If WIP is too high, then the firm can either reduce input levels or increase output levels to reduce WIP. These actions will also reduce throughput times in the facility.

integrated product development See **concurrent engineering.**

intellectual asset Information has value just as materials do—thus, it can be referred to as an asset.

intermittent process layout See **process-focused layout.**

intermodal transportation Two or more modes of transportation are combined to deliver a shipment of goods.

internal barriers to collaboration Can be classified as technological (information system software/hardware) barriers, structural (management hierarchy, goals, procedures) barriers, and cultural (employee values, norms, behavior) barriers.

internal customer service audit Reviewing the firm's current customer service measures, policies, and practices.

internal failure costs The money organizations spend to repair, replace, or discard poor-quality work prior to a customer's purchase.

internal information flow Information flow within the firm.

internal inventory control Methods used to manage inventories from the time parts and materials reach the facility until the time that finished goods are packaged and ready for delivery to customers.

internal process integration Teamwork and collaboration within the firm. To achieve this, firms must break down internal barriers to collaboration, connect departmental and unit information systems, and develop performance measures that encourage departments to work together.

internal supply chain An organization's network of internal suppliers and its internal customers. Internal supply chains can be complex, particularly if the firm has multiple divisions and organizational structures around the globe.

inventory carrying costs See **inventory holding costs.**

inventory holding costs The costs of holding inventory for periods of time, including the costs of warehousing, material handling, shrinkage, obsolescence, labor, and capital costs. Also known as inventory carrying costs.

inventory management The control of all inventories—raw materials, work-in-process, and finished goods—when not in use.

invitation to bid (IFB) Similar to a request for proposal (RFP), suppliers are asked to bid, given certain opening and closing dates of the bid. The basis for awarding a contract is preset and binding. Generally the contract is awarded to the lowest bidder meeting all of the requirements; however, bidders might be told instead that bids will be used as a starting point for further negotiations.

Ishikawa diagram See **cause-and-effect diagram.**

ISO 9000 A set of international management and quality assurance standards for design, development, production, installation, and service, developed in 1987 by the International Organization for Standardization.

ISO 14000 An international set of standards developed by the International Organization for Standardization to help organizations focus on developing and integrating environmental responsibility into their operations.

J

job shop A production facility in which each work center schedules its own production levels and controls the flow of materials. Generally found in organizations offering custom products or services. Production volumes are low but flexibility in accommodating the customer is high. A machine shop is an example of a job shop.

jockeying When customers in one queue leave and join a different queue.

jury of executive opinion Qualitative forecasting method in which a group of experts collectively develop a forecast.

Just-In-Time II (JIT II) A full-time representative of the supplier resides in the buying firm's purchasing department, holding a dual position as both buyer and supplier representative. This person may also contribute to the buying firm's new product development and value engineering/value analysis teams by suggesting modifications or alternate components during the product design phase that customers would not otherwise be aware of.

K

kaizen A Japanese word for continuous improvement.

kaizen investigative teams Cross-functional continuous improvement teams that visit customer sites to discover unmet needs that may not have been verbally communicated before.

kanban A Japanese word for "card," it is a visual tool—often a card in a rectangular vinyl envelope—used in lean production.

key supplier See **supplier partnership.**

L

lateness In scheduling terminology, it is the difference between the completion date and the due date for a job (if a job finishes early, it is still considered "late").

leadership group An organization's senior management team.

lean enterprise Integrating lean thinking practices across all business units.

lean logistics Eliminating as much waste from the supply chains as possible by cutting order lead times, inventory, and excess capacity, for example, to achieve the lowest overall costs.

lean manufacturing See **lean production/ service delivery.**

lean organization Expanding the concepts of lean production/service delivery to the entire business unit.

lean principles Reducing process variance and inventories in actively managed supply chains, by employing just-in-time purchasing, production, and logistics techniques and continuous improvement of processes. Also refers to the application of the Toyota Production System.

lean production/service delivery Organizing work and analyzing the appropriateness of currently operating machines, warehouses, and systems to fit a lean process flow. The goals are to reduce production throughput times and inventory levels, cut order lead times, increase quality, and improve customer responsiveness with fewer people and other assets.

lean supply chain Lean principles are applied cooperatively across the supply chain. Value and target costs for each product or product family are defined jointly among supply chain members. Together, they work to eliminate waste to meet joint target cost and return-on-investment goals. Once target costs are met, supply chain members jointly continue to identify new forms of waste and set new targets. Key processes are aligned across the supply chain, focusing on delivering an uninterrupted flow of goods and services and coordinating inventory policies. Operational information also flows in both directions to ensure transparency of all activity within the supply chain.

lean thinking A philosophy of breakthrough improvement with roots in continuous improvement programs. The goal is to be more productive by doing more, but with less equipment, human effort, time, and space, while at the same time satisfying customers.

legacy systems A firm's existing software applications.

leveraged item A purchased item where unit cost is important because the profit potential is higher, but substitution is possible. For this item, purchasing and supply management personnel seek to exploit their purchasing power to the full extent to obtain the lowest possible prices.

lift See **buy-out.**

line order fill rate A logistics performance measure of the number of line orders filled on the initial order versus the amount of lines ordered.

linear regression analysis A method of estimating the conditional expected value of one variable, y, given the values of some other variable or variables, x.

linear trend forecasting A forecasting method in which the trend can be estimated using simple linear regression to fit a line to a time series of historical data.

load reports Used with MRP and capacity requirements planning systems; load reports compare the required capacity for the given MPS with the projected available capacity.

location planning Making decisions with regards to the size, location, and number of fixed facilities that will be used in a company's supply chain.

logistics customer service The speed and dependability with which items ordered can be made available.

logistics execution suite A blanket term for a family of logistics-oriented software applications, including transportation management systems, warehouse management systems, yard management systems, and returns management systems.

logistics strategy A functional plan developed to support the overall business strategy.

logistics value proposition A logistics alternative that achieves the required customer service levels at the lowest total cost, based on the customer's needs and expectations.

logistics vision What the logistics organization hopes to accomplish in the future, including some goals that go beyond the company's current logistics capabilities.

lost opportunity costs See **opportunity cost.**

lot A production quantity containing a certain number of items.

low-cost leadership strategy Making products and services that sell for lower prices than competitor offerings.

lower control limit A value on a control chart representing the minimum acceptable limit for a sample measure.

M

maintenance, repair, and operating supplies (MRO) Items that are consumed by the business or used to support manufacturing and service processes.

makespan The total elapsed time to complete a group of jobs.

make-to-order replenishment pull system Parts production flows in a first-in-first-out (FIFO) sequence.

make-to-stock replenishment pull system Finished goods or parts are replaced when a customer orders or withdraws them. A store of finished goods is placed at the end of a production line and any parts needed to produce that good are kept within the production area.

Malcolm Baldrige Award A U.S. government award created in 1987 to motivate U.S. companies to improve the quality of their products.

management by constraint See **Theory of Constraints.**

manufacturing execution system (MES) An ERP system add-on that ties management planning to the plant floor.

manufacturing flow management The set of activities responsible for making the actual product, establishing the manufacturing flexibility required to adequately serve the markets, and designing the production system to meet cycle time requirements.

manufacturing resource planning system (MRP II) A software application that has a simulation capability to allow users to perform what-if analyses and gain an understanding of likely outcomes when capacity or production timing decisions are made. Other modules are also included with MRP II systems, enabling various functional area personnel to interact with the MRP II system using a central database. Production, marketing, human resource, and finance personnel can then work together to develop a feasible aggregate plan based on available funds, equipment, advertising plans, and labor.

market return Products returned by an organization somewhere within in the supply chain other than the end user for any number of reasons, including slow sales, quality issues, a need to reposition inventory, or product close-outs.

mass customization The mass assembly of custom products using standardized parts.

Firms produce a number of standardized parts, then delay final assembly until a customer order is received.

mass production High volume production of products using automated equipment.

master production schedule (MPS) Specifies the end products to be made, the dates they need to be completed, and the quantities required. This usually takes the form of a daily or weekly production schedule for each product, which then become inputs to the MRP.

material flow analysis Collecting information and data from the process mapping exercise can guide the process assessment and improvement efforts. Once the data collection phase is complete, the participants in the analysis can compare the current state of the process to a desired or ideal process state based on customer requirements, and rank order the desired process changes based on cost, implementation time, and expected benefit. Process performance measures can then be instituted to track ongoing process capability.

material requirements planning system (MRP) A software application that has been available since the 1970s; it performs an analysis of the firm's existing internal conditions and reports back what the production and purchase requirements are for a given finished product manufacturing schedule.

mean absolute deviation (MAD) An indicator of forecast accuracy based on an average of the absolute value of the forecast errors over a given period of time.

mean absolute percentage deviation (MAPE) An indicator of forecast accuracy based on the true magnitude of the forecast error. The monthly absolute forecast error divided by actual demand is summed, then divided by the number of months used in the forecast to derive an average, and lastly multiplied by 100.

middleware Internal and external application integration software.

mixed-model assembly line sequencing See **mixed model scheduling.**

mixed model scheduling Developing the sequence of products scheduled for assembly while at the same time maintaining a level workload at each work station, which helps production stay within the takt time.

modular-flow warehouse layout Characterized by separate segments that are designed for specific warehouse applications.

modularity Reducing the number of parts used per product.

muda A Japanese word meaning waste or anything that does not add value.

mystery shoppers Paid agents who pose as customers in order to assess the customer service performance of employees and the work environment. Mystery shoppers gather performance information and document employee behaviors, and then create summary reports that are sent to management.

N

neighborhood marketing Identifying and marketing to customers based on geography, where customer segments can be viewed as having similar income levels or ethnic traits.

niche segmentation Identifying groups of customers with similar needs, geographical locations, buying attitudes, or buying habits.

nominal value The central line on a control chart.

non-asset-based 3PLs Supply chain intermediaries that link shippers together with available logistics services. These companies do not own any transportation equipment but may be subsidiaries of companies that do own assets.

non-critical item Purchased item that is thought of more as a commodity—highly standardized and easily substituted. Example: office supplies.

O

on-demand CRM Outsourced or externally hosted CRM services.

one-to-one marketing Offering the right services or products to the right customers at the right time, one at a time; also referred to as individual marketing.

ongoing relationship A buyer/supplier relationship where the same purchase is made on a regular basis even though there are many suppliers available.

open-source communities Internet sites where individuals can share ideas and exchange data and information. One of the world's largest open-source communities is sourceforge.net. This collaboration model is quickly being adopted by millions of workers to generate more innovative solutions to a variety of problems. Users can very quickly mobilize information on any topic, project, or problem in any field. Also see **collaborative environments.**

operating matrix A house of quality matrix that determines the process that will be used to manufacture any required parts for a new product.

opportunity The chance that a defect could occur, such as when process sample measurements are taken or when products are being used.

opportunity cost The monies the firm gives up by having capital tied up in inventory and the land, buildings, and equipment used for storage purposes.

optimizing the supply base Cutting back the number of suppliers and then focusing on improving relations with fewer key first tier suppliers of major subassemblies. Also known as downsizing the supply base.

opt-in/opt-out When customers are asked to either give or not give their consent regarding the use of personal data obtained by a company's website.

order costs The administrative costs associated with purchasing items.

order cycle time See **order lead time.**

order fill rate A measure of the percentage of units available to fill a specific order.

order fulfillment The set of activities that allows the firm to fill customer orders while providing the required levels of customer service at the lowest possible delivered cost.

order lead time The time from initiation of the customer order until the product or service is delivered to the customer. Also known as order cycle time.

order management Managing the procurement of stock-keeping units (SKUs), which will be sold to the customer, and the processing of customer orders.

original equipment manufacturer (OEM) Company that builds components or finished goods which are sold by a reseller. Example: Whirlpool dishwashers are built by Whirlpool, the OEM, and sold by Sears, the reseller.

original parts manufacturer (OPM) Company that builds parts which are sold to original equipment manufacturers (OEMs).

outsourcing When a firm purchases materials or products instead of producing them in-house.

outsourcing customer service When a firm uses another firm to perform customer service activities.

overbooking Refers to accepting more reservations for service than can be provided.

overprocessing Parts are processed on equipment that operates too fast or too slow, or even too accurately, to meet the customer's definition of value.

overproduction An organization produces more products than demanded, or sooner or faster than needed, resulting in excess inventory.

P

pacemaker The workstation that sets the pace of production in a just-in-time environment.

Pareto chart A graph that visually shows the relative magnitude of each quality problem identified using a check sheet; used to identify which quality problem to work on first.

Pareto Priority Index (PPI) A ratio of the benefits versus costs for each potential Six Sigma project.

part record A chart used to track part quantities and their assembly or order activities in the MRP.

performance-based contracts A contract including a set of performance standards for suppliers. These contracts are often used to address issues such as (1) customer satisfaction, (2) product/service quality, (3) end-user satisfaction, (4) process performance, and (5) and other unique aspects of the relationship.

personal knowledge banks Also called customer-managed interactions; when customers are allowed to compile a record of all their interactions across an entire industry and supplement this data with current preferences and plans for future purchases.

piggyback Transportation term referring to the loading of shipping containers or truck trailers on a rail flatbed car (also known as container-on-flat-car (COFC) and trailer-on-flat-car (TOFC)).

pilot customer service initiative A small project that enables management to assess the impact of a customer service idea on customer satisfaction, the real costs involved, and the changes in structure required.

pilot production Occurs once the design-build-test phase is successfully completed. At this point, the new product is produced on a limited basis to determine if full-scale production is possible.

pilot test A preliminary small-scale test or study.

planned order release The bottom line of an MRP part record. It designates when the specific quantity is to be ordered from the supplier or to begin being processed. These quantities also determine the gross requirements of the dependent or "children" parts going into this higher level part or product.

point-of-sale (POS) data Sales data collected at the retailer's sites by scanning products purchased by the consumer.

poka-yoke A Japanese word for mistake-proofing.

poor-quality costs The costs attached to problems in production or service delivery. Can be broken down into three categories: (1) appraisal costs, (2) internal failure costs, and (3) external failure costs.

popularity warehouse storage methodology Places the fastest-moving items in the most accessible warehouse locations, resulting in less picker travel time and decreased warehouse throughput times.

postponement strategy Delaying the final manufacturing, labeling, or packaging of product until it is needed by the customer.

posttransaction customer service elements Customer service activities that occur after the product or service has been sold.

preference matrix A summary of the weighted scores used to select a location.

preferred supplier See **supplier partnership.**

pretransaction customer service elements Occur within the firm prior to, or apart from, the sale of products and services. They involve the firm's ability to support various customer service activities, allowing the firm to position itself such that it can indeed provide good customer service.

prevention costs The money organizations spend to prevent quality problems from occurring in the first place.

priority rules Rules used to determine the sequence in which customer orders will be processed and shipped. Examples: process smaller, simpler orders first; process largest orders (volume or dollar amount are two measures of size) first, or process orders on a first-come-first-served basis.

private carrier A form of transportation owned by a company, such as a fleet of trucks, which is used to ship that company's goods only.

private warehouse A warehouse owned and operated by a company for its own use.

proactive customer service Anticipating customer needs and problems and delivering solutions prior to the time when requests and complaints occur.

probabilistic demand and cycle time reorder point model When both demand and delivery lead times are variable, this model is used; it determines the reorder point based on the expected demand, expected lead time, the standard deviation of lead time demand, the standard deviation of delivery lead time, and the desired service levels.

probabilistic demand reorder point model When demand is variable, this model is used; it determines the reorder point based on the demand, expected lead time, the standard deviation of lead time demand, and the desired service level.

process activity mapping See **process mapping.**

process capability A measure of the uniformity of a process; a measure of the ability of the combination of inputs and resources—employees and other people, machines, methods, and materials—to consistently produce a product or service within design specifications or tolerances.

process capability index (C_{pk}) A measure showing whether the process mean has shifted away from the design target and is off-center.

process capability ratio (C_p) A calculation indicating whether a process can meet design specifications.

process flowcharting See **process mapping.**

process flow diagramming See **process mapping.**

process-focused layout Desirable when many dissimilar products are manufactured, requiring small output volumes or batch sizes. These layouts are designed for manufacturing flexibility and are also called intermittent process layouts. Machines tend to be grouped by function in departments.

process improvement Process evaluations leading to improvements in product cost, quality, and/or customer service.

process mapping Analyzing a given process from order to delivery by making a record of all steps involved in this process in a visual map to eliminate all forms of waste. Also called process activity mapping, process flowcharting, process flow diagramming, and value stream mapping. All of these terms essentially mean the same thing and have the same objective: to understand the material flows within a process, identify the current sequence of activities making up the process, identify and evaluate or eliminate the activities that are not adding value, and then improve the remaining process activities.

process orientation A focus on creating a system of only value-adding sets of activities that are integrated across the firm.

process owner A person who is accountable for the performance of a process and should have a good enough understanding of the process to be considered an expert.

process variation The inherent random changes within a process.

procurement card (p-card) A multipurpose bank card designed to streamline the purchasing and payment processes.

product development and commercialization process The set of activities responsible for developing new products to meet changing customer requirements and then getting these products to market quickly and efficiently.

product flow planning The determination of how products will be moved from the points of origination to demand points. Product flow planning should be used to determine the size, location, and number of fixed facilities in the logistics network.

product focus A philosophy of developing innovative products and services and then attempting to create a market for them.

product-focused layouts Assembly line layouts; used to achieve high volume output of standardized products. Processing steps are standardized, divided into relatively equal time lengths of work, and then assigned to workers, permitting specialization to occur.

production interval A measure of the frequency a product family will be made and the product mix.

production kanban A visual signal used to trigger production of certain components.

production variety funnel A visual representation of the complexity of the supply chain that helps organizations to create a strategy and improve the management of their product lines.

productivity A measure of outputs divided by inputs.

product life cycle The stages of a product's life, which generally begin with development and are then followed by introduction, growth, maturity, decline, and cancellation.

product returns process See **reverse supply chain.**

product structure diagram See **bill of materials.**

profitable customer A person, household, or company that over time yields a revenue stream that exceeds by an acceptable amount the company's cost stream of attracting, selling, and servicing that customer.

profit management automation (PMA) Combines profit planning, activity-based costing, and treasury and audit management into an integrated application suite; it has become a big growth area in the ERP module market.

Program Evaluation and Review Technique (PERT) A form of the critical path network that uses probabilistic time estimates to determine the completion time for a project.

project champion See **team sponsor.**

project milestone The date when a team expects to complete a major portion of a project.

project mission statement Used in Six Sigma projects, it is a brief description of what the Six Sigma team plans to accomplish in relationship to the problem being addressed.

project plan A plan used to run a Six Sigma project; it includes a project problem statement, a project mission statement, and a team charter.

project problem statement A short description of the problem that will be solved in a Six Sigma project.

promotions Special advertising and pricing schemes to increase sales.

psychographics Refers to customer lifestyle choices or personalities.

public carrier A public, for-profit transportation company.

public warehouse A for-profit storage facility that rents space for short periods of time.

pull system An operating system where synchronized work takes place only upon authorization from another downstream user in the system rather than strictly to a forecast.

purchase cost The cost of the items bought from suppliers.

purchasing A major function of an organization that is responsible for acquisition of required materials, services, and equipment.

pyrolysis Also see **gasification.**

Q

quality filter mapping A mapping technique used by organizations to determine where quality problems discovered by the customer are occurring in the supply chain. The map is then used to improve quality.

quality function deployment (QFD) A process to translate customer requirements into measurable engineering requirements, develop part requirements, process steps, and process and quality controls.

quality niche strategy A positioning strategy that identifies those dimensions of quality most important to an organization's customers.

quantity discount model When a supplier offers one or more discounted prices that depend on the purchase quantity, managers use this model to evaluate each of the purchase prices and their impact on total annual costs to determine the optimal purchase quantity.

queue discipline Refers to the policies used to select the next customer in the queue for service.

queuing configuration Refers to the number and type of queues, and the spatial arrangements.

R

radio frequency identification (RFID) A technology that enables a device to read data stored on chips at a distance, without requiring line-of-sight scanning. These chips are typically placed on storage containers and even units of product.

random effects Changes in demand that are impossible to predict and occur at irregular times.

raw materials Purchased assemblies, parts, and materials that are delivered by suppliers and used in the manufacture of finished products or services.

reactive customer service When customers with a problem contact the firm and the firm helps to solve the problem.

reclaim To collect an item for recycling.

recycling The process of returning products for reuse in either the same form, or something completely different through remanufacturing or refurbishment.

refurbishing Restoring a product to like-new condition.

relearning effect When temporary transfers of workers results in a short-term significant loss of service quality or processing capability.

reliability The ability to provide all aspects of the order fulfillment process as promised, including status and location information for any outstanding orders.

remanufacturing Products are disassembled and all parts are examined for their condition, cleaned, repaired as necessary, tested, and reassembled to attain optimal performance.

reneging Giving up and leaving a queue, after entering and waiting for a time.

reorder point (ROP) The inventory on-hand that will be necessary to satisfy demand during the order cycle time period.

request for information (RFI) An informal request to collect general information on price, design, timing, and/or other terms of interest.

request for proposal (RFP) A formal, binding request for pricing used for the more complex critical and bottleneck purchases. The use of RFPs allows the supplier to develop part specifications based on their own knowledge of the materials and technology needed.

request for quote (RFQ) A formal request for pricing from a supplier; commonly used when the purchasing requirements are clear.

response strategy Using a quick, reliable, and/or flexible response to customer demand.

return on assets A financial measure, calculated as after-tax income divided by total assets.

returns allowance An amount of money paid to a retailer or other customer by a manufacturer or distributor and in exchange the retailer/customer deals with any returns problems.

returns authorization (RA) A numbered authorization form used by a manufacturer to permit the return of a product, with screens in place to ensure that the return should be accepted.

returns management Developing and implementing efficient methods for transporting and storing returns while seeking to recover some value, if possible, from the returned items. Returns management activities include environmental compliance with substance disposal and recycling, composing operating and repair instructions, troubleshooting and warranty repairs, developing disposal guidelines, designing an effective reverse logistics process, and collecting returns data.

revenue management See **yield management.**

reverse auction A buying firm runs an online auction using a bidding process with either proprietary software developed inhouse or through a third party. Potential prequalified bidders (suppliers) bid based on given purchase requirements. Bidders log on to a designated website and place their offers, while watching the bids as they come in, and may reduce their own bids until the close of the auction.

reverse logistics A unique form of inbound logistics where returned goods are properly disposed with an attempt to recover some of their original value.

reverse supply chain Also called the product returns process; describes methods used by firms to manage product, parts, and materials returns.

risk management plan A written document that provides details of a Six Sigma project team's risk management strategy.

risk management strategy A plan for mitigating any risks that may materialize during the implementation of a Six Sigma project.

robust When the word is used to describe a product, it means it will work under varied environmental conditions. It is also typically used to describe the EOQ model, meaning that firms can still use the EOQ with a fairly high level of confidence, even though demand, order lead time, order cost, and carrying cost may be only estimated and not necessarily constant.

rolling production schedule In an MRP system, each week the MPS extends its frozen weekly production schedule for the set frozen time period, and then projects a working or rolling schedule for the remaining portion of the year.

running sum of forecast errorsx (RSFE) A measure of forecast bias, that is, whether the forecast tends to be consistently higher or lower than actual demand.

S

safety stock Extra inventory required to minimize the probability of running out during the order fulfillment cycle.

sales and operations planning A joint planning process between sales, operations, and finance to balance production levels and resource requirements with the demand forecast.

sales force estimate A qualitative forecast based on the sales force's knowledge of the market and estimates of customer needs.

sample A quantity of randomly selected observations that represent the population or all observations.

sample coefficient of determination A measure of the variation in the dependent variable that can be explained by the independent variable; the value will range between 0 and 1.

sample correlation coefficient A measure of the strength and direction of the relationship between the independent variable and the dependent variable; the value will range from −1 to +1.

sample size The number of units that will be randomly selected and measured each time a sample is collected.

sampling frequency The time interval between sample collections.

sampling plan A design to collect and analyze samples.

scientific management A management approach to improve productivity through the study of time and motion.

seasonal effects Recurring upward or downward changes in demand within a year.

secondary market Company operating outside the original supply chain.

secondary market brokers Companies that buy returned product and then resell it for a profit.

second-tier supplier The supplier to a manufacturer's supplier.

selective exposure/selective attention A selective internal screening mechanism among consumers to ignore certain stimuli while seeking out others.

selective interpretation/perceptual distortion When consumers interpret various marketing communications, product information, or stimuli differently, based on their predisposition and personality.

self-service Also called the customer participation approach; a standardized service that can be administered with little or no company assistance.

service blueprint Assessing the level of customer contact and control that exists for various service processes, with the objective of separating customers from processes not designed for customer contact.

service capacity bottlenecks Occur when unexpected demand exceeds available service capacity; it is up to management to reduce the likelihood of these occurrences with use of better capacity management and demand management techniques.

service level The probability that an organization will have enough stock on hand to meet customer demand; also defined as the percentage of the area under the demand distribution that is covered by, or to the left of, the ROP.

service process Consists of the servers, the process time distribution, the arrangement of servers, and the server management policies.

service-profit chain Linking the internal environment to employee satisfaction, which leads to customer service value, customer satisfaction, customer loyalty, and finally profitability.

service recovery Remedying a service failure; company personnel in a position to remedy the situation show empathy towards the customer while taking effective and quick actions to fix the situation.

setup activities Machine reprogramming and tool changes, inventory changes, and processing activity changes prior to the start of a new product model run on an assembly line.

setup costs A type of internal order cost; includes writing the production order, preparing equipment for a production run, and setting up the labor for the processing.

shortest process time dispatch rule The job with the shortest process time is selected first.

short payment Paying less than the full invoice amount.

sigma drift The idea that process variations will grow over time as process measurements drift off target.

silo mentality When workers act only in their own best interests, and managers act only in their departments' best interests.

similarity warehouse storage methodology Places items commonly picked together in close proximity within the warehouse.

simple moving average A quantitative forecasting method in which at least two previous periods of actual demand are averaged together to predict the following period's demand.

simulation forecasting method A forecasting model that estimates demand using complex mathematical modeling, role playing without the aid of technology, or some combination of both.

Six Sigma The statistical likelihood that 99.99966 percent of the time, a process sample average will fall below a control limit placed 4.5 standard deviations (or sigmas) above the true process mean, assuming the process is in control, and the process sample measurements are normally distributed around the process mean.

Six Sigma coach A person primarily responsible for providing any required technical expertise to the Six Sigma process owner and team, but also be an expert in change management or process design strategies.

Six Sigma methodology A data-driven framework developed by Motorola, designed to make breakthrough (very significant) quality improvements in value-adding processes. It is loosely based on the quality concepts first developed by Deming, Juran, and others beginning in the 1920s. Also referred to simply as Six Sigma.

size and shape warehouse storage methodology Places heavy or bulky items in easily accessible warehouse locations.

skunkworks Teams that develop new products, usually in a short timeframe, outside the normal rules of an organization.

smart BPM systems Automated systems deployed for a variety of processes in many industries. These are rules-based expert systems, often involving statistical analysis of data, and they typically make decisions in real time after weighing all the data and rules for a particular customer or situation.

smoothing constant The weight used in the exponential smoothing forecasting method; must be between 0 and 1.

social networking technology Helps salespeople figure out who knows who at a prospect organization; these applications allow firms to search for relationships to accounts and contacts within their existing CRM system.

sourcing strategy A long-range plan to manage the supply of purchased items, linked to an analysis and goals, and tied to the corporate and supply chain strategies.

spend category A category of business purchases that has common characteristics such as raw materials, customized items,

standardized items, and services. Each general category may be further divided.

spend management To analyze and hopefully reduce total purchasing costs.

spyware Software used by companies to collect information about a user without his or her knowledge.

stabilize phase Directly after implementation and for a period of perhaps one year, companies familiarize themselves with the ERP system and the process changes that have occurred.

stakeholder An interested party.

standard error of the estimate A measure of the deviation or error; the difference between actual demand and the regression line estimate.

statement of work Written explanation attached to a request for proposal (RFP) of exactly what work will be done and how. Some common services requiring a statement of work include construction, publications, advertising, janitorial services, and laboratory services.

stock-keeping unit (SKU) A single type of product that is kept in stock.

stockout When a company can't fill a customer's order, either partially or at all.

stockout cost When customers cannot buy an item, this results in a lost sale, lost goodwill or damage to the firm's reputation, lost future sales, and possibly a cost to process a backorder.

strategic alliance A strong partnership where buyers and suppliers share information on their long-term strategies and frequently work together as a team to seek out problems and solve them, both from the buyer's and the supplier's perspective. There is a general understanding that process improvements will ultimately benefit both parties.

strategic item A purchased item that is extremely important to production or service delivery because of its unique characteristics. This item is generally managed through closer win/win, partnership-type relationships between the customer and supplier.

strategic quality planning A long-range plan to meet organizational quality objectives.

stretch goals Goals that are not easily attainable.

supplier certification program A program designed to pre-approve suppliers before they are allowed to quote or receive an order. In general the customer firm's representatives will visit the supplier's facilities and observe the supplier's equipment, personnel, facilities, and systems that monitor quality in order to ensure they meet the buying firm's specifications and quality

standards. If those standards have been met, the supplier will be certified.

supplier co-location See JIT II.

supplier development The efforts of a buying firm to improve the capabilities and performance of specific suppliers to better meet its needs.

supplier integration Supplier involvement in the customer's new product development process during planning, design, and/or production stages.

supplier partnership A buyer–supplier relationship that has been more than satisfactory and the two parties see a reason to work together more often and share more information. A means to build stronger, extensive ties between customers and suppliers with the overall objectives of lowering costs and improving quality and customer service.

supplier quality assurance program A supplier's plan to meet set customer performance standards.

supplier relationship management (SRM) Developing strong relationships and partnerships with suppliers based on a strategic perspective, and then managing these relationships to create value for all participants in the supply chain. Also a software application in an ERP system that provides users with analytical tools, tracking capabilities, web services, and reverse auction technologies among other capabilities to improve decision making and control of supplier relationships.

supplier scorecard A performance system used to evaluate suppliers based on the balanced scorecard method.

supply chain event management software Collects real-time data from multiple supply chain sources and converts it into information that gives business managers a good idea of how their supply chains are performing.

supply chain management (SCM) The integration of key business processes regarding the flow of materials from raw material suppliers to the final customer.

supply chain response matrix A mapping technique illustrating the ability of a company to respond to customer demand.

supply management The identification, acquisition, access, positioning, and management of resources the organization needs or potentially needs in the attainment of its strategic objectives.

synergize phase After three years, the ERP system along with its users have reached a level of maturity where system optimization is most likely to occur.

synthesize phase After implementing and ERP system and going through the

stabilize phase, companies seek organizational improvements by improving processes, adding complementary software applications, mastering the ERP system, and gaining additional support for the system.

T

takt time A calculation of how frequently a unit will be produced on an assembly line. Also referred to as assembly line cycle time.

tardiness The amount of time a job finishes beyond its due date (if it finishes early, tardiness is zero).

target cost The product cost (expected production, marketing, and engineering costs) calculated by subtracting the desired profit from the expected selling price.

team charter Used in Six Sigma projects, a document that identifies a Six Sigma team's responsibilities and gives the team authority to pursue its mission.

team leader A person who helps guide a Six Sigma team through a project and is responsible for its completion.

team members People who work for the Six Sigma team leader on a project and are chosen because of their particular expertise for the given project.

team sponsor A member of an organization's leadership group that helps select and provides support for a Six Sigma project. Also known as project champion.

telemarketing Refers to the use of salespeople who use the telephone to identify and qualify potential new customers.

Theory of Constraints (TOC) A philosophy of improvement that recognizes the fact that there will always be limitations to system performance, and that the limitations in many cases can be caused by a small number of process bottlenecks or constraints. Also referred to as management by constraint.

third-party logistics provider See **third-party transportation services.**

third-party transportation services (3PL) For-hire outside agents that provide transportation and other services including warehousing, document preparation, customs clearance, packaging, labeling, and freight bill auditing.

third-tier supplier A supplier to a manufacturer's supplier's supplier.

three-dimensional concurrent engineering (3-DCE) The simultaneous design of a new product, its process, and the supply chain that will be used to deliver product to the end customer.

throughput volume The rate at which materials or people move through a facility.

tiered supply management The integration of a firm's supply management process with its first-, second-, and third-tier suppliers.

time fence A period of time wherein no changes are allowed to the weekly production schedule as used with the MRP. Also known as frozen time period.

time series models Forecasts using past observations of actual demand over a given time period.

top-down forecasting approach Management develops a forecast for each stock-keeping unit and then divides that total demand across its locations.

top-down management approach When the expertise and resources needed for administrative improvements requires the involvement of middle and upper management. In these cases, upper and middle management take the initiative to propose and implement structural solutions.

total cost of ownership See **total life cycle cost.**

total inventory costs The sum of inventory carrying costs, order costs, stockout costs, and purchase costs.

total landed cost The purchase cost plus the transportation cost, tariffs and duties, return of parts cost, repair cost, late delivery costs, and follow-up costs.

total life cycle cost (TCO) Total costs incurred to purchase, maintain, and dispose of a product. Also known as total cost of ownership.

total preventive maintenance See **total productive maintenance.**

total productive maintenance (TPM) A plant-floor based system to prevent equipment-related accidents, defects, and breakdowns. Also known as total preventive maintenance.

total quality management (TQM) A philosophy encompassing a collection of processes that seek to assess and improve quality continuously to please customers, reduce costs, and ultimately, create competitive advantage for the firm.

total resources method A process used to track the costs of poorly performing processes; the total resources used within a cost category are identified and then a percentage of those resources used are allocated to activities associated with fixing the effects of poor quality.

total supply chain material costs A measure of the monies spent for purchase and use of materials, including any additional funds spent due to defective materials along the supply chain.

tour A network or sequence of pickup and delivery stops, including the origination point.

tour improvement When solving a vehicle routing problem, this occurs when one or more nodes are switched to another vehicle's tour, such that vehicle capacities are not exceeded, and total distance of all tours is reduced.

Toyota Production System A methodology created by Toyota Motor Co. in the 1950s. The idea is to make best use of an organization's time, assets, and people in all processes in order to optimize productivity.

tracking signal A measure of whether a particular forecasting method is accurately predicting the changes in demand; the number of mean absolute deviations (MADs) the forecast is above or under actual demand.

transaction elements of customer service Are associated with, and occur during the order cycle; assist the firm in the successful delivery of purchased products and services.

transit time The time from the point where an order leaves the shipper's dock until the time it arrives at its destination.

transportation inventories Inventories owned by the firm and in-transit inbound to the firm or outbound to the firm's customers.

transportation management Overseeing the movement of raw materials and parts to a warehouse or storage facility within a manufacturing site as well as movement of finished goods and supplies to distribution centers and retail sites.

transportation management system (TMS) A software application that allows firms to select the best mix of transportation service and pricing to determine the best use of containers or truck trailers, to better manage transportation contracts, to rank transportation options, to clear customs, to track product movements, and to track carrier performance.

traveling salesman problem The simple case of one vehicle starting and ending at the origination node, with a network of pickups and deliveries to make. The idea is to find a route that minimizes the time, mileage, or cost objective.

trend-adjusted exponential smoothing method A quantitative forecasting method that adjusts an exponentially smoothed forecast for an expected trend; two smoothing constants are used.

trends Long-range changes in sales over an extended time period.

Type I error When a process is mistakenly thought to be out of control and an improvement initiative is undertaken unnecessarily.

Type II error When a process is thought to be exhibiting only natural variations and no improvement is undertaken, even though the process is actually out of control.

U

unit cost method A process to allocate the resources used to fix poorly performing processes by identifying the number of times deficiencies occur, along with the average cost to fix each deficiency.

upper control limit A value on a control chart representing the maximum acceptable limit for the sample plot.

upselling Providing an opportunity to let a customer return a product in exchange for an upscale model to avoid a full return and lost revenue.

U-shaped warehouse layout Items flow in a u-shaped pattern from receiving to cross-docking to shipping, or receiving to storage to picking to sorting and to shipping. The advantages of a u-shaped warehouse layout include efficient utilization of receiving and shipping docks (since they can share the same dock space), dual capabilities of storage and cross-docking, and better security (since entry and exit are on the same side of the building).

V

value-added network (VAN) A provider of a private network that allows for secure electronic transmission of documents between organizations; used when computer documents are incompatible with a trading partners' computers.

value-added per employee (VAE) A financial measure; calculated as sales minus costs (of materials, supplies, and outsourcing costs), divided by the number of employees.

value engineering An analysis and selection of materials, processes, and products during the design phase to achieve the desired function at the lowest overall cost consistent with performance.

value stream A set of all actions, both value and non-value added, required to bring a specific product (whether a good, a service, or some combination of the two) through the (critical) main flows.

value stream mapping See **process mapping.**

variable A factor that can be measured on a continuous scale, such as weight, time, and length.

variable data Data that can be measured on a continuous scale.

vehicle routing problem Assigning pickups and dropoffs to multiple vehicles, with variable demands at each node, and multiple vehicle capacities.

vendor-managed inventory (VMI) A progressive partner-based approach to controlling inventory and reducing supply chain costs. Customers provide information to the key supplier, including historical usage, current inventory levels, minimum and maximum stock levels, sales forecasts, and upcoming promotions, who then takes on the responsibility and risk for planning, managing, and monitoring the replenishment of inventory. The supplier may even own the inventory until the product is sold.

verbal quote An oral request for prices for items, generally for lower cost, non-critical purchases.

versioning When catalog and magazine publishers offer personalized publications that appeal to individuals or very small market niche segments.

vertical e-marketplace E-marketplace that serves businesses within the same industry.

viral marketing When companies form online user groups where owners can share their experiences and ideas, creating direct online information sharing. Also referred to as bottom-up branding.

virtual call center When an organization's call center agents are located around the world, connected by an information system and the Internet; allows the center to be managed and utilized as a single entity.

virtual queue When a firm uses some form of automation to place customers in a computer queue so they don't have to physically stand in line. Restaurants located in malls, for instance, might provide customers with pagers, allowing the restaurant to track their place in a virtual queue while allowing customers to walk around or even shop while waiting for a table.

Voice Extensible Markup Language (Voice-XML) Uses standards for building telephone speech applications to improve the effectiveness of touchtone customer service capabilities.

Voice over Internet Protocol (VoIP) A method for taking analog audio signals (such as talking on the telephone) and turning them into digital data which can then be transmitted over the Internet.

W

warehouse management The proper storage and movement of inventory and minor manufacturing such as assembly or labeling activities within the warehouse, and movement of shipments onto the transportation carrier.

warehouse management system (WMS) A software application that tracks and controls the flow of goods from the receiving dock of a warehouse or distribution center, until the item is loaded for outbound shipment to the customer.

web mining Similar to data mining, companies use customer data collected from web sites to identify hidden patterns of behavior or common interests among their customer group.

web portal A website that provides secure access to data, applications, and services to business partners.

web services Websites that let applications communicate with one another without the need for custom coding, eliminating barriers caused by incompatible hardware, software, and operating systems.

weighted moving average forecasting A quantitative forecasting method that allows greater emphasis to be placed on more recent data to reflect changes in demand patterns; weights tend to be based on the experience of the forecaster.

white belt Six Sigma team member that can lead Six Sigma projects considered too small for a Black Belt or a Green Belt. Have at least 40 hours of Six Sigma training.

Wi-Fi networks Linkages that allow mobile access to the Internet.

withdrawal kanban A visual signal to indicate a container of parts can be moved from one work cell to another.

work breakdown structure (WBS) An account of all work tasks that need to be completed for a Six Sigma project.

work flow The movement or transfer of work from the customer or demand source through the organization according to a set of procedures. Work may include documents, information, or tasks that are passed from one recipient to another for action.

work groups Two or more individuals working together on a common task who generally have computers connected to a network that allow them to send email to one another, share data files, and schedule meetings.

work-in-process inventories (WIP) Items that are in some intermediate processing stage, on their way to becoming finished products.

world-class businesses Firms that manage processes in part by successfully managing inventories, creating long-lasting and mutually beneficial partnerships with suppliers and customers, establishing effective information and communication systems to connect with stakeholders, utilizing JIT practices, and instituting quality management programs to create and deliver products and services customers want, leading to long-lasting success in the marketplace.

X

XML web services The basic platform for application integration; applications are constructed using multiple XML web services from various sources that work together regardless of where they reside or how they were implemented.

Y

yield management Refers to the objective of trying to sell a limited or fixed capacity to the right customers at the right price so as to maximize revenues; also referred to as revenue management.

Z

zero returns policy A rule of not accepting returns or any reason.

Author Index

Subject Index